PRASE FOR *DIDN'T YOU USE T...*

"Mullin has not lost the diarist's touch."
Financial Times

"Another riveting tour de force ... Mullin has not only mellowed
but in retirement become a British institution."
Peter Hain, *The House*

"Lively, lacerating and waspish. A gift for historians, his unique
insights will be studied for decades to come."
Leo McKinstry, *Daily Express*

"Truly perceptive ... in turn reflective and frank, acerbic and
sometimes laugh-out-loud funny."
Julia Langdon, former political correspondent of *The Guardian*

"Chris Mullin's eye for the absurd remains
as keen as ever ... Highly entertaining."
Francis Beckett, *The Spectator*

PRAISE FOR *DECLINE & FALL 2005–2010*

"Mullin's supreme virtues are an eye for the absurd and an incorruptible
independence of outlook ... An indispensable hangover cure for
anyone who has ever been drunk on the idea of power."
Anne Perkins, *The Guardian*

"Witty, waspish and darkly hilarious."
Mail on Sunday

"Funny, redemptive and informing."
Jon Snow, *New Statesman*, Books of the Year

"One of Mullin's charms is his readiness to like
people who don't echo his politics."
Jenni Russell, *Sunday Times*

DIDN'T YOU USE TO BE CHRIS MULLIN?

DIARIES 2010–2022

Biteback Publishing

This paperback edition published in Great Britain in 2024 by
Biteback Publishing Ltd, London
Copyright © Chris Mullin 2023, 2024

ISBN 978-1-78590-915-3

10 9 8 7 6 5 4 3 2 1

A CIP catalogue record for this book is available from the British Library.

Set in Minion Pro and Futura

Printed and bound in Great Britain by
CPI Group (UK) Ltd, Croydon CR0 4YY

FSC
www.fsc.org
MIX
Paper | Supporting
responsible forestry
FSC® C171272

Once again, to my friends in high and low places with thanks for the pleasure of their company.

CONTENTS

About the Author // page viii
Preface // page ix

Chapter One: 2010 // page 1
Chapter Two: 2011 // page 8
Chapter Three: 2012 // page 18
Chapter Four: 2013 // page 29
Chapter Five: 2014 // page 37
Chapter Six: 2015 // page 77
Chapter Seven: 2016 // page 146
Chapter Eight: 2017 // page 209
Chapter Nine: 2018 // page 266
Chapter Ten: 2019 // page 322
Chapter Eleven: 2020 // page 387
Chapter Twelve: 2021 // page 451
Chapter Thirteen: 2022 // page 513

Acknowledgements // page 547
Index // page 549

About the Author

Chris Mullin was the Member of Parliament for Sunderland South from 1987 to 2010. He is a former chairman of the Home Affairs Select Committee and was a minister in three departments. He is the author of four novels, the best-known of which, *A Very British Coup*, was made into an award-winning television series. More recently he published a sequel, *The Friends of Harry Perkins*. His three previous volumes of diaries have been widely acclaimed.

Preface

When I retired from Parliament in April 2010, I ceased keeping a diary, on the assumption that life would no longer be of sufficient interest to justify doing so. It soon became apparent that I was wrong and so before long I resumed.

As readers of the previous volume may recall, my decision to retire was accompanied by a great deal of angst. I always knew there was a life outside politics, but I wasn't confident that there would be any demand for my services. As I wrote at the time, leaving earlier than I need have done was either the best or the worst decision of my life. I wasn't sure which. As it happens it has turned out well. This past decade has seen some of the best years of my life.

By a huge stroke of luck, I had within months of retirement fulfilled one of my life's ambitions, having acquired a small walled garden in a beautiful part of north Northumberland. It might not have been affordable but for the fact that, also within months of retirement, I sold for the second time the television rights on my 1982 novel, *A Very British Coup*. The subsequent rise of Jeremy Corbyn gave the novel a new lease of life.

The success of my earlier diaries – two were BBC Books of the Week and both made brief appearances in the *Sunday Times* bestseller list – generated a small industry which I spent several years servicing. The Live Theatre in Newcastle produced an excellent play based on the diaries which eventually found its way to London's West End. The great discovery of my retirement, however, has been that the political meeting is not dead. It has simply transferred to the literary festival. I have not kept count, but at a guess I must have taken part in around 200 festivals and other book-related events in places ranging from Lerwick in the Shetlands to Fowey in Cornwall and many in between, attracting paying audiences of anywhere up to 750. Six times I have filled the big tent at Edinburgh. It was never like this when I was in Parliament.

It will be apparent that, although I remain resolutely left of centre in outlook, I do not take the standard liberal-left view on everything. I also have friends of all political persuasions. If these are defects, I plead guilty.

On occasion I have made myself useful, or so I like to think. In 2011 I was a judge of the Man Booker Prize. For six years I was north-east regional chairman of the Heritage Lottery Fund and I am currently a member of the Northumberland National Park Authority. I have also served on various small trusts and charities. I have lectured at half a dozen universities and I was for eight years a council member of the Winston Churchill Memorial Trust. Occasionally my views are still sought on matters political. All in all, this past decade has been what my old friend Tony Benn would have called a blaze of autumn sunshine.

I am under no illusion, however. Despite the occasional moment in the sunshine, I have never been much more than a fleabite on the body politic. On a visit to Parliament a couple of years after retiring I came across a former colleague. He peered at me over the top of his glasses and said, 'Didn't you use to be Chris Mullin?'

'Thank you,' I replied. 'That will be the title of Volume Four.' Here it is. Enjoy.

CHAPTER ONE

2010

Wednesday 1 September

Amid great fanfare, ludicrous security and a certain amount of snide commentary from people who have not yet read them, The Man (aka Tony Blair) has published his memoirs. A handful of the commentariat elite have been allowed a preview, in a sealed room at an undisclosed location. Lesser mortals – I have been asked to review the book for *The Times* – have only a few hours to digest the full 700 pages (shades of Robin Cook and the Scott Report). All one can hope to do in the time available is dip into a few key chapters. My copy was delivered to my publisher's office at about 11 a.m. and I managed to knock out an 1,800-word review in about five hours, having drafted the opening paragraphs in advance. Actually, despite an uninspiring title and a naff cover photograph, it is not a bad book. It is organised in themes. There are chapters on the rise of New Labour, on the intervention in Kosovo, on the Northern Ireland peace process (arguably The Man's greatest achievement), on his fraught relationship with Gordon Brown and even on Princess Diana. The core – four chapters in all – is his account of the Iraq debacle. On the aftermath, he appears to be in denial. Iraq is surely a catastrophe. No weapons of mass destruction. Al-Qaeda, not present before the invasion, now rampant. Iran's influence much increased – that surely wasn't part of the plan. And the human cost, about which he expresses much anguish: tens of thousands dead and maimed, millions displaced, a government that barely functions, to say nothing of the damage done to our standing with friends and allies around the world. By any standards it was a huge misjudgement. The Man himself speaks of his 'colossal isolation'.

There is a frank account of the long war of attrition with Gordon. By 2003, he says, he was seriously thinking of giving up. 'The euphoria, the boundless optimism of the early years had long departed. Instead each day, each meeting, occasionally each hour seemed a struggle, an endless pushing against forces, seen or unseen, that pushed back, sometimes steadily, sometimes violently, but always with what seemed like inexhaustible energy and often malice.'

By and large The Man is unrepentant; the only mistakes he admits to are ones that were generally popular – the ban on hunting with hounds and the Freedom of Information Act. He even comes to the defence of the markets over the global financial meltdown: the fault of governments, he says, for failing to regulate. There is one noticeable absentee – God. Not until we reach page 690 does he tantalisingly remark, 'I have always been more interested in religion than politics.' He does not elaborate. One suspects that had God been consulted about the Iraq enterprise, he might have warned against it. After all, the Pope and the Archbishop of Canterbury were opposed.

Saturday 4 September

Today's *Times* gives the best part of a page to my review of the Blair memoirs. Good to feel relevant again, however fleetingly.

Friday 24 September

Tomorrow we shall find out who is to be the new Labour leader. Although there are five candidates, everyone agrees that it boils down to a choice of Milibands. Until recently it had been assumed that Miliband the Elder would win, but in the past few days the polls have been indicating that Ed the Younger may pip him at the post. I voted for David, though without much enthusiasm. Alan Johnson or Alistair Darling would have been my first choice, followed by either Hilary Benn or Margaret Beckett, but alas none of the above were available. It says much for the narrowness of British politics that it should come down to a choice between two members of the same family, albeit both exceptionally bright and talented.

Saturday 25 September

Ed Miliband is the Chosen One, defeating his brother by a little over 1 percentage point, thanks to trade union votes, which is bound to lead to accusations that he is in hock to them. For the benefit of the cameras the brothers laid on a great display of goodwill, with much hugging, embracing and mutual praise, but there must be considerable tension below the surface. Ed has basically put David out of business.

Friday 1 October

On the road by 6 a.m., reaching Henley in good time for my festival appearance, just after lunch. The event, in a local theatre, attracted a full house, but to my dismay the bookshop was hidden away backstage. The audience entered and departed by the main doors at the front of the building, but to buy a book you had to go out of a side exit, up a passageway and into a backroom. My plea to the organisers to display the books where the audience could see them fell on deaf ears. Result: only half a dozen sales. A complete waste of time. As I am beginning to realise, there is a conflict of interest between authors and the organisers of literary festivals. Organisers think an event a success if they have sold all the tickets. Authors judge success by the number of books they sell. I came away fuming.

Saturday 2 October
Oxford

A depressing lunch with a former *Times* journalist, once a distinguished scholar, whom I have not seen for some years. Now a sprightly eighty-four, he has sadly turned into a Holocaust denier, cheerfully describing himself as an antisemite. He believes that 9/11 was the work of the Israelis and the Americans, that the planes were hijacked by drones and that there is no evidence that any Arabs were even on board. Tragic to hear such rubbish spouted by a decent and intelligent man. Needless to say, he has got it all from the internet, on which, he says, he spends two hours a day.

Tuesday 5 October

A dinner in St James's organised by a firm of headhunters who have taken a fleeting interest in me, courtesy of the diaries. Among the guests Martin Narey, a former head of HM Prison Service. 'When is Labour going to stop beating itself up and start taking on the government?' A good question and one I keep asking myself. For months every Tory MP, from the highest to the lowest, has been pretending that the crisis of 2008 was all Labour's fault and thus far the lie has gone unchallenged.

Monday 11 October

According to the *Mirror*, the Tory elite have been quaffing one of the world's most expensive wines on the fringes of their party conference, currently under way in Birmingham. The event, attended by both Cameron and Osborne, was a party hosted by the outgoing Tory treasurer, Michael Spencer, one of Mrs Thatcher's billionaires. The wine, Château Pétrus, apparently retails for up to £1,500 a bottle. So much for our all being in it together. Useful ammunition for our new leader, if he chooses to use it.*

Wednesday 20 October

To Daunt's bookshop in Marylebone High Street, where I gave my diary talk to an audience of about 120 people. One of the managers, it may have been Mr Daunt himself, remarked that ten years from now, at the present rate of attrition, there would be no independent bookshops left outside of central London, save for a handful elsewhere such as Topping's of Bath.

Tuesday 26 October
Church Row, Hampstead

At breakfast Martin Woollacott, quoting his *Guardian* colleague Larry Elliott, remarked that the Tories have succeeded in turning what is by any measure a crisis of capital into a crisis of the public sector. A remarkable achievement and one which neither Her Majesty's Opposition nor our free press seems able or willing to challenge.

---

* He didn't.

To St Margaret's Westminster for Daphne Park's memorial service.[*] The Marquis of Salisbury, who gave the eulogy, caused a titter when he remarked that Daphne had some very surprising friends. That Chris Mullin, for instance.

Wednesday 27 October

A headline in today's *Times*: 'Reason to be hopeful – growth surprises City'. Well, well. Can it be that the coalition's inheritance wasn't so dreadful after all?

Thursday 28 October

Lunch in the Cathedral crypt cafe at Durham with journalist Ed Pearce, who reckons that David Miliband was wrong to withdraw from British politics and that Labour should have made more effort to cobble together a short-term coalition with the Liberal Democrats. 'Never voluntarily surrender power – you never know how long it will be before your turn comes again.' I don't agree. First, because the numbers didn't add up and second, because the electorate would have wreaked a terrible revenge if by some sleight of hand Gordon had been kept in power so far beyond his sell-by date.

Thursday 25 November

To No. 10 for Tom Fletcher's leaving do. The first person I ran into was David Cameron, to whom I chatted amiably for about five minutes. In passing he remarked how much he liked Angela Merkel. I made so bold as to offer a small piece of advice. 'With all due respect,' I said, 'no more annual reshuffles.' In fairness, I think he had already grasped that point without help from me. A memorable occasion. Both the Prime Minister and Tom made amusing speeches. Tom, who looks youthful and has wisdom and experience beyond his years, is off to be our ambassador in Lebanon. He is bright, capable, well-liked and has worked in Downing

---

[*] Daphne Park was a former MI6 agent who had served in, among other places, the Congo, Hanoi and Mongolia. See *Queen of Spies* by Paddy Hayes, Duckworth, 2015.

Street for three years and under three Prime Ministers, so he knows just about all the people high places. I have high hopes for him.[*]

Thursday 9 December

To a private dining room at L'Etoile in Charlotte Street for lunch with my fellow Man Booker judges. Stella Rimington, whom I first came across when she was head of MI5, remarked, apropos the huge leak of American diplomatic cables that is currently causing a stir, that the Americans were crazy to put them on an intranet to which 3 million people had access. 'You can't possibly call that secret.'

Tuesday 14 December

At the *Total Politics* Christmas party, the following exchange with Deborah Mattinson, until earlier this year a Labour Party pollster.

'Why didn't you get rid of him?' 'Him' being our late, unlamented leader. 'If you had, Labour would still be in government.'

'Surely, January this year' – the last serious attempt at a putsch – 'would have been too late.'

'No, all new leaders enjoy a bounce during their first three months and that would have brought you up to April or May, the month of the election. Labour would have won.'

'With whom should we have replaced him?'

'Anyone,' she said. '*You* even.'

Wednesday 15 December

To the Institute for Government's Christmas party at their HQ in Carlton Terrace. A number of former movers and shakers were in evidence, though not much sign of the current management. Someone in a position to know alleged that Ed Miliband talked David out of running against Gordon in the summer of 2009 saying, 'Your time will come.' And when the time did come, Ed, at the urging of Gordon, ran against him. No wonder David is furious.

---

[*] Tom Fletcher is currently Principal of Hertford College, Oxford.

Friday 31 December

The Times have given me a slot on the op-ed page to offer some, slightly tongue-in-cheek, New Year advice to Ed Miliband. I did so as follows: stop apologising and start talking up the achievements of the previous government. Appeal to the best instincts of the middle classes, rather than the meanest. Above all, counter the Tory lie, by now deeply embedded, that somehow the meltdown of 2008 was all Labour's fault. To coin a phrase, it was the bankers, stupid.

CHAPTER TWO

2011

Tuesday 4 January

St Bede's Terrace, Sunderland

A visit from Michael Chaplin and Max Roberts, who want to make a play out of the diaries. Max is artistic director of the Live Theatre in Newcastle; Michael, a north-east playwright of good repute. Personally, I am sceptical, but they seem keen so, hey, why not?

Friday 14 January

To the Newcastle offices of the Heritage Lottery Fund to be interviewed for the regional chairmanship, a job I really want. Right up my street. Each of the shortlisted applicants was asked to bring along a personal item of heritage which meant something to them. I took the photograph of John Doxford, who lived in our house between 1851 and his death in 1899, and explained how I had come by it. The interview went well.

Wednesday 19 January

A letter from Jenny Abramsky, who heads the Heritage Lottery Fund, offering me the regional chair's job. Marvellous. There is life after Parliament after all.

Friday 21 January

The curse of Murdoch strikes again. Andy Coulson has resigned as

Cameron's press spokesman as the net closes around him re. the hacking scandal.

Tuesday 15 February

To Stella Rimington's house in north London for our first formal meeting of the Man Booker judges. The others are Matt d'Ancona, a likeable Toryish journalist, Susan Hill, a hugely successful writer, and Gaby Wood, literary editor of the *Telegraph*. The entire gathering presided over by the genial Ion Trewin, whose many literary achievements include the little-known fact that thirty years ago, as an editor at Hodder & Stoughton, he oversaw the publication of *A Very British Coup*, which remains in print to this day. They are a good crowd and we all get on well. Our plan is to read the books in approximately the same order (they are numbered) and eliminate the no-hopers as we go along. Altogether we are expecting about 140 entries, which we have to whittle down to a longlist of thirteen by the end of July and to a shortlist of six by September.

Tuesday 22 February

This morning I was loitering at a table in the atrium of Portcullis House when who should come by but Ed Miliband. He was amiable but did say, apropos my New Year article in *The Times*, that if I wanted to offer him advice, I should come in and see him. Later, to an *Oldie* lunch at Simpson's in the Strand, where I sat next to Tony Benn. The audience were prosperous Middle England types who would have run a mile from the Benn of old, but when he got up to speak, within minutes he had them eating out of his hand.

Tuesday 22 March

To the Garrick Club for a meeting of my fellow Man Booker judges. Entries are coming in thick and fast, piled high on the bedroom floor, many in packets still unopened. I am getting to the point where I dread the sight of the postman coming down the garden path carrying yet another bulging padded envelope. I have devised a system for coping. Rather than read them all from cover to cover, if the opening chapters don't grab me,

I put it to one side and if, at our six-weekly meetings, one of the other judges commends a book I have sidelined, I get it out and take another look at it. We make progress slowly. Thus far we have eliminated about a third of the entries.

Wednesday 18 May

To the Live Theatre in Newcastle, where I was treated to a preview of *A Walk-On Part*, Michael Chaplin's play based on my diaries. Astonishingly good and cleverly arranged. Six people play about forty parts. John Hodgkinson, the lead, is on stage for two hours and has a huge amount to remember. Afterwards I was asked what I thought of John's performance and replied that the last person to play me was John Hurt and he was better than John Hurt.[*]

Saturday 21 May

To Sunderland, where, alongside the mayor, I presided at the reopening of Barnes Park in my new capacity as regional chairman of the Heritage Lottery Fund. A welcome chance to demonstrate to the local hierarchy that I am still a feature of the landscape.

Friday 8 July

Murdoch has announced that the *News of the World* is to close as the arrests multiply and advertisers withdraw. Couldn't happen to nicer people.

Tuesday 19 July

Rupert Murdoch and his son James appeared before the Culture, Media and Sport Committee to respond to allegations that their minions have been hacking phones on an industrial scale, including that of the murdered teenager Milly Dowler, which is what has really done for them. Needless to say, they insisted that they knew nothing, which is certainly true in the case of the old man and quite possibly in the case of Murdoch

---

[*] Later, I heard that the other members of the cast made John a T-shirt with the slogan 'Better Than John Hurt' printed on the front, which he proudly wore.

Jr, although the evidence in his case is a little murkier since – latterly at least – he was supposed to be in overall charge of this part of the empire. They were accompanied by a squadron of lawyers, advisers and Murdoch Sr's steely but beautiful wife, Wendi Deng, who sat solicitously behind him, in camera shot throughout. There was a wonderful moment when Rupert interrupted his son to assert, apropos of nothing, that this was 'the humblest day of my life'. A line so out of place and so out of character that it could only have been supplied by one of the legion of advisers. Towards the end of the proceedings some idiot in the public seats threw white foam over Rupert, which detracted from what was otherwise an important occasion. There were complaints afterwards that the committee never really laid a finger on either of the witnesses, but that's not the point. The very sight of the great oligarch, a man of whom generations of British politicians have lived in terror, prostrating himself before the elected is in itself a momentous event. All in all, a good day for Parliament – and for democracy.

Sunday 17 July

Ed Miliband has called for the Murdoch empire to be broken up. The first time a senior politician has dared raise the subject. Not that it requires much courage in present circumstances, but all the same, break-up would be a small step towards the creation of a functioning democracy.

Friday 19 August

A two-page handwritten note from Ed Miliband in response to my sending him a copy of my 1995 Media Diversity Bill advocating the break-up of the Murdoch empire. 'We will definitely look at it,' he says – 'definitely' underlined. He signs off saying that he will ask his office to arrange for us to meet.*

Tuesday 23 August

I did a turn on the *Today* programme from the BBC's Newcastle studio.

---

* Nothing came of this.

The taxi driver who took me home said he had to work forty hours a week just to pay his costs, before he could earn anything. In a good week he averaged sixty-five hours and came clear by £300, which was less than when he started ten years ago. He had been caught three times by speed cameras (always doing less than 35 mph). Once more and he would lose his livelihood – job, home, everything. He reckoned it was only a matter of time, considering he drives about 1,000 miles a week. Unsurprisingly, the poor man was permanently on edge.

A call from Mr Speaker Bercow, who is keen to host a performance of the play based on my diaries but anxious not to give his many enemies another stick to beat him with. We chatted for about half an hour.

Thursday 25 August
Edinburgh

Publication day for *A Walk-On Part*, my third – and final? – volume of diaries. Today, for the second year running, I filled the big tent at the book festival and afterwards there was a decent queue for signed copies. Earlier, in Charlotte Square, I came across Ming Campbell and we discussed John Smith. What if he had lived? Ming reckons Labour would still have won in '97 but not by the same margin. Smith, he said, was socially conservative and wouldn't have been interested in such matters as gay rights, but he did believe in basic social justice. Also, there would have been no love affair with George W. Bush and we wouldn't have joined the Iraq invasion – 'he'd have seen the legal point'. I reminded Ming of his remark at John's funeral: 'He had all the virtues of a Scottish Presbyterian and none of the vices.' Apparently it triggered a number of letters from Presbyterians denying that they had any vices.

Tuesday 6 September

A press conference to announce the Man Booker shortlist. We seem to have upset the London literati by 'excluding' (as they put it) several of their mates and by the suggestion that we have favoured titles that are readable rather than literary. This evening at a reception in the Orangery at Holland Park, one of the said literati approached me and alleged that our failure to shortlist Alan Hollinghurst's latest work was evidence of anti-gay bias. Complete tosh. Not having read his previous works, I had no idea that Hollinghurst was gay until his friends started to make a fuss.

Sunday 11 September

A lengthy piece in today's *Observer* by one Catherine Bennett denouncing what she calls the 'stupidification' of the Man Booker. Stella and I, who both made remarks about the need for readability, are singled out as culprits. Halfway through her diatribe Ms Bennett concedes that she has yet to read the entries. We judges do have one advantage over our critics: we have actually read the books.

Tuesday 27 September

'2011 Man Booker shortlist most popular ever', reads a headline in the current *Bookseller*. Well, well. Our critics, of course, will regard this news as evidence of dumbing down. Personally, I see it as vindication. I have lost count of the number of people who, on hearing that I was one of this year's judges, have remarked, 'I hope you are going to choose something readable this year.'

Tuesday 11 October
Heritage Lottery HQ, Sloane Square

A meeting of regional chairs. The woman from the north-west, who was a Conservative candidate at the last election, remarked, 'The Tories are very grateful for Ed Miliband. Everyone at our conference was talking about him. They were comparing him to Ian Duncan Smith. I hope you won't get rid of him.' I assured her that we wouldn't.

Thursday 13 October

To Ilkley in West Yorkshire for another literary festival. 'We had Alan Hollinghurst here last night,' remarked one of the organisers.

My ears pricked up. 'How many tickets did you sell for his event?' Someone was dispatched to find out. Answer: 210.

'And how many have you sold for my event?' Answer: 420.

Touché.

Friday 14 October
Cheltenham Literary Festival

About 700 people attended my event. One man in the audience referred in passing to 'the tyranny under which we have been living these last thirteen years'. 'Truly,' I replied, 'Cheltenham is another country.' As I was leaving the green room to go on stage, a man remarked that he had enjoyed the diaries, to which I made my usual flippant response: 'Obviously you are man of taste and discernment. What's your name, sir?'

'Mike Atherton,' he replied.

Tuesday 18 October

The Man Booker judges met in secret conclave to choose the winner. All done and dusted fairly quickly. It came down to a choice between two titles, and by three votes to two we chose *The Sense of an Ending* by Julian Barnes, who has been shortlisted on three previous occasions. He wasn't my first choice, but choosing him does have one advantage: we have shafted the London literati by anointing one of their own. How can they accuse us of dumbing down now? Conclave over, we were sworn to secrecy until Stella made the official announcement at a slap-up dinner in the Guildhall at 10 p.m.

Friday 28 October

The lead in today's *Express* begins as follows: 'A French plot to send hordes of unemployed workers to snatch our jobs sparked outrage last night.' Are they just taking the mickey or do they actually believe this nonsense?

Thursday 3 November

Came across a New Labour grandee on the Tube. He said that while Tony Blair was a good man who made mistakes, Gordon Brown was a bad man who was sometimes right – as regards the euro, for example. He reckoned that Gordon knew deep down that he wasn't up to it. 'Self-delusion turned to self-destruction.'

Tuesday 8 November

The Leveson Inquiry has heard from a former *Daily Star* reporter, Richard Peppiatt. His statement at yesterday's session included the following:

> The hate-mongering wasn't even genuine. It was a crude, morally deplorable play on the politics of fear in the pursuit of profit … In approximately 900 newspaper bylines I can probably count on fingers and toes the times I felt I was genuinely telling the truth, yet only a similar number could be classed as outright lies. This is because, as much as the skill of a journalist today is about finding facts, it is also, particularly at the tabloid end of the market, about knowing what facts to ignore. The job is about making the facts fit the story, because the story is almost predefined.

Wednesday 9 November

To the Oxford and Cambridge Club in Pall Mall, where for the second year in succession I talked about my diaries, and then to Parliament for tea with Mr Speaker Bercow, who grows on me every time I see him. Most Tories loathe him, but he has certainly shaken up the place, insisting upon September sittings, granting many more urgent questions and speeding up question time so that more Members can be called. Out of the blue he asked if I fancied attending the questioning of James Murdoch tomorrow and gave instructions that I was to be given a ticket.

Thursday 10 November

Arrived at Portcullis House in good time to be admitted to Murdoch Jr's rematch with the Culture, Media and Sport Committee. He has been recalled because no one quite believes his assertion that he agreed two enormous pay-offs without enquiring what they were for and therefore had no knowledge of what was going on. The empire's initial position being that any misbehaviour was the work of a single rogue reporter, whereas it has since become clear that the practice was far more widespread than they have been prepared to admit. I was ushered to a seat near the front of house, from where I had an excellent view of the proceedings. Although the stakes were high, Murdoch, no doubt well-rehearsed, held his ground and never lost his cool. There was an unfortunate piece of grandstanding from Tom Watson, who until now has been the hero of the hour. Several Members, including Watson, addressed the witness by his first name, which would never have been allowed in my day, and there was a certain amount of pouting and posturing from the likes of Louise Mensch. Overall, however, they never really got under the wire, except – as one Member pointed out – if, as he insists, Murdoch didn't know what was going on, it certainly reflects on his management skills.

Thursday 17 November

To Trinity College, Dublin, where I gave my diary talk. I was well looked after. My host, a pleasant young undergraduate, said that many of the Trinity applicants were Oxbridge rejects. A couple of months ago he had shown round one young freshman and his mother from a posh family with an estate in Norfolk. 'Of course,' remarked the mother, 'Charlie applied to Or-xford, but these days it is impossible for the wealthy to get in. They're only interested in the *dis-ad-vant-aged*.' I must tell Sarah. It will be news to her that she's disadvantaged.

Saturday 19 November

A call from Michael White hotfoot from seeing the stage version of *A Walk-On Part* at the Soho Theatre, who says of John Hodgkinson, 'He is very good, but it's not you.' Contrast this with Sheila Williams, who rang last night to say that he had got me off to a T.

Sunday 20 November

A review of the play in the *Telegraph* comes down on Michael White's side, saying kindly that I am neither nerdish nor twerpish. Whew. That's a relief.

Friday 25 November–Saturday 26 November
Castle Hotel, Taunton

Along with John Gummer, Douglas Hurd, Michael Meacher, Patrick Mercer (and Clare Short, who joined us on Saturday), I am helping to entertain a group of prosperous Middle Englanders who have paid a large sum of money to an upmarket travel agency for a 'politics weekend' in a posh hotel. After dinner on Friday evening I delivered a version of my diary talk, which was well received. On Saturday morning several of us took part in a panel discussion. John Gummer told of an amusing exchange with Margaret Thatcher when he had been Environment Secretary. Representing, as he did, a coastal constituency, he was well aware of the threat posed by rising sea levels and decided to draft a paper on the subject for presentation to the Cabinet. He then rang Thatcher to seek her approval and, when he had explained the gist of it, she replied as follows: 'I agree and, therefore, we are a majority.'

CHAPTER THREE

2012

Wednesday 8 February

After much tidying and cross-checking I submitted my evidence to Leveson, suggesting limits on ownership and a tougher definition of who is a fit and proper person to own a chunk of our media – at least tight enough to disqualify the pornographer who owns the *Express*, *Star* and Channel 5. As for Murdoch, I propose a deal: allow him a bigger share of Sky (subject to its being placed on a similar regulatory footing as terrestrial TV) in return for relinquishing control of all his British titles. I have sent a copy to Ed Miliband.

Thursday 16 February

To Manchester, where I am to have a walk-on part in a new television version of *A Very British Coup*. Not that it bears much resemblance to the original. Even the title has changed (it is now called *Secret State*) and the credits say 'Inspired by...' rather than 'Based on...' This time round the Prime Minister is a one-nation Tory, played by Gabriel Byrne. The forces of darkness are represented by an American multinational and the usual suspects in the British Establishment. Director Ed Fraiman has kindly agreed that I may make a cameo appearance, *à la* Alfred Hitchcock. I thought he might reincarnate me as a backbench MP or even a minister, but instead I am to be the vicar conducting a memorial service for the dead Prime Minister.

Friday 17 February
Alderley Edge

In accordance with instructions, I am on parade sharp at 6.50 a.m. I find myself sharing a car with Charles Dance and Gina McKee. Gina, it transpires, is the daughter of a Durham miner, born in Easington, who for a time lived in one of the long streets in Hendon, about a mile from where I live. We are driven to a leafy part of Cheshire popular with Premier League footballers and delivered to a trailer encampment alongside a decaying walled garden on the AstraZeneca estate.

Each actor is allocated a dressing room. There is a pecking order. The biggest stars get the swishest trailers. I am sharing a small room with an actor who is playing a television political correspondent. Each door is labelled with the screen name of the occupant. Thus Gabriel Byrne's dressing room bears the name of the ill-fated Prime Minister, Tom Dawkins. Mine says simply 'Vicar'.

No sooner am I settled in than a young woman from the costume department appears and instructs me to don the vicar's uniform, hanging in the wardrobe. It is the full Monty: black suit, cassock, white surplice, purple stole, dog collar. Next she produces a bag of polished shoes and invites me to select a pair. Finally, I am supplied with a watch. All vicars wear watches, it seems. Then off to Makeup, where powder is liberally applied to prevent my bald head reflecting in the light.

All organised with military precision. We are each given a production schedule showing who is required where and at what precise time. At 8 a.m. we are bundled into vehicles and driven the half-mile to the fourteenth-century St Mary's Church, Nether Alderley, where we are to film the memorial service (there is no body, since the late Prime Minister has been killed in a suspicious plane crash over the Atlantic). A notice on the church noticeboard informs us that this is the constituency of Mr George Osborne, our beloved Chancellor of the Exchequer, who is, he says, at the disposal of all his constituents, regardless of how they voted. The nearby vicarage, a substantial early Victorian house, was once the home of Neil and Christine Hamilton until they met their nemeses in the shape of Messrs Mohamed Al Fayed and Martin Bell.

The scene that greets us at the church door is one of frenetic activity. Cameramen, sound men, riggers, production assistants – assembling, dismantling, re-assembling, adjusting. In addition to the lead actors there are twenty-eight placard-waving protesters, twenty mourners, ten uniformed policemen and an entourage of drivers and protection officers. Later, there will also be a twenty-strong choir. Somehow all these people have to be dressed, fed and watered, mobilised, organised and directed. Overseeing all this, the director and his assistants, meeting, greeting, cajoling, instructing. Everyone is cheerful and everyone has a function. No bawling, no tantrums, no prima donnas. In the entire twelve hours I did not hear anyone raise their voice in anger. We are a large, happy family.

We are shown into the green room, a seventeenth-century schoolhouse. The actors, all old hands, know each other by sight, if not by name. Charles Dance shakes hands with Lia Williams; her face rings a bell, but he can't quite place her. 'Have we worked together before?'

'Yes,' she replies. 'In Birmingham. I was your wife.' Today she is head of MI5. Charles is the Chief Whip.

Once the demonstrators have been filmed waving their placards and the political correspondent has done his piece to camera, it is my turn. I am to stand at the church gate and greet the mourners. When the grieving widow arrives, I am to take her hand and accompany her to the church door. Next to me stands Rupert Graves. He is a senior member of the government, but he is not sure which one. He buttonholes a passing production assistant. 'One question: am I the Chancellor or the Home Secretary?'

The scene is shot repeatedly, perhaps ten times, and from several different angles. Then we move to the church door where, this time, I am to greet Gabriel Byrne, the acting Prime Minister, who sweeps down the church path, accompanied by a posse of stony-faced protection officers and the head of MI5, with whom he is in a whispered, deeply serious, conversation. The party is preceded by a camera crew, walking backwards. When they reach me, the scrum miraculously parts, conversation ceases and Gabriel looks at me meaningfully. At this point I am to utter the first of my four humble sentences. 'Hello, Charles [the dead Prime Minister] always spoke highly of you.' To which Gabriel replies, 'Thank you, vicar,' and then he moves on into the church, still deep in conversation with the lady from MI5.

After four or five takes, I make so bold as to point out to the director that it is not very likely that a vicar, confronted by the acting Prime Minister, would simply say, 'Hello.' How about, 'Good morning, sir'? At first this meets with resistance, but eventually it is decided to shoot both versions. I wait with interest to see which, if any, survives.

The weather is suitably funereal. Dark cloud hangs heavily all day and from time to time there is a light drizzle. Underfoot it is muddy. My cassock was designed for a taller churchman than I, with the result that to walk anywhere I have (to use a suitably biblical expression) to gird my loins. Occasionally I forget and find myself entangled.

Nothing is left to chance. At the first speck of rain, someone with an umbrella appears and holds it over my head. From time to time a young woman sprays what remains of my hair with lacquer. Someone else brushes the mud from my cassock. And yet another person – from Continuity – snaps away at odd angles with a digital camera.

By afternoon we have progressed to the church. There is an encounter between Gabriel Byrne and his ex-wife (Sophie Ward) which has to be shot many times and then it is my turn again. I have to wait in the church porch until everyone is inside, count to ten and then make my way slowly down a side aisle to the front of the church, pausing to shake hands with a couple of mourners. I now find myself standing at the lectern, facing the congregation, directly opposite the grieving widow. The politicians are on the other side, Gabriel Byrne and Charles Dance at the front.

This is the point at which I have to spout my remaining three lines. A tricky moment. Although I have learned them by heart, I am in fear of drying up in front of the entire cast and crew, thereby destroying what promises to be a promising acting debut. Happily, however, the director slides the relevant page of the script on to the lectern in front of me. As a result I am able to deliver my lines with confidence – and without much more than a downward glance. All over in a single take. Amazing.

Everyone is kind about my performance, but later doubts begin to creep in. The hour was late and the director anxious to wind up. Perhaps he has already made up his mind to drop the scene but can't bring himself to tell me. I shall have to wait until autumn to find out if I have ended up on the cutting room floor.

Saturday 18 February

Breakfast with Charles Dance, who, contrary to his screen image, turns out to be surprisingly left-wing, and then home.

Wednesday 22 February
House of Commons

Wherever I wander I am waylaid by old friends. To walk from the Central Lobby for an appointment in Portcullis House I have to allow at least an extra fifteen minutes for conversations with former colleagues. Tony Lloyd was among those I came across today. He looked at me quizzically and said with a twinkle in his eye, 'Didn't you use to be Chris Mullin?' Thank you, Tony. If there is a fourth volume of diaries, that will be the title.

Wednesday 9 May

Came across Bob Ainsworth* and invited him to disclose the identity of the Cabinet minister who according to Bob failed, despite assurances, to join in Geoff Hoon's coup attempt against Gordon. He said that Hoon had been assured that Alistair Darling would join in, though whether directly by Alistair or by someone else was unclear. He added that Harriet and Jack were deeply involved. They went to see Gordon, who refused to budge, but they 'bottled it' and didn't go public.

Wednesday 18 July

To Durham Castle for lunch with the Queen. Well, a slight exaggeration. Myself and about 100 others, this being the north-east leg of her jubilee tour. She was at the next table. I owed my presence to my chairmanship of the regional lottery fund. I caught her staring at me during the national anthem and half-wondered whether someone had tipped her off that she has a walk-on part in my diaries, including an account of an incident which the *Mail on Sunday* had, much to my embarrassment, plastered over the front of its review section and which she won't have been too

---

* Former Labour Secretary of State for Defence. See entry for 27 January 2010, *Decline & Fall*, p. 416.

pleased about.* After she had gone, I poked my nose into the room where she and the Duke had rested briefly before lunch. Sure enough, there was the statutory half-empty glass of gin and Dubonnet. Afterwards several of us were taken up to the roof of the medieval hall, affording fine views over the green and the cathedral.

Tuesday 24 July

Christmas has come early. Rebekah Brooks, Andy Coulson and six other agents of Murdoch have been charged with conspiring to intercept communications. Brooks and her husband are already awaiting trial on charge of perverting the course of justice. This is shaping up very nicely. Surely the moment is coming when politicians will pluck up the courage to take on the tyrant rather than trying to ride the tiger. Who knows, given political will, we might even see him off the premises altogether.

Monday 20 August
Callaly

The bricklayer working on the retaining wall in our garden used to teach bricklaying at a further education college in Yorkshire. He remarked that the Education Maintenance Allowance, which the Tories have abolished, was one of the best things that ever happened. 'Most kids on the course had nothing. Their parents weren't interested.' Needless to say, the course collapsed as soon as the allowance was withdrawn.

Friday 21 September

Tory Chief Whip Andrew Mitchell has been involved in an altercation with a policeman at the entrance to Downing Street. Apparently he was on his bike and the police refused to open the main gate to let him out. According to today's *Sun*, he called them 'fucking plebs'. He admits swearing and has duly apologised but denies using the toxic word.

---

* A man convicted of murdering the Governor of Bermuda, Sir Richard Sharples, in 1973 was sentenced to death and he appealed to the Queen for mercy. A Privy Counsellor of my acquaintance was dispatched to the palace with the relevant paperwork. Needless to say, the advice was 'reject' and she duly signed away the culprit's life, remarking as she did so, 'Fancy appealing to me for mercy. Do you know he even shot the dog?'

Tuesday 16 October

Tabloid clamour for Andrew Mitchell's dismissal grows apace. The fingerprints of the Police Federation are all over it. Mysteriously (or perhaps not so mysteriously), a copy of the incident report in the Downing Street police logbook has found its way into the press. The row has been simmering for three weeks now and Andrew, who continues to deny that he used the toxic word, is under tremendous pressure. I have published a strongly worded op-ed piece in today's *Times* denouncing the Federation for the bullies they are and saying that they should not be allowed to reshuffle the government.

Friday 19 October

Andrew Mitchell has resigned.

Saturday 20 October

A disc containing a preview of *Secret State* arrives. I log in with trepidation. Am I still there? Sure enough, there are my fellow actors: Gabriel Byrne looking grave and prime ministerial. Charles Dance, Chief Whip, looking suitably sinister. Gina McKee, radiant as the whistle-blowing journalist. The plot races along. Soon we are at the memorial service and there I am in my vicar's gear. The camera lingers for all of five seconds. And that's it. Gone is my much-filmed walk to the door with the grieving widow. Gone, my brief exchange with the acting Prime Minister. Gone, my three precious sentences of dialogue praising the dead Prime Minister. Gone, too, the twenty-strong choir. So that's it. My acting career lasted all of five seconds. But who cares? It's a good film – and it's helped pay for my walled garden.

Tuesday 6 November

To Eton, where I gave my diary talk to the sixth form. I was royally treated. They laid on a dinner, gave me a conducted tour. I stayed with William Waldegrave, the provost. The local branch of Waterstones provided a bookstall. I was afraid that there would be few takers, but at the end of my talk one of the masters got up and said that the bursar had agreed that any purchases could be put on their parents' account, whereupon just about everyone bought a copy. Among those in the queue, a young Harmsworth who I assume will one day inherit the evil empire. Afterwards William and I sat up talking and he revealed that he was the genius who (while working in the Conservative Research Department) dreamed up the poll tax. That was news to me, although I do recall that Ken Baker was once asked whose idea it was and he replied, 'A very clever young man whose name I will give you in a sealed envelope, on condition that you do not open it for thirty years.' William also told me a touching story about a young Palestinian who had been granted a scholarship at Eton. His younger brother, asked what he thought of his brother going to study at a grand school in England replied, 'It means I can sleep on the bed, instead of on the floor.'

Wednesday 7 November

As I was leaving this morning, William introduced me to the chaplain, who turns out to be one of my Hull University contemporaries from the late '60s. He reckons, albeit without malice, that I stole his girlfriend. The young woman's name rang only the vaguest of bells.

Monday 12 November

I fear I am about to be monstered by the *Mail* for the crime of renting my London flat to my successor, Julie Elliott. For several days now a *Mail* journalist has been leaving messages on the answerphone, which I have been ignoring. His latest call contains a hint of menace: 'If I don't hear from you tonight, I will also call your wife on her mobile…' I would dearly like to respond with a short statement pointing out that, far from 'having bought the flat with help from the taxpayer' as the reporter alleges, I paid the entire capital cost. Since I am now a private citizen making no claims upon the taxpayer, why should it be anyone's business who I rent my flat to? I would love to point this out, but Julie – on the advice of the Labour Party press office – says that we should not respond so it seems we must lie back and take whatever the *Mail* dishes out.

Tuesday 13 November

To the headquarters of the Criminal Cases Review Commission in Birmingham at the invitation of the chairman, Richard Foster, where I addressed staff and commissioners. Afterwards I was entertained to lunch at the Hotel du Vin. I had been in two minds whether to go, since two years ago I was turned down (after an admittedly poor interview) for a job on the commission, an organisation that would not exist but for the efforts of myself and a handful of others, but I am glad I did. Several hundred convictions, including some historic miscarriages, have been quashed as a result of the commission's work, but progress is slow and there are tentative signs that the Court of Appeal is reverting to old habits. As for the job, it is just as well I was turned down. I could never have coped given everything else that is going on. Every cloud etc.

Thursday 15 November

To the Stadium of Light, where I presented the prizes at the Sandhill School prize-giving before an audience of parents who, I guess, consisted mainly of *Mail* and *Sun* readers. The deputy head introduced me with kind words about how I was a politician of integrity etc. etc. Even as he spoke, I sat there thinking that, a few days from now, most of these people are going to read in their newspapers that their saintly MP was really some sort of crook after all.

Sunday 18 November

Along with a former colleague, Christine McCafferty, I am the victim of a *Sun* 'exclusive' headed 'Ex-Labour MPs still get thousands on taxpayer'. The report begins, 'Two ex-Labour MPs are making a fortune from the taxpayer by renting their old homes to politicians.'

Wednesday 21 November

And today the *Mail* is at it, adding a bizarre twist of their own: 'Two Labour MPs who kept details of their taxpayer-funded homes secret for 'security reasons' are renting them from ex-politicians, it can be revealed today.' The report is accompanied by a long-lens photo of Julie Elliott, my successor, emerging from my flat in the Lycée, looking like an escaping criminal.

Thursday 29 November

Leveson reported today. He has performed a considerable public service by exposing the modus operandi of much of our free press, but his conclusions are disappointing. Nowhere in his 2,000 pages does he address the concentration of ownership, which he appears to consider outside his remit (which no doubt explains why I wasn't called, although extracts from my diaries were quoted at various witnesses, including Blair and Major). His principal recommendation is a new, independent regulator with powers to impose large fines and to direct the prominence of apologies. Whether anything will happen remains to be seen. My hunch is that as soon as the heat is off, they will revert to business as usual.

Monday 3 December

To a party in Broadcasting House to celebrate the sixty-fifth anniversary of *Any Questions*. I chatted to Rory Stewart, the refreshingly untypical Tory MP who has lived in both Afghanistan and Iraq. Afghanistan, he said, had been badly handled. The Taliban should have been invited to the Berlin Conference. How is he finding life on the Foreign Affairs Committee? 'Frustrating. None of the other members have ever lived abroad, a symbol of our declining influence in the world.'

Tuesday 4 December

To Church House Westminster for the Political Science Association Awards, one of which I presented. I was on a table with, among others, Jon Snow and Ben Bradshaw. Jon invited us to predict the outcome of the 2015 general election. Ben thought a Tory majority, which is really my view, although, not wanting to seem disloyal, I suggested another Lib–Lab coalition. Jon floated the possibility of a government of national unity on the grounds that the economy will be as bad as ever and that, for all the huffing and puffing, there is only about a 1 per cent difference between the parties on what is to be done. An intriguing idea, but given the antagonistic nature of British politics and the genuine class differences (Tory MPs for the most part inhabit a different planet from their Labour colleagues), I can't see it coming to pass, except in the direst emergency.

Wednesday 19 December

There appears to be more to Plebgate, as the Downing Street incident has become known, than meets the eye. Andrew Mitchell has managed to winkle the security tapes out of No. 10 and, contrary to police statements, there are no onlookers, shocked or otherwise, hovering at the gate. Also, Michael Crick of *Channel 4 News* has discovered that the man who wrote a letter to his MP claiming to have witnessed the incident was not only not there but is an off-duty member of the Diplomatic Protection Group, the very unit that guards Downing Street. Curiouser and curiouser.

CHAPTER FOUR

2013

Monday 14 January

This evening Radio 4 broadcast the documentary that Jane Ashley and I have been making on outsourcing. I have enjoyed making it and Jane is a pleasure to work with, but it proved a struggle to get the outsourced to talk since they are in fear of losing their already precarious livelihoods. The most iniquitous examples we came across were care workers, looking after the elderly and demented in Croydon. They had been earning about £11 an hour as council employees and, although their terms and conditions were supposed to transfer with them to the private sector, as soon as they were out of the door their new employer put pressure on them to accept a lump-sum payment in return for tearing up the old contract and being re-employed at about £7 an hour and on much worse terms. Most took the money and left. The handful who refused are in the process of being eased out. Result: work that was previously done by dedicated staff with years of experience is now being done by a workforce that increasingly consists of underpaid, demoralised foreigners. The turnover is high – you don't buy much loyalty for £7 an hour, especially in areas where living costs are high. We interviewed traffic wardens, a cleaner who worked for John Lewis and a care worker in Islington who looked after elderly people in their homes – all of whose jobs had been outsourced. All now working on markedly worse terms than when they had been directly employed. This is the brave new world we are building. Two classes of people living and working alongside each other – one with entitlement to sickness pay, holiday pay, redundancy pay and decent pensions; the other entitled to few, if any, of these benefits. All the great social gains of the twentieth century are at risk.

Tuesday 22 January

To Speaker's House, Westminster, where, courtesy of Mr Speaker Bercow, I gave my diary talk to an audience that consisted mainly of members and servants of both houses. It went down well, except when I referred jocularly to the great expenses meltdown, when an eerie silence befell the gathering.

Monday 28 January

To New Broadcasting House, the BBC's glitzy new palace in Portland Place, to take part in a discussion on George Orwell for *Start the Week*. Fellow guests included the Tory journalist Tim Montgomerie and the wonderful Joan Bakewell, both of whom had more interesting things to say than I. Like Alastair Campbell, Tim pressed me to start using Twitter, but I continue to resist on the grounds that life is too short and the chances of saying something foolish too great, as a number of my former colleagues in Parliament have discovered to their cost.*

Wednesday 6 February

This evening, to the IMAX cinema at Waterloo for the political book awards, where for much of the evening I found myself sitting next to Lord Ashcroft, who was helping to fund the event. Needless to say, he was perfectly charming. How disappointing that one's demons, encountered in real life, so rarely live up to their image. (Hopefully he thought the same of me).

Saturday 23 February–Thursday 28 February

Kempinski Hotel, Jordan. A vulgar, marble palace overlooking the Dead Sea. My room is large enough to accommodate at least two families of

---

* I eventually succumbed and joined Twitter in April 2015.

Syrian refugees. I have been brought here by an agency, funded by the Foreign Office, to take part in a conference on constituency work with MPs from Egypt, Jordan and Iraq, though whether the experience of an elected representative from the UK is of any relevance to the harsh realities of life in their countries is a matter for debate. The Iraqis are confined mainly to the Green Zone and can't go anywhere without bodyguards; even so, one of them described how a colleague was embraced by a constituent who then blew them both to pieces. The Egyptians are besieged by supplicants with years of accumulated grievances. Only the Jordanians have anything resembling a functioning Parliament and that is very weak. Nevertheless, I can't deny that it is pleasant dining al fresco each day in the sunshine, a welcome break from the mist and murk at home.

Friday 1 March–Sunday 3 March
Words by the Water Literary festival, Keswick

For the fourth year running I filled the Theatre by the Lake, this time talking about my novels. On Saturday I scrambled up Skiddaw, which rises just behind the hotel. Unfortunately the top was enveloped in mist, so there was no view. In the evening I interviewed Jack Straw, who has recently published his memoirs. A good book. The only quibble I have, which I didn't pursue, is his suggestion that he was somehow intimidated into voting for Tony Benn in 1981. That's not how I remember it at all. He actually rang me at home a week before the election to let me know that he would be voting for Tony, and that he thought he could bring one or two others over. He also put £50 on Tony to win. A rare example of Jack not being on the winning side when the music stopped. Never mind, I love him dearly. He was an excellent minister and he has always been generous to me.

Thursday 7 March

To breakfast with the chief of the armed forces, General Sir David Richards, and his wife, Caroline, at their apartment in Kensington Palace, another of the little fortified hamlets that house the nation's great and good. I owed my invitation to a chance remark I made about Afghanistan in an interview on the *Today* programme the other day. Caroline runs a charity which helps educate Afghan girls which she wanted to tell me about, though in fact our discussions ranged rather wider. Afterwards she led me down passages and courtyards unknown to the world outside, all with doors leading off to grace and favour apartments ('This one is Prince Harry's' and so on) and let me out of a little door in a wall into Kensington Park Gardens.

Later, to the Garrick Club for lunch with Bill Keegan.[*] While I awaited him, Peter Mandelson came in accompanied by Robert Harris. Peter was friendly, though he did complain mildly about disparaging references to him in my diaries. By way of mitigation, I pointed to the introduction to *Decline & Fall*, which suggests that his third visit to government, in the autumn of 2008, probably made the difference between mere defeat and meltdown.

Friday 15 March–Sunday 17 March

To Chagford on the edge of Dartmoor for a delightful little literary festival. My event, a full house, was in the local church. In the evening, in the village hall, there was a most entertaining performance by a band called Little Machine, who set classical poetry to music. On Sunday morning, Ruth Winstone[†] collected me and we drove to the Flete Estate in south Devon, parked the car outside Flete House and then walked several miles through the woods along the Erme estuary, pausing at Nepean's Cottage, which I and three other trainee journalists rented on a winter let forty years ago. The most beautiful place I have ever lived.

Wednesday 27 March
Sunderland

David Puttnam[‡] gave a talk at the university library. Thoughtful, charming and amusing as ever, but he did lose his audience at the point where he remarked that MPs needed to be paid 'properly'. I bent his ear on the subject afterwards, pointing out that although a salary of £66,000 a year may not seem much in the circles in which he moved, by Sunderland

---

[*] Senior economic commentator of *The Observer*.
[†] The editor of *A View from the Foothills*, *Decline & Fall* and *A Walk-On Part*.
[‡] Academy Award-winning film producer and a Labour peer.

standards it was considerable. He took this with his customary good grace and suggested we have dinner to discuss matters of mutual interest.

Monday 8 April

Margaret Thatcher has died, aged eighty-seven. Appropriately, she died in the Ritz, where she had been living for some time as a guest of the Barclay brothers, an unsavoury pair of tax avoiders who live on a rock in the Channel Isles. David Cameron cut short a foreign visit to lead the tributes: 'She didn't just lead our country. She saved our country.' A rather large claim, considering that many of the bills for the Thatcher decade are still coming in, not least the crisis caused by the sale of council housing. The demutualisation of the building societies didn't work out too well either. Ed Miliband issued a careful and far too wordy statement describing her ambiguously as 'a unique figure who reshaped our politics'. I dropped a note to *The Times* to see if they would take an op-ed piece on the view from Sunderland, but needless to say, they wouldn't.

Wednesday 17 April

Thatcher's funeral. A state occasion in all but name. The coffin, draped in a Union Jack and topped with white flowers, borne on a gun carriage along the Strand from St Clement Dane's to St Paul's, escorted by the Royal Horse Artillery and a military band. The Queen in attendance along with representatives of 170 countries. A huge Tory festival at public expense. Outrageous, considering what a divisive figure she was. Only made possible because, apparently, Gordon Brown, when in office, endorsed the arrangements. Yet another of his many misjudgements.

Saturday 27 April

Dinner at Blagdon at the invitation of Matt and Anya Ridley. Guests included Martin Rees (the Astronomer Royal), James Watson, who won a Nobel Prize for his work on DNA, and the novelist Ian McEwan. Also Peregrine Worsthorne, aged almost ninety and looking very sprightly and elegant, and his eccentric wife, Lucinda Lambton. I remarked to Ian McEwan how much I enjoyed literary festivals, but he replied that he avoids them because authors are exploited. It's true that, having for example filled the big tent at Edinburgh four years running (550 people paying £9 or £10 a head), I have occasionally wondered whether the modest fee is a fair share of the spoils, but, hey, I treat them as mini-breaks, a chance to stay in a hotel that I wouldn't otherwise be able to afford, look up old friends, visit a part of the country I wouldn't normally get to see. Professor Watson recounted that when he had been asked to the Cheltenham Festival he had presented the organisers with a long list of demands, including a five-figure fee, business class air tickets and a week's hotel accommodation for himself and his wife. The organisers had quibbled over the size of the fee, but he got most of what he wanted, which only goes to show there is an inside track for those who are seriously in demand. Seven hundred people attended my last event at Cheltenham, for which I was paid £150 (which took several months and one or two reminders to extract) and no travel expenses. I guess McEwan is right, but of course he is famous and can afford to say 'no'. We lesser mortals have to take our chances wherever they arise.

Tuesday 30 April

Dinner with David Puttnam at Olivio's, a Sardinian restaurant in Eccleston Street, near Victoria Station. He recounted a breakfast with Jonathan Powell at Claridge's in December 2000. Powell was straight off a plane from Washington, where he had been meeting the transition team of incoming President George Bush. According to David, almost Jonathan's first words were: 'They're fucking lunatics. Who knows what they'll get us into?'

Wednesday 15 May

Breakfast with former Labour Transport Secretary Steve Byers at Aubain in Hampstead. He thinks we are in with a chance of an outright win and talked of a plan (whose?) to surround Ed Miliband with heavyweights such as Alistair Darling, Alan Johnson and maybe even Miliband Sr in the run-up to the next election. Alistair would become shadow Chancellor. Steve says Ed Balls would be in no position to make a fuss six months before an election. All sounds very improbable to me and as for Ed Balls going quietly, I wouldn't count on it.

Monday 7 October

To the students' union at Durham University to oppose the motion 'This House believes that Baroness Thatcher was Britain's finest post-war Prime Minister'. After dinner at the County Hotel, we walked up to the union building to find it was packed to the rafters. Hundreds were turned away. David Howell (former Conservative Cabinet minister), Jackie Doyle-Price (a Conservative MP) and Charles Heslop (chairman of the National Conservative Convention) spoke for the proposition. Dave Hopper, Alan Cummings (secretary and chairman of the Durham Miners' Association respectively) and myself opposed. It soon became clear from Howell's speech that his heart wasn't entirely in it, despite (or perhaps because) he had served in Thatcher's Cabinet, so the goal was wide open. Even so, on a show of hands, the audience was more or less evenly divided. Extraordinary the interest Thatcher's name excites among a generation unborn when she reigned.

Saturday 26 October

To the Sage in Gateshead to record a session of *Private Passions*, a Radio 3 version of *Desert Island Discs*. I was initially reluctant on the grounds that, being Radio 3, they naturally favour high-brow classical music whereas the Stones and the Eagles are more to my taste. Nevertheless, with some help and encouragement from the producer, I managed to put together a list which shed a little light on my past without being entirely mislead-ing. Works included the Credo from Mozart's Great Mass in C (theme from the television version of *A Very British Coup*), a piece by a Tibetan singing nun, the Benedictus from the Parliament choir's version of the Coronation Mass, a beautiful piece of traditional Vietnamese music and the choir of Hillview Junior School (which included the famous Emma Mullin) singing a Zulu song, 'Aya Ngena'. Rounded off by the Rolling Stones, accompanied by the Bach choir, singing 'You Can't Always Get What You Want'. A most enjoyable outing.

Thursday 5 December

To Newcastle for the quarterly meeting of the regional Heritage Lottery Fund. HLF is a well-managed, efficient, delightful organisation, engaged in excellent work, but they do love meaningless hyperbole. Every other project is described as 'innovative' or 'iconic'. Every opportunity is described as 'exciting', 'amazing' or 'incredible'. One little goal I have set myself: to stamp out the use of such nonsense.

Friday 20 December

To a church in Harrow to take part in *Any Questions*. One has to make the most of such invitations since there won't be many more. The other guests were Michael Portillo, the former Radio 4 controller Mark Damazer and a businesswoman whose name I didn't catch. Portillo, as ever, was on excellent form. Charming, confident, amusing and frequently applauded. The rest of us were lacklustre. The only question to which my answer rang any bells was whether or not there should be a third runway at Heathrow. The others were for; I was against. So, it transpired, were most of the audience.

Tuesday 24 December

I have another op-ed piece in *The Times*, pointing out that, although it may have come as a surprise to the upper reaches of the Tory Party that the police appear to have misbehaved in the Mitchell case, it is no surprise to those of us with longer memories. The only new development – and I readily concede it is a remarkable one – is that they now appear to have targeted a Tory Cabinet minister.

CHAPTER FIVE

2014

Saturday 4 January
Callaly

Neighbours David Horne, Jonathan Clark, Tony Henfrey and I spent a couple of hours with dismembering and removing the huge beech tree that has come down in the burn. Ngoc brought us coffee and cake. There is something particularly satisfying about this sort of communal activity.

Tuesday 7 January

Dinner with Liz Forgan* and her partner Rex at a restaurant in Primrose Hill. Later we were joined by a friend of the Milibands who said that the rift between the brothers is unhealed. David, he said, should have run against Gordon in the summer of 2009 but bottled it. 'I tried to persuade him, but he said the votes weren't there.' What especially rankles with David is that when the European Foreign Minister's job arose, Ed allegedly encouraged him to rule himself out on the grounds that he would be needed to lead the party after the election. Like Blair aide Anji Hunter, he suspects that Ed may have been pressed by Gordon to run against his brother. Ed, he says, is in terror of GB. One can easily imagine Gordon ringing him night after night and saying, 'You fucking run.' He added that Ed may make a better leader than David on the grounds that he is braver.

---

* A former senior executive of Channel 4 and BBC Radio; chair of the Scott Trust (which owns *The Guardian*) 2003–16; one of my closest friends.

Wednesday 8 January

A coffee with Steve Byers, who says that in the run-up to The Man's departure he was desperately doing the numbers to see if someone credible could be persuaded to run against Gordon. The number of MP nominations needed to trigger a contest was forty-two. About seventy said they would vote for someone other than Brown. John Reid was the clear leader with about thirty-four supporters, but no one would switch. So that was that.

Tuesday 4 February

To Notting Hill to see Tony Benn, bearded, increasingly frail but still generally compos mentis. He has virtually 24-hour care these days. We chortled over a recent YouGov poll which suggested that he was the eighteenth most popular person in the country, ahead of Kate Middleton but behind Nigel Farage. One slight sign of confusion. He appeared to think he still has a room in the House of Commons. 'I still go in every day,' he said. 'Well, not quite every day, but when I feel well enough.'

Later he said, 'My life has been a failure.' I did my best to assure him that this was not so. He had been a successful minister and his nine volumes of diaries had helped illuminate the age in which we live. Above all he had inspired a generation of idealistic young people. But of course, compared to what might have been, he is right.

Friday 14 February

Unsolicited I have received bids from three newspapers – the *Sunday Times*, *Daily Telegraph* and the *Mail on Sunday* – for a piece about Tony Benn to be run after his demise. Gratified though I am, I would prefer to write something for *The Guardian* since it is more likely to be read by sympathisers. I dropped a note to the editor of G2 and he replied at once to say that he was 'definitely interested' but he would need to check with other departments.

Monday 17 February
St Bede's Terrace, Sunderland

Out at 7.30 to bear witness to the collection of our bins. I am making a programme about waste for Radio 4. Producer Jonathan Brunert and I spent the rest of the day tracking what becomes of Sunderland's waste. Tomorrow we are visiting the new state-of-the-art heat-from-waste plant on Teesside.

Thursday 20 February

A call from *The Guardian* confirming their interest in a piece on Tony Benn. I replied that before I turned down the other bids, and in view of past calamities, I wanted an email containing the word 'guarantee'. By return I received an email which read as follows: 'As discussed we guarantee that we will run your piece in G2 or on the Saturday features pages.'

Tuesday 25 February

Lunch with Ruth Winstone at Carluccio's on St Pancras Station and then to Charing Cross Hospital to see Tony Benn. Tranquil, bearded, fed through a tube in his stomach. Still all there, but it can only be a matter of days. Not much chance to talk because Melissa and Stephen were there and later we were joined by his brother David, also frail. The hospital allows the dying to do pretty much as they want. Stephen decided that Tony should be allowed a last puff on his pipe, so we wheeled him down several floors and out on to a terrace where, propped on pillows, Tony tried to draw on his pipe. The trouble was that a light breeze made the pipe difficult to light and he didn't have the strength to suck on it. Eventually we wheeled Tony back upstairs and I took my leave. I would have liked to have thanked him for our long friendship and to have told him he will never be forgotten, but with so many people around there was no space for intimacy. As I left his eyes followed me to the door and he smiled. I doubt I shall see him again.

Friday 28 February
Meckelen, Flanders

The Belgians, particularly the Flemish, take waste recycling much more seriously than we do. Their general waste bins are microchipped so citizens can be charged according to how much they throw away. There is even talk about mining old landfill sites for recyclable waste. This morning we visited a huge factory, the only one of its kind in the world, which extracts valuable minerals from discarded computers and mobile phones. At one end, a mountain of redundant IT equipment; at the other, bars of gold, silver, platinum etc. This, surely, is the future. We just can't keep chucking this stuff into holes in the ground.

Tuesday 4 March

To a posh hotel in St James's to help judge the Political Book Awards. Afterwards I chatted to Iain Dale, the amiable Tory who runs Biteback Publishing and is close to Lord Ashcroft. To my amazement, he asserted with great confidence that Labour would have an overall majority at the next election, in part because many Lib Dem voters will switch to Labour. Apparently Ashcroft's polling shows Labour much further ahead in marginal seats than they are overall. Also, Iain reckons that the Tories' failure to push through another round of boundary changes (which were blocked by the Lib Dems) is fatal to their chances. An hour later I was sitting in the Family Room in the Commons when a Tory MP whose name escapes me came in and started a conversation on exactly the same lines. Many Tories, it seems, loathe Cameron because of his failure to lead them to outright victory against a leader as apparently vulnerable as Gordon. Personally, I am sceptical. In my view an economic miracle will be declared in time for the election and that, combined with a compliant media, is bound to improve their chances, even if it doesn't lead to an overall majority.

I am reading John Campbell's excellent biography of Roy Jenkins, which I am reviewing for *The Observer*.[*] It has taken me a long while to realise what a substantial figure he was. The best Home Secretary of the twentieth century. One of the most successful Chancellors. President of the European Union. Author of several bestselling political biographies. And yet throughout his life he found time for leisurely lunches and affairs with at least two women. To cap all, he had a good death. Jennifer, his wife, asked what he wanted for breakfast. 'Two eggs, lightly poached,' was the reply and when she came back with them, he had gone. On the

---

[*] *Roy Jenkins: A Well-Rounded Life*, Cape, 2014.

downside he was one of the founders of the SDP, which arguably helped keep Thatcher in power for a decade. But there again it was arguably the existence of the SDP that gave rise to New Labour. So indirectly he also played an important role in shaping the politics of the late twentieth century.

Thursday 13 March

At the quarterly meeting of the regional HLF committee someone remarked that No. 10 was taking a close interest in appointments to the national board. There appears to be some sort of unit in Downing Street which is scrutinising all national-level public appointments, presumably with a view to inserting Tories. It has already caused major rows in other areas of public life. The result, so far as HLF is concerned, is long delays in getting appointments approved and on one occasion a job had to be re-advertised (despite 200 applicants) because the government changed the criteria. My source added, 'Some of the recent appointees don't appear to know much about heritage, although that doesn't stop them having strong opinions.' Jenny Abramsky's term as chair expires in the summer. Everyone is waiting with trepidation to see who will replace her.*

Friday 14 March

Awoke to the news that Tony Benn is dead. I rang the *Today* programme to offer my services and they asked me to come on at ten past eight. Within half an hour, however, their plans changed and they wanted me to take part in a discussion at 8.45 a.m. I declined since I had to take Emma to work and in the end they opted for Diane Abbott, who didn't really know him. She was on the bulletins for the rest of the day, saying among other things how well read he was, which is nonsense. He rarely read a book, although he occasionally dipped into one in search of evidence to support of views he already held. Later a call from the editor of the G2 section of *The Guardian* to say that, despite his earlier cast-iron assurances, he could not after all use my tribute to Tony because the editor had

---

* It was Peter Luff, a serving Tory MP. I was sceptical at first, although he turned out to be a good appointment.

decreed that next week's G2 should be handed over to 'The Youth'. Why am I not surprised?

Saturday 15 March

The *Telegraph* ran my piece about Benn the diarist across the best part of two pages and *The Guardian*'s website, no substitute for the paper, published the piece I had written for G2.

Thursday 27 March

Tony Benn's funeral. To the dismay of some, though not I, Mr Speaker Bercow had allowed the coffin to rest in the undercroft overnight, so the procession set off from Westminster Hall. Ruth Winstone and I walked with the family behind the coffin. People, some carrying banners reflecting causes he had supported, lined the street from the Members' entrance to the door of St Margaret's. Around the church the crowd was ten deep. The coffin, topped by red roses, was carried in by his sons and grandsons. Inside there were 800 people and the service was relayed to those outside, triggering the occasional ripple of applause. Mourners included Cherie Blair, Alastair Campbell, Jack Straw, the two Eds – Balls and Miliband – and, of course, Mr Speaker Bercow and his troublesome wife, Sally. Michael Heseltine was the only senior Tory on parade, although Cameron published a little tribute. Also present Gerry Adams, Martin McGuinness and a gaggle of glamorous women who befriended him in his later years – BBC newscaster Natasha Kaplinsky and actors Saffron Burrows and Maxine Peake. Moving, humorous speeches from Hilary and Melissa; Stephen played a madrigal and Joshua read a lesson. Outside I chatted briefly to Ed Miliband, who didn't seem all that pleased to see me.

Saturday 10 May

To Oxford for Sarah's graduation. This morning I took a stroll around as many of the college gardens as I could bluff my way into, emerging from Trinity onto Broad Street to see a man who bore a startling resemblance to Bill Clinton striding alone down the middle of the road. He took a moment or two to register. It was only when I noticed the secret service agents, keeping well clear but deployed discreetly around him, that the penny dropped. I followed him to the Sheldonian, where Hillary was waiting. Later, I heard that Chelsea Clinton is receiving her doctorate today – same place, same day as the famous Sarah Mullin.

Saturday 17 May

Out of the blue a telephone call from David Benn, Tony's younger brother and the last surviving member of his immediate family. Ostensibly it was to say that I shouldn't give up on politics since, along with Martin Bell, I am (in his opinion) a credit to the profession. In passing he remarked that their mother disapproved of much of what he did, in particular shortening his surname. He added that challenging Neil Kinnock for the leadership was a big mistake. 'It damaged his relationship with the parliamentary party and he never recovered. We told him so at the time, but he didn't listen. He always did his own thing.'

Sunday 18 May

Off early with Emma for a flight to Rome, courtesy of Flybe. Forty-five years since I was last this way, driving the old Ford van that I bought in Hull for £80. We are staying in a crowded apartment near the Lateran which an enterprising Hungarian and his Moldovan wife have turned into a hostel for backpackers.

Monday 19 May

We passed the day visiting the Lateran Basilica, the Forum, the Colosseum, Pantheon and Palatine Hill. One can't walk round the Forum without wondering if, a thousand years from now, future generations of tourists will pick their way through the ruins of our civilisation as we now do through those of Rome and Greece. 'This is where the chamber of the House of Commons is believed to have been.' 'These are thought to have been the site of the royal apartments in Buckingham Palace.' 'This is believed to have been the site of the Olympic Stadium…' And so on.

Changes since I was last here: an improvement in the quality of the driving (hardly anyone uses the horn these days) and little or no harassment of young women, a sport for which the Italian male was once notorious. And around tourist hotspots desperate youths from west Africa and south Asia selling sunglasses, umbrellas or useless knick-knacks. We sat and watched them plying their wares outside the Colosseum while we munched our sandwiches. In twenty minutes we didn't witness a single successful sale. I feel so sorry for them. What are they doing here? Italy has no historic relationship with the Congo or Bangladesh. Obviously they are the victims of some great people-smuggling racket, lured here under false pretences, having been sold a dream that has turned to ashes. And there is no way back. They have spent their life savings and perhaps that of their families to get here; many will be in debt for years to come to the racketeers who brought them here. And for what?

Tuesday 20 May

Someone tried to pick my back pocket as I was going through the turnstile at the San Giovanni Metro. I shouted and he quickly withdrew his hand. '*Prego, prego, prego*,' he said, as if it were some kind of misunderstanding. Most of the pickpockets in Rome are alleged to be Romanians, but so far as I could tell this one was Italian. He was with a young woman. I noticed them loitering when we were looking at a map.

Today the Spanish Steps, the Villa Medici and a stroll in the Borghese park. Then to dinner with cousin Margaret in her seventh-floor apartment in the south of the city. Margaret has lived here since the '60s and is for all practical purposes a Roman. Indeed, her parking skills exceed even those of most Romans. No sooner was dinner, a memorable lasagne followed by tiramisu, over than my kidney stone began to reassert itself with a vengeance. I have had the occasional twinge in recent months, but this was something else. Nothing for it but to throw myself on the mercy of the Italian medical service. Margaret duly delivered us to the A&E department of a hospital just behind the Lateran, where, after a wait of two hours and various tests, a young doctor administered an injection and sent me away with a prescription for painkillers of varying intensity.

Wednesday 21 May

To St Peter's Square for the Pope's general audience. The route between the Metro and the Vatican was lined with Bangladeshis selling white and yellow paper flags and Africans selling fake designer handbags. Cousin Margaret had obtained tickets. Ours were numbered in the 17,000s, so we knew there would be a lot of people, but when we got there the tickets were of no relevance. The square was already full. The best part of 100,000 people – a rock concert. A monsignor on the steps leading up to the basilica was reading out the names and nationalities of the various pilgrim groups present and after each one a little cheer would go up from one or other part of the vast crowd. This went on for more than an hour. Huge screens around the square were running footage of a previous audience, which at some point morphed into live coverage of today's event. Suddenly, there was a distant figure in white being driven back and forth through the crowd, occasionally pausing to touch outstretched hands. When eventually he reached the podium, he read out a homily in Italian, occasionally departing from his text to elaborate with hand gestures. Then the priests and bishops congregated around the papal chair took turns to step forward and read out summaries in half a dozen languages. Finally, a queue formed of those who were to be presented, by which time the crowd was beginning to disperse. All this took place miles away from where we were standing, but it was an interesting experience. By the time it was over my kidney stone was giving me pain again, so we went in search of a doctor willing to administer another injection.

Thursday 22 May

By about 4 a.m. the pain was becoming unbearable, so I got up and tiptoed out of the apartment and walked about a mile to the A&E department at the hospital, at this time more or less deserted, where I persuaded a surly nurse on duty to administer another injection. I had come out without the keys, so when I got back to the apartment I had to hang around on the pavement outside for an hour until someone came out. Cousin Margaret thinks I should go home, but I am determined not to let this ruin our holiday. Besides, there isn't a plane back to Newcastle until Sunday.

Today we visited the Vatican, having been advised in advance to pay €30 for a 'skip the line tour'. Even so, it was like Waterloo at rush hour. Led by a competent young woman called Serena, holding up an umbrella and pausing at intervals to count heads, we were herded through frescoed galleries and loggia crammed with ancient statues and sarcophagi, through the Gallery of Maps to the Cappella Sistina, where, amid wall-to-wall crowds, we were permitted ten minutes to gaze upon Michelangelo's masterpiece, all the while being urged to keep moving by smart young men in suits. Finally, we were delivered into the great basilica, where we were left to our own devices.

Friday 23 May

Margaret drove us to Tivoli, where we inspected the remains of Hadrian's vast villa and passed a pleasant afternoon in the gardens of the Villa D'Este. By the time we were done, however, I was practically crying with pain. We purchased syringes and painkillers and the pharmacist found us a doctor who administered the injection. 'How much do I owe you?' I asked. He just smiled and shook my hand. I could have kissed him.

This evening, wandering near the Termini, we came across the Basilica di Santa Maria Maggiore, more or less deserted, and there lying prone in a glass coffin, his thin waxed face tilted slightly towards onlookers, dressed in scarlet and white pontifical robes, the remains of Pius V, the Pope who excommunicated Elizabeth I. You can stand within a metre of him. How spooky is that?

Last day of campaigning for the European elections, which are taken seriously here. We arrived back at our lodging to find the Italian populist Beppe Grillo ranting away in front of a large crowd on a platform in front of the Lateran Basilica. Lord help the Italians if he ever gets to power.

Saturday 24 May

Awoken early by the pain, I persuaded the young man on night shift at reception to administer my injection, which he gamely did, even though he had never done such a thing before. Later, Emma and I caught the train to Castel Gandolfo, the town overlooking Lake Albano which houses the Pope's summer residence. After nosing around the backstreets, we spent most of the afternoon seated outside a cafe in the square outside the papal villa, watching a wedding in the church opposite.

Sunday 25 May

Emma, ever solicitous for my welfare, saw me off at the Termini on the train to Fiumicino Airport and I flew home. At the other end Ngoc drove me straight to the RVI in Newcastle, from which I was transferred by ambulance to the urology ward at the Freeman. I am to be operated on tomorrow.

Monday 26 May

Awoke with tubes hanging out of me, one of them a catheter full of urine and blood. The stone has been removed, thank goodness. That's the good news. The bad news is I have a much larger stone in my left kidney which will require another operation in a month or two. Also, the surgeon has left a plastic stent inside me, designed to make it easier to pee.

Tuesday 27 May

Mr Dorkin the surgeon signed me off and Ngoc came to collect me. As I was leaving, the ward sister handed me a lot of painkillers. 'I won't need those,' I said. 'I think you will,' she replied.

Thursday 12 June

Ed Miliband has allowed himself to be photographed posing with a copy of *The Sun*, triggering a great new wave of derision. Evidence were any needed that one can be clever and stupid simultaneously. A conclusion I reached years ago from close study of Appeal Court judges.

Wednesday 18 June

Emma's nineteenth birthday. We took Bruce, our bedraggled old cat, to the vet in Rothbury for her annual trim and various tests to try to establish what is wrong with her. Much of her hair was shaved off to get rid of the awful matting. She emerged looking a very sad cat. It will be a long time before she recovers.

Saturday 21 June–Sunday 22 June

To Petworth in West Sussex to take part in a festival of garden literature. A touch apprehensive, since I know rather less about gardening than many of those in attendance. The event takes place in the fourteen acres of exquisite private gardens attached to Petworth House. In the evening the owners, Max and Caroline Egremont, entertained us to dinner in the famous Grinling Gibbons Carved Room, adorned with Turner landscapes. Unfortunately, the stent has rendered me practically incontinent and I had to keep dashing out to the loo, which in Petworth House is a long way from the dining room. I tiptoed past fellow guests and, as soon as I was out of sight, ran for it, often arriving with seconds to spare. For much of the weekend, I had to keep disappearing into the shrubbery around the wild garden. I had feared I wouldn't get through my talk, but mercifully there was no accident.

The talk, entitled 'My Walled Garden in Northumberland', went well enough. For the first time I used PowerPoint and when the before and after shots flashed up there was a spontaneous round of applause. Afterwards I was approached by a woman who said, 'I am your new neighbour', which, in a manner of speaking, turned out to be true. She and her husband or partner have just bought Lorbottle Hall, a large, secluded house a mile and a half up the road from Callaly. She invited Ngoc and I to dinner in August adding, 'You will find my other half a bit right-wing.'

Tuesday 24 June

The phone-hacking trial ended today. Rebekah Brooks and her husband have been acquitted of all charges, but Andy Coulson and half a dozen other News International employees have been convicted and can expect to go down. A disappointing outcome, but one that leaves Parliament with a strong enough case for diversifying media ownership – if only they had the guts.

Tuesday 1 July

To Fallodon, once home to the First World War Foreign Secretary Edward Grey, now occupied by a young family called the Bridgemans.

By invitation only. Most of the great and good of Northumberland were there. We sat in Edward Grey's drawing room listening to a talk by Michael Waterhouse, who has written a new biography.* An amusing moment when Waterhouse remarked that the Liberal Party was now more or less extinct in this part of the world and Alan Beith MP, who was sat at the back, piped up, 'We're still here.' For all that he was born into one of the great families of the north, Grey's life was a sad one, overwhelmed by his failure to prevent the outbreak of war. His two brothers died tragically young, both his wives predeceased him, his house burned down (and so did a cottage he owned in Hampshire) and for his last decade or more he was almost blind. His ashes and those of his first wife are scattered in the wood at the end of the garden 'beneath the trees they planted together'. A nice touch, that.

Friday 4 July

To Wansbeck Hospital, where a pleasant young woman plugged me into some sort of computer and stuck rubber monitors all over my torso. All this arising from a claim by the medics at the Freeman Hospital, where I had my kidney stone removed two months ago, to have detected 'a slight abnormality' with the muscles surrounding my heart. I am now well and truly in the clutches of the NHS.

Saturday 5 July

Together with my neighbours David Horne and Tony Henfrey, I spent the morning helping to dismember the huge chestnut tree, half of which has fallen across the path at the end of the third lake. Later, a visit from the lady who runs the National Garden Scheme in Northumberland, who wants to include our garden on her list of local open days. I am sympathetic though sceptical that it is significant enough to be of much interest and, in any case, I know Ngoc won't approve, which is why I arranged for her to call when Ngoc was in London.

---

* *Edwardian Requiem: A Life of Sir Edward Grey*, Biteback, 2013.

Saturday 12 July

Dinner at Chillingham Castle with Sir Humphry Wakefield and about twenty other guests. Flaming torches at the entrance and in the court-yard. As usual I was just about the only one who didn't live in a stately home or a castle. At around midnight, as Humphry was showing me out, we came across a party of ghost watchers and he said wistfully, 'In twenty years from now, I will be one of the ghosts.'

Tuesday 15 July

To St Luke's, a beautifully restored Hawksmoor church in Old Street, Islington, now the HQ of the London Symphony Orchestra, for a confer-ence on heritage organised by HLF. A chat with former MP and minister David Heathcoat-Amory, who has recently joined the board. David, a strong Eurosceptic, believes the EU should be about trade and nothing else. I put it to him that the likely outcome of the promised referendum was victory for the status quo. 'Yes,' he said, 'but we need to scare the Europeans into making serious concessions.'

Later, a drink on the House of Commons terrace. All I had to do was plant myself in a seat and people queued for an audience. John Denham, one of those I chatted with, was surprisingly upbeat about Labour's chanc-es, despite the improving economy. He says that the party's private polls agree with Lord Ashcroft: we remain well ahead in the marginals and on track for an overall majority. Not everyone was quite so happy. One of the brightest women in the class of 2010 remarked, 'There is a very small clique around Ed and it is getting smaller. I don't know what we stand for. On the doorstep people say, "What use are you?" and we have no answer.' She added, 'And what if we did win, what then? There is no plan.'

Tuesday 22 July

To the GP's surgery in Rothbury to discuss the outcome of the cardio-gram, which has confirmed the alleged 'slight abnormality' with my heart muscles. 'Do you need help with the stairs?' enquired the receptionist. To which I replied, 'Not for another twenty years, I hope.'

Thursday 31 July

Opened the new Back on the Map community centre in Sunderland in what was, until recently, the Hendon public library. A nice occasion. I do like opening things. Everyone is so pleased to see you.

Sunday 10 August

Our annual garden party. Twenty friends and neighbours. Ngoc has prepared a magnificent spread. All week we have been watching the weather forecast, hoping against hope that the predicted rain would not arrive on time. We awoke to sunshine, but the rain came just as the guests were arriving. A handful of brave souls sat outside under our new tented gazebo, but most crammed into the living room. In the event it went well, although Humphry Wakefield unnerved Emma by challenging her to name the years in which Chaucer and Shakespeare were born – a test she inevitably failed.

Thursday 21 August–Saturday 23 August

Andrew and Sharon Mitchell are staying. The so-called Plebgate incident still haunts them. Andrew says they have not had a proper night's sleep for nearly two years. He would have gone back into the Cabinet but for a libel action brought against him by one of the policemen involved. Several officers involved have been sacked, nine disciplined and one is in jail. The one who is suing is the only one against whom nothing is proven. The policeman's costs are indemnified by the Federation and so he has nothing to lose. Andrew is also suing *The Sun*, a high-risk strategy if ever there was one. He faces enormous costs if he loses. Even if he wins, he will be out of pocket.

Sunday 24 August

Dinner with Kate Donaghy at Lorbottle Hall, the setting sun illuminating the crags on the hill behind the house. She regaled us with a tale about how, a fortnight ago, two joiners repairing a window in what was once the nursery heard a child's voice, followed by a woman sobbing. It seems that many years ago a child fell out of the window and died. The joiners fled and have not been seen since.* According to Kate, her dog, a black Labrador, recently went doo-lally after apparently detecting something in the cellar.

Tuesday 26 August

A glorious day. Ngoc and I took a picnic and walked through the dunes to Ross Sands, the best beach in Northumberland and one which few people know about. We strolled three miles north until we reached the channel between the mainland and Holy Island and ate our sandwiches perched on a log with fine views toward Lindisfarne Castle.

Wednesday 27 August

This wretched stent is driving me demented. Over the past few weeks I have been reduced to peeing in discreet corners of supermarket car parks, in tubs of flowers on Alnmouth Station and in an alleyway off the main street in Rothbury. Sometimes as much as five times an hour. Sooner or later there will be an embarrassing accident.

Thursday 28 August

A letter from the hospital to say that a CT scan in May has discovered a 4mm nodule on my right lung base. Nothing to worry about, they say, but they recommend another scan in twelve months. Oh dear. Kidney, heart, lungs, where will it end? As someone remarked the other day, 'Once past the age of sixty-five you are in Sniper's Alley. You can be picked off from any angle when you least expect it.'

Friday 29 August

A Tory MP, Douglas Carswell, has defected to UKIP and is resigning to fight a by-election. This can only be good for us. Europe haunts the Tories. However hard Cameron tries, he just can't shake it off.

The first sign of aubergines in the glasshouse. Two so far, but many

---

* They later returned.

more in bud. We already have a bumper crop of tomatoes, half a dozen melons and a good supply of cucumbers.

After a week of autumnal weather, the leaves are beginning to turn on the beech trees. Everything has been early this year.

Sunday 31 August

Ngoc, Emma and I lunched with John Field at Callaly Mill. A contented man who lives in splendid isolation with his books and two cats for company. We took him a basket of vegetables from the garden – tomatoes, courgettes, pink fir apple potatoes and a cucumber. He was for thirty years a teacher of English literature at Westminster School, where his pupils included Nick Clegg and Dominic Grieve. I tried out Humphry's test on him. 'In what years were Chaucer and Shakespeare born?'

Quick as a flash, he replied, '1343 and 1564.'

Monday 1 September

Up at 5 a.m. for the drive to the Freeman for the removal of the stone in my left kidney. This one is too big to remove by keyhole surgery, so the surgeon, Mr Dorkin, is to make an incision in my back. I came round some time in the afternoon feeling nauseous and spent the rest of the day comatose. Apparently, X-rays revealed another stone in my right kidney and two in the left, so he removed those, too. He has also inserted two new stents, so I face several more weeks of incontinence.

Tuesday 2 September

Ward Three, Freeman Hospital, Newcastle

Constipated, drowsy and peeing blood, but well enough to sit up, I spent the day reading the new volume of Alan Johnson's memoir, *Please Mr Postman*, the follow-up to *This Boy*, which has been a huge success. Good, but inevitably not quite as compelling as his earlier volume. Full of little pen portraits of those he worked with as a postman, first in Barnes, then in Slough and finally as a member of the union executive. What's striking is how well read many of them seem to be. One or two capable of reciting large chunks of poetry and even Shakespeare. This, of course, was the post-war generation, who grew up before the era of social media and junk TV. I doubt we shall see their like again. Of my half-dozen hospital companions, all friendly working-class men in their fifties or older, only one brought a book in with him. The others just lie staring into space.

Wednesday 3 September

Mr Dorkin decreed that I can go home. The syringe was taken out of my left hand. Ngoc collected me and within a couple of hours I was sitting in the garden at Callaly. I'm not quite out of the woods yet, however. Still peeing blood and in two weeks I have to return to the hospital to have the stents removed. Plus visits to a cardiologist to discuss the alleged abnormality in my heart muscles. After so many years of good health, I am now deep in Sniper's Alley.

Thursday 4 September

After a brief absence, summer is back. Warm sunshine, a cloudless sky. We lunched on the terrace in front of the glasshouse, the urology ward of the Freeman but a distant memory. I spent the afternoon in the garden reading Dennis Skinner's much-delayed autobiography, which has just arrived. Mainly a tale of his greatest triumphs. His wife of thirty years receives scarcely a mention. Without doubt Dennis is a remarkable figure and his is a life that certainly ought to be recorded, but he suffers from a crippling ego which intrudes on just about every page. 'I' this, 'I' that. Also, one can't help wondering whether Labour would ever have seen the inside of government if all policy decisions had been taken on the basis that what is good for Clay Cross is good for the rest of us.

Islamist terrorists have decapitated another American hostage. They announced the news in another gruesome video fronted by the same masked jihadi who featured in the previous one. A British citizen is said to be next in line. Unimaginable, the terror of knowing you will be next.

Monday 8 September

Sunshine. We drove to College Valley and did a little circular walk up one side of the burn and back along the other, eating our picnic by the babbling brook. Although I have been nominally retired for more than four years, I still can't get used to the idea that I don't have to work every day or that I can read a book that I have not been asked to review, work in the garden or simply chill out. Rarely a day goes by without my plugging away at something.

Tuesday 9 September

An email from my old friend Charles Baker-Cresswell: 'Have the poor Scots gone quite mad – or is it just that the popular press wants any sensation that will sell their products?' This in response to the news that, for the first time, an opinion poll has indicated that the 'Yes' campaign is leading in the Scottish referendum. One consequence has been the re-emergence of our late unlamented leader, Gordon Brown, offering maximum devolution in return for a 'No' vote. A desperate attempt to avert Armageddon. If it works, Gordon will be reborn as the Saviour of the Nation.

Wednesday 10 September

John Major was on the radio this morning, discussing Scotland. He set out the case against independence with beautiful clarity. More lucid than any of our current leaders. A much more substantial figure than he was ever given credit for.

Thursday 11 September

With Emma to the Vale of Lorton to stay with Alf and Ann Dubs. We arrived to find that Alf, aged eighty-one, who is indefatigable, had gone to Glasgow for the day to campaign for a 'No' vote in the referendum. Emma and I went for a three-mile warm-up and were chased by a herd of bullocks. Scary.

Saturday 13 September

With Alf we walked from High Lorton to Buttermere via Ladyside Pike (703m), Hopegill Head (770m), and Whiteless Pike (660m). I was worried that I might not be up to it in view of recent health problems, but I managed to keep up. Descent was much harder than ascent and we arrived worn out, except for Emma, who was streets ahead, but rather than disappearing over the horizon she kindly waited at intervals for the elderly folk to catch up. Alf is in remarkable shape for a man of his years. This evening, over dinner at the Pheasant Inn at Bassenthwaite, we discussed the dilemmas to which a vote in favour of Scottish independence would give rise. Does a majority of a few hundred or even a few thousand justify smashing the union of 300 years? Apparently, yes. Ought Parliament to have required a minimum threshold – say 55 per cent – before permitting a constitutional change of this magnitude? Perhaps, but it's too late now. And what if next May's general election, which will take place before the change comes into effect, returns a Labour government dependent on Scottish MPs? We agreed that the only honourable course for Ed Miliband would be to take office until the separation and then to call another election. Finally, supposing the next election to the Scottish Parliament (due in 2016) returned a Labour majority who refused to implement the result of the referendum? Imagine the fallout.

Monday 15 September

To the clinic at Alnwick to see the cardiologist. A further ECG confirms that my heart has a minor abnormality. I am assured it is nothing to worry about for the moment, but in the longer term who knows?

The fate of Scotland dominates the bulletins. Although the Noes are now said to have a slight edge, all the polls seem agreed that it is too close to call. One suspects that, as usual, the media are hamming it up for the fun of it, but one can't be sure. The political leaders have spent the past two days trying to impress on the Scots that this is not an opportunity for a protest vote that can be reversed if it doesn't work out, as they have been led to believe. This is for ever. But is anybody listening?

Wednesday 17 September

To the outpatient department at the Freeman to have my stents removed. Excruciating, but so glad it's all over.

Thursday 18 September

The Scottish referendum. An ominous grey mist hung over our valley, and indeed the entire east coast, all day. The polls are predicting a narrow victory for the Noes, but that won't be the end of the matter. Recent weeks have seen much pandering by the Westminster Establishment and they will now have to deliver. In particular, the leaders of all three parties, on no one's authority but their own, have promised to maintain indefinitely the iniquitous Barnett formula, which awards the Scots a disproportionate share of public spending while allowing them simultaneously to complain that they are the victims of discrimination. Joel Barnett himself was on the radio the other night saying it high time his formula, which was only ever intended to be a short-term measure, was scrapped.

Friday 19 September

Awoke to the news that the Scots have rejected independence by a wider margin than the polls predicted. Cameron, never one to waste a crisis, immediately announced that he will be proceeding post-haste to devolve greater powers to Scotland while at the same time limiting the role of Scots (and maybe Welsh MPs) over the affairs of England. For the Tories, the prize is a great one: permanent power.

Saturday 20 September

To dinner at Chillingham. The usual eclectic assortment of guests. I was seated between Humphry's bright and amusing daughter, Mary, who works for *The Spectator*, and a beautiful portrait painter who at first glance I would have said was in her mid-thirties but who turned out to have six children, the oldest aged twenty-six. Many of the guests had homes north of the border and there was much talk of the Scottish referendum. Needless to say, they were all strong Noes. Someone remarked that those who thought they had something to lose voted No and those who thought they had nothing to lose voted Yes. Or as the beautiful portrait painter put it, 'everyone in Glasgow' (where a majority voted for independence) 'is on benefit'.

'Come off it,' I said.

'Or they work for the government,' she added, which she appeared to think amounted to the same thing.

Sunday 21 September

To London with Emma and her considerable baggage, a drive of 340 miles, much of it through heavy traffic and roadworks. (If only she had chosen a university nearer home.) We reached Goldsmiths in the early evening. The good news is that she has an en suite room in a pleasant flat on campus, sharing with four others. She is very self-confident and didn't appear in the least fazed by the prospect of leaving home, but I think she will find the reading a struggle. Among the books on her reading list, I noticed *Orientalism* by Edward Said, which I found incomprehensible when I tried to read it years ago, so goodness knows what she will make of it.

Monday 22 September

To the Lycée to prune the roses and inspect our apartment. Then back up the motorway to Callaly. The journey took more than eight hours, allowing for a snooze in a lay-by and a veggie burger in Burger King at Washington. The radio was full of Ed Balls's speech to the Labour conference. This is a new Ed Balls, no longer in denial about the deficit, anxious to convince the nation that he can be trusted with the public finances. After several years of decrying the Osborne cuts, he now appears to be signed up to just about every dot and comma of the government's spending plans. Much talk of 'tough decisions' but no real evidence of any. Just about the only saving he is proposing is a risible 5 per cent cut in ministerial salaries. The sad truth is, of course, that he has little room for manoeuvre. The only way to raise serious money would be to increase the basic rate of tax (overturning the disastrous 2p cut that Gordon made in 2007), but as we all know any tax rise proposed by a Labour government would trigger mass hysteria. Only the Tories are allowed to raise taxes.

Tuesday 23 September

'Chris, it was electrifying.' Thus begins a phoney email purporting to be from the Labour Party general secretary but in practice no doubt drafted by a zealous young intern well before Ed's speech was delivered. In fact, it was a disaster. Full of populist nonsense, promising to spend billions more on the NHS and impose a ludicrous and impractical mansion tax on houses worth over £2 million, the implication being that this would somehow fund the proposed extra spending (which it won't). On top of which he entirely forgot to address the deficit, a detail the media homed in on within minutes. By evening, 'Ed's mistake' was leading the bulletins. This is what comes of attempting to make big speeches without notes. Impressive when it works, but disastrous when it doesn't. Inexplicably, the polls still suggest he could become Prime Minister, if only by default.

Thursday 25 September

Parliament is to be recalled tomorrow to vote on whether or not we should join the Americans and the French in bombing the Islamist barbarians who have taken over much of Syria and northern Iraq. How would I vote, if I were still there? Probably 'Yes', but with misgivings. On the one hand, the destruction of ISIS is a noble cause. On the other, bombs alone won't do the trick. Only ground troops can do that, and we are repeatedly assured that neither we nor the Americans have any such plans. Which means we shall have to rely on the Kurds, the Iraqis (who have so far proved useless) and the murderous Syrians to do the job. The trouble is we are not on speaking terms with the Syrians. Or are we?

Friday 26 September

The vote to join the international effort against ISIS in Iraq went through by a large majority, although many of those voting in favour expressed doubts about the likely impact in the absence of a credible army on the ground.

Tuesday 30 September
London

To London, where, in the courtyard cafe of the British Library, I handed over a memory stick containing my memoir to Caroline Dawnay. We shall see what she makes of it. Although I think it is probably publishable, I hold out no great hopes for it. These days one has to be a celebrity chef or a TV comedian to sell non-fiction.

Wednesday 1 October

Guess what? There is an election coming and after years of austerity the Tories are promising tax cuts for everyone. Addressing the Tory conference, Cameron promised to raise the payment threshold by £2,000 for the lowest paid and by a whopping £8,000 for top-rate taxpayers. And this after years of lecturing us on the necessity of dealing with the deficit and pretending to be the only party prepared to take tough decisions. Indeed, they were at it only this week, in the wake of Ed Miliband's conference speech.

Thursday 2 October

Bright sunshine. We worked all day in the garden and lunched on the terrace in front of the glasshouse. Years ago, by a little stream near Rievaulx Abbey, we came across an elderly couple tending an idyllic garden. That's us now. Such a privilege.

Needless to say, Cameron's promise of tax cuts has been received with rapture by the usual suspects – *The Times*, *The Sun* and the *Telegraph* – exactly the publications that have been lecturing us on the need for fiscal rectitude. Only the *Financial Times* spoils the party by asking where the extra £7.2 billion needed to fund this bonanza will come from and what will be the impact, given that the Tories are already committed to cutting public services by a further £25 billion if they win.

Friday 3 October

Scarcely a week goes by without some new sop to the UKIP wing of the Tory Party. Today the Tories have announced that if they win an outright majority next time, they will withdraw the UK from the European Convention on Human Rights.

This evening I harvested the first of our small crop of Galia melons. The effort to produce them has greatly exceeded the result, but they tasted all the better for that.

Saturday 4 October

Bruce, our cat, grows increasingly stupid. Her eating is intermittent.

Sometimes she gobbles her food and sometimes she refuses to touch it for two or three days, until Ngoc tempts her to resume with a piece of fish or chicken. She demands to be let out even in pouring rain. Because we have no cat flap (which she wouldn't use anyway) she is dependent on us for her comings and goings. If we have gone to bed, she taps on the bedroom door until I get up and let her out. Once out she decides that she wants to come back in again, but by then it is often too late and she ends up camped all night outside the doors into the living room. If I do get up in the night and let her back in, she soon forgets why she wanted to come in and demands to be let out again. We leave the porch door open so she can take shelter, but she ignores that. If I call her, she often looks in the opposite direction and it takes her a minute or two to work out where the sound is coming from. Is she deaf, blind, senile? How old is she? We first acquired her, or rather she acquired us, in early 2002. Before that she had belonged to neighbours who moved and she camped on our doorstep until we took pity on her. Which makes her at least thirteen or fourteen years old. Fairly old for a cat.

Wednesday 8 October

To the Dancehouse Theatre, Manchester, for another Tony Benn talk. It went well enough. I stayed with Ray and Luise Fitzwalter.* Poor Ray is undergoing another bout of chemo, the cancer in his bowel having reappeared. He is in good spirits and the side effects are much better than last time round, but the prognosis is not good. I currently have three good friends stricken by cancer.

Friday 10 October

As expected, UKIP have won their first seat. Douglas Carswell, who defected, was re-elected at Clacton by a huge margin. More surprisingly, they ran Labour a close second in Heywood and Middleton. Should we panic? I think not. The most significant figure in Heywood and Middleton was the turnout – 36 per cent. Come the general election and a

---

* Ray Fitzwalter was the editor of Granada TV's *World in Action* who in the 1980s commissioned me to help make three documentaries on the Birmingham bombings.

higher turnout Labour will do better and Douglas Carswell's majority will tumble, though I expect he will survive.

Saturday 11 October

Cleared one of the compost bins, scattering the contents on the raspberries, and then headed for the Durham Book Festival where, with some trepidation, I interviewed Dennis Skinner. I needn't have worried: Dennis was in benign mode, even treating us to a little sing-song. Someone asked him which Labour leader he most admired and to general surprise he nominated Harold Wilson. Later, I did my Tony Benn speech. Both events were a sellout. In the green room I chatted to Rachel Cooke, a journalist who has written a book about admirable women. She seemed to have read at least my first volume of diaries and enquired about my walled garden. Gradually it dawned on me that she was the author of just about the only unkind remark ever made about the diaries. A throwaway line in the *Evening Standard*, 'Does he know what a berk he sounds? I'm guessing not.' I didn't let on that I made the connection, but I took pleasure in telling her that Volume One was on its fourteenth reprint.

Monday 13 October

To London for dinner with the other HLF regional chairpersons on board HMS *Wellington*, a naval vessel used to escort convoys across the Atlantic in World War II, moored in the Thames at Temple. On the way to the station I ran into Nick Brown, looking sinister in dark glasses but affable as ever. How does he rate Labour's chances? 'We will probably lose. Our numbers one and two are not credible compared to the incumbents. The economy is picking up. Much of what Ed Balls said has proved wrong. The two Eds don't get on.' He added, 'Ed Miliband is a nice chap and would probably make a good university lecturer.' Paradoxically, he also confirmed that most Tory MPs think their party will lose, which is what I keep hearing.

Tuesday 14 October

To HLF for a meeting of the regional chairs. As usual, much talk of the impact of the cuts. Everywhere local authorities are offloading responsibility for parks and museums onto independent trusts. Someone reported that Birmingham Art Gallery and Museums had suffered a 42 per cent cut in its Arts Council grant. According to Colin Bailey (director of corporate services), we are only one third of the way through the government's cuts programme.

Wednesday 15 October

This morning on the radio, an interview with a young female doctor who is helping to grapple with the Ebola epidemic in Sierra Leone. Are you going back, the interviewer asked. 'Yes,' she said, 'as a doctor and a human being, I have to.' So humbling to know that there are such selfless people in this selfish world.

Talking of selfishness, the Tories are once again promising to abolish inheritance tax on estates worth less than £1 million. A repeat of the stunt they pulled so successfully in 2007 – although they promptly forgot about it as soon as they were in government. The beauty of it is that, although only about 4 per cent of estates are affected, just about the entire middle class seem to think they will benefit. But, hey, the trick seems to work so why not? What mugs we are.

Thursday 16 October

Someone, I can't recall who, told me a tale about a friend who had gone on holiday to Spain and attempted to hire a car at Madrid Airport. 'What is your profession?' asked the young woman behind the desk. 'I am a playwright,' he replied. Which was a slight exaggeration. He had written only one play, but it had been well reviewed. She googled him and sure enough up came the details. 'I am sorry, sir,' she said, 'but I can't let you have a car. We have a "No Celebrity" policy.'

Monday 20 October

To Newcastle University, where I gave lectures on the Callaghan and Thatcher governments. It is becoming apparent from the seminars that many of the students have read none of the relevant literature. Today Nick

Randall, the senior lecturer, who is usually very tolerant, finally lost patience. He went round the table asking each what preparation he or she had done and then chucked out all those who admitted to having read nothing.

Tuesday 21 October

An invitation from the BBC to appear on a Christmas edition of *University Challenge*, as part of a team of allegedly distinguished alumni from the University of Hull. I consulted Liz Forgan, who took part last year. She replied by return: 'DO NOT GO ANYWHERE NEAR!!!! … It's ritual humiliation.'

Wednesday 22 October

To Wansbeck Hospital, where various electrodes were attached to me, a blue dye injected and I was fed into an MRI scanner, where I remained for an hour while being repeatedly instructed through headphones to 'breathe in', 'breathe out' and 'stop breathing' while a camera dissected every part of my heart. In the evening to the Alnwick Playhouse, where we watched the film version of John le Carré's thriller *A Most Wanted Man*. Although I guessed the ending from some way off, it had us on the edge of our seats throughout.

I have declined the *University Challenge* invitation.

Wednesday 29 October

To the Tankerville Arms at Eglingham, where I lunched with my delightful old friend Charles Baker-Cresswell. Amusing and affable as usual and a Tory to his fingertips. 'Why do socialist governments always ruin the economy?' he asked, as if the near collapse in the autumn of 2008 had nothing to do with the bankers, hedge funders and derivative traders who, by and large, are not Labour voters. Quite apart from which, as I gently pointed out, the collapse began in the American mortgage market, over which British governments have no influence whatever. Charles replied that it was all Jimmy Carter's fault for encouraging US finance houses to lend to people with no money. Since most of the lending took place after Carter had left office, that too strikes me as a long shot. Later he chucked in a reference to Venezuela and Ecuador and remarked, apropos of nothing in particular, 'We are becoming a fourth-rate nation.' I advised a visit to Liberia or the Congo if he really wants to see a fourth-rate nation and he didn't pursue the point.

Friday 31 October

A lovely, mild day: a temperature of 23° was recorded in the south, the highest on record for this time of year. I spent the day raking leaves and cutting grass, autumn sunshine illuminating the beech trees beyond the mansion. Many of our flowers – roses, fuchsia, cosmos, catmint, marigolds, petunias – are still in bloom. Also, the champagne-coloured clematis, which did nothing in the summer, has suddenly flowered.

Tuesday 4 November

Up at 3.30 a.m. to deliver Ngoc to Newcastle Airport for the early flight to Paris en route to Saigon. Then to Central Station, Newcastle, for a day-return visit to London. Although I was at the station by just after 6 a.m., I was told I could not board any train until 8.25 unless I wanted to pay an extra £200 for an earlier ticket, so I sat and watched four or five half-empty trains pull out and eventually made my way to London. First to the Lycée, the outside of which is being painted, then to a council meeting of Winston Churchill Memorial Trust where the chair, Anne Boyd, told me that she had travelled from Edinburgh at 8 a.m. on a first class advance purchase return which cost her £145, little more than the standard class fare and half what Great Eastern would have charged me for a standard class ticket from Newcastle had I caught an early train. Bonkers. Finally, a hasty supper with Sarah and her boyfriend Nick in an exquisite apartment in the little eighteenth-century courtyard off Brick Lane that Nick is renting until he has completed the purchase of his new flat. Back to Newcastle and from there by car to Callaly, arriving home just as Ngoc was touching down in Saigon. A long day.

Thursday 6 November

This evening a long telephone call to Patricia Moberly, who is dying of lung cancer. Yet another of my friends struck down in Sniper's Alley She sounded as robust and cheerful as usual. Not a trace of self-pity. Interested in everything and everyone. Remarking on her good fortune having a teaching hospital just a short bus ride away. She is still active in her local Labour Party and has recently been conducting interviews for the Judicial Appointments Commission, of which she is a member. She claims to feel fine and says the only ill effects thus far are caused by the chemotherapy, which she has every three weeks. Thus far it is working, but there will come a time when it no longer does. She's ten years younger than Richard and naturally worries about him. 'The order of our lives has been reversed,' she said. 'We always assumed that he would go first.'

Friday 7 November

More rumours of plots against Ed Miliband, whose poll ratings continue to trail those of the party he leads. It's a film we've seen before. Brown, Kinnock, Foot. We ought to have learned by now, but the dear old Labour Party never gets rid of failing leaders. We go down with the ship. In any case, who would we put in his place?

Saturday 8 November

A walk with neighbours John Field, Tony Henfrey and Tony's two little terriers, Boot and Bobby (named after the Duke of Wellington and Robert Peel), up into the hills beyond Alnham. Mostly off-piste, which caused John to turn back after a while, but Tony and I ploughed on. Tony favours withdrawal from the EU. He thinks our future lies with trade agreements without European interference in other aspects of our lives. I replied that a Sunderland businessman to whom I had recently spoken had said withdrawal would lead to a collapse of inward investment and that we might, for example, lose Nissan. He said he thought it unlikely but conceded it was a risk and he could understand that from Sunderland's point of view it might make sense to stay. You bet it does. Three hours of sunshine and a final hour of rain.

Sunday 9 November

Former Thurrock MP Andrew MacKinlay was on the radio at lunchtime calling on the parliamentary party to remove Ed, but there is no sign of anyone else sticking their head above the parapet, despite a good deal of anonymous grumbling. Alan Johnson or Alistair Darling are the most credible alternatives, but Alan has repeatedly made clear that he is not interested and Alistair has just announced his intention to stand down come the election. There's always Hilary Benn, of course. A lovely and most capable fellow, but not ruthless enough when it comes to the upsetting of apple carts.

Wednesday 12 November

A MORI poll puts Labour three points behind the Tories, which is incredible considering that the Tories are about to lose another by-election to UKIP. Repeated assertions by Ed Miliband and his acolytes that not only is he up to the job of Prime Minister but he actually relishes the fight ahead convey an increasing air of desperation. Likewise the suggestion that when the public get to know Ed they will warm to him. Rightly or wrongly the public already feel they know Ed and they have not warmed to him. Despite this there is not the slightest chance that he will fall on his sword. And if he did, what good would it do? The only credible alternatives have ruled themselves out. In any case, Ed isn't our only problem. The plain truth is that we don't have anything sensible and distinctive to say about the economy in general and the deficit in particular.

Monday 17 November

Newcastle

Every Monday for several weeks, walking between Newcastle's Haymarket and the university, I have passed a beggar huddled under a blanket, mostly ignored by the passing students. On first sight I had little sympathy for him, reasoning that he could do more to help himself, but today I stopped to talk. He is a young Bulgarian with sunken cheeks and a desperate air who says he has lost his passport and all other means of identification. He has been in this country for five years and for some of that time worked as a chef in a pizza parlour. Now, without any means of identity, he is homeless, jobless and broke. He said he had family in his country and would like to go home, but without papers that was impossible. In short, he is stuck. I gave him a couple of quid and will contact the North of England Refugee Service to see what, if anything, can be done to help him.

Tuesday 18 November

Friday will be the fortieth anniversary of the Birmingham bombings. I have received requests for interviews from several broadcast journalists but declined on the grounds that hearing from me will only upset the relatives of the victims who are still demanding justice, even though two of the perpetrators are dead and, short of a confession, there is not the slightest chance of holding the other two to account so long after the event. I did, however, attempt to interest *The Times* in an op-ed piece. They appeared interested at first but in the end failed to bite. I suspect there is a fatwa on me at *The Times*. I haven't had an op-ed published since the purge that followed James Harding's dismissal. Book review commissions dried up at the same time, even though the reviews editor, Robbie Millen, is the very person who used to gush with enthusiasm over some of my earlier op-ed contributions.

Thursday 20 November

The cat woke me at 3.40 a.m. and I couldn't get back to sleep so after an hour I got up, read a chapter of Roy Jenkins's wordy but magnificent biography of Churchill, a hardback copy of which I recently found in a Hampstead Oxfam shop, and then a chapter of a biography of Nye Bevan, which I am reviewing for *The Observer*. For the rest of the day I worked in the garden, harvesting the remaining (green) tomatoes from the glasshouse, clearing the redundant tomato and aubergine plants and cutting back the herbaceous border by the house. It was dark when I went in.

Friday 21 November

UKIP have won a second by-election – this time at Rochester – by a margin of just under 3,000 votes, which is unlikely to be enough to hold the seat. Needless to say, the media are getting very excited, but despite all the hoo-ha, my instinct is that come the general election UKIP will win very few seats. What does seem to be happening, however, is that they are now taking votes from Labour as well as the Tories.

Dinner at the Tankerville Arms in Eglingham. On the way home, just before Callaly, I had to stop for a large barn owl sitting on the road staring into our headlights. It stayed put for a full minute before flying leisurely away.

Saturday 22 November

The fallout from the Rochester by-election continues. Strikingly, the media are interpreting it as a disaster for Labour, rather than the Tories, who lost a relatively safe seat. Admittedly, our enemies have been ably assisted by Emily Thornberry appearing to poke fun at the occupant of a house in Rochester plastered with the flag of St George, outside of which is parked a white van. She has duly resigned her place in the shadow Cabinet and apologised, but the damage is done (yet more evidence of the perils of tweeting). 'Labour has lost the working-class vote' says a headline on the front of today's *Telegraph*. The *Mail* is pursuing a similar theme (I had a call yesterday from the *Mail* features desk, asking if I want to address the subject – and even offering to ghostwrite it for me). Several of today's papers carry a photo of the owner of the flag-decked house at the centre of the row provoked by Emily Thornberry – a massive man with a number one haircut, dressed from head to toe in red and white whose hobby is said to be cage fighting. He doesn't look typical of any working class I have ever met. And since when did the *Mail* and the *Telegraph* have the interests of the working class at heart?

This evening to Blyth, where I was guest speaker at the local Labour Party dinner. The MP Ronnie Campbell is a former miner whose roots are deep in the community he serves, and the audience was solidly working class. Labour may have lost the working-class vote in Rochester, but not in Blyth.[*]

Sunday 23 November

'When are you going to make Alan Johnson your leader?' enquired Tony Henfrey, my genial Brexiteer neighbour.

'No chance,' I said.

'You'd win the election if you did.'

---

[*] Ha! In December 2019, Blyth returned a Tory MP for the first time in its history.

Monday 24 November

The Tories have quietly admitted that Cameron's promise ('No ifs or buts') to cut inward migration to below 100,000 a year will not be met. Of course it won't. How can it be, as long as we are signed up to membership of the EU, for which the free movement of people is a core principle? Indeed, far from having been met, the immigration rate is about the same as it was under what they like to call 'Labour's open-door policy'. Just like the deficit, which isn't going down much either. Not that this will stop them repeating their bogus promises in the run-up to the election. Do they think we're all mugs? Perhaps we are.

Tuesday 25 November

To Derby to address a ladies' luncheon club. I duly delivered my diary talk to about a hundred prosperous, retired professional women aged between about sixty-five and ninety. Those who looked after me were pleasant enough, but the indifference was total. It is a talk I have given many times, often to great acclaim, but with a handful of exceptions nothing I had to say rang any bells with this audience. Only at the mention of the Queen did they briefly perk up. At the end, only one question (the usual: 'What do you think of Ed Miliband?') and then they scuttled away. Shades of Tony Blair and the Women's Institute.* A long, despairing interview in today's *Guardian* with the leader of Newcastle City Council, Nick Forbes. Last year the council cut spending by £37 million; this year another £38 million will go. Further reductions of £40 million, £30 million and £20 million are projected for the next three years. The result is likely to be the gradual collapse of funding for most non-statutory services – children's centres, youth centres, litter collection, parks, homelessness, swimming pools, museums and the arts. Other big cities, notably Birmingham and Liverpool, are said to be in an even worse position. The National Audit Office are warning that more than half of local authorities are at risk of financial failure. 'Once the first wave of councils has gone down, somebody, somewhere will have to think again,' says Forbes. But will they?

---

* In June 2000, Tony Blair made an ill-advised speech to the annual meeting of the Women's Institute and was greeted by boos and heckling from some parts of the audience. The incident marked an end to the notion that there was room for everyone in New Labour's big tent.

Meanwhile, all our free press wants to talk about is what we think of Ed Miliband.

Wednesday 26 November

Ngoc returned from Vietnam this evening, bearing 10kg of excellent Kontum coffee and a large box of rambutan.

Thursday 27 November

Andrew Mitchell has lost his libel case against *The Sun*, and the policeman whom he accused of lying has won his case against Andrew after a judge decided 'on the balance of probabilities' that he had used the toxic word. Andrew, with Sharon and the children alongside him, made a dignified statement on the steps of the High Court. There is talk of costs running into seven figures.

Friday 28 November

The media has declared open season on poor Andrew. The first six pages of today's *Sun* are taken up with celebrating the outcome. An extraordinary turn of events. No one can say with certainty what precise words were used, but just about everything that subsequently came to light added weight to Andrew's version of events and detracted from the official version, yet the judge found against him. I emailed my sympathy last night and received a reply within three hours: 'As you can imagine, we are pretty gutted, but tomorrow is another day ... Andrew.'

A call from the *Today* programme asking if I would be willing, in the wake of the Plebgate affair, to take part in a discussion tomorrow morning along the lines of whether or not today's politicians are out of touch with those they are supposed to be representing. I predict nothing will come of it because by tomorrow morning the producers will have found someone more interesting, important or proximate to a BBC studio.* Were I permitted to participate, however, I would make the simple point

---

* Which is what happened.

that if Andrew were all that out of touch, he would have been riding in a chauffeur-driven ministerial car rather than on a bicycle. Had he been, the police would have leapt to open the gates.

Saturday 29 November

As Ngoc and I were setting off for Rothbury this morning we came upon a grey squirrel cavorting by the drive in front of the South Lodge. It was still there when we returned an hour and a half later. It is the second glimpse of a grey in the past few days. They are gradually taking over from our reds, not through aggression but because they spread some sort of fatal virus. We are asked to report any sightings so that a local marksman can shoot them. I duly did so, but not without qualms. Who are we to interfere with nature and, anyway, it is probably futile.

Monday 1 December

A neighbour rang to report that the marksman has been out and bagged two grey squirrels in the woods by the south gate. There are thought to be several more and he will be coming back. So, I have two grey squirrels on my conscience.

Tuesday 2 December

Cousin Tony has sent me one of his little poems:

> West Ham United are fifth in the league,
> A pleasant position – though strange;
> I put it, despite what Big Sam says,
> All down to climate change.

He writes:

I have been lumbered with West Ham all my life: Uncle Peter used to take me, aged about seven or eight to watch home games at Upton Park. He would squash me through the railings so that he did not have to pay for me. Uncle Brian* thought supporting West Ham was useful because you had already done your purgatory on earth.

Wednesday 3 December

George Osborne has delivered his autumn statement, the last before the election. Although cunningly disguised with cuts in stamp duty and the usual pre-election talk of tax cuts, the bleak truth is that the deficit remains stubbornly high and that an eternity of cuts in public services lies before us. Indeed, it has emerged that his long-term aim is to reduce public spending to levels not seen since the '30s, way beyond what is required to overcome the effects of financial crash. For the first time, signs that alarm bells are beginning to ring among those who thus far have gone along with the mantra of inevitability. For the first time, too, one sees a little gleam of light; if only Labour were capable of picking up the ball and running with it. 'Forward to the 1930s' could be our slogan.

Thursday 4 December

Jeremy Thorpe has died. A tragic figure. When I contested him in North Devon in 1970, I was so impressed by his wit, charm and energy, which had galvanised that constituency. The turnout was 85 per cent and huge crowds attended the eve-of-poll rallies and the declaration of the result. I recall, too, how he graciously insisted on a recount in the hope of saving my deposit (the threshold being 12.5 per cent in those days) which I narrowly failed to do. On the wall of my study I have the picture of us taken together on the platform at the count when he scraped home by just 369, defeating a ferociously right-wing Tory. Caroline, his attractive young wife, is on the right of the photo talking to Mrs Prowse, Jeremy's formidable agent. When that was taken Caroline had just days to live.† And after that everything unravelled. In later life poor Jeremy was desperate to be rehabilitated. Twice he wrote asking if I would recommend him for a peerage. This evening I tapped out a few paragraphs for *The Guardian* saying nice things about him which I hope they will use.

---

*   A Catholic priest.

†   She was killed in a car crash shortly after the election.

Saturday 6 December

Four nights of hard frost. I lie awake thinking of the destitute Bulgarian. How can he survive the winter and how can I help him? I emailed the head of the North of England Refugee Service in search of advice, but he has not responded. I tried telephoning, but there was no answer.

We drove to Alwinton and walked four or five miles in the hills. The frozen ground meant almost no mud.

Monday 8 December

To the university for the last of my 'New Labour' seminars. No sign of the destitute Bulgarian who has been much on my mind during this recent cold spell. A relief in a way since I have not succeeded in finding a way of helping him, though I was proposing to slip him £20.

As in previous years, I gave out copies of a redundant edition of *A Very British Coup* to those students (about half) who had stuck with the course to the end. This evening, on the television news, we were treated to the remarkable spectacle of Danny Alexander, the second most senior Treasury minister, who despite being a Liberal Democrat has thus far been an unabashed cheerleader for austerity, denouncing Osborne's proposed public spending plans as based on 'ideology' rather than necessity. Truly, a man with no shame.

Tuesday 9 December

The US Senate has published a detailed report on the CIA's programme of torture, or 'enhanced interrogation' as they prefer to call it, authorised by George Bush in the wake of 9/11. We already knew part of the story, but the details are awful – sleep deprivation (for up to 180 hours), waterboarding, 'auditory overload', 'rectal feeding'. And all this, so the committee says, resulted in no useful intelligence and a number of false leads. Many of the detainees were, in the words of the report, 'wrongfully held', i.e. innocent. There is much breast-beating about how inconsistent this is with American values, but on the contrary it seems to me entirely consistent. The only difference is that until 9/11 the United States government employed foreign torturers to do their dirty work, whereas after 9/11 they did much of it themselves.

Thursday 11 December

I delivered my Tony Benn talk in the Alnwick Playhouse, preceded by Anna Lloyd's excellent obituary film. One hundred and fifteen people attended. Respectable, considering the icy weather and the fact that Alnwick is not exactly a Bennite stronghold.

Sunday 14 December

The Small Intellectual has returned from her first term at Goldsmiths, burdened with an essay to write on the causes of the Chinese revolution. I had feared that a study of international relations would prove too much for one so easily distracted, but on the contrary she seems to be loving it.

Wednesday 17 December

Islamist gunmen in Pakistan have slaughtered 132 pupils and nine teachers at a school for the children of the military. Every newspaper is leading with the story, save the *Mail*, the front page of which is headed: 'Four in Five New Nurses on NHS Wards Are Foreign'.

Saturday 20 December

This morning on the *Today* programme an illuminating interview with a delivery driver for one of the private courier companies gradually undercutting the Post Office. He is employed on a casual contract with minimal employment rights and paid 45p per delivery and, if the recipient is not at home, he is expected to return up to three times (reducing his earnings to 15p per call). He earns about £30 a day. This is what the privatisers will do to the postmen, if we let them.

Tuesday 23 December

Today's *Telegraph* describes as scandalous the discovery that elderly folk living alone and in need of care are receiving no more than a fifteen-minute visit from harassed, underpaid care workers. What do they expect? Curious how the cheerleaders for the slash and burn approach to public spending are so quick to resile from the consequences.

My sister Elizabeth comes to stay, bringing with her a copy of the *Daily Mail*, on page two of which there is a little box headed 'Clarifications and corrections' (a new departure for the *Mail* post-Leveson). They have been asked to make clear, says the 'clarification', that the numbers which formed the basis for last week's screaming front-page headline alleging that four out of five new nursing recruits are foreign are, to put it mildly, 'not strictly comparable'. A more accurate analysis 'shows that in the twelve months to September 7,449 out of 33,838 joiners... were non-British', i.e. about one in four.

Thursday 25 December

Ngoc's sixtieth birthday. As usual, we made our own cards. Mine depicted a small figure in a Vietnamese peasant hat, sitting on a tropical beach, under a coconut palm, drinking an unspecified beverage, gazing out at the blue ocean. And, inside, the caption: 'Life begins at sixty'. The girls had purchased a big photo album and filled it with pictures of Ngoc's life, starting with black and white pictures from her childhood in Kontum. They sat up working on it until the early hours.

Saturday 27 December

'Labour faces Scotland bloodbath,' says the headline in *The Guardian* over a poll suggesting that the Nationalists could win thirty or more of the Scottish seats.

Sunday 28 December

A hard frost and glorious sunshine, light snow on the uplands, a buzzard wheeling in a clear blue sky. Two hours in the hills with Tony Henfrey and his little terrier, Bobby. Tony reckons Boris would make the best Tory leader on the grounds that he is a proven winner and that luck counts in politics as in war, but that Cameron will hold on in the event that the Tories emerge as the largest party. He also reckons that, in the longer term, if the northern English regions start demanding to keep more of their local taxes, London and the south will do likewise, leading to a major redistribution of wealth. 'Be careful what you wish for,' he advised.

CHAPTER SIX

2015

Friday 2 January

Twenty neighbours came for New Year drinks. Someone asked me to predict the outcome of the May election. My prediction, which I note for the record, was as follows: the Tories the largest party, UKIP no more than four seats and possibly as low as one or two, Lib Dem seats halved to around thirty or fewer. Labour loses about twenty seats to the Scot Nats. What sort of government will emerge is anyone's guess. A minority Labour government is unlikely but just about conceivable.

Saturday 3 January

Sarah, Emma and I walked with Joyce Quin* from Prendwick to Ingram and back. Once again, with daylight fading, I got us hopelessly lost on the return journey, thanks to a useless guidebook. Fortunately the girls had a better sense of direction than I.

Sunday 4 January

With five months to go, the opening shots were fired today in the election campaign. Both sides are talking past each other. Labour, having nothing original to say on the economy, wants only to talk about the health service. The Tories want to talk only about the economy on which their

---

* Former MP for Gateshead East, now in the Lords.

record is not as impressive as they like to claim. Unbearable to listen to. And to think we have another five months of this.

Monday 5 January

Predictably – and justifiably – the commentariat are pouring scorn on Labour's ludicrous claim that the Tories are out to destroy the health service. Nick Robinson and John Humphrys were at it on the *Today* programme this morning. I don't complain, but I do wish they would analyse with a fraction of the same rigour the endlessly repeated Tory claims that the crisis of 2008 and all that flowed from it was the result of Labour profligacy. The Tories and their allies have got away with this, more or less unchallenged, for five years.

Thursday 8 January

A massive manhunt under way in France for two masked jihadis who machine-gunned the staff of the satirical magazine *Charlie Hebdo*, killing a dozen people. This comes after a series of random attacks at various locations. Another today at a Métro station in France in which two policemen were killed. I guess we must prepare for much more of this. This evening the head of MI5 said that although the intelligence services had prevented several such incidents in the UK, they will not be able to stop them all.

Friday 9 January

Wall-to-wall coverage of the massive manhunt under way in France. The BBC always goes over the top at times like this. Entire bulletins devoted to the subject, as though nothing else is happening in the world. The same clips of film used repeatedly, often several times in the same news bulletin, one BBC correspondent interviewing other BBC correspondents. All the same, one can't deny the drama. A car chase; two sieges, one in a printworks outside Paris and the other in a Jewish supermarket, brought to an end simultaneously; three gunman dead, along with four hostages in the supermarket; the female accomplice of one appears to have gone on the run. Our tabloids, needless to say, are focusing on stirring up fear and loathing.

Saturday 10 January

An impressive display of solidarity by the French. Massive, dignified demonstrations. Some talk from politicians of the need for 'war' against terror, but precisely how does one conduct a war against home-grown jihadis without provoking more alienated first- or second-generation migrants to avenge themselves on a society which offers them few prospects? At home, the usual suspects are already demanding more powers for our security services – Liam Fox was at it this morning. Several unrelated and reasonable questions: how come French jihadis, mostly amateurs, have access to Kalashnikovs? Why do armed police in democracies feel the need to mimic their opposite numbers in Russia by concealing their faces behind balaclavas?

Tuesday 27 January

Ed Miliband has unveiled plans to employ 20,000 more nurses and 8,000 more doctors, all this to be funded by a so-called mansion tax. Frankly, it just isn't credible. To the Heritage Lottery Fund HQ at Sloane Square, where to general amusement I reported to the board that I had almost succeeded in stamping out the use of meaningless hyperbole from northern region project reports, though we still have some way to go at national level.

Wednesday 28 January

Lunch with Stella Rimington at Kenwood. I mentioned Tony Benn's story about Joshua fixing an alarm to the family rubbish bin and catching someone piling the contents into the back of a smart car at five in the morning. 'Not us,' she said, 'that was Benji the Bin man.'*

---

* Aka Benjamin Pell, who made a living raking through the waste bins of prominent people and law firms representing them in search of incriminating or embarrassing documents, which he sold to newspapers.

Saturday 31 January

The fat cats are turning on Labour. To the delight of the Tories, the chief executive of Boots has described the prospect of a Labour election victory as potentially 'catastrophic'.

Monday 2 February

It turns out that Stefano Pessina, the Boots chief executive, lives in Monaco, a tax haven. Now there's a surprise. Ed Miliband has hit back, saying, 'British people won't take kindly to being lectured by somebody avoiding his taxes on how they should be voting.' No, indeed. Let's have some more fighting talk. Why should we take this nonsense lying down?

Tuesday 3 February

To Simpson's in the Strand for an Oldie lunch. During pre-lunch drinks I was approached by an elderly, well-preserved lady accompanied by a younger German gentleman. 'We decided you looked intelligent,' she said. She introduced herself and I enquired what she did for a living.

'I am an artist,' she said.

'Where is your studio?'

'I have two. One in Holland Park and one in Poplar.'

'You must be very successful to afford a studio in Holland Park.'

She smiled modestly and was taken away to have her photograph taken. 'You don't have a clue who she is, do you?' remarked her companion amiably.

'No.'

'Bridget Riley, one of the greatest living contemporary artists.'

I googled her when I got home. Her paintings sell for millions.

This evening, dinner with My Two Best Friends at the Balham Bowls Club. Sarah, who was coming from Manchester, wasn't expected until nearly nine o'clock, so Emma photographed the menu with her iPhone and sent it to Sarah on the train, who immediately replied with her order, which awaited her immediately on arrival. What modern young people they are.

Wednesday 4 February

Lunch with Jean Corston in a Lords dining room. We ran into Matt Ridley, who told the following tale. He was driving up the motorway when his car phone rang and a voice said, 'I have Mr Murdoch for you.'

The great oligarch himself came on the line. 'Matt,' he said, 'how worried should I be about this Ebola?'

'Where are you?'

'Upper East Side, Manhattan.'

'I think you'll be OK,' said Matt.

Then to Speaker's House for my annual general meeting with Mr Speaker Bercow. He has recently been involved in a row over the appointment of a chief executive in place of a Clerk of the House, a messy business, but it seems to have been resolved. We had a pleasant chat for forty-five minutes. He intends seeking another term, which I am all in favour of. He has shaken up the place and it needed doing. So far he has granted 207 urgent questions compared with only a handful granted by his recent predecessors. The government hate him for it, but in my view he is behaving as a good Speaker should.

Sunday 8 February

Another fat cat intervention in the affairs of the nation. Martin Sorrell (who last year trousered what our City brethren like to call a 'compensation' package worth a cool £30 million, or 780 times the 'compensation' of his average employee) has opined that Labour is 'anti-business'. In fairness he also added that the Tories' proposed referendum on the membership of the EU wasn't good for business either, but needless to say, most of our free press are making much of what he had to say about Labour. The trouble is that these FTSE fat cats confuse their personal interest with those of the nation. Reminds me of the manager of a Sunderland engineering plant who confided on the day after the 1992 election that, if he was honest, a Labour government would probably be better for the economy, but personally he was likely to be better off under the Tories and he had, therefore, voted accordingly.[*]

---

[*] In 1998, the average FTSE 100 director earned forty-seven times the average income of his employees. By 2014, they were earning 143 times average salaries.

Thursday 19 February

Tet, the Vietnamese New Year. Ngoc spent much of the day communicating with her worldwide network of sisters. At 1 p.m. UK time they all agreed to a few minutes' prayer for the family dead – a niece, her brother, grandmother and father – whose spirits are still thought to be wandering. The exercise must be repeated indefinitely on the first and fifteenth of each month.

Tuesday 24 February

To London for a council meeting of the Winston Churchill Memorial Trust and then to Primrose Hill for a meal with Liz Forgan. I related to her my electoral dilemma: that I live in a constituency where, the more votes the Labour candidate gets, the more chance of ending up with a Tory MP. Liz insists that it is no dilemma. 'You *must* vote Lib Dem.'

Friday 13 March

On *Desert Island Discs* this morning an impressive American human rights lawyer, Bryan Stevenson, made the remarkable assertion that a black boy born in 21st-century America stands a one in three chance of being imprisoned.

Tuesday 17 March

To Church House, Westminster, for a memorial meeting for Chris Price. Roy Hattersley spoke brilliantly, but the other speakers were far too long-winded. Memo to my heirs: if you are organising a memorial meeting, please restrict contributions to five minutes maximum. 'Are you Chris Mullin?' asked a young woman from the Cabinet Office. She added, 'Your diaries are much referenced there.'

Later, passing through Speaker's Court at the House of Commons, I noticed that the number of ministerial cars appears to be creeping up again. Can it be that the Government Car Service is stealthily mounting a rearguard action?*

---

* After reading my first volume of diaries, David Cameron reduced the number of ministers entitled to an official car.

Wednesday 18 March

To Buckingham Palace, where the Queen laid on a reception to mark the fiftieth anniversary of the Churchill Trust. The old couple are in remarkable shape. HM (aged eighty-eight) and the Duke (aged ninety-three) stood for an hour while we all filed past, shaking 630 hands. Then, starting in the centre and heading in opposite directions, they worked the room for another hour. 'Do you like my pictures?' I overheard the Queen asking one couple. To which there was only one possible answer. Her favourite, she said, was a luminous Rembrandt entitled *The Shipbuilder and His Wife*. Robert Fellowes, the Queen's former private secretary, told me that the Duke once remarked to him, 'Charm is a greatly overrated virtue.'

Afterwards, walking from the palace to Westminster Tube Station, I came across a woman struggling with her possessions in two wheelie cases and a bulging plastic bag. At first I thought she was an old bag lady, but when I drew closer I saw that she was a young Chinese woman, practically asleep on her feet. No doubt her family think she is studying here, but something has gone terribly wrong in her life and she daren't go home. I should have had the courage to talk to her, but, not wanting her problems to become mine, I walked on looking back to see her struggling in the direction of St James's Park, where she will no doubt spend the night. A few yards on, in the underpass at the end of Whitehall, a young couple were bedding down for the night. A sober-looking woman and an inebriated man, a half-empty whiskey bottle and several beer bottles standing in front of them. Beyond them, a man with no visible means of support and no possessions, apparently oblivious, dancing and watching his reflection in a large Perspex covering of an advert. Central London is filling up with homeless people again, just as it did in the Thatcher era. This time around, many are failed asylum seekers or out-of-work Eastern Europeans, flotsam and jetsam who, lured here on a false prospectus, dare not go home. This is only the beginning of a very large problem.

Thursday 19 March

An interesting *Guardian* article on negative campaigning by Rafael Behr, one of the more perceptive commentators. Imagine, he says, if the big brands marketed themselves in the same way as the political parties. 'If McDonald's and Burger King ran around calling each other's products junk. The result: fewer customers all round.' Meanwhile the Tories are peddling a new catchphrase: 'the chaos that we inherited'. I first heard it the other day from the lips of George Osborne, and other prominent Tories have been repeating it since. The truth is, of course, that they didn't inherit chaos. Most of the difficult decisions had been taken by the time they came to power. What they inherited was a growth rate of 2.1 per cent, which it took them three years to exceed.

Sunday 22 March

To London, where I stayed overnight in Wimbledon with my old neighbours from Brixton Road, James and Margaret Curran. We all agreed we are mystified by polls suggesting that one way or another Ed Miliband could stumble into Downing Street. As Margaret remarked, 'We are all party members and if we don't have confidence in him, why should anyone else?'

Monday 23 March

To the Royal Institute of International Affairs, where I took part in a conference on Africa (nice to be remembered). James Duddridge, latest in a long line of Africa ministers, remarked that he had twice heard the Prime Minister quoting from my diaries.

Wednesday 25 March

To the business school at Edinburgh University, where I delivered a lecture entitled 'The Art of Political Leadership' (my third speech this week). At lunch Professor Chris Carter remarked, apropos the resurgent Scot Nats, 'Nothing ever seems to stick to them.' Ten years ago they were arguing that the pound was holding Scotland back and that membership of the euro was the key to Scots prosperity – a subject on which they have now gone quiet. A year ago they were saying that their share of North Sea oil was going to bring Norwegian levels of prosperity, only to see the oil price plunge. And yet no one ever seems to quote any of this back to them. They sail on regardless.

Chris also quoted Peter Jay, on a visit to the business school last

August, as arguing that there was no need to pay off the debt in a single parliament at a time of 1 per cent interest rates. Why not ring-fence the deficit and pay it off over twenty-five years, as you would a mortgage? If only Labour had the courage to make that argument, praying in aid economists like Jay and Robert Skidelsky, British politics would be transformed.

Thursday 26 March

I am reviewing *Blair Inc.*, an account of The Man's multifarious, secretive and extremely complex business activities since he stood down in July 2007. Estimates of his wealth vary from £20 million to £80 million. No previous Prime Minister (let alone a Labour one) has ever accumulated such riches. Visible evidence includes a five-storey Georgian house (which bears a marked resemblance to No. 10) in Connaught Square, a country house in Buckinghamshire (close to Chequers), a portfolio of flats in Stockport and Manchester, homes at good London addresses for three of his children. Much of his wealth seems to have come from advising unsavoury autocrats in central Asia and the Gulf. He is in almost perpetual motion around the globe, occasionally touching down on British soil to offer unsolicited advice to his successors. He looks increasingly jet-lagged and haunted by the spectre of Iraq. What is the point of all this frenetic activity? The mere accumulation of wealth or a desperate attempt to recreate a life in the stratosphere that he once occupied? There is something tragic about it. Or at least there would be if there weren't so many greater tragedies to worry about. Two days ago a deranged pilot deliberately flew a packed aircraft into a mountain in southern France. The descent lasted eight terrifying minutes. Among the dead, a party of German schoolchildren. I can't get them out of my mind.

Monday 30 March

Chuka Umunna (our next leader?) was on the radio this morning, promising that a Labour government would reduce the £80 billion deficit to zero by the end of this parliament. Exactly what the Tories promised last time round (and have spectacularly failed to do) and what they are once again promising next time round. However improbable, this means there can be no significant difference between the two parties on public spending. For all our protests to the contrary, we are doomed to carry on laying waste to the public sector. Unless, of course, we raise taxes, but we aren't proposing to do that either. Only when someone is brave enough to ask (*à la* Peter Jay) 'Why, at a time of historically low interest rates, do we need to abolish the deficit in a single parliament?' – can the spell of deficit-fetishism be broken. Only by doing so can we escape this self-imposed straitjacket and talk rationally and credibly about the economy. The Tories meanwhile are going about claiming that a Labour government means 'chaos' (that word again) and that it will introduce tax rises of £3,000 per household – a figure plucked from thin air. What a dismal business British politics has become.

Tuesday 31 March

Five weeks to go and both the main parties are still talking past each other. Labour going on about the NHS and the Tories talking only of the economy and the alleged 'chaos' that would ensue if, by some remote chance, Labour were to be elected. We are trapped by the fact that, aside from a bit of tweaking, our economic policy is broadly the same as that of the Tories. Neither party is levelling with the electorate about the cuts and/or tax rises that would be required to clear the deficit within a parliament. In so far as any distinct Labour policies have been disclosed, they are mainly populist wheezes – a mansion tax, a freeze on fuel prices (rendered redundant by the recent fall in oil and gas prices) and most recently a 5 per cent limit on profits from firms doing business with the NHS. All hopelessly impractical. Oh yes, and promises to abolish the hated 'bedroom tax' and to clamp down on zero-hours contracts. Which do make sense.

Wednesday 1 April

A hundred business people, many of them Tory donors on mega-salaries, have signed a letter to the *Daily Telegraph* asserting that a Labour government would threaten economic recovery. For some reason the story, although clearly a put-up job, leads the bulletins as though it is some great sensation, whereas similar nonsense has been a feature of just about every election I can recall. 'A hundred fat cats support the Tories.' What can possibly be newsworthy about that?

Davie Gibson, the tree surgeon, and his men came to cut down the split chestnut and the huge cracked beech by the end of the third lake. I watched the beech fall with a mighty crash, taking with it several lesser neighbours. They brought in a tractor with a long steel cable and dragged the trunk uphill into the quarry, leaving huge furrows in the muddy hillside.

Thursday 2 April

The leaders' debate. I slept through most of it, but the consensus seems to be that Nicola Sturgeon, the Scottish National Party leader, did best. At a university in northern Kenya Islamist barbarians have slaughtered 147 students.

Saturday 4 April

Sarah and her boyfriend Nick are staying.

A man has been released from the American gulag after twenty-eight years on death row, the State of Alabama having finally got round to conducting ballistic tests which showed that he couldn't have committed the murders for which he was convicted. He has spent most of his incarceration in solitary confinement. 'There is a Lord,' were his first words upon release. In his position, I would have drawn the opposite conclusion.

Sunday 5 April

With Sarah, Emma and Nick to Barrowburn, six miles up the valley from Alwinton. We walked up to Uswayford, said to be the most remote house in England, where John Williams and I stayed overnight nearly twenty years ago on our great walk from Holy Island to the Lakes. Then into the dark pine forest beyond in search of Davidson's Linn, an allegedly impressive waterfall. Both the map and the guidebook proved useless. We got horribly lost and spent three hours trudging through dense, impenetrable terrain before eventually finding our way up onto the Pennine Ridge, along which we walked via Windy Gyle back to Barrowburn. Glorious sunshine all the way and views deep into Scotland. About fourteen miles in all, five more than intended. Home tired and dehydrated. My left knee swollen. Nick and the girls remain good-humoured throughout.

Monday 6 April

From Saigon comes word that Ngoc's mother is dying. The poor old soul, crippled by back pain, has been more or less bedridden for years. Ngoc spoke to her by Skype last week and she seemed all there, but a few days ago she closed her eyes and stopped eating. As Ngoc says, a lamp running out of oil.

Lunch in the garden for the first time this year and in the evening I sat outside reading Volume Four of Robert Caro's monumental biography of Lyndon Johnson, as the setting sun illuminated first the pine forest and then the beech wood on the other side of the valley. This evening, while waiting to collect Emma from Barter Books, a chat with a local Tory councillor, who says, 'We have been asked to be nice to the Greens because we want them to attract Lib Dem votes, but I am not supposed to tell you.'

Tuesday 7 April

To Alnmouth Station, en route to an HLF meeting at Auckland castle, only to discover that I had left most of my money and my credit card at home. I explained the problem to the man in the ticket office. Without hesitation he took a tenner from his wallet and pushed it under the glass, enabling me to buy a ticket. Disaster averted. How's that for service?

And how about this for the latest piece of Scottish exceptionalism? Nicola Sturgeon is demanding that Scots be exempted from the proposed increase in pension age on the grounds that they do not live as long as the English.

The return of The Man. Emerging from the stratosphere to touch down briefly in his old stamping ground at Sedgefield, he made a speech saying that another Tory government would be damaging for the economy because they are threatening two years of uncertainty over British membership of the EU. Of course he doesn't carry the same weight as he once did, but it is a useful intervention. Extraordinary that the Tories have been allowed to go about accusing Labour of being anti-business while our free press ignores the elephant in the room.

Wednesday 8 April

According to the polls, the main parties' ratings remain deadlocked, despite weeks of knocking five bells out of each other, Incredibly, one can just about see a scenario where, with the support of the Lib Dems (minus Nick Clegg and Danny Alexander?) and the tacit support of the Scottish Nationalists, Labour might stumble into government. Obvious question: what happens if, by any slim chance, we do win? The support of a mere one third of the electorate is hardly a mandate and we have designed a huge trap for ourselves by promising to reduce the deficit at the same rate as the Tories, which leaves little room for manoeuvre. Also, we are saddled with so many useless or impractical policies.

Meanwhile the Tories (sensing that they might lose?) have reverted to being the nasty party. Michael Fallon has made a speech accusing Ed Miliband of ruthlessly stabbing his brother in the back and preparing to stab the nation in the back by abandoning Trident (if only…). Until now they have been portraying Ed as weak and useless; suddenly the line has changed – he is now a ruthless backstabber.

Thursday 9 April

At noon Hanh, one of Ngoc's sisters, rang to say that their mother is dead. A merciful release given the pain she was in. Her life was not easy. Bringing up nine children during decades of war, nine years a refugee, the family fortunes yoyoing back and forth between prosperity and poverty. In the end, though, she had the satisfaction of knowing that her children's lives were better than hers and she died surrounded by those who loved her. Her photograph has now joined Grandpa's on the little altar in our living room.

Ed Miliband has responded with dignity to the Fallon attack. He is growing in stature. All the signs are that the Tory nastiness has backfired.

Friday 10 April

A Skype with Ngoc's sister Hong in Saigon showing their mother peacefully 'asleep' in her bed surrounded by grieving family. Communication these days is instant, so we are operating in real time. The old lady is now en route to Kontum in the Highlands to be interred alongside Grandpa on a date and at a time deemed auspicious by the officiating monks.

Our battered twelve-year-old Toyota has been consuming oil voraciously. The almost universal advice is to throw it away and get a new car, but I have opted instead to try to prolong its life. Not that we can't afford another car, just that I can't bring myself to throw away something that in any sane world ought to be repairable. So today we took it to Minories in Sunderland to have the engine rebored at considerable expense. The man at Minories was too polite to say so, but he obviously thinks I am mad. So does Ngoc.

Sunday 12 April

Faced with deadlock in the polls, the main parties grow ever more reckless. The Tories, still posing as the party of financial rectitude, are promising to pump another £8 billion a year into the NHS. When asked where the money would come from, they reply blithely that it will come from the proceeds of growth. Labour is promising to fund most of its spending pledges by raising an unbelievable £7 billion a year from clamping down on tax dodgers. As the man from the Institute for Fiscal Studies remarked on the radio this morning, both parties appear to be making up numbers as they go along.

Monday 13 April

Ngoc's mother was interred at 2 p.m. Kontum time (8 a.m. our time). At the appointed hour, Ngoc lit the candles on the little altar in our living room and stood in silent contemplation. I, having misjudged the time, overslept. Tony Henfrey and I spent a couple of hours digging silt from the lake.

Wednesday 15 April

With brazen irresponsibility, the Tories are this morning promising to extend the right to buy, with discounts of up to £100,000, to housing association residents. On past form, about 40 per cent of purchased properties will end up in the hands of buy-to-let landlords, who will jack up rents to the outer limit, thereby increasing the bill for housing benefit, already swollen by their last great giveaway. They have also given another outing to their old promise to raise the threshold for inheritance tax to £1 million. With stunning cynicism, the party of bankers, derivative traders, hedge funders and buy-to-let landlords has proclaimed itself 'the party of working people'. Cameron repeated the phrase eleven times at his manifesto launch today. Should we laugh or cry?

This evening, with Emma's help, I took the plunge and finally embraced the digital age: I have joined the Twitterati.

Thursday 16 April

My email has become clogged with Twitterati. By mid-morning I have more than 500 followers, including two ambassadors, a number of techno-savvy former colleagues and a handful of journalists. Many have sent messages which demand a response. Also, an email from Sheila Williams: 'Have you taken leave of your senses???'

Planted our pink fir apple potatoes, garlic and onions, only to find the forecasters predicting frost.

Friday 17 April

Sure enough, awoke to find the lawn white with frost. Mercifully, it doesn't seem to have caught the blossom on the espaliered fruit trees, which, in the absence of bees, we have been tickling with a rabbit's tail.

One by one the dice are falling in the Tories' favour. This morning the IMF chief Christine Lagarde, with George Osborne sitting alongside her, heaped praise upon the government's management of the economy, even going so far as to say they had got right the balance between spending cuts and tax rises. This was followed by the news that, for the first time in years, wages are rising and so too are the number of people in work. Although the polls remain deadlocked, it is hard to believe that all this won't have an impact. The most likely outcome of the election is more of the same (even if Lib Dem numbers are halved). An outright Tory victory, though unlikely, cannot be ruled out.

Saturday 18 April

With John Field and Tony Henfrey to the Breamish Valley, from where we walked, via Linhope Spout, over the hills to Low Bleakhope and back in a circle, encountering skylarks and oystercatchers. Tony, once a Tory, now a free-thinker with Ukippish tendencies, used words like 'barmy' and 'irresponsible' to describe the Tories' promised sale of housing association properties, which he fears, combined with new freedom to draw down pensions, will fuel a new buy-to-let boom.

Monday 20 April

A boat containing at least 800 refugees has gone down in the Mediterranean with only a handful of survivors. The latest of a series of such tragedies since the EU cut back its funding of the Italian rescue operation. The Italians, struggling to cope with the increasing flow of refugees from Syria and Africa, are becoming increasingly desperate. Thus far, however, not much sign of any of the much-vaunted European solidarity. This latest catastrophe has led to a good deal of hand-wringing, but it remains to be seen whether it will lead to action. The root cause seems to be the activities of ruthless people-smugglers who are exploiting the chaos in Libya. No amount of rescuing is going to solve this problem. Much more drastic action is called for. I favour establishing an enclave on the Libyan coast, under UN mandate, and using it as a base from which to process migrants and crack down on the whole rotten trade.

Tuesday 21 April

To the RAF station at Boulmer with Tony Henfrey and a couple of friends, as guests of the commanding officer, who turns out to have attended my talk on Tony Benn at Alnwick Playhouse a few months back. He gave us a tour of the underground bunker from where he and his colleagues are in charge of monitoring aircraft movements in this part of the country and intercepting Russian bombers attempting to probe British airspace. Last week's Russian incursion was apparently targeted on Sunderland. There have been a spate of stories in the press recently, following Russian aggression in Ukraine, suggesting a revival of the alleged Russian threat. Interestingly, however, our host remarked that, despite reports to the contrary, there had been no increase in Russian incursions. He added that we do the same to them.

Thursday 23 April

Robert Caro's account of the Kennedy presidency, which I am currently reading, scrupulously documents the endless humiliations that Kennedy and his arrogant courtiers inflicted on Vice-President Johnson, once he had outlived his usefulness as a vote-winner in the southern states. The President himself was outwardly smiling and courteous, leaving it to his spiteful and vindictive brother Bobby and the underlings to do the dirty work. Shades of the New Labour court and Blair's advice to David Miliband after David had been selected in South Shields: 'Go round smiling at everybody and leave it to others to shoot your enemies'. It belatedly occurs to me that this may be how Peter Mandelson came to acquire the code name 'Bobby' during Blair's leadership campaign. Can it be that The Man and Peter consciously modelled themselves on the Kennedys?

Friday 24 April

Today's headlines:
'Labour's £1,000 a year tax on families' (*The Times*)
'Miliband will bring back uncontrolled immigration' (*Mail*)
'Labour minister attacks Miliband' (*Telegraph*)
This last being a reference to Digby 'Motormouth' Jones, who has never voted Labour in his life and whose brief visit to government was one of Gordon's foolish wheezes. Aren't we lucky to have a free press?

Saturday 25 April

Nick Clegg has ruled out Lib Dem support for any party that doesn't have an outright majority of seats or votes or which is in any way dependent on the Scot Nats. Which would seem to put an end to whatever slim chance Labour has of forming a government.

Sunday 26 April

The Tories and their friends in the media are warning of a major constitutional crisis if the SNP hold the balance of power. Is it my imagination or are they hinting that they won't accept the outcome?

With Tony Henfrey, I walked from Barrowburn to Davidson's Linn, the waterfall above Uswayford that the girls and I spectacularly failed to find over the Easter weekend. The reason we couldn't find it is that the footpath sign had snapped off and was lying concealed in the grass.

Wednesday 29 April

Awoke to the news that the Tories are promising 'within 100 days' to pass an act prohibiting them from raising income tax, VAT or National Insurance. Surely the most ludicrous, irresponsible, outrageous undertaking of any made so far in this most dismal of election campaigns. And one they would abandon at the drop of a hat, if it suited them. Both sides appear to believe that the result of the election can simply be purchased. As someone remarked the other day, this election is like a Moroccan *souk*, full of dodgy salesmen offering unbelievable bargains. I am due to give my 'In Defence of Politics' talk in Newcastle on Sunday, arguing that politics is at heart an honourable profession, but the argument becomes less credible with every day that passes. The polls, meanwhile, are beginning to show the Tories moving ahead. A minority Tory government, perhaps with support from the surviving Lib Dems, now looks almost certain. The prospect of a Labour government dependent on the Scot Nats, which the Tories have been hammering for days, seems finally to have tipped the balance.

Thursday 30 April

On BBC's *Question Time* this evening, Ed Miliband allowed himself to be trapped into forswearing, in terms that seemed unequivocal, any arrangement with the SNP, even if the alternative was another five years of opposition. Unless I've missed something, that would seem to put an end to any slim chance of ousting the regime. Watching the programme, in which all three leaders were questioned separately by a deeply cynical studio audience, one is struck by how deeply the lie that Labour collapsed the economy has become ingrained. So much so that Labour leaders no longer attempt to rebut it. The notion that the bankers had something to do with the crisis of 2008, or that the crisis was Europe-wide and began in the American mortgage market, is simply not mentioned. Likewise the easily rebuttable assertion that the previous government recklessly overspent is simply met with a promise that it won't happen again. Rarely does anyone bother to point out that the deficit was primarily caused by a collapse of tax revenues triggered by the reckless behaviour of the bankers and at the time even the Tories were signed up to match Labour spending on health and education 'pound for pound'. Of course, that stupid note left behind by Liam Byrne for his successor, saying, 'I'm afraid there is no money'* (all Tory candidates are armed with a copy) hasn't helped. I now suspect that the 'Don't knows', of whom there are said to be unprecedented numbers, will come down heavily in favour of the present management and that the Tories will be close to an overall majority.

The Vietnam War ended forty years ago today. On this day in 1975, Ngoc and her family were huddled on the ground floor of their house on Le Van Sy listening to the rumble of North Vietnamese tanks heading into the city centre from the airport. One, on the lookout for snipers, put a shell clean through the upper floor of their house. Ngoc says that, by lying flat on the tiled floor and looking under the shutters, they could see that the boots of the southern army had given way to the rubber sandals of the *bo doi*, the army of North Vietnam. When they eventually felt secure enough to open the shutters, they found the street littered with abandoned military uniforms. From that moment their lives changed for ever.

Saturday 2 May

Kate Middleton was delivered of another royal baby, providing a welcome distraction from the dismal business of politicking.

Sunday 3 May

To Hexham Book Festival, where I gave my speech on the art of political leadership to an audience of just over 200, including Tony Blair's former henchman Jonathan Powell. I signed some books and had my photo taken with the Labour candidate. Then to the Live Theatre in Newcastle, where I gave my 'In Defence of Politics Speech' to a disappointingly small audience, about seventy people. Meanwhile the election campaign gets

---

* It was meant as a joke, but the Tories exploited it mercilessly.

sillier. Miliband, to widespread derision, unveiled an eight-foot block of granite on which were etched Labour's six 'key' pledges, which he says he will erect in the garden of No. 10 if and when he gets there. Personally I would attach it to the neck of whichever young master strategist came up with the idea and throw it in the Thames.

Monday 4 May

A day spent scouring the verges of the A1 and A19 for litter, having persuaded regional BBC television to make a brief documentary about the disgraceful state of the region's roadsides. However, by the time the Beeb got round to giving the idea the go-ahead, the hedgerows had blossomed and the annual clear-up had taken place, with the result that much of the litter had either been collected or was no longer visible. We just about managed in the end. Next step to challenge the highway authorities as to why they don't accord the issue higher priority. Something I've been itching to do for years.

Thursday 7 May

To the village hall in Whittingham to cast my vote and then to London. Whisper it quietly, but for the first time in my life I voted Lib Dem on the grounds that, in this constituency, it is the only chance (and a slim one, at that) of defeating the Tory. The polls are predicting a close result, but I don't believe a word of it. At best we are in for more of the same, a Tory government propped up by the surviving Lib Dems. Our free press have excelled themselves. Only the *Mirror* and *The Guardian* advocated a Labour vote. As Ian Gilmour once remarked of the press under Thatcher, it could hardly be more supine if it were state-controlled.

In the late evening to BBC Broadcasting House, where, along with former MPs Sarah Tether and Richard Ottaway and *The Economist*'s Anne McElvoy, I spent six hours in a World Service studio opining as the election results came in. Arrived to find an exit poll saying, contrary to all previous predictions, the Tories would be within a whisker of an overall majority, the Lib Dems would be slaughtered and that (as predicted) the SNP would sweep Scotland. And so it proved. To bed at 5.30 a.m.

Friday 8 May

Great indeed was the slaughter. Awoke at noon to find that the Tories, exceeding all expectations, have an overall majority. The Lib Dems are all but wiped out and in Scotland every Labour MP bar one has been put to the sword. Among the casualties Douglas Alexander, Jim Murphy and Ed Balls. Just about the only Labour gains came from the Lib Dems plus a couple of London seats. Hampstead Tube Station was closed, half a dozen police cars outside. A person under a train, explained a London Underground man. 'Deliberate,' he added. (A distraught Liberal Democrat?) I walked up to Fenton House and sat for half an hour in sunshine among the apple blossom. How are we to explain the outcome? First, a fair swathe of the public bought the lie, so assiduously peddled, that Labour destroyed the economy when, as we all know, it was the bankers. Second, Tory scaremongering about the prospect of a Miliband government propped up by the SNP spooked the English electorate. Finally, of course, 'Red Ed' (although he came across reasonably well during the campaign) was never a credible leader. By the time I got home he had resigned, along with Nick Clegg and Nigel Farage. It rained all night.

Saturday 9 May

I dropped a line to Andrew Mitchell, who may well feature in the new government, remarking that, for the first time since 1973, I now live in a Tory-held constituency. 'It will be good for you,' he said. I replied, 'Actually, it's raining heavily at the moment.' Also my runner beans, planted last Wednesday, caught an election night frost and died – a portent of things to come?

This evening, to dinner at Chillingham. Guests included Matt and Anya Ridley and several amiable and obscure aristos, some with pedigrees stretching back into the Middle Ages. Just about all Tories, I guess, but no triumphalism re. the election outcome. Katharine Wakefield told a nice little story, against herself. 'We were on a train, in a coach filled with rugby players, and as we were about to get off I called out in my cutglass accent, "Humphry, you've left your hat." Everyone in the carriage fell about laughing. Nothing to be done, except to join in.'

Sunday 10 May

A big bout of navel-gazing under way. Chuka Umunna, almost certainly our next leader, was on the *Andrew Marr Show* exuding an Obama-like calm, talking big tents and recapturing the middle ground. The trouble is that the lie that Labour bankrupted the country is so deeply ingrained that it will take years to eradicate. One can hear it being repeated everywhere and rarely challenged. Much of it is down to that damn Liam Byrne letter, which Cameron read out everywhere he went. Also clear that UKIP is turning out to be more of a problem for Labour than for the Tories and it is hard to see how those votes can be regained by pandering to the middle ground. Never having heard of her, I googled Liz Kendall, one of the contenders for the Labour leadership. Even with her picture, her face rang no bells. We are in deep trouble.

Monday 11 May

A long chat with Ray Fitzwalter, who is on his second big bout of chemotherapy. He put on a brave face but sounds very down. He expressed amazement that Labour never made any serious attempt to rebut the Tory/Lib Dem lie that we collapsed the economy. If we are not careful, this falsehood will haunt us at the next election too. We discussed leadership candidates. I expressed the view that Chuka was our best hope. Ray sounded sceptical. 'I've never seen him smile.'

London

Headline in tonight's *Standard*: '£500 million home buying frenzy after Tory win – prices could rise by 10 per cent, estate agents predict'.

Tuesday 12 May

To Sloane Square for a meeting of HLF regional chairs with our new national chairman, Peter Luff, until the election a Tory MP. He said his daughter was telephone canvassing for the Tories in Battersea and under instructions to play up the supposed SNP threat. 'She didn't like doing it, but it was very effective.'

Then to Parliament, where I passed a couple of hours soaking up the atmosphere in the atrium of Portcullis House. Everyone (on our side) shell-shocked. No great enthusiasm for Chuka, but no sign of a serious alternative and recognition that Scotland is lost for at least a decade. This evening a dinner in the Kennington Tandoori with Ann Grant, a delightful woman who I first came across when she was our High Commissioner in South Africa. At the next table, a cabal of celebrating SNP MPs, including Alex Salmond. Among them one of their new intake, Tasmina Ahmed-Sheikh, a former Tory candidate, in which capacity she once had some very disobliging things to say about Alex (whom she was now sitting opposite). Before that, she was in the Labour Party. Third time lucky, I guess.

Wednesday 13 May

For all Cameron's one-nation talk, the Tories have plans for widening the divide. Cheered on by the Murdoch press, they are also said to be intending to do down the BBC, just about the only significant part of the media not already under the control of their friends. 'Payback time,' according to *The Sun*.

Sunshine. Everywhere blue wisteria and scented azalea in full bloom. The gardens in London are about a month ahead of ours. I passed a pleasant couple of hours in Hill House Gardens, finishing the fourth volume of Robert Caro's Lyndon Johnson biography. This afternoon, to a girls' high school at Aylesbury, in leafy Buckinghamshire, where I gave my 'Rise and Fall of New Labour' talk to sixth form history and politics students. Pinned to the noticeboard were the results of a mock election where it seems the girls voted pretty much along the same lines as their parents (Tories 38.9 per cent, Labour 16, UKIP 10). The only exception was a surge for the Greens (20 per cent), although, as I pointed out to them, the bins in the sixth form centre were overflowing with unsorted waste. No point in talking the talk if you are not willing to walk the walk.

Thursday 14 May

A damp day. With David Fraser to lunch at the Hurlingham, then to the nearby former palace of the bishops of London (an almost empty shell without original contents, although the walled garden is in the process of being restored). Then across the bridge to the church at Putney, which hosted the famous Leveller debates. Finally, to dinner in Kennington with

Sally Banks and Patricia Moberly. Patricia, who has perhaps only months to live, was in remarkable shape. Interested in everyone and everything, talking about the future as if she will be part of it, which of course she won't.

Friday 15 May

Breakfast with Steve Byers at Carluccio's in Hampstead at which we agreed that the rise of Chuka was probably inevitable and then home on the 11.30 train to discover that, a mere three days after having declared his candidacy, Chuka has withdrawn from the Labour leadership election on the not very believable grounds that he doesn't want to inflict press intrusion on his family. Which leaves Labour in a deep, deep hole. All the other candidates are second-raters. As someone remarked to me the other day, the next Labour Prime Minister may still be in primary school.

Meanwhile at Callaly, following several days of intermittent rain, an army of slugs has emerged from the long grass, heading in the general direction of my lupins and delphiniums. I spent an hour scooping them up and deposited them on a tree trunk at the end of the third lake.

Sunday 17 May

The woods at Callaly are carpeted with wild garlic forget-me-nots and yellow leopard's bane. Today we harvested our first strawberries from the glasshouse.

Monday 18 May

Awful scenes from the Andaman Sea, where boatloads of starving, dehydrated Rohingya fleeing persecution in Burma are being pushed back out to sea by amoral and ruthless Thai and Malaysian border police. Meanwhile in Burma, the saintly Aung San Suu Kyi is all but silent on the fate of the Rohingya, no doubt fearful of undermining her political base. What a world we live in.

Tuesday 19 May

A new media game is under way. Candidates for the Labour leadership are being pressed to renounce Ed Miliband and embrace the market. Unfortunately some of our number have fallen for it. Yvette Cooper has launched herself as the pro-business candidate, dissociating herself from Ed Miliband's distinction between predatory and productive capitalism and claiming that Labour under previous management was perceived as 'anti-business, anti-growth and ultimately anti-worker'. All of which plays straight into the Tory narrative. Oh Yvette, must we really become the party of Wonga, Sports Direct, FTSE fat cats and buy-to-let landlords? And if so, what's the point?

Wednesday 20 May

Our gas contract has come up for renewal – Flogas, the company we have been with for the past four years, were demanding 44p a unit. Initially they were unwilling to negotiate until Ngoc rang Calor and was quoted 37p plus a bonus of £250 worth of gas. She rang back Flogas, who immediately agreed to renew our contract on similar terms. I suppose we should be overjoyed at the workings of the market, but the outcome is that the poor, the inarticulate and the uninformed pay more than the prosperous and the pushy.

Yesss. Once again Sunderland's benighted football team have survived relegation by a hair's breadth, an inglorious nil–nil draw against Arsenal being sufficient to earn the one point they needed to survive. Supporting Sunderland is a white-knuckle ride.

Thursday 21 May

Out at 4 a.m. to deliver Mrs Very Big Boss to the airport. She was issuing instructions and advice right up to the moment she disappeared into the departure lounge. As the day for her departure approached, the flow of advice/instructions/reprimands intensified. Including repeats, they amounted to perhaps twenty or thirty a day. Lately she has taken to waving her finger at me as she speaks. Among the last-minute decrees, an email (repeated several times orally) insisting upon a minimalist funeral in the event that she doesn't come back. We went out into a beautiful dawn chorus which we are not usually awake in time to hear.

Six banks – including Barclays and RBS – have been fined a record

£3.7 billion for rigging the foreign exchange markets, only the latest of a long series of scams involving erstwhile masters of the universe. 'Yet another blow for the integrity of the banks,' says one commentator. I don't suppose the Tories will have a lot to say on the subject and Labour will presumably be keeping its head down for fear of being denounced as 'anti-business'.

Saturday 23 May

To the Harthope Valley, from where I walked over the hills to the abandoned hamlet at Old Middleton and then back via Middleton and Langlee Crags, about eight miles in all. At Old Middleton I came across a man who, on seeing my guidebook, remarked that it was unreliable and often got him lost. So it's not just me. Sure enough, just as the track entered a vast conifer forest, the guidebook became unhelpfully vague. Mindful what happened last time, I steered round the forest and made my way back to Harthope under my own steam. A difficult journey home. The plastic mudguard covering the sump became dislodged and I had to drive out of the valley at snail's pace with the mudguard dragging along the ground, people staring as I passed. At Wooler I managed a temporary repair and just made it home to Callaly before it fell off again.

Wednesday 27 May

To Auckland Castle to announce the award of a £9 million lottery grant to help fund restoration. A great project, inspired and driven by a delightful philanthropist, Jonathan Ruffer, who is using his considerable fortune not just to restore the 900-year-old Bishop's Palace but to help revive Bishop Auckland, a down-at-heel market town which has suffered more than most from the decline of traditional industries. Mr Ruffer is a man who thinks big. In addition to the castle and its contents, he's bought two hotels in the market square and turned a disused bank into an outpost of Madrid's Prado gallery. He's leased a town centre car park, bought the Roman baths at Binchester and is now restoring the derelict four-acre walled garden. If it works, and I think it will, this will become a visitor attraction of national and possibly international significance. Then to the Freeman Hospital in Newcastle for a scan, to see whether the tiny lump detected a year ago on one of my lungs is anything to worry about. Home in time to see myself on the regional television news predicting great things for Bishop Auckland.

Thursday 28 May

With our neighbours John and Gilly Nicholls for lunch in Bamburgh. We drove home via Chillingham, where a visitor to the castle commiserated with me for having recently broken my wrist. It took a moment for the penny to drop, but gradually it dawned on me that he thought I was Sir Humphry Wakefield. Not since someone mistook me for Norman Tebbit have I been so misidentified.

Monday 1 June

To Wallington, where the National Trust are scratching around for ideas of how to use the wing recently vacated by the death, aged ninety-seven, of Sir Charles Trevelyan's last surviving daughter. A public consultation is under way. Visitors were asked to choose between half a dozen fatuous options. The only option that didn't seem to have occurred to anyone was using it to raise some badly needed funds. On my Post-it note I wrote: 'None of the above. Do it up and rent it out.'

Friday 5 June

Mrs Very Big Boss returned from Vietnam this evening, as usual complaining of the heat and the chaos, and laden with coffee, ground nuts and mangoes. A major cleaning preceded her arrival; even so, I am sure to fail the inspection.

Sunday 14 June

To College Valley, where we celebrated Charles Baker-Cresswell's eightieth birthday. We picnicked among the great and good of North Northumberland. James Joicey, wearing a badge commemorating the anniversary of Magna Carta, remarked that his ancestors weren't present at the signing. 'No,' I replied. 'But I bet one or two of our fellow guests' families were represented.' Sure enough, within sixty seconds, we were joined by a man whose ancestors had been at Runnymede.

Tuesday 16 June

An irate email from Charlie Gow, son of the late Ian, a housing minister in Mrs Thatcher's government, who has made a fortune buying and letting former council houses. During the run-up to the election, I denounced him on Twitter. 'Are you seriously suggesting that my late father's position … has anything whatsoever to do with me owning hundreds of ex-council properties? I was fourteen years old when the right-to-buy was introduced…' I replied as follows:

> No slur on your father intended, but yes I do suggest that the policy he oversaw has proved disastrous – one of the bills coming in for the Thatcher Decade. Where you are concerned, my only error has been to understate the size of your portfolio, but then I prefer to err on the side of caution.

Tuesday 23 June

Awful scenes on the television news as desperate migrants, taking advantage of a strike by French ferry workers, lay siege to the terminal at Calais, only to be beaten back by French police. Several thousand migrants are camped in squalor on the French coast and thousands more on the way with no solution in sight. Talk of sending them home is pointless, many coming from countries to which they cannot be removed. EU solidarity is in meltdown. Leaders running round in circles, no idea what to do. The UK, of course, is seeking exemption from any solution that involves admitting more than a relative handful – and in any case taking in a few thousand solves nothing. The problem needs to be addressed at source.

Wednesday 24 June

An interesting piece in the *New York Times* by the Nobel Prize-winning economist Paul Krugman:

One important factor in the recent Conservative election triumph was the way Britain's news media told voters, again and again, that excessive government spending under Labour caused the financial crisis. It requires almost no homework to show that this claim is absurd on multiple levels. For one thing the crisis was global; did Gordon Brown's alleged overspending cause the housing busts in Florida and Spain? For another, all these claims of irresponsibility involve rewriting history, because on the eve of crisis nobody thought Britain was being profligate: debt was low by historical standards and the deficit fairly small. Finally, Britain's supposedly disastrous fiscal position has never worried the markets which have remained happy to buy British bonds … Nonetheless that's the story repeated, not as opinion but as fact. And the really bad news is that Britain's leaders seem to believe their own propaganda.

Required reading for any Labour leadership candidates tempted by a policy of appeasement.

Friday 26 June

An enjoyable day touring HLF-funded projects in the spectacular Allen Valleys and then over the hills into Teesdale. Highlights included my first ever trip on an electric bike, which sure takes the pain out of cycling. Home, via Otterburn and Elsdon, to news of new atrocities by deranged Islamists in Tunisia, Kuwait and France.

Wednesday 1 July
Beamish Hall Hotel
On tour with Peter Luff, the new chairman of the Heritage Lottery Fund. We took in the lottery-funded projects at Durham Cathedral (lunch in the spectacular solarium in the Dean's house), Barnes Park in Sunderland and Auckland Castle. The afternoon was enlivened by a sudden electric storm, forked lightning splitting the horizon. In the evening I hosted a dinner for the heads of seven or eight big regional heritage projects. We arrived at the hotel to find that a thunderbolt had knocked out the

electricity. Then, during dinner, a biblical hailstorm. Chunks of ice the size of golf balls bouncing on the lawn.

Thursday 2 July
Beamish Hall

Awoke to news of another mega-thunderstorm during the early hours, which I slept through, though no one else seems to have done. Peter said he had never seen anything like it. Hotel still operating on emergency generator. Reports of thunderbolts, burned homes, smashed glasshouses and damaged vehicles. Mercifully, the storm didn't touch Callaly.

We were collected by horse-drawn charabanc and treated to a conducted tour of the Beamish Museum – which attracts more than 600,000 visitors a year and no longer requires public subsidy. Luff, a decent, one-nation Tory, treated everyone courteously, asked lots of sensible questions and generally made a good impression.

Friday 3 July

Ray and Luise Fitzwalter are staying. Although at first glance he seems fairly robust, Ray is not long for this world.

Sunday 5 July

Ray, afflicted by intermittent pain and lack of sleep, has spent much of the weekend resting. Yesterday we visited the Alnwick garden and by shuffling from seat to seat just about managed to get round. This afternoon Luise and I visited Shawdon Hall, the garden of which opens once a year for the hospice. The owner, Major Robin Cowen, an upright old gent aged ninety-six, was much in evidence. 'Never thought I'd make it to 100,' he said, 'but I guess the odds are getting better.'* He showed us round a barn next to the house, which contained a display of his pastel drawings, including passably good portraits of his late wife, landscapes and on the back of the door a beautiful young woman in a red dress. 'Been a lot of fun,' he kept saying. 'A lot of fun.'

---

* He died eight months later.

Monday 6 July

The turbulent Greeks have voted, by a wide margin, to reject the EU's terms for a bailout. Unclear what happens next. Their economy is in meltdown, their banks have run out of cash and the EU has run out of patience.

Wednesday 8 July

A remarkable budget and one that Labour will find difficult to counter. As expected, Osborne has announced the phasing out of Gordon Brown's tax credits, but to general surprise he also announced a 34 per cent increase in the national minimum wage over the next four years (this from a party that opposed tooth and nail the introduction of any minimum wage – they have travelled quite a distance). Predictable squealing from the business sector, but it surely makes sense for the taxpayer to cease subsidising the lowest-paying employers and at the same time reduce the numbers dependent on the state. I recall Alan Milburn advocating this years ago. 'A big philosophical difference with Gordon,' I remarked. 'It is,' he said. The problem with Gordon was that, combined with a genuine desire to help the impoverished, he wanted everybody to be grateful to him and so set up a fiendishly complex system of tax credits that left too many people dependent on the largesse of government while at the same time giving the worst employers a free pass. The big question is: will the proposed wage increase make up for the loss of benefits? I suspect not.

As predicted – and disgracefully – Osborne has offloaded the cost of free TV licences for the over-75s onto the BBC. Also, as widely predicted, he has raised to £1 million the threshold at which the value of a principal residence is liable for inheritance tax, but he is cleverly paying for it by reducing tax relief on pensions for top earners. Hard to object to that. Finally, Osborne has quietly extended his target for deficit reduction by a further year – something that only a few weeks ago he was denouncing as irresponsible. One has to pinch oneself that this is a man who came to power promising to balance the books within a single parliament. Then it was two parliaments. And now it is two parliaments plus one year. Basically, though no one is ever going to concede the point, he has followed Ed Balls's advice. It seems there was a plan B after all.

Thursday 9 July

An anonymous Cabinet minister is quoted by Tim Montgomerie in this morning's *Times* as saying, re. the budget, 'We have given lazy British business a kick up the arse.' Something no Labour government would ever dare admit to. And which of the three respectable candidates for the Labour leadership would have dared suggest a 34 per cent increase in the minimum wage? Even so, it appears Osborne is taking away more than he is giving.

Friday 10 July

High Lorton

Emma and I are staying in the lakes with Alf and Ann Dubs. We drove to Haweswater and inched our way up the Straits of Riggindale onto High Street. The cloud at the top had lifted by the time we got up there. Alf continually apologising for lagging behind, but he's amazing for a man of eighty-two. I very much doubt I will be capable of anything like that when I am his age.

Saturday 11 July

Osborne's budget is unravelling. The Institute for Fiscal Studies has published figures showing that, even allowing for the proposed increase in the minimum wage, 3 million of the poorest families will be at least £1,000 a year worse off and almost everyone else will be out of pocket except those in the second wealthiest decile. Thus the great Tory tradition of redistributing wealth from the poor to the prosperous continues, albeit heavily disguised.

Sunday 12 July

Last day at Lorton. Awoke to rain which soon lifted. Alf, Emma and I set off for a seven-mile circuit of Loweswater, the so-called coffin walk. On the way home Emma and I stopped at Naworth Castle, where the laird, Philip Howard, treated us to tea and a tour. Naworth, not open to the public, is a fourteenth- and fifteenth-century gem. Libraries lined with portraits of ancestors, a magnificent great hall, the gnarled remains of a hanging tree on which border reivers, including, over the years, eighty-three members of the same clan, were dispatched. Ancestral souvenirs include a sword from the Flodden, where Philip's ancestors presided over the annihilation of the Scots, and a spear from the Battle of Omdurman, where his ancestors also performed. Among the signatories of the visitors' book, a Mr Walter Disney. The library includes a dozen volumes from the Duke of Windsor's library, signed by Nixon, Churchill etc... and two volumes of my diaries, which I duly autographed. I will send him the third.

Monday 13 July

Harriet Harman is in trouble for announcing, apparently without consulting anyone, that HM Opposition would not be opposing Osborne's proposed benefit cap or his plan to restrict child benefit to a maximum of two children. 'Labour needs to get back in touch with the voters on the economy and on benefits,' she said. Two of the four leadership candidates have dissociated themselves and a U-turn is under way.

Tuesday 14 July

Sure enough, 'a source close to Harriet' is letting it be known that her remarks on Sunday were 'an attitude' rather than a statement of policy and she would be 'happy' (I bet) to see it overturned by whoever is elected leader. A pity she has blotted her copybook; she had been doing well thus far.

The Tories have unveiled a bill tightening the screws on trade unions, taking up where Thatcher left off. It includes a clause requiring payers of the political levy to opt in, rather than out. A measure which threatens to bankrupt Labour while leaving Tory mega-donations unscathed. Trade union funding is hardly the great scandal that it's made out to be – several million people paying £3 *a year* into a political fund, not all of which goes to Labour, is the nearest thing we have to mass politics in this age of indolence. And to think, when in office, we held off for years from introducing measures that would affect the Tory funding base on the grounds that, by convention, amendments to the law on such matters are supposed to require all-party consensus. *Consensus*, my foot.

Wednesday 15 July

Emma posted on Facebook a note in praise of Jeremy Corbyn, eliciting the following response from Gordon Castle, the genial, mild-mannered Tory councillor who is her immediate boss at Barter Books:

> I do hope Labour go for him. That should pave the way for many more years of Socialism in the wilderness. Far too much use by Corbyn of 'devastating' for consequences that are inconvenient for some but … are only unfair if you believe the state has unlimited means and, therefore, unlimited obligations … Corbyn is another bewitched believer in the magic money tree, an illusion that the election should have dispelled.

Thursday 16 July

Amid talk of 'blackmail', comparisons with the Treaty of Versailles and a hail of petrol bombs (which tend to figure at an early stage of any political disagreement in Greece), the Greek Parliament has voted through the draconian package of reforms imposed upon it by the Eurozone finance ministers. It is widely thought to be undeliverable – a view compounded by the discovery of an IMF memorandum saying exactly that. The trouble is that, after years of dodging any serious reform, no one trusts the Greeks. Even now most of them prefer to blame Germany for their troubles rather than concede the slightest responsibility of their own. Whatever view one takes, the Greek crisis has highlighted the perils of life in the Eurozone and the fact that, like it or not, Germany is once again the major power in Europe and prepared to act ruthlessly in support of its interests. All hail the once-mighty Gordon Brown for keeping us out of the euro.

Friday 17 July

The more one reflects, the more one comes to realise that George Osborne is the malign genius of the regime. With cynical brilliance he has converted what was by any measure a crisis of capitalism into a crisis of the public sector. Now he is busy painting Labour into a corner over welfare. As someone wrote the other day, he is quite happy to let the victims of his latest round of benefit cuts go running to Labour, because that only adds weight to the warped picture he is trying to paint of Labour as the party of welfare and the Tories as the party of enterprise. So successful has he proved that he has convinced not only a large swathe of the public but even most of the contenders for the Labour leadership, who, even though they may not agree with his analysis, feel powerless to resist. Hence all this apologising and appeasing. Having won the economic argument, the Tories are now getting to work on the power structure – witness the tightening of the screws on the BBC and the proposal to cut off much of Labour's trade union funding. Clearly, despite an overall majority of just twelve, they are working to a plan. If only Labour governments were so bold.

Monday 20 July

The campaign for the Labour leadership is heating up. To the dismay of the Establishment candidates, Jeremy Corbyn is doing surprisingly well and as a result some old smears we haven't heard since the days when Tony Benn threatened to upset the Establishment apple cart are being trotted out. 'Trotskyite', 'hero of the International Marxist Tendency' and so forth. Andrew Rawnsley, who should know better, was at it in yesterday's *Observer*. There is even talk of staging some sort of coup, were Jeremy to win. As it happens, I share the view that Jeremy, principled and decent man that he is, would render Labour unelectable, but I see no evidence that any of the other candidates is a winner either. Like many of their generation, Sarah and Emma are impressed by Jeremy and say they will vote for him.

Tuesday 21 July

A large brown and yellow hornet with a terrifyingly long sting in its tail has taken up residence in the glasshouse. Yesterday it was parked on a bamboo cane holding up a tomato plant. Today it had moved to the rear wall. Later it disappeared and is no doubt lurking amid the tomatoes.

Wednesday 22 July

Jeremy appears to be comfortably ahead in the race for the Labour leadership. Amusing to hear the New Labour elite and the media, with every day that passes, growing shriller in their denunciations (shades of the Great Benn Panic in '81). One former bottle washer at No. 10 is quoted as describing those MPs who nominated Corbyn for the sake of ensuring a free election as 'morons'. Imagine the hysteria were he to win. It is almost worth hoping for just to see the look on their smug faces. Seriously, though, what is interesting about the momentum that Jeremy is generating is what it tells us about the other candidates. Jeremy is the only one with anything interesting to say and so far he has conducted himself well. A small part of me says if we are destined to lose anyway (and I fear we are), we might as well be led by someone authentic.

An unsolicited email from the letters editor of *The Times* inviting me to send him a letter responding to an editorial in today's paper denouncing Labour for its apparent death wish. Good to know that someone on *The Times* cares about balanced reporting, but I have decided to lie low, so I declined his kind offer.

Today, at what looks like a rather small gathering put together short notice, The Man fired a warning shot about the dangers of abandoning the middle ground. Much of what he had to say made sense, but he went a wee bit too far, remarking that anyone thinking of voting with their heart should get a transplant.

Thursday 23 July

Emma reports that her Facebook page is filling up with messages from Tory colleagues cheering on Jeremy and even asserting that they will pay their £3 for temporary membership in order to vote for him. Although still a Corbyn fan, and deeply unimpressed by the other candidates, she is beginning to ask herself why the Tories are so keen on a Corbyn victory.

Sunday 26 July

Espied a red squirrel in the garden. The first for months.

Monday 27 July

To the Live Theatre in Newcastle for a North of England Civic Trust board meeting. On the way to the station I came across Alan and Ruth Milburn, strolling along the quayside. Alan reckons we will be out of office for at least another decade and that none of the candidates for the leadership has what it takes to lead us back to the high ground. 'You and I are lucky to be out of it,' he said. A sentiment I share.

Tuesday 28 July

More extraordinary scenes at Calais, where the wretched of the earth are laying siege to Fortress Britain. Several thousand desperate migrants have stormed the entrance to the Channel Tunnel, causing havoc. In Kent, lorries are backed up for miles along the motorway leading to the tunnel. On the evening news, calls for the army to be deployed. Only a taste of what is to come if the world beyond our smug little enclave continues to disintegrate.

Rain all day. It has been raining since Sunday afternoon. Garden looking sad.

Saturday 1 August

At the Edinburgh Book Festival. Many of the questions were about the remarkable rise of Jeremy. Most of those present thought a Corbyn-led Labour Party would be an excellent idea. I gently pointed out that, saintly man though he is, Jeremy is unelectable, but that wasn't what they wanted to hear. Even Kate Donaghy, who is no socialist, remarked yesterday that at least Jeremy would help the Labour Party regain its soul. John Field said something similar the other day.

Sunday 2 August

A clutch of emails – including one from the *Today* programme – asking if it is true that, prompted by the rise of Jeremy, I am planning a sequel to *A Very British Coup*. As it happened, unprompted by Jeremy, I have tapped out the first 5,000 words of exactly such a novel. If I could only set aside all other distractions and get on with it.

Emma, serving behind the counter at Barter Books, reports that a man bought a copy of *A View from the Foothills*. Upon being told that I was her dad, he asked her to sign it, which she duly did.

Thursday 6 August

Turned over our three compost heaps, disturbing a family of toads and several mice in the process. Meanwhile migrants continue to lay siege to the Channel Tunnel at Calais. The television news depicts nightly scenes of chaos. One man, a Sudanese, is reported to have walked almost the entire length of the tunnel with trains missing him by inches. The Greek islands nearest Turkey are overwhelmed with migrants, mainly from Syria and Iraq. So far this year 124,000 have reached Greece, and the Greek bureaucracy, incompetent at the best of times, cannot cope. Meanwhile the rhetoric from the Tory tabloids is turning nastier. The word migrant has become a term of abuse. Cameron was on the news this evening promising more security guards and razor wire, as if that solves anything.

Friday 7 August

A call from a former colleague mightily upset about the rise of Corbyn. She said 'sensible' MPs were busy signing up friends and relatives in a desperate attempt to hold the line. Meanwhile party officials are trawling through the flood of new members weeding out Trots and Tories. She thought a Corbyn victory possible since many of the second preferences wouldn't be used.

Saturday 8 August

Awoke to find a family of red squirrels helping themselves to hazelnuts from the feeder I attached to a tree near the house. It has taken them several months to find, but hopefully they will now become regular visitors.

Monday 10 August

To London to record a programme about the Birmingham bombings for Radio 4, part of the *Reunion* series fronted by Sue MacGregor. It's forty years this month since the trial and the aim was to bring together some of those most affected by the disaster. The men falsely convicted were represented by Paddy Hill, along with Breda Power and Ann McIlkenny (daughters of Billy Power and Richard McIlkenny). Brian Hambleton, whose sister

Maxine was killed in the explosion, represented the victims who are demanding a new inquiry. It was a real dog's dinner, taking two and a half hours to record, although the producer assured me that they could sort it out. I was wary of appearing with Mr Hambleton, who is spraying around accusations of cover-ups and betrayals. He refused to shake my hand or to even look at me and, once on air, launched into a long denunciation. His rant is unlikely to make the final cut, but it wasn't pleasant.

Afterwards, to the Naval and Military Club in St James's Square (a little part of the Establishment underworld that I haven't previously penetrated), where I was interviewed by John Ware, who is making a programme for *Panorama* about the rise of Corbyn.

Tuesday 11 August

Increasingly, Jeremy Corbyn and Harry Perkins, the hero of my 1982 novel, are mentioned in the same breath. I am receiving a steady trickle of media requests. Today's *Guardian* gives prominence to my light-hearted op-ed piece, written at their request, on the likely reaction of the Establishment to the election of Corbyn, increasingly seen as a strong possibility. The immediate result is likely to be a crisis in the parliamentary party, where he has only a handful of supporters.

To Profile Books to discuss my proposed volume of memoirs, provisionally entitled *Hinterland*. While there I received a request from Radio 4 for a light sketch imagining a Corbyn triumph in the general election of 2020. I duly tapped out 600 words and took it round to Broadcasting House to record. The only line they weren't happy about was a reference to 'the King'. Apparently the BBC top brass go all wobbly at the suggestion that HM may be mortal.

An email from Andrew Mitchell, who is, as he puts it, on a tour of his socialist friends in France. Today, he is staying with the author Robert Harris. He writes:

> I don't know why – it has nothing to do with my Conservative politics – but I feel a spring in my step at the prospect of Jeremy's elevation. As a member of the Establishment, I like to see a little frisson disturbing the champagne and canapé … Authenticity matters in politics today – Boris,

Sturgeon, Farage – so I raise my glass to Comrade Corbyn, and not because I am a Tory.

Wednesday 12 August

To the Assembly Rooms in Edinburgh to deliver my speech entitled 'The Art of Political Leadership', which has acquired a new topicality in the light of recent events. On arrival I could find no evidence that I was expected until a woman pointed out my name and photo displayed at ankle height on a show board in the foyer. I needn't have worried, however. About 200 people (paying £12 a head) turned out and the event went well. Afterwards, to Edinburgh University Business School to see Mr Speaker Bercow perform. He was in excellent form and later, on a taxi ride across town, treated us to some brilliant mimicry (he has added a very good impression of William Hague to his repertoire). Later, to the Balmoral Hotel for a dinner in his honour, following which he was interviewed by Jim Naughtie. Finally, a long drive home through the Border back roads, headlights on full beam most of the way, at one stage not encountering another vehicle for thirty miles, reaching Callaly at 2 a.m.

Thursday 13 August

A Corbyn victory is beginning to look inevitable. An astonishing 360,000 people have joined the Labour Party as either new or temporary party members and they are predicted to be overwhelmingly Corbynista. The Labour top brass are in panic mode. The Man himself wrote a hard-hitting piece in yesterday's *Guardian* warning that, come the next election, a Corbyn-led Labour Party faces not merely defeat but 'annihilation'. My feeling, too, but nobody's listening.

Friday 14 August

Email from Sheila Williams: 'Since Jeremy Corbyn has single-handedly revived your literary career, I think you should vote for him.'

A call from the *Mail on Sunday* suggesting a piece about Jeremy for which they would no doubt pay handsomely. I will not vote for him, but I ain't going to denounce him, especially in the *Mail*.

Sunday 16 August

Radio 4 broadcast my spoof account of Jeremy's first day as Prime Minister, *à la A Very British Coup*. It was well trailed and there were plenty of plugs for the novel. A lot of people seem to have heard it.

Monday 17 August

Gordon Brown has intervened in the Labour leadership election, adding to the growing list of warnings from on high that Jeremy is unelectable. Just how the membership will react to being lectured, not least by an ex-Labour leader whose own reign wasn't exactly a triumph, remains to be seen. Jeremy meanwhile continues his triumphal progress around the country. A truly extraordinary turn of events.

Tuesday 18 August

The red squirrels come every morning now, lifting the lid of the feeder and emptying it one hazelnut at a time.

Wednesday 19 August

John Williams is staying. With our neighbour John Field, we set out to complete the ten-mile stretch of St Oswald's Way between Rothbury and Felton. A couple of miles along the old railway line we were joined by two dogs, a dark brown Labrador with a little terrier trotting along behind. The terrier imitated the bigger dog's every move. When the Labrador stopped to investigate some interesting patch of vegetation, the terrier did likewise; when he sniffed, the terrier sniffed. After a couple of miles we realised we were never going to shake them off and called on a farmer's wife, who took them off our hands, promising to call the owner. Just before Weldon Bridge a border collie appeared out of nowhere and attached itself to us. For the rest of the way it trotted along happily in front of us, with occasional diversions, once to chase a rabbit, once to round up a flock of sheep, once to plunge into a pond, upsetting two fishermen in whose lines he became entangled. We did our best to shake him off, but to no avail. He was still with us when we climbed into John Field's car and drove away, leaving the poor dog to chase us down the road at high speed.

Thursday 20 August

One by one the New Labour elite have been queuing up to warn the party of the dire consequences of a Corbyn victory, but no one is taking any notice. A thousand people attended his meeting in Newcastle the other day and tickets sold out well in advance. On the same day just sixty turned out for a visit from Yvette Cooper. Until now the campaign has been fairly good-natured, but lately there are signs that the gloves are coming off. The Israel lobby is accusing him of associating with antisemites and the list of eligible voters is being purged by the apparatchiks at Labour HQ.

Saturday 22 August

Labour Party staff and volunteers are said to be working day and night to purge from the 360,000 people who have signed up to vote in the leadership election anyone suspected of having supported another party. Not just people who have stood against the party or nominated rival candidates but even those guilty of tweeting or retweeting anything that implies dissent from the One True Path. Social media is being trawled for signs of deviancy; party loyalists are being invited to shop alleged infiltrators. Although some Tories have been weeded out, there is a growing suspicion that this is about stopping Jeremy. All very distasteful. The one thing that would tempt me to vote for him is if I thought the election was being rigged.

Tuesday 25 August

For weeks now the bulletins have been showing footage of desperate, exhausted Syrian migrants flooding across the Greek border into Macedonia, border police trying to beat them back as though they were rioters. 'We are people, not animals,' said one. Many are young men avoiding the draft, but there are also families with small children. Mainly they are middle-class people who once led lives like us. Teachers, doctors, nurses, engineers, students. All reduced to this. They have been on the move for weeks, from Turkey to the Greek islands, and now they are heading north, goodness knows where to. Germany and Sweden seem to be the only countries willing to accept them and they are becoming overwhelmed.

The Hungarians are building a fence to keep them out, not that it will. We, needless to say, have yet to take a single one. And even if we did, it would make little or no impression, since behind these are several millions more. One feels so useless seeing this. Supposing it were us?

Wednesday 26 August

'Perhaps we could sponsor a Syrian family,' Ngoc remarked tentatively this morning. Of course we can't. There is no mechanism.

Friday 28 August

Seventy migrants have been found suffocated in the back of a truck with Hungarian plates parked in a lay-by in Austria. Another 200 are thought to have perished off the coast of Libya. For how much longer can we go on pretending that this is none of our business?

This evening a beautiful full moon in a clear sky rising over the wooded hills to the south of our valley.

Sunday 30 August

Yet another warning from Blair that Corbyn is unelectable.

Wednesday 2 September

A message from a Tory aristocrat of my acquaintance: 'You would not believe the amount of nobs who have signed up to the Labour Party...' – apparently with a view to voting for Jeremy.

Each evening, awful scenes on the television news. Today two small Syrian boys washed up dead on a Turkish beach. On the border with Macedonia, crowds of Syrians, some carrying young children, being beaten back by riot police. And thousands more camped outside the main railway station in Budapest, prevented by riot police from boarding trains for Germany. All over Europe, migrants – Sudanese, Eritrean, Bangladeshi, but above all Syrians – are camped out along roads and railway tracks. The EU is paralysed; no one has an answer. Admit a million and a million more will come. The wretched of the earth are no longer remote, shadowy figures occasionally glimpsed in some TV documentary or in the bottom half of a news bulletin. They are here, in Europe, battering at our gates. I have long known this day would come, but I thought that climate change rather than the collapse of the Arab tyrannies was the more likely cause.

Thursday 3 September

Decision day. The ballot paper arrived a week ago and must now be completed. There is a case for voting for Jeremy on the grounds that of the four candidates he is the least likely to make it to the general election, in which case we will be given another go at getting it right... whereas any of the other three will be with us for the duration. In the end I played safe and plumped without enthusiasm for Yvette, but I am not advertising the fact.

Friday 4 September

The death of the two small Syrian boys and their mother has increased pressure on the government to admit some of the tens of thousands battering on the gates of the EU. Church leaders, UN spokesmen, NGOs, Yvette Cooper and even a couple of Tory MPs have been demanding action. The signs are that Cameron will back down, though the policy he has pursued so far – massive aid to the camps in Turkey and Jordan, a camp-based asylum process that seeks out the most vulnerable – is surely right. To be sure, there is scope for taking more of the vulnerable than the handful we have so far taken, but not the thousands of (mainly) healthy young men fleeing Turkey, not Syria. Is it right to favour those with the energy to breach the walls of Fortress Europe, as opposed to the sick, the weak and the tortured? Or should we just cherry-pick the engineers and doctors? What is urgently needed is pressure on the Turks and Libyans to round up the people-smugglers who are preying on this misery. Not to mention Bulgarians and Romanians, EU members whose only contribution so far has been to provide many of the people-smugglers.

Saturday 5 September

Having tried for days to detain and register the river of Syrians passing through their country, the Hungarians have finally given in and allowed

them to board trains and buses to the Austrian border. To the consternation of other EU members, Germany has made clear that they will
take anyone who makes it across their frontier, with the result that no
one wants to go anywhere else. Admirable though the German stance
is, they have aroused hopes that cannot be fulfilled. They have triggered
a great migration, as the camps in Turkey, Jordan and Lebanon are
emptying of able-bodied young men (and in some cases entire families),
all determined to make it to the Promised Land. For how long can this
go on?

Monday 7 September

Andrew Mitchell was on the radio this morning calling for a UN enclave
to be established in Syria to cater for the millions of displaced. As John
Humphrys repeatedly pointed out, any such enclave would require the
endorsement of the Russians and their Syrian clients, but it's worth a shot.
No one else has a better idea. And in fairness, the Russian assessment of
the likely consequences of the so-called Arab Spring (rapidly becoming
the Arab Winter) has always been more realistic than our own.

This evening, a walk-on part in a *Panorama* programme on the rise
of Jeremy Corbyn. After I had paid tribute to his decency and general
saintliness, I was asked if I thought he was electable. After a slight hesitation I replied, 'Frankly, no.' Which is bound to get me into trouble with
the Corbynistas.

Tuesday 8 September

My first hate mail for some years. It comes from someone in the East
End of London who claims to be a former Labour councillor. 'Watching
you on *Panorama* seemed to be just another reminder of your political
morphing into an out of touch old windbag. It probably started when you
accepted your thirty pieces of silver from the murderer and war criminal
Tony Blair.' 'Windbag' is putting it a bit strongly, given that the phrase that
seems to have upset him consists of just two words. He goes on:

> You are out of touch with the 5 million people who stopped voting
> Labour in 2001, the 4 million who voted UKIP ... and the 5 million plus

under-thirties who have never voted, but who support ... Jeremy Corbyn's policies. They are the people who, given a fair choice, will elect a majority Labour government with JC at the helm and policies to match. Tony Benn would see you as a traitor. That is exactly what you are.

A call from the *Sunday Times* asking for a long piece – up to 3,000 words – imagining the first 100 days of a Corbyn government. Sceptical that anything I write could get past the censors at Murdoch Towers, I took care to nail down terms. To check that we are on the same wavelength, I also took the precaution of sending over the first 700 words. The response was as follows: 'Thank you for your rip-roaring start to the Corbyn 2020 victory. It's great fun and made me laugh.' Suitably encouraged, I ploughed on.

Wednesday 9 September

Sent over my *Sunday Times* piece. It contains the odd hand grenade which may not get past the censors. Although I didn't mention Murdoch by name, I appointed Tom Watson Secretary of State for Culture, Media and Sport and Vince Cable director general of Ofcom. I have a feeling their sense of humour won't stretch that far.

Thursday 10 September

No word from the *Sunday Times*. No doubt they are busy commissioning a replacement from someone more ideologically reliable. I emailed asking for an acknowledgement of yesterday's slightly amended draft and back came a single word: 'Thanks.'

Saturday 12 September

At 11.30 a.m. we turned on our television to see Jeremy Corbyn sweep the board, with nearly 60 per cent of the votes, comfortably winning in all categories bar the parliamentary party. His victory speech was inept, entirely directed towards the party rather than the nation, with scarcely a nod in the direction of unbelievers. He enumerated and thanked each of the trade unions which backed him and went way over the top in his thanks to Ed Miliband, who, after all, played a big part in bringing us to our present pass. Tom Watson was elected deputy and gave a better speech. In my heart I still believe Jeremy can't possibly lead us to victory, but I have to admit to butterflies in my stomach as the moment approached and a tear welling up when the margin of his victory became apparent. A truly astonishing result. We live in extraordinary times. If only my old friend Tony Benn had been alive at this hour.

After three days of silence, a bland little email from the *Sunday Times* saying that they won't be running my first 100 days piece, after all. (I had worked that out several days ago; the only question was how long they would take to level with me.) They have agreed a substantial rejection fee. I shall now offer it elsewhere.

Sunday 13 September

To Stansgate with Ruth Winstone for the interment of Tony Benn's ashes. A simple, informal, delightfully chaotic little event. No one dressed up. Lots of Benns of all ages, shapes and sizes ranging from Tony's (very frail) brother David to great-grandson Ollie, aged eleven months. We sat in rows on the stone steps leading up to the plinth upon which stands the park bench on which Tony proposed to Caroline in Oxford in 1948. Purchased by Tony, it stood for years in the front garden of 12 Holland Park Avenue. Now refurbished, it overlooks their final resting place. A tranquil nook, with a fine view of the spectacular Blackwater estuary. A place where generations of Benns have played. The little brick chamber containing Caroline's ashes had been prised open. Eldest son Stephen and Uncle David – the last survivor of Tony's generation – made brief speeches. A wooden box with Tony's ashes was placed next to Caroline's and the heavy granite slab, etched with their names and dates, manoeuvred back into place. Then we went indoors and ate pizza while a cricket match got under way on the lawn. All the talk was of the new Labour leadership. Hilary is awaiting a call from Jeremy to see whether he is still shadow Foreign Secretary.

Monday 14 September

To lunch with Jack Straw, back in civvy street for the first time in almost forty years, at Gandhi's in Kennington and finally to Millbank for a brief interview with *Channel 4 News* before catching the evening train to the north. In between I spent an hour and a half in the Commons, where the general feeling seems to be that Jeremy isn't going to make it to the election. I put that to a respected lobby journalist and he replied, 'I haven't come across anyone who thinks he will.'

Tuesday 15 September

The Guardian has splashed my 'Corbyn's first 100 days' piece across the G2 section. Very satisfactory in the light of last week's *Sunday Times* debacle. Lots of favourable reaction including enquiries from two film companies about the possibility of a sequel to *A Very British Coup*. All good fun, but of course, of no relevance to reality, which grows grimmer with every passing hour. Most of the parliamentary party are sulking. Jeremy appears to be at odds with his deputy (Tom Watson) over Trident and with his shadow Foreign Secretary (Hilary Benn) over the EU. His appointment of John McDonnell as shadow Chancellor has been badly received, although McDonnell gave a very competent interview on Channel 4 last night and, as Ken Livingstone pointed out, he was once chair of the GLC finance committee, managing a £1 billion budget – rather more experience than George Osborne had prior to becoming Chancellor. Today Jeremy is in trouble for failing to sing the national anthem at a Battle of Britain memorial service. At the meeting of the parliamentary party last night he was asked if he proposed to wear a red poppy at the Cenotaph in November and gave an equivocal reply which only dug the pit deeper. By today he had confirmed that he will. Tomorrow he has his first Prime Minister's Questions. Oh yes, the learning curve is steep.

The Hungarians have sealed their border with Serbia, leaving thousands of migrants stranded.

Wednesday 16 September

The *Today* programme has become a parade of Labour spokesmen being pressed to dissociate themselves from whatever Jeremy has said or done the previous day. No matter what the issue – the migrant crisis, benefit cuts, EU membership – the line of questioning is always the same: do you agree with Jeremy?

Today was his first PMQs. Another milestone, awaited with apprehension. He slipped into the chamber almost unnoticed and simply read out a series of unrelated questions sent in by punters and failed to follow up on any of them. He just about got away with it, but I can't see it working in the longer term. The next big hurdle is the speech to conference.

The sun shone all day. I spent seven hours in the garden collecting poppy seed, lifting the onions and mowing the lawn.

Thursday 17 September

I have been sent a review copy of Vince Cable's latest work, *After the Storm*. The following passage, on page 287, caught my eye: 'It is not true that the Labour government grossly mismanaged the public finances in the run-up to the 2008 crisis. There was a small structural deficit, but the Conservative narrative of spendthrift incompetents is simply wrong.' So much for all that nonsense peddled by Osborne and his playmates about 'Gordon Brown's debt', 'the mess that Labour left us' and 'the chaos we inherited'. Prominent Lib Dems, notably Nick Clegg and Danny Alexander, were at it, too.

For good measure, Cable adds that household debt is a much bigger problem than public sector debt. If only he had been Chancellor.

Friday 18 September

The trees in the beech avenue are beginning to turn. A man from the BBC came from London to interview me about *A Very British Coup*, which is enjoying a new lease of life, courtesy of Jeremy.

Sunday 20 September

An anonymous serving army officer is quoted in today's *Sunday Times* as saying there would be mutiny if Jeremy becomes Prime Minister. 'The military just wouldn't stand for it. The general staff would not allow a Prime Minister to jeopardise the security of this country and I think people would use whatever means, fair or foul, to prevent that.' Cf. pages 164–5 of *A Very British Coup*:

> If anyone had suggested to the air marshal that what he was engaged upon was an act of treason, he would have replied crisply that, on the contrary, he was engaged in an act of patriotism … In one way or another such arguments were to be heard around the dinner tables and in the drawing rooms of gentlemen's clubs the length and breadth of St James's. They were to be heard in the officers' mess at the Army Staff College at Camberley. And in the boardrooms of some of Britain's grandest corporations. They were even, on occasion, to be heard between the four walls of a permanent secretary's office in Whitehall.

John Field came for supper this evening with the former Attorney General, Dominic Grieve, who used to be a pupil of his at Westminster. Dominic, one of the most admirable Tories, has just been made chair of the Security and Intelligence Committee, to which the spooks are nominally accountable. I suggested he ask MI6 what Gaddafi's head of intelligence, Moussa Koussa, told them about Lockerbie. And if they didn't ask him, why not?

Monday 21 September

A call from *The Jeremy Vine Show*. Would I like to respond to the *Sunday Times* interview with the anonymous serving general? The result was a bit of a shouting match with a retired colonel who simply repeated, as if it were fact, all the recent tabloid nonsense about Jeremy – IRA supporter, friend of Hamas, pacifist etc., – and then accused me of insulting him. More heat than light, I am afraid.

Wednesday 23 September

To Sunderland for the opening of the newly refurbished Roker pier and lighthouse. Lunch with Kevin Marquis, my former agent, who remarked that, seasoned campaigner though he is, he was taken aback by the virulence of the media assault on Corbyn.

Thursday 24 September

Calum strimmed the overgrown wildflower section, accidentally disembowelling two large toads in the process. I spent the day raking up after him, building a large haystack in the trees outside our back gate. Huge crops of pink fir apple potatoes, onions, garlic and tomatoes; some good red cabbages and (from the main garden) smaller crops of apples, damsons, raspberries, figs. For the time being we are living off the land, but luckily we are not dependent for survival on what we grow, otherwise we'd be dead by the end of October.

Friday 25 September

A fascinating discussion on the *Today* programme between our former US ambassador Christopher Meyer and the historian Margaret MacMillan, the gist of which was that our international institutions, the EU, UN and the World Trade Organization, are beginning to unravel. Meyer said the situation was worse than at any time in his life. MacMillan said the problem was that they had been set up in the wake of world wars and that today's generation couldn't recall why they were necessary. For the first time, I am beginning to think there is a possibility that, come the EU referendum, we may vote for withdrawal.

Saturday 26 September

A chilling, haunting, sickening story in the current issue of *The Week* about a twenty-year-old Saudi youth, in custody since the age of seventeen, who has been sentenced to be beheaded and crucified for alleged anti-regime activity. He apparently wasn't present at his trial. The report is accompanied by a picture of an innocent-looking boy in a school blazer, no doubt educated at one of our public schools, and while his classmates are enjoying themselves at university, this is his fate. My God, he is just Emma's age. I emailed our ambassador in Saudi asking what representations, if any, he and his colleagues are making.[*]

---

[*] He did not respond.

Sunday 27 September

The Labour conference opens today. Here are the headlines: '"Punishment beatings" to split Labour' (the *Sunday Times* headline over a confected lead story alleging that MPs who don't support Corbyn will be purged). 'Revealed: Corbyn's top team encouraged street riots' (*Sunday Telegraph*). Thank heavens for *The Sun*: 'My Twenty Sex Romps With Kyle Wife'.

I drove to Newcastle and did ten minutes on Radio 4 about what Jeremy should say in his first speech to conference. My advice, for what it is worth: 'Address the nation, not the party. And learn to use an autocue.'

Monday 28 September

This morning's headlines: 'Corbyn and comrades reveal plot to hammer middle classes with tax raids' (*Telegraph*); 'Tax war on middle class' (*Mail*); 'Secret plot to oust moderates' (*The Times*). All dismissed as fantasy by a cheerful, somewhat bemused John McDonnell, who is coming over remarkably well, remaining calm and good-humoured in the face of every provocation.

And from my publisher, Andrew Franklin, an email saying he has ordered another reprint of *A Very British Coup*. The second in three weeks. Thanks, Jeremy.

Tuesday 29 September

Jeremy's big day at the Labour Party conference. I caught ten minutes of the speech on *Channel 4 News*. It was mercifully free of the old Blairite razmataz. No glossy pre-speech video. No choirs of angels. No little wife rushing up on stage afterwards to shower kisses upon him. Instead he was introduced by an impressive young woman from his constituency. From what I could see he did pretty well, looking very trim and buoyant. He even seems to have mastered the autocue. At this stage, of course, no specifics are required, just some warmly worded anti-austerity rhetoric, though he did reaffirm his opposition to nuclear weapons, which will upset some of the boys and girls in the parliamentary party, who appear to be more in love with the bomb than ever. I heard later that Sky News, straining to find something negative to say, reported that 'only' 53 per cent of those interviewed and who heard the speech thought Jeremy has what it takes to be Prime Minister.

Wednesday 30 September
Westminster

To Portcullis House to be interviewed by a young journalist. I was intercepted by Tristan Garel-Jones, once one of Mrs Thatcher's most Machiavellian whips, who is these days reduced to loitering in the corridors and tea rooms of Westminster. 'If you see Jeremy,' he said, 'I have a message for him.'

'Oh?'

'The bourgeoisie united will never be defeated.' And off he went, chortling.

Then to St Martin's in the Fields for Ion Trewin's memorial service. An impressive turnout of literati and a sprinkling of literate politicians. (I sat next to former Tory Home Secretary Ken Baker.) A wonderfully uplifting service. Two choirs. A mix of hymns, songs from Rodgers and Hammerstein musicals and tributes from, among others, Judi Dench (read for her), Julian Fellowes, Thomas Keneally, Michael Palin and Ann Widdecombe (looking like a fearsome Victorian matron, dressed in black, her white hair tied back in a tight bun), all authors he had nourished. I owe Ion two great debts. First, thirty-four years ago he published *A Very British Coup*. Second, he invited me to take part in judging the Man Booker Prize, one of my most enjoyable post-retirement incarnations.

Finally to lunch in Kennington with Patricia Moberly and Sally Banks. Sally, who was at the Labour conference in Brighton yesterday, reckons we are in deep trouble. Actually, she put it more robustly than that.

Friday 2 October

Glorious sunshine. It's been like this for a week or more. I finally got around to lifting the remaining potatoes – a bit late, some had been nibbled by mice. Then we picked our very fine crop of pears. John Field called round to pick up some damsons and we had a mug of tea on the glasshouse terrace. Lunch in the garden, after which I sat in the sunshine watching a red squirrel cavorting on the lawn and reading Adrian McKinty's latest, *In the Morning I'll Be Gone*. Good stuff. Vivid, sharp, up there with Elmore Leonard. McKinty's just beginning to attract the attention he deserves. Later, when shade fell across the garden, I went and sat reading on the slope on the south side of the big house, where the sun lingers for another hour and a half.

Saturday 3 October

To the Marquis of Salisbury's vast palace at Hatfield for the festival of garden literature, where I am to present a slideshow entitled 'My Walled Garden in Northumberland'. This evening a reception in the King James Drawing Room. A near life-size statue of the said King over the mantelpiece, every inch of wall space crammed with masterpieces. Shades of Downton, Lady Molly, the dowager, aged ninety-three, petite and elegant, floated gracefully among us. Lady Salisbury gave Evan Davis and myself a tour of the Long Galley. 'That', indicating a throne-like armchair, 'is where Queen Anne rested after her coronation.' 'And in that', indicating an ornate wooden cradle, 'supposedly', is where Charles I was rocked. As last year at Petworth, there is a pecking order. The elite are accommodated in the big house. Evan and I, alas, are lodged at a comfortable but soulless hotel in a business park two miles down the road.

Sunday 4 October

One of the guests in the big house reports that the aged dowager appeared at chapel this morning shrouded in a black lace mantilla. As soon as Lord Salisbury, always the last to enter, takes his seat, the service begins. In this little air pocket of tranquillity, adjacent to a brutalist new town and the busy A1, everything is as it has always been. My event, in which I shared the platform with two other speakers, took place in the great hall of the Old Palace, once home to Mary and Elizabeth, the children of Henry VIII. The marchioness, the dowager and the amiable second son, Lord Charles, in the front row, applauded politely, but a one-acre walled garden must seem very small beer to them.

That old flamethrower Denis Healey has died, aged ninety-eight, triggering a predictable bout of nonsense from the commentariat about 'the greatest Prime Minister we never had'. I don't buy it. Remarkable he may have been, but he was also an uncouth bully who rarely took account of the views of others and never owned up to mistakes. We had to wait thirteen years before he finally conceded, in a throwaway line buried on page 381 of his memoirs, that he had been wrong to deliver us into the hands of the IMF, thereby triggering the sequence of events that brought Mrs Thatcher to power. 'If I had been given accurate forecasts in 1976, I would never have had to go to the IMF at all.'

Tuesday 6 October

Defence Secretary Michael Fallon has announced the deployment of 100 British soldiers to the Baltic states, a move he describes as 'further reassurance for our allies in response to Russian provocation and aggression', as if 100 British soldiers will deter the might of the Red Army. Meanwhile the Americans are reported to be sending 250 tanks and other equipment to Poland, Romania and Bulgaria 'to counter the Russian threat'. One can't help wondering where all this is leading.

Wednesday 7 October

To London, nose buried in the second volume of Charles Moore's widely acclaimed biography of Thatcher, which I am reviewing for *The Observer*. This evening a disturbing *Newsnight* report depicting growing unrest in Germany over the influx of migrants, which is giving the far right a new lease of life. Hostels firebombed, crowds chanting 'send them home' and, scarier still, calls for the return of the Sudetenland and Silesia.

Thursday 8 October

To the *Guardian* offices at King's Cross to help judge the Prison Reform Trust's annual competition for prison writing. Then to Wimbledon for the literary festival, where I gave my speech on 'The Art of Political Leadership' to an appreciative audience of about 300. A long queue for the book signing. Afterwards, supper with James Curran and Margaret Hung, with whom I stayed overnight. To my astonishment, Margaret recently visited a friend in Damascus who was once a tourist guide ('I was her only tourist'). Apparently life is surprisingly normal in the Alawite enclave, disturbed only by the distant boom of cannon fire.

Saturday 10 October

To the Durham literary festival, where I interviewed Vince Cable before a capacity audience in the old town hall. An impressive man, thoughtful, balanced, sensible. He foresees a long period of one-party rule and reckons there is a 40 to 60 per cent chance that the great British public will vote for EU withdrawal. If we do, the Scots will of course want another referendum. What a mess. Cameron has lit a long fuse.

Monday 12 October

To the university at Newcastle, where I delivered two lectures and took part in three seminars. Then to London for tomorrow's meeting of regional chairs of the Heritage Lottery Fund. My fourth trip south in two weeks, every train ride taken up with frantic reading of books sent for review within tight deadlines. Last week Ashcroft's biography of David Cameron and Seldon's account of the Cameron government, both 500-pagers. This week Volume Two of Charles Moore's mammoth biography of Thatcher. All that, and three festivals – in Hatfield, Wimbledon and Durham. Nice to be in demand, but I am so tired.

Monday 19 October
Haymarket, Newcastle

A chat with a young homeless man, huddled against the railing by the footpath on the way up to the university. He was holding out an empty paper cup. At first, I thought he was the Bulgarian I talked to last year in the same place, but he turned out to be local. His parents had been travellers. He had been in care and chucked out as soon as he turned eighteen. Lately he'd had spent two months in hospital after being glassed while intervening to save the Bulgarian, who had been knifed. He claimed to have woken up in the morgue, having been declared dead. He was remarkably cheerful given his dire circumstances and not unintelligent. All he wanted was three quid, which he said would enable him to obtain a sleeping bag. I didn't quite follow why, but I gave it to him. Hard to say without knowing the full story, but I couldn't help feeling that with support he could be saved.

Tuesday 20 October

On this evening's television news, a clip of a somewhat uncomfortable Jeremy Corbyn, clad in white tie and tails, being shown to his place at the state dinner for the President of China. A seminal moment in British politics. Jez we can. Oh, that I should live to see this day.

Wednesday 21 October

To Sunderland, where I spent an hour being grilled by students in the university's media studies department, returning home to the astonishing news that my friend Michael Meacher is dead. He had been ill for some time, apparently, but had kept it quiet. Dear Michael. Even forty-five years in Parliament failed to temper his idealism, energy and boyish enthusiasm. Above all, he never succumbed to cynicism.

Sunday 25 October

The Hungarians and Macedonians have sealed their borders, leaving thousands of desperate migrants stranded in mud and rain on the wrong side of the razor wire. Awful scenes on the bulletins. Mostly young men, but there are also families with children, grandmas, people in wheelchairs marooned in mud and rain. Some of the children are clutching dolls, all that remains of the world they left behind. And still they come. Nine thousand a day are reported to be reaching the Greek islands. They think the worst is over when they have made the sea crossing from Turkey, but in reality the worst is yet to come. Fortress Europe has closed its doors. They can't go back and they can't go forward. Soon it will be winter and they are going to start dying.

Tuesday 27 October

To the House of Commons, where I ran into a prominent Tory who remarked that Jeremy is doing reasonably well at Prime Minister's

Questions. 'Several of us thought he won the last round.' Our side not so upbeat, though. 'He just sits there like a lemon at meetings of the parliamentary party,' remarked one of our former top brass. Another of our number talked of 'a pervasive sense of gloom'. Then to the Athenaeum, where I delivered a talk entitled 'The Challenges Facing Labour' to a fairly sympathetic audience of elderly professional people, members of something called the Romney Street Group. Afterwards Anthony Sampson's widow took me upstairs to the drawing room, where I last set foot in 1982 when Ion Trewin arranged for me to be smuggled in to get some colour for the opening chapter of *A Very British Coup*. Then back to the House for a drink on the terrace with Labour peer Bruce Grocott, who roundly rejected any suggestion of an electoral pact with the Lib Dems. I quoted 1906 at him and he replied, 'That's what led to the destruction of the Liberal Party. If we help them recover, they will supplant us.' Bruce is also in favour of withdrawal from the EU. 'Please don't give me that old argument about the likely flight of capital. That's what they said would happen if we didn't join the euro.'

Thursday 29 October
Callaly

With each day that passes, the view from my study window grows more wondrous as the autumn sunshine sets ablaze the beech avenue on the south side of the mansion, the splash of gold, red and yellow contrasting with the dark pine forest higher up the hill. A privilege to live here.

Sunday 1 November

The number of people earning less than the living wage (£9.40 an hour in London and £8.25 elsewhere) has risen by 580,000 in the space of a year, according to a report by the accountants KPMG. Should we be surprised? For all the rhetoric to the contrary, government pressure on local authorities to outsource is driving wages down, not up. Given the relentless Treasury pressure on local authority budgets, where on earth is the care industry going to find the wherewithal to pay the living wage, which is supposed to replace the tax credits that the very same Treasury is committed to phasing out?

A lovely, mild autumn day. Sunshine, not a breath of wind. We made a circuit of the Hulne Park, picnicking on the bench outside the old priory overlooking the Aln.

Monday 2 November

Another week, another dictator. No sooner have the flags in Whitehall been taken down after the visit by the President of China than we are putting them out again. This time for General Abdel-Fattah el-Sisi, Egypt's latest military ruler, whose notorious jails are crammed with opponents of his regime and who is threatening to hang his predecessor. Distasteful though it is, one can just about understand the rationale for kowtowing to the Chinese, but beyond a general desire not to see Egypt descend into chaos, it is hard to discern an argument for laying out the red carpet for this puffed-up autocrat, unless of course we have received instructions from Washington to be nice to him. Yet again we are about to be treated to a demonstration of Cameron's infinite capacity for flexibility. Five years ago he was strolling through Tahir Square congratulating the Egyptians on having overthrown their last dictator. Now he is welcoming the new one.

This evening to Islington for dinner with Andrew and Sharon Mitchell. The other guests were that most intelligent and admirable of rock stars, Bob Geldof, and his wife, Jeanne; also, Health Secretary Jeremy Hunt and his wife, Lucia. For a man with one of the most demanding jobs in government (he is presently embroiled in a row with junior doctors over their contracts), Jeremy seems remarkably relaxed. He has a modest, pleasant disposition and comes over well on the media. Much of the evening was taken up with an exchange between Bob G and Sharon about the causes of depression in middle-aged males, but there were many lighter moments. Later, a quiet chat with Bob, who described his various encounters with George W. Bush. Like others who have dealt with Bush one to one, he describes him as likeable and easy going. 'He just should never have been President.'

Thursday 5 November

A day out with my old school friend David Fraser. We walked through the parks to the Royal Academy for lunch, then through rain to the National

Portrait Gallery, where we browsed for a couple of hours, then for a drink at the East India Club in St James's Square and, finally, to Chatham House to attend a debate on whether or not the UK should withdraw from the European Convention on Human Rights. One of the speakers was Keir Starmer, the former Director of Public Prosecutions and now a Labour MP whose name is sometimes mentioned as a possible future leader. Why not? At least he has a hinterland.

Saturday 7 November

Today's *Telegraph* carries my review of a Daphne Park biography. A glance at the rest of the paper affords a glimpse into the mindset of that part of Middle England mired in self-interest, oblivious to the wider world. The lead is a report that 'senior military figures' (as usual they are anonymous) are objecting to proposed cuts in the defence budget, which, among other things, will deny members of the armed forces the automatic pay rises they have come to expect. A familiar story – the officer class of the armed forces vote overwhelmingly for the party which promises to cut taxes and public spending and then demands exemption from the consequences. Meanwhile the front page of the financial section is devoted to an article headed 'Wave goodbye to income tax – forever', explaining how 'by exploiting an array of new tax breaks you will soon be able to draw an annual income from your investments of £98,100 – tax free'. The property section features an article on ski chalets in the French Alps and advertises retirement apartments at prices ranging from £1.3 million for one bedroom to £2.45 million for three bedrooms. And the travel section is stuffed with adverts for luxury cruises at five or six thousand pounds a time. The *pièce de résistance* is a feature on an inside page of the financial section depicting a smug-looking sixty-year-old Middle Englander astride one of his six Japanese motorbikes. It is headed 'We have £1m – we want to spend every penny'. Tempting to predict that there will be social unrest if this carries on, but in truth I see absolutely no sign that there will be, such is the tyranny of the fortunate.

Friday 13 November

To St Mary's Church, Wimbledon, which was packed for Michael Meacher's funeral. He would be chuffed to know that he attracted a full house, including Jeremy Corbyn and Ed Miliband, who arrived together. Some nice tributes, one of which I delivered. Smiles of recognition all round when I talked of his engaging naivety. Len McCluskey said to me afterwards, 'You got him just right. I wanted to applaud, but I wasn't sure it would be right.' Afterwards a brief chat with Jeremy, who seems in good spirits despite the slings and arrows that rain down upon him.

Saturday 14 November

Awoke to the awful news that jihadis, armed with explosives and Kalashnikovs, have killed at least 130 people and injured 200 others at a concert in Paris. Later, to St Peter's Church, Monkwearmouth, where I gave a public lecture entitled 'The Changing Face of Sunderland' to mark the publication of Victoria County History's volume on the city. A number of familiar faces in the audience, including a couple who told us that a boy in their daughter's year at Durham University has lost both his parents in the Paris slaughter.

Sunday 15 November

Those responsible for Friday's outrage in Paris are all said to be either French or Belgian citizens. The jihadi virus has well and truly taken root in the soil of Europe. We're in for years more of this.

Monday 16 November

Corbyn is in trouble for saying that he is not keen on shoot to kill as a means of dealing with suspected terrorists. Bad timing, but the sentiment is not unreasonable – remember that unfortunate Brazilian electrician gunned down at Stockwell Tube Station after being mistaken for a jihadi? Jeremy may be the victim of a BBC sting. A favourite trick among BBC political correspondents is to get someone to say something controversial on air and then ring round likely suspects inviting them to denounce the hapless interviewee. On this occasion no one seems to have done so publicly, but, as the later bulletins gleefully reported, Jeremy was given a hostile reception at this evening's meeting of the parliamentary party.

Wednesday 18 November

Awoke to news of a gun battle in northern Paris as police laid siege to an apartment in which one or more of those responsible for Saturday's slaughter were reported to be lying low. It ended when a woman inside the flat apparently blew herself up. Other bodies are said to be in the wreckage.

Thursday 19 November

Much speculation that, in the wake of the Paris massacre, Cameron will have another go at persuading Parliament to let him do some bombing in Syria. As several people have pointed out, it doesn't appear to be part of any strategy, just a general desire to be seen as relevant. The truth is that only ground troops can clear the Islamists out of Syria and Iraq and there are not many volunteers for that.

Monday 23 November

Newcastle

An icy wind. Eddie, the young homeless man I came across the other day, was sitting shivering by the footpath leading up to the university, a few coins in his paper coffee cup. 'Are you going to sit here all winter?' I asked. He replied that a hostel place cost £16.50 a night and that he could rarely raise the money and anyway there were often no beds available. When I got to the university, I rang the homeless unit in the civic centre and they said they would send someone to see him. Later, I had an email saying blandly that he was known to them, but that's not good enough. He needs help. So far as I can see there is no issue with drink and drugs, though by his own account he has been in trouble with the police, for over-retaliating against assailants, or so he says.

Tuesday 24 November

An email from an official at Newcastle Civic Centre: 'The Outreach Team have been out to look for Eddie, but he was not at the location you reported...' She added, 'The next time the team see Eddie they are going to allocate him a worker from the Multiple Exclusion Team who will offer him appropriate support.' I replied pointing out that he was still there when I left the university just after 4 p.m. yesterday afternoon and offering to pay his lodgings for a few days, until more permanent arrangements could be made.

Wednesday 25 November

To the Stadium of Light Sunderland, where I stood in for the chancellor, Steve Cram, at the university's graduation ceremony. My role, clothed in academic finery, is to shake hands, wish them good luck and make a short, hopefully uplifting, speech. Surprising how many students don't know how to shake hands, some just holding out fingers for me to clutch, and some of the hands are like wet sponges. No wonder the Queen always wears gloves.

An email from a 'temporary accommodation manager' in Newcastle Civic Centre promising to make Eddie an offer of place to stay but suggesting that in the past he has rejected help. I have asked to be kept informed.

Osborne's long-awaited financial statement. Cuts to local authority budgets will go ahead as planned but, lo, he has dropped entirely his plans to do away with tax credits. Amusingly, the Tories cheered the restoration of tax credits as loudly as they did when he announced a few weeks ago that he was doing away with them. He has also abandoned plans to impose cuts on the police and is proposing to spend much more on the military. All possible, apparently, because he has discovered the existence of £27 billion that, as recently as July, he didn't know he had. A curious business, high finance.

Thursday 26 November

Ngoc collected a box of Christmas decorations from the garage, took the box to the living room and when she opened it, out leapt three mice.

As expected Cameron is having another go at persuading Parliament to authorise the bombing of ISIS, having failed two years ago to persuade MPs to let him bomb Assad. This time it looks as though he might get away with it. He fed them some cock and bull story about how it's part of a wider strategy, and a majority appear to have fallen for it, even though it is completely pointless without troops on the ground and goodness knows how many civilians are being killed. Corbyn, who is opposed, is heavily outnumbered in the shadow Cabinet, and no doubt in the parliamentary party, which seems to grow more reactionary with every day that passes. There are already quite enough people dropping bombs on Syria without us having to join in, but we just can't bear to be left out. If I were still in Parliament, I would certainly have something to say on the subject.

Friday 27 November

The wheels are coming off the Corbyn leadership. Members of the parliamentary party are queuing up to denounce him. Shadow Foreign Secretary Hilary Benn – who much to my disappointment favours bombing – was on the evening bulletins disagreeing with his leader. Also, John Spellar and Paul Flynn, an unlikely duo, demanding that Jeremy goes. The irony is that, for all his ineptitude, Jeremy is right on Syria.

Saturday 28 November

The plotting and scheming has begun. Today's *Times* leads with a story saying that 'senior Labour figures' are seeking legal advice as to whether, in the event that Jeremy is overthrown, his name would automatically have to appear on the ballot paper for a new leadership contest. The problem being, of course, that if a free election were permitted, Jeremy would be overwhelmingly re-elected. The gap between the leaders and the led has never been wider. 'Is there not', asks Matthew Parris re. Syria, 'a *Through the Looking-Glass* quality to the spectacle of the media, the Tories and Mr Corbyn's own shadow Cabinet in full cry against an opposition leader who has said something that tens of millions of people on both sides of the party divide suspect to be true?' Indeed there is. The parliamentary party appears to be in the grip of neo-cons.

Sunday 29 November

Bruce, our skeletal, bedraggled old cat, appears to be on her last legs. These past few days she has hardly eaten and is increasingly wobbly. I fear the end is nigh.

Monday 30 November
Newcastle

Eddie, the homeless man, still in his usual place, shivering in the drizzle. He reported that, following my intervention last week, someone from the homeless unit had taken him to a local hostel, only for him to be told once again that there are no beds. When I got to the politics department, I sent another email enquiring what their plans were. There may be something I don't know, but I am beginning to suspect they may be useless.

Tuesday 1 December

Bruce weaker than ever. Following us around the house in search of food, but rarely eating what is put in front her. The time has come to bite the bullet. I rang the vet and arranged an appointment for 10.30 a.m. tomorrow. When I put the phone down, tears welled up. She has been part of our lives for fourteen years and this is the last day. How on earth do we break the news to Emma?

Every so often I catch myself humming a happy tune and then I look at Bruce curled up in her basket by the fire and think, 'How can I be happy when this is the last day of her life'? This evening, just before I went to bed, she abandoned her basket by the stove and curled up on the carpet in my study.

Wednesday 2 December

Dawn: Bruce, a little bag of bones, hobbling around as usual, no inkling of what is to come. Overnight her appetite seems to have perked up. I put her on my lap and stroked her while she purred gently. Three hours to go, two, one…We loaded her, unprotesting, into the cat box and drove to the vet in Rothbury. He examined her briefly, weighed her and said, 'Time to let her go.' A consent form was produced. I signed through tears. The vet disappeared into a back room and emerged with a syringe of anaesthetic. We stroked her as she lay on the table and slowly went to sleep. A second dose and she was gone. We continued stroking for another five minutes and then left. I never realised how much I loved her until today. The bill said: 'Cat euthanasia, £79'. She will be returned to us as ashes one week from now.

This evening the Commons voted overwhelmingly to launch air

strikes in Syria. The BBC are making a great fuss, running extended news bulletins, hamming up the significance for all its worth, but for all the synthetic drama, the decision is of little relevance to the world outside our self-centred little bubble. The highlight was a *tour de force*, attracting prolonged applause from all sides, from Hilary Benn, who wound up the debate in favour of bombing and in defiance of his leader. Although I disagree with him on this issue, he is the obvious choice to replace Jeremy when the time comes.

Thursday 3 December

An email from the letters editor of *The Times*: 'Might I tempt you to write a short succinct letter … in response to yesterday's debate – perhaps on Hilary Benn's speech?' The second such missive I have received this year. Are they hard up, or what? As before, I politely declined.

Friday 4 December

No doubt to the disappointment of Jeremy's many detractors, the result of the Oldham by-election was remarkably good for a wet Thursday in December; Labour's share of the vote actually increased on a respectable 40 per cent turnout. Oldham is not typical of anything, of course, but the result should buy Jeremy some respite from the plotters and schemers, at least until the local elections in May.

A call from my GP to say that she has spotted a small patch on my recent chest X-ray which needs investigating. Have I ever smoked? No. Or worked anywhere unhealthy? No. Or had pneumonia or whooping cough? Yes, both as it happens. Well, that might explain it. Nothing to worry about, she says. All the same, she's ordered a CT scan.

Saturday 5 December

Twenty-four hours of rain and howling gales, the trees in the shelter belt swaying ominously, the drive outside our gates scattered with twigs and branches up to ten feet long. The villages between here and Wooler, ten miles north, are without electricity. On the periphery of the estate a large beech has crashed through the ancient stone wall.

Sunday 6 December

Awoke to find that, after thirty hours, the storm had abated. The silence audible, the ground sodden, the burn swollen. Cockermouth, Keswick and several other Cumbrian towns are underwater, despite millions spent on flood defences. I spent the day clearing leaves from the gutters and gullies. According to the forecasters, more rain on the way.

Monday 7 December
Newcastle

Eddie, the homeless beggar, in his usual place by the path leading up to the university. Three weeks since I first contacted the council's homeless unit and nothing much seems to have happened. He says that someone called Dave took him to a couple of hostels last week, but he was turned away. Why? 'Because I don't have a drug problem.' That may not be the whole story, but thus far I have failed to get any sense out of anyone.

Wednesday 9 December

A call from the head of the homeless unit in Newcastle regarding Eddie. Apparently there is more to his case than meets the eye. He has turned down several offers of accommodation. It doesn't quite add up, though I don't think I can do much more.

Thursday 10 December

Three hours chopping wood, which Ngoc arranged into an impressive pile in the garage.

On today's bulletins, a distraught Syrian who has lost his wife and seven children, aged between twenty days and nine years, trying to cross by boat from Turkey to Greece.

Sunday 13 December

Talked to Patricia Moberly, who despite having recently embarked on a second bout of chemo seems in her usual good spirits. She says that since Jeremy's election many of the old Lambeth Trots who disappeared during the New Labour ascendancy are back. Even 'Red Ted' Knight has resurfaced in Norwood. Should we be pleased?

Tuesday 15 December
London

To the Hampstead Waterstones, where I bought half a dozen novels (Hemingway, Greene, Orwell) as Christmas presents for Sarah and Emma. Then to Millbank, where I passed a happy hour as guest of the day on the *Daily Politics* show, at last managing to float my suggestion for a an electoral pact between Labour, the Lib Dems and the Greens as the only hope of taking on the Tories next time around. Although, as Vince Cable pointed out, before there can be a pact, the parties concerned will have to come up with a common offer and there is no chance of that while Labour's current turmoil endures. Today we have an idiot Labour MP threatening to 'stab Jeremy in the front' if he doesn't deliver to her satisfaction. Lord spare us.

Saturday 19 December

We are said to be on course for the warmest December on record. Temperatures nudging 16°. Daffodils blooming in the south. In our garden a handful of lupins and a clematis still in flower and a crop of roses almost as fine as in June. An aberration or evidence of something more serious?

Sunday 20 December

An article in today's *Observer* by Peter Hyman, a former Blair speechwriter, suggesting that disaffected Blairites should consider setting up a new party allied to the Liberals. Actually, Peter, in case you had forgotten, this is a film we've seen before – and it didn't work out too well. Remember?

Monday 21 December

A call from the GP. The result of my chest X-ray shows no cause for alarm, although there are signs of congestion. Chronic bronchitis, she thinks. More tests required.

Tuesday 22 December

Rain all night. Ground sodden. The burn a raging torrent. Teams of tits, occasionally assisted by a woodpecker, working their way through the peanuts on the bird feeder.

Saturday 26 December

Rain, rain, rain, drumming on the roof, puddles in the fruit cage. In the park around the big house the fourth lake, said to have been filled in in the 1890s, has reappeared and the burn is racing through the grounds, crashing over the sluices.

Sunday 27 December

Sunshine, a cloudless sky, in stark contrast to yesterday. We scattered Bruce's ashes, a surprisingly small quantity, but then there wasn't much of her in the end, among the lupins, where she used to lie for hours in warmer weather. Sarah and I walked about eight miles through Eslington, up through Great and Little Ryle and back in a circle, sticking to the lanes to avoid becoming bogged down. Water pouring off the hills, through the fields and ditches, along the lanes, sweeping top soil and detritus before it. The ford at Eslington was impassable and several large trees have fallen, but we have got off lightly. From York, Manchester and Leeds reports of floods and evacuations.

Monday 28 December

Right on cue, the *Telegraph*, *Mail* and *Sun* all carry articles calling for the overseas aid budget to be diverted to help with UK flood relief. As if we, one of the world's richest countries, can't afford to fund flood relief and meet our international obligations.

CHAPTER SEVEN

2016

New Year's Day

Awoke to wintry sunshine and a light frost. Sarah, Nick, John Field and I drove to the end of the Breamish Valley and walked up Hedgehope, the second highest Cheviot summit. Fine views, but a vicious, icy wind and light covering of snow. John turned back two thirds of the way up, but the rest of us carried on to the top, slipping and sliding in the ice and bog. We ate our sandwiches huddled in the shelter of the huge cairn and then scuttled back down into the valley.

Sunday 3 January

The Saudis have celebrated the New Year by beheading forty-seven alleged terrorists, including a prominent Shia cleric. Needless to say, this latest atrocity (as with their indiscriminate bombing of Yemen) has provoked scarcely a word of criticism from their gutless friends in the West, even though, as one of today's newspapers remarks, the only difference between this outrage and those of ISIS is the absence of an official video.

Meanwhile Jeremy Corbyn is said to be planning to strengthen his grip on the shadow Cabinet with what our free press are calling a 'revenge reshuffle'.

Monday 4 January

A third continuous day of rain. The burn (usually no more than three feet wide) now extends to 30ft in places, flowing over rather than under the bridge in the lawn and over the sluices. Meanwhile an impressive waterfall has formed between the first and the newly formed fourth lakes. According to the forecast there is no end in sight.

Tuesday 5 January

To Sunderland, where I am fronting a little film for the regional BBC. Much of the filming was out of doors and we got soaked, which won't do my bronchitis much good. Lunch in a little seaside cafe watching angry waves crashing over the pier, the beach littered with driftwood. Still raining when I drove home, water bubbling up from drains and streaming down both sides of the road, at times almost impassable. When will it stop?

Thursday 7 January

Corbyn's reshuffle, for all the fuss, turned out to be a damp squib. One new face in the shadow Cabinet and one out. Plus a few minor changes in the lower ranks. None of which has stopped the so-called Blairites from behaving badly, touring the studios sounding off. One junior spokesperson, whom I had never heard of, resigned live on TV.

Monday 11 January

The musician David Bowie has died and news of his death has dominated the bulletins all day, with many anchors behaving as though they have suffered a personal loss. Radio 4 seems to have been taken over by 5 Live for the day. Someone on the *Today* programme remarked that there was a little bit of Bowie in all of us. Not in me there wasn't. I find the whole business utterly bemusing. Now if it had been Mick Jagger...

Wednesday 13 January

To the surgery at Rothbury, where a friendly nurse bade me blow repeatedly into a gadget called a spirometer. I didn't do well. Each blow ended in a coughing fit. Then to Sunderland to finish the BBC documentary. In keeping with these populist times, I had to stand in the street outside the Bridges shopping mall and ask people what they thought of the city centre. A pointless exercise since everyone gave contradictory answers. Only one person recognised me and he turned out to be deranged. We ended up on the beach with me saying that there is much that is attractive about Sunderland but perhaps we need to shout about it a bit more.

Sunday 17 January

Jeremy Corbyn was on *The Andrew Marr Show* this morning, saying that maybe we could keep the nuclear submarines without the warheads. A ludicrous proposition inviting ridicule, which is duly being delivered by the shovel load. No doubt he has been driven to this by the fact that several of the big unions are saying that doing away with nukes will cost jobs. Sooner or later the bullet will have to be bitten. Either we are in favour of keeping the damn things or we are not.

To London on an afternoon train. I am staying with John and Sheila Williams in Clapham. Peter Tatchell, still living in a council flat in Bermondsey, came to dinner. He estimates that over the years (though not recently) he has had bricks or stones through the window on about fifty occasions as a result of the tabloid campaign of hate during that infamous by-election in 1982. Resilient and completely lacking in bitterness, he would have been an excellent MP, though perhaps not the ideal choice for Bermondsey. His life could have been much different but for Michael Foot's foolish denunciation of him, which triggered the whole thing.

Monday 18 January

To the Winston Churchill Trust, where I spent the day interviewing candidates for travel scholarships. Then over the road to the Cinnamon Club for dinner with Michael Jay.* He kept a diary of his years as ambassador in Paris (he was there when Diana died) and wants my advice about publishing. I am sure there would be interest, he writes well, but it's a pity that he didn't keep it up for the rest of his career, which would have included the build-up to Iraq and the aftermath. I put it to him that Iraq

---

* Lord Jay, head of the Diplomatic Service 2001–06.

was an intelligence screw-up and he recounted a top-level meeting he had attended in July 2003, three months after the invasion, at which Richard Dearlove, who until then had been insisting that it was only a question of time until Saddam's weapons of mass destruction were uncovered, suddenly blurted out, 'Maybe there aren't any.' Said Michael, 'There was a palpable silence around the table.'

Tuesday 19 January

Sure enough, Corbyn is getting his leg pulled about his suggestion that we could keep the submarines and get rid of the nukes. His suggestion that we need to talk to ISIS isn't going down too well either. Dear Jeremy, I fear, is hopelessly unsuited to the realities of power.

Lunch with Jean Corston in the Barry Room at the House of Lords. She says she is trying to persuade our masters, so far without success, to start referring to housing benefit as 'landlord subsidy', which is a more accurate description. I always enjoy a visit to the Lords because at every corner one comes across old friends and even the occasional former enemy, but there is absolutely no malice. They have closed their eyes and woken up in heaven. The old jealousies and resentments have disappeared; all is well with the world. Unlike the Commons, no one in a hurry, everyone pleased to see you and time to chat. Among those I came across today Peter Hennessy, Tommy McAvoy and Lord Lloyd, the judge who quashed the Birmingham Six convictions. Oh yes, and Bill Cash (still in the Commons) holding court in the Family Room to a delegation of bemused Norwegians who, he assured me, all shared his view of the EU. Some things never change.

On the way out I came across a long-serving Labour Party staffer who remarked of the current management, 'If only they would lead, instead of being reactive all the time; the Tories are getting away with murder.' By way of evidence she cited the trade union bill, the principal purpose of which seems to be to drastically reduce the number of political levy payers in the hope of bankrupting the Labour Party.

This evening to Houseman's bookshop, near King's Cross, where I gave a light-hearted talk on *A Very British Coup* to a small audience composed mainly of eccentrics.

Wednesday 20 January

From John and Sheila's window an aerial view of two remarkably healthy foxes, basking on the roof of the garage in winter sunshine. We breakfasted on Craster kippers which I brought with me from Northumberland. Then to a three-hour lunch with Melissa Benn in a branch of Pizza Express near the British Museum. Increasingly people are talking about Hilary as the next leader, but we agreed that he mustn't get involved in any of the scheming and plotting. Jeremy must be given two full years and then, if we appear to be facing annihilation rather than mere defeat, that will be time to talk about the succession.

In a speech of blood-curdling stupidity and pig-headed ignorance, Sarah Palin has come out for Donald Trump, which with any luck will prove as fatal to him as her support for John McCain. But not immediately, one hopes. The best outcome would be for Trump to win the Republican nomination and then to be trounced by Hllary Clinton. Although that's a slightly risky strategy since Americans do not love Hillary and once the full Fox News hate machine is unleashed upon her she may prove vulnerable. President Trump, just imagine.

Thursday 21 January

I have been reading Piers Morgan's American diaries,[*] a second-hand copy of which I found in Barter Books. It pains me to admit, but they are strangely addictive. To be sure he is brash, vulgar and celebrity-obsessed and name-drops on an industrial scale. But he is also amusing, self-deprecating and surprisingly perceptive. Politically, too, despite spending much of his time in the company of the super-rich, he has managed (more or less) to keep his feet on the ground. There is a fascinating interview with Donald Trump, dated 22 August 2008. Trump says of George Bush:

> He has set back the country by fifty years. We were a great country before he became President. A respected country. Whether you like Clinton or whether you don't like Clinton, we had no deficit for the first time in many years and were doing well economically. And then Bush came in and wrecked it. After 9/11 America had a chance to be the most popular

---

[*] *God Bless America*, Ebury Press, 2009.

country in the world and instead, in a matter of weeks, that man destroyed it ... We have been seriously hurt by Bush and his cronies.

On Iraq, says Trump, 'He invaded a country that had nothing to do with 9/11, absolutely zero. He purposely lied and lied badly and his lies got us into a war.' Can it be that beneath that ludicrous exterior there lurks an intelligent human being? As someone recently remarked, 'Say what you will about Trump, he's not stupid. He is a smart man with a deep understanding of what stupid people want.'

Friday 22 January

A dire warning from the French Prime Minister, Manuel Valls, that the migration crisis could destroy the EU: 'If Europe is not capable of protecting its own borders, it is the very idea of Europe that will be questioned.' I have long thought that the flow of migrants from failed states could bring down our fragile social systems, particularly those in southern Europe, but I didn't think it would happen this quickly. Despite the onset of winter, 2,000 refugees a day (mainly from Syria, Iraq and Afghanistan) are still arriving on the Greek islands. Another forty, including many children, are reported to have drowned last night. Even Germany is overwhelmed. Meanwhile the migration crisis is pushing European politics steadily to the right. How will it end?

Thursday 28 January

A message from a friend in Boston reporting that he has just come across a black taxi driver who says he supports Trump. Why? 'Because he is the only politician who dares say what ordinary Americans think.' Presumably he means as regards Muslims and Mexicans, not blacks.

Friday 29 January

All over Europe attitudes towards migrants are hardening. The Danish Parliament has voted to confiscate the assets of asylum seekers valued in excess of $1,000. How can that be justified? The Swedes are talking of deporting up to 80,000 failed applicants and the Dutch have come up with a plan for immediately returning to Turkey those making the perilous journey to the Greek islands. And these are some of the most liberal countries in the EU. Meanwhile the bulletins are showing families trudging through snow across the Balkans towards Germany, children sometimes smiling at the camera as though they are on some great adventure; little do they know what awaits them.

Wednesday 3 February

After an existence of barely eighteen months, Active Northumberland, the charitable trust to which Northumberland County Council outsourced its libraries and leisure centres, is appealing to the council for a £1 million bailout. My guess is we are going to see much more of this as Osborne's budget cuts take hold. If this goes on, all over the country, libraries, leisure centres, youth clubs – any service which local authorities are not obliged by law to provide – will be wiped out.

Thursday 4 February

This evening's *Newsnight* was entirely devoted to a debate about whether or not to renew Trident (at a minimum cost of £30 billion). The usual suspects were on parade: Defence Secretary Fallon talking up the Russian threat, Admiral Lord West saying how shocked the Americans would be if we were to dispense with our nukes. Then up popped the former US ambassador to the UN Nancy Soderberg, who quietly and calmly disposed of all the nonsense in a few crisp sentences. Trident, she said, was of symbolic value only. Its disposal would not make Britain vulnerable since we are under the American nuclear umbrella and always will be. And, far from being shocked if we were not to renew, the United States government would welcome a reduction in the number of nuclear nations because it was hard to persuade the Iranians that they didn't need a nuclear weapon when countries like Britain and France had them. For good measure she added that she thought Trident would be phased out sooner or later anyway.

Friday 5 February

Ngoc is chasing pheasants. Every few minutes she goes outside, shouting dementedly and waving a long bamboo cane with a bin bag attached at the wretched birds who come daily to raid the bird seed and peck the tops of emerging bulbs. All this commotion doesn't seem to make much impression on the pheasants, but it's driving me mad.

Sunday 7 February

Tet, the Vietnamese new year. A time for remembering ancestors. Ngoc has placed a basket of fruit and four lighted candles on a table in front of photos of her late parents. Meanwhile the North Koreans have succeeded in test-firing a rocket with a range of 6,000 miles, which means they are getting closer to the day when they can nuke the USA. As if the world doesn't have enough to worry about.

Monday 8 February

Calum turned up with a large wire cage to trap the pheasants who are laying waste to our garden. I scattered a few sunflower seeds inside it and within ten minutes we had our first catch, which he promptly deported to the furthest corner of the estate. By the end of the day we had trapped and removed three of the blighters.

Tuesday 9 February

To College Valley for a three-hour walk with Tony Henfrey, a right-of-centre libertarian who lived for years in Texas. He says, 'My friends in Texas talk of the US as though it is a failed state. Many of them are still in denial about Obama's right to be President.' He thinks Obama has been a good President, considering the hand he was dealt. 'His mistake was not to have lowered expectations early in his presidency, but I think history will be kind to him.'

Wednesday 10 February

A call from *The Guardian*. Would I like to write a piece about the demand by relatives of the victims of Birmingham pub bombings for yet another investigation? Actually, I wouldn't. Every time I open my mouth on the subject it just upsets people. During the past few days I have declined half a dozen requests for interviews. However, after initial reluctance I agreed to tap out 800 words setting out my take on the matter. Within an hour the shilly-shallying starts. Well, it might only be for the online edition. I should have pulled out at this point, but instead I ploughed on. 'Nice piece,' comes the reply after I sent it over, 'we're hoping to launch it by sixish.' 'Launch'? Does this mean that it isn't going in the paper after all? 'Sorry, another piece came in that has to go in tomorrow's paper, so we'll be running yours online only.' What a mug I am. I should have realised by now that a request to write an op-ed for *The Guardian* is really only an invitation to put your name in a lottery in which the dice are heavily loaded because most of the available space is already mortgaged to the paper's legion of regular columnists, some of whom have little to say but are capable of saying it at some length. Every time I fall for this, I tell myself this is the last time, but it never is. Never mind, I have a nice piece in *The Spectator* this week.

Sunday 14 February

A light covering of snow. Ngoc is in London, visiting the girls, and I am enjoying the rare privilege of doing whatever I like without having to account for my actions. This afternoon, in a sunny interval between sleet showers, I went litter-picking on the lane between the Eslington estate and Whittingham. In the space of no more than a mile I filled three black bin bags. Incredible. Who are these barbarians who drive around the lanes routinely tossing their rubbish out of their vehicles? Presumably the same handful of people will go on doing so for their entire lives. What do they think becomes of their detritus? Who do they think will pick it up? Stupid questions. I doubt they give the matter a second thought.

Monday 15 February

Having run out of other things to do, for the first time since September, I finally managed to knock out another 2,000 words of the long-awaited (by me at any rate) sequel to *A Very British Coup*.

Wednesday 17 February

En route to collect Ngoc from the station, I passed the huge barn owl who lurks nightly on the edge of the beech wood sitting on a fence post – at 2.30 in the afternoon. Usually we only glimpse him in darkness, no more than a ghostly flapping of wings, but here he was in broad daylight.

Thursday 18 February

Sunshine. A cloudless blue sky. Snow-streaked hills. We drove to the Breamish Valley, climbed to the hillfort at Brough Law and walked round in a little circle. Home to find two more pheasants trapped in the cage. That's six we have caught so far.

An email from a west London Brahmin quoting Philip Collins, once a New Labour courtier, in the latest edition of *Prospect*: 'Perhaps we should be thankful that, in thirty years of political protest, Corbyn has no achievements to his name at all ... His causes are things he has no capacity to change...' My correspondent writes, 'Quite why the Labour Party persists with this essentially very dim fellow is beyond me. Any ideas?' Actually I do have one: Iraq. This was Corbyn addressing the million-person anti-war demonstration just before the invasion: 'Thousands more deaths in Iraq will set off a spiral of conflict, of hate and misery that will fuel the wars, the conflict, the terrorism and the depression of future generations.' I wonder if Philip Collins was so prescient. Or for that matter the aforesaid Brahmin.

Saturday 20 February

After twenty-four hours of wrangling in Brussels, Cameron has declared a great triumph and announced to no one's surprise that he will be campaigning for a 'Yes' vote in the EU referendum, which will now take place on 23 June. A reckless game of brinkmanship, for the sole purpose of papering over divisions in the Conservative Party. We've got another four months of this and the outcome is by no means certain.

Sunday 21 February

After weeks of prevarication, Boris Johnson has finally come down in favour of Brexit. Far from being some great principled stand, his announcement reeks of calculation. When has Johnson ever done anything against his own self-interest? Although he no doubt expects the Leave campaign to lose, he presumably believes his heroic stand will ingratiate him with the Tory faithful, which will pay dividends when the time comes to choose a new leader.

Monday 22 February

To the James Cameron Memorial Lecture at City University. While waiting to go in, I was waylaid by a sixty-something zealot. He didn't introduce himself, though he was apparently a member of the Islington North Labour Party. 'Do you support our leader?' he demanded. I replied that, while I didn't believe in undermining Jeremy, he was unlikely to win an election. 'The Labour Party is finished. It will never win another election,' he said vehemently.

'And you think that doesn't matter?' I replied.

'The Blairites made Labour unelectable,' he sneered and with that he slunk off. One begins to realise that for True Believers the election of Corbyn was an end in itself. Winning elections is of little or no relevance. After all, government means compromise and these people do not do compromise. They come from the world of glorious defeats.

Afterwards, with Martin Mori and Hella Pick we went for a fish supper. Hella, once *The Guardian*'s diplomatic correspondent, said Boris Johnson, who in those days was based in Brussels for the *Telegraph*, was notorious for the myth-making half-truths that infected much of his reporting. 'He had his own agenda and often gave a slant to stories that bore little resemblance to reality.' She made another interesting point. 'Why aren't those Brexit supporters who are so concerned by our pooling of sovereignty in the EU equally concerned about the reduction of sovereignty implied by our membership of NATO, which, after all, could drag us into a nuclear war?' A good question. Could it be that for most Little Englanders the Americans don't count as foreigners?

Tuesday 23 February
Church Row, Hampstead

What is Labour's position on the EU? For the moment it may make sense to sit back and let the Tories tear themselves apart, but sooner or later we will have to take a stand. Martin reckons Labour's line should be: 'We are not keen on Cameron, he has got himself into a mess, but it is our duty, in the national interest, to help him out.' In other words make the government dependent on us. As indeed they are, given the mayhem in their own party.

As usual, I am making the most of my time in London. A dozen engagements in three days. Today began with a visit to the publishers to sort out photographs for *Hinterland*, then to Kennington for lunch with Ruth Winstone. After which we visited Patricia Moberly, who remains cheerful and outgoing, though noticeably frailer, wearing a woollen hat to conceal her loss of hair. I put it to Patricia that she should let me write her obituary. Hers is a life that ought to be recorded and that is all I can do for her. She made a little show of reluctance, but I suspect she quite likes the idea. Whether or not she will cooperate remains to be seen. She is rapidly becoming drained of energy. Then to Seven Sisters to see Max Stafford-Clark, a theatre director who wants me to write a play for him. We had a friendly chat, but writing for the stage is absolutely not my thing. Finally, to dinner with my friends Hélène Mulholland and Alan Simpson in their new home on the frontier of Dulwich. Other guests included David Edgar, the playwright; Tony Travis, an LSE professor of politics; Andrew Sparrow, who works for *Guardian* online. Professor Travis remarked that Blair had made a mistake agreeing to forgo the moratorium on freedom of movement for citizens of the East European accession states. True, but I couldn't resist pointing out that the decision was made on the basis of a study by two foolish academics which concluded that the numbers seeking admission were unlikely to exceed a few thousand a year.

Wednesday 24 February

A pleasant two hours at Company Pictures chatting with Jason Newmark, who produced *Secret State*, and two engaging, high-powered female producers. They are keen to make a drama exploiting the window of opportunity opened up by the rise of Corbyn but are not quite sure how. We reached no particular conclusion, though I would like to interest them in my sequel to *A Very British Coup*, but at the moment I am not sure where that is going either. I could do with some help from one of those clever American screenwriters from the talent pool that produces series like *Homeland* or the Netflix version of *House of Cards*. Then to a council meeting of the Winston Churchill Trust and finally to Hove to speak at a chaotic Labour Party fundraiser in an Indian restaurant. Party membership in Brighton has apparently doubled since Corbyn was elected. I put it to them that Labour's only hope in the foreseeable future was a pact with the Lib Dems and the Greens. In Brighton, where the Greens are strong, one of the three seats would have to be conceded in the event of a pact. Needless to say, they were having none of it. As so often with the dear old Labour Party, a lifetime of opposition is preferable to compromise.

Thursday 25 February
Church Row, Hampstead

To Church House for farewell drinks for Robert Fellowes, who is retiring after fifteen years as a Churchill trustee. A lot of Churchills present, including Nick Soames, who treated me to an amusing account of his son's progress at Eton. 'Costs £25,000 a half,' he boomed. 'Ask him how he's getting on and he replies, "Cool." How did his exams go? "Cool." Are the teachers any good? "Cool." £25,000 a half and that's all I get out of him.'

Friday 26 February

An hour browsing in the Hampstead Waterstones before taking the train to the north. A visit to Waterstones can be a depressing experience. So many good books by so many brilliant authors. What chance have my own humble works?

A male nurse from Tamil Nadu, an intelligent young man in his thirties, was sitting next to me on the train. He's working at a hospital in King's Lynn but was previously at Broomfield in Chelmsford. I asked how standards here compared with those in the large private hospital in Chennai where he had been trained and he said they were similar, but he remarked on the waste in the NHS, the tendency to throw away equipment that could easily be reused.

Sunday 28 February

Awoke to a hard frost. We walked in bright sunshine up to Yetlington and back and then for the first time this year lunched in the garden.

Monday 29 February

To Newcastle on Heritage Lottery Fund business. I bought a *Big Issue* from a street seller. A Romanian who spoke no more than five words of English. What is he doing here?

Tuesday 1 March

The migration crisis grows worse by the day. Last night's television news showed hundreds of young Syrians and Iraqis attempting to batter their way through the razor-wire fence erected along the Macedonian border only to be met with tear gas. There are now thousands camped out in the fields of northern Greece and more arriving every day, only to find that the route is blocked. Meanwhile in Calais police have begun destroying a large part of the makeshift encampment known as the Jungle, which is full of desperate migrants trying to get to Britain. All over Europe, hearts are hardening. Only the Germans are doing their best to cope; everyone else is putting up barriers. If anything can drive us out of the EU, it is this.

Wednesday 2 March

Still no sign of the Labour leadership's position on the EU. Every day the bulletins are full of Tories arguing for one side or the other, but from our side only silence. To be sure, a few of the New Labour elite – Mandelson was on the radio this morning – can be heard arguing that withdrawal will be bad for business, but no one currently in authority is making the case with any passion. Jeremy, in particular, is said to be lukewarm. It's not hard to make a case for staying in. On workers' rights, environment, investment, there is much to be said, but nobody on our side is saying it.

Thursday 10 March

To Newcastle, where I chaired a five-hour meeting of the Heritage Lottery committee despite a sharp pain in my right kidney. Not another stone, surely?

Saturday 12 March

Shadow Chancellor John McDonnell has made a remarkable speech asserting that a future Labour government will exercise iron discipline over the public finances. Much talk of 'wealth creators' and 'what business wants'. Shades of Gordon Brown, circa 1995. Quite how this squares with ending austerity is unclear, but it is interesting to behold. He was on the radio this morning sounding very New Labour. Quite unlike the McDonnell of old. The transformation is remarkable, if not entirely credible.

Tuesday 15 March

To Bury to visit Ray Fitzwalter, another of my dying friends. The medics have given up trying to reduce the tumour; from here on in it is just pain relief. We managed a pleasant little walk, but afterwards he had to go for a lie down and missed supper. His quality of life is ebbing. I don't think he'll see out the year.

Wednesday 16 March

A report in today's paper says that the Arctic temperature is a staggering 10° above average for this time of year.

Friday 18 March

To the Star Inn at Netherton for a drink with my neighbour John Field. The pub was built in anticipation of a railway that never came. Vera, the formidable landlady, elderly, stooped, white hair dyed blonde. Her family have owned the Star since 1917, but it is unlikely to survive her. A distinctly no-frills operation: no draught beer, no food, no dogs, no children; just bare boards and a selection of bottles on a trolley. Everyone sits in a circle and chats; Vera presides from a wooden armchair by the fireplace (no fire). The only other customers were a local farmer and a man who works for the national park, though several others trickled in as we left. On the way home, John reported a call from a prominent Conservative politician of his acquaintance who remarked that the atmosphere in the Tory Party is so poisonous that he can't see how they can continue to function as a government after the EU referendum.

Tuesday 22 March

George Osborne's recent budget is spectacularly imploding and with it his chances of succeeding David Cameron. Yesterday the Treasury announced they will not be proceeding with the planned cuts in disability benefits, leaving the Chancellor with a large hole in the public finances – which he will no doubt try to fill by a further assault on local government, given that he has already pledged to ring-fence the budgets of the other two big-spending departments, health and education, and refuses to do anything which adversely affects the interests of the prosperous elderly. Meanwhile the Tory high command are loudly protesting their commitment to one-nation, compassionate Conservatism. Time to start counting the spoons.

Suicide bombers in Brussels have detonated bombs on the Métro and at the airport. At least thirty dead.

Saturday 26 March

In today's *Times*, Matthew Parris on Boris Johnson:

> There's a pattern to Boris's life, and it isn't the lust for office, or for applause, or for susceptible women, that mark out this pattern in red ink. It's the casual dishonesty, the cruelty, the betrayal; and, beneath the betrayal, the emptiness of *real* ambition: the ambition to do anything useful with office once it is attained.

Sunday 27 March

Spent much of the day reading David Laws's *Coalition*, an insider's account of the Lib Dems' alliance with the Tories which ended so badly for them, which I am reviewing for *The Observer*. He quotes an interesting memo, written as long ago as 1998, from Lib Dem strategist Chris Rennard predicting that coalition (in this case with New Labour) without electoral reform would be political suicide. This being so, a better title for Laws's book might have been 'Chronicle of a Death Foretold'.

Tuesday 29 March

Ngoc's mother died a year ago today. She placed a large bowl of fruit on a table in front of the little altar in our living room; this evening she will light candles.

Finished David Laws's book. A blend of anecdote and forensic detail. Some nice pen portraits. Cameron: bright, personable, devoid of ideology, a short-term thinker; to quote Nick Clegg, 'so busy wondering how he is going to get through the next few weeks that he could endanger Britain's international position for decades'. Osborne: shrewd, pragmatic, ruthless, cynical, relentlessly focused on party advantage. Gove: a courteous, amusing ideologue and, according to Cameron, 'a bit of a Maoist'.

Wednesday 30 March

This evening, news that Joe Homan* has died. I have volunteered an obituary to *The Guardian*, but it remains to be seen whether they will bite. Sadly I have reached the age when my friends are increasingly beginning to pop their clogs, some – Patricia Moberly and Ray Fitzwalter – dying slowly and painfully, others – like Joe – going quickly and quietly. A decent obit, ensuring a record of their lives, is the best I can do for them.

Thursday 31 March

An email from someone at the *Mail on Sunday*: 'As a former DfID minister, do you agree with the fixed 0.7 per cent aid obligation?' For a fraction of a second I thought perhaps they were looking for someone to present the other side to the argument they have been maliciously peddling in recent months, that we should scrap our overseas aid obligations, but of

---

* A former teacher of mine who migrated to southern India in the 1960s, where he set up a series of villages to house and educate destitute and impoverished children.

course, that is not the *Mail*'s style. I sent a single-word reply, 'Yes.' Back came a one-word reply, 'Ta.'

Friday 1 April

The possibility of a Trump presidency grows scarier. His latest pronouncements include a statement that he is relaxed about the possibility that Japan, South Korea and even Saudi Arabia might acquire nuclear weapons. Asked if he would consider using tactical nuclear weapons in the Middle East, he replied, 'I wouldn't rule it out.' He said the same when asked about using nuclear weapons in Europe. The other day he upset all sides by suggesting that women who have abortions should be punished, a position from which he swiftly retreated when he realised that not even most pro-lifers were up for that. There are tentative signs that the Republican hierarchy may move to deny him the nomination after all. Not necessarily good news. Hillary Clinton is vulnerable to even a halfway sane Republican.

Sunday 3 April

The Observer have published my review of the David Laws book. At the newsagent's, I glanced at the front page of the *Mail on Sunday*. Sure enough, the paper leads with a renewed assault on the overseas aid budget, which they claim could be used to bail out the steel industry. This at a time when tens of thousands of destitute Syrians, Iraqis and Afghans are camped out in the rain and mud of northern Greece and millions more are trapped in desolate camps in Jordan, Lebanon and Turkey. The very notion that this is the time to slash the aid budget makes one ashamed to be British.

Tuesday 5 April

An email from Luise Fitzwalter: 'Ray left us yesterday at one o'clock.'

Friday 8 April

A great new feeding frenzy has developed around David Cameron following the discovery that his late father set up an offshore trust, based in Panama. Personally, I can't see that there is much to get excited about. Cameron admits to being a minor beneficiary but sold his shares before becoming Prime Minister and paid tax on the proceeds. True, it took several days to wring the truth out of him, but as several people have pointed out, he can hardly be held responsible for his father's tax affairs. Others are naively commenting that this only goes to show that we are not all in it together, but you have to have fallen off a Christmas tree to believe we ever were. For me, the clarifying moment came six years ago when the Tory elite celebrated their election victory with a party funded by a billionaire at their conference in Birmingham, at which they cracked open bottles of Château Pétrus at £1,500 a bottle, an incident that never had the attention it deserved.

Sunday 10 April

David Cameron has bowed to pressure to publish his tax returns, which at first glance seem innocuous enough but which, needless to say, have generated a vast new feeding frenzy, including demands that other politicians do likewise. Meanwhile opposition spokesmen are still going around claiming piously that he has 'more questions to answer'. Which only goes to show that there is no level of transparency that can satisfy the mob in this age of gotcha journalism. Were the position reversed, of course, the Tories would do the same to us, with knobs on, but that doesn't excuse this behaviour. In the end the entire political class ends up being tarred with the same brush. Freedom of information is all very well, but it does presuppose a degree of maturity and goodwill on the part of those receiving the information as well as those providing it, and that, I am afraid, is absent.

Monday 11 April

Dinner with Sally Banks at the Kennington Tandoori. Among our fellow diners, Ken Clarke. 'One always gets a little semi-detached in one's last parliament,' he remarked. To which I responded, 'You were always semi-detached, even when you were at the centre of government.' It's true. Ken always looked as though he was enjoying himself at the dispatch box, however rough the going got – and during the final years of the Major government it got very rough indeed.

Tuesday 12 April

To the Heritage Lottery Fund HQ at Sloane Square for a meeting of regional chairs and then to the House of Commons for a coffee with Adrian McKinty, who writes gritty, violent, addictive thrillers set in Northern Ireland. On the way out I ran into Rob Marris, one of Wolverhampton's MPs, who gloomily predicted victory for the Brexiteers resulting in Cameron's departure and an October general election in which he, Rob, would lose his highly marginal seat. I put this to Andrew Mitchell, over dinner in Islington, and he pointed out that an autumn election was out of the question since the 2011 Fixed Term Parliament Act decreed five-yearly elections and could only be overturned by a two thirds majority, which is not very likely whatever the outcome of the referendum. Andrew predicts a narrow victory for the 'Yes' camp. He says that if the Brexit camp win, Cameron 'will be gone by the following weekend' and Boris would be most likely to succeed. 'I might well vote for him,' he added.

Wednesday 13 April

Lunch in the Adjournment Cafe with Lisa Nandy, one of the rising stars of the new generation of Labour MPs. She has already caught the eye of The Man, who from his place in the stratosphere continues to take an interest in the doings of lesser mortals. Apparently he checked her out over a cup of tea in his suite at Grosvenor Square. Appropriately, she says the flag of the United States embassy billows outside his window and the only photographs in the outer office are of The Man and various US politicians, Clinton, Obama, Kerry etc. She thinks that Corbyn will stand down before the election. 'He never bargained for this. His wife's unhappy. He's not happy.' Potential successors include Heidi Alexander, Stephen Kinnock, Keir Starmer and, of course, John McDonnell. A McDonnell succession would require a lowering of the nomination threshold, but manoeuvring to that end is already said to be under way. On the EU she thinks the 'Yes' camp will win on the back of Scotland, Wales and

London, 'which will only lead to greater alienation in Labour's northern strongholds, where old loyalties are breaking down'.

Thursday 14 April

The London mayoral campaign is turning ugly. The front-page story in last night's *Standard* was headed 'Exclusive: Zac Blasts Sadiq Over Extremists – "he hides behind Muslims and brands critics Islamophobes"'. The story was bylined Joe Murphy, the paper's political editor, but it ought to have been attributed to Lynton Crosby. He, after all, is running Goldsmith's mendacious campaign. Meanwhile Sadiq's literature promises that he will be 'the most pro-business mayor ever'. Really? Are we that desperate?

Monday 18 April

To the cemetery at Ramsbottom to see Ray Fitzwalter's coffin lowered into the Silence. A simple little ceremony, no God, a few words from a moderator and that was it. Luise distributed daffodils she had picked this morning from their garden and we each dropped one into the open grave. Ngoc and I were the only non-family members present. Then to a nearby hotel, where 150 of Ray's friends and former colleagues had gathered for a memorial meeting. I gave the main tribute and others followed. Afterwards a good lunch, Lancashire hotpot followed by apple pie and custard, and then the long journey home through the Northumberland wilderness, along the Roman Wall, through Redesdale, Otterburn and Coquetdale, evening sunshine highlighting every ancient hummock and furrow. By a happy coincidence, today's *Guardian* carries my obituary of Ray.

Meanwhile Project Fear gathers pace. The Treasury has published a report alleging that EU withdrawal would cause the economy to shrink by 6 per cent, requiring a hike in income tax of 8p or further drastic cuts in public spending (no prizes for guessing which Osborne would choose). If the consequences of withdrawal are really as bad as Cameron and Osborne now allege, one wonders what on earth possessed them to gamble so recklessly on the outcome of a referendum in the first place.

Wednesday 20 April

Eight former US Treasury Secretaries have written to *The Times* advising against British withdrawal from the EU. On which side of the Atlantic was that conceived, I wonder?

To Blyth, wearing my Heritage Lottery Fund hat, for a visit by Sophie, Countess of Wessex, to the tall ship project which we help fund. There is only so much excitement that a visit from the wife of the eleventh in line to the throne can generate, but it was a good effort – flag-waving primary schoolchildren bussed in from local schools, a male voice choir – and the sun shone. Sophie, a handsome woman in white, was accompanied by the Duchess of Northumberland, elegant as ever in a body-hugging and no doubt *très* expensive ankle-length pink overcoat. The project itself, run by a charismatic former Royal Marine, is impressive. Young apprentices, in an area of high unemployment, refurbishing an elderly Danish sailing ship in which they plan, in due course, to sail to Antarctica to commemorate the 200th anniversary of a voyage by a local explorer.

Thursday 21 April

Another 500 – yes 500 – refugees are said to have drowned in a single incident off the coast of Libya. Such incidents are becoming so commonplace that they no longer dominate the news. Much hand-wringing, but no one has a solution. A UN spokesman talks vaguely of letting everyone in, but that is nonsense. There are millions more in the pipeline. Migrants are being ferried in truckloads across the Sahara from Niger, Nigeria, Eritrea, Sudan, Somalia. It's big business and the more we let in, the more will come. Libya is the weak link and given that thus far there is absolutely no sign that Libyans are capable of governing themselves, one possibility worth considering is that Libya, or at least a substantial coastal enclave, should be taken over by an international force and governed indefinitely under a UN mandate. Refugees could be processed there, without having to entrust their lives to racketeers, and those who don't qualify (the overwhelming majority) should be returned forthwith to their country of origin. That's the only way the flow will stop. It has to be said that there is no sign whatever that anyone is thinking along these lines. Our main contribution so far has been to hand over £10 million to an outfit calling itself the Libyan government whose writ does not run beyond the naval base to which it is confined.

Saturday 23 April

The Remain camp has received a big boost from Barack Obama, who has touched down briefly in London. Don't imagine, he said soon after emerging from No. 10, that if the UK were to withdraw, the US would be in any hurry to negotiate a new trade agreement. America's primary objective is an agreement with the EU and anyone else would have to go to the back of the queue. The fact that he used the English word 'queue' rather than the American word 'line' has led suspicious minds to suggest that this is yet another wheeze dreamed up in Downing Street rather than Washington. In the last week alone, the IMF, eight former US Treasury Secretaries, our own Treasury and now the US President himself have weighed in on the side of the Remain camp. These interventions have all the hallmarks of a somewhat cynical and carefully orchestrated campaign, but it is sure to have an impact. I no longer think there is any danger of a vote to leave.

Thursday 28 April

To Ealing Town Hall, where I delivered my 'Art of Political Leadership' speech to 150 Third Agers, and then to King's Cross for the train back to the north. I am reading the diaries of Ivan Maisky, the extraordinarily well-connected Soviet ambassador through the appeasement era and the first three years of war. What comes over most vividly is the Soviet resentment at Churchill's repeated postponement of plans for a second front in France, preferring instead to concentrate on north Africa and Italy, while Russians died in their millions in the East. No wonder there was such distrust. Some nice vignettes. This, for example, after observing a debate in the Lords: 'Never in my life have I seen so reactionary a gathering … The mould of the ages lies visibly upon it. Even the air in the chamber is stale and yellow … The light through the windows is gloomy.' Arrived home to find the plum blossom, daffodils and lupins drooping and miserable under a thin layer of snow. *Snow*, for goodness sake, and we are almost in May.

Friday 29 April

Just as Labour seemed poised to recapture the London mayoralty, it has become embroiled in a new and largely (but not entirely) self-inflicted crisis. The young Asian woman who defeated George Galloway in Bradford has been accused of antisemitism for retweeting what one suspects was a light-hearted suggestion, made in the heat of the moment two years ago when Israel was laying waste to Gaza, that the Israelis ought to be rehoused in the USA, leaving Palestine for the Palestinians. Never mind that the offending tweet was posted well before she was elected to Parliament. Or that she has issued a grovelling apology. Or that most of the indignation appears to be coming from people who have little or nothing to say about Israel's various crimes in Gaza and the West Bank. Labour, which has always run scared of the well-organised Israel lobby, suspended her and then, to make matters worse, Ken Livingstone jumped in with a comment about Hitler having once been a Zionist and now he's been suspended too. Tonight's television news shows a lengthy clip of Livingstone being harangued and denounced by ultra-loyalist headbanger John Mann, whose interventions are rarely helpful. Result: massive distraction from the matter at hand. Labour's many enemies making hay.

Saturday 30 April

The slow-motion car crash continues. Never mind that the Tories are systematically strangling local government. Never mind that an entire generation has been priced out of the housing market. Never mind that our schools are being forced to become centrally controlled academies, whether they want to or not. Local elections are due in five days, but all anyone wants to talk about is whether Labour is antisemitic or not. Jeremy has announced an inquiry, a code of conduct, training for parliamentary candidates. We are becoming engulfed by the toxic politics of race and the Middle East.

Friday 6 May

Sadiq Khan has been comfortably elected mayor of London. A rebuff to the Tories for their despicable campaign, trying to present Khan as some sort of Muslim extremist; they even targeted Sikhs and Hindus with their odious message, which has, happily, backfired. Even Tory candidate Zac Goldsmith's sister Jemima appeared to dissociate herself. It remains to be seen where Khan will take us. Despite a great backstory (one of eight children of an immigrant bus driver), he is entirely lacking in charisma and does not appear to stand for very much. The result will be a disappointment for those who were hoping for a bad outcome to provide them with an excuse for having another bash at Jeremy, though they will take heart from the rest of the local election results, which are poor, though not disastrous. Even as the votes were being counted some of the more brazen were taking to the airwaves demanding a coup.

Monday 9 May

A letter in the *Daily Telegraph*: 'I would appreciate some clarity on how to voice disapproval of Israel's treatment of the Palestinian people without being labelled a racist.'

Tuesday 10 May

Almost unnoticed, the migrant crisis sweeping the EU has claimed its first head of state. The Austrian Chancellor has resigned following a disastrous showing for his party in recent elections.

Wednesday 11 May

Sunderland's benighted football team has pulled off its annual miracle, ending a dismal season by defeating, in the space of four days, Chelsea and then Everton, thereby hauling themselves clear of relegation. Newcastle, by contrast, have fallen into the abyss.

Wednesday 18 May

To Church House for the presentation of medallions to recipients of Churchill scholarships and then to the House of Commons, where I was visited by a bright but politically clueless young woman who wanted advice on how to get elected to Parliament. I gave my usual advice: go away and do something else first and then you will be more useful if and when you are eventually elected, but it wasn't what she wanted to hear. I wouldn't be at all surprised to see her wafted into Parliament on an all-woman shortlist two or three years hence.

Sunday 22 May

Headline in today's *Express*: '12 million Turks say they'll come to UK once an EU deal is signed'.

Donald Trump has moved ahead in the polls for the first time. Hillary Clinton is in trouble over leaked emails and may even be charged with an offence. Ominous.

Friday 27 May

With my good friend Claes Bratt, who is visiting from Bangkok, to Edinburgh where the castle, shrouded in mist, was all but invisible. We walked in a loop around the New Town and then up the Royal Mile, rounding off with a visit to the Scottish National Gallery. Claes regaled me with an account of his clandestine trip into eastern Tibet, in October 1991, to film the return of an incarnate lama. Late one night in the remote town of Dege he was summoned to the presence and found the said lama, who had lived most of his life outside Tibet, in a small room illuminated by a single bare light bulb, receiving homage from a stream of supplicants. 'It was a scene from 1,000 years ago. The lama was seated cross-legged on a bed, at the end of which was a small table. The chanting supplicants crawled towards him on all fours, never looking him in the eye. Each in turn placed a handful of money on the table, the lama touched them on the head and they withdrew, still on all fours. And all the while the lama, who spoke perfect English, was recounting what a great, tax-free, deal he had got on his video camera at Hong Kong Airport.'

This evening I found a baby rabbit ensnared in the netting around Ngoc's sweet peas. I cut the culprit loose and deported him to the wood outside the gate.

Wednesday 1 June

All day a stream of requests for interviews and articles after the

Birmingham coroner decided to reopen the inquest into the deaths of the pub bombing victims, saying that there is 'a wealth of evidence that has still not been heard'. I did an early morning turn with John Humphrys on *Today*, tapped out an op-ed piece for *The Guardian* and ignored the rest, except for a request for 1,500 words from *The Sun*, which I had particular pleasure in declining.

The EU debate grows daily more toxic. Both sides making wild, dishonest claims. The Tories are in a dreadful mess, but we seem unable to take advantage of their discomfort. Jeremy is all but invisible. The Brexiteers and the tabloids are focusing on immigration while the Remain camp stick to the economy. Polls indicate that the Leave camp may be edging ahead, although my instinct is that, when the chips are down, there will be a majority for staying put, not out of any love for the EU but due to fear of the unknown.

Sunday 5 June

David Fraser and I are walking St Cuthbert's Way, from Holy Island to Melrose. As we approached Jedburgh this afternoon we enquired of an old countryman whose land we were on. After a moment's thought he replied, 'It's either the Duke of Buccleuch, the Duke of Roxburghe or the Marquess of Midlothian.' Some things never change.

Friday 10 June

At last rain – the first for ten days. A grey mist hangs over the hills. This afternoon to Chillingham for the annual meeting of the Wild Cattle Association. Nigel Vinson,* a strong Brexiteer, says that if there is a narrow victory for the Leavers, he would expect renegotiation followed by a second referendum. He added, 'In most countries a constitutional change of this magnitude would require at least 60 per cent.'

Saturday 11 June

Dined with Kate Donaghy and Jeremy Hosking at Lorbottle Hall. Jeremy,

---

* A former businessman, philanthropist and Conservative peer.

who is funding a Brexit poster campaign, agrees with Nigel Vinson that if the Leavers win, there will be a period of renegotiation and then another referendum. For this reason, he says, anyone in favour of reforming the EU, whether they want to leave or not, ought to vote 'Out', because that is the only way of inducing the Europeans to negotiate seriously. Personally, I don't buy it. The prospect of a second referendum promises years more turmoil, not to mention shouts of 'betrayal' from hardline Brexiteers.

Monday 13 June

Another mass shooting in the USA, fifty dead. Killed by a lone gunman in a gay nightclub in Orlando, Florida. Apparently he had mental health issues, but that of course was no bar to him acquiring automatic weapons.

A depressing little clip on this evening's Radio 4 news, recorded in a social club in Sunderland. The punters, working-class retirees, Labour voters all, declared they would be voting to leave the EU. Why? Migration, of course. 'Many migrants in Sunderland, are there?' enquired the interviewer. 'Er, no.' 'Had migration had any impact on their lives?' 'Er, no.' But they were voting 'Out' anyway. And this is the city with the Nissan car plant upon which perhaps 20,000 jobs depend. Which only goes to show that turkeys can be persuaded to vote for Christmas. We creep ever closer to the abyss.

Thursday 16 June

To Newcastle, where I chaired the Heritage Lottery Fund committee. Two little straws in the wind. Darlington Council is said to have slashed its budget for non-statutory services from £12 million to £2 million. And Sunderland City Council is proposing to stop locking its parks at night in order to save on security. Barnes Park, in which the HLF recently invested £7 million, is particularly vulnerable to vandalism. Every day the noose tightens. Osborne's much-trumpeted austerity is gradually strangling the public sector.

Jo Cox, an up-and-coming Labour MP, has been shot and stabbed by a deranged gunman shouting nationalist slogans. Later it was confirmed that she was dead and all parties suspended their referendum campaign. She leaves a husband and two small children.

Friday 17 June

Liz Forgan is staying. We went straight from the station to Howick Hall, where we trailed around the garden in the damp and in the evening dined at the Angler's Arms, where she had her wallet stolen, apparently by the woman sitting next to us, who disappeared rather abruptly. Liz handled the crisis with admirable calm, cancelling credit cards, informing the police and so on, but it made a damp day even damper.

Saturday 18 June

This evening, with Liz, to dinner with Matt and Anya Ridley at Blagdon. Fellow guests included Nigel Lawson, Owen Paterson, the journalists Andrew Knight and David Rose and their spouses. Although I overlapped with Lawson for five years, when he dwelt in the stratosphere and I in the lower foothills, this was our first encounter. We chatted amiably about his house in Gascony, my children and his grandchildren, the impact of Brexit and so on. He was dismissive of the suggestion that, whatever the outcome, the Tory Party is damaged beyond repair and didn't think the Nationalists in Scotland would be in any hurry to hold another referendum, given the collapse of the oil price. Although most of those present were Brexiteers, the subject was not laboured. Liz said afterwards that she had the impression that the wind has gone out of their sails and they now expected to lose. It seems the mood may have changed since the murder of poor Jo Cox, which has been all over the news for three days.

Monday 20 June

A couple of hours pushing Labour's anti-Brexit leaflet through every door in Whittingham. Pleasantly surprised to find three Remain and no Vote Leave posters in cottage windows, albeit displayed discreetly. Meanwhile Parliament has been recalled for tributes to Jo Cox, prompting a complaint from Nigel Farage that Cameron and co. are exploiting her death for their own purposes. There may be something in this, but there is no doubt that the awful death of this lovely young woman has caught the public imagination in a way that gives the lie to the oft-repeated suggestion that the entire political class is loathed.

Tuesday 21 June

Much talk from leading Brexiteers of 'taking back our country', but I notice that many of those deploying this line of argument already seem to own more than their fair share of it.

Wednesday 22 June

Ngoc arrived home from Saigon bearing many kilos of coffee and cashew nuts and telling tales of gross overdevelopment as the gulf between the new rich and everyone else grows unchecked. Entire districts given over to vast, vulgar condominiums, patrolled by security guards and isolated behind coded entry gates.

Thursday 23 June

Referendum day. We cast our votes in the village hall at Whittingham. The polling clerks predicted a record turnout. Alas, most of our neighbours, being prosperous and of a certain age and outlook, are voting Leave, but my hunch is that Remain will win. One thing is for sure: a victory for the Brexiteers will hand the country over to the hard right of the Conservative Party, and they are unlikely to be merciful in victory.

Friday 24 June

Awoke to the shocking news that, against expectations, the UK has voted to withdraw from the EU. Shamefully, but unsurprisingly, Sunderland led the way, voting 61:39 for withdrawal. Migration seems to have been the key issue. There are scarcely any migrants in Sunderland, but there are a lot of *Sun* readers. By breakfast Cameron had announced his intention to stand down, as well he might. A fine mess he's got us into. And there is no going back. This is for ever. The beginning of a long, slow decline into insularity and irrelevance. Boris Johnson and Michael Gove, even in their hour of triumph, looked shell-shocked. Someone remarked of Gove that he looked like a man waking up from a bad trip to find that he had just murdered his best friend.

Other news: Emma arrived home from university declaring that from now on she is a vegan.

Saturday 25 June

An email from David Fraser in London: 'There is a strange feeling of un-reality here, as though there has been a bad accident, which in a way is the case.' Already it is becoming clear that the fallout could extend well beyond our shores. Every little flag-waving nationalist in Europe will soon be on the march. Marine Le Pen, who leads the resurgent French nationalists, says that if she is elected President (which cannot be ruled out), she will hold a referendum on French withdrawal. In one's darkest moments one can see disintegration beckoning. Shades of Europe in the '30s? Exactly what the EU was set up to avoid.

With David Simmonds, a most agreeable neighbour, I walked the Coquet Challenge. A thirteen-mile stroll in the hills above Rothbury and back along Simonside. Heavy rain at one point, but once the rain had cleared the views were spectacular. This evening to a concert in the church at Alwinton. Whatever storms rage elsewhere, all is well in this privileged little cocoon of ours.

Sunday 26 June

Labour appears to be imploding. Hilary Benn has been sacked from the shadow Cabinet after declaring his lack of confidence in Jeremy's leadership. A dozen other frontbenchers have resigned and more resignations are in the pipeline. A motion of no confidence is being tabled at tomorrow's meeting of the Parliamentary Labour Party. It looks like the end is nigh for Jeremy, although he has declared his determination to stay put. Hilary, unfortunately, has ruled himself out of any future leadership contest, even though he is by far the most credible candidate. I rang him this evening and pressed him to reconsider, but he was adamant. On Jeremy, Hilary was scathing: 'A complete absence of leadership.' He also recounted an extraordinary exchange he had recently with a man in Sunderland which gives a flavour of the current madness. The man was lamenting the disappearance of Sunderland's manufacturing base, to which Hilary said, 'You've got Nissan.' The response was: 'They're Japanese.'

A call from Julie Elliott, my successor in Sunderland, who says the Labour vote is in meltdown and that if there were an election tomorrow UKIP would win most of the seats in the north-east. 'Unless we do something radical, we've had it. We can't go on like this. Jeremy has to go.'

Monday 27 June

A *coup d'état* is under way. By mid-afternoon more than thirty Labour frontbenchers had resigned, with further resignations said to be in the pipeline. Jeremy is insisting that he has a mandate from the membership and only they can remove him. Which means the struggle could continue for months while Labour's credibility drains away. Meanwhile the opposition are utterly unable to exploit the mayhem in the Tory Party. Blair would have murdered them by now. If there is another election, assuming some halfway credible candidate emerges, Jeremy could well lose. Many of the £3 members who helped elect him have drifted away and his support among paid-up members must be eroding. He can't be enjoying all this, but I guess he would be happy to go down fighting. He is, after all, a veteran of so many glorious defeats, and the history of the Labour movement is littered with them. The evening bulletins showed him addressing an impromptu rally of supporters in Parliament Square. It was noticeable that several of them were carrying 'Socialist Worker' placards.

Meanwhile Michael Heseltine has suggested that Parliament may refuse to endorse whatever withdrawal terms are obtained by the Brexiteers and that there may have to be another referendum. Already the *Mail* is reporting a poll suggesting that 7 per cent of those who voted Leave have changed their minds.

As if all this wasn't bad enough, England's overpaid, overhyped football team have been knocked out of the European Cup by a team of amateurs from Iceland, a country with a population the size of Croydon. Unf***ingbelievable. Truly, the gods have abandoned us.

Tuesday 28 June

Diane Abbott, one of a rapidly diminishing band of loyal Corbynistas in Parliament, was on the radio this morning lamenting the behaviour of her colleagues (two thirds of the shadow Cabinet have gone) and repeatedly stressing that it was up to the party, not MPs, to decide Jeremy's fate. Of the electorate she made no mention. What a mess. The economy and the Tory Party are in meltdown and Her Majesty's Opposition has gone AWOL. All of which only goes to highlight the folly of electing a leader who has little or no support among his or her parliamentary colleagues. When all this is over, Labour is going to have to look at our system for electing leaders. I say this as someone who played a part in the setting up of the present, convoluted system. Maybe we should adopt the Tory model, whereby the parliamentary party presents two candidates, both of whom have a following in Parliament, to the wider membership.

Wednesday 29 June

Labour is facing what commentators are increasingly referring to as an existential crisis. Yesterday, by a margin of more than four to one, the parliamentary party passed a motion of no confidence in the leader, but Jeremy is sticking to his guns: he was elected by the membership and, in the event of another leadership election, he will be a candidate. A long and bloody battle beckons with no sign of a credible alternative in sight. Angela Eagle is said by some to be next in line for the poisoned chalice. An intelligent, decent woman, but she radiates gloom, exactly what we don't need.

On the radio this morning John Mills, a lifelong Labour-supporting Brexiteer and a successful businessman to boot, remarked that perhaps we didn't need to be in the single market. The tariffs that would be imposed if we didn't join are only about 3 per cent and these would easily be offset by the fall in the value of the pound, which, he asserted, is still too high.

Thursday 30 June

Another astonishing development. Boris Johnson, who was widely expected to be the front runner for the Tory leadership, suddenly announced that he will not be running after all. He has been shafted by Michael Gove, who, against expectations, announced that *he* would be standing. Boris, who is not as popular with his parliamentary colleagues as he is with the rank and file, apparently concluded that he no longer had enough support from fellow MPs to get his name on the ballot paper. Obviously there has been an epic bust-up behind the scenes. One suspects, and no doubt Gove and his playmates also suspect, that Boris, despite his starring role in the Brexit campaign, is not actually in favour of withdrawal and never anticipated that this would be the outcome. He simply calculated that by placing himself at the head of the Leave camp he would sufficiently endear himself to the Tory rank and file to win any subsequent leadership election, which he expected to be two or three years down the line. Cynicism of a very high order. Well, for once he has miscalculated, big time. As for Gove, he isn't going to win because card-carrying Tories will not back someone who has knifed their hero. Which means the odds are now firmly on Theresa May.

Meanwhile Jeremy, trapped in his bunker and pounded by artillery from all sides, is showing no sign of surrender.

Friday 1 July

The 100th anniversary of the battle of the Somme. Twenty thousand dead in the first few hours. Ultimately, a million casualties. Their ghosts are all around us on war memorials in every town and village, on quad walls at Eton and Oxbridge colleges. Poignant reminders of that unlucky, doomed generation. Someone had the bright idea of marking the anniversary by getting young men dressed in First World War uniforms to wander silently through city centres the length and breadth of the country. Oddly affecting. You could see tears trickling down the cheeks of passers-by as the ghosts mingled silently with the living.

Sunday 3 July

After three fruitless years we have our first peaches. The bad news is, however, that some wee beastie is nibbling them. Yesterday we found three on the ground in the glasshouse. Today another three. We spent half an hour trying to cover the remainder with a net, but there are still many holes.

Monday 4 July

To London on the 09.00. At Westminster Tube Station I was waylaid by Tory MP and Norfolk squire Henry Bellingham, who said, 'I am furious with the Prime Minister for going. He could have toughed it out for another eighteen months.' Meanwhile every conceivable card is being played in the campaign to destroy Jeremy. I came across a copy of last Friday's *Mirror*. The headline: 'Under Corbyn Labour is not a safe place for Jews.'

Some of those who voted Leave appear to be under the impression that they voted to kick out all foreigners. The police are reporting a big rise in racially motivated incidents since the Brexit vote. Anyone remotely foreign is being asked, 'When are you going home?' Polish and even Asian shops have been vandalised. Nor are the French exempt. My friend Hélène Mulholland reports the following exchange while queuing to pay at her local supermarket: 'At last we've got rid of the Frogs.' To which she responded, 'No you haven't. There's one behind you.' And at her hairdresser, to whom she has been going for years, she made some casual remark about the weather, to which the hairdresser replied with a slight edge in her voice, 'Are you criticising *our* weather?'

Tuesday 5 July
Westminster

After a morning interviewing for a Radio 4 documentary, lunch at one of the tables in the atrium of Portcullis House, where I received a constant stream of visitors. One, a Cabinet minister, said firmly that he would be supporting Theresa May but there was a danger that the membership would go for Andrea Leadsom. 'And then we'd be in the same situation as you are, a leader who lacks support in the parliamentary party. We tried that with Iain Duncan Smith and look what happened.'

Earlier, I came upon Kelvin Hopkins, a genial but obscure old leftie. 'I am in the shadow Cabinet,' he beamed. 'For twenty-four hours I was the oldest frontbench appointee since Gladstone, until I was trumped by Paul Flynn.' Flynn, aged eighty-one, is currently shadow Leader of the House. So few people are willing to serve that Jeremy is having to scour the hedgerows, but still he shows no sign of surrender to the baying mob.

Wednesday 6 July

The long-awaited Chilcot Report on Iraq. As expected, Blair gets a roasting, but to the disappointment of some he is accused of exaggerating, not lying. Richard Dearlove and John Scarlett, the former intelligence chiefs, don't come out well either, but inevitably the focus is on Blair. He gave a two-hour press conference, voice breaking, apologising and yet not apologising. But for the catastrophe of Iraq (and it is a big 'but') he would be viewed in an entirely different light. I feel sad about it.

This evening, to a party given by Andrew and Sharon Mitchell at the Vintner's Hall in the City. Among the guests Charlie Falconer, Geoff Hoon, Chris Huhne, Jeremy Hunt, the former chief of the armed forces David Richards and a subdued-looking Boris Johnson. I bent General Richards's ear on the subject of Trident, on which Parliament is shortly due to vote. He said he was instinctively anti, providing that some of the savings were used to bolster spending on conventional forces. He seemed only vaguely aware of the history (the fact that it was only ever about keeping in with the Americans, who never wanted us to have nuclear weapons in the first place). I suggested he needed 'a line to take' and he promised to read up on it. I will send him the relevant references. Anyway, it's too late now. Parliament will vote to go ahead regardless.

Thursday 7 July

Andrea Leadsom, until recently an obscure junior minister, has made it into the final two in the ballot for the Tory leadership. Theresa May, the other candidate, has far more MPs in her camp, but it is the members in the shires who will take the final decision and they could well back Leadsom. As expected, Michael Gove's campaign imploded amid allegations of 'betrayal' for knifing Boris.

Friday 8 July

Ngoc has discovered who it is that is nibbling at our precious peaches: red squirrels whom we have kept fed all year with hazelnuts. Ungrateful beasts.

There has been a terrible accident at a recycling centre in Birmingham. All the victims are Gambians, but what caught my ear was a passing reference by the reporter to the '10,000-strong Gambian community in Birmingham'. What on earth are 10,000 Gambians doing here?

Monday 11 July

Andrea Leadsom has withdrawn from the Tory leadership election, which means Theresa May is our next Prime Minister and the Tories will soon get their act together. Labour meanwhile is still marching steadily towards the machine guns.

A day spent weeding – five barrow loads – in anticipation of a visit from *Gardeners' World* next week.

Tuesday 12 July

To Sunderland for a meeting of the steering group on the city's bid to be the 2021 UK City of Culture. One of the proposed themes, diversity, has taken a bit of a knock, given that Sunderland has just voted overwhelmingly for Brexit, mainly on the grounds that most locals are not keen on foreigners. General agreement that the issue can't just be brushed under the carpet but will have to be met head on. It prompted the city's chief executive, Irene Lucas, to come up with an interesting new piece of jargon: 'decatastrophising'. Inevitably, it originated in America.

The Chinese have reacted with imperialist arrogance to a ruling by a UN panel that disputes their claim to 90 per cent of the so-called South China Sea. They are in dispute with just about all their neighbours, which in due course could lead to war.

Wednesday 13 July

Theresa May entered Downing Street this afternoon, making a one-nation speech that might have done justice to Blair circa 1997 ('the government I lead will not be driven by the interests of the privileged few'). As with the early days of New Labour, there seems to be room for everyone in Theresa's big tent. Which is just as well because, the way things are going, Labour isn't going to be in a position to do much for the marginalised in the foreseeable future. This evening the first Cabinet appointments: Osborne is out, replaced by Philip Hammond, economically dry but calm and unshowy and, unlike his predecessor, not given to cynical, mendacious gimmickry of the 'strivers versus skivers' variety. To general amazement Boris Johnson is to become Foreign Secretary, but the Brexit negotiations will be in the hands of David Davis, a tough cookie. There is no doubt now that it will happen.

Just three weeks since the referendum and the Tories have got their boots on. Labour meanwhile hasn't even decided whose names should go on the ballot paper.

Thursday 14 July

Eighty-four men, women and children, celebrating Bastille Day in Nice, have been mown down by a lorry, driven by a deranged Islamist. Poor France. It's coming down hard.

Monday 18 July

The long-awaited visit from Joe Swift and the *Gardeners' World* team. I had been concerned (a) that they might be disappointed with my relatively puny (one-acre) garden compared with some they feature and (b) that the weather would let us down, but I need not have worried. They were full of enthusiasm and the sun shone. They were here all day, even though they are only making a six- or seven-minute cameo. After they had gone, I picked the last half-dozen peaches from the tree in the glasshouse.

Meanwhile Parliament voted overwhelmingly to blow a minimum of £30 billion on renewing Trident. Completely bonkers. People keep asking if I miss politics. Not a bit.

Tuesday 19 July

Angela Eagle has withdrawn from the Labour leadership race, after being out-nominated by Owen Smith, a Welshman of whom I had never heard until he announced his intention to run, but that may reflect more on me than on him. This evening to London, where I am staying with John and Sheila Williams in Clapham. Sheila reckons the revolt against Jeremy is media-generated hysteria, but there is surely more to it than that.

Wednesday 20 July

To the BBC at Millbank, where I interviewed a woman whose young son is serving life for his part in a brutal attack which he insists he had nothing to do with. One of a growing number convicted under the controversial joint enterprise rules, which allow for the prosecution of members of a group for murder when it cannot be proved which member inflicted the fatal blow, his case is all the more remarkable given that the boy is registered blind and there is no evidence that he took part in the assault at all. Dignified, intelligent and articulate, his mother has been thrust into the limelight by the disaster that has overtaken her family. Apparently the killing took place when Cameron had launched his cynical 'Broken Britain' campaign and he used the case to illustrate his bogus argument, thereby generating tabloid hysteria. He even went so far as to make the wife of the victim a peer.

Lunched at the House, where the feeling is that Jeremy will win again. The big question, of course, is what happens then, given his inability to form a functioning opposition? Some headbangers in the parliamentary party are talking openly of a split, but the precedents – 1931 and 1981 – are not good. The good news is that Labour Party coffers are several million pounds better off as a result of the recent influx of members.

Thursday 21 July

To Westminster, where I interviewed Alan Beith (former chairman of the Justice Select Committee) and Dominic Grieve (former Attorney General) for my Radio 4 miscarriage of justice documentary. Afterwards lunch with a bright young MP from the north-west, not a particular fan of Jeremy but not a headbanger either, who said his party was split 50:50 and the leadership ballot could go either way. He thinks that if Jeremy wins again, the MPs have a duty to try to make it work but says there are seventy or eighty kamikazes who are convinced that they will either be deselected or lose their seats come the election and who therefore have nothing to lose by continuing the mayhem.

Friday 22 July

To dinner with Nigel and Yvonne Vinson in their beautiful, remote house on the edge of the Cheviots, down a mile and a half of single-track road, with panoramic views towards the Vale of Whittingham. Nigel proudly showed us his apricot tree, espaliered along the wall of his glasshouse, only three years old, with about 200 plump fruits. He denied possessing any magic formula, but there must be something he knows that we don't.

Sunday 24 July

Poor Jeremy is coming under unrelenting attack, much of it fuelled by headbangers and grandstanders in the parliamentary party, who appear oblivious to the damage they are doing. Yesterday a letter signed by forty or so of his female 'colleagues' demanding that he do more to dissociate himself from alleged incidents of bullying and intimidation (many of which, I suspect, are wildly exaggerated). This despite the fact that he has repeatedly dissociated himself from such behaviour and is himself the subject of all kinds of abuse to which he never responds. If the stakes weren't so high, I would be tempted to vote for Jeremy regardless in the face of this avalanche of nonsense.

Monday 25 July

To Sunderland, where I spent three hours helping Sky Television with a documentary on why a city that has done so well out of the EU should have voted so heavily for Brexit. Then to Newcastle for a meeting of the North of England Civic Trust, whose finances are increasingly parlous. And finally to London, where I am again staying with John and Sheila. This evening, on *Newsnight* an interview with Owen Smith, the fluent but slippery Welshman who is challenging Corbyn for the Labour leadership. Like many a Welsh politician on the make, he lays claim to the mantle of Nye Bevan, although it is far from clear that Nye would be keen on a former drug company lobbyist. He also claims he would have voted against the Iraq War, although he was conveniently not in Parliament at the time and someone has unearthed an interview he gave at the time which seems to suggest the opposite.

Tuesday 26 July

To Sloane Square for the board of the Heritage Lottery Fund, where I was required to give a short presentation. The finance director remarked that the Treasury 'have been taken aback' by the amount of EU funding the UK has received. Ought it to have come as a surprise? Surely someone had done the sums before the vote? Apparently not. Later the chairman, Peter Luff, said that in Worcester High Street last Saturday he had spotted what purported to be a Labour Party stall displaying a placard saying

'Support Jeremy, defeat the Blairites'. He was incredulous that Labour members should flaunt their disagreements so publicly. It occurred to me that perhaps they were not long-term members but recent arrivals from a distant planet.

Wednesday 27 July

A YouGov poll in *The Times* gives the Tories a twelve-point lead and ominously suggests that 2.5 million of the 9 million or so people who voted Labour at the last election believe that Theresa May will make a better Prime Minister than Jeremy Corbyn.

Thursday 28 July

Hillary Clinton has formally received the Democratic nomination for the US presidency, the first woman to do so. Given the competition she ought to be a shoo-in, but incredibly Donald Trump is ahead in some polls. We are entering the era of post-truth politics, in which hope and optimism are capped by fear and loathing.

Friday 29 July

To tea with Humphry and Katharine Wakefield at Chillingham, where Ngoc and I were treated to a tour of their magnificent border and Humphry's extraordinary, eclectic collection of ancient artefacts. Among them a portrait of an Elizabethan lady purchased in New York for $150. He brought it home and hung it on the wall opposite a portrait of Mary, Queen of Scots but says that it kept falling off. On one occasion the wire was cut clean through. Later, he found the original at Longleat, which identified the woman as someone who had fallen out with Mary. He hung the portrait elsewhere and there has been no trouble since. That, anyway, is Humphry's story.

Saturday 30 July

An email from a fan of the diaries: 'You could have been the first natural leader the country has ever had or ever likely to have. Please don't give up!' Ah, but I have.

Sunday 31 July

A round robin email from Owen Smith promising pay rises for public sector workers and an utterly incredible '£200 billion New Deal for schools, hospitals and infrastructure'. Not a word about where the money will come from. The man's a shyster. Apart from his not being Jeremy Corbyn, it is hard to think of a reason why anyone should vote for him.

Monday 1 August

Corbyn, not to be outdone, is promising a £500 billion investment programme backed up by a national investment bank (shades of Harold Wilson circa 1960s). The bank will apparently have £100 billion capital, which is expected to leverage another £250 billion. From where is unspecified. The magic money tree, no doubt.

Wednesday 3 August

The Met have announced they are putting 600 more armed police on the streets of London 'to reassure the public'. Cue pictures of Commissioner Bernard Hogan-Howe against a background of men in balaclavas cradling state-of-the-art weaponry. I don't know about the terrorists, but they scare the hell out of me. Why do anti-terrorist police need to wear balaclavas?

Thursday 4 August

John McDonnell was on the radio this morning justifying his plans for the economy, which involve an enormous increase in borrowing, taking advantage of record low interest rates, in order to boost infrastructure investment. He comes across as fluent, competent and good humoured, although one suspects that behind that genial exterior he is quietly compiling a list of enemies to be summarily dispatched come the revolution.

Friday 5 August

Headline in today's *FT*: 'Carney issues stark warning with package to ease Brexit downturn'. Meanwhile the lead in that parallel universe that is the

Daily Express begins: 'Britain will prosper out of the EU, the Bank of England confirmed yesterday'.

Wednesday 10 August

A book review payment from the *Irish Times*. The usual fee, £235, is reduced to £197, hard evidence of the impact of the Brexit vote upon the value of sterling.

Friday 12 August

This evening, a seven-minute slot *on Gardeners' World*, taking us into new territory. A flood of friendly emails from friends and neighbours. Even one from someone who says he was in my class at school and another who remembered me from childhood in Dorset Avenue, Chelmsford.

Saturday 13 August

One of our red squirrels is dead. The young one with the light tail. I found him about twenty minutes ago, stretched out by the side of the drive, as though he was asleep. A mystery as to what killed him. He was alive and well as recently as this morning, when I watched him darting up and down our Prunus tree, taking hazelnuts from the feeder.

Sunday 14 August

With every day that passes, Labour's civil war is hotting up. Tom Watson, the supposed deputy leader, is going on about Trotskyite infiltration. Undoubtedly there has been, but it doesn't begin to explain Labour's 200,000 new members. Michael Foster, a Labour donor, writes in today's *Mail* an article headed: 'Why I despise Jeremy Corbyn and his Nazi storm troopers' (did he really write that or was it one of the *Mail*'s team of ghostwriters?). Various Blairistas sounding off, without reflecting that it was their hero's adventure in Iraq that brought Jeremy to office in the first place and that many of those flooding back into the party are not Trotskyites but former members who left in disillusion. It's becoming clear that, even if he wins again, and the expectation is that he will, Jeremy will not be allowed to lead. For many of his opponents, scorched earth is the name of the game. They are willing to destroy the party rather than allow him to form a functioning opposition.

Another day out in the Borders. This time to Manderston, the last great house to be completed before the long party enjoyed by the Edwardian upper classes was brought to an abrupt end by the First World War. We came across the laird, Adrian Palmer, wandering through the servants' quarters. A lonely figure, his children grown up and flown the nest, two wives divorced. Unless I am mistaken, he lives alone in that vast palace. 'Were you brought up here?' I asked. 'My father used to go on "grand tours" and I was sent up here to my grandmother, but she just looked into the nursery every day to check that I was still alive.' He added, 'When I go, the only thing I'll miss about this place is the gardens.'

Tuesday 16 August
Vale of Lorton, The Lakes

Emma, Alf Dubs (aged eighty-three) and I completed the Fairfield Horseshoe (873m). Eleven miles, temperature in the mid-twenties and a difficult descent. Poor Alf was all in by the time we came down but in remarkable shape for a man of his years.

Saturday 20 August
Callaly

Hilary and Sally Benn, holidaying in Northumberland, called in. Like just about everyone I know, Hilary is resigned to another Corbyn victory and a long period of impotence. He says Corbyn was useless in the shadow Cabinet, offering no leadership, having little to say on anything and often deferring to John McDonnell. Remarkably, however, he has met people who genuinely believe that by some miracle Jeremy is going to lead us to victory. Like the Tory Party, we have been taken over by a cult.

I gave them a tour of the estate and mentioned that the Browne family, the former lairds, used to have their own train. Hilary said that when he was Secretary of State for Environment, the Prince of Wales had invited him to accompany him to the Lakes on the royal train. Charles had even offered to send the train to Ealing to collect him, an offer that Hilary wisely declined. (Imagine the fun the tabloids would have had with that – 'Royal train diverted to pick up Labour minister'.) His suite had its own bath, of which he took advantage, if only to say that he had made full use of the facilities.

Sunday 21 August

The Labour leadership ballot opens tomorrow. Jeremy addressed a rally in London, where a couple of thousand supporters chanted his name, but as we have learned to our cost over the years, big rallies are no substitute for a credible programme, and that is utterly lacking. Time for a tweet: 'Much as I respect Jeremy, I shall not be voting for him. To do so risks annihilation…' Within minutes it was trending.

Monday 22 August

Among the many responses to my Corbyn tweet one that reads, 'Anni hilation by whom?' To which I have replied, 'The electorate. Remember them?'

Tuesday 23 August

To the Edinburgh University Business School (of which I am 'an associate') to hear Professor Chris Carter interview Sky political supremo Adam Boulton. I asked Adam if he agreed that Jeremy Corbyn owed his election to New Labour's adventure in Iraq. He gave a long-winded answer and then said, 'The short answer is "yes"'. Afterwards we talked of what might happen if, as seems likely, Jeremy wins again. There is one intriguing possibility: if a majority of the parliamentary party decided to defect, the Speaker may be obliged to recognise them as the official opposition. Ruinous, of course, because come the election there would be two Labour candidates vying for every seat, leading to a catastrophe of 1931 proportions.

Wednesday 24 August

A big row over pictures of Jeremy crouched on the floor between carriages on a Virgin train bound for Newcastle. Allegedly because he couldn't find a seat, although CCTV footage appears to show there were plenty of free seats. His spokesmen have offered a number of explanations, none entirely credible. The suspicion is that it was an attempt to justify his plans for renationalising the railways. If so, it has backfired. A stunt worthy of New Labour at its most devious.

Monday 29 August

To Edinburgh for the book festival, where I more or less filled the big tent. I was sitting in the authors' yurt chatting to a man whose name I hadn't caught when Gordon Brown, Special Branch men fore and aft, suddenly appeared. 'What are you doing here?' he asked, more or less affably.

I explained that I was in the big tent after him.

'So we are in competition?'

'If so, you'll win easily.'

'What are you talking about?'

'My memoirs, coming shortly.'

He, with a just a hint of bitterness, 'That'll make a change from writing about me.'

It turned out that I was sitting with Gordon's older brother, John – refreshingly normal, down-to-earth man who wangled me a ticket to Gordon's show. Gordon was on good form, relaxed, humorous, speaking without notes for thirty minutes, answering questions with good humour. His argument was that, rather than the Scots declaring independence (which they can't afford), there should be a new settlement between England and the regions. Some sort of federal arrangement. He was well received, attracting several spontaneous rounds of applause. It may be my imagination, but I sense that Gordon, by living modestly and devoting himself, *à la* Jimmy Carter, to good works, is gradually being rehabilitated in public esteem.

Thursday 1 September

A good harvest. Abundant crops of peas, pink fir apple potatoes, beetroot, onions, tomatoes, courgettes, half a dozen large red cabbages and runner beans, plums by the kilo and good crops of pears and apples, the latter still on the small side. We are eating our way through as much as possible and giving away plums to friends and neighbours. The rest Ngoc is stewing and freezing for consumption in the long winter months. This weekend we must lift and store the potatoes.

Saturday 3 September

To lunch with friends in Rothbury. One of those present reminisced about Major Browne, the last inhabitant of Callaly Castle before it was converted. Everyone agrees he was a delightful old boy, despite dwelling on another planet from most of the world around him. His sixty-year lairdship was devoted mainly to hunting. He did little in the way of repairs or maintenance, planted no trees and sold a farm whenever he ran out of money. By the end it came down to just him and one servant rattling around in the great house while everything around him declined. In his latter years he was often to be seen speeding around the lanes in an electric scooter. Around his neck he wore a Second World War gas mask case, which was, as he put it, 'worn according to the 1940s regulations'.

'What have you got in there?' my informant enquired.

'Everything I need.' Whereupon the major opened his gas mask case to reveal his pipe, a tobacco pouch, a box of Swan Vesta matches, half a bottle of whisky and a small pair of binoculars.

Sunday 4 September

Keith Vaz has been outed by the *Sunday Mirror* for, apparently, entertaining two male prostitutes while posing as a washing machine salesman. Although he is made of Teflon, I have long thought Keith would come to a sticky end, but thus far he has always survived. He surely won't be able to wriggle out of this. Meanwhile, at the G20 summit in China, the Japanese have fired a warning shot across the bows of the Brexiteers by pointing out that their companies account for 140,000 jobs in the UK and that they expect tariff-free access to the EU to be maintained…

Wednesday 7 September

My recently launched memoir, *Hinterland*, is proving a hard sell in the face of stiff competition from bigger fish than me, but today brought one little sliver of good news. The journalist John Crace said on the BBC's *Daily Politics* that, of the current crop of memoirs, mine was the best.

Thursday 8 September

Jeremy Corbyn and Owen Smith were on the telly tonight, answering questions from a live audience in Oldham. Corbyn – smooth, relaxed, well-informed – completely outclassed Smith, but Jeremy's insurmountable problem is that he has so little support among his colleagues in Parliament. Anyway, it is not good for Labour to be washing so much dirty linen on primetime television.

Incredibly, Donald Trump appears to be moving ahead of Hillary in the polls. A call from M, my well-connected Washington friend, who describes Trump as 'a lying psychopath'.

Meanwhile Theresa May, so soon after proclaiming her desire to help those at the bottom of the pile, has announced her first concrete measure: more grammar schools.

Saturday 10 September

Walls are going up all over Europe, and not just on the southern frontiers. The French are building one around the port at Calais to keep desperate migrants at bay. Even the Norwegians are building one across their frontier with Russia, above the Arctic Circle.

Thursday 15 September

Up at 3 a.m. and then to the airport with our friends Aidan and Jill Harrison, where we caught the 06.00 flight to Toulouse, via Amsterdam. On the second leg Aidan found himself sitting beside a massive, moustachioed, garrulous American, an expert on bees, who regaled him on the virtues of a Trump presidency. The second time this week that I have come across Americans abroad who are Trump supporters. The point is these are some of the 18 per cent of Americans who own passports. Unlike most of their fellow countrymen, they know about Abroad and yet they are still Trumpistas. The more I hear of this, the more I begin to think that Trump may win.

Friday 16 September–Monday 19 September
Abbaye de Camon, Ariège

Candlelit corridors paved with fifteenth-century terracotta tiles, breakfast on the terrace overlooking forested hills with a distant view of the Pyrenees. We are here as guests of our generous neighbours, Tony and Mary Henfrey. About twenty in number, among them a couple from Texas who appear to be Trump sympathisers, all friends of the Henfreys, who have taken over the hotel for the weekend. During the day we are free to explore the surrounding countryside and each evening we dine together. This is Cathar country, a place of deep gorges and ruined castles perched on precipitous crags. The Cathars were a peaceful people whose only offence was not to believe in priests, for which heresy they were ruthlessly suppressed on the orders of Pope Innocent III, tens of thousands of men, women and children slaughtered in cold blood, 220 burned at the stake (and we think ISIS is evil). Jill, Aidan and I explored Foix, Ax-les-Thermes and the fortress city of Carcassonne. What strikes one driving around this relative backwater is how well maintained the roads and other public infrastructure are compared with in the UK. Whatever their economic problems, the French do believe in public works.

'Whatever you do, please don't elect Trump,' I remarked to the couple from Texas as we were departing. 'Hillary's the problem,' he replied.

Wednesday 21 September

To Westminster, where I was guest of the day on BBC 2's *Daily Politics* show. They ran a little piece about *Hinterland*, beginning with footage, which I didn't know existed, of a young, naive me, with hair on top, from the 1970 election campaign in North Devon. Later an interview with Adam Boulton on Sky, after which I ran into the former Tory Education Secretary Ken Baker, who says he is opposed to May's plan to re-introduce selection at eleven, although he wouldn't oppose it at the age of fourteen, providing there were more technical schools available for those who were not academic. He asked how old I was and, when I told him, smiled and said, 'The best is yet to come.'

Saturday 24 September

Corbyn has been re-elected leader by an even wider margin than before. That surely resolves the leadership issue for the foreseeable future. We just have to grit our teeth and soldier on. Above all, the boys and girls in Parliament must either step up or pipe down. We can't have another year of posturing and plotting.

A friendly *Hinterland* review by Robert Shrimsley in today's *FT*. 'Reading his diaries', he writes, 'left me to regret that, in my decade as a political reporter, I had lazily bought into the stereotype of Mullin as a Bennite headbanger and never bothered to get to know him.'

Thursday 29 September

To *The Guardian* to judge a writing competition for the Prison Reform Trust. On the Tube I ran into former Defence Secretary Geoff Hoon. Apropos the failed coup attempt that he and two others launched against Gordon in January 2010, I enquired if he had been expecting to be joined by bigger fish. 'Yes,' he said. 'There was a call from Harriet Harman on the Sunday evening saying that, if we went public, she and Jack Straw would tell Gordon that he had to go. Our mistake was that we never checked with Jack, who denied being part of any such plan.'

Wednesday 5 October

An old-school journalist from the *Journal* came to interview me. We sat out in the garden. As is the way these days, he took his own photographs and described how, for the most part, the paper's coverage was determined by clickbait. The daily editorial conference is dominated by a discussion of what's trending on the internet (a theft of jewellery from Kim Kardashian is the current front runner) and the paper's declining staff of journalists are expected to write accordingly. He added, 'They will judge this piece about you by how many clicks it gets.' In which case I am doomed.

Thursday 6 October

Up at 3.30 a.m. to drive Mrs Very Big Boss to the airport, en route for Vietnam. As ever she left behind many instructions and much advice. She also, bless her, left a dozen packs of homemade pasta bake and casserole to sustain me during her absence.

Saturday 8 October

Donald Trump appears to be imploding. A tape has surfaced, recorded eleven years ago, in which he talks in the crudest terms about his predatory attitude to women, causing many senior Republicans to dissociate themselves and prompting that rarest of political phenomena, a Trump apology. This, surely, is the tipping point.

Monday 10 October–Tuesday 11 October

To London for what is likely to be my last meeting with the Heritage Lottery Fund top brass. We dined in what was once Battersea Town Hall, a relic of the days when local government exuded confidence and civic pride (who would want to be a local councillor in these days of year-on-year cuts?), now reborn as the Battersea Arts Centre. Then to Birmingham for a literary festival. About 150 people attended my event. The man who ran the bookshop reported that *Hinterland* had sold well at the Tory conference last week.

Wednesday 12 October

Home to find a robin trapped in the house. It must have slipped in as I left two days ago. The poor thing had lost half its bodyweight and was frantically flying from window to window in search of an escape route. Another few hours and it would have been a goner.

Thursday 13 October

At short notice, an invitation from Sir Humphry to dine at Chillingham. Just two other guests, Lord Astor (Willliam Waldorf Astor IV) and Michael Waterhouse, a well-connected author. Lord Astor, amusing, deceptively youthful and with a mischievous twinkle in his eye, has been in the Lords since the age of twenty-one and is acquainted with or related to just about everybody who matters in public life. He is also Samantha

Cameron's stepfather. A whip in the last months of Mrs Thatcher's reign and a junior minister in John Major's. He said David Cameron once remarked to him that, had he been up against Hilary Benn, he would have found the going much harder. Despite Labour's present difficulties, he does not foresee a Tory landslide. Instead he predicts an early general election brought about by the government's inability to get Brexit through Parliament ('your lot will find some excuse to vote against it').

Saturday 15 October

Armed with my National Trust card, I set out on a six-part tour of festivals and bookshops in the Welsh borders and beyond. First stop, Chester, a prosperous little city which, improbably, returns a Labour MP. I addressed about 100 people in the old town hall, signed about twenty books and then, in twilight, completed a circuit of the ancient city walls. They have put me up in a nice hotel, which served an awful fish and chips, the fish consisting mainly of batter. When the manager asked if I had enjoyed my meal, in that insincere way that they do, I complained, but she merely said she was sorry and quickly skedaddled. She was followed by a vapid youth who asked the same question, to whom I gave the same reply, which he affected not to hear. Why ask, if you are not interested in the answer?

Wednesday 26 October

Still feeling dizzy after a recent episode, so I paid a visit to the doctor, who diagnosed high blood pressure and made an appointment for me for a brain scan at the stroke unit at the Wansbeck. This evening, to the airport to collect Ngoc, home after three weeks in Vietnam. Meanwhile the post-Brexit pound continues to plummet. The thieving airport cash machines are offering £1 for 98 cents against the euro.

Friday 28 October

A computerised call from the 'elderly care' department of Wansbeck Hospital to confirm that I have an appointment next Friday. I am asked to press 1 to confirm that I will be attending and then to press 1 again to confirm that I understood the implications of pressing 1 the first time (with the elderly I suppose you can never be quite sure).

Saturday 29 October

Incredibly, with days to go until the US presidential election, just as Hillary Clinton seemed to be coasting to victory, the FBI have reopened the investigation into her emails, injecting new life into the Trump campaign. No suggestion yet that they have even looked at the new tranche of emails that have suddenly and mysteriously become available. This is what American psephologists call an October Surprise. Predictably, Trump has declared that this is bigger than Watergate, and the baying crowds at his rallies are chanting 'lock her up'. My guess is that Hillary will, just about, manage to ride this out but that the Republicans will ensure that the so-called email 'scandal' haunts her through her presidency.

Sunday 30 October

Some weeks ago my publisher Andrew Franklin sent me a copy of Alan Bennett's latest diaries, *Keeping On Keeping On*, which I put to one side on account of it being 700 pages long and having much else to do. This morning, however, prompted by hearing his voice on the radio, I looked myself up in the index and came across the following reference to *A View from the Foothills*. He writes (in part), 'What comes over very plainly is Mullin's fundamental decency and honesty. He's so patently a good man that one feels he's taken on board the government simply because (and having voted against the war) he adds moral weight.' He goes on:

> Paradoxically one of the uplifting features of the diaries is the ordinariness of his complaints: he doesn't let his position … set him apart from the common man. I hope I meet him one day if only to tell him how clearly his voice comes through and to say (though I don't think I would ever dare) never to underestimate the good he has done in his life.

Hallelujah.

Monday 31 October

To London. A low mist filling the valley, hilltops floating above the cloud. And in the lane through the beech wood a hawk brazenly tucking into a dead pheasant. I sat and waited until he deigned to move – and then only to the nearest tree. This evening a conversation with Peter Hennessy in the Boothroyd Room in Portcullis House. Enjoyable though it was, the turnout was dismal, coinciding as it did with a one-line whip. Afterwards a drink on the terrace (yes, it is still mild enough to sit outside) with one of the brightest of the up and coming Labour MPs. He reckons Theresa May could go for an early election. How so, given that these days a two-thirds majority of MPs is required to trigger a dissolution? He said many of his colleagues would go for it in the hope of putting an early end to the Corbyn regime. A tad reckless given our low poll rating, I ventured. 'They don't care.' Would he support an early election? 'I might.'

Tuesday 1 November

A council meeting of the Winston Churchill Memorial Trust, held in the boardroom of the Engineering Employers Federation in Tothill Street. Three boffins were invited to make short presentations on how they saw the future. Two of them made the point that capitalism was undergoing a crisis of legitimacy. Matthew Taylor, one-time head of the No. 10 policy unit, said, 'Capitalism isn't working for ordinary people and there will be consequences' – the rise of Donald Trump (currently neck and neck with Hillary Clinton) was one. Brexit, I suppose, is another.

Thursday 3 November

The High Court has unexpectedly ruled that Theresa May does not have the power to unilaterally trigger Article 50 of the Lisbon Treaty, which takes us out of the EU, and that it is a matter for Parliament, triggering howls of outrage from the Brexiteers and their media friends.

Saturday 5 November

The *Mail* has unleashed upon the judges the sort of treatment usually reserved for the likes of Arthur Scargill or Ken Livingstone. 'ENEMIES OF

THE PEOPLE' screams yesterday's front page under pictures of the three High Court judges who delivered Thursday's verdict. Meanwhile *The Sun* has vented its fury on the woman who brought the action, a 'foreign-born multi-millionaire' (just like *The Sun*'s owner, one is tempted to add, but *The Sun* doesn't do irony). Already threats of rape and murder are pouring in from online trolls. Early days yet. There is an appeal pending in January, but the decision has fuelled talk of an early election.

Wednesday 9 November

Awoke to the extraordinary, unbelievable, awful, terrifying news that, against all odds, Donald Trump is to be the next President of the United States. Republicans will now control both houses of Congress, the Supreme Court and the presidency. There is no hiding place from this, the mother of all political upsets. As they say in Tibet, the earth has changed places with the sky. A man uniquely unqualified has become President without having previously held any public office. A serial bankrupt who has no plan, only slogans. Who has talked of building walls, tearing up trade agreements, doing away with environmental treaties and reigniting the nuclear arms race. And yet, within an hour of victory, this man, who ran on stirring up fear and loathing and jailing his political opponent is talking unity, bringing people together and thanking Hillary Clinton for her long record of service. The only glimmer of hope is that there is no reason to believe a word he says.

To London, where I am staying with John and Sheila Williams. Sheila says she has placed a bet on Corbyn succeeding Theresa May as Prime Minister, thinking that she would get odds of hundreds to one. To her surprise, the best she could get was 9/2. The bookies must know something we don't.

Thursday 10 November

Trump's election is a bad dream. You wake up thinking it hasn't happened, but it has. The Republicans, many of whom repudiated him when he appeared to be leading them to destruction, are now suddenly clambering back on board. The Speaker of the Senate was on the radio this morning saying that his first priority was to repeal Obama's health reforms. In other words they are going to take medical insurance from 20 million of

America's poorest people, many of whom no doubt voted for Trump in the foolish belief that he offered them a better life.

Saturday 12 November

Sunshine, blue skies, no wind, a light dusting of snow on the Cheviot. We drove to Boulmer and walked along the cliff towards Craster, until we found our path blocked by a herd of bullocks, forcing us to retreat to the Fishing Boat Inn for lunch.

Sunday 13 November

Jeremy Corbyn, interviewed by Andrew Marr this morning, came over well. He's getting better, though nothing can save us.

This evening a call from Pat Hall in the North Lodge to say that a dozen wild horses, installed by our laird on the moors above Callaly, have escaped and are currently parading up the lane by the north gate.

Mum died ten years ago today. How time has flown.

Monday 14 November

The day began with Donald Trump pledging to remove 'or incarcerate' 2 million of the estimated 11 million illegal immigrants who, he claims, are drug dealers and rapists. 'After that, we'll see about the rest.' Quite how he is going to achieve this feat without concentration camps and mayhem in the ghettos remains to be seen. By this evening the talk was of his intention to renege on America's commitments to reduce global warming.

Tuesday 15 November

The escaped wild horses have been corralled in a field about a mile up the road, but no one has the slightest idea how to get them back onto the moor.

Wednesday 16 November

Dug out a couple of compost heaps and scattered the contents on the garden. Then to St Peter's School in York (alumni include the late Mr Guy Fawkes), where I gave my book talk to a very friendly audience numbering about 200. An angry-looking man near the front asked why I thought my former constituency had voted so heavily for Brexit. By way of reply I made my usual crack that, although immigration was clearly the main issue, there weren't many immigrants in Sunderland but there were a lot of *Sun* readers, whereupon he denounced me for sneering at the electorate. He's right, of course, one can't just blame it all on the tabloids, but neither can one pretend they are of no relevance. Someone else asked why, in retirement, Tony Benn and I (to a lesser extent, it must be said) had become national treasures. That's easy to explain: because nowadays we pose no threat to the established order. Afterwards, in the long queue for books, several people remarked, 'I don't share your politics, but…' which makes me all the more annoyed that none of the Tory papers thought *Hinterland* worth reviewing.

Thursday 17 November

Today's newspapers record a large fall in unemployment to 'only' 1.4 million (a level that would have been considered intolerable forty years ago). The bad news is that most new jobs appear to have gone to foreigners, which no doubt helps explain the growing demands to 'control our borders', even at the risk of collapsing the economy.

Saturday 19 November

In defiance of the odds, Ed Balls has survived eight rounds of *Strictly Come Dancing*. The transformation is remarkable, from political bruiser to national treasure. This evening he was lowered from the rafters of the Winter Gardens in Blackpool, playing what appeared to be a blazing piano, to the tune of Jerry Lee Lewis's 'Great Balls of Fire'. This is the man who might have been Chancellor of the Exchequer had the cards fallen differently. Instead he will be remembered as an awful dancer but a good sport. At least he seems to be enjoying himself and is amusing people along the way, but tonight's spectacle reminds me of the tragic tale of the Rector of Stiffkey, the Norfolk vicar who, having been defrocked, earned his living delivering sermons from inside the cage of a lion called Freddie who eventually killed him.

Tuesday 22 November

Lunch with Bruce Grocott in the Adjournment. As ever, we talked of the *ancien régime*. 'Whatever you say about Tony,' said Bruce, 'he didn't surround himself with sycophants.' Anji Hunter, Jonathan Powell, Alastair Campbell and Bruce himself were all capable of telling him what he didn't want to hear – and they did. Bruce describes Alastair as

> one of the most remarkable people I've ever met in politics. Honest about his weaknesses, utterly driven, astonishing work rate. Decides he's going to run the marathon and gets into shape, running into work by 7 a.m. and home again, often at midnight, then he sits down and writes in minute detail everything that happened that day.

His marathon run raised more than £250,000 for cystic fibrosis research. He even tapped George Bush for a contribution.

Like many politicians of our vintage, Bruce laments the way Parliament's so-called 'family-friendly' hours have drained the life out of the place. 'Many of the new generation of MPs turn up for little more than two days a week. They arrive on Monday afternoon and go home after Prime Minister's Questions on Wednesday. They seem to think they can change the world by tweeting.'

Wednesday 23 November

A chat with Steve Byers, who reckons recent reports that The Man may be about to re-enter politics are serious: witness the fact that he appears to be winding up his extensive commercial activities. Extraordinary if true. He must surely know that since Iraq he's a busted flush. And yet, and yet. We all know that if Blair had been in the front line these past few months he'd have murdered the Tories over Brexit. Steve, by the way, reckons that Keir Starmer is a credible future Labour leader. One hears his name mentioned increasingly.

Thursday 24 November

Several of today's papers carry a picture of John McDonnell responding to the Chancellor's autumn statement, noting that about half of the serried ranks of Labour Members sitting behind him seem to be playing with their mobiles. My goodness, what a shell Parliament is becoming.

Saturday 26 November

Fidel Castro is dead. A big tree in the forest falls.

Sunday 27 November

Cambridge

The Backs. Sunshine illuminating the gothic stonework of St John's. Courtyards, cloisters, a bridge over the canal beneath which punters glide. Bowler-hatted proctors guard the rear entrance to Trinity. Then to the Union building, where the festival is based. Denizens of the green room include Charles Clarke, Margaret Hodge, Alan Johnson and Margaret Drabble. Alas, my event was held in a lecture theatre about a quarter of a mile away, down an alleyway, across a road, down another alley, around a little square, up a staircase… More than once I pointed out to the nice people organising the festival that the distance between my event and the bookshop all but kiboshed the book-signing, but they were in denial. I was interviewed brilliantly by Melissa Benn in front of an enthusiastic audience. Unsurprisingly, however, only five people made the complex journey to the book signing. No doubt the organisers consider the event a success since they sold all the tickets. Everyone went home happy, except me.

Monday 28 November

To the Freeman Hospital in Newcastle for my annual kidney stone check-up. An X-ray, a brief chat with the consultant, who gave me the all-clear for the second year running. All done with Rolls-Royce efficiency. Within an hour I am on my way home. The NHS may have its problems, but it's coping very well here.

Friday 2 December

The Tories have lost the by-election in Richmond, which they held at the general election with a majority of 23,000.

Saturday 3 December

The lead headline in today's *Times*: 'Labour has few safe seats left, MPs warn'. Maybe, but it takes some ingenuity to come up with this the day after the overturning of a 23,000 Tory majority. I have written to congratulate the editor, but I suspect *The Times* is too up itself to do irony.

Several hours spent chopping logs and clearing leaves.

Sunday 4 December

Some unlikely followers on my Twitter account. To clear up any confusion, I posted the following: 'For the avoidance of doubt, I am not the American basketball player of the same name.'

Tuesday 6 December

Sure enough, my Twitter following has suffered a slight fall since I revealed that I was not the American basketball player.

Wednesday 7 December

'Under attack. Nowhere to go, every minute feels like death. Pray for us. Goodbye.' This message from Bana al-Abed, a seven-year-old and her mother trapped in the rubble of eastern Aleppo as regime forces close in. On *Channel 4 News* last night a distant, fleeting, hazy glimpse of four or five small children on a balcony waving towards the camera, as though they were riding the big dipper in an amusement park. From north-east Nigeria, where several million refugees from Boko Haram face starvation, the constant wail of emaciated, hungry children. From Yemen, an almost forgotten war fuelled by our Saudi allies, an entire country about to run out of food and water and little or no help in sight. From the hermetically sealed Rakhine state in western Burma, reports of mass rape and burned out villages as the country's murderous military cleanses the country of Rohingya Muslims. These, for those who can be bothered to watch, are the images flashed into our living rooms every night. Has the world ever been in such a state or is it just that, almost in real time, we can now see what is happening to people who were previously remote? Meanwhile, when not obsessing about the minutiae of Brexit, much of our free press is demanding an end to – or at least a drastic reduction in – the overseas aid budget. To crown all, today comes news that Donald Trump has appointed a climate change denier to head the US Environmental Agency. And all I can do in my beautiful bubble is rake leaves, dig weeds, make the occasional speech and deliver the occasional lecture, my irrelevance growing with every day that passes. Not that I would be of much relevance were I still in Parliament.

Saturday 10 December

Boris Johnson is in trouble for criticising our much-loved allies the Saudis for what they are up to in Yemen. Someone has written, 'Amazing that after years of unalloyed codswallop, the thing that finally gets Boris into trouble is telling the truth.'

Monday 12 December

My sixty-ninth birthday. We walked, in sunshine, along the beach from Craster to the Ship Inn at Newton-by-the-Sea and back, past the stark, jagged ruin of Dunstanburgh Castle – six miles in all. Beats working for a living.

Saturday 17 December

Awful scenes from Aleppo, where tens of thousands of exhausted, terrified people remain trapped after the fall of the last remaining eastern enclaves to the regime and its Iranian allies. A recent clip of film from a hospital shows a terrified, bewildered, dust-covered, silent little person aged about two with a great mop of thick hair, forehead caked in blood, recently plucked from the ruins in which his family perished. A woman howls that she has lost all her children; beside her, a boy of about twelve is cradling his baby brother, who, according to the commentary, is dead but he won't let go. Another woman is guiding two small children through the chaos, searching for their mother. Their father is said to be dead. Much hand-wringing from well-meaning people who say the West should have intervened at the outset, but so far as I can see there has been too much rather than too little Western interference. Posturing by Western governments gave Syrian dissidents the false hope that if they held out long enough, the international community would come to their rescue and now, of course, they feel betrayed.

Tuesday 20 December

A lorry has been driven at high speed into a crowded Christmas market in Berlin, killing at least twelve people and injuring fifty others. The incident appears to be the work of an Islamist terrorist. The perpetrator is still at large. Already critics of Angela Merkel's asylum policy are using the incident to undermine her. Early days yet, but this has the potential to bring down Europe's strongest leader.

Saturday 24 December

To Cheswick House, a beautiful gothic mansion near Berwick, for Christmas drinks with former neighbours. R, a mysterious and obnoxious neighbour who never bothers to conceal his loathing of me, was there sporting what he said was a 45 Commando tie. He claims to have been at Oxford University, to have been in the Marines and to have served in Ireland and Vietnam in some unspecified top-secret capacity, but none of it quite adds up. I find the best way of dealing with him is to take the mickey. Today we had the following exchange. He, affecting his most pompous voice, said, 'When I was young my grandfather said to me, "This country is best governed by aristocrats." I didn't agree with him at the time, but ten years later, I realised he was right.' In response I smiled benignly and replied, 'And then they let the likes of me into government and everything went haywire.' Whereupon everyone except R fell about laughing. Later, too late, I thought of an even better response: 'Oh you mean like my old friend Viscount Stansgate.' Tony Benn, needless to say, is another of R's hate figures.

Tuesday 27 December

For those with an eye on posterity, Christmas is a good time to die. The bulletins are chock-a-block with tributes to George Michael, Carrie Fisher and other alleged cultural icons who have sadly died in the last few days, meanwhile interest in the outside world has declined almost to zero.

Thursday 29 December

Debbie Reynolds, the 1950s actress mother of the *Star Wars* actress Carrie Fisher, who died a few days ago, has also died. In keeping with our burgeoning celebrity culture, which infects even Radio 4, news of her death occupied the first third of the bulletin and tributes filled a chunk of the subsequent programme. These past few days the *Today* programme has become an extension of Hollywood. Syria, Yemen, the famine in northern Nigeria have all disappeared from the bulletins. No mention either of those poor people in the shanty towns of Manila who the other day were reported to be facing a 140-mph typhoon. The insularity is stifling.

A letter from the stroke doctor to whom I was referred following a spell of dizziness in October. He reports that a recent brain scan revealed nothing out of the ordinary 'apart from a moderate degree of generalised atrophy'. Oh, oh. So 'generalised atrophy' is where I am headed, unless overtaken by something worse.

Friday 30 December

Obama has expelled thirty-five Russian diplomats in revenge for Russia's alleged interference in the US presidential election. Arguably Trump owes his election to the hacking by the Russians of Hillary Clinton's emails and the FBI's cack-handed intervention. Extraordinary. The stuff of thrillers. Perhaps surprisingly, Putin has decided not to retaliate, for now at least, and instead wished Obama and the American people a happy new year. Unusually sophisticated for the Russians.

Saturday 31 December

So ends 2016, truly an *annus horriblis*. The year of Brexit, Trump, Syria and the rise of populist parties all over Europe. As for me, I sink ever deeper into obscurity. My greatest fear – indeed terror – is of having nothing useful to do for the last years of my life. I am not at that point yet, but one begins to glimpse the looming void.

CHAPTER EIGHT

2017

Sunday 1 January

To Harbottle with Nick and Sarah. We walked in sunshine up to the Drake Stone and then followed a muddy path through the pine forest and back along the track by the Coquet into the village. Five miles in all, reaching the car just as the rain started.

In Istanbul a gunman has murdered thirty-nine New Year revellers at a night club. Some reports suggest he was dressed as Santa Claus.

Monday 2 January

An email from a reader in Australia drawing my attention to a long-forgotten entry, dated 22 January 2006, in *A Walk-On Part*. It quotes an unnamed 'Labour veteran' as follows:

> Mark my words, in twenty years' time, when I am in my grave, fascism will start coming back. The Single Market is what started it. A single currency follows as night follows day. What's going to happen when people find they can't legislate to solve their own problems? Fascism will come back if politicians fail.

If memory serves me, the author of these prophetic words is Doug Hoyle, father of Mr Speaker Hoyle. Happily still very much alive and now in the Lords. I shall remind him if and when our paths next cross.

Saturday 7 January

The new, improved Ed Balls was on the radio this morning sounding remarkably normal. Providing he can keep it up, it occurs to me that we could do worse than choose him as our next leader when the time comes. Always assuming he's interested, of course. Many years of opposition beckon and Ed is, above all, a creature of government. It is one thing to be a national treasure and quite another to be leader of the Labour Party in opposition.

Tuesday 10 January

Dinner with Jean Corston in the Barry Room at the House of Lords. The press have taken to calling Theresa May 'Theresa Maybe', but as Jean remarked, this is just because (unlike her predecessor) she declines to feed the lobby with a daily sound bite. Whatever her other deficiencies, I rather approve of this way of operating.

Wednesday 11 January

A day at Church House, Westminster, interviewing candidates in the 'migration' category for Churchill scholarships. Admirable though they were, everyone took it as read that it was our job to integrate every new applicant for asylum into the British way of life. The possibility that for many the kindest way forward would be to look for ways of humanely repatriating those who don't qualify had not occurred to anyone.

Thursday 12 January

Lunch with Cousin Jo and then back to the north on the 14.30 train. The man (inevitably from Eastern Europe) collecting rubbish on the train was wearing a jacket emblazoned with the slogan 'Committed to enhancing your experience'. A new piece of corporate doublespeak. I hope the agency employing him, no doubt at or near the minimum wage, has enhanced his experience. Talking of such nonsense, a cheerful young woman who served me in a coffee shop on Clapham Common the other day invited me to 'have a wonderful evening'. To be wished a pleasant evening would be quite enough. 'Wonderful' would be a night with Julia Roberts or Saffron Burrows – a mite ambitious at my time of life.

Friday 13 January

I've been reading *Do No Harm*, a brilliant, utterly gripping account of the life of a brain surgeon, Henry Marsh. From time to time, like others of our generation, he laments the growth of political correctness in his profession. This, for example, is his account of being obliged to take a day off from his duties to attend a seminar on Customer Service and Care:

> How strange it is, I thought as I listened … that after thirty years of struggling with death, disaster and countless crises and catastrophes, having watched patients bleed to death in my hands, having had furious arguments with colleagues, terrible meetings with relatives, moments of utter despair and profound exhilaration – in short, a typical neurosurgical career – how strange it is that I should now be listening to a young man with a background in catering telling me that I should develop empathy, keep focused and stay calm.

Wednesday 18 January

A telephone chat with Cousin Tony, who has been undergoing treatment for bone cancer. Aged eighty-three, he is my oldest surviving relative. Now that all the uncles and aunts have gone, it is the turn of us cousins. 'Officially, I am the next to go,' he said cheerfully.

Friday 20 January

To Murton for the funeral of former colleague John Cummings. A fifth-generation miner, one of the last of an almost extinct species. A man who lived all his life in the same small, close-knit community. He didn't make much impact in Parliament, but at home he was 'Mr Murton'. A big turnout of locals, plus a dozen or so past and present parliamentary colleagues, two of whom are receiving treatment for cancer. Then to Newcastle University to discuss the lectures I have been asked to give next month. Finally, back up the A1 listening to Donald Trump's inauguration. A remarkably uncompromising speech, making little attempt to reach out either to the world at large or to his political opponents at home. Obama and the other ex-Presidents sat impassively as he trashed their legacy and that of the entire political class. America über alles was the theme. Within hours it was reported that the climate change page on the White House website had been deleted and replaced by one with an 'America First' energy policy. And the civil rights page had been replaced by one entitled 'Supporting Our Law Enforcement Community'. We are entering a dark era.

Sunday 22 January

An amusing little spat has broken out over the size of the crowd attending Donald Trump's inauguration on Friday. The White House press spokesman, Sean Spicer, asserts that it was 'the largest inauguration audience ever', but photographs taken from the rear of the crowd appear to show that it was much smaller than that which gathered to see Obama anointed. Later another Trump aide brushed aside a suggestion that Spicer had been lying, saying instead that he had just been presenting 'alternative facts'.

Tuesday 24 January

An email from Andrew Mitchell, attaching a report of his recent visit to Yemen. Among the places he visited, a school in north-west Yemen destroyed by bombs supplied to the Saudis by the USA and Britain. Ironically, he also came across a former British Army officer, funded by the British taxpayer, helping to defuse unexploded ordnance, and a hospital feeding malnourished children, also part funded by the UK. So we are helping both to destroy and to clear up afterwards. Meanwhile in tabloid Britain the only serious political pressure on the government is to end our aid programme, not to stop selling warplanes and bombs to the Saudis.

Thursday 26 January
Hôtel La Louisiane, Rue de Seine, Paris

As recommended by John and Sheila, clean, central, cheap – and *très* basic. Alleged once to have been a haunt of such cultural luminaries as Hemingway, Sartre and Quentin Tarantino (the WiFi password is Pulp-Fiction), but these days lacking any trace of its former clientele. Indeed, lacking in character of any sort, save threadbare carpet on the stairs and in the narrow corridors. Apart from a brief ministerial visit in 2004 (when my feet barely touched the ground), it is more than forty years since I last set foot in Paris. A cold, bright day. I walked to the Louvre, through the gardens of the Tuileries (the ponds frozen), to the Place de la Concorde and beyond. Then back across the river to La Tour Eiffel, via the Quai d'Orsay. First impressions: relentless traffic, bars thronged with prosperous young people, elegant women, folk of every ethnic origin – and many beggars. Just around the corner from the hotel, a swarthy couple with two small children, huddled under blankets, woolly hats and a large suitcase. 'Where are you from?' I asked. 'Syria,' they said, but are they?

Friday 27 January
Versailles

Luxury coaches disgorging Chinese tourists by the thousand. Already they are hard at work with their selfie sticks. Even on this cold January morning the queue stretches more than 100 metres from the gold-topped gates of the great palace. Cobbles flecked with a light covering of frost. After a wait of half an hour we are admitted. To begin with, the scene resembles rush hour at a Chinese railway station, but gradually the congestion dissipates. Everywhere gold and glass, vast galleries and painted ceilings. Louis XIV was the Donald Trump of his day. Except that he reigned seventy-two years, and the reign of Trump, please God, will be somewhat shorter. Talking of which, Theresa May is in Washington today, paying homage to The Donald. Why do we always have to be the first? Why can't we maintain a dignified distance, like the French and Germans? So humiliating.

Back to Paris, in fading daylight, exploring Notre-Dame and the Île de la Cité. On one of the bridges, I spy the refugee family I came across last night camped out with their begging bowls. The children ought to be in school, or playing in the parks, not living like this. What is to become of them?

Saturday 28 January
Paris

Through the galleries of the Louvre, so vast that they are capable of absorbing armies of Chinese tourists. I had feared it would be too crowded to enjoy, but most of the Chinese seemed only to be interested in taking selfies in front of the Venus de Milo and the Mona Lisa. Having ticked those boxes, they melted away. So great is the accumulation of statuary looted from ancient civilisations that it is a wonder there is any left *in situ*. I tramped the halls for five hours before leaving the rest unvisited (one can only take so many paintings of Madonnas with fat babies and grisly crucifixions) and coming up for air. Then to the pedestrian streets around the Élysée and the US and British embassies, patrolled by surly gendarmes, cradling machine pistols (mind, all the security in the world is of no use if the President of the Republic insists on travelling by Lambretta to visit his mistress). Then up the Champs-Élysées to the Arc de Triomphe, everywhere eastern-looking beggar women thrusting paper coffee cups under the noses of elegant promenaders. Then to Montparnasse, where I clambered up the 300 or so steps to the Sacré-Coeur with its night-time views across the city. Finally, back to my Left Bank garret in the Rue de Seine, to rest aching joints.

Sunday 29 January
Paris

A little googling reveals that most if not all of the beggars pretending to be Syrians are in fact Romanian or Bosnian Roma. Some genuine Syrian refugees in the city are mightily indignant at the pretence and have been campaigning to expose the fraud. There is even a suggestion that the children are farmed out and sometimes even drugged to render them quiescent.

Monday 30 January
Hôtel La Louisiane, Rue de Seine

A creepy place, this. In four days I have caught no more than fleeting glimpses of other guests. Until this morning, when I came across a friend of Sheila's, I had met no one else at breakfast. Creaking floorboards, the sound of a toilet being flushed or a bath being filled are the only evidence of life. And yet the streets all around here hum with life and the price is attractive,

---

* In January 2014, a French magazine published photos of President François Hollande being dropped off by scooter outside the apartment of his mistress, Julie Gayet.

compared to neighbouring hostelries. This morning I toured the Jardin du Luxembourg and then to the Panthéon, the vast, cold mausoleum housing the remains of the heroes of France. Later, on the train to the airport, a well-dressed young man distributed a little notice claiming to be a refugee with a family to support. A nice try, but there were no takers. Ngoc says she came across the same thing when she was in Paris, a year ago.

Wednesday 1 February

A brief interview, via Skype, with a BBC journalist making a programme for Radio 4 about whether, with the rise of Trump, real life has overtaken fiction. It sure has. Who, even a year ago, could have imagined that this would be the outcome and that Russian manipulation (with a little help from the FBI) may have determined the outcome? Truly, the stuff of thrillers.

This evening the Commons voted by a large margin – 498 to 114 – for the second reading of the Article 50 Bill. Only one Tory, Ken Clarke, voted against, along with about forty Labour MPs, mostly those whose constituencies voted Remain. Had I still been there, I am afraid that, no doubt after a certain amount of agonising, I'd probably have felt obliged to vote with the majority, given the way Sunderland voted.

Thursday 2 February

A call from Ian Blair, a former Commissioner of the Metropolitan Police, to discuss an alleged miscarriage of justice. We talked of rogue police squads. In his experience, he said, the clue that there was something wrong was often an unusually high success rate. It applied in other walks of life, too, such as banking. Nick Leeson's bosses at Barings ought to have noticed that he was making far more money than could reasonably be explained.

'I have admired your work from a distance,' he said.

'Not many policemen say that to me,' I replied.

'I was referring to your diaries,' he said cheerfully.

Saturday 4 February

An essay in the review section of today's *Guardian* prompted by the rise of Trump contains the following quote from a *New York Times* journalist:

'When and if fascism comes to America, it will not be labelled "made in Germany"; it will not be marked with a swastika; it will not even be called fascism; it will be called, of course, Americanism.' This was written in 1938.

Monday 6 February

John Bercow has set the cat among the pigeons by announcing, rather theatrically, that he will not be issuing an invitation to Donald Trump to address both houses of Parliament, despite May's offer of a state visit. The news was applauded by Labour MPs while the Tories sat in stony silence. Much as I admire Bercow and agree with his sentiments, the way in which he has gone about it is unfortunate. If I were him, I would have discussed the matter quietly with the Lords Speaker (who appears not to have been consulted) and with the Chief Whips on both sides and then privately informed the government that The Donald will not be welcome. As it is, he has played into the hands of those who argue that he is too partisan. I fear he may provoke the Tories into making another attempt to remove him.

Tuesday 7 February

A pleasant day touring Heritage Lottery Fund projects, starting with the wonderfully restored 1830s glasshouse at Felton Park, then on to the der-elict Cresswell Tower and finally to a new visitor centre at the Hauxley wildlife centre, still under construction. My time with HLF comes to an end next month. I shall miss these little outings.

Friday 10 February

To Newcastle University, where I delivered two lectures to third-year stu-dents who proved surprisingly appreciative. Much to my embarrassment there was even a modest round of applause at the end.

Monday 13 February

To Alnmouth Station for what was supposed to be the 13.00 to London but, owing to a points failure further north, the trains were completely up the creek. In the best British tradition everyone was polite and stoic. The poor chap behind the glass screen did his best to keep us informed, but he had little useful information to impart. What was really annoying, indeed apoplexy-inducing, was the endlessly repeated stream of insincere pre-recorded apologies, accompanied by inaccurate information, emitted by an annunciator which in the best Orwellian traditions was coming from a distant command centre and could not be controlled or even adjusted locally. It was more than three hours before the first train broke through, and that only went as far as Newcastle. An eight-hour journey door to door. I am staying with John and Sheila. Sheila predicts that Trump won't make it through his first term. I think he will. The question is, will we?

Wednesday 15 February

After less than a month in power, Trump, looking increasingly embattled, is picking fights with everyone. He's already lost his national security adviser and his relationship with Russia is coming under increasing scrutiny. Much talk of congressional inquiries and fanciful suggestions that this could be bigger than Watergate. We mustn't get too carried away, but maybe there is a god, after all.

Thursday 16 February

Trump has given a bizarre 75-minute press conference in which he accused the media of being dishonest and out of control and claiming that his administration, far from being in turmoil, is a finely tuned machine. After less than a month in office he already sounds like a man urgently in need of therapy.

Friday 17 February

The Man has re-entered British politics with a powerful speech on the need to reconsider Brexit if the terms we are offered for departure aren't right, which they almost certainly won't be. A glimpse of the Blair of old. Crystal clarity, common sense, making one nostalgic for the glory days. Problem is he's a busted flush.

Monday 20 February

Dinner at the House with Lisa Nandy, who talks of absolute demoralisation in the Parliamentary Labour Party. Later, I ran into John Cryer, chairman of the parliamentary party, who reports that some MPs are getting nasty threats. I thought it was exaggerated, but John, who has seen much of the material, says not. Lisa, too, said she's been threatened and one colleague has round-the-clock police protection. Where is this poison coming from? The answer seems to be a toxic mix of Trotskyite headbangers and ultra-nationalists like the one who murdered poor Jo Cox – the latter emboldened by the recent Brexit vote.

Tuesday 21 February
The Oxford and Cambridge Club

Breakfast in a vast, chandeliered dining room under life-sized portraits of William of Orange and one of the Georges. Uniformed servants, foreigners every one, glide noiselessly between tables. The man at the next table is reading the *Daily Mail* (very un-Oxbridge) lingering over a story headed 'I had sex with her when she was drunk and asleep'. After breakfast I whiled away a couple of hours in the morning room, hung with portraits of vice-chancellors. For much of the time the only other occupants were a couple engaged, *sotto voce* (everyone seems to whisper in this place), in a blazing row. Then my *Hinterland* talk to an audience of sixty or seventy, mainly retired folk, and afterwards a healthy queue for the book signing. My fourth appearance at the Oxford and Cambridge Writer's Club, which, according to the chairman, is a record equalled only by Douglas Hurd.

Wednesday 22 February
Church Row, Hampstead

Out early. Just about everyone on the Tube at 6.30 is of foreign origin, mainly Eastern Europeans, part of the vast army of minimum-wage cleaners, labourers and baristas upon whom our economy now depends. To Aylesbury High School, where I delivered my 'In Defence of Politics' lecture to 200 sixth-formers, followed by a history class where I answered questions about Margaret Thatcher (now ancient history and so part of the syllabus). The teacher, Ian Ochiltree, remarked that the 1990s had seen the end of what had once seemed to be the three great, immutable certainties of his lifetime: the Berlin Wall, apartheid in South Africa and the war in Ireland.

This afternoon to Primrose Hill, where I spent a pleasant ninety minutes in the company of the great Alan Bennett. I had always thought of him as a shy man and feared that conversation would be difficult, but on the contrary, it flowed easily. We talked of Northumberland (he has been to Barter Books), literary festivals, the fate of the Labour Party and much else. Although Alan denies being a technophobe, he still writes in longhand, possesses no email address and gets around on an elderly bicycle which was chained to the railings outside his house.

Friday 24 February

To Linlithgow for Tam Dalyell's memorial service. About a thousand people, including many former colleagues from the lately annihilated Scottish Labour–Liberal elite – including Alistair Darling, Douglas Alexander, Jim Murphy, David Steel and Ming Campbell. No one anticipates that the tide will turn in Scotland in the foreseeable future and when it does it will not necessarily be to our advantage. For the first time in decades the Tories seem to be picking up votes north of the border. As if to underline our plight, Labour lost yesterday's by-election in Copeland to the Tories (the first such gain by a governing party since 1982), though mercifully we held Stoke against what had been billed as a strong UKIP challenge.

Sunday 26 February

Open season has been declared on Corbyn in the wake of the Copeland result. On every bulletin he is surrounded by a baying mob of hacks demanding to know when he'll go. Unfair in a way, since the decline of Labour's support among the working classes was under way long before he became leader. Likewise the loss of Scotland and the collapse of the Lib Dems are nothing to do with Corbyn. So far he shows no signs of budging, but my guess is he won't make it to the election.

Monday 27 February

Gerald Kaufman has died. He had been in Parliament forty-six years, part of that unlucky generation of Labour politicians whose careers peaked during the eighteen-year Tory interregnum. A serial loyalist, witty, waspish, vain and (as one obituarist put it) untroubled by self-doubt. He it was who dubbed the 1983 Labour manifesto 'the longest suicide note in history'. I recall one occasion, at a meeting of the Parliamentary Labour Party meeting when Blair was under pressure to stand down, he quoted a Broadway producer who was asked by a disaffected actor, 'Who do I have to sleep with to get out of this show?' To which said producer replied, 'The same person you slept with to get into it.'

Friday 3 March

Yet another trip to the doctor, this time regarding a bulge that has appeared just above my groin. He confirmed that it is a hernia and says it will require an operation eventually. Spent most of the afternoon pruning roses accompanied by a woodpecker drilling into an adjacent oak.

Tuesday 7 March

To the museum of working-class history at Beamish, where, in the boardroom of the old bank and after six most enjoyable years, I chaired my last meeting of the Heritage Lottery committee. Everybody was very kind. Last night there was a dinner at the home farm where speeches were made and where, despite my insistence that I did not want a leaving present, I was presented with a carefully wrapped box tied with ribbon containing a stainless steel gardening fork and trowel. I must find something else useful to do. There are currently two vacancies on the board of the national park. Last time I applied I didn't even make the shortlist. Even so, I will give it another shot.

Friday 10 March

A lot of jumping up and down over Chancellor Philip Hammond's proposal, in his recent budget, to equalise National Insurance payments for the self-employed with those of the rest of the working population on the not unreasonable grounds that they enjoy similar benefits. A modest tax increase, to be phased in over several years, affecting only 15 per cent of the workforce, about half of whom will be better off. Tory MPs are against on the grounds that it 'discourages enterprise'. A lot of angry white van men have been interviewed, bleating about 'betrayal'. And Labour, scenting an opportunity, have climbed on the bandwagon. Meanwhile every news bulletin is a parade of people demanding that more public money be spent on whatever public service they happen to work for (this morning it was head teachers), social care is said to be in crisis and scarcely a day passes without carefully selected footage of patients awaiting treatment in hospital corridors. And yet, whenever anyone so much as hints at raising taxes to pay for any of this, hysteria is organised. Labour's position is particularly cynical given that party spokespersons are to be found on every bulletin demanding more spending. Really, it's time that we all grew up and recognised that, if we want north European standards of public services, we will have to pay north European levels of taxation.

Saturday 11 March–Sunday 12 March
Lizzick Hall Hotel, near Keswick

A weekend in the company of such luminaries as the BBC's John Simpson, the environmentalist George Monbiot, journalist Christina Lamb (who has spent thirty years reporting on Afghanistan) and their spouses. We are here for the Words by the Water festival, always one of the most enjoyable because we are so well looked after. Full houses all round. Lots of books signed. Everyone happy. John Simpson told of BBC research in 2005 to discover which of their correspondents, in the opinion of viewers, had performed best reporting from the Iraq War. John came second with 30 per cent. The winner was Kate Adie, who scored 60 per cent – except that she no longer worked for the BBC, having retired two years previously. So much for market research. Also, I met the man with the best job in the world: Chris Somerville, who writes the weekly walks column for *The Times*. Previously, for seventeen years, he did the same for the *Telegraph*. Together with his wife, Jane, he travels the length and breadth of the country searching out walks of between seven and ten miles – and gets paid for it.

Wednesday 15 March

Remarkably, the Tories have backed down on their plans to equalise National Insurance contributions in the teeth of a fierce backlash from their friends in the tabloid media and the meaner parts of Middle England. Which only goes to prove the point that in 21st-century Britain it is virtually impossible, save in the face of dire emergency, for a governing party to increase mainstream taxes. The Tories, of course, are caught by the fact that they go into every election pretending to be the party of low taxes, but this raises a serious issue, highlighted the other day by Theresa May herself. Namely, that our increasingly casualised workforce is gradually eroding the tax base, which in the long run may render our main public services unsustainable. This is something even the Tories can't ignore and yet, in seeking to address it, they have backed down at the first whiff of grapeshot.

Friday 17 March

To general astonishment George Osborne has been appointed editor of the *Evening Standard*, although he is not proposing to stand down from Parliament. An insult both to his constituents and to the very concept of a free press. He's already picking up £650k a year for four days' work a month with BlackRock, a global hedge fund. Despite everything that has happened, the City is still taking the rest of us for fools.

Sunday 19 March

The Man, taut, tense, tanned, was interviewed by Andrew Marr this morning, making a thinly disguised argument for a second referendum once the Brexit terms are known. One yearns for the quality of leadership that he once provided.

Monday 20 March

Lunch in the garden, watching two small red squirrels competing to raid the hazelnuts in the feeder. We were sitting less than three yards away, but they ignored us, racing off in different directions with their prize and returning a minute later for more. At one point a scuffle broke out.

Tuesday 21 March

The Man was on the radio this morning, paying tribute to Martin McGuinness, who has died. He had a nice line about the Irish peace settlement: 'Just occasionally politics actually works.'

Wednesday 22 March

This evening an apparent terrorist incident in which a man drove a car into pedestrians on Westminster Bridge and then tried to gain access to Parliament through the Carriage Gates, stabbing and killing a policeman before he was shot dead. Meanwhile yesterday near Raqqa a coalition aircraft is said to have bombed a school, killing more than thirty displaced people, mainly women and children. Not a single line on our television bulletins. Hard to avoid concluding that, compared to ours, these small lives don't matter.

Thursday 23 March

Massive bout of me-tooism under way regarding yesterday's incident at Westminster. Everyone who's anyone getting in on the act, even though there is little new to say. As is often the case on big occasions, the BBC has gone overboard, unable to talk about anything else. Even that most intelligent woman Mishal Husain is struggling to ask sensible questions. I sent an email to the *Today* programme enquiring if they had any plans to report the bombing of that school in Raqqa on Tuesday but just received the standard response saying they didn't have time to reply but thank you for writing, so I copied it to Nick Robinson, who acknowledged immediately. The domestic bulletins have become so stupidly insular that one has to turn to Al Jazeera to find out what else is going on in the world.

Friday 24 March

To Newcastle University, where I delivered a lecture on the House of Lords. Afterwards, I went in search of the post office, which turned out to have been subsumed into a branch of WHSmith. Although there was no queue for the counter, a pleasant young woman directed me to a digital franking machine, which, inevitably, I required assistance to operate. 'You realise that this is designed to do you out of a job?' I said.

'Oh, don't say that…'

She guided me through a complex process necessary to frank the envelope, which took far longer than it would a counter clerk. 'How do I pay for the envelope?'

'Ah, you can't do that here.' Instead I was directed to the nearest WHSmith till, some distance away. So, a transaction that under the old system could be carried out by one person now (under this allegedly more efficient system) requires two people and a machine. Never mind, I expect it enables someone somewhere to tick a box.

Monday 27 March

To Venice. Mrs Very Big Boss produced, from a secret wardrobe, clothes that I didn't know I possessed. I am kitted out in a beige safari-type waistcoat with half a dozen pockets, of the sort that foreign correspondents in hot countries wear, an expensive bush hat, which according to the label 'floats, ties on, repels rain, blocks UV rays, won't shrink and comes with a four-page owners' manual'. Also, a pair of lightweight walking shoes. As usual, I could not have been consulted in advance of purchase, because of my habit of declaring myself happy with what I already possess.

At the WHSmith in the departure lounge at Newcastle Airport, a shelf labelled 'Fresh Talent' which contains, among others, the following titles: *Jane Eyre*, *Catcher in the Rye*, Sherlock Holmes and the works of Anthony Trollope.

Venice

Oh, what joy. A city consisting entirely of pedestrians, not a single vehicle, even a bicycle. And without a trace of junk architecture. The waterways alive with traffic. Wonders around every corner, ancient palaces, exquisite churches, pavement cafes. 'Just let yourself get lost' was the advice from friends. Not difficult. Signs on every corner point either to San Marco or the Rialto, but they are apt to disappear at crucial junctions, with the result that within minutes one is hopelessly, irretrievably lost.

Tuesday 28 March

Piazza San Marco

The clock high on a building overlooking the basilica strikes noon, whereupon two life-size bronze statues come to life, hitting the huge bell with hammers. The sound reverberates around the square, half of which is in sunshine, half in deep shade. A continuous procession of visitors snakes through one entrance to the basilica and out of the other. Ubiquitous Chinese tourists, armed with selfie sticks, photograph themselves in front of every conceivable landmark, even the pigeons. Hopeless African migrants attempt without success to foist red roses on to tourists. Above the entrance to the basilica, half illuminated by sunshine, the four bronze horses, kidnapped by Napoleon and repatriated after his downfall. Soldiers, accompanied by an elegant *carabiniere*, mingle with the crowds, cradling machine guns. In cafes around the square, immaculate, handsome, white-jacketed waiters gliding between the cloth-covered tables. No ordinary waiters these, they are the cream of their profession, exuding an air of superiority. Ordering a coffee here could easily set you back €10. 'Something that you must do once and then you can frame the receipt and hang it on your wall,' remarked a Finnish woman we encountered yesterday while changing planes at Amsterdam. We decide to forgo the experience and make do with stone seats on the base of *Il Campanile*.

Later, we stroll for hours back into the maze of streets and alleyways, with no particular aim except to soak up atmosphere. In the poshest part of town we come across a woman with a selfie stick photographing herself in front of shops with luxury brand names – Gucci, Chanel, Tiffany. A handbag here can set you back €1,800. This is a city of surprises: even the meanest, narrowest alleyway can suddenly open onto a marble church, illuminated by evening sunshine. After dark we return to San Marco. Two lights on in an upper floor of the Patriarch's residence, adjacent to the basilica. This house has been home to two saints in the past 120 years – Popes Pius X and John XXIII, the latter one of my early heroes. A pianist and a pair of classical violinists are playing in one of the open-air cafes, although one does not have to buy an expensive coffee to benefit from their music. The desperate Africans are still peddling their roses, but now they have been joined by others selling little plastic helicopter devices which they catapult high into the air and which then slowly drift back to earth, purple parachutes luminous against the night sky. Never once did we witness a sale and yet they persevere.

Wednesday 29 March

A day devoted to extracting maximum value from our 24-hour water bus passes. First, we sped across the lagoon to the islands – Murano, Burano and Torcello, this last with fewer than sixty inhabitants and a seventh-century church, from the bell tower of which there are fine views over vineyards and orchards and across the lagoon. On Burano, an island of lace makers and brightly painted toy townhouses, we witnessed an amusing little drama. A young Chinese woman had accidentally dropped her selfie stick and its attached mobile phone into the murky waters of the canal, from where a water taxi man was gallantly attempting to retrieve it. Then to Murano and from there to the Piazzale Roma, from where we caught a vaporetto along the length of the Grand Canal and out across the lagoon to the Lido, where, al fresco, we ate lasagne and strolled along the promenade, lined with 1920s villas. All in all a brilliant day. I calculate that we did €49 worth of travel on each of our €20 passes.

Thursday 30 March
The Rialto

Alone at 9 p.m., Mrs V. B. Boss having retired early.

A crescent moon. The bridge crowded. Beggars (elderly Italians) accompanied by healthy-looking dogs guard the steps at either end. The Grand Canal alive with traffic, even at this late hour. Half a dozen gondolas, moored to stakes by the promenade, bob up and down on the swell caused by a passing vaporetto. A homemade banner displayed above a pizzeria on the quayside reads: 'NO MAFIA! VENETCIA E SACRE'. Hotels apart, many of the buildings are in darkness, save, here and there, for a light in an upper window indicating the residence of some privileged citizen. A desperate north African, clutching a bunch of red roses, approaches a courting couple. He gives a rose to the young woman, who hastily tries to hand it back. No, no, he insists. Take it, a gift. She clasps the rose but doesn't get the hint: for all his protests, she is supposed to pay. For her, a few euros is nothing; for him, it is about survival. He tries another tack: 'Are you married?' 'No,' says the woman. 'Not yet,' says the man. The north African's English is apparently good enough to detect the nuance. With a pretence of great joy, he thrusts the entire bunch into the young woman's hands. Again she tries to resist, but he insists, pretending that he wants nothing in return, making a little show of walking away. But he doesn't go far. He can't afford to lose his roses; so he hovers. It ends badly, of course. They are not his friends after all. The roses are returned and the couple do not part with a single cent. Off he slinks to begin the whole rigmarole over again.

Tuesday 4 April

With Ngoc and Emma to the Hirsel, where we wandered in sunshine amid hosts of golden daffodils, around the lake, along the Leet Water and back around the boundaries of the big house. Some time ago I sat next to Caroline Douglas-Home, Sir Alec's daughter, at dinner in Chillingham. She said that when the old man was dying, they asked what he would like to do. And he said, 'Fish.' So, with difficulty, they loaded him into a boat on the lake, where he surprised everyone by catching a huge trout.

Wednesday 5 April

Another chemical attack in Syria. Many children among the dead. At the UN, the US representative holds up pictures of dead children, trying un-successfully to shame the Russians (although the Americans have killed many more in their recent bombing of Mosul). The Russians are saying, improbably, that the explosion was caused by the bombing of a terrorist arms dump, but one does wonder why Assad would act so completely against his interests. Trump is blaming Obama for backing down last time, but it is far from clear that anything can be done aside from adding this to the charge list against the day when Assad and his cronies are eventually called to account.

Thursday 6 April

Bloody pheasants. They have decapitated almost every one of our fritil-laries and all the tulips in the grounds of the big house.

Friday 7 April

Awoke to the news that the US has fired fifty-nine Cruise missiles at an airbase in Syria. It amounts to an overnight change of policy. Until last week, Trump's line was that we could live with Assad. Whether this is a one-off or the beginning of something bigger remains to be seen, but whatever else one can say about Trump, it is decisive. No doubt Pyongyang is taking careful note.

Friday 14 April

Ngoc and I were married in Ho Chi Minh City thirty years ago today.

Tuesday 18 April

Theresa May has unexpectedly announced a general election for 8 June, having previously ruled one out on the grounds that the country needs political stability. I guess the open goal presented by the chaos on the Labour side has proved just too tempting. Apparently the services of Mr Lynton Crosby have been retained for the duration, thereby proving once again that whenever the chips are down, the 'Nasty Party' resurfaces.

Meanwhile tension is mounting in Korea. Trump, having rocketed Syria and dropped a 20,000-pound bomb in Afghanistan, has now turned his attention to North Korea. He and his deputy, Mike Pence, are saying their patience is at an end and that if the Chinese don't sort it, they will. The North Koreans, meanwhile, are talking nuclear war. This is shaping up to be the biggest game of brinkmanship since the Cuban Missile Crisis.

Wednesday 19 April

MPs have voted by 522 to a mere thirteen in favour of holding a general election. Just why Labour MPs think an early election is in their interests, or indeed in the national interest, is beyond me. Some, no doubt, see it as an early opportunity for regime change, though many of them won't live to see the day. The Labour leadership, I guess, doesn't want to be accused of being frit, though given everything else they've been accused of, I don't see why that should worry them. Instead they have walked into a great big trap.

Thursday 20 April

John Field came to lunch with old Bill Hugonin (former agent to the 10th Duke of Northumberland). I asked if the story were true that when, just after the war, the old Duke ('my Duke', as Bill calls him) wanted to propose to the daughter of the Duke of Buccleuch, Scotland's largest landowner, he mounted his horse and rode across his estates to the Buccleuch residence at Drumlanrig, a distance as the crow flies of more than 100 miles, without once leaving land owned by one or other of the estates. Bill confirmed the story about the Duke riding to Drumlanrig but was uncertain about the second part, although he did say it would have been technically possible in those days.

Bill knew Callaly in the 'good old days' when Major Browne was in residence. He agreed that the Major, although a charming old gent, didn't do much in his sixty-year lairdship 'except expound his political views at considerable length', which were, said Bill, with a twinkle in his eye, 'unenlightened'.

Saturday 22 April

The one great advantage of the Tories' huge poll lead is that they don't have to pander to the meanest instincts of their supporters. Yesterday they announced that, despite speculation to the contrary, they will not abandon the commitment to spend 0.7 per cent on overseas aid. Today they are talking of breaking the so-called triple lock, which guarantees pensioners (many of whom are among the most prosperous people in the country) year-on-year above-inflation pension increases. There are also signs that they may abandon their usual mendacious promise not to increase tax. Labour, needless to say, are grasping none of these nettles, making wildly extravagant spending promises and suggested they can all be paid for by increasing taxes on the rich when in truth only an increase in the basic rate of income tax (26 per cent when Mrs Thatcher left office; 20 per cent today) will enable us to go on living in the style to which we have become accustomed.

Saturday 29 April

For the first time an honest discussion about tax on the radio this morning. Perhaps because no politicians were involved. Meanwhile Sunderland's wretched football team have got their relegation in early this year. A one–nil defeat to Bournemouth sealed their fate with weeks still to go before the end of the season.

Monday 1 May

On this day twenty years ago, New Labour was swept to power on a scale hitherto unimaginable and amid scenes of near universal rejoicing. For twenty minutes or so I was the only MP in the country and my little victory speech went out live on all channels. So much water under the bridge since those heady days. Truly, the past is a foreign country.

Tuesday 2 May

An email from Nicholas Soames in response to mine expressing the hope that he would again be favouring the nation with his candidacy (on the grounds that in these difficult times we need all the one-nation Tories we can get). 'If it is of any interest to you,' he writes, 'you are much missed in the House … I take no pleasure in the implosion of your party.' He ends with a characteristic flourish, 'Place me at the feet of Lady Mullin.'

Thursday 4 May

The Duke of Edinburgh has announced that he is withdrawing from public life. A cantankerous old buffer he may be, but you have to admire someone who considers ninety-six a reasonable retirement age.

Friday 5 May

Local elections have resulted in the predicted Labour meltdown. Naturally it is all being blamed on Jeremy (and he is certainly a factor), but in truth the election was all about Brexit and any Labour leader would have struggled in this fraught climate. The only good news is that UKIP has disappeared in, to quote Robert Harris, 'a puff of sulphurous smoke'.

Saturday 6 May

To Hexham, where I addressed 200 people at the book festival. Inevitably the first question was about Jeremy. By now I have perfected my answer: lovely fellow, decent human being, right about Iraq, but high risk choosing a leader who enjoys the confidence of only 10 per cent of the parliamentary party. No one challenged this and we moved swiftly on to other matters.

Thursday 11 May

Labour's draft manifesto has been leaked, disclosing a giant wish list of supposedly populist policies with massive spending implications, inviting comparisons with 1983. Most of it is irrelevant anyway because all anyone seems to want to talk about is Brexit. I feel sorry for Jeremy because, despite everything, he's actually coming over well: good-humoured, articulate and, above all, authentic. Unfortunately, he is fatally hobbled by his past and the fact that he is a believer in the magic money tree. Meanwhile the nation – or that part of it which gives a fig – is in receipt of daily anodyne tweets from Chuka Umunna, who is clearly on manoeuvres.

Asked what he thought of Labour's draft manifesto, Ben Bradshaw, the Labour candidate in Exeter, replied, 'Let's get real. We are twenty points behind in the polls. It's the Tory manifesto we need to focus on. We need to save as many good MPs as possible so we can have some sort of opposition.' A grim but realistic assessment of our plight.

Friday 12 May

To York to be interviewed for a place on the Northumberland National Park Authority. Ngoc and I decided to make a day of it, visiting the Treasurer's House and walking the walls. Later, in town, we came across a pale, exhausted-looking young woman crouched in a doorway on a filthy sleeping bag. I bought her a sandwich. She was about Emma's age. Once upon a time, like Emma, she was perhaps the apple of her daddy's eye. At what point did it all go wrong? And how will it end?

Headlines in today's papers:

'Labour fights civil war over hard-left manifesto' (*Times*)

'Labour MPs ditch Corbyn manifesto' (*Telegraph*)

'Corbyn's Fantasy Land' (*Mail* – plus a strapline asserting that it would cost £4,000 per household and an unflattering picture of Jeremy)

'CRASH, BANG, WALLIES' (*Sun*)

'Labour's £50 billion wish list' (*Indy*)

Sunday 14 May

A call to Emma, who having completed her studies is volunteering in a community garden in Deptford and earning a few quid cleaning. How I love hearing her cheery voice.

'How are you, Sunny?'

'OK. Just got to figure out what I am going to do with the rest of my life and I'll be fine.'

Monday 15 May

Despite everything Jeremy looks as though he is enjoying himself. This evening, interviewed on *Channel 4 News*, he was relaxed, amusing, well informed, refusing to be provoked. He is attracting large friendly crowds wherever he goes. Today he was in Hebden Bridge, where a remarkable one in ten citizens are said to be members of the local Labour Party. It's a film we've seen before, of course. Michael Foot, circa 1983, was well received on the stump… but, as we have learned to our cost, come the day it's the silent majority who count. And their minds appear to be made up.

This evening a long talk with a former colleague, who sounds very down. She reckons we could lose a minimum of six seats in the north-east and maybe more. Bishop Auckland, Darlington and Hartlepool are all considered to be lost causes. Even Tony Blair's old seat, Sedgefield, is said to be wobbly. Brexit's not the problem, she asserts. It's Corbyn. 'He's toxic.' She says she has come across lifelong Labour voters who are switching to the Tories solely on account of Corbyn. I did gently put it to her that in these difficult times we'd be in trouble whoever our leader was, but she doesn't buy that. As far as she's concerned, Corbyn is the problem – and who am I to contradict her, not having knocked on any doors for seven years?

Tuesday 16 May

The much-leaked Labour manifesto was published today, promising everything to just about everyone – all based on some rather dodgy costings which Labour spokesmen have spent the day struggling to explain. They are planning to take the railways, Royal Mail and the water industry back into public ownership, requiring a huge increase in borrowing. Jeremy launched the manifesto in front of an audience of impressionable young folk at the University of Bradford who cheered him to the rafters. Come 9 June they will wake up with sore heads.

Wednesday 17 May

Up early. I put out beer out for the slugs and then to London. The Tories are alleging there is a £58 billion black hole in Labour's spending plans, which is a bit unnecessary since there are no shortage of holes to pick without having to make them up. 'Labour's Plan to Bankrupt Britain' is the *Mail*'s considered opinion. One other item of interest on this morning's news: Lloyds Bank is back in private ownership, having repaid the £23.3 billion bailout and delivered a £890 million surplus for the taxpayer. So much for all that Tory nonsense about 'the mess that Labour left us' and 'Gordon Brown's debt'.

Saturday 20 May

Fly poster seen in Islington: 'Deport thy neighbour. Vote Conservative.'

Monday 22 May

Today the Tories are playing their 'Corbyn is a friend of the IRA' card. 'Corbyn kick in the teeth for IRA victims' screams this morning's *Mail*. The *Telegraph* is at it, too, with 'Corbyn engulfed in IRA row'. Actually, despite everything, Jeremy is having a good campaign. Night after night the bulletins show him drawing large, enthusiastic crowds. At the weekend he addressed 20,000 young people at a pop concert on Merseyside who chanted his name. He was in his element, relaxed and happy. Theresa May, by contrast, is usually pictured addressing ticket-only audiences, packed with prosperous-looking but not particularly enthusiastic Middle Englanders. She had a bad day today, apparently reversing a commitment made only days ago to place a cap on the funding of social care, which has led to much mockery about her oft-repeated claim to provide strong and stable leadership. Can it be that talk of a Tory landslide is premature?

Tuesday 23 May

Awoke to the awful news that a suicide bomber has blown himself up at a concert in Manchester, killing twenty-two people and injuring many others. Among the dead a shiny-faced little girl called Saffie. I thought about her all day.

Wednesday 24 May

The bomber has been identified as a 22-year-old British-born Libyan whose family came to this country as refugees from Gaddafi and have since returned to Libya. The feeling is that he cannot have acted alone and that others are still at large. Police and the army on high alert. We live in fear of another atrocity.

Monday 29 May

On Twitter up pops a photo of an IRA funeral, masked men firing shots over the coffin. A large arrow directs the viewers' attention to a bearded man standing behind the coffin. 'Let's play a game of Where's Jezza?' says the caption. Actually it's fake. The man in question turns out to be a leading Sinn Féiner.

Tuesday 30 May

To the Playhouse in Alnwick to see the film version of Julian Barnes's *A Sense of an Ending*, which won the Man Booker in the year I was a judge, a decision from which I and one other dissented. The film was better than I expected and, having seen it, I feel better about the book.

Wednesday 31 May

A massive bomb in the embassy quarter of Kabul has killed at least ninety people and injured 400. How long before Afghanistan disintegrates?

Thursday 1 June

Working in the garden, still thinking of little Saffie in her cold box when she should have been out in the sunshine playing with other little nuggets. Her sister and mother were also seriously injured. The mother, who has been in a coma, has only just been woken and told that Saffie has gone.

This evening Trump announced to general consternation, but to no one's surprise, that he is withdrawing America from the Paris agreement on climate change.

Friday 2 June

Today's headlines:

'Fake web accounts boosting Labour vote' (*Daily Telegraph*)
'Corbyn's sly death tax trap' (*Mail*)
'Corbyn's magic money tree will cost families £3.5k a year' (*The Sun*)
'We will use SNP to give us power say Labour' (*The Times*)

Obviously there is no central guiding hand from Tory central office today, so they've had to make it up as they go along.

Sunday 4 June

Winchester Speakers Festival: I gave my *Hinterland* talk. First question from an Alan B'Stard-type Tory in the front row: would I care to dissociate myself from Jeremy Corbyn's support for the IRA? I pointed out that this was fake news of the sort that demeans politics, but the point was lost on him. He just sat there looking pleased with himself. Then someone asked if the Labour Party is finished and I did my best to assure him it isn't, though I do sometimes wonder. After signing a few books, David Fraser and I commenced the South Downs Way, a 100-mile stroll through the heart of Tory England.

Another atrocity: deranged Islamists, armed with twelve-inch knives, have run amok on London Bridge and in Borough Market, killing at least half a dozen young people and injuring many others.

Monday 5 June
Milbury's Inn to Buriton

Rolling hills, chalk soil, rich green pasture, chocolate-box villages, distant spires. Only a handful of other walkers, one a burnished man carrying a huge load who started from Southwold in Suffolk and who plans to continue to north Wales, via Offa's Dyke. 'Heavy and persistent rain' was forecast, but mercifully it held off until early evening, though we were soaked by the time we staggered into our resting place.

Tuesday 6 June
Buriton to Cocking

Rain all night, although fortunately the chalk soil drains easily. An unseemly numbers game is under way in the wake of Saturday's atrocity. Labour is promising to restore the cuts in police numbers over which Theresa May presided while Home Secretary, even though there is not the slightest evidence that shortage of resources is the problem when it comes to fighting terrorism, although it does seem that both the Manchester and the Borough Market attackers were known to the authorities. The dilemma is what to do about jihadi suspects who have committed no offence. I fear we may be lurching towards internment.

Another dozen or so miles tramping the hills, pausing at Uppark, the National Trust house destroyed by fire in 1989 and since wonderfully restored. We encountered few people. A lone fell runner, a few day trippers, one or two cyclists, a posh lady on a fine horse. Our landlady has a Labour poster in her window, one of several I have seen in unlikely places.

Thursday 8 June
Amberley

Election day. (In case anybody's wondering, I voted by post.) Today's *Telegraph* contains a front-page article by the former head of MI6 Richard Dearlove headed 'Jeremy Corbyn is a danger to this nation'. Until now I had thought the spooks had given up interfering in domestic politics, but after reading this I am not so sure. Dearlove writes, 'In the past MI5 would actively have investigated him … Britain would be less safe with him in No. 10.' How dare he? This from one of the men who gave us the Iraq War, on the basis of flawed intelligence. An issue on which Corbyn's judgement proved superior to that of almost all his critics, including Dearlove. Our host, a Tory but not a particularly rabid one, thinks the election result will be close on account of the widening gap between rich and poor, news of which seems to have reached him even here in deepest Sussex.

Friday 9 June
The Rising Sun, Upper Beeding

Awoke to the astonishing news that Labour has gained thirty seats. Against all predictions, Theresa May's gamble has backfired spectacularly. Far from the strong and stable government we were promised, it seems that we now face a Tory government propped up by the Democratic Unionist Party. Overnight the tables have turned. Now it's May's future that's in doubt and Corbyn is secure. It's becoming clear that half the country simply didn't fall for all that 'friend of the IRA, Hamas, Hezbollah, you name it' nonsense. In Scotland, the Nationalist bubble appears to have burst. They have lost twenty-one seats and suffered huge swings against them, even in seats they held.

I am on my own now. As planned, David and I parted company at Amberley.

Saturday 10 June
Chestnuts Tea Rooms, Alfriston

Only seven miles today. Here by noon. I purchased a copy of *The Times* and sat reading it in the garden of the Clergy House, the National Trust's first acquisition. There are some truly remarkable results. Labour has captured Canterbury and even Kensington, average household income £148,000. Vince Cable is back in Twickenham, Nick Clegg out in Sheffield Hallam. David Winnick lost Walsall North and Alan Meale is out in Mansfield. Both hitherto safe Labour seats. The consensus seems to be that the youth turned out in unprecedented numbers, but that the

Sun-reading, Brexit-voting end of the white working class actually swung to the Tories. In seats where there are large number of young folk we have piled up huge majorities. The Labour candidate in Bristol West has a *majority* of nearly 40,000. Unbelievable. Just one cloud on the horizon: this remarkable result was achieved by promising just about everything to just about everyone and saying someone else will pay for it. Goodness knows what would have happened if we'd actually won.

Alfriston was once home to Edna and Denis Healey. I found their graves in the churchyard. He has a modest stone in line with all the others. No hint that this was a man who led a big life.

Sunday 11 June

What a fine mess the Tories have got us into. 'They have utterly trashed this country,' Robert Harris tweeted. First with that stupid referendum and now by holding a wholly unnecessary election that has rendered the country ungovernable. And both were about sorting out internal party differences. Absolutely zilch to do with the national interest.

A grey mist lingered. I walked twelve miles over the Seven Sisters and Beachy Head, arriving in good time to catch a train to London and then home to the north. Some kind person on the Tube offered me a seat, but since I had just walked 100 miles, it didn't seem necessary.

Wednesday 14 June

Fire has engulfed a 24-storey block of council flats in west London. A vast inferno. Awful scenes. People glimpsed at high windows begging for help. Entire families incinerated. Hundreds unaccounted for.* Tonight the fire was still burning.

Thursday 15 June

John McDonnell is calling for a million people to take to the streets to force another election, thereby confirming suspicions that he doesn't quite get this democracy lark.

---

* The death toll was eventually put at seventy-two.

Friday 16 June

Angry scenes in London in the wake of the Grenfell Tower tragedy. Much shouting and ranting. The usual quota of Socialist Worker placards. A mob stormed Kensington Town Hall and Theresa May's car was surrounded by a baying crowd when she attempted to visit one of the churches housing the victims. This evening there were demonstrations in Whitehall demanding that she go, though it is hard to see how she can be blamed for this, even if her initial response was cack-handed. The government are making rash promises, at one point saying they will rehouse everyone within three weeks in or near the area they came from, thereby raising expectations that cannot possibly be fulfilled. There is a danger that this awful tragedy will become an excuse for a summer of looting and burning.

Saturday 17 June

To the Borders Book Festival in Melrose. One of my favourites. Fellow guests include the ubiquitous Jim Naughtie, Richard Ingrams (late of *Private Eye* and *The Oldie*), that most unusual Tory MP Rory Stewart (currently one of my many successors as Africa minister – the fifth in seven years), thriller writers Ann Cleeves and Val McDermid, Rory Bremner, Michael Parkinson and son (who flew to Edinburgh in their own plane) and Carol Klein from *Gardeners' World*. Also John Smith's daughter Sarah and her husband Simon, who works for the Halo Trust, the de-mining organisation. As ever we are well looked after, dining together around the big table in Harmony House. I am lodged, together with the Parkinsons and Carol Klein, in a beautiful country house in Gattonside.

Sunday 18 June

To the Duke of Buccleuch's great palace at Bowhill, where he entertained festival authors and organisers to a delicious brunch. The Duke, who is not only the country's but Europe's greatest private landowner, is one of the most likeable, down-to-earth aristocrats I have ever met. I came across him carrying a copy of *Hinterland* and four signed copies of Carol Klein's gardening book.

'Why four?' I enquired.

'One for each of my head gardeners.'

About 200 people, the Duke included, attended my talk. Afterwards I sat in on a discussion between Jim Naughtie and the *Sunday Times* political editor, Tim Shipman, who has written a book about Brexit. Shipman said that he had put it to a Conservative MP that no Tory in his right mind would want another election just now, to which the said Tory had replied, 'The trouble is that about a third of my colleagues are clinically insane.'

Saturday 24 June
Kells Festival, Ireland

An enjoyable evening in the company of the film director Stephen Frears, whose many triumphs include *The Queen*. He said Robin Janvrin, who as deputy private secretary had been at the Queen's side throughout the Diana crisis, remarked to him afterwards, 'You got everything wrong, but you got it right.' Meanwhile our beloved leader has been addressing festivalgoers at Glastonbury, where he was received with rapture. Jeremy has become a cult figure, though the magic may in due course evaporate when they realise that he, too, is at heart a Brexiteer.

Monday 26 June

Far from damping down the tension over the Grenfell Tower tragedy, Labour's new masters are ramping up the rhetoric. Yesterday John McDonnell remarked that those who died were 'murdered by political decisions'. Which tends to confirm suspicions that underneath that remarkable veneer of contrived affability that he has displayed of late there lurks the same irresponsible headbanger.

Saturday 1 July

An ugly tabloid-inspired blame culture is sweeping the country. The immediate response to any disaster is to look for someone to blame. Journalists descend in packs upon hapless victims and invite them to vent their spleen on whatever target is nearest to hand. Up pop unelected representatives of 'the community' (whose credentials are rarely questioned) expressing their lack of confidence in the efforts of the elected, demanding apologies, resignations and 'a say' in what is to be done. The BBC has become one of the worst offenders. Whenever the Prime Minister emerges from Downing Street, a journalist shouts a hostile question at her, not because he or she is expecting a reply but merely to get on record the smear of the hour. This non-exchange is then broadcast to the nation. A High Court judge is appointed to lead the inquiry and almost immediately the self-appointed are given a platform to question his suitability. Yesterday the leader of Kensington and Chelsea Council was forced to resign in the wake of the Grenfell tragedy and the television news depicted him driving away with a reporter chasing him down the road, shouting hostile questions, as though he were an escaping criminal. Today there are demands that the council be taken over and run by commissioners. Then up pops a 'representative of the community' demanding a say in precisely which commissioners should be appointed. I am sorry to say that Labour politicians are playing the game, too, oblivious to the fact that were we in office, the tables would be swiftly turned. This madness is getting worse with every new incident and it is undermining confidence in the democratic process. Indeed, in all our institutions.

Monday 3 July

Emma Mullin (hitherto known as The Small Intellectual) has been awarded a first-class degree in politics and international relations. She is now officially the 'intellectualest' member of our family.

Tuesday 4 July

Finished reading *Called to Account*, Margaret Hodge's memoir of her five years chairing the Public Accounts Committee, a shocking tale of official incompetence: massive overspends, tax forgone, wasted public money and evasion of responsibility on the part of those in power. She writes, 'A common feature of all the disasters we examined was the frequent change of personnel.' Not just ministers, but officials. Rare it is for the person in charge at the beginning of some great public spending programme to be there long enough to see it through. She gives one example of a project that was led by ten different people in five years.

Thursday 6 July

To Longridge Tower, a private school in a Hogwarts-type, mid-nineteenth-century Borders mansion, where I handed out the prizes and gave a short speech containing the usual simple messages that I reserve for such occasions: happiness comes from doing stuff, not buying stuff; be aware of your good fortune; pay your taxes (when the time comes); and remember there is more to life than shopping. This evening, the air being fresh and unusually bug-free, I sat outside for an hour reading *A Buyer's Market*, part of Anthony Powell's brilliant but inconsequential series *A Dance to the Music of Time*.

Tuesday 11 July

Much to my surprise, Michael Christopher Hayes, one of the prime suspects in the Birmingham bombings, identified as Z in my book, has given an on-camera interview to Kevin Magee, a Belfast-based BBC journalist who came to see me a couple of weeks ago. He refused to own up to his precise role in the pub bombings but claimed to have defused the third bomb that night, which was left in a doorway of an office block in Hagley Road. The interview triggered a brief flurry of interest, including a call from the *Today* programme, who scheduled an interview for 7.15 a.m. this morning, but their boredom threshold is high and the appointed hour passed without their coming back to me. Someone later rang to apologise.

Saturday 15 July

The Man, sounding a wee bit hyper, was on the radio this morning arguing that the French and the Germans might, after all, be prepared to cut us some slack on free movement in order to keep us within the single market. A long shot, but worth a throw of the dice.

Monday 17 July

An American academic interviewed this evening by the BBC cited polls suggesting that a significant minority of the UK population and about half of US citizens would be content to live under military rule. Which model they would prefer, I wonder? Chilean, Argentine, Salvadorean, Brazilian or Turkish? With or without death squads?

Tuesday 18 July

A letter from one of my Tory friends who attended our garden party the other day (up here people still write thank-you letters). In passing he writes:

> The only shadow, which is everywhere, is Brexit. Isn't it amazing how divisive it is – it comes between families and friends and husbands and wives … I can hardly bear to read the papers and as for looking at the television news… Too awful. It is so annoying to listen to 'The people have spoken' argument. They spoke on a certain day with a very uncertain note. 48:52 on a bum prospectus which would have been challenged in a court of law if it had been a commercial transaction.

Wednesday 19 July

To the great hall in Goldsmiths College to see the dearest, amusingest, intellectuallest Emma Mullin (once known as The Tiny Tyrant) receive her first-class degree. This evening we celebrated with a meal at the Drapers Arms in Islington with our friends the Woollacotts, who have always taken a close interest in our daughters.

Thursday 20 July

Today's *Guardian* contains a picture of a Grenfell Tower protester brandishing a placard asserting that 'Tories have blood on their hands'. If you look carefully, you can just make out that the words 'Socialist Worker' have been torn off.

Friday 21 July

This evening Nigel and Yvonne Vinson came to dinner with Frank Field, who has just been elected for a second term as chair of the Work and Pensions Select Committee. Although he's a bit right-wing for my taste, I do so admire Frank. In Parliament eight years before me and there eight years after I departed, he is still finding useful things to do. He it was who successfully put pressure on the odious Philip Green to do right by the British Home Stores pensioners.[*]

Sunday 23 July
The Old Hall, Buxton

Breakfast with Erwin James, whom I first came across ten years ago on the board of the Prison Reform Trust. A most remarkable man who had a horrendous upbringing and served twenty years of a life sentence for a brutal double murder, a rare case of a man emerging from prison utterly transformed – for the better. He has written an account of his colourful life[†] which is in many ways on a par with the first volume of Alan Johnson's memoirs, although sadly it hasn't attracted anything like the same attention. Later we both spoke at the *Oldie* lunch. The journey home took three trains and six hours.

Wednesday 26 July

Today was the funeral, in a wicker coffin covered with red roses, of Saffie, the beautiful little victim of the Manchester bombing. It had been delayed so her mother, who was seriously injured, could attend. Unspeakable, the sorrow of losing a much-loved child to such a random act of barbarism.

Saturday 5 August

In the review section of today's *Guardian* a piece by the author James Kelman, who makes the extraordinary claim that at any given time he has around 150 stories in process – 'plus essays, plays and novels'. He says, 'Writer's block is an economic luxury.' How true. The '80s, when I was lean and hungry, was the most productive period of my life. *A Very British Coup* was written in perhaps thirty days (the last third in seven) and

---

[*] Following an investigation by the Work and Pensions Select Committee, Sir Philip Green agreed to pay £363 million to the pensions regulator after the collapse of British Home Stores with the loss of 11,000 jobs and a pensions deficit of £571 million.

[†] *Redeemable*, Bloomsbury, 2016.

my other two novels in several sittings amounting to not much more, even though there was much else going on in my life. Today, when I have money in the bank and time on my hands, I am far less productive. My attempt to produce a sequel to *A Very British Coup* has run into the sand. Alan Bennett, when I visited him the other day, said that when he came to a blockage he simply skipped a few chapters or scenes and came back to them later. I may have to try that if I am ever to get started again.

Wednesday 9 August

North Korea is alleged to have constructed a small nuclear device which it is proposing to fire in the general direction of Guam. Unclear whether this is fake news or not, but Trump has responded anyway, promising to respond with 'fire, fury, the likes of which the world has never seen'. Scary. Unclear who is the bigger lunatic – Kim Jong-un or Donald J. Trump.

Thursday 10 August

To the University Business School at Edinburgh, where I was interviewed by Professor Chris Carter on the theme of 'Great Political Disasters'. My list included the Balfour Declaration, Indian partition, Suez, Harold Wilson's failure to devalue in 1964, Denis Healey's trip to the IMF in 1976 (which triggered the Winter of Discontent and the election of Margaret Thatcher and which Healey eventually admitted was unnecessary), the poll tax, Iraq and the Brexit referendum. Re. partition, I came across the following quote from Mountbatten, a man of staggering complacency:

> I shall see to it that there is no bloodshed and riot. I am a soldier and not a civilian. Once partition is accepted in principle I shall issue an order to see that there are no communal disturbances anywhere in the country. If there should be the slightest agitation, I shall adopt the severest measures to nip it in the bud.

Sunday 13 August

Corbyn is being assailed by Tory commentators for his failure to condemn the disastrous Maduro regime in Venezuela. Thus far he has confined himself to condemning violence by both sides, which is not, of course, the required answer. 'Condemn' is a favourite Tory game. Mrs Thatcher used to play it on Neil Kinnock ('Today, Neil, we are going to condemn Brent Council…') and more often than not he used to fall for it. Amusingly, to-day's *Telegraph* contains a photograph from Venezuela of a fearsome-look-ing thug wearing a steel helmet and a gas mask, holding a petrol bomb. The caption describes him as 'opposition activist'. Which does not quite fit with the official line that the violence in Venezuela is all on the government side.

Tuesday 15 August

To Alnham for lunch with Chris and Christine Nicholson, who live in a nineteenth-century house attached to a medieval pele tower next to the church. Chris, a handsome, cultured man, worked for the *Express* in the last days of Beaverbrook, who, he says, was always referred to as The Lord. One was always given advance notice of a call from The Lord in order to allow time to go to one of the two telephones in the office that were attached to a recording device. This was so that the minions would have a precise record of The Lord's every word. Chris also worked as a leader writer for the *Mail* under the tyrant Paul Dacre, who, he says, despite his fearsome reputation, was capable of generosity and also rather prudish. A funny old world, this, that I should find myself getting on so well with a former *Daily Mail* leader writer. One never ceases to be surprised by who one comes across hidden away in the wilds of Northumberland. My enemies, of course, will ascribe this to my having gone soft in old age, but it is not so. I simply refuse to accept that one can only engage with people who are on the same political wavelength. In any case, were I to do so, I would have very few friends up here.

Friday 18 August

A demented Islamist has mown down a hundred or more people in a crowded street in the centre of Barcelona, leaving thirteen dead and many injured. Later, another incident at a town south of Barcelona, where Spanish police shot dead all five attackers.

Saturday 19 August

An email from Liz Forgan on North Ronaldsay:

> Everyone at Neven is reading *Hinterland* this summer and my stock has SOARED due to your lovely words … It's been lovely here. The weather forecast has said hail and tempest and every morning the sun has beamed down. Exciting event was the late laird's wife's ashes being shot off in a specially constructed firework, let off on Nouster beach. All perfect until a young couple went walking with their dog the next morning and were horrified to have him deliver the unexploded nosecone full of ashes. They then decided that burial at sea was the only appropriate course of action, only for Hector (the dog) to dash obligingly into the waves to retrieve it again…

Sunday 20 August

Today's *Sunday Times* has run, across two pages, my article about the garden, illustrated by a nice picture of Ngoc and I standing by the gate in the historic wall. Perhaps unwisely, I circulated details to friends who I thought might be interested and received several replies from purists admonishing me for having any dealings with the Murdoch press. I am on a bit of a roll at the moment, having also written this week's *Spectator* diary, plus there was an interview in last week's *Sunday Telegraph*. Object in each case: to alert the world to recent publication of *Hinterland* in paperback. Only *The Guardian*, my natural territory, has so far proved impenetrable.

Tuesday 22 August

The bulletins are awash with pictures of yesterday's total eclipse across America. Some wag has erected a makeshift roadside hoarding which read: 'Dear Lord, Is it time to impeach? Send us a sign. Blot out the sun.'

Wednesday 23 August

Out with neighbours Kate Donaghy, Jeremy Hosking and their black Labrador Fergus. We did the nine-mile circuit over the hills from Prendwick to the Breamish Valley via the abandoned farm at Chesters, my favourite walk. One or two nervous moments when we had to divert around herds of cattle, who eyed us warily. Jeremy, a fund manager, remarked that the markets were soaring, despite Trump and Brexit. Although there is the little matter of the 15 per cent post-referendum devaluation of sterling, but somehow that doesn't seem to be upsetting people, although I guess it would if it had occurred under a Labour government (remember 1967, the pound in your pocket and all that?). Jeremy, who during the recent general election controversially offered a £5,000 contribution to the election expenses of any Tory fighting a seat with a Brexit-voting electorate and a Remain-supporting incumbent, says that eighty of the 140 eligible candidates took up his offer but only four were successful. Not one of his better investments.

Friday 25 August

To dinner with Stuart and Mary Manley, owners of the celebrated Barter Books in Alnwick, and a dozen of their friends. Stuart says that business is booming. Each year has been better than the last. Currently, the most valuable book in stock is an early edition of Chaucer, going for a cool £37,000. We dined around a table in what was once the station waiting room, décor and much of the furnishing unchanged since the 1880s; the remainder of the vast space was in twilight.

Saturday 26 August

Ngoc arrived in the UK thirty years ago today wearing a purple jumper, a gift from her sister (Emma has it now), and carrying all she possessed in a single suitcase. I met her at Heathrow, an ITN camera crew in tow. Somewhere I still have the video, but she has forbidden me to dig it out. We celebrated with a picnic on Ross beach. Five miles of sand with a castle at either end, though the castle on Holy Island is in the process of being re-roofed, half-clothed in an ugly white canopy visible for miles. Despite this being a bank holiday weekend, we saw no more than a dozen people all day.

Monday 28 August

Jeremy Hosking and I traced the rarely trodden path from Callaly to Debden (near Cragside), where we were picked up by Kate and taken back to the Big Hoose at Lorbottle for a bowl of thick pea soup. Kate's friend Brigitte, once chatelaine of the great house at Bantry Bay, was staying and afterwards I gave her a tour of the grounds at Callaly. Brigitte is Austrian, brought up in Vienna during the post-war occupation. 'What was it like?' I asked. 'Have seen the film *The Third Man*?' she replied. 'Just like that.'

Tuesday 29 August

To the Red Lion at Milfield for lunch with former *Mirror* editor David Banks and his wife Gemma, yet another of the one-time movers and shakers who inhabit these hills. David, a larger-than-life character in every sense, has also edited various Murdoch publications in New York and Sydney and was an assistant editor of *The Sun* under the notorious Kelvin MacKenzie. A genial fellow with a great fund of anecdotes, he told of attending a gathering of Murdoch executives at Aspen, Colorado, in 1992, at which Vice-President Dick Cheney and his prudish wife, Lynne, were guests of honour on whom Murdoch was anxious to make a good impression. A senior Fox Television executive was addressing the gathering when, to Murdoch's consternation, from the back of the hall a male stripper emerged who was, by the time he reached the platform, stark naked. The Oligarch and his guests, needless to say, were not amused and the executive responsible for the stunt, a rising star, was gone by nightfall.

David also recounted his role in the move to Wapping. 'I was lied to. Told that the plan was to launch a new paper, to be called the *Daily Post*. I was to be deputy editor.' He was ordered to get himself over to the US and tour the country, no expense spared, educating himself on the most advanced production techniques in preparation for his new role. After three weeks of this, he rang his masters to say he had seen enough and was coming home but was told firmly to stay away. When he insisted, a senior executive flew to New York and let him in on the secret: there was no *Post*. Wapping was built to house *The Sun* and the *News of the World*. In this brave new world there would be no troublesome print workers and no more hot metal. Journalists and secretaries would input the copy. Top secret. Known only to a handful of senior management. He was to stay away until further notice. They were afraid that word would leak. The rest, as they say, is history.

Thursday 31 August

The bulletins have been dominated for days by news of the hurricane which has been dumping unprecedented rainfall on Houston, Texas. Actually, there are much worse floods in Bangladesh, Nepal and West Bengal, where tens of millions have been displaced and the death toll is many times higher, but such disasters rarely make the news, giving rise to the obvious question: how many dead Bangladeshis equal one dead Texan? Trump, no doubt mindful of the disastrous handling of Hurricane Katrina, got down there quickly, but predictably made an ass of himself, which prompted many of his Twitterati fans to rush to his defence. 'What was Obama doing during Katrina? He was playing golf.' Fake news, of course. Obama wasn't President during Katrina. It was George W. Bush. The ignorance of the average Trumpista is truly staggering.

Tuesday 5 September

War drums beating loudly in Korea. The North, having recently fired a ballistic missile over Japan, has now tested a hydrogen bomb, prompting the US spokeswoman at the UN to say that they are 'begging for war', exactly the sort of irresponsible nonsense we don't need to hear from the world's greatest superpower. Meanwhile the US and the South Koreans are conducting military exercises right up to the North Korean frontier, which only serves to heighten the tension. Only the Russians and Chinese, urging calm on all sides, seem to be talking sense. There is an obvious long-term deal available: US withdrawal from the Korean peninsula in return for nuclear disarmament. The trouble is no one trusts the North Koreans to stick to any agreement and they don't trust us, having seen what happened to Gaddafi once he was persuaded to disarm.

Wednesday 6 September

Much to my surprise, given that I thought the interview was a bit of a car crash, I have received an email from the Environment Department asking if I am willing to serve on the committee of the Northumberland National Park. You bet I am.

Friday 8 September

Awful scenes from Bangladesh, where hundreds of thousands of Rohingya Muslims have been driven out of Burma by so-called nationalist Buddhists. (Who said Buddhism is a merciful religion?) Desperate, hungry, shoeless people carrying small children, aged grannies and all they possess and telling tales of rape and slaughter are making their way out of the hills through mud and rain. Behind them smoke rises from burning villages. Burmese officialdom, meanwhile, is lying through its teeth about what is going on. Aung San Suu Kyi, winner of the Nobel Peace Prize, also appears to be in denial. Bangladesh is the world's most crowded country. What is to become of these people?

Monday 11 September

This evening on BBC News an interview with a traumatised Rohingya woman in an overwhelmed hospital whose two sons have had their legs blown off. What is she to do? She has no means to care for them. No home, no food. No possibility of a wheelchair, even if they survive. Anyway, the terrain is all mud. 'Better for them to die,' she said. And who could disagree?

Wednesday 13 September

To the Palace of Westminster, where the first person I ran into was Neil Kinnock, who stood me a cup of coffee in the Pugin Room and we chatted pleasantly for half an hour, our longest encounter for more than thirty years. Tantalising glimpses of the Kinnock of old – amusing, acerbic, thoughtful – although one senses that resentment still burns not far below the surface. In truth I fear we were unfair to him in the '80s, especially over the miners' strike, where he was dealt an impossible hand. As we walked together down the Lords' corridor a passing friend unwisely suggested I should write a profile of him. 'Done that,' said Neil, 'spray painted.'

Thursday 14 September

A View from the Foothills is prominently displayed in the window of the Oxfam shop in Hampstead High Street.

Thursday 21 September

To the *Spectator* offices in Old Queen Street, Westminster, a house over-looking St James's Park, where I recorded a twenty-minute podcast in conversation with the political editor, James Forsyth. Then to the BBC at Millbank, where I was guest of the day on the *Daily Politics* programme, the main item on the agenda being the latest bout of Cabinet infighting over Brexit. Then to LBC at Leicester Square, where I was interviewed about *Hinterland* and related matters by Iain Dale. Finally, to Hampstead, where I met up with Emma and we repaired to the Coffee Cup for (in my case) a spaghetti arrabiata. Then back to the north on the 18.30 from King's Cross All in all, a good day's work.

Sunday 24 September

Letter in today's *Sunday Telegraph*: 'There must be something seriously wrong with Britain's educational system if we have shortages of doctors, nurses, teachers, engineers, plumbers and bricklayers when nearly 50 per cent of our teenagers are going to university. What are they all studying?' Indeed, by way of illustration, Emma Mullin, the recent recipient of a first-class honours degree in politics and international relations, is cur-rently employed as a waitress.

Monday 25 September

Upsetting news from Germany. For the first time since the war a hardline nationalist party has been elected to the Bundestag. Across the country it has taken about 13 per cent of the vote and much more in the former East Germany. Of course, it's yet another of the bills coming in for mass migration, part of a trend that is sweeping Europe. Impressive though she is, Chancellor Merkel made a big mistake when she said there was room for everyone in Germany.

Tuesday 26 September

A visit from our neighbour Tony Henfrey, a retired businessman and by no stretch of the imagination a Labour supporter. 'Say what you like about John McDonnell,' he said, 'but he's on to something, promising to unravel these PFI contracts. Some of those deals are outrageous. They were all about the government borrowing money without have to put it on the books. In business that would be called fraud.'

After he'd gone, I lifted our very healthy crop of onions and laid them out to dry in the glasshouse.

Thursday 28 September

The Labour Party is in the grip of a cult of the leader unseen since the Blairite heyday. Yesterday's speech by Jeremy to the Labour Party conference in Brighton was received with rapture, wide-eyed, credulous delegates chanting his name, members of the parliamentary party who might constitute a more sceptical audience banished to an upper gallery beyond the reach of prying cameras. All discussion of Brexit banished to the fringe. Jeremy is at the height of his game. Calm and confident. Mobbed everywhere he goes. Rightly or wrongly, the party has convinced itself that we are on the threshold of power. And who knows, we may be. Or could this be peak Jeremy?

Sunday 1 October

A neighbour reports that he spotted a grey squirrel in the wood outside our gate this afternoon. The second sighting in the past ten days. A couple of small reds still come to our feeding box every day, but I fear they may be the last we shall see.

Monday 2 October

A text from Emma Mullin, still employed as a waitress: 'When I have children I will insist they study science and become doctors, not bloody arts and humanities.'

Wednesday 4 October

Poor Theresa May. Her luck has well and truly run out. Everything she does turns to ashes. Her speech to the Tory conference this afternoon went horribly wrong. She was repeatedly interrupted by some stupid comedian trying to hand her a sheet of paper marked P45 and then overtaken by a fit of coughing. Meanwhile her colleagues are noisily protesting their loyalty. Always a bad sign.

Friday 6 October

Bright sunshine illuminating the valley, turning the beech and chestnut leaves to gold. Piteous baying, audible over a great distance, from cows recently separated from their young. So far the calves have only been moved to a neighbouring field, still within sight of their mothers, but soon they will be taken away altogether. How I loathe the meat industry. We walked up the hill to Yetlington and back via Tod le Moor and Lorbottle. Ngoc's last taste of fresh air for three weeks. She departs for Vietnam early tomorrow.

Saturday 7 October

Message from Paris, where Mrs V. B. Boss is changing planes: 'The tablet dispenser in the dishwasher no longer works so you should put the tablet straight in the bottom.' Why do I need to be told? The tablet dispenser has been out of action for at least a year.

Wednesday 11 October

Messages from HCM City:

2.57 a.m. 'If u pack sandwich for yr walk tomorrow, you should use the wholemeal bread, not my soda bread….'

3 a.m. 'Don't 4get spicy tomato soup in second drawer…' In fact I have already consumed three portions. Very good it was.

Saturday 14 October

Trump's latest folly: he has disowned the painstakingly negotiated agreement between Iran and the rest of the world whereby Iran agreed to suspend its development of nuclear weapons in return for an easing of sanctions. He has done so even though the International Atomic Energy Authority, which is tasked with inspecting the Iranian nuclear facilities, says the Iranians are abiding by the deal, and in the teeth of opposition from just about every other country in the world (only Israel and Saudi Arabia have expressed support) and from most of his own advisers. The suspicion is that this has more to do with his determination to trash what remains of Obama's legacy than it does with genuine concerns over the terms of the deal. All he has succeeded in doing is further isolating the US and giving more weight to the view that the US is fast becoming a rogue state.

Sunday 15 October

To Durham for the book festival, where I gave a speech on the prospects for a Corbyn government, gently warning of the dangers of arousing un-realistic expectations and the need to learn to say 'no' now and again. Jeremy (having spent his career supporting every halfway good cause, protesting every closure, appearing on every picket line) has little or no experience of saying 'no'. If and when he becomes Prime Minister, every-one will come knocking. How will he cope?

Friday 20 October

To the Durham University union to take part in a debate entitled 'The United Nations is a failing organisation'. On our side Sir Richard Dalton, a former diplomat; Stewart Wood, a one-time Treasury adviser (now in the Lords); and Patrick Grady the SNP's Chief Whip in the Commons. Proposing the motion three bright young Brexiteers and a former RAF officer who now works for the Royal United Services Institute. Although they were at pains to suggest otherwise, The Three Brexiteers seemed to be arguing for withdrawal rather than reform. We beat them easily, only to turn on the news and discover that the World Health Organization, a UN agency, has just appointed Robert Mugabe a 'goodwill ambassador', despite his having collapsed his own country's health service and much else besides. And we wonder why people are losing faith in the UN.*

---

* The nomination was withdrawn after a widespread outcry.

Wednesday 25 October

Called on old Bill Hugonin and loaned him my copy of *Brief Lives*, W. F. Deedes's elegant pen portraits of the great and the good of his acquaintance – from Stanley Baldwin to Princess Diana. Bill has much in common with Deedes – both gents of the old school, same generation, same patrician sense of decency. He sits in his beautiful house in the Hulne Park, feeling pangs of guilt about his privileged life and worrying about the state of the world, which he says is as bad as any time he can remember. I quoted Noël Coward to him: 'Nothing is ever as bad as it seems at the time.'

Friday 27 October

The Brexiteers are becoming increasingly rabid. One Tory MP has written to a university demanding to know what its students are being taught about the EU. The ensuing row has prompted the *Daily Mail* to call for people to write in with examples of anti-Brexit bias at universities. One wag has tweeted, 'Shocked to discover that the university canteen serves spaghetti bolognaise every Monday.'

Saturday 28 October

Catalonia has declared independence from Spain on the basis of a referendum that attracted a turnout of 43 per cent and in defiance of the Spanish constitution. A big confrontation brewing. If they get away with it, populists all over Europe will be demanding the right to set up their own little statelets. No doubt the Walloons in Belgium and the Northern League in Italy are watching closely. Could it be that the sixty years of peace and prosperity that the EU has brought us is about to disintegrate into squabbling, warring fiefdoms?

Monday 30 October

Yet another feeding frenzy under way at Westminster. A list is said to be circulating of MPs alleged to have engaged in – to use a word beloved of the politically correct – 'inappropriate' behaviour. The charges vary from the serious (an allegation of rape) to the unspeakably trivial. At the lower end of the scale the Defence Secretary, Michael Fallon, is said to have touched the leg of a female journalist fifteen years ago. He apparently apologised to her soon afterwards and the woman concerned is said to be untroubled by the incident. But that has not stopped hysteria being organised.

This afternoon to Churchill College, Cambridge, where I attended a lecture on travellers in 1930s Germany and was afterwards entertained to dinner at High Table and put up for the night in one of the college's luxurious guest rooms.

Tuesday 31 October
Churchill College, Cambridge

Alan Packwood, the archive director, gave me a tour of his domain, which contains not only Churchill's papers but those of Jock Colville, Thatcher, John Major, Neil Kinnock and Robin Cook. Peter Mandelson's and Gordon Brown's papers are said to be promised. I was shown a manuscript of Jock Colville's marvellous diaries, all neatly handwritten in a lined exercise book, including the page in which he recounts the Norway debate which brought down the Chamberlain government (he was Chamberlain's assistant private secretary at the time). That day's entry begins, 'Rode at Richmond under cloudless skies.' Politics was so much more laid-back in those days. The *pièce de résistance* was the dinner menu at the Potsdam conference signed by everybody present, including Churchill, Truman and Stalin.

Then back to London for a council meeting of the Winston Churchill Memorial Trust and finally to a church in Barnes, where I gave my book talk in aid of a Tibet charity, which raised £3,700.

Headline in today's *Sun*: 'Shock confession on sex pest dossier implicates SIX Cabinet ministers: FALLON: 'I FELT RADIO HOST'S KNEE'.

Wednesday 1 November

To the House of Lords for lunch with Jean Corston. I came across Shirley Williams, who is looking frail, and reminded her of the time we stayed at David Steel's house in the Borders. Before leaving David had insisted we each write few lines of the poetry in the visitors' book. Mine read:

> Who should have guessed,
> That I should be blessed,
> To spend a night in the tower,
> With the beautiful Shirley Williams.

Her only comment at the time was: 'It doesn't scan.'

This evening, to a dinner at the lavish offices of Linklater's, a firm of City solicitors, organised to celebrate the twentieth anniversary of the Criminal Cases Review Commission, a body I had a hand in setting up. I found myself sitting next to the recently appointed Lord Chief Justice, a pleasant, refreshingly normal man, ten years younger than me. These days almost all the world's great public servants are younger. I only await the election of a younger Pope and then I will know the game is up.

This evening we heard that Michael Fallon has resigned.

Thursday 2 November

Much talk of an 'alcohol-fuelled toxic culture' at Westminster. Which only goes to show what a sheltered life I have led. In twenty-three years in the Commons no one ever made a pass at me, nor I at them. Nor (although one did occasionally come across evidence of alcoholic excess) was I aware of the debauched culture that, if our free press is to be believed, stalked the bars and private recesses. Believe it or not, however, before I was elected I was once stalked by a young woman with whom I was vaguely acquainted through the Campaign for Labour Party Democracy. On one occasion she turned up at midnight on the doorstep of my flat with a long sob story about having missed the last bus home and demanding to stay the night. Unfortunately a neighbour had already let her into the hall and short of physically evicting her there was no way of getting her out. With a minimum of ceremony I conducted her to the spare bedroom, although she barged into my room several times during the night. Next morning she departed, having sprayed the inside of my shoes with scent. Later, she wrote me a number of obscene letters which I hung onto for several years by way of evidence in case she ever went public with the (false) suggestion that we were in some kind of relationship. I heard later that she went off in pursuit of Chris Smith, who she decided looked like me. Tony Benn had a woman who haunted him for years. She used to turn up at his house with love letters. In politics, harassment can be a two-way street.

Today's news is that a journalist and Tory activist in her thirties has accused Damian Green, the Deputy Prime Minister, of touching her knee two years ago, 'so fleetingly as to be almost deniable'. He is also said to have sent her a faintly risqué email after she was photographed for *The Times* wearing a corset. Unlike Fallon, Green is fighting back.

Monday 6 November

A hard frost last night wiped out the cosmos and most of the remaining colour in the garden, which until yesterday was extensive.

Wednesday 8 November

To Wansbeck Hospital for surgery on my hernia. Awoke feeling very sore. Sent home with a supply of painkillers, a six-week ban on table tennis, no driving for a fortnight and no labouring in the garden until goodness knows when.

Home to find that Priti Awful Patel has resigned as International Development Secretary after accusations that she has been conducting a foreign policy of her own, involving undisclosed meetings with the Israelis. Having been let off with a caution on Monday, it appears there were other undisclosed meetings that she forgot to mention when she was supposedly 'fessing up. Were it up to me, I'd reappoint Andrew Mitchell, one of the few Tories with a serious interest in the developing world. Of course, there would be a great shout of 'Plebgate' from the Twitterati, which I guess the government is too weak to weather. The only other suitable candidate who comes to mind is Rory Stewart.*

Sunday 12 November

Tapped out a review of Gordon Brown's memoirs for the *Irish Times*. The centrepiece is a detailed account of his role in preventing the meltdown

---

* In the event, the Prime Minister appointed Penny Mordaunt, whose principal qualification appeared to be having worked in a Romanian orphanage in her gap year. Stewart was eventually appointed but lasted less than three months.

of the global financial system and in persuading other world leaders to pump liquidity into their economies in order to prevent a recession. Without doubt his finest hour and no one can take that away from him. 'This was the fallout from the years of greed,' he writes and who can disagree? Given that this is so, however, one wonders why throughout his years as Chancellor he appeared to buy into the City's own estimation of itself. One has only to read his annual Mansion House speeches (which he does not cite) to appreciate the scale of the delusion. As to his personal inadequacies, which became so obvious once he was Prime Minister, he acknowledges that he might not have been temperamentally suited to the top job. 'In a far more touchy-feely era, our leaders speak of public issues in intensely personal ways ... For me, being conspicuously demonstrative is uncomfortable.' One understands why he wouldn't wish to dwell on the subject, but there is surely more to it than that. How does one explain the volcanic rages, the chronic indecision, the desperate, backfiring gimmicks and his inability to engage with all but a handful of colleagues? In the twenty-three years that our parliamentary careers overlapped Gordon rarely acknowledged my existence. On the two or three occasions he visited Sunderland he appeared not even to notice my presence in the room. More than once I introduced him to people with whom he struck up a conversation lasting several minutes without ever acknowledging that I was standing next to him. Weird or what? My guess is that he never forgave me for publicly taking Blair's side in 1994. Presumably he behaved in the same way towards others on his blacklist – at least until things got so desperate that he had to send for help.

For all that, however, and the fact that The Man was an incomparably more accomplished politician than Gordon, he may well be better remembered. Blair, of course, will be haunted by Iraq whereas Brown may be honoured principally for his role in averting global meltdown. Also, perhaps, because in retirement he has chosen to lead a modest life, devoting time to his family and to good works, in contrast to the glitzy lifestyle of his predecessor.

Monday 13 November

On the spur of the moment I tapped out 900 words on the role of the feeding frenzy in modern British politics and pinged it off to Mary

Wakefield at *The Spectator*, who replied saying they would use it. After lunch I walked up through the beech woods to Castle Hill, only to be roundly told off on my return by Mrs V. B. Boss for over-exertion when I am supposed to be convalescing.

Thursday 16 November

To Sunderland for the funeral of council leader Paul Watson. A big turnout, about 400 people, including the Lord Lieutenant, mayors from neighbouring authorities and the three local MPs. That's what happens when you die in office. Personally I will settle for another twenty years and a small turnout at my funeral. Afterwards a chat with Michael Mordey, who used to work for me and is now a senior councillor. He says the social fabric in some of the poorer parts of the city is once again rapidly deteriorating. Youth projects have been closed and gangs of feral youths are once again causing havoc. Entire streets are becoming uninhabitable and may eventually have to be demolished. A re-run of what happened at the height of the Thatcher decade. Michael added, 'This time round the Tories have managed to achieve in five years what took Mrs Thatcher ten.'

Sunday 19 November

This morning, two fat grey squirrels in our garden. This is surely the end of the reds.

Friday 24 November

A cold, clear day. John Field, John Williams and I drove to East Ord near Berwick, scrambling along a badly eroded path on the south side of the Tweed until we crossed over into Scotland via the chain bridge, then back along the north bank in bright sunshine, through the Paxton estate, at one point losing our way and having to divert along a dangerous road. The river was in full spate and rich in birdlife – ducks, swans, Canada geese, oystercatchers, egrets – and also, unfortunately, plastic bottles caught up in the brash on the river bank. What are we going to do about plastic?

Saturday 25 November

A new edition of *A Very British Coup* arrived in today's post. Profile are hoping to ride the Corbyn bandwagon and have designed a cover dressed up like the front page of a newspaper. 'The novel that foretold the rise of Corbyn' reads the strapline and on the back in large letters 'PREPOS-TEROUS', *Daily Telegraph*. It is the tenth printing since Profile bought the rights seven years ago. I wish I could persuade them to reprint my other two novels, which are actually better, though not so topical.

Wednesday 29 November

To Sunderland for the university's winter graduation ceremony. The high-light was the awarding of an honorary degree to Lt Col Mordaunt Cohen, aged 101, said to be the last surviving officer from the Burma campaign and once one of the city's most prominent citizens. He's fairly deaf and confined to a wheelchair but otherwise all there. After the presentation he was wheeled to the microphone and, without notes and in a strong, clear voice, proceeded to deliver a beautifully crafted fifteen-minute speech, a perfect blend of humour and seriousness. At first the audience didn't seem to realise quite how old he was. It was only when he referred in passing to 'my hundredth birthday last year' that the penny dropped, re-sulting in an audible gasp and a prolonged standing ovation.

Friday 1 December

Today's news: a retired police forensics expert has told the BBC that he found thousands of pornographic images on Damian's Green's computer when his office was raided nine years ago in connection with a Home Office leak inquiry. Naturally Green is denying all, but he is unlikely to survive.

Monday 4 December

Davie Gibson, the tree surgeon, and his merry men came to give our huge willow tree a long-overdue and rather drastic haircut, leaving us with a huge pile of firewood and a vast supply of wood chippings. 'Do you still go to London?' Davie enquired. 'Yes, I am going tomorrow,' I replied. Whereupon he revealed that he hadn't set foot in London since 1979 and one of his men remarked that he had never been, except in transit to Heathrow en route to Greece. One forgets how irrelevant London is for many country folk. When I was on the *Mirror*'s journalism training scheme in Devon, I lodged in a farmhouse where, in July 1971, the farmer's wife came across me loading up my old Ford van. 'Where are you going?' she enquired. 'London,' I replied. 'Oh,' she said, duly impressed, 'I've never been there.' I hadn't the heart to tell her that I was actually en route to Peking.

Tuesday 5 December

To London on the 11.00. 'How you doing?' asked the friendly ticket collector? To which I gave my usual facetious reply, 'So far, so good, but the day is young.' Sure enough, within minutes it was announced that we would have to disembark at Newcastle owing to a body on the track near Durham. Instead we were bussed to Darlington and put on to another train. It was all handled with great efficiency, but that didn't stop a spoiled youth next to me muttering, 'This is beyond a joke.'

'Someone has been killed,' I said. That shut him up.

Wednesday 6 December
Westminster

Our crumbling Parliament is becoming a vast building site. A huge tower of grey plastic rises besides St Stephen's entrance, the clock tower is swathed in scaffolding and may not be seen again for years, inner courtyards are crammed with temporary structures. There is talk of the entire building having to be evacuated. Many existing Members may never work there again. I am fortunate that I served my time while Parliament was still venerable and recognisable and while it was still possible to walk the corridors trod by Disraeli, Gladstone, Lloyd George, Churchill et al.

Thursday 7 December

Lunch at the Travellers Club with Alastair Papps, a former senior official of the Prison Service, an admirer of my various works. I have now made my way down Pall Mall and up into St James's and Mayfair courtesy of the diaries. Clubland is a world of its own, unknown to most outsiders, peopled by obsequious servants and immaculately tailored elderly gents, some with vaguely familiar faces to whom one can't quite put a name. The only one I recognised was Terry Waite.

Friday 8 December

Today's *Spectator* published my piece on politics as a game of gotcha, a reference to the various media feeding frenzies that sweep through like Atlantic hurricanes leaving corpses in their wake. Recent casualties have included Michael Fallon and Priti Patel. Damian Green is likely to be next.

Tuesday 12 December

My seventieth birthday. Ngoc made a delicious banoffee pie, in which, for the rest of the year, I am strictly forbidden to indulge. We lunched with neighbours at the Fishing Boat Inn, overlooking the sea at Boulmer. If I am lucky, I may have another fifteen years of reasonable health, though bits of me are gradually seizing up.

Thursday 21 December

Damian Green has been sacked, the third and by far the most senior minister to go in the past month.

Friday 22 December

The Brexiteers are exulting over the impending return of old-style British passports, possession of which may well make travel rather less convenient than the current EU passport, but hey, they are British and that's what counts. The irony is that since we are still bound by EU procurement rules, it may not even be printed in Britain, which has triggered yet another bout of apoplexy in the *Mail*.*

---

* They were designed in France and printed in Poland.

Saturday 23 December

Headline in today's *Daily Telegraph*: 'Exclusive: Nigel Farage snubbed for knighthood for services to Brexit – again'. Good old *Telegraph*, as reliably barmy as ever.

Thursday 28 December

Today's madness: fifty Tory MPs are demanding the construction of a new royal yacht, funded by the National Lottery, 'to showcase Brexit Britain'. Needless to say, the *Telegraph* is the vehicle they have chosen to launch this bold initiative.

Friday 29 December

The former international footballer George Weah has been elected President of Liberia at his third attempt, in place of the formidable Ellen Sirleaf Johnson, whose time is up. Not good news. I met him once, in 2004 – at a dinner for presidential candidates given by the US ambassador in Monrovia. He arrived accompanied by a couple of dodgy-looking businessmen and, despite the ambassador's best effort to draw him out, appeared to have nothing to say about anything. One other ominous straw in the wind: his Vice-President is the wife of former President Charles Taylor, currently resident in HMP Frankland, serving fifty years for war crimes.

Saturday 30 December

Snow still lying at Callaly, but it has more or less disappeared a mile or so down the road. We took a picnic to Warkworth and walked north along the beach, eating our sandwiches on a dune overlooking the Aln estuary, six or seven miles in all. Emma, who has a history of falling into water, tried to jump a stream and fell in.

Emma is in the process of applying for a US visa. Among the questions to which she is required to answer 'yes' or 'no' the following: 'Do you seek to engage in or have you ever engaged in terrorist activities, espionage, sabotage or genocide?' Reminds one of Graham Greene's reputed response, in the '50s to a similar question: 'Do you intend to subvert the US government?' to which he is said to have replied, 'Sole purpose of visit.'

CHAPTER NINE

2018

Monday 1 January

A New Year message from the Chinese. From today they are refusing to take any more of the plastic waste that, until now, we have been exporting to them in great quantities. Which means we are going to have to get serious about disposing of plastic.

Saturday 6 January

The *Guardian* feministas are becoming more ludicrous by the day. Today's crop includes a three and a half-page feature in the review section devoted to 'Six remarkable women and the food they ate'. In the news section there is a page lead headed 'Government accused of "institutional" gender bias in art acquisitions'.

Monday 8 January

A hard frost, bright sunshine, snow on the Cheviot. We walked up to High Houses and back via Cross Fell and Dancing Hall. On the way we were overtaken by a convoy of shooters in black land cruisers. They turned into a little valley below Cross Fell, but, to judge by the intermittent gunfire, most of the pheasants have already been shot or are lying low – some in our garden.

Tuesday 9 January

London: dinner with Jon Lansman, now back in the public eye after a 35-year absence, as the man in charge of Momentum, the Corbynite praetorian guard. I employed him at *Tribune* in the '80s and we were both involved in the Bennite uprising. In those days he was young and strikingly handsome, but he is now a slightly overweight, sixty-something Jewish gentleman with a white beard and a flat cap (I didn't recognise him at first). Far from being a zealot, he is – unlike some of his flock – rational and sensible. Momentum has an office in Aldgate. He is unpaid. He says they have 11,000 subscribers. Their funding comes from supporters. During the election they had a couple of £20,000 donations but those apart have never received anything over £1,000. Their aim is to keep the Labour Party on the One True Path (my words, not his). He is open about wanting to change the composition of the parliamentary party, but I didn't get the impression he has plans for a purge. Instead he is focusing on getting sympathetic candidates into vacancies where they arise. I put it to him that a Lib Dem revival in areas like Cornwall would be greatly in Labour's interests, but he begged to differ, saying that Labour was in with a chance of winning two seats in Cornwall, which I regard as fanciful. We talked about Israel. Jon lamented the fact that the present younger generation of Israelis has little or no contact with Palestinians. 'Some have opinions that are frankly racist.' He did not dispute the use of the word 'apartheid' to describe the present state of affairs. He had an aunt living in the south of Israel. 'When I visited her years ago she used to mix freely with Palestinians, exchanged banter with shopkeepers, even invited labourers into her house for tea. That's impossible nowadays.' Just about the only Palestinians his cousins had ever encountered were during their military service, frisking them at army checkpoints.

Wednesday 10 January
Piccadilly

Homeless people every twenty yards. Almost as bad as in Thatcher's day. I put my head round the door of St James's Church only to find four homeless men stretched out on pews, sound asleep, one snoring loudly. Then to the National Portrait Galley. The most striking image, a bromide print of an emaciated Philip Gould, one of the architects of New Labour, standing on the plot in Highgate Cemetery that he had selected for his grave. 'A nice spot,' he is quoted as saying. 'It has to be. I am going to be here for a very long time.' He died nine days later.

Thursday 11 January

Lunch at the House of Commons with Mark Hosenball, the American journalist who was expelled from the UK in 1977 by the then Labour government for writing about GCHQ at a time when its very existence was top secret. He has subsequently worked for *Newsweek* and is now employed by Reuters. On return to the UK he was given a tour of the new GCHQ and treated as an honoured guest. What goes round comes round. Mark thinks it unlikely that Trump will win a second term but says much depends on the mid-term elections – and the Democrats coming up with a credible candidate.

Friday 12 January

A day at the Winston Churchill Memorial Trust, interviewing for travel scholarships. As usual some impressive candidates, but it is extraordinary how many are stumped by the simple question we always ask at the end. 'If someone asked you "Who was Winston Churchill?", what would you say?'

One slightly dreamy woman, after long hesitation, said 'he was a wonderful man'.

'What was wonderful about him?'

Stunned silence. And then: 'Haven't I already answered your question?'

Monday 15 January

Time to evict the pheasants before they destroy the garden. I put out the cage, baited with bird seed, and trapped two, whom Calum then deported to the furthest end of the estate.

Tuesday 16 January

Carillion, one of the behemoths that have been hoovering up outsourced public sector contracts, has gone bust, leaving many of its 20,000 employees out of work and threatening the livelihoods of many more in their long chain of unpaid suppliers. As usual in such cases the pension fund is also massively in deficit and the top brass have escaped with huge bonuses and salaries that will continue to be paid until long after the receivers move in. The fallout will be huge. Carillion have their fingers in everything: schools, hospitals, prisons, roads. Remarkably, the government has been pushing more contracts their way even after it was widely known they were in trouble. This, surely, ought to bring an end to the orgy of outsourcing that successive governments have pursued, but I wouldn't count on it.

Wednesday 17 January

Awoke to a winter wonderland. Ankle-deep snow, shrubs, trees and hedges outlined in glistening white, hills illuminated by winter sunshine. We made a circuit of the lakes, the only tracks being those of deer, hare and the ubiquitous, accursed pheasants. Later, I walked alone up the lane to the Mill for a coffee with John Field. He is reading *Durgan*, a novel by Edward St Aubyn, yet another famous alumnus of Westminster School. 'At one time I had three former pupils in the Cabinet,' he remarked (Nick Clegg, Dominic Grieve and Chris Huhne). On the way back, three deer emerged from Cabin Wood and crossed the road in front of me.

Friday 19 January

A cold, clear day. The snow still lying. We drove three miles up the Breamish Valley and took a short walk along the river but were beaten back by icy winds. This afternoon I tapped out another thousand words of a little short story I am writing, 'The Man Who Shot the President'. I don't suppose anything will come of it, but it whiles away the winter days.

Sunday 21 January

John McDonnell gave an impressive interview on the *Andrew Marr Show* this morning. One doesn't have to agree with him or believe that he is a loveable human being to see that he is up to the job of being Chancellor.

Monday 22 January

As if the situation in Syria isn't already catastrophic enough, Turkey has launched an attack across its border into the enclave controlled by the

Kurds, who have done more than anyone to defeat the Islamists. This evening to Barter Books, where I gave my talk on 'Great Political Disasters I Have Known'.

Wednesday 24 January

A man came to see me today who recounted a recent exchange he had with Michael Howard.

He: 'What do you think of Theresa May?'

MH: 'I don't know her. Nobody does.'

Wednesday 24 January

A reporter from the *Financial Times* has infiltrated a vulgar, men-only event at the Dorchester which, although it raised large amounts for charity, also appears to involve a good deal of misbehaviour towards young female hostesses. Result: an enormous hoo-ha. Great Ormond Street Children's Hospital immediately announced it would be not only refusing £500,000 they were expecting to help fund a new intensive care ward for chronically sick children but also returning all previous donations, which apparently amount to about £2 million.

Friday 26 January

The fallout from the alpha male event at the Dorchester continues. The organisation behind the event has been wound up. The Charities Commission has announced an investigation. A huge bout of what has become known as 'virtue signalling' under way. Politicians are jumping up and down; children's charities due to benefit from the £2 million raised are vying with each other to demonstrate feminist purity. One small charity is said to have laid off three staff members because, having rejected donations from this tainted source, it can no longer pay their wages. I know I shall get into trouble for even thinking this aloud, but what sort of world are we living in when the interests of chronically sick and deprived children are swept aside in a tide of feminist outrage? If no one in this country wants their money, I suggest the organisers give it to those trying to help the desperate Rohingya children on the Burma–Bangladesh border.

Saturday 27 January

For the first time since we moved here five years ago I bought a copy of the *Northumberland Gazette*, our local newspaper. There is a touching innocence about it compared to most local papers, which are a parade of crime and underclass mayhem. The following paragraph, reporting the monthly meeting of Wooler Parish Council, caught my eye. It is headed 'Four crimes since last meeting' and reads as follows:

> Police reported there had been four recorded crimes since the previous parish council meeting. There had been 'a heated exchange', a car's windscreen wiper had been damaged, crops had been damaged, likely by a poacher, and a racial slur had been written on a bench.

Sunday 28 January

To the students' union at Northumbria University in Newcastle to take part in a live edition of BBC 1's *The Big Questions*. The issues included alleged antisemitism in the Labour Party, safe injecting rooms for heroin addicts (which the Home Affairs Committee recommended under my chairmanship fifteen years ago) and pornography. I've always been nervous of these live audience shows ever since appearing on *Kilroy* some years ago, which consisted of a lot of people, egged on by the host, shouting at each other. This, however, turned out to be a good, balanced discussion, ably hosted by Nicky Campbell (one of the heroic six BBC male anchors who have voluntarily taken big salary cuts to bring them into line with their female equivalents). Predictably, it was antisemitism that generated most heat, although nobody misbehaved. Like most of our universities, Northumbria appears to have been swept by political correctness. There were three toilets: male, female and 'inclusive'. This last had a sign on the door with male, female and transgender symbols.

Monday 29 January

A long email from a Jewish woman, a former neighbour in Brixton Road, questioning my characterisation (on TV yesterday) of Israel as being in the process of constructing an 'apartheid' state. One can argue about the use of the word 'apartheid', but she defended just about everything, even going so far as to suggest that talk of mass casualties the last time Israel pulverised Gaza was 'Hamas propaganda'. It never ceases to disappoint that so many people of Jewish origin, who on most issues tend to be liberal and left of centre, have a complete blind spot when it comes to Israel. I remember sitting next to Maureen Lipman at the Man Booker Prize dinner a few years ago and she was perfectly sensible until Israel came into the conversation. Increasingly, it seems, many conflate criticism of Israel with antisemitism. Lately, it's become yet another stick with which to beat Corbyn. I take comfort, however, from the fact that a significant minority of Israelis are just as critical of their government as any of us.

Thursday 1 February

To Sunderland for a preview of a brilliant, uplifting BBC2 documentary about the city. Among those present, a local teacher who remarked that for the first time in her life she is encountering what she called 'fascism' from some of her pupils. She attributes this to the sentiments unleashed by Brexit.

Friday 2 February

Brexit, Brexit, Brexit. That's all the media seem to talk about these days. I wake up in the morning, turn on the *Today* programme and all the talk is of Brexit. I go to bed at night listening to the *News at Ten* and it's all Brexit. Theresa May has been in China for the past three days and, as all Prime Ministers do, took the lobby hacks with her and all they wanted to talk about was Brexit and how long she is likely to survive. Every day anonymous Brexiteers are calling for her head (what a miserable job being Prime Minister has become). Years more of this lie ahead.

Ngoc spotted two grey squirrels in the garden this morning. The reds haven't been seen for a month.

Saturday 3 February

'There was a time when Eurosceptics revered British democracy,' writes George Eaton in the current *New Statesman*. 'Its sovereign parliament, its independent judiciary, its neutral civil service. But the Brexit referendum created an alternative centre of power: the people. Rather than loyalty to the constitution, institutions are now judged according to their loyalty to the *demos* (nearly half of whom voted to Remain).'

Northamptonshire County Council has declared a state of emergency, banning all but statutory expenditure and announcing the possible sale of its headquarters. Is this the beginning of the long-awaited collapse of local government? Fortunately it is Tory-controlled; otherwise it would be dismissed as a consequence of Labour profligacy.

Sunday 4 February

An email re. Corbyn from Andrew Mitchell: 'If I'd bet you he'd be elected leader of the Labour Party, you'd have given me odds of 500/1; now what are the odds on him becoming PM?' Actually, I still think it unlikely – we are still not ahead despite the mess the Tories are in, – but you never know. Stranger things have happened in this topsy-turvy world.

Monday 5 February

Increasingly it becomes apparent that there are two John McDonnells: the one who pops up from time to time on the *Today* programme and the *Andrew Marr Show* being calm, reasonable, self-deprecating, moderate even. And the other, who when addressing meetings of the converted behind closed doors clearly has a problem with parliamentary democracy. This weekend, in the wake of a recent incident at the University of the West of England in which Jacob Rees-Mogg was shouted down by a bunch of masked, hooded Momentumists, someone has dug out a clip of McDonnell saying, 'I want to be in a situation where no Tory MP … can show their face anywhere in public without being challenged by direct action.' It is unclear when it was recorded or when, but, needless to say, the Tories are enthusiastically peddling it around the Twittersphere.

Saturday 10 February

To Chillingham for dinner with Humphry and Katharine Wakefield and half a dozen aristos. An enjoyable evening, but an undercurrent of unease about the prospect of a Corbyn government. 'Is he a communist?' someone asked. She added, 'My parents suffered badly under communism.' I did my best to explain that Jeremy is modest, down to earth and more green than red, but it didn't cut much ice. The fact that he was so keen on the Chávez regime in Venezuela was cited as evidence for the prosecution. Home at midnight through driving rain and sleet and flooded lanes.

Thursday 15 February

Headline in today's *Sun*: 'CORBYN AND THE COMMIE SPY: Shock Claims in Secret File – "Briefed" Evil Regime'. Apparently Jeremy some years ago was visited at the House of Commons on a couple of occasions by a Czech diplomat who unsurprisingly turned out to be an intelligence officer. The story appears to be based on an anodyne report from the archives of the old Czech security service. Quite where has come from is unclear, though a professor connected to an organisation calling itself the Oxford Intelligence Group is quoted. Usual suspects up to usual tricks, I guess.

Saturday 17 February

Today's headlines: 'Corbyn was Cold War source says Czech spy' (*Telegraph*). 'Corbyn "the Collaborator"' (*Mail*). The *Mail*'s story suggests he was 'a paid informant', which I would have thought was actionable. The obvious question arises: what possible use would Corbyn, who for the first thirty years of his time in Parliament was a man of absolutely no influence and entirely without access to any secrets, have been to an East European intelligence agent?

Sunday 18 February

The silly season has come early this year. 'Corbyn's Soviet [*sic*] spy links should be investigated by Parliament' (*Express*). Today's *Telegraph* has upped the ante: 'Czech agent claims fifteen Labour MPs met spies'. Just like old times. Meanwhile, in the Czech Republic, where higher standards of reporting prevail, the story is beginning to unravel. The head of the Czech Security Services Archive is quoted as saying that Corbyn was neither a spy nor a collaborator and that if he had been, the records of his meetings with a Czech diplomat who, unknown to him, worked for the Czech security service would have been filed elsewhere. The agent himself, one Jan Sarkocy, is making increasingly improbable claims. His latest is that the Czechs funded Bob Geldof's Live Aid concert. Even the most gullible *Sun* reader may have trouble swallowing that one. On the spur of the moment I devoted several hours to tapping out 2,400 words on Labour and the Red Menace, using this latest nonsense as a peg, which I will offer to the *London Review of Books*.

Wednesday 21 February

Corbyn spy mania has reached new levels of insanity. The focus has now switched to East Germany, where Jeremy apparently went on a motorcycle holiday in 1977. 'Corbyn urged to reveal his Stasi file' is the lead in today's *Telegraph*. Even though the Germans are saying there isn't one. Meanwhile Jan Sarkocy, the former Czech agent who started all this, is making wilder and wilder claims. His latest is that fifteen Labour MPs were paid up to £10,000 to meet Eastern bloc spies. John McDonnell, who wasn't even in Parliament at the time, is said to have met a KGB agent in, of all places, Guildford. The Tories meanwhile are shamelessly demanding select committee inquiries. One has even libellously compared Corbyn to Kim Philby. I suspect that even those making these claims don't believe them. They just hope that if they go on spraying mud, enough of it will stick, and I am sure it will. Today's *Guardian* quotes Radek Schovánek, an analyst with the Czech defence ministry, as calling Sarkocy a 'liar'. He goes on, 'I personally don't like Corbyn. I'm Roman Catholic and conservative, but I think we have to defend people against a lie.'

Saturday 24 February

The *London Review of Books* is running my piece on Corbyn spy mania, which is being much retweeted. The good news is that, faced with a threat of libel action, one foolish young Tory MP has issued a grovelling apology to Jeremy, along with solicitor's costs and a donation to charity. At last a fightback.

Wednesday 28 February

To Parliament for lunch with Bruce Grocott, one of a handful of Labour peers who are Brexiteers. He takes the view that the governing classes are hopelessly out of touch with the common man and that Brexit was the latter's revenge. 'Despite agreement among the leaders of all parties, most commentators and just about everyone who was university-educated, the people came to a different conclusion.' On the recent allegations of sexual harassment in Parliament, he thought, like me, that we were in for another feeding frenzy, akin to the great expenses meltdown. 'That's what the media were hoping for, but I was surprised how little of it there was.'

Later, half an hour with Mr Speaker Bercow, who continues boldly to assert the primacy of Parliament over the executive. Only yesterday he delivered a memorable bollocking to a minister who was getting above herself and when the Chancellor of the Exchequer, who was seated beside her, raised an eyebrow he was told to 'stick to his abacus'. He told me proudly that, thus far in his reign, he has granted 439 urgent questions, compared to only a handful granted by his predecessors. That, plus the absence of a government with an overall majority, has completely altered the relationship between Parliament and the executive. No wonder most Tories loathe him, although a couple remarked to me that they had changed their minds about him on account of his defence of the rights of backbenchers.

Afterwards, having an hour to spare, I took coffee in the atrium of Portcullis House, which was crowded with staffers but scarcely any MPs – at four o'clock on a Wednesday. Increasingly, so far as Parliament is concerned, Members are on a two-day week. They arrive at lunchtime Monday and depart after Prime Minister's Questions on a Wednesday. For the rest of the week the chamber is almost dead. The absence of votes and the introduction of so-called 'family-friendly' hours have killed most evening sessions, with the result that ministers no longer bother to socialise with backbenchers. Unless they are making statements or answering questions, most just stay in their departments, complete their boxes and return to either their homes or their lodgings. The evening economy of the building has all but collapsed. And this despite the best efforts of Speaker Bercow to liven up the place. If MPs don't take Parliament seriously, why should anyone else?

This evening to Islington, where I dined with Andrew Mitchell, much in demand recently, being one of the few Tories willing to speak up in favour of overseas aid. He is also a closet admirer of Jeremy Corbyn, who, he thinks, will become Prime Minister. Theresa May, he says, is competent, hard-working and good at mastering detail 'but has not a sliver of leadership in her DNA'.

Thursday 1 March

To the George Hotel at Lichfield, once upon a time represented in Parliament by a Major-General Sir James d'Avigdor-Goldsmid, a magnificent ruling-class specimen of whom it was remarked that 'if there was a canal in Lichfield, he'd sail a gunboat up it'. I am to perform the local literary festival tomorrow. Icy winds from Siberia are bringing more snow. It is being dubbed the Beast from the East. A great British panic is under way.

Friday 2 March

An email from Mrs Very Big Boss, who says that there has been more snow at Callaly and that I should not attempt to travel home. It ends: 'Listen to me for ONCE.' The bulletins are full of horror stories about people spending the night in cars and trains. Sadly for the festival organisers, a number of authors had heeded the warnings and cancelled. Much to my surprise, however, I had a more or less full house and sold a reasonable number of books. I then set out on the long trek home.

Saturday 3 March

A mile short of home the road was under several feet of snow and the digger trying to clear it had broken down. Nothing for it but to head back to Whittingham and try the lane to the north gate, which, happily, had been cleared. So, home by 3 p.m. after a 26-hour journey involving four trains, one bus, one taxi and a short hitch-hike. I am due to go south again on Tuesday.

Sunday 4 March

Icicles dripping from gutters. Desperate blackbirds hovering around the feeder in the hope of catching seed spilled by the smaller birds. A buzzard swoops in an unsuccessful attempt to catch one for breakfast, sending the smaller birds scuttling for shelter in the bamboo. I spent an hour carving a path from the gates to the top of the steps, the snow so compacted that I had to cut it out in blocks like those with which Eskimos build their igloos. An email from the Speaker's office inviting me to give a talk about *Hinterland* in Speaker's House.

Monday 5 March

A ghostly grey mist hangs over the valley, obscuring the hills behind the mansion. The snow, although still deep, is beginning to recede. Every-where the sound of dripping water. We walked down the lane to the Mains for my weekly game of table tennis with John Nicholls and this afternoon I walked a five-mile circuit through Whittingham, snow drifts on the south road still piled up to eight feet high; the fields a vast, white panorama, broken only by hedgerows and woodland. An email from the *Sunday Mirror* asking me to expand from 800 to 1,200 words a piece they commissioned some time ago for a feature they are doing on the deep state and how it might react to a Corbyn government. A later email adds, 'but not too much about the media, please!' What sensitive flowers they are.

Tuesday 6 March

As the snow melts, so come the floods. The stream is a raging torrent of muddy water crashing through the estate, spilling across footpaths and into the lakes. The lawn behind the mansion has been transformed into a huge icy lake. The pipe bridge has disappeared under water and the other bridges are threatened. Remarkably, the snowdrops are resurfacing, still flowering and none the worse for having been buried this last week. Fortunately the roads are passable.

Wednesday 7 March

A former KGB agent living in Salisbury, who came to the UK as part of a prisoner swap, and his daughter have apparently been poisoned by nerve gas.

Monday 12 March

To the Lakes for the Words by the Water festival, my fifth appearance

The 2011 Man Booker judges. *Left to right*: Matthew d'Ancona, Stella Rimington, CM, Gaby Wood, Susan Hill and Ion Trewin. We did have one advantage over our critics: we had actually read the books.

Standing in for the chancellor at the University of Sunderland. My message to the newly graduated: 'Remember, there is more to life than shopping.'

In debate with Alastair Campbell.

Star of stage and screen. On set with the stars of *Secret State*. I thought they might make me a backbench MP or, who knows, even a minister. Instead they made me a vicar. *Left to right*: Charles Dance, CM, Gina McKee and Gabriel Byrne.

A poster advertising Michael Chaplin's play based on the diaries, which made its way to London's West End.

By Tony Benn's grave at Stansgate on the day his ashes were interred.

ABOVE The 2017 election: peak Corbyn. I have known Jeremy for forty years. He would have been a hopeless Prime Minister, but he is a thoroughly decent human being.

© Jeff J. Mitchell/Getty Images

LEFT John McDonnell: one can't help feeling that beneath that carefully cultivated benign exterior, he is drawing up lists of those to be shot on day one of the revolution.

© Hollie Adams/Getty Images

© Leon Neal/Getty Images

Keir Starmer, taking the knee and flying the flag. Singing Corbyn's praises and then denouncing him. No bandwagon unclimbed upon.

Before and after: my walled garden in Northumberland, as seen on *Gardeners' World*.

Six times I have filled
the big tent at Edinburgh.
The political meeting
is not dead. It has
merely transferred
to the literary festival.

Sir Humphry Wakefield
in his natural habitat:
'In twenty years I shall
be one of the ghosts.'

My Learned Friend John
Field, late of Westminster
School: 'I am reading
cantos of Byron's Don
Juan aloud to the cats …
They haven't yet objected.'

The Lord of Chaos, Boris Johnson. In the words of fellow Tory Andrew Mitchell, 'Boris is like the James Bond villain who quits the sinking craft in his escape pod, stroking his white cat, leaving the rest of us to clear up the mess he's left behind.'

Prince Philip: 'Charm is a greatly overrated virtue.' Whatever opinion one has of him, it is impossible to withhold a grudging respect from someone who considers ninety-six an appropriate age to retire.

The beautiful Sarah Mullin marries the handsome Nick Hamilton.

The Tiny Lord and his entourage.

Emma Mullin (aka The Small Intellectual) and her dad.

Outside the Old Bailey after a judge refused an application by West Midlands Police for an order under the Terrorism Act obliging me to disclose sources in the Birmingham pub bombings case.

Ngoc and I at the garden gate.

Over and out. Elderly Has-Been celebrates his seventy-fifth birthday at the Ship Inn, Newton-by-the-Sea, Northumberland.

there. Among those at dinner, Phil Collins, who used to write speeches for Tony Blair and has a regular column in *The Times*. Like just about every other pundit, myself included, he was wrong about the outcome of the last election, but he thinks we might have reached peak Corbyn. So do I.

Tuesday 13 March
Lyzzick Hotel

A warm, clear day, the first for some time. I listened to Phil Collins talking about his book on great speeches and then took a stroll up Catbells with its fine views over Newlands Valley, Derwent Water and the snow-streaked fells beyond. This evening I delivered my 'Remarkable Rise of Jeremy Corbyn' speech to a packed house (about 400 people). It went down well, but book sales were a disappointment. What appeared to be a triumph was in fact an abject failure – from my point of view, at least.

Wednesday 14 March

The government have announced the expulsion of twenty-three Russian 'spies' in retaliation for the attempted poisoning of the former KGB agent and his daughter in Salisbury. It isn't clear that it was officially authorised, but the Russians have made no attempt investigate or to account for the incident, instead brazenly painting themselves as victims of a Western conspiracy. Corbyn under fire for failing to join in the big bout of me-too-ism about Russia.

Thursday 15 March

Headline in today's *Daily Mail*: 'Corbyn the Kremlin stooge'.

A foolish Labour backbencher has fuelled the fire by tabling a motion endorsing the government's expulsion of Russian diplomats. It is aimed at Corbyn, of course, not Putin. About twenty Labour members have signed. A poll suggests that Labour has slipped three points. Meanwhile Gavin Williamson, our flyweight Defence Secretary, a bigger embarrassment to HMG than Boris Johnson, made a speech telling the Russians to 'shut up and go away'.

Friday 16 March

Corbyn has an article in today's *Guardian* attempting to repair the damage from his lacklustre response to Theresa May's robust statement on Wednesday. He belatedly endorses the expulsion of Russian diplomats and makes the reasonable point that previous bouts of me-too-ism, all supported by intelligence, have got us into calamitous wars in Iraq, Libya and Afghanistan. It may well be that the Russian state is not directly responsible for the incident in Salisbury, but nothing can get us round the fact that the Russians have yet to offer *any* serious explanation as to how their nerve gas came to find its way to Wiltshire. They have a record of lies and prevarication on a range of other issues, too – the systematic doping of their athletes, the shooting down of a Malaysian airliner over Ukraine, and at least one other poisoning. Meanwhile a second Russian exile has been found dead, allegedly strangled and his death made to look like suicide. Previous cases of dead Russians, of which there have been rather a lot (fourteen in all), are being reopened.

Tuesday 20 March

Tremendous hoo-ha over Cambridge Analytica, a tech company which has mined a huge amount of Facebook data and allegedly used it to manipulate elections, including, it is claimed, the last US presidential election and the Brexit referendum. Interesting, but I can't get too excited. Who needs Cambridge Analytica when we have the Murdoch press, the Harmsworths, the Barclay brothers and Richard Desmond? An online article by Brian Cathcart,[*] based on an interview with a man who used to bug telephones and bank accounts for the *Sunday Times*, alleges that the entire Blair Cabinet was targeted.

Wednesday 21 March

After fifteen years and 150,000 miles of loyal service, my old Toyota has finally given up the ghost. I drove to Hexham for a meeting of the National Park Authority and the gearbox went into meltdown half a mile short of my destination. It now sits, forlorn and immobile, in the yard behind

---

[*] A professor at the University of Kingston and a founder of Hacked Off, an organisation that campaigns against abuses of press freedom.

the Old Motor House in Rothbury. Russell, the mechanic, advises that it is not worth repairing. No sympathy from Ngoc, who has been telling me for years that we need a new car.

Thursday 22 March–Sunday 25 March

To Amsterdam. A belated seventieth birthday present from My Two Best Friends. We are staying, courtesy of Airbnb, in the upper two storeys of a maisonette with vertiginous stairs in a townhouse in the upmarket Jordaan area, a cross between Venice and Hampstead. We whiled away many pleasant hours wandering the canal paths, catching the occasional whiff of dope. Everywhere museums of this and that… tulips, cheeses… even a Museum of Bags and Purses. Here, as in Hanoi forty years ago, the bicycle is king. People of all shapes and sizes pedal (for the most part) gracefully along lanes that are almost vehicle-free, save for trams. In front of the main railway station, a four-storey bicycle park containing perhaps 10,000 bikes. We spent a pleasant day in Delft and in Amsterdam visited the Rijksmuseum and Rembrandt's house. On the last evening I went alone (there being only one ticket available) to Anne Frank's house. The tiny room she shared with her sister, featureless except for pictures cut from newspapers of her favourite film stars, still exactly as she left them. Pencil marks on a wall, where every few months her father, Otto, record-ed her height (she grew thirteen centimetres in their two years of con-finement). Standing in that small space, looking at that bright little face, I find it hard to think of her without welling up. She and her family so nearly made it. They were on the last train that left Holland for Auschwitz and even then she survived until February 1945. Were she alive today, she would be eighty-eight.

Monday 26 March

Another anti-Corbyn feeding frenzy under way. This one triggered by a letter from the Board of Deputies of British Jews accusing Labour of 'an institutional failure to tackle antisemitism' and describing Jeremy as 'a figurehead for an antisemitic political culture based on obsessive hatred of Israel'. By evening Jeremy had issued a long conciliatory letter, offering to meet with Jewish leaders, but I doubt whether anything he can say or do will appease them. This evening rival groups of Jews – pro- and anti-Corbyn – were demonstrating outside Parliament. Several of the usual suspects (and one or two who are not) in the parliamentary party were on parade, stirring the pot. All very unfortunate and undoubtedly damaging. Although Jeremy is no antisemite, he does if truth be told bring with him considerable baggage which is being assiduously mined with a view to inflicting maximum damage.

Tuesday 27 March

On the radio this morning, a scientist calmly explaining that it is necessary to colonise the moon and Mars in order to preserve the human species in the event of extinction. Give me extinction any day.

Saturday 30 March

Out of the blue an email from the journalist Tom Bower, enclosing an article by Howard Jacobson in the *Jewish Chronicle* which cites a recent tweet of mine in defence of Corbyn. Bower, a dangerous man who specialises in hatchet-job biographies, is presently writing a book on Corbyn which will no doubt be serialised by the *Mail* in due course. A month ago he asked me for an interview and I politely declined. Today's exchange was follows:

CM: 'Thanks for drawing this to my attention. Toxic subject. Wish I hadn't got involved.'

TB: 'The problem is you would not have said the same about Muslims or Blacks, therefore it is assumed you are an antisemite.'

CM: 'Can't stop people assuming whatever they want to assume, but I am content to be judged by those who know me.'

TB: '…I have thought about your reply. The remarkable feature is that you do not deny you are an antisemite.'

CM: 'Of course I am not an antisemite. What I am not keen on is the Tom Bower school of journalism – of which this appears to be an example. That's why I declined to see you.'

And there, for the time being, the matter rests.

Saturday 31 March

Israeli snipers have shot dead sixteen Palestinians and inflicted life-changing injuries on many other foolish youths who were demonstrating and throwing missiles over the border fence between Gaza and Israel. The Foreign Office has issued the usual bland little statement urging everyone to be nice to each other, but hardly anyone on the Labour side dares say anything for fear of being accused of antisemitism. Jeremy, meanwhile, is reduced to issuing a fatuous video wishing the Jewish community a happy Passover.

Sunday 1 April

Headline in today's *Sunday Times*: 'EXPOSED: CORBYN'S HATE FACTORY'. Surely, if one were interested in hate factories, one need look no further than the Murdoch empire, the Harmsworth Lie Machine or Richard Desmond's odious *Express*?

Monday 2 April

The great film director Stephen Frears and his lady friend whom I first met at a festival in Ireland last year called in. I had been intending to give them a tour of the estate, but as it was snowing we just sat by the fire and talked. I asked about the meaning of that scene in *The Queen* where she come across a great stag which is later shot by a hunter on a neighbouring estate, but he didn't seem to know beyond saying that the stag, like her, was an imperial figure. He has just made a three-part drama for BBC on the scandal that brought down Jeremy Thorpe which will be showing shortly.

Tuesday 3 April

Corbyn under fire again this morning. This time for meeting the wrong type of Jews. He recently attended a Passover celebration in Islington with a Jewish organisation, some of whose members apparently take the heretical view that the present row is a cynical attempt by his political enemies to undermine him. Jon Lansman was on the radio this morning trying to douse the fire, conceding that Labour does have a problem with antisemitism and that it is larger than he had at first realised but calmly pointing out that criticism of Israel is not antisemitism. Jon, of course, has the great advantage that he's Jewish and therefore harder to shout down.

Saturday 7 April

Our neighbour Tony Henfrey, a former Conservative parliamentary candidate, came for supper. He remarked, apropos HS2 and Hinkley Point power station, 'Tory governments are at least as capable as Labour ones of pissing away large amounts of public money.' He also said that he thought Theresa May had consolidated her position and that he wouldn't be surprised if she led the Tories into the next election.

Wednesday 11 April

War drums beating again. Trump threatening fire and brimstone after the Syrians appear to have used chemical weapons in the final stages of a battle for the Damascus suburb of Douma last week. France and Britain keen to join in. May has consulted the Cabinet, but she is apparently reluctant to consult Parliament, presumably for fear of getting her fingers burned as Cameron did three years ago The Russians, as usual, are lying and blustering. Even so, it is far from clear what our objective should be. Few people now think that overthrowing Assad is a good idea given the catastrophic outcome of our previous adventures in the Middle East. This crisis has the added danger of a direct clash between the US and Russia. A dangerous moment.

Friday 13 April

Came across the following from the American poet Robert Lowell, quoted in an article by the late Christopher Hitchens: 'I am glad I was not a revolutionary when young, because it prevents me from becoming a reactionary bore in old age.'

Saturday 14 April

Awoke to the news that US, French and British forces have launched missile attacks on three targets in Syria, 'assessed' to be places where chemical weapons are stored. A much smaller operation than Trump's early rhetoric implied, suggesting that the few remaining adults in the regime (notably Defence Secretary Mattis) have prevailed. Fallout so far limited. Quite what difference this will make is unclear, beyond salving Western consciences. Several commentators have made the point that whether we like it or not, Assad, helped by the Russians and Iranians, has won – though with the country in ruins and a third of the population displaced, that depends, I suppose, on your definition of victory. The BBC's respected correspondent Frank Gardner went so far as to say this morning that 'without Russian intervention Damascus might have fallen to the jihadis'.

Thursday 19 April

To Kendal with fellow members of the National Park Authority to see what we might learn from our opposite numbers in the Lake District National Park. My star is high here, having been the minister who banned speed boating on Windermere. Like all national parks, the Lakes have had their funding cut by a third and are desperately trying to commercialise in order to make up the difference. Some of the schemes are a bit tacky, but, as the man in charge said, after years of cuts, 'we don't think the government is going to give us any more money, so we have no choice'. Among the plans, a scheme to launch its own currency, a Lake District 'pound', spendable in local businesses. I wish them well, but it seemed a bit of a scam to me since, as it was explained to us, much of the potential for profit is based on the hope that tourists will buy the currency but not spend it.*

Friday 20 April

Stonecross Manor Hotel, Kendal

Breakfast with Glen Sanderson, the charming and excellent chair of the Northumberland National Park Authority, who is also a Tory county councillor. He quizzed me about my erstwhile friends in high places. What did I think of Tony Blair, Peter Mandelson, David Cameron, Jeremy Corbyn, John McDonnell etc? I gave the nuanced replies I usually give

---

* The scheme was wound up after two years.

when the subject crops up at literary festivals, after which he said, 'Well done. You managed all that without being nasty about anyone.'

Wednesday 25 April

To Hexham for a meeting of the National Park Authority and then to Northumbria University to hear a talk by the north-east playwright Michael Chaplin about his father, Syd Chaplin, who was also a well-known regional writer. At supper afterwards I was approached by a professor of something or other who took my hand and said, 'Every Irishman must shake hands with Chris Mullin.' It is twenty-seven years since the Birmingham Six were released and still the warm glow lingers.

Friday 27 April

Awoke to find the little robin which follows me round the garden caught by a leg in the trap we have installed in the hope of catching rats which have tunnelled under the bird feeder. No choice but to kill the poor thing. Been feeling sick about it all day. The bloody rats, meanwhile, are keeping a low profile.

Saturday 28 April

To Hexham for the book festival, where I interviewed Alastair Campbell and Paul Fletcher, the latter a former Burnley footballer, who have together written a very readable thriller involving the IRA and a struggling football team with an alcoholic manager whose only chance of survival is to pull off a win against Chelsea in the FA Cup. Once we'd discussed the book, the conversation inevitably turned to Brexit and Corbyn. Alastair expressed despair about what he regarded as a complete absence of political leadership: Theresa May was embarked on Brexit, which she knew was against the national interest, and Labour under Corbyn incapable of challenging her. At one point he asked the audience, which was overwhelmingly composed of Remainers, to raise their hands if they thought May was doing a good job. No hand went up. Then he asked who thought Corbyn would make a better Prime Minister. Again, no hand went up. There, in a nutshell, is Labour's dilemma.

Still haunted by that little robin that I murdered yesterday and the thought that, instead of killing, I should have released it and given it a chance to survive on one leg.

Monday 30 April

With Ngoc to the Alnwick Castle garden, where we picnicked in the spectacular cherry orchard, which, underplanted with daffodils, is in full bloom. Disappointing local election results at a time when Labour should be rolling up the map if it is to stand a chance of winning a general election. Confirms my suspicion that we have reached peak Corbyn and if nothing changes, we are heading for yet another glorious defeat.

Sunday 6 May

To a somewhat upmarket literary festival at Dumfries House in Ayrshire, the Adam mansion rescued by the Prince of Wales just as it was on the point of being sold off. At lunch I briefly found myself sitting next to Judy Murray, mother of tennis champion Andy. She has a strong accent. 'I have to check on my appearance,' I understood her to say as she was leaving.

'*You* don't need to check on your appearance,' I responded.

What she had actually said was, 'I have to check on my parents.'

Friday 11 May

To Holy Island with Hélène Mulholland and Alan Simpson. Much to my disappointment, Lindisfarne Castle, although open, is still swathed in scaffolding and devoid of contents, replaced by a so-called art exhibition by an 'internationally acclaimed artist' which consists of oak frames draped with coloured blankets. Really, this is too much. There is no shortage of local artists, several living on the island, whose works they could have displayed. What are the National Trust playing at? I shall not set foot there again, until normal service is resumed, disgusted of Callaly writes…

Monday 14 May

In scenes reminiscent of Sharpeville, the Israelis have shot dead more than fifty Palestinians demonstrating against the border fence with Gaza on the day when the United States opened its new embassy in Jerusalem. Last night's television news also showed thousands of flag-waving Zionist zealots marching through the narrow streets of Jerusalem's Arab quarter intimidating residents, just as Unionist bands used to do when they marched through Belfast's Catholic ghettos.

Friday 18 May

At the entrance to Clapham Common Tube Station, a young homeless woman of about Emma's age, seated cross-legged on the pavement, displaying a piece of cardboard upon which was scribbled 'Help the Invisible'. It's true, the destitute are becoming invisible: they are to be found camped out in every high street, in alleyways and outside closed shopfronts, some too far gone to beg. At first it is a shocking sight, but after a while, one no longer sees them. A phenomena I first noted in Calcutta, nearly fifty years ago. How quickly they become the norm. In Calcutta, of course, they were families with children and it has not yet come to that here, but, who knows, it may do so in due course.

Sunday 20 May

To Heathrow, which I have managed to avoid for almost ten years, for a flight to Lyon. At the security counter a woman tipped out the contents of my wash bag and put them in a transparent plastic bag. 'Next time you'll know what to do,' she said.

'Yes,' I replied, 'not travel from Heathrow.' She looked hurt and I felt a bit of a cad. She had not been in the least officious.

David Fraser met me at Lyon and we drove up into the mountains, where he has an apartment.

Monday 21 May
Les Allues

From David's balcony, a view across a deep valley to forested hills interspersed with tiny hamlets, beneath snow-capped mountains. Today is a public holiday and just about everything is *fermé*. Meribel, further up the valley, a town almost entirely dedicated to skiing, is also well and truly *fermé*, indeed almost a ghost town. Knight Frank have an office in the main street, offering a clue as to the type of clientele to be found here during the season. We walked up the hill behind David's apartment to the Col de la Lune (1,785m), past the Refuge du Christ, where there is talk (God forbid) of building a helicopter landing pad to enable fat cats to dine without the inconvenience of having to walk up from the valley. From the Col we sat for a while peering into a neighbouring valley and then made our way back down.

Tuesday 22 May
Les Allues

We drove to the end of the valley and walked up a steep track to the Refuge du Saut (2,126m), the last few kilometres slipping and sliding through snow, jagged mountains towering above us, streams plunging vertically into the roaring river. Marmots, emerging from hibernation, bounding over rocks; last year's cowpats and the occasional footprint emerging from beneath the receding snow. In places where the snow had receded, the ground was covered by a carpet of small white crocuses. The refuge was also *fermé*. No sign that anyone else has made it up there so far this year. At least that's what we thought until a lone skier emerged from a misty cleft high above us and disappeared down the valley in the direction from which we had come.

Wednesday 23 May
Les Allues

Awoke to a vast white cloud drifting out of the opposite valley and into ours, as though emanating from a huge explosion. Fortunately it had cleared by the time we set out up a precipitous road to a hamlet, from where we followed a steep track zigzagging up to the Refuge de la Glière (2,010m). The track was strewn with rubble from recent rockfalls and in places blocked by mini glaciers. Above us rutting ibexes dislodged stones, one of which just missed my head. We met no one all day and, as before, the refuge itself was snowbound. We ate our sandwiches watching melting snow tumbling out of the mists on the mountain above us, streaking into the river far below.

Thursday 24 May
Les Allues

Staying below the snowline, we crossed the valley and followed a steep path up through the woods to distant hamlets visible from David's balcony. Unlike those in Les Allues and Méribel, most of the houses here are weather-beaten and show signs of being occupied all year round, each with its store of logs and adjacent vegetable patch. A glimpse of Alpine life before the coming of the skiing fraternity.

Friday 25 May

We drove to Lyon Airport, returned the car and took the Métro into town, then via the funicular railway up to the basilica and down through gardens to the old city. My memories of Lyon are not good. I was last here in 1966, hitch-hiking to Rome on a shoestring budget. My night en route was spent shivering, *sans* sleeping bag, in a small park by the river and on the way back, already having spent a night without sleep near the top of Mont Cenis and suffering from sunstroke, I was locked out of the youth hostel by the fascist in charge, so exhausted that I was hallucinating. Happily, today's visit to this beautiful city went without a hitch. In the evening we flew back to London and treated ourselves to a pizza in Notting Hill.

Saturday 26 May

My annual general meeting with Claes Bratt, who has recently arrived from Bangkok. We completed a circuit of the royal parks, putting the world to rights and lunching in the cafe at the end of the Serpentine. On the north side of the lake a massive piece of floating junk art is in the process of construction, consisting of 7,500 red, mauve and blue barrels and rising twenty metres. The author of this monster, I hesitate to call him an artist, is a Bulgarian called Christo whose previous works include wrapping the Reichstag in polypropylene. Asked what it's all about, he is quoted as saying, 'I cannot explain my art. Everything I do is irrational and useless.' I'll second that. What I don't understand is why we indulge these people.

Wednesday 30 May–Saturday 2 June

To north Devon to stay with Ruth Winstone and then to Ilminster to speak at the local festival. On the way to the station in Barnstaple, Ruth took me to the vast pannier market, which is still flourishing despite the havoc wreaked on local high streets by the ubiquitous out-of-town shopping centres. It was here forty-eight years ago that I stood alongside Jeremy Thorpe at the declaration of the 1970 general election result. Afterwards we went up to the mayor's parlour and waved to the crowd from the window. I remember little of it, except that the local newspaper the next day featured a picture of two girls fighting, the only time in my life that I have ever been fought over by women.

The Italians have elected a populist government with a programme which includes a pledge to expel half a million migrants.

Monday 4 June

To the doctor in search of an answer to the early morning bouts of dizziness that have afflicted me of late. He asked me to lie down and twisted my head to one side, causing the world to start spinning so rapidly that I pleaded with him to stop. Apparently it has something to do with crystals in my inner ear. He thinks it will go away after a while, but I am not so sure.

Wednesday 6 June

House of Fraser have announced that they are closing thirty of their high street stores; this follows a recent announcement from Marks & Spencer that they are closing 100 of theirs. All part of the long hollowing out of our town centres caused by the rise of online shopping and decades of planning approvals for out-of-town stores. How did the planners think it was going to end? Or didn't they think?

Thursday 7 June

To Belfast for a literary festival. The taxi driver who drove me into town from the airport remarked that he was too young to remember the Troubles and that he and people of his generation wanted nothing to do with sectarianism. I am not so sure. Stormont has been suspended for months and local politics is dominated by issues such as whether the Union Jack should be flown from Belfast City Hall and whether the Irish language should be part of the school curriculum.

Tuesday 12 June

Donald Trump and Kim Jong-un have met in Singapore and Trump has declared a great triumph, though it is hard to see that anything concrete has been achieved. On past form, however, they may have done enough to earn themselves a Nobel Peace Prize.

Saturday 16 June

Peter Oborne in today's *Daily Mail* has this say about our beloved leader:

> When the history books come to be written, and the path to Brexit analysed, Jeremy Corbyn's role will be seen as crucial. Historians will recall how he took on and defeated his powerful internal opposition, including his shadow Brexit Secretary, Keir Starmer, and Tony Benn's son Hilary. Not all Brexiteers may like Jeremy Corbyn. But this weekend they have good reason to raise a toast of thanks to the grizzled Labour leader.

Hmmm. That's praise he could well do without.

This afternoon, to Melrose for my favourite literary festival to deliver my 'Remarkable Rise of Jeremy Corbyn' talk. I have toned it down a bit as I fear the shine has come off our Jeremy in the year since I drafted it. We are way past peak Corbyn now. Instead Labour is trapped in a twilight zone from which there is no obvious escape. History tells us that Labour usually needs to lose three or four elections before a little light comes on and thus far it has only lost two and a half.

Saturday 23 June

To Blagdon to celebrate Matt Ridley's sixtieth birthday. A party like no other – champagne, canapés, a Northumberland piper, a sit-down meal for 430 guests, cabaret, music, dancing. Everyone accommodated in a series of marquees arranged around the reflective pool on the south lawn. The forty tables bore labels such as Pessimists, Optimists, Lost Causes, Free Trade, Brexit, No Brexit, Trump, No Trump... I sat next to a man who remarked that his wife had been one of a party of tourists I took to Tibet in 1980. 'What do you do?' I enquired. 'I was a photographer,' he said modestly. 'And now?' 'I manage a large house in North Yorkshire.' He turned out to be the reigning member of the Howard family and the property in question was Castle Howard, one of the country's great treasure houses. Among the Brexiteer elite David Davis, Archie Hamilton, Owen Paterson, Bernard Jenkin. Plus Nick Soames, a Remainer, and the sole representative from the Labour side, my friend Joyce Quin. We were driven home after midnight in a minibus organised by our generous neighbours at Lorbottle Hall, a streak of midsummer light still illuminating the horizon.

Wednesday 27 June

Given that we appear to have reached peak Corbyn, I have taken to asking former parliamentary colleagues of all parties to name any credible alternative, bearing in mind that such a candidate has to be acceptable to both the Parliamentary Labour Party and the membership as whole, not to mention the electorate. Emily Thornberry, my best guess, attracts surprisingly little support. Several people mentioned Angela Rayner, who wasn't there in my day. Some older guard still cling to the idea that Yvette Cooper is electable, but I don't buy that. Hilary Benn and Alan Johnson are often mentioned, but only as evidence of what might have been. Chuka Umunna's name also features, but he is far too smooth and Blairite to win support from the wider membership. Who knows, someone may come out of nowhere, but we still have a mountain to climb. This afternoon, a visit from the Cottage Garden Society, mainly ladies of a certain age. I enjoy showing people the garden. What's the point of having a beautiful garden if you don't share it?

Thursday 28 June

No rain for almost two weeks. Temperature in the high twenties. Computer temporarily kaput. Nothing to be done except to sit in the shade and read. These past two days I have read Robert Harris's *Munich* and the latest John le Carré, *A Legacy of Spies*. Aged eighty-seven, the master is still on good form. In the evening, much watering. The soil so dry that you can hear it drinking.

Sunday 1 July

The heatwave continues. The Lancashire moors are on fire, enveloping Manchester and surrounding towns in great clouds of smoke. In Belfast and the Home Counties there is talk of hosepipe bans. At Callaly we are fortunate in having our own water supply, which thus far shows no signs of drying up, though the water in the burn is lower than ever.

Thursday 5 July

To Sunderland for a dinner in honour of the departing vice-chancellor. I am to give the graduation speech at the degree ceremony tomorrow. The event takes place in the stadium and I usually open my remarks with a line about the magnificence of the stadium not being matched by the quality of the football, but after two successive relegations the situation is beyond a joke. A note from the university's director of marketing says, 'The vice-chancellor has requested that we refrain from mentioning Sunderland AFC and their recent performance please!' Earlier I called on Julie Elliott, my successor, who like many of her colleagues, especially the women, is on the receiving end of threats from internet trolls. Members of an outfit called National Action are currently on trial at the Old Bailey for allegedly planning to murder Rosie Cooper, a Lancashire MP. One had even bought a machete with which to do the deed. 'I am not worried about the trolls,' says Julie, 'but my fear is they might prompt some unstable person to do something stupid.' Brexit has made it worse, she says. 'It has given people permission to say things they would never have dared say previously.' Apparently a mob recently went in search of Julie's home address, which fortunately they didn't find. The police are taking it seriously.

Friday 6 July

To the Stadium of Light, home of Sunderland's benighted football team, where I stood in for chancellor Steve Cram at the graduation ceremony. I shook more than 500 hands and made two speeches, dutifully avoiding all mention of football. The morning shift consisted mainly of young Arabs, Asians and Africans graduating in technical subjects such as computers and cyber security; the afternoon of young local women graduating in subjects such as social work, childcare and primary education. What shocked me, as I watched them wobbling across the stage, was how obese so many of them are. How can they be role models for those in their care if they can't manage their own lives? Meanwhile the Cabinet have been meeting in conclave at Chequers, where Theresa May is attempting to sell them her plan for a Brexit that doesn't crash the economy. They emerged this evening having agreed a plan which seems to involve signing up to the EU rules for goods but not for services. Now all she has to do is sell it to the Tory Party and the Europeans.

Saturday 7 July

It is reported that Cabinet ministers at yesterday's meeting had their phones confiscated on arrival to prevent leaks. Exactly as I envisaged in *The Friends of Harry Perkins* when the shadow Cabinet assembles in a country house on the South Downs to discuss Labour's proposed U-turn on EU membership. A scene I wrote only last Thursday.

Sunday 8 July

Our annual garden party. Tables, chairs, crockery begged and borrowed from neighbours. Ngoc was up at 5.30 and produced an enormous spread, on the leftovers from which we shall be feasting for the next week. I talked weddings with Barbara Baker-Cresswell. She said that on the way along the A66 to her wedding at Catterick in a chauffeur-driven Rolls-Royce, the driver had a sudden heart attack and died at the wheel. She had to lean over the dead driver and steer while her father climbed onto the passenger seat and switched off the engine. Even so, the car carried on for some distance. They laid out the body behind a hedge and her father stayed with it while she (in her wedding dress) hitched a lift to the church at Catterick, stopping at Scotch Corner to dial 999. Her father didn't make it to the church in time and she had to be walked down the aisle by her brother. Anyway, it doesn't seem to have been an inauspicious omen. She and Charles have been happily married for fifty-six years. Pity about the poor chauffeur though.

Monday 9 July

Awoke to the news that Brexit negotiator David Davis has resigned on the grounds that the strategy painstakingly hammered out at Chequers last week gives too much away too soon. It remains to be seen what damage, if any, this inflicts on Theresa May. To the BBC at Newcastle to be interviewed by David Aaronovitch about how the Establishment is likely to react to a Corbyn government. I am slightly wary of Aaronovitch, who makes a living debunking leftist myths for readers of *The Times* and who I fear wants to present me as a conspiracy theorist, but he was on his best behaviour today and the interview went well. Home in time to hear that Foreign Secretary Boris Johnson has resigned.

Wednesday 11 July

'Is Theresa May guilty of treason? Plenty of readers think so. Politicians would be wise to listen up'. Headline over a characteristically barmy op-ed article in today's *Daily Telegraph*. British politics is turning nasty. As someone pointed out, this is the sentiment that led to the murder of poor Jo Cox.

Friday 13 July

Donald Trump, on his much-anticipated state visit, has given an interview to *The Sun* in which he rubbishes Theresa May's Brexit strategy, sings the praises of Boris Johnson and pours cold water on the prospect of a post-Brexit trade deal with the US. Amusing to hear ministers, notably Alan Duncan, on the radio this morning trying to put a brave face on it. This evening to Fallodon, where Lucia and Mark Bridgeman hosted my *Hinterland* talk in aid of the hospice (we raised more than £1,200). Fallodon was once the home of the First World War Foreign Secretary Sir Edward Grey, and the London–Edinburgh main line railway runs across the estate, which in the good old days gave him the right to stop trains when he wanted to travel to London. Lucia gave me a copy of a remarkable handwritten letter, dated 22 September 1911, which Grey wrote to the Liberal Chief Whip regarding arrangements for Lloyd George to stay at Fallodon en route between Scotland and London. It reads as follows:

> My dear Elibank,
>
> Lloyd George can stop either the 12.50 or 7.45 from Edinburgh by telling the guard he is coming to me and wants to be put down at Fallodon station. I sent him full particulars by letter.
>
> As to going away – to catch the 10 o'clock to Newcastle on Sunday, he would have to leave here by 7.16 in the morning. That can be done, but isn't comfortable for him. If he prefers it, I will stop the midday express for him from Edinburgh on Sunday. It passes here about 2 o'clock and gets to London 9.40 p.m.
>
> But the most comfortable way is to go by night, which I am going to do on Sunday night. It means walking in to a sleeping berth here about 10 p.m. and getting out of it at King's Cross at 8 a.m. next morning.
>
> He can settle what he likes after he gets here.
>
> Yours sincerely,
>
> E Grey

He adds a postscript: 'To prevent any difficulty about stopping trains I enclose an order which Lloyd George can present at Berwick Station, where they know about my right of stopping trains at Fallodon.'

Those were the days.

Saturday 14 July

To dinner at Chillingham. I arrived early and whiled away fifteen minutes in the garden, the only sounds birdsong, the hum of insects and trickling water, with the last sun illuminating the castle. What makes this garden different from so many others is that the long herbaceous border against the crenelated wall is wide enough for flowers to be allowed to grow to their natural sizes, making the entire border larger than life, as though in some tropical rainforest. At dinner I sat next to Diana Cavendish, a great-great-granddaughter of Robert Peel. 'Of course,' she said apropos a fleeting mention of Attlee, 'his big mistake was not to abolish the public schools.' Hang on a minute, I thought. That's not a sentiment one hears very often around this table. I looked to see if the chandelier was swaying and it may have been. 'They are so divisive,' she added. 'If the middle classes had been obliged to send their children to state schools, they would have demanded better.' Someone commented on her elegant gown. 'I had it made for the film premiere,' she said. My ears pricked up.

'A film? What about?'

'Oh, my life – and that of my husband. He had polio.'

'Who played you?'

'Claire Foy.'

'The actress who played the Queen in that Netflix drama *The Crown*?'

'Yes, that's the one.'

When I got home, I googled her and sure enough there she was at a film premiere swathed in the same elegant gown as she had been wearing at this evening's dinner. Soon after they were married in the '50s, her husband contracted polio, became paralysed from the neck downwards and was confined to an iron lung. Far from letting this tragedy destroy their lives, they rose above it. In defiance of medical advice, she insisted on caring for him at home and they become campaigners for severely disabled victims of polio, who at that time were usually confined to hospital for life. Against the odds, he survived another thirty-four years. An uplifting story of unconditional love and steely determination overcoming unspeakable adversity. The film is called *Breathe*. I shall order a copy.

Sunday 15 July

Trump has departed for Helsinki, where he is due to meet Putin. General relief that he has gone, not least from Theresa May. She looked almost demob happy when she appeared on the *Andrew Marr Show* this morning. The drought continues. Apart from one or two light showers there has been no rain for weeks. No need for holidays in Tuscany; Tuscany has come to us. According to the radio, there has been no rain in London since 29 May.

Tuesday 17 July

The tree in our glasshouse has produced about twenty juicy peaches. We have been eating them every day this week.

Thursday 19 July

Another day, another Brexit scare. Today's bulletins report that the EU is preparing for the possibility that the UK may crash out without an agreement. A possibility that can't be entirely excluded, but where the EU is concerned there is a long history of scare stories which usually end with compromise after all-night negotiations that go to the wire. Keep calm and carry on, that's my motto. We harvested our first potatoes, beetroot and tomatoes and put up a net to protect our outdoor peaches from the birds.

Friday 20 July

Simon Jenkins in today's *Guardian* pours cold water on the latest bout of Brexit scare stories, which he labels 'Project Fear Mark 2'. If there is no agreement by the deadline, he says, we will simply revert to WTO rules and life will go on as normal. This evening, to dinner with the Vinsons and Frank Field, who is on his annual visit. Frank recounted how a television company had recently come to his flat to interview him and two of their cameras mysteriously blew. The most likely explanation is that his flat is bugged – probably as a result of a run-in he had with Robert Maxwell years ago. He was warned at the time to get it swept for bugs but never did.

Saturday 21 July

The long run of good weather has revived Mrs Very Big Boss's interest in gardening. Always a dangerous moment. Her opening line this morning was, 'I'll tell you what I am going to do and even if you say "no", I'll still do it.' She then set about cutting back the lady's mantle, which is still in bloom, and is threatening to do the same with the catmint.

Tuesday 24 July

An email from a Labour Party activist in south London inviting me to add my name to a campaign for the abolition of the monarchy. I declined on the grounds that were Labour daft enough to adopt such a policy, it would be the one cast-iron way to ensure election defeat. Plus, I don't believe there is a problem that needs fixing. President Boris, anyone? Be careful what you wish for.

Wednesday 25 July

Having no articles to write, books to review or engagements to fulfil, I am free to take advantage of this glorious weather (which surely cannot go on much longer), spending entire days out of doors. Usually I start with a little light gardening, cutting back, deadheading or trimming, and then retire to the shade of the summerhouse to read. Currently I am reading Alec Douglas-Home's autobiography. A more substantial figure than I ever realised, having been in office almost continuously from the early 1930s to the mid-1970s, once Prime Minister, twice Foreign Secretary, flipping between the Lords and the Commons. A one-nation Tory, many of his judgements are sound and generous, though occasionally naive or disingenuous. He seemed to think that the Russians were primarily responsible for sabotaging the 1954 Geneva Convention, thereby triggering the Vietnam War, whereas the Americans refused to sign and began sabotaging it before the ink was dry on the grounds that Ho Chi Minh would have won a free election. No excuse for not knowing: it's all in the Pentagon Papers, published several years before he wrote his book. Also, while laying the blame for the Cold War entirely on the Russians, he does not refer to the fact that in 1955 they withdrew from Austria in exchange for agreement that it should remain neutral and had earlier offered a similar deal on Germany which the Allies rejected. One curiosity: like many posh people of my acquaintance, he refers throughout to the Labour Party as the Socialists (with a capital S). Hardly ever, if at all, does he refer to Labour by its proper name, which dates back to the party's foundation in 1900.

Thursday 26 July

This evening to the Mill for drinks with former Attorney General Dominic Grieve, his wife Caroline and their son James, who are staying with John Field. Dominic says a *Daily Mail* photographer has been photographing his house in France, presumably with a view to outing him as a dangerous Europhile whose loyalty lies elsewhere. I asked what he thought the eventual outcome of the Brexit debate would be. A soft Brexit is, he thinks, the most likely, which will ironically leave us signed up to the customs union and the single market and the jurisdiction of the European court, but with no power to influence the rules, perhaps with some restrictions on immigration as a sweetener. He thinks a second referendum is a possibility or, failing that, a general election. The crisis, he says, is likely to come to a head before Christmas.

Friday 27 July

After two months in which there has been scarcely any rain, the long spell of hot weather ended this evening with a spectacular thunderstorm, bright blue flashes lighting the sky, followed by heavy rain which means we won't have to water the garden for the foreseeable future.

Tuesday 31 July

The assault on Corbyn for his supposed tolerance of antisemitism is unrelenting. On some days it leads the bulletins. This morning he was having to apologise for appearing on a platform eight years ago with someone who allegedly compared Israel's treatment of the Palestinians to Nazi treatment of the Jews. It turns out that the individual concerned is a Holocaust survivor, Dr Hajo Meyer, but no matter, he's the wrong kind of Holocaust survivor.[*] Meanwhile the Corbyn haters in the parliamentary party are scenting blood, openly denouncing him regardless of the damage they are doing to the party and its prospects. Tonight – from his luxurious billet in New York – David Miliband has joined in. It's true that the issue has been mishandled, but it has also been blown out of all proportion by people who do not have Labour's interests at heart. Poor Jeremy is just a rabbit in the headlights. I begin to think he isn't going to make it to the election. The obvious successor is John McDonnell, but for all that he is a shrewd performer he, too, comes with baggage.

Thursday 2 August

Encouraged by the long run of warm weather and the absence of work,

---

[*] Dr Meyer was quoted as saying, 'An antisemite used to be a person who dislikes Jews. Now it is someone whom Jews dislike.'

my life has assumed a pattern. In the morning I write. This week an essay entitled 'The Queen and I' and now a long piece entitled 'The Men Who Bombed Birmingham', both of which I will offer to the *London Review of Books* in due course. Whether any of it will see the light of day, I have no idea, but the words flow effortlessly and I am content. In the afternoon, after the shadow falls over the west side of the garden, I sit outside the summerhouse in a canvas chair and read; my current book is Adam Nicolson's *The Gentry*. From the summerhouse there is a view along the narrow grass path between the wild flowers towards the white bench on the far side of the garden. Butterflies flit through the flowers. A woodpecker taps away on the big oak tree in next door's garden. It is good to be alive.

Friday 3 August

Jeremy is reported to be negotiating with the Jewish Museum with a view to making a speech there next week. Big mistake. No amount of pandering will appease the Corbyn haters. His best course would be to stopping faffing, sign up to that darn antisemitism declaration, change the subject and move on. As if to prove the point, the UK's three Jewish papers today publish a joint editorial claiming that a Corbyn government would pose 'an existential threat to Jewish life in this country'. Anyone who believes that must be off their rocker. No hope of sensible dialogue with this mindset.

Sunday 5 August

A walk along the Simonside Hills with my friend and neighbour the arch-Brexiteer Jeremy Hosking, who is talking of setting up a new party which would run 200 candidates against Remainer MPs at the next election. A good way to pour your fortune into a deep black hole, I suggested. A first-past-the-post electoral system makes it almost impossible for a third party to break through. The fate of the SDP should be a warning to anyone tempted. No new party had a more favourable wind and more credible leadership than they, and look what became of them. It appears I am not the only person to have made these points, but I suspect he may go ahead anyway. The sun shone; the views were spectacular. What an unlikely pair we make.

Monday 6 August

Adam Nicolson's brilliant book about the long decline of the English gentry follows the fates of fourteen families between the fifteenth and twenty-first centuries. The most remarkable statistic appears on the last page. Until 1914 the gentry owned about half of the land of England. Today they have only 1 per cent. If so, many of the survivors must live up here. Our laird still has 5,500 acres. So do the Carr-Ellisons on the other side of the main road. Duncan Davison up the road is said to have almost 40,000 acres and the Duke (who of course doesn't count as gentry) has around 100,000.

Friday 10 August
The Lakes

Rain, which had eased by midday. Emma and I drove to Glenridding, caught the boat to Howtown and walked back along the edge of Ullswater. Our friends the Saudis, meanwhile, have bombed a school bus in Yemen, killing twenty-seven children and injuring goodness knows how many more. Who supplied the missile, us or the Americans?

Saturday 11 August

Here we go again. 'Corbyn wreath on graves of Munich terrorists' is today's *Mail* front page. My heart sank when I read it. If true, this surely is fatal, but is it? Turns out to be a rerun of an old smear. The photo accompanying the story was taken in 2014 when he was attending a conference organised by the Palestinian Liberation Organization in Tunis, where a wreath was laid on a memorial to the more than sixty people, many of them Tunisians, killed when the Israelis bombed the PLO headquarters in Tunis. An act of Israeli, rather than Palestinian, terrorism and one which, at the time, even Margaret Thatcher condemned.

Monday 13 August

'MUNICH MASSACRE WIDOWS RAGE AT CORBYN'. Yes, the *Mail* is still on the case. Today's edition leads with interviews with relatives of the Israeli athletes murdered at Munich. How much more of this unrelenting assault can Corbyn take? If I were him, I would want to crawl away and die. And yet, and yet, it never pays to appease the mob. But he must know he can't be elected. What is his plan? Does he have one? Or is he going to take us all down with him?

Tuesday 14 August

Today's *Mail* devotes nine pages to its assault on Corbyn, much helped by the fact that Israeli Prime Minister Netanyahu has joined the fray, straightforwardly accusing him of laying a wreath on the grave of one of those involved in the 1972 Munich attack. The *Mail*, however, has retreated slightly from yesterday's position, accusing him only of 'standing near' the grave of one of the Munich terrorists. If only because it appears that none of the perpetrators are buried in the same cemetery, although at least one of the alleged organisers is and there was a wreath on his grave. Jeremy himself hasn't helped himself by responding in a BBC interview, 'I don't think I was actually involved in laying it.' '*I don't think*'. Oh dear.

Wednesday 15 August

The Times has opened a new front: 'Jeremy Corbyn faces inquiry after failing to declare Tunisia visit expenses'. We will see where that leads. Meanwhile on the front page it is business as usual: 'Corbyn: I did attend wreath ceremony for Munich killers'. This last has prompted the following response from a Labour spokesman: 'Jeremy Corbyn said no such thing. Those who carried out the Munich massacre are not buried in the Palestinian National Cemetery and there was no ceremony for them.' Also, there seems to be a proliferation of anonymous websites devoted to spreading poison – Corbyn's Lenin Cap, Mr Corbyn and *The Times*. Who is behind these? This is surely the greatest assault I have ever seen on a senior politician – even the monstering of Tony Benn in the early '80s never plumbed these depths.

Thursday 16 August

Reading Max Hastings's superb account of his ten years as editor of the *Daily Telegraph*, during which he fought to drag the paper from the eighteenth to the twentieth century, I came across the following assessment of Rupert Murdoch:

Murdoch, as always when I have encountered him, cut a curiously joyless figure. He appeared to have no life beyond his business, no cultural or aesthetic interests. He conveyed no sense of pleasure in anything beyond the deal of the moment. That he is a kind of genius, few can doubt. No newspaperman of the twentieth century displayed a more brilliant understanding of popular taste. But Murdoch will leave this planet having added precious little to the store of decency, culture, humanity that sustains civilised societies.[*]

Hastings himself comes over as a decent one-nation Tory with sound instincts on apartheid, the death penalty, Thatcher and even Trident. Our paths crossed only once, on a panel at Chatham House in May 1975, discussing the Vietnam War, which had just ended. We were both young and callow and fell out so badly that I thought at one point he was going to hit me, but I suspect that were we to meet today, we would get along.

Friday 17 August

Labour is at last fighting back, with complaints to the press regulator about alleged falsehoods in six newspapers. The BBC, which after initial reticence had enthusiastically followed the *Mail*'s lead, has also gone quiet. This will be an interesting test of the new press regulator's credibility.

Monday 20 August
Charlotte Square, Edinburgh

To the Edinburgh Book Festival, where I delivered my 'Remarkable Rise of Jeremy Corbyn' talk to a full house – 550 people. I had feared that the discussion afterwards would be hijacked by the antisemitism row, but in the event the subject was hardly mentioned. Afterwards I signed the best part of 100 books. Other guests at the festival included Chelsea Clinton, who apparently did not quite rule out that she might one day run for office. Also the former Greek finance minister Yanis Varoufakis, who seems to have become a bit of a rock star. A small crowd gathered to watch him being interviewed for television and applauded when he had finished.

---

[*] *Editor: A Memoir*, Macmillan, 2002, p. 154.

Tuesday 21 August

William Sutcliffe, an author of children's books who attended last night's Edinburgh Book Festival event with Jeremy Corbyn, has tweeted as follows:

> I've always felt Corbyn is maligned by the mainstream media, so I went to hear him speak in a non-confrontational setting. What I learned from this is that he is flat, uninspiring, repetitive, dreary, inarticulate and vague. Bitterly disappointing... I honestly don't know why so much effort has gone into smearing him, when the best way to make the guy look bad is just to hand him a microphone.

Much the same was said of Attlee, of course, but someone else commented that a more appropriate comparison is with George Lansbury rather than Attlee. Fair comment, I am afraid.

Thursday 23 August

One of our laird's partridges, camped in our garden, has eaten the white onions stems. For some reason he doesn't seem interested in the reds.

Saturday 25 August

The lead in today's *Times* is headlined 'Far right comes out for Jeremy Corbyn'. What will they think of next?

Sunday 26 August

The *Times of Israel* has followed up with 'Corbyn praised by former KKK grand wizard'. Oh, please.

Tuesday 28 August

Out of the blue, an email from the features desk of the *Daily Mail*: 'Would you be up for heading to Venezuela tomorrow and doing a dispatch for us? We're after a prominent lefty to visit the country and do something about how far it is from a left-wing utopia.' It promises 'a nice fee' and concludes, 'I realise it's an absolutely bonkers proposal, but I reckon it could be a really fantastic, moving piece.' I have replied as follows: 'Thanks for thinking of me, but as you say it is an absolutely bonkers proposal. I am proposing to mow my lawn instead.'

Wednesday 5 September

Yesterday, after several hours of wrangling, the Labour national executive committee finally signed up to the official definition of antisemitism and all appendices, despite fears that it outlaws criticism of Israel. Unfortunately Corbyn muddied the waters by a attempting, unsuccessfully, to attach a lengthy 'clarifying' statement. Predictably, most of those who have been campaigning for the declaration to be signed in full have immediately returned to the offensive. Margaret Hodge on the radio this morning said, 'This is only the beginning…' Indeed, this will go on until Jeremy has gone and that is only likely to happen after another election defeat.

Thursday 6 September

A terrible night retching and vomiting. The world spinning. I had to crawl to the bathroom to avoid being sick on the bed. Not even water would stay down. I spent the day wrapped in blankets sitting by the electric heater. Ngoc went to the doctor and got some tablets to control the nausea and by evening I was capable of holding down two small crackers spread with Marmite washed down with a mug of herbal tea. Goodness knows what's caused this. It doesn't seem to have been anything I ate. Tony Blair leads this morning's bulletins saying that he believes that the Labour Party is lost to moderates. He doesn't go so far as to call for a new party, but that is the implication.

Saturday 8 September

Lead headline in today's *Telegraph*: 'Iranian regime has infiltrated Labour'. Truly, the world has gone mad.

Sunday 9 September

The Swedish general election: a right-wing populist party with alleged neo-Nazi roots has gained 18 per cent of the votes and holds the balance of power. A similar trend across most of Europe. All driven by the migrant influx. The liberal left ignore this at their peril. Those who refuse to recognise the problems posed by mass migration are aiding and abetting the far right.

Friday 14 September

To Carluccio's on Waterloo Station for a late breakfast with Ann Grant, our former High Commissioner in South Africa. She volunteers one day per week at Citizens Advice in Peckham, dealing with a steady stream of indebted, impoverished victims of the gig economy. Most are in work, she says, but don't earn enough to pay the bills. Theirs is a world of total insecurity – no sick leave, no holiday pay or any of the other benefits we used quaintly to associate with civilisation. No one is a member of a union; few if any are in work long enough to qualify for employment rights. When they can't pay bills, the first thing to be cut off is the mobile phone contract, which means they can't respond to other demands for payment, all of which these days come by email. And all the while we keep hearing that more people are in work than ever before. Yes, but what kind of work?

Then to lunch at the terrace cafe in the House of Lords, where I was joined by Andrew Adonis, who these days is much preoccupied with stymying our exit from the EU. 'The more I think about it, the more I admire Harold Wilson,' he said. A reference to Wilson's handling of the divisions in the party over the common market – to which I added, 'And for keeping us out of Vietnam.' 'Yes,' says Andrew. 'Tony would have got us into Vietnam, without hesitation.' He added, 'George Bush was Tony's downfall. If Al Gore had won, Tony would have been an environmentalist.'

Wednesday 19 September

First, the bad news. Winds of up to eighty miles an hour – Storm Ali – have brought down the magnificent copper beech which has dominated the main lawn at Callaly for 150 years. The good news is that Simon &

Schuster have bought *The Friends of Harry Perkins*. Suddenly there is a spring in my step.

Friday 21 September

Theresa May's much-trumpeted Brexit plan has been rejected out of hand by the EU heads of government meeting in Austria, several barely concealing their contempt. 'Brexit is the choice of the British people,' said French President Macron, '…pushed by those who promised easy solutions.' For good measure he added, 'Those people are liars.' *The Sun* is apoplectic. 'EU DIRTY RATS' screams the front-page headline. It goes on, 'We can't wait to shake ourselves free of the two-bit mobsters who run the European Union.' If only we could liberate ourselves from the two-bit mobsters who run *The Sun*.

Tuesday 25 September

Keir Starmer, speaking at the Labour Party conference in Liverpool, has set the cat among the pigeons, saying, to the evident surprise of the Labour leadership, that 'nobody is ruling out Remain as an option'. He was greeted with a partial standing ovation, though some notables remained firmly in their seats. On Brexit, Labour is almost as divided as the Tories and suddenly the mask has slipped.

Thursday 27 September

For the first time I can remember, Labour has had a good conference. Corbyn's speech has been widely praised, even by critics, and whether one agrees with them or not, the party has a more or less coherent set of policies. Unlike the Tories, who are bogged down in Brexit, from which they appear to have no escape route.

Friday 28 September

To *The Guardian*, where I help to judge entries for the Prison Reform Trust's annual writing competition for prisoners. This year's theme: 'What is prison for?' One of the winning entries, written by a young woman, begins as follows:

The word 'prison' terrified me as a child when we'd go to visit my big brother ... I'd always ask my mam, 'Why is my brother staying here?' and 'Why can't he come home with us?' She'd reply, 'He's been a naughty boy and he has to stay here until he's good again.' I'd break my heart leaving him sitting there. All the way home I'd tell my mam, 'I promise I'm never going to get into trouble' ... and how I would never ever leave her. Yet here I am. Sitting in my cell, writing this...

Monday 1 October

Still much colour in the garden. Outside the kitchen window, a mass of pink and white cosmos; in the pots that line the steps, most of the petunias are still healthy; and in the bed by the path, a blaze of yellow rudbeckia. In the herbaceous borders, there are pink and white anemones, various shades of phlox, fuchsia and even a deep blue Jackmanii clematis enjoying a second flowering. By the glasshouse, a good display of roses. Our fruit trees are laden with pears and apples and in the glasshouse there are many tomatoes still to come. Any day now, a frost will put paid to the flowers, but it is good, living as far north as we do, to get this far into autumn with so much of the garden intact.

Tuesday 2 October

John Ware's programme on the Birmingham bombings, which purports to identify the surviving suspects, was broadcast last night. I am shown resisting his attempt to persuade me to disclose the name of the so-called young planter, on the grounds of undertakings I gave at the time. It's bound to lead to a further bout of hate mail.

Wednesday 3 October

Sure enough, my refusal to name the younger of the two planters has produced a trickle of low-level Twitter abuse: 'scumbag', 'paedo' etc.

Saturday 6 October

A letter from a solicitor acting on behalf of the Birmingham coroner, asking for a statement summarising my three interviews with Michael Murray, the man who made the Birmingham bombs and placed the botched warning call. No problem about complying with this, but I fear I may be sucked into the forthcoming inquest, which relatives of some of the victims see as an opportunity to identify the culprits, although the courts have ruled against them. To judge by some of the abuse directed at me, anyone would think I planted those damn bombs myself, when in reality I am just the guy who helped clear up the mess.

Monday 8 October

Scientists at a UN conference on climate change have warned of catastrophic consequences unless global warming is kept below 1.5° by 2030. In reality there is not the slightest chance of this happening. Neither the public nor our politicians have the will. Eventually catastrophe beckons, but it is the rice farmers in the great river deltas who are the first to suffer and most people in the rich world don't care about them, unless of course they start migrating to Europe. Mercifully, I will not live long enough to see the consequences, but Sarah, Emma and their children will.

Tuesday 9 October

'Multimillionaires are setting up offshore investment accounts or shifting the location of UK-registered trusts holding their wealth to outside the country, in anticipation of higher tax rates and potential capital controls should Labour seize power.' So says a recent article in the *Financial Times*. I guess we can all live with the departure of a few oligarchs and their ill-gotten gains, but it is disappointing to see our most respectable national newspaper suggesting that Labour will 'seize' power. If Corbyn becomes Prime Minister, it will be because he has won an election and for no other reason.

Monday 15 October

A huge row is developing over a US-based Saudi journalist, Jamal Khashoggi, who disappeared two weeks ago after visiting the Saudi consulate in Istanbul. All the signs are that he was murdered and dismembered by a hit squad of Saudi agents who arrived by private jet in Turkey the day before his disappearance and departed soon afterwards. The incident has triggered much huffing and puffing from Washington and other Western capitals, but I doubt anything much will happen. Although particularly blatant, this is the least of Saudi crimes.

Thursday 18 October

To Sheffield, the home of Harry Perkins, where I gave my *Hinterland* talk at the local literary festival and signed about forty books. Afterwards a drink with local MP, Paul Blomfield, and his wife, Linda, a member of the European Parliament. Paul said that following the rise of Corbyn, membership of his constituency party has swelled from 350 to more than 2,000, but the new members are mostly invisible. When he recently circulated an email asking for help with leaflet distribution, two thirds didn't even open the email. They seem only to have joined to vote for Jeremy. I hear this wherever I go. Strikingly, according to Paul, far from being Trotskyites (though some are), the influx consisted mainly of people aged sixty-plus, former members who had deserted the party over one or other of its alleged 'betrayals'. Some had deserted as far back as 1983, when Neil Kinnock became leader.

Friday 19 October

On the train this morning I helped a woman with her suitcase and she said, 'You sound like Chris Mullin.' Turned out she had read and enjoyed all three volumes of the diaries but had found Alastair Campbell's heavier going, although she admired him for his candour on mental health. This sparked a lively discussion in which we were joined by a man who turned out to be the BBC's health correspondent, Dominic Hughes, who among other things had reported from Iraq in the aftermath of the invasion. None of us had bookings and the train was crowded, so we had to keep changing seats. The woman, who was on her way to a poetry writing course, got off at Leeds, but the BBC man continued to Newcastle. Later he tweeted, 'Very much enjoyed my journey from Sheffield to Newcastle this morning where I found myself sitting opposite the fascinating @chrismullinexmp and was privileged to pick his brain on all sorts of topics. Thanks for the company.'

Monday 22 October–Saturday 27 October

To Cornwall, where, together with my good friend Professor Chris Carter and his friends Andy and Sarah, I knocked off the remaining stages of the coastal path walk. On Thursday we had a day off visiting Antony, a magnificent early eighteenth-century National Trust property, where we were shown round by Sir Richard Carew Pole, a delightful patrician Tory, whose family have owned the estate for the best part of 500 years. One of his ancestors signed Charles I's death warrant and, come the restoration, was duly butchered. Afterwards Sir Richard and his wife Mary took us to lunch in a local pub. He recounted an exchange he had years ago with a neighbouring landowner, following the return of a Labour government. 'I said, "It will be the ruin of us." "Nonsense," he replied. "The things that can bring us down are bad marriages, adultery, gambling and alcohol. All much bigger threats than a Labour government."'

Sunday 28 October

On *The World This Weekend*, Chancellor Philip Hammond, due to deliver his budget tomorrow, referred in passing to the crash of 2008 as 'Labour's recession'. Disappointing that one of the more credible ministers should still be peddling that old Tory lie. It was the bankers, stupid.

Monday 29 October

Awoke to a hard frost which has finally killed off the huge display of cosmos in front of the kitchen window. To general surprise, Hammond's budget includes a massive spending splurge, with much more promised over the next four years and no tax rises. Nothing for local government, however, which is in desperate straits, and no talk of benefits uprating. As one commentator remarked, it seems to be aimed mainly at those who are concerned about the impact of austerity as opposed to those who are actually hit by it. Overall, however, it seems that – like Jeremy and his friends – the Tories, too, believe in the magic money tree.

Monday 5 November

To my old stamping ground, the Foreign Office, for the launch of Simon

Jenkins's latest book, *A Short History of Europe*. I chatted to Jonathan Dimbleby, who recounted a tale told him by Justin Welby, who recently lunched with the Pope. Jonathan asked what they had talked about and Welby said he had asked how the Pope dealt with the obstructionists in the Curia. 'I pray that they will be enlightened,' Francis replied with a twinkle in his eye.

'And if that doesn't work?'

'Then I pray for their immortal souls.'

Tuesday 6 November

A deliciously barmy tale from Cragside, the National Trust property just down the road from us. The politically correct people at head office have decreed that their staff should look for ways of celebrating the lives of women associated with the properties entrusted to them. At Cragside it was decided to focus on the life of Lady Armstrong, rather than her husband, the great Victorian engineer. So far so good, except that they decided to do so by covering up the pictures and statues of men in the house. So great was the outcry from visitors that the comments box was filled to overflowing, resulting in a rapid uncovering of the said artefacts. This latest insanity follows a hastily rescinded decree earlier this year from HQ requiring all volunteers to wear Gay Pride badges and the exhibition of junk art by an 'internationally acclaimed' artist in Lindisfarne castle. Meanwhile from Southampton University, another piece of bonkers feminism. The young female president of the student union demanded that a mural in the Senate building be removed on the grounds that it portrayed only white men, even threatening to paint over it herself, until it was gently pointed out to her that the painting commemorates Southampton students who were soldiers killed in the First World War.

Sunday 11 November

Today is the 100th anniversary of the Armistice that brought the World War I slaughter to an end. All week the television has been replaying footage of unspeakable horrors and interviews with the last survivors (all now gone) who lived on into this century. Even now there are a handful of people alive who, while not old enough to have served, are old enough to remember. One woman, aged 112, recalled with absolute clarity the day the postman knocked with a letter to say her brother was dead. She has lived on into the outer atmosphere and he was gone, aged twenty-three.

Monday 12 November

To Westminster, where, at the invitation of Mr Speaker Bercow, I gave my *Hinterland* talk in the state rooms at Speaker's House, my third such event in recent years. At Westminster Tube Station I came across a senior *Guardian* journalist who shares my view of the paper's growing obsession with identity politics. He said a recent editorial which deviated marginally from LGBT purism had resulted in a letter to the editor from the paper's large LGBT chapter expressing 'outrage' at the line taken. These days mere disagreement is insufficient. Nothing less than outrage will do.

Wednesday 14 November

A five-hour meeting of the Cabinet to discuss Theresa May's Brexit strategy, which has apparently been agreed with the Europeans. At length she emerged saying everyone had gone along with it, but have they? We shall see.

Thursday 15 November

The resignations have begun. So far two Cabinet ministers – including her latest Brexit Secretary – two junior ministers and a handful of parliamentary private secretaries. Only a smattering of Tory MPs spoke up for her when she presented her deal to Parliament this morning and there is talk of a challenge to her leadership, though it is hard to see how anyone could dig the Tories out of the large pit they have dug for themselves – and the nation. Robert Harris tweeted, 'No group of politicians has done more damage to this country than the 50 or so hardline Tory Brexiteers. They have infected the UK with their poison, concealed their real aims, evaded all responsibility, and now knife their own leader for failing to deliver their fantasy.' 'And so the great unravelling begins,' tweeted Paddy Ashdown, harking back to the great Tory split over the Corn Laws. One of my Brexiteer neighbours made a similar point the other day. I am not so sure, although a Tory split is not inconceivable. In the meantime they have rendered the county ungovernable.

Friday 16 November

Unfashionable though it may be, I am developing a grudging respect for Theresa May. Despite being assailed from all sides, she ploughs on resolutely, calm, courteous, unruffled, refusing to be provoked or distracted. Andrew Mitchell once remarked that she didn't have an ounce of leadership in her DNA and that may have been true – until now. Also, she appears to have noticed that the public have grown weary of the antics of Jacob Rees-Mogg and his pals and just want the issue settled, which may work in her favour. The tricky moment will come when Parliament votes, because the narrowness of her majority means that hardliners hold the balance and unless help comes from an unexpected quarter, she will almost certainly lose.

Sunday 18 November

Dinner with my neighbour Jonathan Clark in the South Wing of the big house. We ate at a small table by the fire in his grand salon, illuminated only by the light of the fire and two candles. The talk was mainly of Brexit, Jonathan being a keen Brexiteer. Needless to say, we do not see eye to eye, but relations remain cordial.

Monday 19 November

Ngoc, who is visiting family in Vietnam, has sent a photograph of the three adjacent houses in the main street in Kontum, where her father and his two surviving brothers lived side by side, where she was brought up along with her eight siblings and many cousins. Between them, her father and his brothers had thirty-four children. The family house is now eclipsed by a giant neon Samsung hoarding, three storeys in height. Uncle Three's house is still owned by his family and Uncle Eight's is now in the hands of strangers. Of the family's once thriving coffee plantation, on the outskirts of the city, she says there is no trace. Much of the space is now occupied by a petrol station.

Tuesday 20 November

Despite much hype, the Tory Brexiteers have failed to muster the forty-eight signatures necessary to hold a vote of confidence in Theresa May. Perhaps now we can be spared Jacob Rees-Mogg's daily press conferences, given that he has turned out not to be quite such an influential figure as we have been led to believe. The respite, however, is only temporary. There is no way May can get her Brexit plan through the House and what will happen then is anyone's guess. Meanwhile the stone in my right kidney is beginning to play up.

Wednesday 28 November

Mrs Very Big Boss returned from Vietnam today. A major clean-up preceded her return.

Thursday 29 November

Despite my valiant efforts yesterday, the hearth and the kitchen floor were deemed unsatisfactory and had to be cleaned again.

Friday 30 November

Finished reading Ian McEwan's *Sweet Tooth*. Elegant, clever, but slightly overwritten. His best line concerns the central character's father, an Anglican bishop: 'The reason he wouldn't be drawn into political or even theological debate was because he was indifferent to other people's opinions and felt no urge to engage with or oppose them.'

Saturday 1 December

Theresa May lost another minister this morning, the eleventh since she announced her Brexit plan and the twenty-first to go on her watch.

Tuesday 4 December

Awoke to a hard frost which lingered all day, although I managed a couple of hours in the garden. Meanwhile Parliament has found the government to be in contempt for refusing to disclose the Attorney General's advice on Theresa May's Brexit deal, which bodes ill for next week's big Brexit vote. And in France, following a bout of rioting, arson and general mayhem, the government has been forced to back down on plans to increase taxes on fossil fuels. Everywhere chaos beckons. Or so it seems.

Wednesday 5 December

This morning on *Today*, a long sad interview with a working mother and her daughter, turned out of their lodging because she can't afford the rent. This was followed by an interview with a woman from Shelter who said that what is needed is a big new social housing programme. Nobody was indelicate enough to mention that the crisis might have something to do with the sale of council houses, 40 per cent of which are now in the hands of buy-to-let landlords. Not that there would be any point in building more social housing if we continue to sell them.

Saturday 8 December

This morning, an interview with a prominent Norwegian about the possibility, increasingly floated, that if all else fails the UK may opt for what's becoming known as 'the Norway option'. 'No,' she said. 'We don't want you. It's not in our interests. It would be like having an abusive partner, spiking the drinks. You would mess it up for us in the way you have messed it all up for yourselves.' A light-bulb moment. 'An abusive partner'. How disappointing for the more thoughtful Brexiteers to discover that foreigners don't seem to have such a high opinion of us as we have of ourselves. Or perhaps they haven't noticed.

Monday 10 December

A call from Sarah in London, who says she came across both yesterday's Brexit marches – Remainers demanding a second referendum and hardline Brexiteers shouting betrayal. The Remainers, she said, looked happy and prosperous, their slogans light-hearted. The Brexiteers, by contrast, were older, maler, angrier, poorer, heavily policed and carrying a mini gallows complete with a dangling noose.

Tuesday 11 December

Much excitement at Westminster. The Tory Brexiteers have triggered a vote of no confidence in Theresa May. The virulence of the language is extraordinary. Philip Hammond is publicly referring to leading Brexiteers as 'extremists' and some leading lights in the European Research Group, the organisation at the core of the uprising, have been overheard referring to their headquarters as 'the kill zone'. Shades of Labour's disastrous internal strife in the late '70s and early '80s. The pit is deep and they are furiously digging.

Wednesday 12 December

My seventy-first birthday. Emma has given me a CD of *Desperado* by the Eagles, which I played as I drove across the moors to Hexham and back for a meeting of the National Park Authority. Also, I won a pair of stainless steel balti dishes complete with a packet of basmati rice and a jar of curry paste in the authority's Christmas raffle. Theresa May, meanwhile, survived her vote of confidence by 200 votes to 117. Now what?

Monday 17 December

To Chillingham on a cold, pitch-dark night for an al fresco carol service. Local gentry, citizens and retainers in attendance, about fifty in all. We assembled in the courtyard of the castle, illuminated by flaming torches and warmed by three braziers. The service was led by a lady vicar, Sir Humphry in a magnificent brown greatcoat (made, he said, for his uncle in 1912) presided. Carols alternated with readings from the scriptures. Mine an obscure, incomprehensible text from the prophet Micah. The singing a tad desultory, but the occasion memorably atmospheric. By the end my feet were numb with cold.

Tuesday 18 December

An irresponsible, expensive game of brinkmanship is under way. This morning the Cabinet upped preparation for a no-deal Brexit. Several thousand troops are to be placed on alert and the government have magicked up £4 billion to be invested in preparations for a cliff-edge departure, with businesses being urged to stock up. No one seems to believe it will actually come to this. The aim appears to be to frighten dissenters into voting for Theresa May's deal when the vote is eventually held, in mid-January. If she loses again, she could well resign, in which case the most likely candidate to take over is the weaselly Gove. Meanwhile, despite the turmoil, Labour still lags in the polls. Fear of Corbyn is just about the only card that the Tories have left to play, but thus far at least it seems to work.

Wednesday 19 December

Out of the blue an email from someone calling himself SirKidMarx: 'No one will ever forget your despicable failure to publish the register of Freemasons as promised. You failed. You are a Blairite weasel consigned to the trash can of failed Labour politicians who betrayed the working class of England.' Why now? It is getting on for twenty years since I last had anything to say about Freemasonry and when I did it was the opposite of what this deranged tweet implies. Yet more evidence that all over the country there are people in basements and bedsits raving away at ancient grievances, real or imagined. In years gone by it might have meant a letter scrawled in green ink, but usually the mood would have passed before they could summon the energy to get together a stamp and an envelope and walk to the postbox. Now you just press a button and whoosh…

Thursday 20 December

A damp, grey day, the mist briefly lifting. Emma and I drove to the Breamish Valley and completed a circuit of the Iron Age hill forts before it again descended.

Saturday 22 December

Brexit will go ahead if Labour wins a snap election, Corbyn tells today's *Guardian*. There was, however, just a chink of light. He did not quite rule out the possibility of another referendum but said his first move would be try to persuade the EU to let us remain in the customs union. The first sliver of evidence of a credible Labour policy?

Sunday 23 December

Paddy Ashdown has died. A politician with hinterland. A man of substance in a profession where substance is in increasingly short supply.

Monday 24 December

This evening, with Sarah and my sister Liz to St Michael's at Alnham, a remote hamlet on the edge of the Cheviots, for a carol service. Enjoyable but slightly chaotic, children running hither and thither, a microphone which didn't work rendering most of the readings inaudible. The Bishop of Berwick, resplendent in a cloak of gold and scarlet with a mitre to match, presided. 'I bet you are thinking two things,' he said. '"Isn't he young for a bishop?" and "I didn't know Berwick had a bishop."' A bull's eye. Both thoughts had passed through my mind in the preceding ten minutes. As we were driving home, Sarah texted her fiancé, Nick, a junior surgeon who was still at work. 'Been to a carol service. What are you doing?' Nick replied, 'Just drained an abscess.'

Tuesday 25 December

'I am all alone (poor me) in the White House waiting for the Democrats to come back and make a deal on desperately needed border security,' tweets Donald Trump. The economist Paul Krugman has retweeted commenting as follows: 'People, time for an intervention. This guy has nukes.'

Saturday 29 December

Someone has tweeted 'where's @chrismullinexmp when you need him?' To which I have replied, 'In my walled garden, awaiting The Call. Alas, no sign so far.'

Monday 31 December

Ngoc has spent much of the week engrossed in Michelle Obama's memoir, which is proving to be a huge bestseller. This afternoon she drew my attention to a passage recounting Mrs O's visit to her youngest daughter's school. On the classroom wall were children's essays entitled 'What I Did in My Summer Vacation'. Sasha, aged eight, had written, 'I went to Rome and met the Pope. He was missing part of his thumb.'

CHAPTER TEN

2019

Friday 4 January

A YouGov poll of 1,200 Tory Party members suggests that 63 per cent are delighted/pleased/relieved at the prospect of a no-deal Brexit. The comparable figure among the public as a whole is 18 per cent. And they have the nerve to suggest that it is Labour that is in the grip of extremists.

Saturday 5 January

A sign of the times. I picked up a glossy magazine left behind by my sister which contains a feature on the rejuvenation of Bylaugh Hall, a country house in Norfolk. Its new owners are turning it into a training establishment for modern domestic servants. How fitting that the rise of Mrs Thatcher's billionaires should revive the market for domestic servants, which mostly died out in the early 1940s.

Sunday 6 January

Reading Ian McEwan's *Amsterdam*, written in 1998, I came across the following exchange at an editorial meeting of his fictional newspaper, *The Judge*, which is looking for ways to arrest a declining circulation:

'It's time we ran more regular columns. They're cheap and everyone else is doing them. You know, we hire someone of low to medium intelligence, possibly female, to write about, well, nothing much. You've seen the sort of thing. Goes to a party and can't remember someone's name. Twelve hundred words.'

'Sort of navel gazing,' Jeremy Ball suggested.

'Not quite. Gazing is too intellectual. More like navel chat.'

'Can't work her video recorder. Is my bum too big…?'

Then I turned to yesterday's *Times*. The entire cover of the weekend section is taken up with a rear view of Boris Johnson's sister, Rachel, in tight purple slacks. The caption, in large letters, reads: 'Does my bum look bigger in this?'

Thursday 10 January

Jaguar Land Rover has announced more than 4,000 redundancies in the British operations. Various reasons are given – falling demand in China, reduced sales of diesel engines, but also Brexit, about which the company has been warning for some time. Ominously, they have also announced that they are opening a plant in the Czech Republic for which they are recruiting 3,000 new workers. Meanwhile there are reports that Ford at Dagenham and elsewhere are about to cut jobs.

Sunday 13 January

'A Very British Coup'. The headline is emblazoned across the entire front page of today's *Sunday Times* over the suggestion that a handful of Remain MPs are 'plotting' with the Speaker to seize control of the Brexit agenda. Grateful though I am for the attention, the parallel is not exact. My novel is about the unelected seizing power from the elected whereas what appears to be exercising the *Sunday Times* is that the elected may be 'plotting' to take back control (to coin a phrase) from an incompetent executive. 'Do you receive royalties every time the phrase is used?' enquires one of my Twitter followers. If only…

Tuesday 15 January

After months of ministerial writhing, wriggling and clarifying, the House of Commons has thrown out the government's proposed Brexit deal by an incredible 432 votes to 202. A margin of defeat unprecedented in modern times. How can a Prime Minister, even one as resilient as Theresa May, survive so great a humiliation? But it seems she might. Tomorrow there is to be a vote of confidence and just about all of tonight's rebels are expected to clamber back on board the government's rickety bandwagon. After which search parties will be sent out in pursuit of compromise, if there is one to be found. Right now there doesn't appear to be a majority for anything. In the name of providing 'strong and stable government' the Tories have rendered the country ungovernable.

Wednesday 16 January

To London, where I spent two hours at Simon & Schuster going over plans for marketing the new novel, then to the City for a brief meeting with a lawyer acting for the coroner who will preside over the long-postponed inquest into the Birmingham pub bombings and finally to Westminster for a BBC interview. College Green, the patch of grass opposite the Victoria Tower, is now a tented village where the world's media were awaiting the result of a vote of no confidence in the government following last night's debacle. Predictably, the government won easily, all yesterday's rebels having scuttled back into line.

Friday 18 January

Today's *World at One*, in which I was allocated a minor role, was broadcast from Sunderland. Part of a belated but laudable effort by the BBC to explore territory deep behind the Brexit lines, *terra incognita* for most of the chattering classes. The programme included vox pops with random citizens. One remarked indignantly, 'When I voted Leave, I expected we would be out in two or three days,' an illustration of the staggering levels of ignorance we have to confront.

Sunday 20 January

Prince Philip, aged ninety-seven, has been spotted driving without a seat belt, three days after he was involved in what could have been a very serious accident. He took delivery of a new car within about twenty-four hours of the incident, while the injured were still in hospital. I was inclined to be sympathetic at first, but this is a provocation too far. Time the silly old buffer was relieved of his licence.

Monday 21 January

A call from a Lucy at *The World at One*: they are considering exploring the notion, popular with hardline Brexiteers, that the attempt by Parliament to influence the negotiating process is some sort of 'coup', with reference to my 1982 novel. She asked a number of questions and to each answer replied, 'Fantastic.' There then followed the usual rigmarole. Could I come to the studio? No, on account of my living 350 miles north of London W1. How about Newcastle, a return journey of eighty miles? 'No.' Then she rang to say they were sending a radio car. Then to say that the radio car was stuck in traffic and wouldn't make it in time. Where was it coming from? No wonder, it was coming from Leeds, 150 miles away. (The geography of the UK north of Watford has never been a strong point in the Home Counties.) Then we tried Ngoc's 4G telephone, on which she manages to communicate clearly with relatives all over the world, but for some reason they could not use that. Nor was the landline satisfactory. Eventually they managed to get through on Skype. With five minutes to go and the studio on the line, Lucy rang again. Very sorry, the editor had decided, 'in view of the technical difficulties' (which had by now been resolved), not to go ahead. Fantastic.

Wednesday 23 January

Despite the predicted Armageddon, I begin to see a possibility that there might, after all, be an orderly Brexit. Just about all negotiations with the EU (as with those to do with Northern Ireland) go to the wire. Could it be that as the deadline (which will surely be postponed) approaches, both sides will suddenly find that they can, after all, modify the Irish backstop? At which point the surly Unionists will grudgingly come aboard, bringing with them (most of) the Tory Brexiteers. Result: bingo. This only works, of course, if the threat of a so-called cliff-edge Brexit is kept hanging over all concerned until the last possible moment. For all her much-criticised stubbornness, Theresa May's approach may be right.

Friday 25 January

To the Salvation Army Hall in Millfield, Sunderland, for the funeral of Derek Foster, the former Labour Chief Whip, a good, honest, straight-forward man. Some nice tributes and rousing music from the Sally Army band. Jeremy Corbyn, John Prescott and a big crop of north-east MPs were in attendance. Afterwards, a long, friendly chat with Prezza, who was on good form, still talking nineteen to the dozen, among other things complaining that the weekly meetings of the Parliamentary Labour Party increasingly resembled a student debating society. This was my first ever Salvation Army event. They do not use the word 'death'. Instead they call it 'promotion'. So Derek did not die. He was promoted. Later, an email from a friend who was also at the funeral which ends, 'Long may we stay unpromoted.'

Sunday 27 January

An email from a famous film director to whom I sent a proof of my new novel. 'Your book is terrific, measured, heart-stopping, exciting, moving, calm, perceptive.' He asks if I want him to direct a film/TV version (you bet I do). He goes on, 'I could name five or six people who would love your book and I could easily start a bidding war.' Mustn't get too excited. In the world of films there is many a slip between cup and lip, but it is a good sign.

Wednesday 30 January

Brexit, part ninety-two… the Commons last night voted by a narrow ma-jority to send Theresa May back to Brussels to reopen negotiations about the backstop. Of course, the EU are saying they will do no such thing, but I suspect they might as the abyss draws nigh. A cold, hard frost which stayed all day. The snowdrops are out.

Friday 1 February

Awoke to a carpet of snow. John Field and I walked up through the woods to Castle Hill and then on to the crag and round in a four-mile loop. To the north a white landscape dissected by hedgerows, sunlight illuminating the Cheviot, every branch on every tree etched in white. Besides ours the only footprints were of the occasional deer and a fox. A fine walk through a pristine landscape. John said, 'I am seventy-eight tomorrow and, if this is the last walk I ever do, I shall be happy.'

Sunday 3 February

Nissan announced that it is cancelling a previously announced decision to build its X-Trail model in Sunderland. Declining demand for diesel engines seems to be the main factor, but there was also a reference to Brexit which has sent a little shiver through the dovecotes.

Tuesday 5 February

To London on the 09.00. Dinner in Islington with Andrew Mitchell, who reckons that there is significant investment waiting offshore to see which way the Brexit wind is blowing and that, if there is a deal, the stock exchange will suddenly soar. So it is possible that Theresa May emerge alive, after all. In the last month or two Andrew has had direct dealings with May, Cameron and Blair and reckons that when it comes to leadership skills Blair is head and shoulders above the others. On a scale of 1–10 he rates them as follows: May 1.5, Cameron 7, Blair 11.

Wednesday 6 February

To the offices of the *London Review of Books* in Bloomsbury, where I corrected the proofs of a lengthy piece about the Birmingham bombings which is scheduled for their next edition. Then to Carluccio's on St Pancras Station for a long lunch with Stephen Frears, who offered much useful advice on the film possibilities for *The Friends of Harry Perkins*. In a nutshell, 'if you can bag a great actor, everything else will follow'. We agreed that Michael Sheen would be ideal for the lead. If only… This evening to the basement of a pub in Cavendish Square, where I took part in a lively debate organised by the Manchester University Alumni Association. The motion was 'This House would move Parliament to Manchester'. I, needless to say, led for the opposition. We won, but only by a single vote.

Friday 8 February

John McDonnell was interviewed by John Humphrys on the radio this morning. Humphrys threw everything at him – Brexit, Venezuela, anti-semitism, and to each he responded calmly and reasonably. Humphrys's final throw was 'Can you name one country that has ever made socialism work?' to which McDonnell replied, 'The UK, 1945.' And then went on to enumerate the achievements of the Attlee government. Game, set and match.

Sunday 10 February

Here we go again. Today's *Mail on Sunday* devotes an incredible thirty pages to serialising Tom Bower's book on Corbyn. So far over the top that it resembles a *Private Eye* spoof. The headline gives a flavour: 'Jeremy Corbyn's 40 years of plots, lies, intimidation and chaos: chilling biography tells how Labour leader followed Lenin and Trotsky's bloody footprint – seize power, purge moderates, crush dissent and leave the dirty work to others'. Whew. Just as well I didn't soil my hands by talking to the loathsome Bower, not that I was ever tempted.

Monday 11 February

The Tories are after the aid budget again. Bob Seely, a member of the Foreign Affairs Committee, has written a pamphlet arguing that the definition of what it can be spent on should be relaxed to include funding the BBC World Service, peacekeeping missions and generally promoting British interests abroad. Boris Johnson has piled in, saying it should be reduced from 0.7 to 0.5 per cent of GDP. Goodness knows what will happen if the serially incompetent MoD ever gets its hands on the aid budget. Everyone seems to have forgotten that the reason it was ring-fenced in the first place is because previous Tory governments were using the aid budget as sweeteners for trade deals. Alas memories are short. When Clare Short enshrined the internationally accepted definition of aid into law, the Tories – anxious to prove that they were no longer the 'nasty' party – couldn't sign up fast enough.

Tuesday 12 February

Olly Robbins, the chief British Brexit negotiator, has been overheard in a Brussels bar saying that, despite all the scaremongering, there will be no hard Brexit. Instead MPs will in due course be faced with a choice of accepting Theresa May's deal or a lengthy extension to the deadline for withdrawal. So there.

Friday 15 February

Ngoc delivered me to Newcastle Airport, from where I flew to Bangkok via Dubai for a month travelling to places from which I once reported as a young journalist in the 1970s.

Monday 18 February

From home comes news that seven Labour MPs, led by Chuka Umunna, have defected to set up their own little party. Foolish man. I thought he had more sense.

Monday 4 March

Here is the news, courtesy of *The Guardian*'s website: 'Non-binary trans author nominated for women's fiction prize.' Meanwhile our ludicrous MP, Anne-Marie Trevelyan, has warned of 'riots' in her constituency if Brexit is thwarted. Riots in Berwick-upon-Tweed? The mind boggles…

Saturday 16 March

Home to Brexit Britain. A 26-hour journey starting with a taxi ride at snail's pace through the heat and fumes of Bangkok's merciless traffic and finishing with a drive back to the fresh air of Callaly through a light covering of snow. I doubt I shall ever return to Asia, except perhaps for a farewell tour of Vietnam. What a mess the Asians have made of their cities. All concrete and glass skyscrapers, shopping malls and choking traffic. I count myself lucky for having seen Beijing, Rangoon, Hanoi and Saigon before the coming of market forces, in the days when the bicycle and the cyclo were king. A world that Graham Greene so brilliantly captured in *The Quiet American*. As my friend Claes remarked the other day, 'We were lucky. We just caught the end of it.'

Monday 18 March

Mr Speaker Bercow has chucked a potentially large spanner into the Brexit works, saying that he will not allow the government to come back to Parliament for a third vote unless the motion is significantly different. Meanwhile the Brexit deadline creeps ever closer.

Wednesday 20 March

To a meeting of the National Park Authority in Rothbury and then to Birmingham, where I have been summoned to give evidence at the inquest into the Birmingham pub bombings. Slight trepidation since for some time I have been on the receiving end of some unpleasant and delusional tweets from an outfit calling itself Justice4the21.

Thursday 21 March

The Coroner's Court, Birmingham. Several cameras and a handful of placard wavers at the public entrance, easily avoided since, as instructed, I entered by another door fifty yards down the street. I am met by three G4S security men and shown to a small room on the sixth floor. One of the guards remains posted outside the door. It turns out that there is another witness before me, Kieran Conway, a former IRA man, giving evidence from Dublin by video link, with the help of a technician. Accompanied by two security men who remain present throughout, I am shown into a room full of journalists who are watching the live feed. Conway, who was close to the IRA leadership at the time of the pub bombings, is a good witness – succinct, frank about his own past and adamant that the targeting of civilians was not IRA policy and that the pub bombings were a disaster for the IRA which the Dublin leadership had nothing to do with. One light moment in an otherwise sombre session. After a couple of hours the witness requests a brief adjournment in order that he can go and feed the parking meter. 'Isn't there someone else who can do that for you?' asks the coroner. After a brief pause someone is found and duly dispatched with a handful of coins. Mr Conway resumes his evidence, but after a few minutes there is a technical hitch. 'Where is the technician?' asks the coroner. 'Gone to feed the meter,' replies the witness.

Contrary to expectations, Mr Conway's evidence is destined to last all day and my services will not be required until tomorrow, which means that I can scuttle back to London in good time for a long-planned event at the British Library devoted to my diaries and those of Tony Benn. The panel, ably chaired by Peter Hennessy, consisted of Melissa Benn, Ruth Winstone and myself. The event, which attracted 230 people, paying £15 a head, was a huge success. Much good humour and laughter amid some serious points. One of the highlights was a delightful audio clip of Tony recounting lunch with the Duke of Edinburgh back in the late '60s when he was in the Cabinet. The entire evening recorded for posterity.

Meanwhile Theresa May has dug the pit deeper by seeking to blame what she calls 'political games' by MPs for the delay to Brexit. She surely cannot be long for this world.

Friday 22 March

Back to the Coroner's Court in Birmingham only to discover that they still weren't ready for me. Once again I am escorted to a small room on an upper floor, given a cheese sandwich and a banana and told to await the court's pleasure. Care is being taken to keep me apart from the relatives of the victims, some of whom seem to be under the illusion that I am some sort of spokesman for the IRA. At one point I was ambushed by a man who demanded to know why I was telling 'lies'. Eventually I was ushered into court at around 14.30 and was taken through my statement describing my three encounters with the bomb-maker Michael Murray by a courteous but rigorous barrister. He was principally concerned to discover whether Murray had intended to kill civilians and whether the wholly inadequate warning was a deliberate ploy. I did my best, without wanting to appear to be defending Murray, to assure him that in my view it was a cock-up rather than a conspiracy, but it wouldn't surprise me if the jury found otherwise. Inevitably, my two hours in the witness box barely scratched the surface and I am asked to return again next week. Really, this is too much. Today I have spent eight hours on trains and just two in court.

Saturday 23 March

The Friends of Harry Perkins is published next week. A trawl of the internet unearthed reviews in three of today's papers – friendly in *The Guardian*, disappointing – verging on malicious – in *The Times* and neutral in the *Irish Times*. This is going to prove a harder sell than I thought. Personally, although it is much the shortest, I regard it as perhaps the best of my four novels and certainly the most topical. However, my opinion is not what matters. I dropped Jim Naughtie a note asking if he could help penetrate the wall of indifference at the BBC. He replied promising to make enquiries.

The campaign for another referendum is building a head of steam. Today the best part of a million people marched through London calling for one. Inevitably it was dominated by the metropolitan middle classes. Someone remarked that it looked like a long Waitrose queue.

Sunday 24 March

Rumours of an impending Cabinet coup to oust May. It may just be the Sunday lobby at work, but the end is surely nigh. Most likely she'll be gone by the end of the week.

Monday 25 March

The *Mail* website carries a photo showing me being escorted into court on Friday by what it calls 'three burly minders', though one of them was smaller than me. It also says I have received death threats. If so, no one has told me.

Tuesday 26 March

To Westminster for an interview on Sky with Adam Boulton. In Parliament Square a man standing on a traffic island is holding a placard which says 'JUST HOOT, WE VOTED LEAVE'. Nobody was hooting. Among the Remain placards one saying 'We didn't vote to be poorer'. Oh yes we did. The media village on College Green is besieged by rival camps of protesters. Someone has attached EU flags to the barriers which thus far are unmolested. After Millbank I went to Simon & Schuster, where I signed 500 books in an hour and a half and then to lunch with an engaging woman from the *Sunday Times* who interviewed me for one of those intrusive Q&A features entitled 'Fame and Fortune'. Then to a studio in Wardour Street to record my introduction to the novel for the audiobook and finally back to Birmingham for what will surely will be my last appearance at the pub bombings inquest.

Wednesday 27 March
Coroner's Court, Birmingham

The best part of three hours in the witness box. A succession of barristers acting for the families floated various ludicrous theories while at the same time half-heartedly trying to paint me as the villain of the piece for refusing to divulge the name of the so-called young planter. I replied that I had given repeated undertakings not only to the guilty but to innocent intermediaries and that I could not now renege just because it was convenient to do so, adding that without those undertakings no one would have cooperated with my investigation. The point I should have hammered home but didn't was that, but for a chain of events that I unleashed, six innocent people might still be in jail and no one, victims included, would be any the wiser about what happened to their loved ones. Indeed, the fact that the names of four of the five culprits are now public knowledge is mainly down to my efforts. There was a brief drama towards the end of my evidence when Julie Hambleton, whose sister died in the atrocity, stormed out shouting that I was 'a disgrace'. Later, when I left the court, accompanied by three minders and a policeman, four members of the Hambleton family launched an assault. The incident appeared to have been staged for a television camera which was in attendance. The minders walked with me all the way to the station, where they handed me over to the transport police, who saw me safely onto a train.

Other news: Theresa May has announced that she will resign as soon she gets her Brexit deal through. The ultimate sacrifice, but even that may not be enough.

Thursday 28 March

To St Peter's School, York, where I gave my 'Great Political Disasters' speech to an enthusiastic audience of about 250. Perhaps surprisingly, considering the low esteem in which politicians are held, the organiser said that my event and an earlier one with Alan Johnson attracted a much larger audience than big-name fiction writers like Joanna Trollope and Kate Mosse, who were also in the programme. Earlier, on the way to Alnmouth Station, I gave a lift to a scruffy old boy whom I often find hitch-hiking in the lanes around Callaly. 'Something big is going to happen tomorrow,' he said. 'There's a word for it, but I can't remember.'

At first I thought he was talking about the weather, which we had just been discussing, but then I twigged. 'Do you mean Brexit?'

'Yes, that's it. I first heard about it in January.'

'January? It's been around for a couple of years. Haven't you seen the TV?'

'Don't have a TV.'

'Or radio?'

'I hate radio.'

A pause and then, 'What does it mean?'

Have I just met the only person in the UK who doesn't know what Brexit means?

Friday 29 March

And so to Glasgow for the Aye Write festival, where I took part in what was billed as 'The Great Brexit Debate' at the Royal Concert Hall. 'Debate' was a misnomer since all three of us on the panel were Remainers and on a show of hands only one member of the 230-strong audience, an incomprehensible Scotsman, admitted to being a Brexiteer.

Meanwhile in London tens of thousands of almost exclusively white, mainly male, flag-waving Brexiteers, led by Unionist pipe bands, descended on Parliament shouting 'betrayal' and 'treason'. The UKIP part of the crowd was addressed by Tommy Robinson, a far-right extremist. Parliament has rejected Theresa May's deal for the third time, this time by a majority of fifty-eight. She is now threatening a fourth vote and, failing that, a general election. Who knows, she may just wear them down in the end.

Saturday 30 March

Glasgow

Today's headlines:

'The Great Betrayal' (*Mail*)

'We'll never give up on the Brexit we voted for' (*Express*)

'BREXSICK – Shame on MPs who have betrayed the 17.4 million' (*The Sun*)

Monday 1 April

David Runciman has published a long piece about my new novel in the current edition of the *London Review of Books*. Disappointingly non-committal, however, nowhere saying what he thought of it. In Glasgow the other night he remarked that the novel was 'haunting'. Now if he'd said that… However, there was a very useful full-page Q&A in yesterday's *Observer* and we have unsolicited media interest from the US, Germany and Ireland. Only the BBC remains impenetrable.

Thursday 4 April

Up at 5 a.m. and then to Newcastle for a turn on the *Today* programme, prompted by some foolish British soldiers who have been using a poster of Jeremy Corbyn for target practice. The taxi driver was Polish and had lived here for fourteen years. A chef by profession, he had worked first at a caravan park in Seahouses, then for a company in Houghton-le-Spring that makes car seats for Nissan and now has his own taxi business. His wife works in a care home and they have two children. He wasn't worried about Brexit but said that some of his countrymen were going home and that the recent announcement that Honda is leaving was making some of his English Brexiteer friends jittery. He also said that about 2 million Ukrainians have migrated to Poland in search of work. Now that's something we haven't heard about.

Friday 5 April

The Birmingham inquest has concluded that the pub bombings victims were unlawfully killed; the verdict is likely to lead to renewed efforts to bring the surviving culprits to justice. Julie Hambleton, the most outspoken of the victims' relatives (indeed just about the only one doing any talking), is denouncing me at every opportunity to a compliant media, including, I am sorry to say, in *The Guardian*, which ought to know better. I received an email from a *Guardian* journalist asking if I'd like to comment and replied as follows:

> Until I came on the scene no one was doing any investigating. The only reason the bereaved relatives now know the names of four of the five people responsible for the bombings is as a result of my investigation… Far from obstructing justice, I am the person who helped clear up the mess and it would be nice if some of those concerned could bring themselves to acknowledge that.

Six hours later *The Guardian*'s website story had still not been amended. This the second such story in the past few days. Their last effort was headed 'Pub bombings sister brands Chris Mullin a disgrace'. There was a time when *The Guardian* took this story seriously, but these days it's full of brash young millennials who think that history started when they came of age. The West Midlands BBC, which was never very brave, meanwhile has run a story headed 'Ex-MP called "scum" for pub bomb name silence'. It then refers to the incident in which I was ambushed by the Hambletons outside court last week and says 'he appeared shaken as crowds shouted "scum" and "disgrace"'. Actually, there were no crowds, just four members of the same family plus a television camera.

Dinner with neighbours. Home to find a message from a reporter on BBC *Breakfast* saying they were interviewing the Hambletons tomorrow morning and would I like to respond to what they were saying about me. I duly fired off my little statement, only to realise that the reporter concerned had gone home. It was after midnight when I managed to get through to someone on the news desk who promised to include my response in the interviewer's brief.

Saturday 6 April

Julie Hambleton and her brother duly appeared on *Breakfast* and seemed at first to be on their best behaviour. When my name came up, the interviewer put in a word for me causing her to respond that 'he did a fantastic job' before going on to repeat her earlier denunciation. Also an email from a *Guardian* journalist apologising for overlooking my response to his earlier missive and promising to make amends. Later, ominously, a recorded delivery letter arrived from West Midlands Police giving me seven days to produce all material relating to my interviews with the so-called young planter, including original diagrams used during the course interviews, 'in particular those annotated or touched by YP'. How ironic if the only successful prosecution arising from all this were to be of the person whose efforts led to the overturning of the wrongful convictions.

Monday 8 April

To the Crown Court at Durham to see Peter Candler installed as High Sheriff. Apparently it used to be one of the duties of the High Sheriff to organise executions. The judge who presided today said that in bygone years it was not unknown for the Sheriff to invite friends to attend. One such invitation read, 'Hanging at eight, breakfast at nine.'

Tuesday 9 April

Rang the university archivist at Hull History Centre to enquire why so many of my papers are listed as being subject to a 75-year embargo. Apparently it is in order to ensure privacy for individuals mentioned in them, although it looks to be using an unduly cautious interpretation of the data protection regulations. 'People have a right to be forgotten,' the archivist said, adding that he had been advised that even MPs might want to be forgotten.

'In my twenty-three years in Parliament I have never come across an MP who wanted to be forgotten. Most struggle to be noticed.'

'That's what we were advised.'

'By whom?'

'The Information Commissioner.'

Oh, please…

Thursday 11 April

The EU have grudgingly extended the Brexit deadline to 31 October. It remains to be seen whether the Tories will use the time wisely or fritter it away trying to displace Theresa May. As former EU Commissioner Lord Hill remarked with admirable clarity on the radio this morning, 'The choice is clear: We have first to make up our minds which is more important, reasserting control of our borders or maintaining tariff-free trade, and then we must choose. But we can't have both.'

Sunday 14 April

Today's *Telegraph* reports that, were there an election tomorrow, Labour would emerge as the largest party and the Tories would lose about sixty seats. The only flaw in this story is that there isn't going to be an election now. At the very least not until someone else is in charge and probably not even then.

Sunday 21 April
Easter Sunday

In Sri Lanka a series of horrendous explosions in churches and luxury hotels have killed several hundred people.

Tuesday 23 April

A conference call with lawyers and an official from the National Union of Journalists about how to respond to the letter from West Midlands Police demanding that I surrender my notes of interviews with the Birmingham bomber. The NUJ have agreed to fund the cost of legal advice. I have drafted a response which one of the lawyers will amend as he sees fit and come back to me tomorrow. He is of the opinion that were the police were to apply for a court order forcing me to disclose, they would lose on the grounds that they have only just got round to it after thirty-three years.

The death toll from the Sri Lanka explosions has topped 300.* Although no one has claimed responsibility, it appears to be the work of jihadis intent on creating yet another failed state. A clip of CCTV film on this evening's bulletins showed an apparently ordinary young man with a large rucksack on his back casually strolling into a crowded church,

---

* Later revised down to 253.

pausing as he did so to pat the head of a passing child. Seconds later the screen erupts in a huge explosion. What possesses these people?

Wednesday 24 April

Dispatched my carefully drafted response to West Midlands Police. We'll see what happens next.

Our friends the Saudis have beheaded thirty-seven condemned prisoners in a single day, many arrested while still in their teens, all allegedly tortured. The body of one was crucified.

Thursday 25 April

The other day I came across an extraordinary little snippet, first reported in August last year but which somehow escaped me. According to their accounts for 2017, the Tories received more in legacies from dead members than they did in donations from the living – £1.69 million and £835,000 respectively. The party of the dead? Now there's a thought.

Friday 26 April–Sunday 28 April
Beaufort Hotel, Hexham

To the Hexham Book Festival, where I was involved in three events: on Friday I gave a talk entitled 'If I were Prime Minister', on Saturday I was interviewed about the new novel and on Sunday I interviewed Ian Fraser, a Scottish journalist, who has written a brilliant book about the collapse of the Royal Bank of Scotland.* The figures are astonishing: the bailout cost the taxpayer £45 billion. Even now, a decade after the collapse, the bank is still 62 per cent state-owned with no prospect that the government will get back its money. The loss is likely to be in the region of £26 billion. The whole thing was a giant Ponzi scheme – the bank had 300 subsidiaries in tax havens, most of the 16,000 small businesses which were ruined or seriously damaged have not been compensated and it is still putting the squeeze on local authorities with outstanding loans, the government having given priority to ruthlessly getting back as much as possible of its

---

* *Shredded: Inside RBS, The Bank that Broke Britain*, Birlinn, 2019 (second edition).

investment. Ian quoted from an internal memorandum which said that the borrowers would have to 'go hang'. Some, no doubt, have.

Wednesday 1 May

To the Freeman Hospital for my annual kidney check-up. En route I stopped at Waterstones and signed some books. While doing so I was approached by an elderly woman who smiled sweetly and said, 'I am a Labour Party member and I have bought your book.' So far, so good, I thought. She then paused and added, 'I voted Leave and I didn't like it.' With that she walked away without making any attempt to engage. The stone in my right kidney is 8mm, up from 5mm last year.

Saturday 4 May

The Tories have received a drubbing in the local elections, losing more than 1,300 seats, but the big winners are not Labour (which also lost seats) but the Lib Dems. Of course the result is being interpreted as punishment for lack of progress on Brexit, which may well be true in the north, but the surge in Lib Dem support further south suggests the opposite. Personally, I find it hard to be disappointed that the Lib Dems are at last seeing some reward for their honourable and consistent stand over Brexit.

Dad died fifteen years ago today.

Thursday 16 May

After months of pressure Theresa May has agreed to step down if, as widely expected, Parliament rejects her fourth and last attempt to force her Brexit deal through the Commons. Boris Johnson, Lord help us, is the overwhelming favourite to succeed among the elderly Brexiteers who make up most of the Tory membership, though he may struggle to get on the ballot paper since he is not popular with Tory MPs and only the top two names go forward to the members.

Saturday 18 May

To dinner with Jonathan and Katherine Clark in the 'Big Hoose'. Among the guests the regional chairman of the Northumberland Conservatives, who says there is talk among the faithful of changing the rules to ensure that Johnson gets on the ballot for the new Tory leader. The plan is that, instead of the top two, the top four candidates in a ballot of MPs would be put to the membership, which would almost certainly result in Johnson becoming Prime Minister. Another guest, whose husband made a film about Johnson some years ago ('when he was strongly pro-EU'), said she had got to know him fairly well at the time and that he lacked the ability to concentrate on anything for more than about ten seconds. Meanwhile the British entry came last in the Eurovision Song Contest. A humiliation that will be as nothing compared with the rise of Boris.

Wednesday 22 May

Open season on poor Theresa May, who is making her fourth attempt to get her Brexit deal through the Commons. 'Desperate, Deluded, Doomed' (*Telegraph*), 'Theresa's Gamble Too Far' (*Mail*), 'You'll be Gurn in the Morning' (*Sun*), 'Besieged, Theresa's Last Hurrah' (*Express*). Meanwhile British Steel is on the verge of collapse.

Thursday 23 May

To the House of Lords in anticipation of lunch with Peter Hennessy, only to discover I had got the wrong date. The first person I ran into was a prominent Lib Dem. 'Who's your next leader?' I enquired. 'The choice is dire,' he replied gloomily. 'There are only two candidates: Jo Swinson, who I would not trust with a single pound of my money, and Ed Davey, who is boring.' So, it seems that all parties are in trouble. Meanwhile, despite everything, Boris Johnson is emerging as the Tory favourite to succeed May.

Friday 24 May

Theresa May has at last announced her intention to resign. This evening we harvested the first strawberries from the glasshouse.

Thursday 30 May

To London, where I stayed with John and Sheila Williams. The first time I have seen John since he was diagnosed with a cancerous tumour on his spine. Until now, though both in their eighties, John and Sheila have been ageless. Unfailingly generous. A fund of good humour. Excellent company. Always there. Always the same. Permanent, unchanging features of my life. Now for the first time they are beginning to look their age. Sheila has lost weight, which is worrying, and John, who until a year or two ago was capable of walking ten or twelve miles carrying a heavy backpack, now walks with a stoop and uses a walking stick.

Friday 31 May

To Broadcasting House for a much-postponed appearance on Radio 4's *Loose Ends*. As I was leaving this morning, John said to me, 'My advice to you, Chris, is don't get old.' Uncle Peter said much the same when he was dying. Among my fellow guests on *Loose Ends*, Armistead Maupin of *Tales of the City* fame; Renée Fleming, a beautiful American opera singer; and the singer P. P. Arnold, whose 1960s classic 'Angel of the Morning' I still play. I made a point of having my photo taken with her and tweeted it. To my surprise, she has only a couple of thousand Twitter followers. I guess her star, like mine, is fading.

Tuesday 4 June

To London on an early train and then to Simpson's in the Strand for an Oldie literary lunch. One of my fellow authors, who has just published a biography of Peter Carrington,* described how, when Lord Carrington was on his deathbed, his son went in to give him the news that Boris Johnson had resigned as Foreign Secretary. The old fellow was comatose and the news had to be repeated. When finally it registered, he suddenly came alive, raising his arm and punching the air. An hour later, he died.

---

* Christopher Lee, *Carrington: An Honourable Man*, Viking, 2018.

Wednesday 5 June

What a dismal business the Tory leadership election has become. Sajid Javid proclaiming his love of country, Dominic Raab promising tax cuts while his rivals demand more spending on the police and the military, even as the social fabric crumbles. Of the dozen or so declared candidates, only Rory Stewart is making any serious attempt to appeal to the dwindling one-nation constituency. One anonymous Tory is quoted in *The Times* as saying that the parliamentary party has lost its political and moral compass. Lunch at the House of Lords with the historian Peter Hennessy, who suggested I write a book about great lives that have overlapped with mine, along the lines of Roy Jenkins's *Nine Men of Power*. I will think about it, but as things stand a fourth volume of diaries, if there is any interest, is likely to round off my literary career, bringing my total output to ten books, a satisfyingly round number.

Thursday 6 June

D-Day as was. Even as world leaders and aged veterans are gathering in Normandy to celebrate the anniversary, Tory blogger Guido Fawkes opened a new front: 'Corbyn argued for Appeasing Hitler and Disarming DURING the Second World War'. Did he? Does anybody care any more? We've had Corbyn the Marxist, Corbyn the antisemite, Corbyn the Soviet agent, Corbyn the friend of terrorists. Surely we have reached saturation point. Meanwhile the country sinks deeper into the Brexit nightmare and none of the eleven candidates for the Tory leadership offers any credible way out. One of the front runners is even talking of proroguing Parliament in order to force through a no-deal Brexit.

Friday 7 June

To general astonishment, Labour have won the Peterborough by-election. Quite an achievement considering that, if the polls and pundits are to be believed, our unloved leader is plumbing new depths of unpopularity, not to mention that the citizens of Peterborough are overwhelmingly Brexiteers and the by-election was triggered by the jailing of the previous Labour MP for being a serial liar. Perhaps there is something in Corbyn's strategy of trying to focus on other issues besides Brexit. Could this be peak Farage?

Saturday 8 June

'New Labour MP "must be suspended"'. So says the front-page headline in today's *Times* over a report of yesterday's surprise Labour victory at Peterborough. Yet again Labour's enemies have been provided with a stick with which to beat us by those two zealous dames, Louise Ellman and Margaret Hodge. This latest assault has been prompted by the discovery that some weeks ago the new MP, Lisa Forbes, unwisely 'liked' an antisemitic Facebook post without apparently having read it properly. On the surface it was expressing solidarity with the victims of the massacre in Christchurch, New Zealand, but there was an unpleasant message attached it. Yet another illustration of the perils of social media. No matter that Ms Forbes has been profuse in her apologies. No matter that she has only been elected for a matter of hours. That is not enough for The Dames. The poor woman must be immediately cast out.

Sunday 9 June

Ngoc has come across a diary that Sarah wrote, aged eleven, when we visited her cousins in Vietnam eighteen years ago. It contains the following line: 'Dakla and Bop think Emma [then aged six] is cute, but I know better.'

Monday 10 June

Boris Johnson now seems certain to become Tory leader, but he still feels obliged to make undeliverable promises. This morning, with gobsmacking cynicism, he promised to raise the threshold at which the higher rate of income tax is paid from around £50,000 to £80,000. A naked attempt to purchase the votes of the leaner, meaner elements of the aged Tory membership, many of whom are in the upper tax bracket. Cynical not least because as he well knows there is not the slightest chance he could get such a measure through Parliament either now or in the foreseeable future. Dog-whistle politics of this sort bear the fingerprints of Lynton Crosby, who, according to a senior Tory I came across in Westminster the other day, is advising Johnson. The strategy is entirely transparent. He's smartened himself up – haircut, new suit – and has for the past two weeks kept his head down for fear of alienating fellow Tory MPs whose votes will count in the first stage of the selection process. Having secured the necessary nominations, he has now turned his attention to the members.

The *Washington Post* reports a leaked tape of a meeting between the US Secretary of State, Mike Pompeo, and unspecified Jewish leaders. It is unclear whether any of those present were British. Question: 'Would you be willing to work with us to take on actions if life becomes very difficult for Jews in the UK?' Answer:

> It could be that Mr Corbyn manages to run the gauntlet and get elected. You should know we won't wait for him to do those things to begin to push back. We will do our level best. It's too risky and too important and too hard once it's already happened.

Apparently this was met with 'fervent applause'. Shades of Kissinger and Chile. We know what our American 'friends' had in mind for Chile. What have they in mind for us?*

A spectacular display of lupins in the garden, now alas at risk from the wind and rain forecast for the next few days.

Tuesday 11 June

A BBC journalist came to discuss making a programme about threats and abuse targeted against MPs, which he wants me to front. It prompted me to look up the latest tweets directed at me over the Birmingham bombings case: 'You are filth,' from someone who styles himself a supporter of justice for the twenty-one murdered victims. And this from another, 'The specimen Mullin is a disgusting arrogant scumbag.' Both within the past twenty-four hours.

Wednesday 12 June

After a period of uncharacteristic silence, Boris Johnson launched his leadership campaign. We are being invited to believe that this is a new Boris. Not the irresponsible scoundrel with the attention span of a gnat

---

* On 27 June 1970, Kissinger told a meeting of the 40 Committee for Covert Action on Chile, 'I don't see why we need to stand by and watch a country go communist due to the irresponsibility of its own people. The issues are much too important for the Chilean voters to be left to decide for themselves.'

who has led a life of total self-indulgence that we have all grown used to. No, that Boris has gone. At least for the moment. In his place we are being offered a sober, clean-living, thoughtful statesman who alone can save the Tories from oblivion and rescue the nation from the morass of Brexit, which (in his previous incarnation) he has done so much to bring about.

Thursday 13 June

Another day in the life of Brexit Britain and the pit gets deeper. This morning the UK's outgoing High Commissioner in Singapore is reported as saying that Singaporean leaders are 'mystified to how our political leaders have allowed things to get to this pass'. He goes on to say that a nation Singaporeans once 'admired for stability, common sense, tolerance and realism grounded in fact', they now see 'beset by division, obsessed with ideology, careless of the truth, its leaders apparently determined to keep on digging'. Rain all day, beating down my beautiful lupins and laying waste to much of the wild flower area.

Saturday 15 June–Sunday 16 June

To my favourite literary festival at Melrose in the Borders. What makes it so enjoyable is the feeling that it is so intimate and the authors are made so welcome. We are encouraged to stay the weekend, bring partners and attend each other's events. We dine together around a communal table in the aptly named Harmony House and are luxuriously accommodated. As usual, that most genial of aristocrats, Richard Scott, aka the Duke of Buccleuch, who sponsors the festival, was much in evidence. This year's cast list included old favourites Jim Naughtie, Jan Ravens, Sandy McCall Smith. Among the newcomers Dominic Grieve, who is saying he will vote to bring down the government if Boris attempts to take us out of the EU without a deal, and David Nott, a modest, soft-spoken surgeon who has worked voluntarily in many of the world's most terrible war zones. He was rewarded with a heartfelt standing ovation.

To Bowhill on Sunday morning, where the Duke, wearing a dark green velvet frock coat and open-neck shirt, entertained a hundred or so of us to his traditional brunch. Afterwards he treated some of us to a whistle-stop tour of the principal rooms, adorned with the portraits of illustrious ancestors and the occasional Canaletto. In the little library beyond the morning room he plucked from the shelves signed first editions of the Waverley novels and *The Wealth of Nations* and handed them around for us to admire. 'Which of your principal residences is your favourite?' I enquired. 'Oh, I love them all. I would never prefer one over the others. It would upset those who look after them.'

At dinner someone remarked firmly that 'not one person who has had direct dealings with Boris Johnson believes he is fit to be Prime Minister'. Maybe, but, barring miracles, it will come to pass. The expectation is that as soon as he meets obstruction from Parliament he will call a general election to free himself from dependence on the Ulster Unionists, and the odds are he will win. A poll suggests that 47 per cent would contemplate voting for him even though 59 per cent of the same sample say they would not buy a used car from him. Such is our national loss of self-esteem.

Monday 17 June

A tweet I posted on Saturday defending the achievements of the Blair government by reference to the impact on the poorer parts of Sunderland has taken off, attracting 4,300 likes and 1,100 retweets. Can it be that, the Iraq catastrophe notwithstanding, there is growing nostalgia for the relative calm of the *ancien régime*?

Wednesday 19 June

An astonishing YouGov poll published this morning suggests that more than 60 per cent of Tory Party members would accept the loss of Scotland and Northern Ireland as a price worth paying for Brexit. A similar number would accept significant damage to the economy and 54 per cent would even accept the destruction of the Conservative Party. If YouGov is to be believed, almost half of them would even accept Nigel Farage as leader. All of which suggests that the Tory Party is in the grip of an extremist cult, although most of our free press, so busily searching for extremists in the ranks of the opposition, don't seem to have noticed.

Sunday 23 June

Among our visitors this morning a man who had once been a neighbour of Boris Johnson's in Islington, who said his abiding impression was one of chaos. Boris would emerge each morning looking scruffy, hair unkempt, stained suit. He had once owned a camper van which was frequently towed away because it lacked the necessary residents' parking permit, for which he seemed incapable of applying.

Monday 24 June

This evening I watched the last of three excellent programmes about the growing tide of plastic waste under which we are sinking. The presenters, Hugh Fearnley-Whittingstall and Anita Rani, persuaded the residents of a street in Bristol to turn out all the plastic in their houses and then set out to show where this stuff is coming from and what happens to most of it. Fearnley-Whittingstall travelled to Malaysia, where much of our waste has simply been dumped in the rainforest. He then visited those struggling to deal with the waste in the UK, and finally INEOS, which manufactures on a vast scale the raw ingredients of much of our plastic and has plans to double production. Rani visited the head offices of some of the big polluters in an attempt to get them to face up to their responsibilities. With the exception of INEOS, which at least engaged, the brazen arrogance of the other corporations was shocking. Despite mission statements full of warm words professing their love of the environment and a commitment to sustainability, faced with difficult questions they simply retreated indoors and pulled up the drawbridge, putting out bland little press releases claiming always to act within the law. Predictably, the most brazen was McDonald's, which gives away useless, unwanted, unrecyclable plastic baubles with their children's meals. When Rani, accompanied by two bright-eyed small people, aged seven and nine, who had collected 160,000 signatures on a petition calling for an end to the practice, visited the McDonald's headquarters to deliver their petition, the staff on reception simply summoned a security guard who ordered them off the premises. You could see the disappointment in the little girls' faces on discovering that their effort was wasted. For them an early lesson in the workings of the market. The moral is clear. For all their PR bullshit, most big corporations and their top brass don't give a fig about the damage they are doing to the planet. They will only act when forced by governments to do so. Bring it on, I say.

Friday 28 June

To London for *the* wedding. For weeks Mrs V. B. Boss has talked of little else. My former colleague Joyce Quin was on the train as far as Newcastle. Joyce, a fervent Remainer, remarked, 'I laugh when I hear Brexiteers like Matt Ridley and Jacob Rees-Mogg talking about the metropolitan elite. Which one of us went to Whitley Bay High School?' In fairness to Matt, who inevitably went to Eton, he would probably see the joke. Not sure about Jacob, though.

Saturday 29 June

This morning, with Andrew and Diana Hamilton, our new in-laws, we made our way to Islington Town Hall to bear witness to the marriage of the beautiful Sarah Mullin and her handsome fiancé, Nick Hamilton. A simple, intimate little ceremony conducted in the mayor's parlour. Aunty Liz and Emma the only other relatives in attendance. Afterwards we walked back to the happy couple's flat, pausing en route to buy a takeaway lunch at the local Ottolenghi. I slept for two hours in the afternoon and in the evening flew to Dublin for a festival in Kells.

Sunday 30 June
Kells

Another of my favourite festivals, everyone so hospitable and friendly. A relatively small event, only about 100 people, but they bought a lot of books. This evening, to Newcastle, courtesy of the loathsome Ryanair, who fined me €55 for failing to check in more than two hours in advance. I was driven to the airport by a former Fine Gael MP who remarked that while Brexit was generally bad for Ireland, there was a silver lining: 240 companies had migrated, partly or wholly, from the UK to Ireland.

Meanwhile *The Times* has opened a new front on Corbyn. Yesterday's paper leads with the suggestion that neither his physical nor his mental health is up to the top job. 'Corbyn too frail to be PM, fears civil service' is the headline over a lengthy report quoting anonymous 'mandarins'. As several people have tweeted, this could be a scene from *A Very British Coup*.

Monday 1 July

An amusing little bidding war has broken out between the two final candidates for the Tory leadership, both vying to spend the supposed £26 billion which the Treasury is said to have put aside (though actually it is extra borrowing) to deal with the fallout from the hard Brexit that they are both now threatening. As someone pointed out, both Labour and the Tories are now dancing around the magic money tree.

Thursday 4 July

I am going off Jeremy Hunt. When I met him at dinner in Andrew Mitchell's house a couple of years back, I rather warmed to him, but this Tory leadership election is bringing out the worst in him. Although at heart a Remainer, he is becoming increasingly reckless in an attempt to out-Brexit Boris. That I can live with, though I don't approve. Yesterday, however, he managed to get a reference to Auschwitz and Jeremy Corbyn into the same sentence, which is utterly beyond the pale.

Saturday 6 July

An interesting intervention from John Sawers, former head of MI6, on the *Today* programme this morning. The UK, he said, is going through a political nervous breakdown. In what appears to be a reference to both Johnson and Corbyn, he said:

> We have potential Prime Ministers being elected … who do not have the standing we have become used to in our top leadership … We have taken a huge risk with our international standing, to the strength of the British economy … It is not surprising that people who have devoted their lives to serving the interests of the country are concerned about the direction the country is taking.

How should democrats respond to this? He's right, of course, and his former colleagues are entitled to their views, but at the end of the day in a democracy the electorate is paramount, whether we like it or not. As it happens, Sir John's view of the way things are going is shared by security chiefs in *The Friends of Harry Perkins*. Life imitates art. I wonder if anyone will notice.

Sarah's Wedding Party, Callaly

A hundred and something guests, including relatives from as far away at Calgary, Alberta; Boston, Massachusetts; and Malaysia. The radiant bride, on the arm of her old dad (who has been awarded a new suit for the occasion), was preceded by a kilted piper and five bridesmaids, each bearing posies cut from our garden this morning. We made our way across verdant lawns to the edge of the lake, where an exchange of vows took place. This evening, a slap-up meal in a vast marquee decorated with Vietnamese lanterns, erected on the croquet lawn to the east of the big house, above which (courtesy of our neighbour Tony Henfrey) flies the flag of Vietnam. The bride, her sister and her mother dressed in elegant *ao dai*. Three good speeches. A massive quantity of alcohol consumed – mercifully purchased in Calais by the in-laws at an advantageous price (thank goodness we are still in the EU). Followed by a ceilidh. Just before midnight the happy couple were driven away by Tony in his Rolls-Royce, wearing his chauffeur's cap. The sun shone, no one misbehaved, the neighbours were tolerant. A great relief that it is all over and we can now talk about something other than weddings.

Sunday 7 July

After the party, the clear-up. Emma and I made a trip to the recycling centre in Alnwick with a car-load of detritus. More will follow next week. So much for living sustainably.

Wednesday 10 July
Ways With Words Festival, Dartington

John Major was on the radio this morning talking sensibly about Brexit. He even went so far as say that if Boris tried to prorogue Parliament in order to get through no-deal, he would personally seek a judicial review.

Later, Melissa Benn, who like me is here for the festival, remarked that it comes to something when, in the absence of leadership on our side, we find ourselves cheering on the likes of John Major, William Hague, Michael Heseltine and Philip Hammond. To which list I would add Rory Stewart.

After breakfast I strolled along the river into Totnes and back. A couple of hundred people attended my event in the Great Hall this afternoon.

Other news: Britain's ambassador in the US has resigned following a leak of his emails criticising Donald Trump.

Thursday 11 July
Dartington

Breakfast with Melissa Benn. We both reckon that Jeremy has been un-fairly traduced over antisemitism (last night's *Panorama* was devoted to the subject). Nor is it helpful to have his supposed deputy, Tom Watson, popping up every five minutes saying how shocked/chilled/appalled he is. Oddly enough the wider public doesn't seem to share the media obses-sion with the issue. The subject arose briefly at my session yesterday and no one argued with my response: that there is a problem and it may well have been mishandled, but it is a small problem that has been blown out of proportion by those who have a different agenda.

London

To Clerkenwell for the Profile Books summer party. Among the guests the historian Margaret MacMillan, who speculated that next time around Trump may choose Ivanka as his running mate and that he will stand down halfway through his term so that she can replace him and pardon his many crimes. An amusing fantasy. Or is it?

Tuesday 16 July

To Committee Room 4a in the House of Lords, where I was guest speak-er at the annual meeting of the Association of Former MPs. A generally good-humoured affair, though one or two old codgers are still fighting the battles of the 1980s. This was followed by a reception in Speaker's House, after which I dined with Andrew Mitchell in Islington. Andrew has come out for Boris Johnson. Why? Because rightly or wrongly he believes he has influence with Boris, having apparently extracted an assurance that he will not let the Foreign Office recapture the aid budget (which they are itching to do). Also, I suspect, he believes there is a prospect of a return to office under Boris, albeit a slim one. That would be no bad thing.

Wednesday 17 July

To Primrose Hill to see Liz Forgan. We walked to Regent's Park and whiled away an hour in the rose garden. Liz remarked how impressed, despite obvious misgivings, she is with John McDonnell. Is it all a front or is he really the charming, self-deprecating pragmatist who comes over so well on the *Andrew Marr Show*? The short answer seems to be that whatever his instincts, John is smart enough to realise that in the unlikely event that Labour does by any chance stumble into government, it will be in no position to enact a revolution and has adjusted his rhetoric accordingly.

Thursday 18 July

Chennai (formerly Madras), a city of 8 million people, is reported to have run out of water.

Saturday 20 July

Today is the fiftieth anniversary of the moon landing and there is talk of spending billions on another space race. Even India, which has 600 million people without toilets, is joining in. We should surely sort out this planet before conquering another one.

Tuesday 23 July

As expected, Boris Johnson today became leader of the Conservative Party and will tomorrow enter No. 10 as Prime Minister. There is a certain poetic justice in the fact that it now falls to him to clear up the mess that he has done so much to create. His bluff is about to be called.

Thursday 25 July

Johnson's new Cabinet: in the words of Alastair Campbell 'post-truth, post-shame, Trumpian'. With a handful of exceptions, who have run up the white flag, it is shorn of unbelievers. Sajid Javid, Chancellor; Dominic Raab, Foreign Secretary; Priti Patel, Home Secretary; Michael Gove, Cabinet Office; Jacob Rees-Mogg, Leader of the House. Humphry Wakefield's fractious son-in-law aka Rasputin, Dominic Cummings, is to be a special adviser in No. 10 – bets are already being taken on how long he will last. Nick Boles, a dissenting Tory MP, commented, 'What this establishes beyond any shadow of doubt is that the Conservative Party has been taken over by the hard right, turning themselves into the Brexit Party in order to fend off Nigel Farage.'

A heatwave. Down south the temperature has touched 38°. Up here a very reasonable 25. I passed most of the day in the garden, reading.

Friday 26 July

Already the first little cracks are appearing. Headbanger Steve Baker has turned down a job in the Brexit department on the grounds that, since primary responsibility for Brexit now resides with Dominic Cummings in No. 10, he would be powerless. As today's *Times* recalls, there is no love lost between Baker and Cummings, who is on record as describing the European Research Group, of which Baker is a leading light, as 'a narcissistic-delusional subset' and a 'metastasising tumour' that needs to be excised. All of which sounds promising.

Saturday 27 July

The heatwave is over; thunderstorms and heavy showers deluged the garden. A grey mist shrouds the hills.

Sunday 28 July

Some unkind person has written of Jo Swinson, the new Lib Dem leader, that 'she can't shake that terrible, pious, illiberal, ultra-Liberal tendency to look astonished, truly shocked, and appalled when encountering opinions other than her own'. There is a grain of truth in this, but liberal intolerance is just one symptom of the age in which we live. Nor is such intolerance confined to liberals. Witness the boundless 'outrage' of our right-wing tabloids. As for Jo Swinson, in the absence of the Labour Party from the field of battle, she is well placed to lead a Lib Dem revival.*

Friday 2 August

The Lib Dems have won the Brecon and Radnorshire by-election, but not by the expected margin considering that the Tory candidate, the former sitting MP, was an expenses fiddler. On this result the Tories will regain the seat at the general election. Labour came fourth, after the Brexit Party. Ngoc packed a picnic and we drove to St Boswells, from where we walked along the Tweed to Dryburgh, pausing to eat our lunch on a bench by the river. Then to the Duke of Sutherland's garden at Mertoun, where we wandered for a pleasant two hours. Despite this being the height of the holiday season, we were the only visitors.

Saturday 3 August

'I WANT CRIMINALS TO BE TERRIFIED'. The front page of today's *Mail* over an interview with our ludicrous new Home Secretary in which she promises a return to zero-tolerance policing, whatever that means. I tweeted that she appears to be utterly out of her depth and this morning comes an email from a former Permanent Secretary of my acquaintance: 'I completely agree with your tweets on Priti Patel … I don't think I have ever seen a Secretary of State look so completely out her depth – and so quickly.' He added, 'I greatly enjoyed *The Friends of Harry Perkins*, though bittersweet.'

Sunday 4 August

According to today's *Sunday Times*, several leading Brexiteer hedge funders have made huge bets against the share price of British companies in the expectation of a no-deal Brexit. One of them, Crispin Odey, who helped fund Boris Johnson's leadership campaign, is already said to have

---

* Ha!

made £220 million on the outcome of the 2016 referendum and stands to make another fortune if the economy takes another hit as a result of Brexit. 'This absolutely stinks,' tweeted Sarah Wollaston, a former Tory MP. I'll say.

Tuesday 6 August

A wake-up call from Larry Summers, former US Treasury Secretary. On the *Today* programme this morning he described the idea that Britain will secure an early and advantageous trade agreement with the US as 'delusional'.

> Britain has no leverage. Britain is desperate … The last thing you do is quit your job before you look for a new one. In the same way, establishing absolutely, as a matter of sacred principle, that you are leaving the EU has to be the worst way to give yourself leverage with any new partners.

This despite a letter from forty-five Republican senators expressing confidence in an early agreement.

Rain for much of the day. And the lawn mower is refusing to start.

Saturday 10 August

Still raining. The burn has turned into a raging torrent, crashing over the sluices and the waterfall. A large new lake has appeared on the lawn where a month ago we held Sarah's wedding. How lucky we were to get away with it. Three of the five Saturdays since then have been washed out. The show at nearby Glanton, a highlight of the local social calendar, has been abandoned at the last minute. The marquee stands empty and forlorn in a waterlogged field. 'The worst August weather in living memory', according to the message announcing cancellation.

Sunday 11 August

Every day a new crowd-pleasing announcement from our new masters, all from the Lynton Crosby playbook of so-called dog-whistle issues: more money for the NHS, 20,000 more police officers, longer prison sentences (an old Tory favourite when all else fails) and today 10,000 more prison places. Unclear as yet where the money is coming from or even if much of it will come to pass. Everything points to an early election – before the consequences of a no-deal Brexit kick in.

Wednesday 14 August

To Edinburgh, where I did a turn at the festival. A just about full house, 750 people and the book-signing queue took almost an hour to clear. Among those in the queue a couple from northern California who are spending the summer in Scotland to escape the smoke from the forest fires that engulf their small town during the dry season. My first encounter with climate change refugees. Afterwards a pleasant walk with Emma around the Old Town and along the Water of Leith, which was flowing heavily following the recent rain.

Thursday 15 August

Jeremy Corbyn has written to the leaders of other opposition parties and 'senior backbenchers' suggesting they form an alliance to vote down the government and replace it with 'a strictly time-limited temporary' administration which would apply for an extension of Article 50 to allow time for a general election. The letter concludes, 'In that general election, Labour will be committed to a public vote on the terms of leaving the EU including an option to Remain.' Theoretically a credible initiative, but for one large fly in the ointment – Jeremy is not a unifying figure. Witness that Jo Swinson, the Lib Dems' pious new leader, responded with an immediate denunciation and it is stretching the imagination to believe that the Tory dissenters could ever pluck up the courage to support even the most temporary government led by Jeremy.

Friday 16 August

Much fanciful talk of a caretaker government led by the likes of Ken Clarke, Harriet Harman or Margaret Beckett. Other names in the ring include Yvette Cooper or Hilary Benn. Team Corbyn would never go for either of the last two on the grounds that their appointment would in effect amount to a coup. To stand a chance of acceptance by most Labour members, the nominee has to be someone who has no ambition to lead their party into a general election. Like it or not – and I don't – that's Jeremy's job.

This afternoon to the Freeman Hospital in Newcastle to prepare for yet another kidney stone operation. An X-ray, an ECG and then a long interview with a delightful Filipina nurse who took samples of my blood urine and asked many questions, including, 'Can you walk up two flights of stairs?' She was taken aback by the news that I had been known to climb 3,000ft hills in the Lake District.

Upon discovering that I was married to a Vietnamese woman, she asked how we met and what I was doing in Vietnam in the '70s and '80s. 'I was a journalist,' I said.

'Are you famous?'

'No.'

'Have you appeared on television?'

'Yes.'

'Then you are famous.'

We left it at that.

Tuesday 20 August

Three years after the referendum, Project Fear is in full swing. Every day a new scare story. Tonight's television bulletins are led with a suggestion that the UK's oil refineries could be put out of business by cheaper oil imports. Meanwhile the regional news, never knowingly outdone, is leading with heart surgeons saying that Brexit could mean fewer heart transplants. Don't ask me why.

Friday 23 August

A call from the hospital. As I suspected, my latest kidney stone appears to have passed naturally. Operation cancelled. Yessss.

Sunday 25 August

Another little heatwave. We packed a picnic and drove to Warkworth, from where we strolled under cloudless skies three miles or so along largely deserted beaches towards Alnmouth, all the while remarking on our good fortune at being able to enjoy Caribbean sunshine and empty beaches without having to stray more than a few miles from home.

Meanwhile the Brazilians are burning down the Amazon rainforest, their government brazenly oblivious.

Monday 26 August

Belatedly, prompted by the fact that our paths are likely to cross again in October, I have been reading William Waldegrave's autobiography, *A Different Kind of Weather*. An account of a golden life, rich with glittering prizes (he had two first-job interviews on the same day – one with the Governor of the Bank of England and the other with Lord Rothschild), only made bearable for us ordinary mortals by a healthy dose of self-deprecation and some shrewd judgements such as, 'It is wrong that the Ministry of Defence is the promotional arm of British Aerospace.'

Wednesday 28 August

The government has prorogued Parliament in order to prevent the opposition – and some of their own – from resisting a no-deal Brexit, resulting in howls of outrage from Remainers and some constitutionalists. You have to hand it to these guys, they are nothing if not ruthless. Imagine a Labour government daring to pull a stunt like this?

Friday 30 August

Brexit has become a shouting match with two rival camps each talking past each other. The decision to prorogue Parliament has spurred Remainers to new heights of apoplexy, while Leavers think it is a perfectly reasonable way of breaking the deadlock. Much foolish Remainer talk of taking to the streets which is only likely to further polarise opinion and scare away the centrists, if there are any left. Meanwhile the polls show the Tories well ahead. One, asking who would make the best Prime Minister – Johnson, Swinson or Corbyn – even has Jeremy lagging behind the Don't Knows. In a choice of three he came fourth. Oh dear, oh dear. Where are we headed?

Monday 2 September

Belatedly I came across the following from a contemporary of Boris Johnson's at Eton:

> Johnson ... looked pretty much the same at 15 as he does at 55, and was a familiar sight as he charged his way around the college lanes. The big-foot stoop (he was known as 'the Yeti'), the bumbling confidence, the skimmed-milk pallor, the berserk hair, the alarming air of imminent self-harm, which gave the impression that he had been freshly released from some protective institution: all was already in place.[*]

Tuesday 3 September

What times we live in. Corbyn and McDonnell in Salford last night demanding a general election. Tony Lloyd, a member of the shadow Cabinet, this morning saying that Labour will not be daft enough to agree to an election this side of Brexit (wanna bet?). Tory whips openly threatening dissenting MPs with deselection. Philip Hammond, until recently Chancellor of the Exchequer, on the radio this morning saying that his party has been taken over by entryists and incomers. (Dominic Cummings, the man at the centre of the mayhem, is not even a member of the Conservative Party.) Meanwhile sterling sliding towards parity with the euro. This evening in the House of Commons the government were defeated by a surprisingly wide margin – twenty-seven votes.

Our Brexiteer neighbour Tony Henfrey joined us for dinner this evening, unruffled by the turmoil at Westminster. 'This is the democratic process working exactly as it should,' he says cheerfully. As for scare stories about the dire consequences of no-deal, he dismisses these, saying that investment will flood in and the value of sterling will rebound once there is clarity. He might be right. Andrew Mitchell says the same. It is the long-term impact that I fear.

Wednesday 4 September

To Sunderland for the funeral of former council leader Bryn Sidaway, one of my earliest supporters. A Tory councillor in attendance divulged

---

[*] James Wood, 'These Etonians', *London Review of Books*, 4 July 2019.

a snippet of which I was previously unaware: in the 1997 general election campaign we were honoured by the presence of one Dominic Cummings campaigning on behalf of the Conservative candidate, a pleasant but ineffectual former RAF officer. Cummings's principal contribution to the campaign seems to have been to draft a lengthy, ludicrous, aggressive speech which, to the embarrassment of everyone present (not least the Tory agent), the said candidate proceeded to read out after the declaration of the result, having just been soundly defeated. He went on for so long that I had to leave the stage while he was still speaking in order to respond for requests for interviews, Sunderland as usual being the first seat to declare. Cummings has obviously honed his political skills since then. As for the hapless ex-RAF officer, he has not been heard of since.

Another crazy day in Brexitland. Last night's Tory rebels – who include four recent Cabinet ministers, not to mention veterans such as Ken Clarke and Nicholas Soames – have been told that they will not be permitted to run again as Tory candidates. Unintimidated they have gone on to defy the government again, voting to make time for a bill which would prevent a no-deal Brexit. Meanwhile Boris Johnson's threat of a snap general election evaporated when it was decisively voted down.

An email from my brother, David: 'Cameron's plan to keep the Conservative Party together seems to be going frightfully well.' Yes, indeed.

Friday 6 September

Out of the blue, an email from the musician Brian Eno. 'Over the years I have often had cause to admire your work ... and now I discover we were at school together.' Indeed we were. He is just about the school's only famous alumnus. Was it I, he enquires, who 'felled the quasi-psychotic Brother X with a well-aimed blow to the stomach ... As a pacifist, it probably isn't something I shouldn't be celebrating ... Were you the Mullin?' As it happens, I wasn't. Nor do I recall any such incident. Or indeed the existence of any other pupil with a similar surname.

Saturday 7 September

Suddenly Boris Johnson looks vulnerable. What briefly looked like a bold and brilliant strategy no longer looks so clever. He has lost control of both the election timetable and the timetable for EU withdrawal, outmanoeuvred by the combined forces of the opposition and rebels in his own party. He can have an election, but only if he agrees to ask Brussels for a three-month extension of the withdrawal timetable, which would be a humiliation. This may only be a temporary respite, but it is a moment to savour.

'The Conservative Party is dying,' says Matthew Parris in today's *Times*. I doubt it. On another page in the same paper the psephologist John Curtice says that if there were an election in the near future, the Tories would still win. A measure of the depths to which the Corbynistas have led Labour.

Sunday 8 September

Another brick falls from the arch. Amber Rudd has resigned from the Cabinet and announced that she is leaving the Conservative parliamentary party.

Monday 9 September

Mr Speaker Bercow announced today that he will stand down on 31 October. In my view, for all his various shortcomings, he will go down as a great champion of Parliament. The fact that he is loathed by the executive counts in his favour.

Wednesday 11 September

To dinner at the Mansion House in Newcastle, an Edwardian Gothic pile that once housed the city's Lord Mayor, where I entertained members of the Pen and Palette Club. One of the guests told me that he knew of a Japanese businessman working for one of Nissan's local suppliers who is currently scouring Europe for an alternative base in the event that Brexit turns out badly. Another ominous little straw in the wind.

Thursday 12 September

In the wake of a decision by the Scottish court that the proroguing of Parliament was illegal, the Remain media are obsessing about whether Boris

Johnson lied to the Queen about his reason for closing Parliament. If even I, a Remainer, find this nonsense irritating, imagine how Joe Public must feel. One keeps hearing our unloved legislators popping up in the media expressing faux outrage at the premature closure of Parliament and demanding that 'we be allowed to do our jobs'. Ha, if only. In recent years we have all become used to the spectacle of ministers addressing a near-empty chamber. By Thursday on any given week the place is deserted.

Saturday 14 September

David Cameron's long-overdue memoirs are serialised in today's *Times*. He lays into Boris Johnson, Michael Gove and Dominic Cummings and expresses remorse about his mishandling of the referendum and its outcome, but – shades of Tony Blair and Iraq – can't quite bring himself to say the whole thing was a mistake. On Brexit he says, 'I worry about it a lot. Every single day I think about … the things that could have been done differently, and I worry about what is going to happen next.' He concludes, 'I deeply regret the outcome and accept that my approach failed. The decisions I took contributed to that failure. I failed.' Who says Etonians don't do remorse? In a way it's sad because Cameron wasn't a bad man. Intelligent, moderate, liberal, but like Blair he made one massive misjudgement which will hang round his neck for the rest of his life.

Monday 16 September

The Lib Dem conference has voted to reverse Brexit without bothering with another referendum 'if we form a majority government'. Fantasy politics, of course, given that they currently have just thirteen elected MPs plus a handful of defectors, but it gets them noticed. Jo Swinson is bright and articulate, but there is an air of the student politician about her which she can't quite shake off.

We drove to Etal and picnicked in sunshine by the river Till.

Thursday 19 September
Coniston Hotel Skipton
A two-day conference of delegates from national park authorities. This

morning, at the final session, much beating ourselves up about how old and white we are. Later we were addressed, among others, by a right-on, tattooed young woman who urged us to set up a committee to examine the problem. Personally I found her a bit of a pain, but it would never do for a white, balding man of my vintage to say so out loud, so I kept my mouth firmly closed. Later, however, I discreetly sounded out several of the women and to my pleasant surprise they concurred.

Friday 20 September

For all the talk of 'crashing out' and the dire consequences of no-deal, there are tentative signs that the regime may reach a last-minute deal with the EU – something along the lines of a border in the Irish Sea. Anathema to Unionists, of course, but lately they have been making conciliatory noises and as for the Tory hardliners, most of them are now inside the tent and may be reluctant to rock the boat. My guess is that Johnson will offer to rehabilitate the expelled Tories, if they vote the right way. That plus the fact that Labour will struggle to find a reason to vote against any halfway credible deal and even if the leadership did, many Labour MPs may vote for it anyway, meaning that a soft landing can no longer be ruled out. In which case an enormous triumph will be declared.

Saturday 21 September

Corbyn's poll rating is down to 21 or 16 per cent, depending on which page of today's *Times* you believe.

Sunshine – likely to be the last for a while. We drove to Druridge Bay and ate our picnic in the dunes, overlooking a vast empty expanse of sand.

Tuesday 24 September

The Supreme Court has unanimously and sensationally annulled Boris Johnson's prorogation of Parliament, which, among other things, has had the welcome effect of diverting attention from the mayhem at the Labour Party conference. Although this doesn't change the politics, it's a major blow to the credibility and self-confidence of the current management.

Johnson, who is at the UN in New York, was looking distinctly chastened this evening. Not least because he has had to telephone the Queen, presumably to apologise for dragging her into this mess.

Wednesday 25 September

Now what? Parliament has been hastily reassembled, thanks to the judges. Our Prime Minister, brazenly unrepentant, has had to cut short his visit to the UN and race back across the Atlantic to face the music. Sound and fury on all sides, but very little light. The question arises: how are our underworked legislators going to occupy themselves in these extra weeks they have been gifted?

Sunday 29 September

'No. 10 probes Remain MPs' "foreign collusion"' – the wonderfully bonkers front page of today's *Mail on Sunday*. Needless to say, it is labelled 'Exclusive'. How could it be otherwise? An inside headline reads, 'The government is working on an extensive investigation into Dominic Grieve, Oliver Letwin, Hilary Benn and their involvement with foreign powers and the funding of their activities … Nobody knows what organisations are pulling the strings'. This is the first instalment of what the paper calls 'a thirteen-page crisis special' under the logo 'DEMOCRACY IN MELTDOWN'. One shouldn't laugh, of course, because it means a lot more hate mail and perhaps worse for the MPs in question.

Tuesday 1 October

To London on the 09.00. A great new fuss about a claim by a female journalist that Boris Johnson squeezed her inner thigh nineteen years ago. I am inclined to treat the matter lightly – and so it seems is most of the public, but my politically correct friend Hélène Mulholland, with whom I lunched at St Pancras, assures me it is a serious issue.

Wednesday 2 October

Boris Johnson has unveiled what is dubbed his final offer to Brussels

– Northern Ireland would leave the EU with the rest of the UK, there would be no hard border but EU regulations would somehow continue to apply to agricultural and other products and the Unionists would be given a veto which would have to be voted on by Stormont every four years. Initial reactions from Brussels and Dublin are sceptical, but the Unionists appear to be on board and most Tory MPs seem to be up for it so it might just slip through Parliament.

Friday 4 October

I have been sent the third volume of Charles Moore's monumental biography of Margaret Thatcher. In many ways a masterpiece, which has met with near-universal acclaim, but despite it being a thousand pages long he can find no room for any consideration of the consequences of her long rule. Most of his sources appear to dwell in the comfortable world in which he himself lives; a surprising number are fellow Etonians. Not a word about the impact of mass unemployment on places like Sunderland, the resulting breakdown of the social fabric and soaring levels of crime and yobbery that accompanied the Thatcher decade. Nor does he have much to say about the shameless enrichment of the middle classes through the sale of public assets at knockdown prices. And was the enforced sale of local authority housing such a triumph given that 40 per cent of ex-council houses are now in the hands of rapacious buy-to-let landlords, leaving us with a housing crisis the like of which we haven't seen for decades? And did her so-called Big Bang make us more vulnerable than our European neighbours to the 2008 crisis in the US mortgage market? I don't allege that these arguments are necessarily correct, but one would at least like to see them addressed. Given that Moore himself concedes that she was a divisive figure, one might expect him to be curious about why. It's not as though he didn't have the space. His three volumes taken together amount to more than 2,800 pages.

Tuesday 8 October

Seen in Alnwick this morning, a billboard advertising passport photos: 'Is your passport BREXIT READY? Under new passport validity rules you will need six months left on your passport to travel abroad.'

Wednesday 9 October

Turkish troops are poised to invade eastern Syria following Donald Trump's announcement, in a tweet, that he is abandoning America's Kurdish allies. The Kurds have been working for years with the Americans against Islamic State. They have borne the brunt of the fighting on the ground, suffering heavy casualties, and now overnight they are to be left to the tender mercies of their traditional enemies. Quite apart from which, the Kurds hold several thousand IS prisoners who are liable to take advantage of renewed chaos to restart their war. An epic betrayal. Of all Trump's crimes, this is surely the worst.

Thursday 10 October

The Turks are raining shells down on the Kurdish enclave in Syria, thousands of distraught civilians are fleeing into the desert, and President Erdoğan (again) is threatening to unleash a new wave of refugees into Europe if EU governments don't stop complaining. In Washington, Trump is talking gibberish about the Kurds not having helped the US in World War II… Awful, awful, awful.

Friday 11 October

To the literary festival at Ilkley, one of about ten speaking engagements this month. Having checked in at the theatre, I went for a walk round town, where I came across a group of people trying to help a woman who had collapsed in the street. They had covered her with their coats and were trying to make her comfortable. 'We need a woollen hat,' said one. Immediately I took mine off and handed it over. 'The ambulance will be here in five minutes, then you can have your hat back.' When I returned fifteen minutes later they were still there. No sign of an ambulance. I began to suspect that this might be some sort of student prank and hung back watching discreetly from the other side of the road. After a while, realising that it wasn't, I crossed over and said to one of the young women that I was due on stage in the theatre in fifteen minutes. 'So am I,' she replied. She was taking part in the poetry event downstairs. All ended well. Eventually an ambulance took the casualty to hospital, where she was found to have broken her shoulder. My hat awaited me at the box office after the show.

Sunday 13 October

Quentin Sommerville, a BBC reporter, has discovered three traumatised British orphan children, aged six, eight and ten, who, having emerged from the hell of Raqqa, are now living in desperate squalor in one of the prison camps for the families of Islamic State fighters in northern Syria. He interviewed the ten-year-old, a girl, who said that their parents and three of their siblings had been killed. Of Raqqa, the child said, 'There was a little house and a big dusty mountain. Behind it everybody was dead. We were going to pack our stuff and get out, but the aeroplanes came and bombed. So then my mum died, my littlest brother, my little brother, my sister…' She had grandparents in England but couldn't remember their names. Her memory of life in England was hazy: 'We used to go to restaurants and funfairs.' She and her siblings had been in Syria for about five years. By now they will be engulfed in a new nightmare as the Turks spread yet more chaos. What will become of them?*

Thursday 17 October

To Eton, where I gave a talk to members of the political society and stayed overnight with the provost, William Waldegrave. En route, having time to spare, I strolled around Windsor. The Royal Standard was flying above the castle, indicating that HM was in residence. On trying to gain entrance to the precincts, I found the way barred by an outrageously camp, charming man in a red cape and top hat who said that it was past closing time, 'unless', he added with a conspiratorial smile, 'you are going to the service'.

'Service? Ah yes, I am.' And so I found myself in St George's Chapel listening to a choir of angelic boys singing the *Magnificat and Nunc Dimittus*.

Friday 18 October

Our Prime Minister, hotfoot from Brussels, boasting of a great triumph. He has, so we are told, secured a deal which will enable him to fulfil his promise of leaving on 31 October. This is a film we have seen countless times before. All he has to do now is get his deal through Parliament.

---

* At the last moment, UN officials rescued these children and about twenty other orphans.

Saturday 19 October

Despite much fanfare, today's debate turned out to be a damp squib. By 322 votes to 306, MPs passed an amendment tabled by Oliver Letwin refusing to endorse withdrawal until they have seen the bill giving effect to it. A not unreasonable proposition, given that this is legislation that will shape the future of the country for years to come. On reflection it seems incredible that our masters could ever contemplate pushing through such a measure without disclosing the details. Is this what is meant by 'taking back control'?

Sunday 20 October

Boris Johnson is taking the mickey. He's sent two letters to the EU President. One, unsigned, asking for an extension to Article 51. The other, signed, saying why he doesn't think it is a good idea. Another trip to the courts beckons. As for yesterday's huge Remainer demonstration demanding another referendum, I fear it will have done no good. The public are getting heartily sick of this and another referendum will almost certainly reaffirm the result of the first.

Monday 21 October

To London for an evening book event in Kennington. This afternoon to Primrose Hill, where I passed a pleasant two hours in the company of Alan Bennett. No longer as fit as he was since a heart operation in May, but still as bright as a button. His bicycle chained to the railings but no longer in use. We talked Brexit, literary festivals and diary-keeping. Much laughter and good humour. As I was leaving, I mentioned my friend Liz Forgan, who lives round the corner. 'A life enhancer,' I said. 'So are you,' he replied.

Tuesday 22 October

Maybe it is my imagination, but there seem to be more beggars in London than ever. They vary from the usual ruined, damaged old men hovering in alleys and doorways to more or less respectable-looking young folk outside supermarkets and Tube stations, wrapped in sleeping bags, possessions in a rucksack. In Notting Hill the other day, I passed a young woman sitting calmly reading a novel, disinterested as to whether or not anyone was putting coins in her paper cup. Begging is becoming more common on the Underground, too. Usually the supplicant begins with a pathetic little speech while passengers avert their eyes. This morning on the Northern Line a dark-skinned man silently distributed a little piece of paper on which was written, in clear English, a message saying he was unemployed and homeless. He hovered for a moment at one end of the carriage to see whether he had hooked anyone, but nobody flinched, so he simply retraced his steps, collecting up his precious bits of papers, and moved to the next carriage. Sometimes, from a train, one glimpses people camped under railway bridges and in London one comes across solitary bundles of possessions wrapped in blankets or a duvet stored in a sheltered place, awaiting the return of their owners. And not just London. Beggars are becoming a prominent feature of most British cities. The foreigners, I guess, are failed asylum seekers who have simply dropped below the radar to avoid removal. As for the young Brits, aside from those brought low by drug addiction, they must be people who don't have the Bank of Mum and Dad to sustain them.

This evening the House of Commons voted down the government's proposed timetable for consideration of the EU Withdrawal Bill, which kiboshes Boris Johnson's much-trumpeted but wholly artificial 31 October deadline. The Brexiteers are champing at the bit for a Parliament versus the People general election, but the opposition parties will surely not be so foolish as to give it them. Were it up to me, I would leave Boris and his mates gently swinging in the wind for as long as possible. The likelihood is yet another extension.

Thursday 24 October

The bodies of thirty-nine people have been found in a refrigerated trailer at Grays in Essex. At first they were thought to be Chinese, but it seems they may come from Vietnam.

Friday 25 October

Signs that the regime is beginning to panic. From Boris Johnson, fascistic talk of the need to 'release the people from subjection to a parliament that has outlived its usefulness'. A bit rich coming from someone who was chosen to rule over us not by 'the people' but by Conservative Party members, a relatively small and not very representative organisation, the members of which would, in the words of Chris Patten, fit into Wembley Stadium ('although some would need help with the stairs'). Meanwhile that utter charlatan Sajid Javid was all over the airwaves this morning demanding the opposition agree to a general election on 12 December and hinting that the government will boycott Parliament if they don't get their way. All Jeremy Corbyn's fault apparently. Javid must have mentioned Corbyn by name twenty times, repeatedly referring to a 'zombie' parliament. Easy to see what's happening. Having flunked their precious 'Brexit or bust' deadline, the Tories are desperate to get an election out of the way before Farage accuses them of betrayal and runs candidates against them. They have got themselves into this mess. Why should anyone want to bail them out?

Saturday 26 October

A haunting last text message from a young woman whose body was among those found the other day in the freezer truck in Essex: 'I am so sorry Mum and Dad. My path to abroad doesn't succeed. Mum I love you and Dad so much. I am dying because I can't breathe. Mum, I am very sorry.' Her name was Pham Thi Tra. She came from a town in Ha Tinh, one of Vietnam's northern provinces.

Sunday 27 October

My neighbour Tony Henfrey says he recently came across Peter Mandelson at a dinner at St Catherine's College, Oxford, of which they are both alumni. 'He's not very keen on you.' Er, no. Over the years I had noticed.

Monday 28 October

The EU have graciously granted us an extension of the Brexit deadline to 31 January and, rather less graciously, Boris Johnson has been obliged to accept. So much for all that 'do or die' nonsense he has been spouting for the past few weeks. Most satisfyingly, the commemorative 50p pieces minted to mark the occasion have had to be melted down. A metaphor for the whole miserable business. Meanwhile tens of millions of taxpayers' money spent preparing for a no-deal Brexit has been squandered. Now Johnson is continuing to press for a December general election and tonight there are signs that, for entirely cynical reasons, the SNP and the Liberal Democrats may be about to oblige him.

Tuesday 29 October

There is to be an election after all. Our third in four years. We are becoming like Italy. The Liberal Dems and Scottish Nationalists, having reversed their positions overnight, suddenly announced that they now favour an election, and this has spooked Labour into going along with it for fear of appearing frit. A big mistake which almost certainly condemns the country to five more years of the present management. On the evening bulletins Corbyn and the shadow Cabinet were shown trying to sound enthusiastic at the prospect of an election, but the expressions on their faces did not match their slogans. Jeremy is talking of delivering the 'most transformative, radical and exciting programme ever put to the British electorate', but it is hard to think of anything more likely to frighten the wits out of the middle classes. What he doesn't seem to grasp is that most people in the UK would run a mile at the thought of revolution. For Johnson, meanwhile, Christmas has come early. The opposition has fallen headlong into his trap.

Friday 1 November

This was the day when, not for the first time, we were supposed to leave the EU come what may, but it turned out to be just another milestone in this interminable saga. Meanwhile Nigel Farage has challenged the government to abandon the deal agreed with Brussels last week, failing which he is threatening to run Leave candidates in 500 seats. Go for it, Nigel. You are Labour's best hope of avoiding meltdown.

Saturday 2 November

No sooner had I listened to the BBC's chief political adviser, Ric Bailey, piously expounding the Corporation's election guidelines than I turned to the *Today* programme to hear Andrea Leadsom being allowed to refer – unchallenged – to 'the mess that Labour left us in 2010'. It didn't occur to the interviewer, the normally robust Mishal Husain, to point out that the public debt was incurred bailing out the bankers – which the Tories were keen on at the time. For good measure Leadsom was also allowed to say that 'Labour governments always raise taxes' – and by implication Tories always cut them. Which Chancellor (foolishly in my view) was it who cut the basic rate from 22 to 20 per cent in 2007? And which Chancellor almost doubled the rate of VAT in 1979, having previously denied any intention of doing so?*

Sarah (known to her dad as 'Billie the Beautiful') is thirty today.

Monday 4 November

An email from a City economist of my acquaintance who is in the process of moving to Berlin, not necessarily because of Brexit but 'more the dreadful debate around it'. He asks, 'Isn't there a feeling inside Labour that with Corbyn you have blown the greatest opportunity for decades to defeat the Tories…?' A good question, but given that so many Labour voters are Brexiteers, any Labour leader would have found the job difficult. The only thing we can be sure about is that Jeremy's leadership guarantees defeat.

Lindsay Hoyle has been elected Speaker. Decent, dull, safe. Perhaps he's what's needed after the colourful reign of Speaker Bercow, but I hope he doesn't reverse Bercow's reforms.

Wednesday 6 November

On my way through Green Park this morning I passed David Cameron, the architect of our current woes, discreetly trailed by a couple of protection officers. He was wearing a tracksuit and seemed to have been jogging. He looked very down, as well he might. I should have stopped and said hello, but what would one say after that? Later, to Kennington,

---

* Gordon Brown cut 2 per cent of the basic rate of income tax in his last budget as Chancellor; Geoffrey Howe raised VAT from 8 to 15 per cent in his first budget while at the same time cutting 3 per cent off the standard rate of income tax.

where I inspected the flat and pruned the roses. Afterwards, I was idly glancing in the window of a local estate agent when suddenly there was a great kerfuffle inside as all the staff rose and rushed to the window, peering after two young women who moments before had been standing alongside me. One even came outside and stood watching them disappear into the distance. 'Who are they?' I asked. '*Love Island*?' 'You've got it,' she beamed. How's that for a guess, considering I have never even seen the blasted programme? This evening to Islington, where I had dinner with Sarah. Scribbled in felt pen on a whiteboard at Angel Station was the following Thought for the Day: 'Before you judge a man, walk a mile in his shoes. After that, who cares? He's a mile away and you've got his shoes.'

Thursday 7 November

What a dismal game British politics has become. A constant stream of demands that X, Y, Z apologise, repent, resign for slights, real or imagined. The main political parties and various interest groups have taken to trawling through the Twitter accounts of their enemies in search of evidence of momentary foolishness or political incorrectness which can be used to fuel ever more intensive bouts of synthetic indignation. This is being done scientifically and the slightest error of judgement, no matter how trivial or ancient, can be turned into a national scandal overnight. This is especially true of anything that gives offence to the hyper-sensitive MeTooists or the Israel lobby. Thank goodness I am not a candidate today. I would surely fail the test.

Friday 8 November

I am staying with David Fraser in Notting Hill. We spent the day exploring the City and arrived home to find a Lib Dem canvasser on the doorstep. He pressed upon us a leaflet which made the usual mendacious claim that the Lib Dems were in sight of victory in the Kensington/Notting Hill constituency. On the back page was one of those fraudulent graphs in which the Lib Dems specialise, purporting to prove the point. I asked if he knew how many votes their candidate received last time and he didn't. After he'd gone I looked up the figures. Last time round the Lib

Dem received 4,724 votes against around 16,000 each for the Labour and Conservative candidates. Labour has a majority of just twenty votes. It is the most marginal seat in England. The slightest swing to the Liberals will deliver the seat to the Tory, a hardline Brexiteer who works in 'finance'.*

Sunday 10 November

Having failed to persuade the Treasury to publish its own analysis of Labour's spending plans, the Tories have produced their own fanciful version, which, sure enough, is splashed all over the front pages of the right-wing press, as though they are for all practical purposes wholly owned subsidiaries of the Tory Party. One might imagine that some minimal degree of self-respect on the part of those who work in such places would make them want to put a little distance between themselves and the ruling party, but apparently not. Anyway, why exaggerate? Labour's spending plans *are* preposterous, but then so are those of the Tories. We are in the midst of a cynical bidding war, the only impact of which is to demean politics and politicians. Meanwhile David Blunkett, from the comfort of his billet in the House of Lords, complains in the *Telegraph* about what he calls the thuggery and antisemitism in the Labour Party. Why now, David? And why in the Torygraph? Can't you just say 'no' when they ring up? I do.

Monday 11 November

Nigel Farage, who only last week was proclaiming his intention to put up Brexit candidates in almost every constituency, has suddenly (and much to the relief of the Tories) announced that he will now be doing so only in Labour-held seats. As recently as last week he was describing Johnson's Brexit deal as 'a gigantic con'; now he is suddenly prepared to go along with it. What has brought about this remarkable volte-face? Rumour has it that he has received a call from his mate Donald Trump. If so, it isn't only the Russians who are interfering in our elections.

Home on the 09.30. As we approached Doncaster at 11 a.m. – the eleventh hour of the eleventh day of the eleventh month – the train guard

---

* Which is exactly what happened: the Lib Dem share of the vote almost doubled and the Tory defeated the sitting Labour MP by 150 votes.

announced a two-minute silence. I googled Wilfred Owen's 'Anthem for Doomed Youth' and thought of all those names carved on village memorials and college cloisters the length and breadth of the country.

'What passing-bells for these who die as cattle,
Only the monstrous anger of the guns...'

Wednesday 13 November

A Conservative majority after the election would be 'disastrous for the prosperity of this country', according to David Gauke, who was a member of Cabinet until a few months ago, now standing as an independent. Gauke claims there is a strong possibility of a hard Brexit at the end of next year, which, he says, could render whole sectors of the economy 'unviable'. Ordinarily, coming as it does from a former Chief Secretary to the Treasury, this ought to be gold dust for any half-decent opposition party, but alas our own economic policies are so incredible – and grow more so with each passing day – that we are in no position to take advantage of it. Meanwhile Tom Harris, once a Labour MP, was on the radio this morning urging listeners to vote Tory on the grounds that Labour's economic policy would be ruinous. The second former colleague to do so in the past few days. What a topsy-turvy world we live in.

Saturday 16 November

The pre-election bidding war grows more ludicrous each day. A Tory announcement that they will plant 30 million trees to combat climate change is immediately capped by the Lib Dems promising to plant 60 million. Labour, for once, declined to play, saying only that they will 'follow the science'. Meanwhile Prince Andrew has given a car-crash interview to the BBC in an attempt to rebut the allegation that he had sex with an American teenager twenty years ago. Big mistake.

Tuesday 19 November

The Lib Dems, no strangers to the magic money tree, are promising to spend a mythical £50 billion which they claim would be the proceeds of growth were we not to leave the EU.

Wednesday 20 November

The Tories have been caught relabelling their official Twitter account 'Fact Check UK' and using it to pump out propaganda. Despite universal condemnation they are shamelessly refusing to admit to wrongdoing, pointing out that for those with sharp eyes the account contained a minuscule CCHQ logo. These are people not easily embarrassed.

Friday 22 November
Church Row, Hampstead

To Broadcasting House, where I was interviewed by Mark Mardell for a *World at One* profile of Jeremy. Among the questions, 'How would Corbyn adapt to life at No. 10?' A tad hypothetical in the circumstances, but should that day ever dawn I imagine he would find it extraordinarily difficult. Expectations have been aroused that cannot possibly be fulfilled. Policemen, nurses, doctors, teachers, local government workers, pensioners: they will all come knocking, each with a list of impossible demands. For the first time in his life Jeremy will have to start saying 'no'. Disappointment followed by disillusion will set in quickly. He will find that very hard to cope with and, like Thatcher in her third term, will soon find himself in opposition to his own government.

Saturday 23 November

The girls and I drove to Chelmsford, where we laid flowers on Mum's grave. Emma remarked, 'Why is everyone so down on Jeremy? In my little bubble everybody loves him. I don't know anyone who doesn't like him.'

Sunday 24 November

'MI6 CHIEF: CORBYN IS SECURITY DANGER' screams today's *Mail*. Yes, Richard Dearlove, one of the men who got us into Iraq (a feat for which he has not received sufficient credit), is at it again. MI6 and the *Mail*, the team that brought us the Zinoviev letter, still together after all these years.

With Nick and the girls to Highgate, where, in Dickensian gloom, we were treated to a guided tour of the closed west cemetery among higgledy-piggledy crumbling tombs, scarcely a space between them. Afterwards, alone, I toured the east side, where I found the graves of two people I once knew – Paul Foot and my former literary agent, Pat Kavanagh. Someone had left a note on George Eliot's grave which read, 'Blessed is the man who, having nothing to say, abstains from giving us wordy evidence of the fact.'

Monday 25 November
Church Row, Hampstead

Through the door comes a newsletter from the local Liberal Democrats claiming that their candidate is running neck and neck with Labour in the Hampstead and Kilburn constituency. Needless to say, there were no figures, just the usual dodgy graph which among other things purported to show the Tories on just 2.5 per cent. I googled the 2017 result. Sure enough, it shows Labour on 34,400, the Tories on 18,900 and the Lib Dems on 4,100. What a shameless bunch they are.

Tuesday 26 November

The unrelenting assault on poor Jeremy continues. Today it is the turn of the Chief Rabbi, who has written a strident piece in today's *Times* alleging that 'the overwhelming majority of British Jews are gripped by anxiety' at the prospect of a Labour victory and urging people to 'vote with their conscience'. Inevitably the bulletins are leading with this and no one of any significance dares counter it for fear of being smeared with the antisemite brush. Thus far no one has even been allowed to make the very simple point that most of the antisemitic abuse directed at Jews in general and Jewish Labour MPs in particular comes from the far right. Michael Heseltine, who is urging a vote either for the Lib Dems or for the handful of Tory dissidents, brushed aside with magnificent disdain the Tories' repeated assertion that a Lib Dem vote could put Corbyn in Downing Street as 'a traditional reds under the beds scare that has existed in every election I've ever fought'. Yes indeed. A card that Hezza himself has been known to play in days gone by, but he has been so outstanding on Brexit that we will draw a veil over that.

Wednesday 27 November

Allegations of Labour antisemitism continue to dominate the bulletins. Nothing Jeremy can say will satisfy his persecutors. The game now is to try to get him to apologise, but as anyone with the slightest political nous knows, any apology would be rammed straight back down his throat. Not to be outdone, many prominent Muslims are alleging that the Tories are infected with Islamophobia, but that is not an issue in which our free press is much interested, having indulged in a certain amount of it themselves. Even the Hindus have been trying to clamber on the bandwagon with a claim that Labour's lack of enthusiasm for India's takeover of Kashmir amounts to discrimination against them. Meanwhile the Tories sail blithely on. The whole thing is a nightmare.

Saturday 30 November

A crazed Islamist wearing a fake suicide vest stabbed two people in London yesterday and was shot dead by police on London Bridge. Within the hour a fake post appeared on Twitter and WhatsApp purporting to come from Jeremy Corbyn. It read, 'A man was murdered by British police in broad daylight.' What Corbyn actually tweeted was, 'Shocking reports from London Bridge. My thoughts are with those caught up in the incident. Thank you to the police and emergency services who are responding.'

Friday 6 December

Owen Jones, the Corbynite social commentator who has a huge social media following, has retweeted one of the many threatening messages he receives from angry white males. It reads, 'One day I will find you and beat the living shit out of you. Mark my words, watch your back, bitch.' Remarkably, far from being anonymous, the sender has tweeted under his own name and his profile photo shows a pleasant-looking man with his young son. What sort of example is he setting to the boy? 'That's the most disturbing part of it,' says Jones. Meanwhile a senior British diplomat in our Washington embassy has resigned, saying she is no longer willing to peddle half-truths on behalf of a government she does not trust.

Monday 2 December

'NEW BLITZ ON FREED JIHADIS' screams this morning's *Mail*, alongside photographs of the two young people who died in the recent terrorist incident. The *Express* is playing the same game: 'BORIS BLITZ ON FREED JIHADI BEGINS'. 'Don't use my son's death, and his and his colleague's photos, to promote your vile propaganda,' tweets David Merritt, father of one of the victims of the London Bridge killings. 'Jack stood against everything you stand for – hatred, division, ignorance.' His tweet has gone viral. Not to be outdone, Tory central office has put out a photo of Johnson overprinted with the words 'TOUGH ON TERRORISTS'. Next to it a photo of Corbyn overprinted with the words 'SOFT ON TERRORISM'. Truly, there are no depths to which they will not sink.

Tuesday 3 December

This morning, out of the blue, comes the following:

> I'm sitting in a cafe in Loughborough reading 'A View from the Foothills'. My mother is being discharged today from hospital after weeks, frail and weak. My dad is blind and frail. Both refuse to contemplate a care home. Dad refuses care. I live 100 miles away. I keep reading snippets about your parents and think, 'Oh yes. I am not the only one.'

A chat with my successor in Sunderland, Julie Elliott, who is very pessimistic. 'What are people saying to you?'

'It's all Corbyn, Corbyn, Corbyn.'

I take this with a pinch of salt. 'That's what you said last time and you got a reasonable result.'

'But last time they just didn't vote. This time round they are switching to the Tories.'

The Tory candidate in Sunderland Central is a 21-year-old from Surrey, which won't play well with the locals. Corbyn or not, Julie will survive.

Saturday 7 December

The last week of this miserable election campaign. Last night the two leaders were in a televised head to head. I couldn't bring myself to watch it, but the consensus is that Jeremy held his own. His problem, and it is unsurmountable, is that he is saddled with an absolutely undeliverable programme, which would soon become apparent if by any fluke he were to find himself in the top job. I can't help feeling that he will be relieved when it's all over and we go down to yet another defeat. Unfortunately, the price of his adventure is many more years of Boris and his friends.

Monday 9 December

To Borrowdale in the Lakes, where after a pleasant dinner in a good hotel I was invited to entertain national park chief executives with tales of life in the lower rung of government. Meanwhile Boris Johnson has been ambushed by an ITN journalist who showed him a picture of a boy with pneumonia sleeping on a pile of coats on a hospital floor, with a drip in his arm. The hack kept demanding that he apologise and Johnson kept dissembling. Needless to say, the incident has been seized upon by those who allege the NHS is on the brink of collapse, but it makes me uneasy. This is lazy, cheap journalism. You take a one in a million incident like this, suggest that it is typical and pretend that whoever happens to be in government at the time is personally responsible. I don't like it. It demeans both journalism and politics.

Tuesday 10 December

Home via Naworth Castle, where I lunched with Philip Howard. 'Who's that?' I enquired of the portrait of a grand lady on his kitchen wall.

'That', he replied, 'is my wicked aunt who broke every one of the Ten Commandments.'

'Including "Thou shall not kill"?'

'Yes, at least twice.'

Philip is nervous about what a Corbyn government might portend for him and his class. I related Richard Carew Pole's story about gambling, alcohol and bad marriages being a much greater threat to the landed classes than a Labour government, which he immediately relayed to his cousin's wife, the chatelaine of Castle Howard. Meanwhile Labour's health spokesman, Jonathan Ashworth, has been surreptitiously recorded saying that Labour is doomed. He's right, of course, but it is not very helpful.

Thursday 12 December

Election day. Only the scale of the slaughter remains to be determined.

Friday 13 December

The carnage is considerable. The Tories are now the party of the white working (and non-working) class. Ashfield, Bassetlaw, Blyth, Bolsover – yes Bolsover – Darlington, Durham North West, Grimsby, Mansfield, Redcar, Sedgefield, Stoke-on-Trent, Workington and Wrexham are among their trophies. Most of these places have not returned a Tory MP in living memory, if at all. It is striking how many are former mining areas. In Sunderland the three Labour MPs held on – just. David Gauke, Dominic Grieve, Anna Soubry and Sarah Wollaston – the last of the Tory dissidents – were annihilated. Only in multicultural London and the university cities, where Remainers have held on, is there any sign of resistance. In Scotland the SNP have once again just about swept the board. Nationalists now hold sway north and south of the border.

Inevitably, many of The Fallen are blaming the debacle on Jeremy, and of course he and his blinkered supporters bear a heavy share of responsibility, but it is apparent from the wide variation in results that Brexit was a bigger factor. The Tory slogan 'Get Brexit Done' found a ready audience in the Labour heartlands. Corbyn just provided a convenient alibi. Whatever one thinks of Jeremy, he has behaved with dignity throughout, despite the extraordinary quantity of shite that has rained down upon him these past four years, much of it from people unworthy to tie his shoelaces. I put out a tweet to this effect and by this evening it had been liked and retweeted more than 12,000 times.

Sunday 15 December

Magnanimity in victory. Herewith the *Mail*'s considered verdict on the election (ironically handed down to us from their fortress in Kensington High Street): 'This is not the internet obsessed, twittering, fanciful Britain imagined by the vain, secluded elites of London. This is the Britain of normal people living in normal places and dealing with all the hard-edged problems of real life, clear-thinking and unsentimentally patriotic.'

Monday 16 December

'I am a socialist now,' says Ngoc, recently returned from Vietnam. Until recently she has always been a bit iffy on the subject given that she lived for twelve years of her life under communism and, in many minds, the two philosophies tend to be confused. Her conversion, if that's what it is, has come about after bearing witness to the growing gulf between the arrogant nouveau riche in her home country and the all but invisible underclass who cling to life on the margins. She describes an encounter with an impoverished woman who scrapes a living collecting plastic bags for recycling. On a good day the poor old soul, who was little more than skin and bones, can collect ten kilos, for which she earns about 3p; enough for two bowls of *pho*. Ngoc left behind £50 for her sister to discreetly hand over after she departed.

Simon Jenkins has a hard-hitting piece in today's *Guardian* saying that the Lib Dems' only significant achievement in recent years has been to help deliver four successive Tory victories by splitting the anti-Tory vote. He suggests that the party ought to disband and allow its members to exercise a moderating influence on the two main parties. Fat chance.

Tuesday 17 December

According to YouGov, a mere 14 per cent of people aged seventy and over voted Labour in the recent election. At the opposite end of the spectrum the picture is reversed – 56:21 in Labour's favour. The trend in favour of Labour continues until somewhere in the mid-forties, when the balance tips. Unsurprisingly, those most rabidly hostile are also exactly the demographic who receive most of their information from a daily reading of our free press. Meanwhile, in response to the news that defeated Tory Zac Goldsmith is to be elevated to the Lords and will continue in his existing ministerial job, someone has tweeted the following:

> Zac Goldsmith, what a story. Son of a humble billionaire, at 23 made editor of a magazine (owned by his uncle), gets the Tory nom for leafy London seat at 32, loses the seat twice in 3 years (also losing London mayoral election). Elevated to the House of Lords. Truly, the British dream.

I had a wisdom tooth removed today by a very efficient dentist with a Russian-sounding name. A bit sore, but not as grisly as I had anticipated.

Wednesday 18 December

A call from a neighbour (who I doubt has ever voted Labour in his life but who loathes the current government). 'Your friend Lisa Nandy was on the TV this morning. She came over very well, but there's no way she could stand up to Johnson. You should go for Keir Starmer.' He may well be right. I had thought until now that we needed to look for a woman, preferably from the north, but of course an ability to ruthlessly expose Johnson's bluster is the primary qualification and there are few obvious candidates. Emily Thornberry is the only woman who fits the bill, but from a northern perspective a transfer of power from Islington North to Islington South might not look like change. The Corbynistas, meanwhile, are promoting Rebecca Long-Bailey, which would be suicide.

Thursday 19 December

To Sir Humphry's carol service at Chillingham, where I was once again asked to read an incomprehensible text from the prophet Micah. Mercifully the service was indoors this year. Afterwards, as we munched our mince pies in front of a roaring log fire, a charming Tory lady of my acquaintance said that although she had voted Remain, she was now of the opinion that leaving might not be such a bad idea after all, adding brightly that she thought the EU would eventually collapse, 'it's so corrupt'.

Friday 20 December

A man from a farming family in the neighbouring valley came with his heavy-duty digger to scoop up the roots of the big bamboo cluster just inside the garden which was spreading out of control. In passing he described an exchange with the local vicar, who had come upon him, cigarette in one hand and a pint of beer in the other, and jokingly remarked, 'Stephen, you'll never get to heaven.' To which he replied, 'I don't want to. I wouldn't know anyone there.'

Saturday 21 December

In Australia, a series of vast infernos are consuming the outback and beginning to threaten the cities. Homes have been incinerated. No end in sight. The skies around Sydney and Melbourne are darkening under a pall of ash. Widely believed to be a consequence of climate change (temperatures in excess of 40° are now the norm), although the Aussie government remains in denial. One hesitates to say so, but it is good that this is happening in a rich, first-world country. If climate change affected only the poor, no one would notice.

Sunday 22 December

Two crumbs of comfort that help put the recent election in perspective. First, Remain-supporting parties received around 2 million more votes than Leave-supporting ones. Second, Labour under Corbyn received 10.3 million votes, more than Blair in 2005, Brown in 2010 and Miliband in 2015. The big difference this time around is the collapse of the Lib Dems. They increased their vote by enough to deprive Labour of a number of seats without making any significant gains themselves. Not that this absolves the Corbynistas, since it implies that almost all ex-Lib Dem voters were so scared of Labour that they turned into Tories.

Monday 23 December

'Pressure builds for a Lavery/Butler ticket* as pledges mount,' tweets Squawkbox, a Corbynite fanzine. One is tempted to dismiss this as a spoof, but there again it might not be. Fiona Millar, Alastair Campbell's partner, has retweeted it with the comment, 'Laugh or cry?' Indeed, there is much to cry about, to judge by some of those putting their names forward in the hope of leading us to the Promised Land. I had thought the next Labour leader was bound to be a woman, but as a number of sensible women – not least Sarah Mullin – have pointed out, an ability to take on Boris Johnson is the key consideration which takes precedence over all else. Keir Starmer's name crops up repeatedly as the only one who

---

* Ian Lavery and Dawn Butler, MPs for Wansbeck and Brent Central.

qualifies. Never mind that he is white, male, middle aged, metropolitan and not overly charismatic. He has a sharp brain and he has been tested in the front line. The key question, of course, is of whom – if anyone – are the Tories most afraid? Once again the path leads back to Sir Keir. There is also the not entirely irrelevant point that, as a knight of the realm, he is less vulnerable to a tabloid monstering. Not that any of this will necessarily cut any ice with the new breed of party members, of course.

Tuesday 24 December

An email from Claes in Bangkok to which he has attached a photo of a young anti-government demonstrator holding up a placard in Thai hieroglyphics. It translates as follows:

> 'There are two flames burning in the human heart:
> The flame of anger against injustice,
> And the flame of hope that you can build a better world.'
> – TONY BENN

I forwarded it to Ruth Winstone and various members of the Benn clan.

CHAPTER ELEVEN

2020

Wednesday 1 January

New Year messages: Boris Johnson upbeat and conciliatory, reaching out to the vanquished and promising, however improbably, a decade of prosperity; Jeremy dour and downbeat, talking of 'resistance' and 'campaigning every day'. As someone remarked, he sounds like the Japanese soldier who hid for twenty-nine years in a cave on an island in the Philippines, refusing to accept defeat.

Friday 3 January

Awoke to the news that the Americans have assassinated the Iranian general thought to be responsible for much of Iran's activity in Iraq, Syria and elsewhere. There will be consequences. We hold our breath as we wait to see when and where.

Saturday 4 January

Jess Phillips, a somewhat louder than life Birmingham MP, has announced that she is running for the leadership. Her pitch is that she uniquely capable of understanding the concerns of 'ordinary' people. By 'ordinary' she appears to mean working-class Brexiteers. To illustrate the point, she chose to launch her campaign in Grimsby, where she was filmed attempting ostentatiously to schmooze with several somewhat startled 'ordinary' citizens ambushed in the local fish market. I am all for listening to the concerns of ordinary folk and attempting to address them where reasonable, but I do not favour pandering to their basest prejudices, which I suspect is what Ms Phillips has in mind. At dinner with neighbours this evening, a local landowner asked why it was that all Labour governments leave the country worse off than they found it. A common myth among Tories of a certain ilk (usually owners of 5,000 acres or more) and one that needs to be regularly rebutted.

Sunday 5 January

Keir Starmer has entered the Labour leadership race with an impressive interview on the *Andrew Marr Show* and a carefully crafted video (fronted by a former miner with a strong northern accent) detailing some of the causes – locked-out print workers, striking miners, poll tax rioters – to whom he gave pro bono legal advice in their hour of need. A naked appeal to erstwhile Corbyn supporters who still make up the bulk of Labour Party members and must somehow be persuaded to vote for him if he is to stand a chance. The video has provoked a fierce backlash from die-hard Corbynistas, who accuse him of insufficient loyalty to their saintly leader and draw attention to some of his less popular decisions as Director of Public Prosecutions. In his Marr interview, Starmer accepted that Brexit will now go ahead and that the issue from now on will define our post-withdrawal relations with the EU – or, to put it another way, damage limitation.

Monday 6 January

In anticipation of dinner with Sherard Cowper-Coles, our former ambassador in Afghanistan, later this week I have been reading his account of his three-year involvement with the country, *Cables from Kabul*. The overwhelming impression one gets is the sheer futility of it all. Taxpayer billions poured into a great black hole, a constant merry-go-round of strategies, a revolving door of brigadiers, special representatives and other visiting bigwigs and still, after getting on for twenty years, no representative of a foreign power dare set foot outside his fortified compound without armed guards. The only question is how to get out without the roof falling in.

Tuesday 7 January

Ngoc remarked this morning that the older she gets, the more she finds herself thinking fondly of her parents. Me too. What a disappointment we Mullin children must have been to poor Dad, a brilliant scientist, when three out of four of us (myself included) failed the eleven-plus. But he never let on. And how did Mum cope bringing up four young children, alone for months at a time when Dad was working in the US, in an age before dishwashers and washing machines? And as for Ngoc's parents, they brought up nine children in a war zone and somehow managed to get them all well educated. Our lives have been so easy by comparison.

Wednesday 8 January

To London on the 09.00 for two days of interviewing fellowship candidates for the Winston Churchill Memorial Trust. The big news today is that Prince Harry and Meghan have announced that they wish to become semi-detached from the royal family and live for much of the year in Canada or the US. Despite their apparently golden lives they appear to regard themselves as victims. Harry, who had already made something of his life before he met Meghan, has always been vulnerable because of what happened to his mother. My guess is that Meghan, bringing with her a Californian level of entitlement and all the hang-ups of a 'woke' American woman, is the cuckoo in the nest. The couple say they intend to seek financial independence while at the same time keeping one foot inside the royal family. We will see how that works out. I foresee a future involving high-end therapists and soul-baring memoirs, possibly ending in estrangement and loneliness.

A Ukrainian passenger plane has crashed on take-off from Tehran, killing all 176 passengers and crew. The cause is said to be technical failure, but there is suspicion that it might not be.

Thursday 9 January

The first day of interviews at the Churchill Trust. A succession of extraordinarily bright and engaging men and women of all ages and backgrounds. The undoubted star: a stone-deaf woman from an impoverished deaf family in South Shields ('which I don't suppose you have heard of'

– ha, little did she know) whose parents were illiterate and whose education hardly began until the age of eleven. Also, a young man from Somalia who came here from a refugee camp in Kenya not speaking a word of English, who has somehow pulled himself up to the point where he now works for a City law firm. So humbling. One wonders how many other deaf, disabled or otherwise disadvantaged little geniuses there are lurking in slums and refugee camps who, given half a chance, could change the world.

Dinner at Brooks's (which describes itself as 'one of London's oldest and most exclusive gentlemen's clubs') with Sherard Cowper-Coles, a former Foreign Office high flyer who, having read the diaries, has taken a shine to me. As befits his profession, a charming and engaging man. He believes that, given time, the Taliban would have kicked out Osama bin Laden and the other Arab terrorists without having to be invaded. His take on Robin Cook, whose private secretary he once was, was also interesting (a mix of brilliance and insufferable arrogance). Afterwards, a brief exchange with Michael Heseltine, who was dining at the next table. Although we overlapped, Hezza always seemed to me a rather aloof figure and I scarcely crossed his radar. Nevertheless, he sparkled. 'If anyone says we have met, I shall be obliged to deny it,' he remarked with a twinkle in his eye.

Friday 10 January

A second day of interviews at the Churchill Trust. As usual the question that often floors even the brightest applicants is the last one: 'If someone were to ask you "Who was Winston Churchill?", what would you say?' Some are reduced to incoherence, some raid his vast hinterland for scraps that appear to support their own application, some attribute to him politically correct views that he undoubtedly did not possess. Today one woman, a lawyer, referred to him as 'William' Churchill. At first I thought it was accidental, but she repeated her mistake three times.

Home on the 18.30.

Saturday 11 January

After several days of prevarication and denial, the Iranians have finally owned up to accidentally shooting down the Ukrainian passenger plane that crashed on Wednesday. An unintended consequence of the long fuse lit by last week's assassination of their general.

Monday 13 January

Nominations for the Labour leadership have closed. Five names will be on the ballot paper – Rebecca Long-Bailey, Lisa Nandy, Jess Phillips, Keir Starmer and Emily Thornberry. Starmer is well ahead in terms of nominations, but the tricky bit, the ballot of members, is yet to come. There is a school of thought that says we must have a woman at all costs. It would be good if we could, but it would also be nice to be in with a chance of winning an election once in a while.

Tuesday 14 January

Liam Fox was on the radio this morning talking ominously about 'better aligning' the aid budget with our trade interests, with particular reference to Africa.

Wednesday 15 January

An exchange with Andrew Mitchell, who says despite Liam Fox et al. there is no danger of the aid budget being returned to the Foreign Office.

Thursday 16 January

With Ngoc to Sunderland for a solicitor's appointment to update our wills. Afterwards we called at the office of my successor, Julie Elliott. To my surprise, the building has been heavily fortified and all mention that it is the MP's office has been removed: a consequence of the threats Julie has been receiving. As a result, surgeries are by appointment only. According to the office manager, Graham March, who used to work for me, the abuse is far worse than it was in my day (although I attracted my fair share). Angry white men of a certain age, fired up by social media, seem to be the main culprits, prompted no doubt by the fact that the MP is a woman.

Saturday 18 January

Finally, I bit the bullet today and tweeted that having lost four elections in succession, we can't afford even a little punt on the outcome of a fifth; that, desirable though it would be to have a female leader, Keir Starmer stands the best chance of leading us to victory. I was careful not to cast aspersions on any of the other candidates. By nightfall it had been widely liked and retweeted. There were dissidents, however. 'Starmer is such a void, both as a personality and as a political presence,' wrote one. 'You surprise me, Chris. I never thought I'd see you giving up on socialism just for the chance of winning an election,' wrote another, offering a clue to the Corbynista mindset. Someone else accused me of going for 'a posh white man in a suit'.

Sunday 19 January

For all Boris Johnson's talk of healing the wounds, the Brexiteers are planning a massive outbreak of jingoism to celebrate our exit from the EU on 31 January. A clock counting down the final hour is to be projected onto Downing Street, Parliament Square is to be festooned with Union flags, plans for a commemorative 50p coin are being revived and there is talk of firework displays.

Tuesday 21 January

Jess Phillips has withdrawn from the Labour leadership race, giving a boost to Lisa Nandy, a rising star.

Wednesday 22 January

The disease that is sweeping US campuses has reached Sunderland. Today, in anticipation of a public lecture I am due to give at the university in March, comes an 'External Speaker Declaration Form'. The university, it says, is 'committed to providing a forum that facilitates freedom of speech…' So far so good, but there is a catch: '…while providing a safe space for our staff students and the public'. I am, therefore, required to familiarise myself with the following documents: Events and External Speaker Policy, External Speaker Code of Conduct, Code of Practice on

Freedom of Speech. I am also warned that the university thought police reserve the right to postpone or suspend the event with no notice ('even during the event itself'), to impose conditions on the event taking place or to withdraw permission for it to go ahead. I should have told them to fuck off, but I am afraid I meekly ticked the box. Those whom the gods wish to destroy…

Sunday 26 January

A deadly new virus is reported to be spreading in China. The city of Wuhan, where it was first diagnosed, has been locked down and quarantined, but it appears to be spreading.

Wednesday 29 January

I am compiling a souvenir photo album for my good friend and long-time walking companion John Williams, who has spinal cancer. This evening I spent a couple of hours trawling through family albums in search of photos taken on our walks together. The exercise revived memories of when our girls were small – outings to castles and gardens, picnics on empty beaches, walks in hills and forests, the Stone Age house we built on the beach at North Ronaldsay on what I still regard as one of the happiest days of my life. Anyone coming across these in years to come will say, 'What golden lives these people had.'

Thursday 30 January

Nigel Farage and his motley crew of Ukipper MEPs staged a pathetic little farewell demonstration in the chamber of the European Parliament, standing amid a sea of empty seats (few of their fellow MEPs wanted to be seen sitting near them) waving tiny Union Jacks. Someone tweeted, 'God, this is embarrassing.' I'll say.

Friday 31 January

To Newcastle, where I delivered my 'How to Be an MP' lecture to third-year politics students. At Alnmouth Station I ran into one of my Brexiteer neighbours en route to London to participate in the 'Farewell EU' celebrations. 'What will you be doing at 11 p.m. tonight?' he enquired. I shall be in bed.

Saturday 1 February

Our first day of 'freedom'. We are no longer a vassal state. Hooray. The television news is awash with flag-waving super-patriots, rejoicing in Parliament Square last night as the digital clock ticked down. Some ugly scenes on the fringes, shaven-headed men of a certain age trampling the EU flag, one repeatedly chanting, 'Stop turning churches into mosques.' Nigel Farage delivered a triumphalist speech in which he uncharacteristically lavished praise on Boris Johnson. How long, I wonder, before the cries of 'betrayal' resume? At first light this morning my friend and neighbour John Field and I surreptitiously clambered up the spiral staircase to the roof of the big house and raised the EU flag. Only a question of time before we are rumbled, but from our window we could see it happily fluttering all day in the wind. I tweeted a photo with the caption 'Still some pockets of resistance, even in the most unlikely places'.

Sunday 2 February

Our flag was still flying this morning – or rather (in the absence of wind) hanging limply – from the pole on the big house. It is unclear whether anyone has yet spotted it. Our two most fervent Brexiteers have been away these past two days which means there is no one to feign amusement – or take offence.

By lunchtime it had been taken down.

Monday 3 February

A new piece of university madness. In order to be paid for three hours' teaching at Newcastle the other day, I must complete a form of several pages which, among other things, needs to show my passport to prove that I have a right of residence. This despite the fact that I have been teaching at Newcastle University for ten years and provided all these details on numerous previous occasions. Having omitted to take my passport with me, I was advised instead to send a scanned copy of the title page, which I did. Today comes a reply saying that a scan is insufficient and I must present the actual document. The fact that I sat in the British Parliament for twenty-three years, was a member of the government for four years and have taught at the university for a decade is apparently of no relevance. Since a visit to Newcastle is a round trip of eighty miles, I have declined. We will see what happens next.[*]

Wednesday 5 February

A copy of John Bercow's memoir has arrived, which I am eagerly devouring. No doubt it will be excoriated in the Brexit media (Quentin Letts, late of the *Mail*, now of *The Times*, says he's embarrassed to be seen with it). I have been asked to provide a 2,000-word review for *Prospect* by next Wednesday.

Friday 7 February

Awful scenes from Syria's Idlib province, graphically portrayed on Channel 4's evening news. The regime has launched a brutal new offensive aimed at recapturing the last rebel enclave. Indiscriminate bombing and shelling, terrified children, trucks laden with people and possessions jamming the roads with nowhere to run to. All escape routes cut – the Turks having closed the border. By contrast, this morning's BBC television focused on the news that a single British passenger evacuated from a cruise liner anchored off Japan has been diagnosed with the coronavirus. Oh, and also that a minor celebrity has come out as gay. I suppose they know their audience.

Saturday 8 February

The coronavirus appears to be spreading. So far about 35,000 cases have been diagnosed, mostly in China, but twenty other countries are also affected, including the UK. Hong Kong has introduced two weeks' quarantine for travellers from the mainland and 3,000 tourists are marooned

---

[*] They eventually coughed up.

on a cruise ship off Yokohama. It is becoming clear that the authorities in Wuhan ignored early warnings and that, as a result, the genie is out of the bottle.

Tuesday 11 February

This evening the second of an excellent three-part BBC series on universal credit. Tonight's episode featured a job centre in Toxteth, Liverpool. It followed a woman of sixty-two who had been made redundant from her cleaning job and a cheerful unskilled labourer. To remain qualified for benefit they had to attend weekly appointments and prove that they had spent the equivalent of thirty-five hours seeking work in a world where there was very little work available. The overworked staff at the job centre came across as diligent, helpful, humane and yet they are administering a brutal, complex system. The cleaning lady had to find three part-time jobs in order to escape the clutches of the system. The labourer, after weeks of tramping the streets distributing his CV to anyone who would take it, was over the moon to land a job on a construction site, only to be laid off again at the end of his trial period, back where he started. It struck me, not for the first time, how little those of us whose salaries or pensions are paid monthly into our bank accounts know about the world of minimum wages and zero-hours contracts. How precarious life is at that level where you live in fear of every bill for gas, electricity or rent dropping onto the mat. A single slip can send you plunging to the bottom. Perhaps 20 per cent of the population live from hand to mouth like this. They are all around us. Yet they might as well be in Bangladesh for all that most of us know about their lives. A friend who once worked in No. 10 recounted that he had been present at a meeting where George Osborne casually remarked that he didn't know anyone who earned less than £100,000 a year. And that was in 2010.

Thursday 13 February

The charlatans are falling out. To general astonishment, Sajid Javid has resigned as Chancellor. Ordinarily this would be a cause for celebration except that, to his credit, he appears to have resigned on a matter of principle: he was faced with a demand (the unseen hand of D. Cummings?)

that he sack all his advisers and cede control over economic policy to Downing Street. Bizarrely, the Northern Ireland Secretary, Julian Smith, has been sacked after little more than 200 days in the job, where he was widely regarded as a success. And Theresa Villiers has gone after a similar period in office. Priti Awful Patel, however, has survived unscathed.

Friday 14 February

Much the worst of yesterday's appointments is that of our local MP, Anne-Marie Trevelyan, as Secretary of State for International Development, the fifth in four years. She has no known interest in aid policy and her only public utterance on the subject is that 'charity begins at home'. My guess is that the 'nasty party' is looking for ways of siphoning off the aid budget to other departments and she can be relied upon to offer little or no resistance. For all the bogus talk of 'punching above our weight', international development is the one area where we actually do – or did.

Saturday 15 February

Emily Thornberry is out of the Labour leadership contest, having failed to secure enough constituency party nominations. Charismatic, confident, robust – in many ways she might have been the candidate best equipped to take on Johnson. BUT, however unfairly, she is seen as too posh, too metropolitan and too outspoken to have much traction north of Watford. Boris Johnson, of course, suffers from all the same afflictions and a few more besides, but the normal laws of political gravity don't seem to apply to him – yet.

Monday 17 February

This England:

'Which property do you think pays the most council tax,' asks someone on Twitter. 'A 3-bed semi in Hartlepool on sale for £107k or a 10-bed townhouse on Berkeley Square, Westminster, worth £82.5m? Answer: The Hartlepool semi at £1,569 vs £1,507.'

Thursday 20 February

Came across a copy of Piers Morgan's celebrity-obsessed but oddly compulsive diaries in Barter Books the other day. The following passage caught my eye:

> A Prime Minister from one of the Caribbean islands once told me that he'd had dinner with Bush and Blair separately within six months.
>
> 'What was the difference between them?' I asked.
>
> 'Bush looked me in the eye and told me what he knew I wasn't going to like hearing, whereas Blair looked me in the eye and told me what he thought I wanted to hear.'*

More than a germ of truth in this. I remember Jack Straw remarking that Tony was like a man who told several women that he loved them and they went away happy until they got together afterwards and compared notes.

Monday 24 February

To Dublin, through a snowstorm, where I am to deliver a speech on the accountability of the security services at an event which is being billed as 'The National Security Summit'. This evening, participants were entertained to a dinner at a pub on the city outskirts, complete with an excellent folk band and some brilliant Irish dancers. I was seated next to the British ambassador, Robin Barnett, who in my Foreign Office days was in charge of the visa department. He made a short speech concisely identifying future threats to peace and prosperity: climate change, migration, cybersecurity and terrorism. A woman sitting opposite me, a cybersecurity expert, remarked cheerfully that if I knew what she knew, I wouldn't sleep at night.

Tuesday 25 February
The Helix, University College Dublin

We were collected by bus from our hotel and taken to an ultra-modern

---

* *Shooting Straight: Guns, Gays, God, and George Clooney*, Ebury Press, 2013, p. 36.

conference centre on the impressive new campus of University College Dublin. The Irish, for all that they are a small, neutral nation, punch way above their weight when it comes to UN peace operations. As a result they have some very experienced soldiers. I spent some time chatting to a retired colonel who had been a UN weapons inspector in Iraq in the 1990s. He had also served with the UN in Lebanon during one of Israel's so-called incursions. Most of his colleagues, he said, were sympathetic to Israel when they arrived but had changed their minds by the time they went home. The Iraqis, he said, were an unsophisticated people, capable of great brutality, but the threat they posed had been much exaggerated. Tariq Aziz, the apparently urbane front man of the regime, was 'a thug' who had once invited him to an execution (an offer he declined). This evening at dinner I met a former British navy officer (now working for a manufacturer of warships) who had been brought up in Northern Ireland on the estate of the Duke of Abercorn, where his father was the manager. One day in August 1979, aged seventeen, he was working in the grounds when the Duchess appeared in the company of a distinguished-looking Englishman. 'Stephen, have you met Lord Mountbatten?' They shook hands. 'Stephen's going to join the navy,' she said, whereupon the great man delivered an encomium to life on the high seas. It turned out to be the last day of his life. Next morning he was blown up by the IRA.

Thursday 27 February

The virus has spread to every continent except Antarctica. The bulletins are awash with tales of flights cancelled and tourists trapped in hotels and on cruise ships in sunny climes. In this country just sixteen cases, so far. Many more in northern Italy.

Friday 28 February

According to the Electoral Commission, the Tories received £37 million in donations in the last three months of 2019 – more than double the amount received by Labour and the Lib Dems added together. And surprise, surprise, three of their top donors are reported to be in line for peerages.

Sunday 1 March

In an interview with yesterday's *Times* Sajid Javid says that had he remained at the Treasury, he was planning to cut 2p off the basic rate of income tax (at a cost of £10 billion a year). His long-term aim, he says, was to bring the rate down to 15p in the pound by the next election. *The Times*, in a leading article, seems to think this would be an excellent idea, while breezily adding, 'How he proposed to pay for all this we may never know.' In fact it would be an act of gross irresponsibility given the parlous state of our public services. Local authorities are on their knees, having lost 40 per cent of the central government contribution to revenue since 2010.

Monday 2 March

Ngoc and I measured the circumference of the veteran oak in the field behind us, the lone survivor of a much earlier era. Something I have been meaning to do for a long time. It measures 327 inches, making it just over 400 years old.

Wednesday 4 March

On tonight's *Channel 4 News* an interview with a black journalist on the *Washington Post* who remarked that he had recently asked his mother which presidential candidate she was supporting. 'If we want to get rid of Trump,' she had replied, 'I think we ought to go for an elderly white man. After that we can experiment.' A very sensible woman. By the way, Joe Biden, aged seventy-seven, appears to be re-emerging as the front runner for Democratic nomination. Extraordinary that the choice of candidates for the most important job in the world comes down to three white men – Biden, Trump and Saunders – in their mid to late seventies.

Thursday 5 March

We were due to meet our friend and former neighbour Helen Belger for lunch at a pub near Hexham. An hour or so before we set out she rang and explained in a croaky voice that she appeared to have some sort of throat bug, although no temperature. Did we still want to meet up? Since Helen is a doctor and she assured us that it wasn't the dreaded virus, we decided to go ahead. But ever since I have been worrying that we may have made the wrong decision. The virus dominates the bulletins even though, of the 118 UK cases so far, only one has proved fatal. Much panicky talk of an impending epidemic, an overwhelmed NHS and even of suspending Parliament (wouldn't the government just love that?). I can't make up my mind what is worse: the disease or the reaction. Is this a new plague or a symptom of the age in which we live?

Saturday 7 March

In today's *Times* magazine a long interview with Lisa Nandy, who, even though destined to come a distant third in the Labour leadership contest, has had a good campaign and one which has propelled her into the front line of British politics. Should Labour ever again see the inside of government, she could well be the party's first female Prime Minister. Already, alas, there are signs that ambition has got the better of common sense. Asked if she would press the nuclear button, she replies without hesitation that she would. The other day she declared herself a Zionist. Lately she is spouting some populist nonsense about 'moving the No. 10 operation to the north'. On the other hand, she's bright, northern, personable and much of what she has to say is reasonable even if she does occasionally come across as holier than the rest of us.

Monday 9 March

Coronavirus is ravaging Italy. Ten provinces in the north have been declared off-limits. More than 400 dead. Only a question of time until it spreads here, say the experts.

Tuesday 10 March

A year on from the pub bombings inquest I am still the target of regular abuse from members of an outfit calling itself Justice4the21. They also have it in for West Midlands Chief Constable Dave Thompson, whose force is re-investigating the case. Today's offering gives flavour of the intellectual level:

MONGREL & TERRORIST appeaser @chrismullinexmp IS the MOST

Obnoxious, GUTLESS BASTARD I've ever met as well as a fanny mer-
chant who was guaranteed safe passage into Birmingham BOMBINGS
Coroners Court by a CORRUPT and DEPRAVED PROTECTOR of
MURDERERS @DaveThompsonCC 2 LIE & PEVERT [*sic*]

Yesterday came this: 'Mullin is as bad as the cowardly scum who planted
the bombs, absolute low life.'

Mostly they are retweeted by (to judge by the pictures on their Twitter accounts) the same handful of overweight, tattooed white males who
have the look of ex-soldiers or policemen. One of yesterday's tweeters is
an expat Brummie living in Mexico; another is pictured at his holiday
home in Spain. Several describe themselves as Brexiteers; some appear to
be members of a West Bromwich Albion supporters club calling itself the
Democratic Football Lads Alliance. What possesses them? One suspects
that they are the same sort of people who were in denial when I first
suggested that the six convicted men were innocent.

Wednesday 11 March

Our brand-new Chancellor, Rishi Sunak, presented his budget. A massive
spending splurge, all based on borrowing. Gone all talk of austerity. Ostensibly it's about countering the effects of coronavirus and giving effect
to lavish election promises. In keeping with the prevailing ideology, little
or none of it is going to hard-pressed local authorities. Instead most of
the new spending will go towards pouring concrete onto green fields. It
may also have something to do with countering the economic impact
of Brexit. Para 1.12 of the report by the Office for Budget Responsibility
which forms the background to the budget reads:

We estimate that the economic effects of the referendum have so far
reduced potential output by around 2 per cent, relative to what would
have happened in its absence ... Mostly it reflects weaker productivity
growth on the back of depressed business investment and the diversion
of resources from production towards preparing for potential Brexit
outcomes ... Broadly speaking, we believe that around one third of the
long-run hit to productivity from Brexit has already happened.

Needless to say, the Chancellor made no mention of this.

The coronavirus death toll in Italy now exceeds 800.

Thursday 12 March

Donald Trump has banned all flights to the US from Europe, with the exception of the UK. His announcement was made in a characteristically nasty little speech replete with references to a 'foreign virus' and 'America First'. The ban apparently came as a surprise to senior members of the administration. In Italy the death toll has passed 1,000. Here it is just ten, but this may be only the beginning. This evening Boris Johnson, looking and sounding unusually sober, appeared at a press conference in No. 10, flanked by scientific advisers. 'I must level with you,' he said. 'Many more families are going to lose their loved ones.'

Friday 13 March

All over Europe schools and universities closing. Markets plunging. Death tolls rising. One by one all my pathetic little engagements are falling away. Talks, lectures, literary festivals. Everyone is cancelling. Common sense, I know. I shouldn't care about it, but I do. Doing things. That's what I exist for. John Field and I drove to the Harthope Valley and walked three miles over the moor to North Middleton. Lunch at the Tankerville Arms. We had the place to ourselves. This evening a call from our neighbour John Nicholls to say that he and Gilly are self-isolating. Bang goes our weekly game of table tennis. Every time the phone rings it is someone cancelling something.

Saturday 14 March

Every day our little world grows smaller. Messages coming in from friends and neighbours who have gone into hibernation. Yesterday it was announced that all league football is to be abandoned. Now we know it's serious.

The death toll: Italy: 1,266, Spain: 190, UK: 21 (up from 10 yesterday).

Sunday 15 March

Fear spreading along with the virus. Talk of asking those of us aged seventy or over to self-isolate indefinitely – possibly for months. MONTHS! It doesn't bear thinking about. News bulletins showing empty shelves and long queues at supermarkets further south. Airlines and travel companies face ruin as borders close and economic activity grinds to a halt across Europe. Talk of closing down schools and universities – most EU countries have already done so. Meanwhile a new piece of nonsense has entered the political lexicon: 'at pace'. It trips easily from the lips of scientists, businessmen and politicians alike, replacing that other much-used piece of business speak, 'going forward', which has more or less disappeared. Probably because we are going backwards.

Death toll: Italy: 1,806, Spain: 288, UK: 35. In Iran, where the virus appears to be raging out of control, 724 people are said to have died so far.

Monday 16 March

To Morrisons in Alnwick for our weekly shopping, setting out early to avoid crowds. Car park two thirds empty, shelves full. Absolutely no sign of panic despite the best efforts of our most loathsome tabloid: 'VIRUS WILL PUT 8 MILLION BRITONS IN HOSPITAL'. One useful measure to avert meltdown would be to ban the *Daily Express* for the duration.

Tuesday 17 March

A sudden step-change in the official advice. The government now advising us to stay out of pubs, clubs and theatres, where possible to work from home and cease all unnecessary travel. The new advice appears to be based on a gloomy prognosis from the scientists. Imperial College are said to be running a computer model that predicts up to 250,000 deaths on existing policies. Not a good time to be in government. Intractable problems to grapple with, such as how to head off a pandemic without collapsing the economy? Meanwhile, from the US, pictures of Americans queuing to buy more guns. The rest of the world is stocking up on hand gel and toilet rolls and in the US the crazies are stocking up on guns and ammo in anticipation of social breakdown. Donald Trump is not having a good crisis. Rambling, incoherent, contradictory, his pronouncements are frequently having to be 'clarified' by officials. At times like these you need an adult in charge.

This afternoon the Chancellor announced a £350 billion emergency package of loans, tax rebates and grants for businesses in freefall. Also, a three-month holiday on mortgage repayments. All talk of austerity banished. The Tories can certainly rise to the occasion when they want to, but the big unanswered question is what can be done for the several million inhabitants of the so-called gig economy, who mostly live in private rented accommodation and who at the best of times survive from hand to mouth? The world of zero-hours contracts and minimum wages is a foreign country to most Tories, who find it so much easier to empathise with the needs of businessmen and mortagees.

UK death toll: 55. Italy: 2,000-plus.

Wednesday 18 March

In defiance of advice from The Very Sensible Sarah Mullin, who reminds Her Foolish Old Dad that the virus can prove fatal for someone such as he (who has chronic bronchitis), I sped across the moors to Hexham for a meeting of the National Park Authority. A virtual meeting was apparently impossible since the authority had been advised that the budget could only be approved by a face-to-face meeting. Only eight of us attended along with a handful of senior officials, sitting at desks arranged a metre apart. The business was over in an hour and a half. Afterwards we were provided with a packed lunch. I ate mine at Wallington, on the curved bench by the China pond where we used to picnic with Granny and Grandpa. This evening it was announced that from Friday all schools are to close indefinitely, exams cancelled. The UK death toll now stands at 104. In Italy it is over 3,000, a leap of more than 500 in a single day.

Thursday 19 March

Gordon Brown was on the radio sounding statesmanlike and serious, arguing, among other things, for the government to put money into the pockets of wage earners, as the German and Scandinavian governments are doing. Shades of 2008. Nothing like an economic crisis to bring out the best in Gordon. At times like these one misses someone of his stature.

John Field and I drove (in separate vehicles) to the Harthope Valley, from where we walked up to Broadstruther and back along the Carey Burn.

In Italy the death toll now stands at 3,405, greater than that of China, which today reported no new cases. In the UK it is 144. First cases reported in Northumberland.

Friday 20 March

First day of spring. A lone bee has found its way into the glasshouse and is making heroic efforts to pollinate the apricot tree, which for the first time in seven years has a healthy display of blossom. A message from our son-in-law Nick, a medic at a London teaching hospital: 'We are predicted to run out of beds and ventilators between 7 and 14 April.' This morning, an interview with a Spanish barman who has just been sacked without notice by a hotel in the Cairngorms where he has worked for three years. He has also been turned out of his tied accommodation and has no idea where he will sleep tonight. No one from management was available for comment. I bet they weren't. The bastards. A spokesman for the Coylumbridge Hotel in Aviemore, owned by Britannia Hotels, later said that the letter instantly dismissing and evicting temporary staff was 'an administrative error' and should not have been sent. Meanwhile the Chancellor has announced another massive spending round: the government will pay 80 per cent of wages up to £2,500 a month of workers who are at risk of redundancy. Important though this is, it still does not address the plight of the several million inhabitants of that twilight zone that is the gig economy.

Saturday 21 March

Callaly. Breaking news: a family of otters have been spotted in the stream by the third lake.

Sunday 22 March

Mother's Day. This morning a video conference with Our Two Best Friends – Emma, who is on her own in Edinburgh, and Sarah in London.

It may be some months before we meet again. Later, a four-mile circuit of the forested hills above Callaly with Kate and Jeremy from Lorbottle Hall, on account of which I later got a great deal of grief from Mrs V. B. Boss.

Not everyone is entering into the spirit of the occasion. EasyJet, which has given its employees two months unpaid leave, is planning a £174 million dividend payout, including a whopping £60 million for the airline's owner and his family.

The death toll in Italy has risen by 793 in the past twenty-four hours.

Monday 23 March

This evening a new bombshell. We are all to be confined to our homes until further notice. The only exceptions are essential workers. For the rest, we are allowed the occasional trip to the supermarket and to exercise either alone or with one family member for no more than an hour per day. Where necessary these rules will be enforced by the police. A dramatic change of strategy from just a few days ago. It has come about because of the sudden realisation by the government and its advisers that we are on the same trajectory as Italy, where more than 6,000 have so far died and the health service has been overwhelmed. Who knows what the future holds, but the dead could be numbered in tens of thousands. Worldwide, perhaps millions.

Tuesday 24 March

'End of Freedom': banner headline in today's *Telegraph* (where the lunatics are still in charge of the asylum).

Besides a daily stroll and seasonal gardening, I have set myself a couple of small targets for the long weeks of isolation that lie ahead.

1. To complete a couple more short stories that might be entered for next year's BBC short story prize. I am working on one called 'Liberation', loosely based on the experience of Ngoc's family in the years following the fall of Saigon.
2. A rough edit of my past ten years' worth of diaries so that I might be in a position to offer them to publishers when the shutdown is lifted. I had intended to pull stumps next month on the tenth anniversary

of my departure from Parliament, but my thinking for the moment is that I must see this crisis through, at least to the point where there is a sliver of light at the end of the tunnel. We shall see.

Wednesday 25 March

An email from The Very Sensible Sarah Mullin to Her Foolish Old Dad:

> Hello Dad, Just a note, which I know you don't want to hear and that I am sure is being relayed to you on an hourly basis by Mum: please, for the next however many weeks, stay within Callaly and don't have anyone around … You've got the luxury of a whole garden so this is not a very big ask … Yesterday on Nick's ward a non-Covid cancer patient tested positive. They then tested the rest of the people in the ward and all patients in the surrounding beds tested positive. It is astonishing how infectious the virus is…

I immediately came out with my hands up and cancelled this week's planned walks with John Field and Tony Henfrey.

Among today's casualties, the Prince of Wales. Only a mild dose apparently. I wonder when he last saw his mother.

Thursday 26 March

Chancellor Rishi Sunak has announced that the government is extending its wages guarantee to inhabitants of the gig economy. Fiendishly complicated to organise and the snag is that the money won't start to flow until June. How will those on the bottom rung survive until then? So far the Chancellor is having a good crisis. As Michael White, the former *Guardian* political editor, says, Boris was lucky to lose Sajid Javid when he did. Javid, let us not forget, was planning to slash income tax. We won't be hearing any more about that for a long time, although I wouldn't put it past the current management to go into the next election with the usual vague talk of 'aspiring' to cut taxes. When the time comes to recoup this vast expenditure, the Tories may at least rest assured that Labour will not be so cynical as to go into the next election talking of 'Rishi Sunak's debt' or 'the mess that Boris left us'. At least I hope we won't.

The Italian death toll now exceeds 8,000. In the UK, 578, about 100 up on yesterday. Alarm bells ringing here. We are heading down the Italian road.

Friday 27 March

George Monbiot has posted the following on Twitter: 'I have just been in touch with someone whose entire family are self-employed on zero-hours contracts. They won't get anything from the government until June. In the meantime they face destitution. What are they supposed to do?'

When all this is over, we are going to have recognise zero-hours contracts for the social evil they are and put a stop to them.

Today's news: another 900 deaths in Italy; here another 180. Among those who have tested positive: Prime Minister Boris Johnson, Health Secretary Matt Hancock and chief medical officer Chris Whitty.

Saturday 28 March

The Italian death toll now exceeds 10,000. Here we passed the 1,000 mark.

Sunday 29 March

In keeping with the spirit of the times, last week's sunshine has given way to a thin sleet brought to us on a bitter wind. A letter in yesterday's *Financial Times* suggests that the consensus around the government's handling of the crisis is beginning to fray:

> I can't decide which is more astonishing: my incredulity at your pandering editorial 'Johnson is coming to grips with the virus' or at Boris Johnson's earlier blind faith in the herd immunity strategy … The time to wake up and smell the roses was in February, for in truth that is when Britain's darkest hour took hold…

The *Mail*, meanwhile, has excelled itself with a claim that Michel Barnier, who has the virus, may have infected Johnson as part of some wider EU plot. It begins, 'Could this be the ultimate revenge for Brexit?' Happily, this seems to have attracted universal derision. Not even the average *Mail* reader is daft enough to fall for that one.

This morning an hour-long Skype with Our Two Best Friends. Nick says University College Hospital, his place of work, is not yet over-whelmed. Both he and Sarah think they may have had the virus, having suffered mild symptoms last week.

I am reading *The Way We Live Now*, which My Learned Friend John Field assures me is Trollope's best work.

Monday 30 March

A message from John Field, who lives alone in the mill cottage, 600 yards off the beaten track. 'What I miss most about the isolation', he writes, 'is the absence of human voices, including my own. I have a deep dislike of phone calls, which makes it harder to endure. So I am reading cantos of Byron's *Don Juan* aloud to the cats each morning after breakfast. They haven't yet objected.'

Tuesday 31 March

Priceless. Someone has tweeted the following about our sinister Foreign Secretary, who in the absence of the Prime Minister was yesterday's gov-ernment front man: 'Raab always exudes the air of a man rehearsing his story in a service station bathroom mirror with the body of a hitchhiker he ran over in the back of his BMW.'

Wednesday 1 April

Confidence in the government's strategy continues to fray. Much talk of the importance of testing, but little sign of progress. Even normally servile Tory commentators are beginning to ask questions. Stephen Dor-rell, a former Health Secretary, talks of ministers over-promising and under-delivering. Ministers and officials put failure down to a shortage of reagents, but the chemical industry says supplies are plentiful and university labs are saying they could start testing straight away, if given the go-ahead. Also, growing anger in the NHS and care homes about the shortage of masks and gowns. No doubt there will be a public inquiry in due course. Meantime we have no choice but to put our faith in those who govern us. With every day that passes it is becoming clear that – as in 1992 – Labour's recent election defeat may have been a blessing in disguise. If Corbyn were in charge, our free press would have roasted him by now. UK death toll: 1,789, including a thirteen-year-old boy in Brixton. In Italy the number of new infections seems to have peaked, though deaths are still rising. In the US even Trump seems belatedly to have grasped the magnitude of the crisis. He is now talking lockdown, having recently spoken of wanting to see packed churches at Easter.

Spring has brought the garden to life, great swathes of daffodils along either side of the lawn. Sadly, there is no one but us to bear witness.

Friday 3 April

Completed a first draft of 'Liberation' which comes to almost 10,000 words, the upper limit for a short story. Next on the agenda, I shall edit my diaries.

UK death toll: 3,605 and rising. Worldwide more than a million people are known to have contracted the virus and an estimated half the world's population are subject to some form of lockdown.

Saturday 4 April

As anticipated, Keir Starmer was today anointed leader of the Labour Party, thereby bringing to an end Labour's interminable leadership election process. The choice of Starmer represents defeat for the no-compromise-with-the-electorate wing of the party and suggests that four successive election defeats may have caused a little light to come on, even for some Corbynistas. Lisa Nandy came a distant third, though I would not be surprised if she emerged at the top of the pile eventually. Sir Keir's immediate task is to drag Labour back onto the centre ground of British politics and keep it there, while at the same time providing some constructive and intelligent opposition. In the longer run, an assault on the gig economy would not be a bad issue to campaign on. The present crisis has provided fertile ground for that. Hospitals have recorded 700 coronavirus deaths in the past twenty-four hours, bringing the UK total to 4,313. In parts of the US, meanwhile, the virus appears to be raging out of control. And as for the Indian subcontinent, no one knows...

Sunday 5 April

The Queen addressed the nation today and so did I. Her Majesty's four-minute address, delivered from Windsor, struck exactly the right tone and was greeted with widespread acclaim. Mine (on Radio 4's *Broadcasting House* programme) attracted slightly less attention. Nonetheless it represented a triumph of sorts: I have at last mastered the art of being interviewed via Skype.

This evening it was announced that the Prime Minister, who has been suffering Covid symptoms for ten days, has been taken to hospital 'for tests'.

Monday 6 April

Massive outbreak of sycophancy from usual suspects following the Queen's broadcast: 'A magnificent speech by a magnificent monarch. Thank you, Your Majesty – this was your finest hour' (Piers Morgan). 'Perfect ... Long may she reign' (Tim Montgomerie). 'Absolutely brilliant' (Julia Hartley Brewer). And this in the *Telegraph* from the normally sensible Alastair Campbell: 'The Queen is the most remarkable person on earth.' I wonder how the Queen feels about all this nonsense? I bet she doesn't even notice.

Keir Starmer has named his top team. Lisa Nandy becomes shadow Foreign Secretary. Most of the rest I have never heard of, which probably says more about me than it does about them.

Boris Johnson is in intensive care.

Tuesday 7 April

Passengers from a virus-stricken cruise ship marooned off the coast of Florida have been allowed back into the country without an attempt to test them, let alone any suggestion that they should be quarantined. Ngoc's sister in Ho Chi Minh City says people there are amazed to see that we are still allowing new arrivals into the country without automatically isolating them. Vietnam, which from the outset has been isolating all incoming travellers for two weeks, has thus far got off lightly.

Meanwhile, in the Land of the Free, fourteen mainly Bible Belt states have exempted churches from restrictions on movement. A woman interviewed by a CNN reporter as she drove away from a crowded church service said she wasn't worried about the virus because she was 'bathed in the blood of Jesus'. Also, an online clip of a pastor saying that people should listen to Trump because he was appointed by God (but as some wag remarked, 'I'd like to see the paperwork first'). For all their wealth, their space-age technology and their capacity to inflict unspeakable violence on those they perceive to be their enemies, so many US citizens are simpler and more ignorant than the humblest Asian rice farmer.

Another 854 UK hospital deaths recorded today, bringing our total to over 6,000. A report from the Office for National Statistics says that, taking into account delays in recording and those who die at home or in care homes, this may be a considerable underestimate. Boris Johnson, meanwhile, is said to be stable.

Wednesday 8 April

In our little bubble, life is good. Fresh air, sunshine, wholesome food (we are still – in part – living off the fruits of last year's harvest). And yet all around us a life-and-death struggle is under way. Doctors, nurses, care workers are in a daily confrontation with death and bereavement, some at the cost of their own lives. People who lack resources are struggling to survive when, for the likes of us, the only issue is how to amuse ourselves. If only there was something I could do to help, but as a 72-year-old male with chronic bronchitis and no particular skills, other than the gift of the gab, I am an irrelevance.

Today's hospital deaths: a record 938. Total now over 7,000.

Thursday 9 April

Ngoc read my Vietnam short story and wept at the memory of her parents and their hard lives.

Friday 10 April

Boris Johnson is out of intensive care. Allison Pearson, a *Telegraph* columnist, writes: 'It's rare for a politician to inspire such emotion, but Boris is loved – really loved – in a way that the metropolitan media class has never begun to understand.' Truly, the *Telegraph* is a foreign country. They do things differently there.

Today's hospital death toll is 980, more than either Spain or Italy. In New York bodies are being buried in mass graves.

Saturday 11 April

Finished reading *The Way We Live Now*. Although Trollope is writing about the excesses of the 1870s, there are contemporary echoes in the decadent lives of Russian oligarchs, Californian tech billionaires and various other twentieth and 21st-century elites. Augustus Melmotte, the great swindler, is the very image of Robert Maxwell, and the idle young toffs who frequent the Beargarden bring to mind 'Lucky' Lucan and the Clermont set.

Sunday 12 April

Our weekly Skype with the girls and son-in-law Nick. Nick says he gets through up to five sets of single-use masks and gowns a day, which all have to be destroyed. This being so, no wonder we have a shortage. If only the lazy 'gotcha' journalists who from the comfort of their studios demand instant answers to unanswerable questions would do more to educate their listeners on the stark realities of the crisis. Today the UK death toll passed 10,000. We are on the way to becoming world leader. The media have started putting faces to the figures. Grannies, grandpas, uncles, aunts and, most distressing of all, doctors, nurses, care home assistants and even London bus drivers. Some in the prime of life, often with young children.

Monday 13 April

Boris Johnson has been released from hospital and is recuperating at Chequers. This evening he recorded a heartfelt little tribute to the NHS for saving his life and went out of his way to thank by name two nurses who had sat with him through the night, both foreigners. An email from Liz Forgan: 'The government has some tough questions to answer, though I fear Boris has been sanctified.' Yes indeed. He has shared the nation's pain. It will give him new credibility – for the time being at least.

Tuesday 14 April

The UK death toll now exceeds 12,000, not counting those who have died at home or in care.

Thursday 16 April

Awoke to the news that in the absence of any British citizens willing to work for so long and in such poor conditions, six planeloads of Romanians are being flown in to help farmers in the Fens, the heart of Brexitland, with the salad harvest. Someone up there is laughing at us. Meanwhile the government has announced that the lockdown will continue for at least another three weeks.

Friday 17 April

'Around the clock'. Another annoying little phrase which has become a standard feature of official pronouncements. Ministers and officials are apparently working 'around the clock' to attend to the needs of an ungrateful nation. The phrase first cropped up several weeks ago in relation to the repatriation of British citizens stranded abroad. Now it occurs frequently in relation to supplies of personal protective equipment, which despite constant reassurances is still in short supply. I wish they could stop themselves, because constant repetition of vacuous phrases implies insincerity. As in 'the welfare of our customers is our highest priority' or 'your call is important to us'.

Saturday 18 April

Scarcely a drop of rain in the past month and none forecast. The garden is bone-dry, so I am having to hump buckets of water around the fruit trees and the azaleas.

Sunday 19 April

A long and apparently damning article in today's *Sunday Times* documenting the government's alleged failure to get to grips with the virus in the first three months of the year with Johnson largely absent from the front line. He failed to attend five meetings of the government's emergency committee, COBRA, and spent much of February holed up with his girlfriend at Chevening. An anonymous source, described as 'a Downing Street adviser', is quoted as follows:

> There's no way you're at war if your PM isn't there. And what you learn about Boris was he didn't chair any meetings. He liked his country breaks. He didn't work weekends. It was like working for an old-fashioned chief executive in a local authority twenty years ago. There was a real sense that he didn't do urgent crisis planning. It was exactly like people feared he would be.

Also, a growing suggestion that, in the early stages at least, there may have been an ideological problem. Someone has posted a clip of a speech he made in Greenwich on 3 February in which he says:

> And when there is a risk that new diseases such as coronavirus will trigger a panic and a desire for market segregation that go beyond what is medically rational, to the point of doing real and unnecessary economic damage, then at that moment humanity needs some government, somewhere, that is willing at least to make the case powerfully for freedom of exchange ... Here in Greenwich in the first week of February 2020 I can tell you, in all humility, that the UK is ready for that role.

The smoking gun? Not quite. The key phrase is 'beyond what is medically rational'. As long as he can demonstrate that he followed the science, he is safe.

Sunshine all day. This afternoon I climbed up through the forest onto the ridge above Callaly, across the moor, up onto Long Crag, along Coe Crag and back along a little trodden path through an empty little valley. By a stream I came across a lone camper who, in defiance of the lockdown, had driven up from his home in Whitley Bay, where he said he was going 'stir crazy'. After a month of drought the peat was dry and crumbly, the heather brown and parched. My first proper walk for a month. Exhilarating.

Tuesday 21 April

A message from a woman in Ireland, prompted by one of my recent tweets: 'Dragged my teens (one very hungover after raiding the drinks cabinet with her friends the night before) to hear you speak – you not only woke them up, you kept them awake and they forgot that neither of them were speaking to me.'

This evening, having finally managed to connect up the hose, a massive garden watering, just in time to revive the roses.

The hospital death toll seems to have stabilised at around 800 per day. Have we reached peak Covid at last?

Wednesday 22 April

A very much downsized version of Parliament resumed today. Only fifty members allowed in the chamber to bear witness to Keir Starmer's low-key debut and another 120 able to join in via Zoom, should they feel so inclined. General opinion seems to be that Starmer did well. 'Britain now has an opposition again,' tweeted George Osborne. 'Or to put it another way,' replied a cynic, 'we do not see him as a threat or in possession of any ideas that might challenge the status quo.' We shall see.

Thursday 23 April

Donald Trump has suggested injecting disinfectant as a possible cure for coronavirus.

Friday 24 April

The manufacturers of Dettol have issued a statement saying that under no circumstances should their product be administered to the human body 'through injection, ingestion or any other route.'

Saturday 25 April

The weekly Skype with our daughters. Emma, cheerful as ever, despite having been on her own these past four weeks, remarked that 2020 will just be a tiny blip in her lifetime. Yes, my dear, but it will be a considerably larger blip in what remains of mine.

Today the UK hospital death toll passed 20,000.

Tuesday 28 April

A surprisingly low-key reaction to last night's *Panorama*, which alleged that when the crisis broke in January the government's pandemic stockpile contained no visors, gowns, swabs or body bags. Almost the only comment has come from the right-wing blogger Guido Fawkes, who claims that everyone interviewed in the programme was a Labour activist.

Wednesday 29 April

This morning's BBC bulletins report that the US death toll now exceeds the number – 58,000 – of Americans killed in Vietnam. Maybe, but there is still some way to go before it exceeds the Vietnamese casualties. Meanwhile the *Mail*, having purchased 150,000 face masks from China and chartered a plane to fly them in, is engaged in an orgy of self-congratulation ('Mail's £1 million airlift for NHS heroes'). Puts one in mind of their part in that sickening episode in the final days of the Vietnam War – Operation Babylift – when the *Mail* hired a plane 'to rescue orphans from communism.' Boris Johnson's partner, Carrie Symonds, gave birth to a baby boy this morning, thereby providing yet another major distraction from the issues at hand.

Rain. With the exception of one small shower, the first for six weeks.

Thursday 30 April

Life at Callaly has settled into a pattern. I rise at about 7 a.m., read for an hour (currently Orlando Figes's graphic history of the Crimean War). The rest of the morning is spent editing my diaries, which I hope may see the light of day next year. The afternoon is devoted to whatever needs doing in the garden and in the early evening a short walk. Yesterday I climbed up through the woods to Castle Hill and back in a circle along a little-used path which delivered me almost by the gate by the South Lodge. I try, not always successfully, to listen to the news only once a day since it so repetitive, demoralising and insular. What I miss most is the company of friends. Although I do my best to keep in touch by email and

---

* The episode ended tragically when one of the planes – not the *Mail*'s – crashed on take-off, killing 138 people, including seventy-eight children. Many of the evacuees turned out not to be orphans and decades later some were still searching for their parents.

telephone, it is not the same as personal contact. I had thought the lock-down might be over by June, but it is beginning to look as though – for us non-essentials, at least – it will extend through the summer and perhaps into autumn. My engagements diary is a great blank space. Will life ever be the same again?

A slightly breathless Boris Johnson reappeared at the Downing Street press briefing for the first time since he was laid low by the virus, claiming that the crisis has passed its peak and hinting at a cautious easing of the lockdown.

A greater spotted woodpecker appeared on the bird feeder this morn-ing. The first sighting this year.

Friday 1 May

Piers Morgan, never backward at coming forward, lays into our beloved Prime Minister for his handling of the crisis in, of all places, the *Mail* web-site: 'I didn't think it would be possible for any world leader in this crisis to sound more delusional than Trump … The cold hard truth is that Boris Johnson didn't care enough about this virus when it really mattered, and that has made Britain one of the worst coronavirus death-traps.' Unfair? To some extent, yes. True, our casualty rate is among the worst, but it's not far adrift of that in Italy, France and Spain and anyway it is hard to make accurate comparisons given that different countries use different criteria to assess the number of fatalities. When this is over, though, there will need to be some searching questions about our level of preparedness and the long delay in organising a testing regime. Trump, meanwhile, is claiming that the virus may have originated in a laboratory in Wuhan, and in Michigan a band of heavily armed 'patriots' have invaded the State House demanding an end to the lockdown. The official death toll in the US exceeds 60,000.

Health Secretary Matt Hancock proclaimed a near-miraculous rise in the number of coronavirus tests, meeting his much-trumpeted 100,000 target. Cue an outbreak of rejoicing for the Tories and their cheerleaders which instantly evaporated as it became clear that the figures appear to represent test kits dispatched, not those returned. No Labour minister would ever get away with a scam like this.

We drove to Rothbury and ate fish and chips, sitting in the car while outside it rained. Our first outing for a month.

Saturday 2 May

Son-in-law Nick reckons that testing isn't all that important, given only 70 per cent accuracy. More significant, he says, is the progress being made on finding a vaccine.

Monday 4 May

For the first time someone known to us has succumbed to the virus. Judith Crawford, the much-loved former head teacher at our daughters' primary school. One of a handful of inspirational teachers I came across during my twenty-three years representing Sunderland. On one memorable occasion when the school had its annual 'Red and White Day' to celebrate the football team in a city where football is a religion, the children, unknown to us, were supposed to come to school wearing the team shirt and the only child in the entire school who didn't possess one was Sarah Mullin, daughter of the MP. Mrs Crawford came to the rescue. She ordered a search of the lost property basket which was found to contain just one red and white shirt, several sizes too big, but adequate to the needs of the hour. Humiliation narrowly averted. The news of her death comes out of the blue. Ngoc last spoke to her in the first week of the lockdown and there was no hint then of infection, although she had suffered for years from leukaemia and was obviously vulnerable. So now we can put a face to the nightly litany of grim statistics.

Tuesday 5 May

Question: how far should one go, at this time of national emergency, in criticising those poor, inadequate politicians struggling to grapple with it? A tricky matter for any responsible opposition, and of course there is always the question in the back of one's mind: would a Labour government have done any better? With every day that passes it is becoming obvious that there have been some big blunders on the timing of the lockdown, non-availability of protective equipment and testing delays, but how much of this is hindsight? That said, however, there is a growing body of evidence that suggests the crisis could have been better handled. 'If the lockdown had been brought in earlier,' Professor Sir David King, a former chief scientific adviser to the government, was asked on television this morning, 'might the UK have had a lower death toll by now?' He replied, 'I don't think there is any "might" about it. Of course it would.'

Wednesday 6 May

Gary Lineker (7.5 million Twitter followers) has highlighted a string of mysterious Twitter accounts – there are said to be more than 700 – all parroting a more or less identical message: 'Journalism is missing the "mood" in this great country of ours. We do not want or need blame. We do not want constant criticism of the government who are doing their very best in a very difficult and unprecedent global emergency.' I opened a handful and they come up with messages such as 'this account does not exist' or 'there is unusual activity on this account'. Some appear to have been in existence for several years but have few, if any, followers. There is an unseen hand at work.

Today the UK death toll passed 30,000. The highest in Europe.

Thursday 7 May

The Bank of England is predicting the worst recession since the South Sea Bubble. If Labour were especially cynical, it might contrive to lay the blame for the crisis wholly or mainly at the door of the government. It would not be hard for opposition leaders to sit around a table and come up with suitably mendacious slogans: 'Boris Johnson's debt', 'failing to fix the roof while the sun was shining' and so forth. Of course, we'd never get away with it, would we? Our free press would never allow it.

Friday 8 May

Today we celebrate the seventy-fifth anniversary of VE Day. Another broadcast from the Queen which perfectly caught the mood of the hour. All the more so because she was there on the day. The odd thing is that the more distant the event becomes, the more enthusiastically we celebrate. At first I was inclined to be churlish about it, but then, as Matt d'Ancona points out, we are actually celebrating victory over fascism in a war in which more than 70 million people died. The one thing that does grate is the posh, patronising stream of jingoist drivel from 1940s broadcasters. As Martin Bell once remarked, 'officers addressing the other ranks'. Were they all like this, treating the population as idiots to be force-fed? How did it seem at the time? Surely people must have wearied of having this diet of ludicrously over-the-top propaganda thrust down their throats every night.

This evening, at a suitable distance, drinks with neighbours from the Big Hoose. The woods around the lake are carpeted with bluebells and wild garlic. No one has told nature that the world is in crisis.

Sunday 10 May

Awoke to find (not for the first time) one of the laird's pheasants trapped in the wire cage under the bird feeder. The same stupid bird has been stuck there several times before but, despite a great panic, appears to have no memory of previous incidents. Last night, for the first time in weeks, a healthy shower of rain. With the rain, of course, come the slugs. Our cabbages are beginning to look very sorry. This evening another prime ministerial broadcast which was billed as a loosening of the lockdown but which seems only to have sown confusion. Of more than academic interest to us since Emma Mullin, now in London, starts her new job today, which involves a lengthy commute by public transport.

Tuesday 12 May

We have become so insular. Everything is about the virus and how it impacts on *us*, the media straining to find new angles. Of the wars in Syria and Yemen, conditions on the Greek islands where tens of thousands of migrants are stranded, the plague of locusts devastating crops in east Africa, we hear little or nothing. The Israelis are in the process of stealing another large chunk of the West Bank and nobody even dares to raise the subject. And in the Bay of Bengal 700 Rohingya migrants are said to be trapped in appalling conditions on three boats, no country willing to accept them. All we know of this is that the UN has said they will die unless one of the neighbouring countries relents.

Wednesday 13 May

Snow on the Cheviot.

To our favourite garden centre, open for the first time in six weeks. Surprisingly relaxed and uncomplicated. Hand gel on a table by the entrance. In one door, out the other. Arrows on the floor indicating direction of travel. The other customers, like us, people of a certain age, some masked, some not. Staff on the tills separated from customers by Perspex. On the way home we stopped at Heighley Gate, a much more commercial operation. A long queue, staff in high-vis jackets regulating the flow. The man on the fruit and veg stall said the lockdown had cost his business about £150,000.

Thursday 14 May

The new Labour leader is attracting rave reviews for his performance at PMQs yesterday. This from the *Telegraph*: 'Keir Starmer took Boris Johnson apart like a Duplo train set … Labour's new leader is calm, polite, and utterly merciless. He doesn't rant or shout putdowns. Instead he asks factual questions designed to establish whether or not the Prime Minister knows what his own government is doing.'

Other news: the Vietnamese and US navies are to mount a joint exercise in the face of growing aggression from China, which has claims on the territory of all its neighbours, but Vietnam is the most vulnerable since – unlike Japan, Taiwan and the Philippines – it has no defence treaty with the US. Lately Chinese gunboats have been attacking and sometimes detaining Vietnamese fishermen. The Vietnamese government has kept very quiet for fear of inflaming the situation, but it is a sign of how worried they must be that they have agreed to this. In the medium to long term, I don't rule out another war.

Friday 15 May

The weekly trip to the fish and chip shop in Rothbury has become a highlight of our much-reduced – that is to say non-existent – social life. Not much of a queue. One in, one out. We place our order fifteen minutes in advance and then proceed to the local Co-op store for a little light shopping before collecting our meal. Then home via Cartington Bank, where we eat our dinner (a single portion between two) in a place with a fine view across the Vale of Whittingham towards the Cheviot. Illuminated by evening sunshine.

Saturday 16 May

The teaching unions are objecting to government plans to reopen schools next month, ostensibly on health grounds. They may well be right, but my suggestion via Twitter that perhaps one solution would be for teachers to take their summer leave in June and July and bring schools back in August when the risk will hopefully be much lower has triggered a tsunami of outrage from members of the profession who insist that they have been working hard throughout the lockdown (which no one disputes) and that, anyway, their contract only pays them to work 195 days a year (true for teaching assistants, but not for full-time teachers). Many go on about their pay (which surely isn't the issue right now – or is it?). One claims to be earning less per hour than a supermarket shelf-stacker (a nonsense I first heard years ago from an angry police officer). The scale and irrationality of the response is extraordinary, given that all that is being suggested is that, for one year only, they align the English school timetable with that of their Scottish colleagues, who have long taken holidays in June and July and returned in August.

Sunday 17 May

My post about bringing the schools back in August seems to have touched a raw nerve. By this morning it had been liked or retweeted 2,300 times and attracted 350 replies, mostly from hostile teachers or teaching assistants. If any conclusion can be drawn, there seems to be a divide between the teachers and the rest of us. The Twitter spat raged all day. The intemperance of the reaction, the determination to wilfully misunderstand the proposition and the eagerness to take offence suggest that one has come up against a mighty vested interest, as when, some years ago, I took on the Police Federation. Also a certain amount of ignorance. Several respondents seem to be under the impression that I am still in Parliament.

Today's *Mail* features a lame attempt to monster Keir Starmer. 'Man of the people? New Labour leader Sir Keir owns land worth up to £10 million.' This turns out to be a seven-acre field behind the home of his late parents in Surrey which Starmer purchased twenty-five years ago to enable his disabled mother to open a donkey sanctuary. Since the land is green belt, it cannot be built on anyway. A statement from Sir Keir says the field is not for sale and no one, developer or otherwise, has been shown around it. To judge by the derision the story has attracted, it has backfired.

Tuesday 19 May

To Alnwick for a mega shopping. The first in several weeks. A slight increase in footfall, given the easing of the lockdown, but people eyeing each other cautiously and giving a wide berth. Everywhere employees in high-vis security jackets directing, advising, assisting. Then to the recycling centre, which despite notices warning of queues was more or less empty. A surly jobsworth guarding the entrance demanded to know my business before reluctantly granting admission, eyeing me suspiciously until I was off the premises.

Wednesday 20 May

To the coast with John Field. We parked along the road near Craster and walked three or four miles to Boulmer along the coast. Temperature in the low twenties, people enjoying the sunshine, families camped on little beaches and rocky coves. John said, 'I can't tell you how liberating it is to see the sea, after eating 200 meals at home alone.'

Thursday 21 May

Curiously, the government has yet to publish the Intelligence and Security Committee's report on Russian interference in British politics, which was delivered to the Prime Minister as long ago as last autumn. After sitting on it until the election was out of the way, Boris Johnson announced in mid-December that there was no reason on security grounds why it should not be published and yet, five months on, there is no sign of it. The suspicion is that it suggests that the Russians have been channelling money into the Tory Party via the friends or relatives of oligarchs who have adopted British citizenship. I dropped a note to a friend in the shadow Cabinet, suggesting that he prompt Keir Starmer to pursue the matter at PMQs or, failing that, to feed a question to a sympathetic backbencher.

Saturday 23 May

A great hoo-ha under way following the discovery that Dominic Cummings drove 250 miles to his sister's home in County Durham, where he, his wife Mary Wakefield (Humphry's daughter) and their young son spent the lockdown. Tempting though it is, I shall not be joining in. First because, thus far at least, the details are obscure and secondly because there are obvious mitigating circumstances. Both he and Mary (and maybe the child) were infected with the virus. They couldn't have known how it would turn out, may well have feared the worst and urgently needed help with childcare. As yet there is no evidence that they did anything which could have led to the spread of the virus and it is far from clear what law, if any, has been broken.

Sunday 24 May

Knives well and truly out for Dominic Cummings. Massive feeding frenzy under way. No shortage of the virtuous (and not so virtuous) casting stones. Opposition parties and even some Tory MPs participating. Inevitable, I suppose, for a man who has accumulated so many enemies. Boris is sticking by him for now.

Monday 25 May

Open season on Cummings. 'A CHEAT AND A COWARD' (*Mirror*), 'WHAT PLANET ARE THEY ON?' (*Mail*), 'No apology, no explanation: PM bets all on Cummings' (*Guardian*). A mob of journalists laying siege to his home. The Twittersphere has gone bananas. Yet, deep down, all is not as it seems. Like most things in British politics, Brexit remains the dividing line. A pollster on the radio this morning reckoned that the government, though damaged, is still well ahead of the opposition, and most of the Brexit media is still onside or at least soft-pedalling: 'DEFIANT

BORIS STANDS BY HIS MAN' (*Express*), 'He has acted responsibly, legally and with integrity' (*Telegraph*), 'Bo Jo stands by top aide' (*Sun*). Maybe Boris will tough it out after all, but whatever happens the brand is surely tarnished and no doubt behind the scenes knives are being sharpened. This afternoon a soberly dressed, somewhat chastened but unapologetic Dominic Cummings gave a press conference in the No. 10 rose garden, setting out his version of events. The weakest part of his case is not the drive to Durham but a thirty-mile family outing to Barnard Castle on Easter Sunday, where they were spotted sitting by the river.

Tuesday 26 May

For the fourth day running our media are still wallowing in the Cummings story, scouring the highways, byways and even the beaches in search of indignant citizens, of whom there is no shortage in these days of instant outrage. Every rent-a-quote in the land is being given airtime. No other story gets a look in. Classic lazy journalism. I can't stand listening to it.

Wednesday 27 May

The Cummings inferno rages unabated. Mobs of feral hacks and virtuous Twitterati gather outside his house each day, so much so that he now requires a police escort to get in and out. I have even received queries asking if it's true that he has been seen at Chillingham and in Wooler (I am sure it isn't). Perhaps, like Martin Bormann, he is destined to be 'sighted' all over the world for years to come.

Thursday 28 May

Durham Police have sensibly concluded that while the Cummings outing to Barnard Castle (though not his drive north) breached the lockdown rules, no one was endangered, and they therefore propose to take no further action. No doubt this will come as a disappointment to the virtuous, who will now have to find some other target for their boundless outrage. How the police must resent being used by people playing politics. Meanwhile, on *Channel 4 News*, a rare glimpse of life beyond our first-world bubble. A ten-minute documentary following a destitute Peruvian mother and her three young children (one a babe in arms) attempting to walk and hitch-hike the 300 miles from Lima to their home 4,500 metres high in the Andes. They made it after seven days and nights, sleeping out in the open and with, one suspects, a little help from the film crew. Just some among millions of penniless hungry migrant workers whose livelihoods have disappeared. Still no word in our free press of what is happening in Syria, in Yemen or among the Rohingya camped along the Burmese border, nor even what has become of those in the path of the typhoon which swept Orissa, Calcutta and the Bay of Bengal last week.

In the US the death toll has passed 100,000.

Saturday 30 May

Andrew Adonis has written an excellent biography of Ernest Bevin, one of the twentieth century's great men, which I have been asked to review by *Prospect*. Reading it, I came across the following in a letter from Sarah Churchill to her father in July 1945:

> Socialism as practised in the War did no one any harm and quite a lot of people good. The children of this country have never been so well-fed or healthy. The rich did not die because their meat ration was no larger than the poor and there is no doubt that this common sharing and feeling of sacrifice was one of the strongest bonds that unified us. So why, they say, cannot this common feeling of sacrifice be made to work as effectively in the peace?

Sunday 31 May

My Learned Neighbour John Field has fallen on the dunes near Bamburgh and fractured his femur.

Monday 1 June

This morning a cautious attempt to reopen primary schools in the teeth of disagreement among teachers and scientists as to whether it is safe to do so. Meanwhile in the US yet another blatant killing of an unarmed black man by a white police officer, triggering a wave of angry demonstrations, accompanied by an outbreak of arson and looting by usual suspects. One man interviewed this morning said, 'Our ancestors slaved to build this country. We've got a right to burn it down.' Just the sort of sentiment that could get Trump, who is busy fanning the flames, re-elected.

Wednesday 3 June

To Wansbeck Hospital to collect John Field, whose leg has been bolted back together following his fall on Sunday. He is a man with many friends and there was competition for the honour of collecting him.

Sunday 7 June

The fallout from the death of George Floyd, the unarmed black man killed by police in Minneapolis, continues. In Bristol a mob tore down a controversial statue of an seventeenth-century philanthropist who owed his fortune to the slave trade. The fall of the statue was accompanied by much righteous whooping and dancing, reminiscent of the scene in Baghdad when Saddam's statue fell. For my part a feeling of unease. Bristol is not Baghdad. There may well be a strong case for removing the statue, but in a democracy that ought to be a decision for the elected, not for the mob. What next? Churchill's statue in Parliament Square perhaps? Already someone has daubed it with the world 'Racist'. Among the righteous such qualms are brushed aside with contempt. As regards the Bristol statue, even my dear daughters, whom we Skyped this evening, disagree with their fuddy-duddy old dad.

Tuesday 9 June

Self-styled anti-racists are reported to be drawing up lists of more statues for demolition. As many as sixty are said to be in the firing line and new ones are being added daily. Meanwhile politicians have been scrambling to ride the tiger, but, as some are discovering, the tiger cannot be ridden. In Minneapolis, where all this began, the young mayor was booed off the platform because he would not commit to closing down the entire police department. Here Keir Starmer and Angela Rayner were pictured looking somewhat ridiculous in an empty room 'taking the knee' in tribute to

George Floyd. Floyd, though no one can excuse the manner of his death, is a dubious icon. Although in recent years he seems to have turned his life around, he had a string of convictions, including one for an armed robbery in which he burst into a home and held a woman at gunpoint, demanding to know where she kept her jewellery. Lucky there isn't a film of that.

Monday 22 June

Dad would be 100 years old today. When he was dying, he said to me, 'I am nearly a hundred, you know.' 'Nonsense, you're eighty-three,' I replied. Well, Dad, you've finally made it.

Tuesday 23 June

The government has announced that from 4 July, and subject to strict conditions, pubs, restaurants, cinemas etc. can reopen. The announcement is accompanied by warnings from scientists that there is still a good chance of a second spike, in which case we will have to return to lockdown.

Yesterday's death toll was 171, bringing the UK total to almost 43,000. Along with Russia, the US and Brazil, we are among the world record holders.

Wednesday 24 June

To Durham to see my good friend Peter Candler, who is slowly recovering from a severe stroke. Afterwards Ngoc and I took a walk along the river and ate our sandwiches in a green space beside Prebends Bridge, where once we picnicked with Granny, Grandpa and the small people. The hottest day of the year so far. The temperature touched 30°.

Thursday 25 June

Dominic Grieve, former Attorney General and hero of the Brexit resistance, came with his son James for a socially distanced al fresco glass of champagne. They are staying with My Learned Neighbour John Field.

Dominic now chairs an outfit called the Conservative Group for Europe (president: Ken Clarke) which he says has about 300 members, just seven of whom are sitting MPs, who in the current climate presumably have to move from house to house under cover of darkness. He says that, contrary to speculation, the Intelligence and Security Committee's much-delayed Russia report, which was drafted on his watch as chairman, contains nothing very explosive – which makes the refusal to publish it all the more puzzling.

Friday 26 June

The perils of tweeting, part ninety-five: Keir Starmer has sacked Rebecca Long-Bailey for retweeting – and refusing to retract – an interview by the actress Maxine Peake which is said to contain antisemitic sentiment. Meanwhile the housing minister Robert Jenrick, a well-upholstered lawyer, is in trouble for overruling the planning inspectorate to fast-track approval of a £1 billion luxury housing development in the Isle of Dogs part-funded by Richard Desmond, the former pornographer who used to own the *Daily Express*. Although Jenrick hastily rescinded his approval, it turns out that Desmond, a Tory Party donor, had personally lobbied him. Two weeks later, Desmond donated £12,000 to the party. Jenrick is staying put. These guys are not easily embarrassed.

Sunday 28 June

The great gardens are reopening. Yesterday we visited Fallodon. Today I went alone to Lilburn Tower. The new regime is hedged around with rules. All bookings must be online via the National Garden Scheme and are accompanied by a long list of dos and don'ts: arrive at the allocated time, stay no longer than one hour, no picnics etc. The reality, however, was quite different. No one checked our tickets. Picnics (at Fallodon) were encouraged. And we could stay as long as we liked. It was much the same at Lilburn, minus the picnics. Afterwards to tea with Humphry and Katharine Wakefield at Chillingham. Humphry still smarting from recent adverse publicity on account of his being the father-in-law of Dominic Cummings.

Tuesday 30 June

'Build, Build, Build.' Armed with his new slogan, our beloved Prime Minister has made a rare foray beyond the Home Counties, in this case to rain-soaked Dudley in the West Midlands, where he was pictured astride a dumper truck wearing a high-vis jacket, after announcing a blizzard of initiatives designed to dig us out of the deep, dark pit into which the post-Covid economy has sunk. Much of it – 'forty new hospitals', 'more affordable housing' – has been announced many times before. Some (the housing budget, for example) amounted to an actual reduction on what had previously been pledged. Some, if deliverable, makes sense: easing of planning restrictions to enable the conversion of commercial property to residential, for example. On planning, though, one suspects that the real goal is to concrete over every available blade of grass, with a view to ensuring a continuing flow of funds from the construction industry into Tory Party coffers. As with so much of what Boris says, one can never be sure how much is windy rhetoric and how much has a basis in reality. To quote *Guardian* columnist Rafael Behr, the speech had 'a make-believe quality, as when a child gets more play out of the packaging than the gift'.

Wednesday 1 July

The government have announced, in response to China's crackdown in Hong Kong, that the more than 3 million Hong Kong citizens with British passports will be free to settle in the UK. A foolish piece of opportunism from a party which regularly plays the immigration card. Not hard to guess how the Great British Public will react, if it comes to pass, to the possible arrival of several hundred thousand Hong Kong Chinese at a time of record unemployment, though Labour is in no position to take advantage since it supports the policy. The unpalatable truth is that the young extremists leading the protests in Hong Kong, smashing up the legislative assembly, attacking public buildings, lobbing petrol bombs – have brought this on themselves, playing into the hands of Chinese hardliners. The move is being compared to the admission of Ugandan Asians in the early 1970s, but there is no comparison. First because it involved much smaller numbers and second because the Ugandan Asians faced much more immediate threat. Were it up to me, I would offer asylum only to those most directly at risk rather than opening the floodgates.

Friday 3 July

Occasional speculation among the Twitterati that rather than suffer the humiliation of defeat Donald Trump may simply decide not to contest November's presidential election and walk away, all the while complaining about how he was robbed. He looks increasingly depressed. Defeat is the one thing he couldn't cope with.

Saturday 4 July

From today – in England (other parts of the UK are doing their own thing) – an easing of the lockdown. Pubs, hotels, restaurants, cafes, museums, hairdressers etc. will be allowed to reopen, subject to strict rules about social distancing. Also, air travel will now be permitted to fifty-nine countries that are deemed safe. All this is accompanied by stern warnings that the lockdown will be reimposed if (as experts predict) there are signs of a new spike. Meanwhile, from around the country, reports of misbehaving youths holding street parties, leading in some places to riots and knee-deep litter.

Sunday 5 July

A telephone chat with Martin Woollacott. We agreed that we have both become old fogies. Awful though the death of George Floyd was, neither of us are comfortable with the orgy of virtue signalling to which it has given rise. As regards Hong Kong, we are both of the view that the young extremists have played into the hands of the hardliners on the mainland. Neither of these views would find favour with the current management of *The Guardian*, where Martin worked for more than forty years and to which I have occasionally contributed over the same period.

Tuesday 7 July

I am reading Shirley Williams's autobiography, which I came across in Barter Books the other day.* Although we have had our differences, it confirms my impression when I briefly came to know her eight years

---

* *Climbing the Bookshelves*, Virago, 2009.

ago: a thoughtful, principled, intrepid woman who, despite a privileged upbringing, has had her share of life's setbacks. In her early twenties she was briefly a reporter on the *Mirror* and when it came to expenses she had exactly the same experience as I on the very same newspaper twenty years later. 'My expenses came to less than a quarter of those of most of the other reporters. My colleagues told me I had to pad them out or else they would all have been in trouble.' Like me, she then received a short course in how to construct fraudulent expenses. Again, as I did, she threw away the revised expense sheet when her colleagues weren't looking.

Wednesday 8 July

We are losing track of time. We went through yesterday believing it to be today and only realised our mistake this morning. This is what comes of having a blank diary, stretching way into the future. Yesterday Tony Henfrey and I drove to Redesdale and walked along a little-used path following the river, which was fairly full after recent rain. Afterwards lunch in a pub at West Woodburn. Two days since the lockdown ended, but there were only a handful of other customers. We had to complete a form with our name and address in case we brought the lurgy with us and needed to be traced.

Thursday 9 July

Chancellor Sunak, who is having a good crisis, has unveiled a £30 billion package to help revive our rapidly shrinking economy. It includes cuts in VAT and a £10 a head subsidy for every midweek meal purchased in a pub or restaurant. The total cost so far of his virus-related spending plans is said to be £190 billion, the biggest government intervention since the war. 'I am unencumbered by dogma,' he told the House of Commons yesterday. Which, if true, distinguishes him from many of his colleagues.

Friday 10 July

Mum was born 100 years ago today.

It rained on and off all day. In between the showers there was sunshine. I dug up some potatoes, which we ate for lunch, seeded the bare patches on the lawn and in the afternoon sat in the glasshouse reading Hemingway's *A Farewell to Arms*. I cried when I got to the end, even though I saw it coming some way off.

Saturday 11 July

Tweeted a picture of the fine display of lavender in the border just outside our window. It included the double doors which lead into our sitting room. Among the comments one from the very wicked Nicholas Soames: 'Love the entrance to the visiting valets' card room.'

Sunday 12 July

The government has announced that it will spend £700 million on new customs and border infrastructure in anticipation of a no-deal Brexit. So much for the Brexit savings.

Wednesday 22 July

Keir Starmer has settled libel actions brought against the party by the journalist John Ware and seven former Labour Party staff members who were featured on *Panorama* alleging that Labour under Corbyn had been dragging its heels on dealing with complains of antisemitism. They subsequently claimed the party had defamed them in its response to the programme, which had argued that their criticisms were politically motivated. This settlement will spare them the embarrassment of having to explain the huge tranche of ferociously hostile internal emails that were leaked earlier this year. The settlement is expected to cost the party about £600,000 and was made despite legal advice that the party stood a good chance of winning. Whatever the rights and wrongs, one can't blame Starmer for wanting to draw a line under this damaging episode, but has he? The plaintiffs were represented by an Israel-based no-win, no-fee lawyer who claims to have another thirty-two cases in the pipeline. One anonymous litigant has been quoted as saying, 'If it bankrupts the Labour Party, so be it.'

Saturday 8 August

A visit from Our Two Best Friends. Not wanting to infect their old dad and mum, they are staying in a local B&B.

Sunday 9 August

To Ross Sands, Northumberland's finest beach, with Sarah and Emma. Five miles of sand with a castle at each end. After our picnic and a stroll along the sand, Ngoc, Sarah and I dozed off. Emma photographed the scene and later tweeted it with the caption, 'An exciting day on the beach with the Mullins.'

Monday 17 August

Andrew and Sharon Mitchell stopped by for lunch, en route from a holiday in Scotland. Andrew reports that there is growing unhappiness with Boris in the Tory parliamentary party.

Thursday 10 September

To Durham to see Peter and Jeana Candler. Afterwards we ate our sandwiches by the river. A commercial waste bin was resting conspicuously on the weir below the cathedral, not a good look for a world heritage site. Reminds me of the story told years ago by former Durham MP Gerry Steinberg. Apparently when the council was interviewing for a new environment director the candidates were asked what would be the first thing they did if they got the job. One of them replied, 'Have you noticed that shopping trolley that's been in the river below the cathedral for the last few months? I'd remove it.' He got the job.

Saturday 26 September

Tony Henfrey and I drove to the Harthope Valley and walked up through the wilderness to the shooting lodge at Broadstruther. As we sat on the doorstep munching our sandwiches, I found myself thinking of the little family who must have lived here in years gone by. No electricity or running water, maybe five or six children and a walk of several miles to the nearest primary school. How different their lives were from ours.

Thursday 29 October

An email from Hong Kong inviting me to be the guest speaker at a dinner which is apparently to be attended by 'international celebrities and world-renowned entrepreneurs' in aid of a charitable foundation whose alleged mission is to help disadvantaged children. I replied saying that I didn't think flying me halfway round the world and paying a no doubt substantial fee would be the best use of their funds. Suspect they may have confused me with my namesake, the former US baseball star.

Friday 30 October

Keir Starmer has withdrawn the whip from Jeremy Corbyn for suggesting, in response to a report from the Equalities Commission, that allegations of antisemitism in the Labour Party have been exaggerated by people with a different agenda. As it happens, I agree with Jeremy. The proposition is not difficult to illustrate. To take but one example, most of those named in Margaret Hodge's much-publicised dossier of alleged antisemites turned out not to be members of the Labour Party. What's more, the handful of cases highlighted by the commission's report as having been mishandled occurred at a time when party headquarters was firmly in the hands of Corbyn's sworn enemies. I feel angry about this. Corbyn was never leadership material, but he is a good and decent man and it upsets me to see him cynically thrown to the wolves. For the first time in more than fifty years, having stuck with the Labour Party through thick and thin, I begin to wonder if I still belong in it.

Tuesday 3 November

The US presidential elections. Results awaited with trepidation. The polls put Joe Biden well ahead, but as we've seen before, that's no guarantee of victory.

Wednesday 4 November

Awoke to the news that, against predictions, Trump has won Florida. Although Biden is ahead in the popular vote, the delegate count is neck and neck. Is history about to repeat itself? This afternoon to Chillingham, where Humphry described how he once arranged a test-firing of one of the two cannon, originally from Nelson's flagship and rescued by Humphry from Sebastopol, which now stand on the terrace in front of the castle. A ball was loaded, what was thought to be an appropriate quantity of explosive inserted and the fuse lit. The resulting explosion lifted the three-ton cannon clean off the ground. The ball flew down the long tree-lined avenue, over the equestrian statue of one of Humphry's kinsmen, over the railings, across the road and came to rest harmlessly in a nearby field. Heaven knows what might have happened had a vehicle been passing. A damn close-run thing, as the Duke of Wellington might have said.

Thursday 5 November

7 a.m.: Biden 4 million votes ahead but still short of the magic total of electoral college delegates: 270. As we saw last time round, it is possible for the Democratic candidate to be several million votes ahead and still lose. Those wretched founding fathers have a lot to answer for. Six states are still to declare. Trump is ahead in several of them, but his lead is expected to erode as the postal ballots are counted.

Friday 6 November

Delegate count: 253:213. Biden now has narrow leads in Arizona, Georgia, Nevada and Pennsylvania which, if sustained, would take him past the winning post, but the margins are tantalisingly close – a fraction of 1 per cent. He has yet to claim victory, restricting himself to dignified little speeches calling for calm and healing. Trump is talking fraud and lawyers. Donald Jr is calling for 'total war', which has to be taken seriously given that Trump supporters are heavily armed. Hardcore Trumpistas have been gathering outside polling centres chanting 'Stop the Count', except in Arizona, where the postal vote may go in their favour. There they are chanting 'Count the Vote'.

Saturday 7 November

By 7 a.m., Biden's delegate count was still stuck on 253. Trump on 214, having picked up Alaska. Biden's slender lead is gradually widening as the postal votes are counted. There seems no doubt that he has won, but in America it is not over until the networks 'call' the result and they have not yet pronounced. You have to hand it to old Joe Biden, he is behaving with great dignity.

A light mist which by midday had given way to sunshine. Neighbours Kate Donaghy, John Field and I walked up through the forest onto the crag and back in a circle. Fine views across the valley to the Cheviots. By the time we came down, the networks had declared Biden the winner. Even Fox News has accepted the result. A good day to be alive.

Monday 9 November

Light at the end of a long, dark tunnel? The US pharmaceutical giant Pfizer has announced that, together with a small company in Germany, it has developed a vaccine for the virus which tests have shown to be 90 per cent effective. The demise of Trump and the discovery of a vaccine in the space of just two days. Almost too good to be true.

Friday 13 November

Turmoil at the heart of government. Relations between Boris Johnson and two of his key henchmen are reported to have gone over a cliff edge. First Lee Cain, director of communications, flounced out of No. 10 after being turned down for the post of chief of staff, and last night Dominic Cummings, in a carefully staged exit, emerged carrying his possessions in a cardboard box. Both men are core Brexiteers and know where the bodies are buried. They could be dangerous enemies.

Saturday 14 November

Fascinating piece in the current *LRB*:

> Covid-19 has revealed the depth of cronyism and clientelism in British public life. More than almost any other comparable state, Britain – or,

more accurately, England – has outsourced swathes of its pandemic response, often to companies with strong links to Conservative politicians but little obvious relevant experience.[*]

A shocking story, with plenty of chapter and verse. Something any halfway decent opposition should be getting its teeth into.

Sunday 15 November

A new civil war brewing in northern Ethiopia, which, after a turbulent history, was on course to become one of Africa's most successful economies. Reports of massacres and refugees pouring into Sudan. Twenty years ago I flew up from Djibouti to Addis Ababa in a light aeroplane and was taken to see Prime Minister Meles Zenawi. 'Spectacular country,' I remarked, 'but difficult to govern.' 'Spectacularly difficult to govern,' he replied.

Meanwhile in the La-La Land that the USA has become, Trump has yet to concede defeat and the crazies are out in force. What is most remarkable about the recent election is not Joe Biden's victory but the fact that so many people still support Trump. Only a handful of Republicans have publicly conceded the result and they are still solidly entrenched in the Senate and Supreme Court. Enough, should they so choose (as they surely will), to render the country ungovernable. Poor Joe Biden will find the going very tough.

Tuesday 17 November

A belated outbreak of common sense. Corbyn has been reinstated as a Labour Party member after 'clarifying' his position. It remains to be seen, however, whether he will be allowed back into the parliamentary party.

Wednesday 18 November

Margaret Hodge has tweeted, 'I simply cannot comprehend why it is acceptable for Corbyn to be a Labour MP if he thinks antisemitism is

---

[*] 'Cronyism and Clientelism' by Peter Geoghegan, *London Review of Books*, 5 November 2020.

exaggerated…' I took a deep breath and responded as follows: 'Dear Margaret, a question: how many of the people who featured in your famous dossier of alleged antisemites turned out to be members of the Labour Party?' The abuse started within minutes. A sample: 'Complete scumbag', 'Were you always a deranged offensive shit…?', 'Chris Mullin has long been a cretinous, unpleasant, individual', 'Why are you bullying Margaret Hodge?', 'Alexa, what is Jew baiting?' And so on. No one actually addressed the question. The answer, according to Jennie Formby, Labour's general secretary at the time, is that of the 111 individuals named in Hodge's dossier, only twenty were party members and not all of the complaints against them were upheld. Meanwhile Keir Starmer has announced that Corbyn will not be readmitted to the Labour Party. It may appease the mob, but it is an act of moral cowardice.

Thursday 19 November

The row over Corbyn's suspension from the parliamentary party still rages. This morning, yet again, Margaret Hodge was given the freedom of the airwaves to pronounce on the subject. Steve Richards, whose judgement I respect, says that Starmer has made a major strategic error.

Friday 20 November

Biden has again been declared the winner in Georgia after a recount. He is now almost 6 million votes ahead of Trump, who is still refusing to concede and is said to be planning a legal onslaught. The official Republican Party remains eerily silent. Increasingly one hears the word 'coup' being used to describe what is happening. Personally, I think not, but it sure sets a bad example to all those third-world rulers for life who have to be prised out of presidential palaces when the day of reckoning comes. Trump has made America a laughing stock.

Saturday 21 November

In today's *Telegraph*, a joint plea to the government from Tony Blair and David Cameron not to slash the aid budget, one of the few areas where the UK can still hold its head high in the international arena. To renege on our existing commitment would, they argue, be 'a moral, strategic and political mistake'. Development aid, they say in language that *Telegraph* readers ought to be able to understand, is not charity but enlightened self-interest. David Richards, the former armed forces chief, backs them up. Aid, he says, is 'much cheaper than fighting wars'. Alas their pleas are likely to fall on deaf ears. And anyway, most *Telegraph* readers tend to be keen on war.

Sunday 22 November

This evening to Lorbottle Hall, where our neighbours Kate and Jeremy have set up what they call the 'Covid cafe' in an enclosed courtyard at the rear of the house, heated by a fire in a large steel bowl. We sipped wine and gossiped for two hours oblivious to the fall in temperature. Only on leaving did I find that the car windows had frosted over.

Wednesday 25 November

Chancellor Rishi Sunak announced his spending plans. As expected, he is cutting the overseas development budget from 0.7 to 0.5 per cent of GDP and increasing military spending by about the same amount. The Tories have correctly calculated that this will do them no harm with the electorate, who, egged on by our loathsome tabloids, are deeply hostile to spending public money on impoverished foreigners. Overall borrowing, mostly pandemic-related, now stands at an astonishing £400 billion, besides which the bailout of the banks and the Corbyn magic money tree pale into insignificance. So far not a hint of how all this is to be paid for. A tricky issue for a party which is forever proclaiming its love of low taxes. Labour, too, seems anxious to avoid the issue while simultaneously demanding yet more spending. No mention of Brexit or its likely impact on the economy. It was left to the Governor of the Bank of England to point out that a no-deal Brexit would inflict greater damage than Covid.

Saturday 28 November

A cold clear day, −4° when I left home. Kate Donaghy, Caterina Leigh-Pemberton, Jean Matterson and I drove up Coquetdale, walked up to the border ridge and round in a circle. About seven miles, wonderful views stretching north, all the way to the Eildon Hills and into deep, empty valleys. Behind us, on the Otterburn range, red warning flags were up and the army were pounding away at goodness knows what with their heavy guns, muzzle smoke rising from a distant valley. As we ate our packed lunches on Windy Gyle, Kate pulled out a huge, shiny apple. 'Where did that come from?' I enquired, thinking perhaps the Co-op at Rothbury. 'From our local grocer's – Fortnum and Mason,' she replied.

Sunday 29 November

A note from My Learned Friend John Field, accompanied by a dozen bottles of beer from the little brewery at Elsdon. It reads, 'Thank you for your support and encouragement in this difficult and estranging year. This is not a Christmas gift, does not set a precedent, and reciprocation is not permitted.'

Monday 30 November

The Israelis – or is it the Americans? – appear to have assassinated another of Iran's nuclear scientists. Presumably with a view to wrecking any chance of a renewed deal with Iran once Biden takes office. As usual with such events, the international community's calls for 'restraint' seem mainly to be directed at the victim rather than the perpetrator. The UK has so far confined itself to 'urgently trying to establish the facts'. Ho, ho.

Wednesday 2 December

With colleagues from the National Park Authority, a couple of hours tramping the muddy wilderness just north of Hadrian's Wall, inspecting the site of yet another proposed Sitka spruce plantation, part of a vast, unstoppable army that is advancing through the park. Already about 20 per cent is covered in the dreaded, deadening spruce and we are powerless to stop it, the Forestry Commission being under no obligation to do any more than consult. What is particularly maddening is that this is funded by the taxpayer. It costs the landowner little or nothing and the resulting timber is of such poor quality that most of it ends up as wood chips or fence posts. I drove home across the moors chasing a huge, vivid rainbow which seemed to rise from the hedgerows only to evaporate every time I thought I had caught up with it.

Thursday 3 December

To Waterstones in Newcastle to spend an eighteen-month-old book token on Christmas presents. My first train journey for almost a year. Rail travel these days is very different from how it used to be. No more just turning up and boarding the first available train. Seats have to be reserved in both directions. The man behind the counter ostentatiously rinses his hands before handing over the tickets. The seats in the waiting room are taped off. A loudspeaker voice reminds us at intervals that the wearing of masks, even on the open-air platform, is compulsory. At Newcastle the station was eerily quiet. The bookshop, however, was bustling. Everyone, without exception, masked. Likewise most people in the street. All transactions are by credit card. Cash has become almost redundant, which must make life even harder for the handful of homeless people and *Big Issue* sellers. Today the death toll passed 60,000.

Friday 4 December

We spent the morning signing Christmas cards, scenes of Callaly in the snow. Reading through our address list, I am struck by how many names we have had to cross out as the years pass. Men, mostly. So many of our friends are widows. One day, perhaps in the not-too-distant future, Ngoc will be sending cards that no longer bear my name.

Saturday 5 December

An email from a bigwig at the BBC to whom I complained about its increasingly insular news coverage. He talks of 'a life-and-death battle for the BBC's future' and says:

> The depressing fact is that the BBC is in a serious financial crisis and this shows itself most obviously in the most expensive area of our operations, foreign news. The limitations are drastic: essentially no one is travelling

anywhere. The US election mopped up what little cash there is and it will take months before we get our head above water, assuming we do.

This is all part of George Osborne's poisonous legacy, forcing the Corporation to fund the World Service and free TV licences for the over-75s. Though goodness knows why the Beeb didn't mount stronger resistance, instead of coming out with their hands up at the first whiff of grapeshot.

Sunday 6 December

Trump, campaigning in Georgia, where a struggle for the two remaining Senate seats is under way, is still in denial about the election result. So are many of his supporters. A poll suggests that only 28 per cent of Republicans accept the result. Vox pops with people at his rally suggest that many believe he won by a landslide.

Tuesday 8 December

The first Covid vaccinations. A moment to celebrate, though it may be many months before normal life resumes. A BBC bulletin solemnly informed us that the Queen and the Duke of Edinburgh would wait their turn on the vaccine priority list – slightly unnecessary since, aged ninety-four and ninety-nine respectively, they are likely to be fairly high without having to pull rank.

Wednesday 9 December

Following a routine visit to the surgery yesterday I have been asked to take my blood pressure twice daily for a week. Early readings worryingly high. Stroke territory. Boris Johnson flew to Brussels tonight for what is being billed as last-ditch talks with EU President Ursula von der Leyen.

Friday 11 December

Blood pressure readings still alarmingly high, with inexplicable variations. Why? I am not overweight, eat little or no meat, don't smoke, consume little alcohol and get plenty of fresh air.

Growing pessimism about the possibility of a trade deal with the EU, although I still think a rabbit will be pulled out of the hat at the last moment. What a mess the posh boys have got us into. Meanwhile the following account has emerged of Johnson's dinner with Ursula von der Leyen. The source is said to be a former MEP with contacts in Brussels:

> Despite a belief on the EU side that Mr Johnson had come to make peace, he went into the pre-dinner *à deux* meeting with all guns blazing, urging her to side line Michel Barnier ... He also made an embarrassing crack about Barnier being French, and both the British and the Germans knowing how difficult they could be. VDL, who was cool, made it clear that Barnier's mandate from the EU was solid. She called his bluff and asked if he had any fresh proposals. He did not. After that, the dinner was an exercise in studied politeness, but Johnson did not appear to notice the offence he had given and continued to make facetious comments. Several people asked afterwards whether he realised how serious the situation had become.

Saturday 12 December

Here is the news:

'Gunboats To Guard Our Fish' (*Express*)

'We'll Send In Gunboats' (*Mail*)

'Shove your cake, Mr Macron. And your bloody croissants' (*The Sun*)

'Areas of the north and Midlands that backed Boris Johnson's Conservatives at last year's election are among areas of Britain with the highest share of jobs in sectors most at risk from the combined impact of a no-deal Brexit and the Covid pandemic' (*Financial Times*)

Monday 14 December

David Cornwell, otherwise known as John le Carré, has died. One of my small pantheon of literary heroes. How I would have loved to have met him. The closest I came was a couple of years ago when staying in Hampstead with the Woollacotts. One evening Martin said, 'I ran into John le Carré in the high street this morning and we went for a coffee at Maison Blanc.' He recounted once sharing a taxi with le Carré and Timothy

Garton Ash. Garton Ash was dropped off first and, as he got out, said something in German at which le Carré laughed and replied, 'Oh, I don't think we can guarantee that.' Asked what Garton Ash had said, le Carré replied that he had used a well-known German expression which meant, 'Speak well of me after I have gone.'

In the US the electoral college has finally confirmed Biden's election. Trump and most of his supporters are still in denial.

Wednesday 16 December

This evening a Zoom meeting with John and Sheila Williams, Adrian and Kathy Ham for our weekly version of *Mastermind*. My turn to set the questions, Kathy's turn to answer. Her special subject: Princess Margaret followed by a couple of minutes of general knowledge. Our version is not quite so rigorous as the real thing, since the contestant tends to argue with the moderator.

Friday 18 December

The online news agency Middle East Eye has published my lengthy piece on the weaponisation of antisemitism which in the current climate could never be published in the UK. Comments so far generally favourable. My Tory friend Andrew Mitchell writes: 'A superb piece venturing where most fear to tread and elegantly navigating the rapids without ducking the issues.' But there was also this: 'I am so disgusted with Mullin that I threw all his books away. Didn't even take them to a charity shop. I'll never buy another.'

Saturday 19 December

Christmas is cancelled. Faced with a sharp rise in Covid infections, the government has reversed its previous plan to relax travelling restrictions over Christmas and imposed a lockdown on London and much of the south, which means Our Two Best Friends and their partners will not be visiting us after all. They had planned to rent an apartment in a big house nearby and only outdoor activity was planned. Ngoc has been preparing Vietnamese delicacies, the fridge and freezer are full, all in vain. It is three months since we last saw them and maybe several more before we can meet again, by which time Sarah, seven months pregnant, will have given birth. Disappointing, but what can you do?

Sunday 20 December

I am reading Barack Obama's account of his presidency, a gift from my generous American neighbour, Katherine Clark. It's 750 pages and only covers his election campaign and first two years in office. I had intended only to dip into it, but it is so compelling and well-written that it is hard to put down. What's astonishing is that he came out of nowhere. A series of lucky breaks, plus his own extraordinary charisma, propelled him into the Senate and within two years he was on the road to the presidency. Talk about seizing the moment. Had he hesitated, we might never have heard of him. Like all good memoirs, it is not just about what happened but about what it felt like to be there and the impact on his young family. 'Have you won?' his youngest daughter asks as the votes are being counted. 'Yes,' he says. To which she replies, 'It says on the television that there is going to be a big party, but I don't think anyone will turn up. The streets are empty.' When they got to Chicago's Grant Park, there were 200,000 people waiting. What a night. And what an inheritance. An economy on the brink of collapse (it was the height of the banking crisis) and two unwinnable wars. All that plus a paralysed political system. For his first two years Obama had a majority in the Senate but not enough to overcome filibusters, a Republican speciality. I used to think that he squandered his first two years by being too consensual, but what choice did he have?

Tuesday 22 December

Massive queue of trucks at Dover. Caused by Covid, not Brexit, but a foretaste of what may be in store if there is no deal. A wake-up call for our masters.

Wednesday 23 December

Humphry Wakefield's Christmas card: a long-distance aerial view of his estate captioned: 'Chillingham Castle – at a social distance'.

Thursday 24 December

Surprise, surprise. A last-minute Brexit deal is rumoured. Stand by for a massive bout of tabloid triumphalism. Things not going so well at Dover, though. The best part of 6,000 trucks are stuck, many of the drivers without food and water. The French have lifted their blockade, but the jam will take days to clear. The mood is ugly.

Friday 25 December

A cold, clear, crisp day. Sunrise briefly cast an eerie pink glow over the land. We Skyped with the girls and then walked up to High Houses, the hills blanketed in snow. Today being Ngoc's birthday, I bought her a Val McDermid thriller. One of about thirty Val has written, but it turned out to be the only one Ngoc had read. Just my luck. This afternoon and evening several hours in an armchair by the fire with the Obama memoirs.

Sunday 27 December

Former *Sun* editor Kelvin MacKenzie has chosen to celebrate the Brexit deal as follows: 'The Establishment was against it. Parliament was against it and at least two Tory Prime Ministers were against it. And yet we won. An astonishing victory. Now for a referendum on the death penalty. There would be the same barriers. Stay strong. Murdering scum should not live.' When it comes to the gallows, MacKenzie has form. This is what *The Sun*, which he then edited, had to say about the Birmingham Six in January 1988: 'If *The Sun* had had its way, we would have been tempted to string 'em up years ago.'

Meanwhile someone has posted a shot of a 1970 National Front poster headed 'Put Britain First'. It sets out the party's programme as follows: 'Stop immigration, Reject Common Market, Restore capital punishment, Make Britain great again. Scrap overseas aid. Rebuild our armed forces.' We are not quite there yet, but it is a work in progress.

My Middle East Eye article on Labour's antisemitism crisis has been shared 10,000 times.

Monday 28 December

From Michael Gove, one of the Brexit architects, a hint that there may, after all, be a downside to the brave new world we are about to enter. We must, he says, be ready for 'some' disruption. Travellers to the EU are advised to take out comprehensive insurance, pet passports will no longer be valid and there may well be a sharp hike in roaming charges for mobile phones. Businesses are advised to make sure they have the right paperwork. But never mind all this. The good news, so we are told, is that we are about to take back control of our borders. Albeit that an extra £705 million has had to be spent on extra personnel and infrastructure, not to mention £80 million on new customs facilities to enable us to fortify our new freedom. One would like to think that sooner or later a little light will come on, but it won't.

Tuesday 29 December

Finished the Obama book. Like all the best memoirs, it is the incidental details, the small observations, the light and shade which bring his extraordinary story to life. Thoughtful, self-deprecatory, amusing, beautifully written. The pace never slackens. Three thoughts occur to me:

1. That intellectually and morally this man is head and shoulders above any other US President in my lifetime (although as regards morality honourable mention must also be made of Jimmy Carter).
2. For all the general paralysis, dysfunction and downright corruption that infest the great cesspool of US politics, there must be something to be said for a political system that, once in a while, throws up a man of his stature.
3. Given the obstacles both constitutional and political, not to mention the sheer weight of the forces of reaction, it is remarkable that any centre-left politician in the US can hope to achieve anything worthwhile. And yet he did.

Thursday 31 December

10 p.m.: In two hours from now we leave this miserable, dreadful year behind. Good riddance, I say. I am off to bed.

CHAPTER TWELVE

2021

Friday 1 January

A grey, damp day. We set up our two braziers on the patio and several neighbours joined us for a socially distanced al fresco glass of champagne. Later I worked on a big piece about Tory plans to neuter the BBC. This evening I watched the third part of an excellent documentary series on the rise, via social media and reality TV, of generally mindless celebrity culture and how it has begun to infect politics: witness Donald Trump, Boris Johnson and even, to a lesser extent, Jeremy Corbyn. Much of the world's youth are, it seems, lounging in their bedrooms, playing with their smartphones, their brains otherwise anaesthetised. Maybe, like most fads, this one will crash and burn. Can it be that those whom the gods want to destroy, they first make mad? But then I am just an old has-been. What do I know?

Sunday 3 January

A medic of our acquaintance says that the hospital in which he works is overwhelmed with Covid patients. Intensive care units are overflowing and doctors are having to make decisions about who can be saved and who can't. Apart from cancer, all other treatments have stopped. Almost without exception, he says, those worst affected are obese.

Monday 4 January

The *Washington Post* has published a remarkable hour-long tape in which

Trump tries to browbeat the governor and chief election officials in Georgia into reversing the result in their state. He complains of ballot rigging, box stuffing, rigged counting machines, dead people voting – all allegations that have been comprehensively investigated and rebutted. Much of it is delusional: 'There's no way I lost Georgia ... I won by hundreds of thousands.' The Georgia secretary of state, a Republican, remains calm: 'Mr President, the data you have is wrong,' but Trump ploughs on relentlessly: 'I just want you to find 11,780 votes...' The call was made on Saturday. The interesting point is that even if Georgia were to roll over, that would not give Trump enough electoral college votes to overturn the result, so the odds are he is making similar calls to officials in other key states, too. More such tapes may yet emerge. Meanwhile the stakes are getting higher. Eleven Republican senators are saying they will challenge the result when the Senate is asked to ratify Biden a few days from now. Other news: all ten living former Defence Secretaries, most of them Republicans, have responded to the suggestion that Trump may declare martial law, with a joint statement saying that the military should not become involved in electoral politics. Yes indeed. The problem is that America's military have long been involved in politics. The military-industrial complex is the core Republican base.

This evening Boris Johnson announced a new lockdown, which will continue until at least the last week of February. This only twenty-four hours after he was insisting that schools must reopen today. As is the way with ministerial announcements these days, the Union flag was conspicuously on display behind him.

Wednesday 6 January

After consulting a lawyer, whose services are thankfully paid for by the National Union of Journalists, I dispatched a brief reply to the 10 December letter from West Midlands Police, saying that I am not able to provide further assistance. After months of gentle sparring, we are reaching endgame. The next time I hear from them they may well be armed with a court order. I have not yet broken this news to Ngoc. She will not be amused.

This evening, extraordinary scenes from Washington, where several thousand Trump supporters stormed the Capitol in an attempt to stop the Senate ratifying Joe Biden's election victory.

Thursday 7 January

The news from Washington: four dead, one from gunshot wounds. Trump, who earlier in the day had been inciting the mob, whom he calls 'patriots', finally got round to appealing for them to go home, but not before he had repeated his claim that the election was fraudulent. Twitter and Facebook, mindful no doubt of the possibility that the incoming administration may take an interest in the part they have played in all this, have temporarily suspended his accounts. Most, but not quite all, Republican leaders have sullenly accepted the election result. Meanwhile Georgia, a former slave state, has by the narrowest of margins, returned two Democrat senators (one of them black), giving the Democrats control of the Senate on the casting vote of the Speaker. The impact of all this on the Republican Party remains to be seen. A permanent split between moderate Republicans (if there are any left) and extremists would be the ideal outcome, but I am not holding my breath.

Friday 8 January

Awoke to a winter wonderland – four inches of snow.

The mayhem in Washington seems have backfired on Trump. Abandoned by his Vice-President and the Senate majority leader, cut off from his social media accounts and no doubt prompted by rumours that his Cabinet may seek to remove him, he is now talking of an orderly transition. Today's Trump couldn't be more different from yesterday's. 'My focus now turns to ensuring a smooth, orderly and seamless transition of power.' Two members of his Cabinet have resigned and there has been a trickle of other resignations. This, of course, is leaving it a bit late to go straight. Someone has dubbed it 'the phenomenon of elite defection in the end, when their personal safety is in peril'. Here, too, some tricky footwork required from the English nationalists. People are posting footage of Boris, Gove, Farage, Rees-Mogg et al. singing Trump's praises in the days when it was fashionable to do so.

Saturday 9 January

7.10 a.m. Sarah rang to say that her waters have broken – six weeks prematurely.

−6°. Bright sunshine. Out along the north drive, up the track to the Mill, crunching through the ice and snow. Over the gate, through the fields by Whittingham wood and across to the beech avenue, the trees casting long shadows on the pristine snow, the surface broken only by the footprints of deer, hare and maybe a fox.

Wednesday 13 January

Today's Covid deaths: 1,564. A new record for a single day. Total UK death toll: 84,767. Temporary morgues are being set up to cope with the bodies.

Thursday 14 January

To paraphrase Margaret Thatcher, 'We are a grandfather.' A tiny person, six weeks premature, came into this world after a long labour at 7.47 this evening. He weighs 5lb 4oz. With average good fortune he will live into the twenty-second century. I looked at the photo of Mum on the mantelpiece, taken with the girls when Sarah was about nine and Emma four, and said, 'Well, Mum, you are a great-grandma now.'

Friday 15 January

The new arrival has been named Ralph Christopher James Hamilton.

A hard frost which stayed all day. John Field and I made a circuit of the lakes, frozen snow crunching under foot. I passed the evening with John Preston's riveting biography of Robert Maxwell, which I am reviewing for the *Times Literary Supplement*.

Tuesday 19 January

Finished reading David Cameron's autobiography. A better book than most of his critics were willing to concede. Honest, self-deprecating and down to earth. The general impression is of a humane and decent man whose otherwise golden life was irrevocably changed by two great events. One, an act of

God: the birth of a severely disabled son. The other, self-inflicted: that god-damn referendum, although given that he had the bad luck to hold office when his party was in the process of being captured by English nationalists, perhaps it was inevitable. There is also a certain amount of jingoist bullshit, de rigueur for the average Tory politician, about Britain being 'the greatest country on earth'. I do have one big bone to pick, however. He appears genuinely to believe all that 'broken Britain' claptrap that we heard so much of in the run-up to the 2010 election. One can only conclude that, like so many of his class, who by definition tend to represent the more prosperous parts of the country, he simply had no concept of the scale of the social breakdown inflicted upon poorer areas during the Thatcher decade, and when he did become aware, he assumed it was of more recent origin. He also seems to have convinced himself that he inherited an economy in meltdown due to Labour profligacy (though he does fleetingly concede that the financial crisis had something to do with the US mortgage market). The reality is that most, though not quite all, of the difficult economic decisions had been taken by the time he took office. The main decision for him and Osborne was how far and how fast to run down the deficit, and they certainly got that wrong. If I run into him again, I will bend his ear on the subject.

Wednesday 20 January

To a worldwide sigh of relief, Joe Biden was today sworn in as the 46th President of the United States. An uncharacteristically subdued Donald Trump left town ahead of the ceremony. He is rumoured to be planning to set up a Patriot Party. My initial reaction was that this would surely be excellent news. Rather like the so-called bad bank to cope with the fallout from the 2008 financial crisis, it could soak up all the racists, screwballs and super-patriots who have inflicted such damage on American public life. With any luck it would split the Republican Party and keep them out of power for a generation. On the other hand, it may be too much to hope for. This is what some people hoped UKIP would do to the Tory Party, only for us to wake up and discover that it had taken over.

Friday 22 January

Prompted by a discussion on the radio the other day, I reread *The Great*

Gatsby, which caused me to reflect that unrequited love is the most enduring because it never crashes against the harsh rocks of reality. As I get older and have more time on my hands, I think back more and more to the mistakes of my younger days. There is a good story to be written on this theme, but it would be self-indulgent and hurtful to people I care about, so I must resist the temptation.

Nissan has announced that, after several years of uncertainty, it will be staying in Sunderland thanks to the recent trade deal with the EU. No doubt the Brexiteers will be chortling 'told you so', but the fact is that they took a hell of a risk. Anyway, I am glad it has worked out.

Saturday 23 January

Despite the vaccine, the scientists are calling for the lockdown to be extended, maybe for several more months. There is talk of spring or perhaps even the autumn before life returns to something approaching normal. No one yet knows for how long the vaccine confers immunity or whether it prevents transmission.

Sunshine, a hard frost. I walked up through the forest onto the ridge, through patchy snow and puddles of melting ice. From the top, fine views across the green valley to the snow-covered hills beyond. I came across our laird's Exmoor ponies standing motionless, bunched together making the most of the winter sunshine in preparation for another long, hard night.

Monday 25 January

'Angela Merkel is more responsible for Brexit than any other political figure in Europe, on either side of the Channel,' writes Ambrose Evans-Pritchard in today's *Telegraph*. To which a writer named Otto English has responded, 'They finally did it. They blamed Germany for Brexit. The circle of life is complete.'

Tuesday 26 January

Another grim milestone. The UK's Covid death toll has passed 100,000.

Wednesday 27 January

Chopped logs from a chestnut tree which has come down in the castle grounds and then drove to Roddam with a card and a bottle of champagne to mark Nigel Vinson's ninetieth birthday. Yvonne answered the door. 'He's out,' she said.

'Where is he?'

'He's gone riding.'

I did, however, manage to intercept him on the way back. What extraordinary shape he is in. Cheerful, optimistic and looking a generation younger than he actually is. The product of a golden life. I can't help but compare him to those broken old ruins many years younger who used to shamble into my surgeries, weighed down by the cares of the world. 'We are so lucky', he remarked, 'to have lived in this seventy-year slot of history.' Then he glanced up at the sky and said with a mischievous grin, 'Thanks, Guvnor.'

Saturday 30 January

An unseemly spat has broken out between Britain and the EU, and for once we seem to have the high ground. The Brussels bureaucracy has only just got round to approving the use of the AstraZeneca vaccine (which our regulators approved three months ago), with the result they have fallen to the back of the queue for supplies from AZ factories in the UK. Rather than acknowledge their own incompetence, the EU then started demanding that AZ reduce supplies to the British market in order to meet demand on the Continent. It has also blocked the export of vaccines from the EU to the rest of the world and at one point was threatening to reimpose a hard border in Northern Ireland. Result: the Brussels bureaucrats have supplied our Brexiteers with a rich new seam to mine. *Financial Times* journalist Robert Shrimsley, a Remainer, tweeted, 'Fair play to the Commission, it's damn sporting of them to work so hard to make Brexit look like a reasonable idea after all.'

Sunday 31 January

'Rain was the natural state of Glasgow. It kept the grass green and the people pale and bronchial.' *Shuggie Bain*, page thirty-nine. I read the first sixty pages and gave up. I'm sure it says more about me than the novel, but I just couldn't cope with all that unrelenting Glaswegian squalor.

Monday 1 February

This evening, a Labour Party political broadcast. Keir Starmer in front of a Union Jack (ugh), which I gather is known in PR circles as 'Fatherlandism'. Why can't we leave phoney patriotism to the Tories?

Tuesday 2 February

Grey skies, raining slush and sleet. My Learned Friend John Field is eighty today. We celebrated with a socially distanced glass of champagne in his barn. Long may he be spared.

Thursday 4 February

George Osborne has announced that he is standing down as editor in chief of the London *Evening Standard* to become a partner in a firm of Mayfair consultants specialising in mergers and acquisitions, where the top-earning partner trousered a whopping £27.8 million in 2019. Osborne has much to answer for. 'Rarely has one man left so indelible a mark,' says Polly Toynbee in today's *Guardian*. As shadow Chancellor he risked spooking the markets with blood-curdling warnings of an imminent collapse of sterling and hair-raising visions of Britain on the verge of bankruptcy. None of it was true. Interest rates were at record low levels; we could easily have borrowed more. Instead he used the excuse of debt arising from the banking crisis to inflict lasting damage on public services. His axe fell on the weakest, poorest and sickest, leaving Middle England unscathed. And all the while he stirred up fear and loathing with spurious talk of idle scroungers lying in bed with the curtains drawn while honest folk went to work. And it didn't work. The deficit remained stubbornly high and the overall impact was to choke the recovery. Today, with a sensible Tory in charge of the Treasury, we suddenly find that the sky's the limit when it comes to borrowing our way out of a crisis at a time of record low interest rates.

Friday 5 February

A third day of unrelenting rain. Roads flooded, ditches overflowing, a lake has appeared on the north lawn and the burn is a raging torrent crashing through the sluices. What with Covid and long, empty days, this is the most miserable winter I can remember.

Saturday 6 February

To Rothbury along flooded lanes for my Covid jab, administered by a cheerful young medical student from Newcastle. The Coquet, ordinarily a harmless little river, has turned into the Mississippi, swamping the entire valley. A long list of questions before I can be jabbed. To be answered thrice: once over the telephone and twice at the surgery. My favourite: 'Are you pregnant?', which since I am in the over-seventies cohort doesn't seem of much relevance to the women, let alone the men. By the time we set off for home, the rain has turned to sleet and a thick grey mist shrouds the hills, in keeping with the spirit of the age.

Thursday 11 February

Today's *FT*: 'Amsterdam surpassed London as Europe's largest share trading centre last month as the Netherlands scooped up business lost by the UK…' Another little straw in the post-Brexit wind. Temperature this morning: $-7°$.

Friday 12 February

Vietnamese New Year – the year of the water buffalo. Ngoc lit candles and placed flowers and a large bowl of fruit on a table in front of the little shrine to her parents in the living room.

Prompted by signs of suspicious activity, Calum unscrewed a panel in the garage and out jumped two large rats. Meanwhile the snow lies deep and crisp and even. It's been with us all week.

Martin Woollacott has an inoperable tumour. Another of my dearest friends cut down in Sniper's Alley.

Saturday 13 February

Predictably, Trump has been acquitted on the second attempt to impeach him, though he has undoubtedly been damaged by it.

Tuesday 16 February

The first rumble of discontent from the friends of Keir Starmer about what they see as his lacklustre leadership. Writing in today's *Guardian*, Tom Kibasi, a former director of the Institute for Public Policy Research, who claims to have been 'the strategic architect' of Starmer's campaign, criticises Starmer for wasting so much time dissociating himself from Corbyn. 'It was … strategically foolish to expend so much political capital making that negative point rather than positively defining the new leader of the party.' He goes on, 'If Starmer were to depart as leader tomorrow, he would not leave a trace of a meaningful project in his wake … The country cannot afford for Starmer to waste another year being hard on Labour and soft on the Tories.'

Monday 22 February

Our neighbour Keith Hann, head of public relations at a national super-market chain, has lost his job as a result of a tongue-in-cheek blog he wrote six years ago – three years *before* he took up his present employment – making fun of the Welsh language. Keith, who describes himself as 'a poor man's Rod Liddle', found himself dubbed an anti-Welsh bigot and on the receiving end of a great deal of abuse from righteous Twitte-rati. He writes:

> I recognise that my humour is not to everyone's taste. I am an elderly (sixty-six), white, middle-class, Oxbridge-educated, libertarian Geordie who grew up on the humour of Hancock, *Round the Horne*, *I'm Sorry, I'll Read That Again*, Monty Python and – yes – Benny Hill and Bernard Man-ning. There are plenty of things I still find funny that could never make it onto terrestrial TV, even with a long prior apology and a trigger warning…

Boris Johnson has made a long-awaited statement setting out a timetable for a gradual end to the lockdown. Schools will go back on 8 March, non-essential shops and beer gardens can reopen on 12 April, pubs on 17 May and all restrictions will lifted on 21 June. The announcement is accompanied by warnings that this could all be reversed if there is a resurgence of the virus, but thanks to the vaccine, hopes are higher this time than on any previous occasion.

Tuesday 23 February

From Myanmar (née Burma) reports of daily demonstrations against the recent military coup. I fear it is only a question of time before the killing starts. The Burmese military are particularly effective against unarmed civilians. They have been at war with their people for more than sixty years.

Wednesday 24 February

We are in receipt of daily bulletins, usually accompanied by mobile footage, on the progress of our little grandson. Ralph being fed, Ralph's first outing, Ralph awake, Ralph sleeping etc. It is seven weeks since he was born, but thanks to Covid it may be some time before we are able to meet the Little Lord in person.

Thursday 25 February

A call from my dear, generous, wise friend Martin Woollacott, who has been sent home to die, after his cancer was deemed inoperable. He is camped in the dining room downstairs and attached to a long tube administering painkilling medicine. He sounds calm and reconciled. My first instinct was to get on a train to London and pay him a visit, but of course that's forbidden under the present rules. I may never see him again.

Friday 26 February

Sylvie Bermann, a former French ambassador to the UK, has predicted that Boris Johnson, whom she describes as 'an unrepentant and inveterate liar', will attempt to hide the cost of Brexit 'under the Covid carpet'. I am sure she is right and he will be aided and abetted by much of our free press.

Sunday 28 February

Lunch in the garden for the first time this year.

Monday 1 March

Prince Philip, who has spent the past few days in the King Edward VII Hospital being monitored for an infection, has been transferred to St Bartholomew's, which is NHS. Apparently there is a problem with his heart. This could be the end. A friend points out that were he to die before the lockdown is lifted, only eight people would be allowed to attend his funeral – and of course the royal family would be obliged to stick to the rules that apply to everyone else.

Tuesday 2 March

The government has announced it is cutting aid to Yemen by half, at the very moment when the country is facing a catastrophic famine. The UN secretary general described the decision as 'disappointing'. 'Unimaginable,' says Andrew Mitchell, a former DfID Secretary. What have we become?

Wednesday 3 March

Budget Day. An increase in corporation tax to take effect two years from now and a five-year freeze on income tax thresholds, but by and large steady as we go, despite the record deficit. The fact that most Tories are – rightly – content to live with the deficit at a time of low interest rates exposes George Osborne's lie that it was necessary to lay waste to much of the public sector in order to pay down it down within one parliament – which he didn't manage anyway.

Thursday 4 March

The unexpurgated Chips Channon diaries, a mighty thousand-page doorstopper, arrived today. I have to produce 2,000 words for *Prospect* by next Wednesday.

Saturday 6 March

A long, emotional call from Martin Woollacott, his voice distorted by morphine. He has received the little photo album we compiled of all the happy times we spent together. Such small gestures are all I can do for my dying friends.

Monday 8 March

Meghan Markle and Prince Harry have been parading their victimhood in a much-trailed interview with the US celebrity talk show host Oprah Winfrey. Meghan clearly the main mover, Harry very much second fiddle. She played all the cards: woman, race, mental health. How long, I wonder, before the marriage ends in tears and Harry comes limping home?

Tuesday 9 March

Ms Markle's allegation that, when she was pregnant, a member of the royal family speculated about her baby's likely skin colour has gone viral. Although we don't yet know what was said or by whom, her version of events has been accepted without question and every professional anti-racist in the country is pronouncing on the subject. Even if true, depending on the context, there is another possibility. I am married to a Vietnamese woman and from time to time, over the years, people have remarked, without being in the least offensive, that they can see evidence of Vietnamese blood in Sarah. The palace has issued a conciliatory little statement which says simply that 'while recollections may vary' they will address the issue within the family, of which, it adds, Harry and Meghan remain much-loved members. Oh yeah?

Friday 12 March

The public space is getting narrower for us men of a certain age. Self-styled anti-racists are being given airtime to argue that no white person is entitled to express scepticism about Meghan Markle's version of events because ours is not her 'lived experience'. An angry young zealot called Aaron has tweeted, 'You're all middle-aged white men whose ideas of mental health and race are too out of date to have a place in the normal. Your privilege creates you a safe space for cultivating bigotry.' To which Colin Brazier, who has resigned from Sky News along with Piers Morgan, replied, 'Hi Aaron, I'm a single parent of six young kids. Have been since my wife died a couple of years ago. That's my "lived experience". Tell me about yours.'

Sunday 14 March

The Birmingham Six were released thirty years ago today. What a moment. Even today, so long after the event, ripples still spread outwards.

Monday 15 March

The fallout from the Meghan interview still reverberates. A YouGov poll indicates that while those in the eighteen to twenty-four age bracket are overwhelmingly sympathetic to Meghan, the opposite is true among those aged sixty-five and over. Which broadly reflects the division of opinion between Emma Mullin and her boring old dad.

Tuesday 16 March

We seem to be going backwards. The government has announced a proposed 40 per cent increase in our stockpile of nuclear weapons 'in recognition of the evolving security environment'. How long before someone suggests they should be decorated with a Union Jack?

Friday 19 March

Meanwhile in La-La Land: 'Outcry as sneering BBC presenters mock minister over Union flag' (*Daily Telegraph*). English nationalists are intensifying their war on the BBC. Every ministerial interview now includes a Union Jack as a backdrop.

Saturday 20 March

Breakfast news presenter Naga Munchetty has been ordered to apologise for 'liking' a tweet which poked fun at flag-wavers, or 'flag shaggers', as some call them. Undeterred, newsreader Huw Edwards, a Welshman, has bravely tweeted, 'Flags are now mandatory – very pleased with my new backdrop' together with a picture of himself in front of the flag of Wales. He has been ordered to delete it. Yesterday's *Telegraph* published an article by Simon Heffer headed 'The BBC must stop employing those who despise their own country'.

We drove to Craster and sat in the sunshine by the harbour eating fish and chips purchased from a van outside the Jolly Fisherman.

Tuesday 23 March

At a hearing of the Public Accounts Committee, James Wild, a Norfolk Tory MP, indignantly pressed the BBC director general to explain why the Corporation's annual report failed to display an image of a Union flag. 'My constituents would expect to see more than one flag,' he says.

Wednesday 24 March

Katy Woollacott rang to say that Martin died this morning.

Someone asked the other day if I think about death. I do. Two thoughts: 1. When a good friend dies, I move up one place in the queue. 2. Mum was eighty-six when she died, Dad eighty-three. Split the difference and I might make it to eighty-four – another eleven years. Extrapolating backwards that takes me to 2010. Not so long ago.

Thursday 25 March

A new virus is taking hold. Culture Secretary Oliver Dowden has decreed that henceforth the Union flag will be flown from every government building. And Local Government Secretary Robert Jenrick has written to all local authorities encouraging them to fly the flag on all their buildings. Meanwhile our own ludicrous MP, Anne-Marie Trevelyan, has been pictured sitting next to an outsize Union Jack and wearing what appears to be a tastefully tailored jacket with a collar in colours matching the flag.

Saturday 27 March

Finished reading *The Anarchy*, William Dalrymple's masterful account of the rise of the East India Company, a blood-soaked period of our history – and India's – about which I was totally uninformed. Echoes the present-day rise of aggressive multinational corporations more powerful than the states in which they operate. Like our bloated banks, the East India Company was 'too big to fail'. It had to be bailed out by the government in 1772, by which time its debts amounted to a quarter of Britain's GDP. As the author says, 'The East India Company remains today history's most ominous warning about the potential for the abuse of corporate power – and the insidious means by which the interests of shareholders can seemingly become those of the state.' Think Boeing, Halliburton, British Aerospace.

Sunday 28 March

More rumblings of discontent with Keir Starmer reported in today's *Observer*. Some apparently coming from members of the shadow Cabinet, unhappy that after a year in office Labour's poll ratings are as dismal as Corbyn's.

Friday 2 April

The latest YouGov poll puts the Tories on 42 per cent and Labour on 32. As someone commented, 'It took a relentless campaign of lies and vilification to drive Corbyn's Labour down to this level in the 2019 general election. Impressive in a way that Starmer's Labour has dipped this low without the Establishment laying a finger on him.' Cruel but true. All the more impressive considering that one of Boris Johnson's former girlfriends has been revealing details of her four-year affair with him, which threatens to reopen the investigation into how a large dollop of public money found its way into her business while Johnson was Mayor of London. A serial liar he may be, but no one seems to care.

Saturday 3 April

Sarah, Nick and our little grandson, Ralph, arrived last evening. Our first encounter with the chubby-cheeked Little Lord, aged eleven weeks. He sleeps, eats and occasionally gurgles while everyone oohs and aahs. House chocker with first-world baby paraphernalia.

Tuesday 6 April

'Nursery teachers should be trained in "understanding white privilege" according to new guidance…' A report in today's *Times*.

Wednesday 7 April

An email from Cousin Margaret in Rome, where she has lived and worked for decades. She has just had her post-Brexit right of residence accepted by the Italian authorities on payment of a fee of €30. By contrast, she says, her nephew's wife, who is of foreign origin, will have to pay £5,000 over five years to have her right of residence in the UK officially recognised.

Thursday 8 April

Prompted perhaps by a recent outbreak of mayhem in the Loyalist ghettos of Ulster, someone has posted a photo of a hoarding with the following message: 'DUE TO COVID WE ARE ASKING RIOTERS TO WORK AT HOME AND DESTROY THEIR OWN STUFF.'

Friday 9 April

The Duke of Edinburgh has died, two months short of his 100th birthday.

Saturday 10 April

The BBC has gone into overdrive with its coverage of Prince Philip. Last night's schedules were cleared on all channels for wall-to-wall tributes, prompting comparisons with North Korea. 'Embarrassing', 'servile', 'counter-productive' are some of the more printable comments. My view is more nuanced. His was a big life which deserved to be commemorated, but this is overkill. A complete misjudgement which is going to alienate yet more licence payers at time when the Corporation needs all the support it can get. As someone said, 'Thank fuck for Netflix.' Or in my case Al Jazeera.

Sunday 11 April

Complaints pouring in about the over-the-top coverage of Prince Philip.

A big fall in ratings, not just on BBC but on ITV too. The irony is that Philip, who was famously plain-speaking, would have loathed it. Goodness knows what will happen when the Queen goes.

Monday 12 April

Another tentative step towards normality. From today, non-essential shops can reopen and pubs and restaurants can serve food and drink outside.

Tuesday 13 April

Shirley Williams has died. Although we were on different sides in the struggle for the soul of the Labour Party in the '70s, I came to know her briefly in later years and much admired her.

Wednesday 14 April

Five successive nights of hard frosts have laid waste to my wonderful display of daffodils, though miraculously, after a few hours of sunshine, most rise again – only to be mown down when the next frost descends.

Thursday 15 April

I have been reading *Whittingham Vale*, David Dippie Dixon's history of our valley, published in 1895. He gives this account of a false alarm on 31 January 1804, when the beacon on Ros Hill was lit, indicating that Napoleon had invaded. The militia were hastily assembled, but some amusing excuses were given:

> Tom Bolam had a pain in his breast, but three glasses of whiskey … soon cured him, and then he was open to fight 'Bonny' or any other man … Willie Middlemas was seized with a violent pain … but no sooner did it become known that the alarm was false than Willie at once set forth and joined the troop in time for dinner at Collingwood House. At Collingwood House there was plenty of good cheer and … the troopers felt so much relieved that they had not to fight the French they partook largely

of eatables and drinkables set before them, and very soon their spirits rose beyond all bounds.

And this account of the 1826 general election, contested by various local gentry:

> Cartloads of voters and their friends out of the valleys of the Coquet and Aln travelled daily back and forward to Alnwick ... to be feasted and refreshed by the Tories one day [and] by the Whigs the next. After being feasted and refreshed at the expense of each party alternately, they voted for their man on the very last day of the poll with feelings of regret that the glorious campaign had come to an end.

These days there are too many voters to make it worthwhile trying to bribe them individually. Instead it makes more sense for the seriously rich to bankroll an entire party.

Friday 16 April

Brexit news: UK banks and insurers are reported to have moved about £1 trillion of assets out of the UK because of Brexit, according to a report by a City think tank. Around 7,400 jobs have also gone. Dublin, Paris, Amsterdam and Frankfurt are said to be the preferred destinations, with Frankfurt expected to be the biggest beneficiary in the long term.

Saturday 17 April

The Duke of Edinburgh was interred in St George's Chapel, Windsor, this afternoon. A dignified, beautifully understated service strictly in compliance with Covid regulations and his own wishes, his four children following the coffin on foot down the slope from the castle. The service, attended by just thirty people, all wearing regulation black face masks. No eulogy, a four-person choir, a blessing from the Archbishop, a magnificent, kilted bagpiper playing 'Flowers of the Forest', a trumpeter sounding the Last Post. Most poignant of all, the Queen, a tiny, hunched woman in black, sitting alone in front of the flag-draped coffin, quietly saying goodbye to her husband of seventy-three years, knowing that she will shortly be following him into the Great Silence that awaits us all, high or low.

Wednesday 21 April

To Holy Island with My Two Best Friends, the Little Lord Ralph and Emma's boyfriend, Ed. We made a circuit of the island in perfect weather, clear views south across the empty Ross Sands to Bamburgh Castle and the Farnes. The Little Lord, in a sling around Sarah's neck, slept soundly throughout. Notices attached to every other lamp post telling us to stay at home, despite the success of the vaccine, the easing of the lockdown and the reopening of pubs and cafes. Home over the hills via Chillingham, arriving in good time for my weekly Mastermind session via Zoom.

Friday 23 April

No rain for more than a month. This evening a lengthy hosing in an attempt to save the garden. We appear to have lost the three Ceanothus, the Hebe hedge looks parched and everything else is wilting.

Saturday 24 April

Suddenly the phrase 'Tory sleaze' is back in fashion again and there is no shortage of ammunition. According to his erstwhile sidekick Dominic Cummings, Boris Johnson devised an 'unethical, foolish' and 'possibly illegal' scheme for funding the renovation of the Downing Street flat. Meanwhile David Cameron has been vigorously lobbying on behalf of a bankrupt finance company. Not forgetting the Covid-related procurement controversies of the past year. Commentators are beginning to join the dots. I have mixed feelings about 'sleaze mania', since such rows tend to demean politics as a whole, but for the moment at least the regime looks vulnerable. The Cummings intervention is the most serious yet. What else does he have up his sleeve?

Sunday 25 April

'No. 10 fears bombshell dossier'. Headline in today's *Telegraph* regarding a supposed treasure trove of documents that Dominic Cummings is proposing to make public next month. Boris Johnson increasingly looks besieged. Lots of shrill calls for inquiries by opposition spokespersons, but I would not get too excited. If the worst comes to the worst, the Tories will simply change their leader and move seamlessly on.

Monday 26 April

Early this morning on Al Jazeera, a depressing documentary on the dark side of the supposed green revolution. Solar panels, wind turbines and electric cars are not, it seems, our salvation. They all depend on massive quantities of rare minerals being mined in countries like China, Chile and Bolivia without regard for the environmental and social consequences. Hard to reach any conclusion other than that the human race is heading helter-skelter towards catastrophe. I look at our little grandson, Ralph, aged fourteen weeks, lying beside me on the sofa. With average good fortune he will outlive me by at least eighty years. To what horrors will he bear witness?

Tuesday 27 April

'BORIS ON THE ROPES' – this morning's *Daily Mail*. And it's true, his troubles are accumulating. The row over who paid for the renovation of the Downing Street flat is not going away. He has picked an unnecessary fight with his former bosom buddy Dominic Cummings and now he is being quoted as having once said that he would 'rather see bodies piled high in their thousands' than order another lockdown. Everything is denied, of course, but as even his friends concede, his career is built on falsehoods. Former Attorney General Dominic Grieve describes him as 'a vacuum of integrity'. Johnson's problem is that he doesn't think the rules apply to him. Never forget what that far-sighted Eton schoolmaster wrote about him forty years ago: 'Boris sometimes seems affronted when criticised for what amounts to a gross failure of responsibility … I think he honestly believes that it is churlish of us not to regard him as an exception, one who should be free of the network of obligation that binds everyone else.'

Wednesday 28 April

It seems the mystery funder of the refurbishment of the Downing Street apartment is one Lord Brownlow, a recruitment agency tycoon and a mega-donor to the Tory Party. Just why it's been hushed up is a mystery since sooner or later it will have to be declared to the Electoral Commission anyway. In any case, the trail leads back to his girlfriend, Carrie Symonds. As Liz Forgan says, 'I doubt whether Boris took much interest in how the flat was furnished.' Carrie is proving to be a bit of a liability. She is also alleged to have triggered the row that led to Dominic Cummings's unceremonious departure from No. 10, which is coming back to bite them.

Meanwhile, herewith the latest piece of bonkers wokeism from *The Guardian*: 'Justin Bieber accused of cultural appropriation over hairstyle.'

Friday 30 April

I have been reading the diaries of Alan Duncan, a former Tory minister and one-time colleague of Boris Johnson at the Foreign Office. Initially Duncan flirted with Brexit, but he soon went off the idea when he saw the people he was mixing with. On the capture of the Tory Party by English nationalists, he has this to say:

> Somewhere along the line from the early 1990s the cause of honest and thoughtful Euro-scepticism mutated into a form of simplistic nationalism ... There was a rational and pragmatic case to be made for leaving the EU, but few bothered to make it. Instead we faced a wave of populist nonsense, emotive platitudes and downright lies.

Boris Johnson he describes as, 'a self-centred ego, an embarrassing buffoon, with an untidy mind and sub-zero diplomatic judgement ... an international stain on our reputation ... a lonely, selfish, ill-disciplined, shambolic, shameless clot'.*

---

* Alan Duncan, *In The Thick of It*, William Collins, 2021, pp. 2–3, 228.

Saturday 1 May

The Little Lord, his two principal servants and his vast baggage train departed this morning after a month at Callaly. Actually, it's been a joy having them with us. A chance to get to know the little fellow before he departs for America.

Sunday 2 May

According to an obituary of Helen McCrory, a brilliant actress who has tragically died prematurely of cancer, her father was a diplomat who had served in Tanzania. That rang a bell, so I did a bit of googling and realised that I stayed a couple of nights with her family in Dar es Salaam when I first visited Africa in 1976. I have no memory of her, but she would have been about eight at the time.

Tuesday 4 May

Finished reading Jill Lepore's masterpiece, an 800-page history of the United States, *These Truths*. Perhaps the most striking theme is the central part that race and white supremacy have played throughout the entire US history. Forces that seemed to have been buried with the election of Barack Obama were disinterred by Donald Trump. On the rise of populism, she has this to say: 'Nationalists, who had few proposals for the future, gained power by telling fables about the greatness of the past.' However, she does not spare the liberal left either for their retreat into identity politics, generating 'sentimental, meaningless outrage and sanctimonious accusations of racism, sexism, homophobia, and transphobia.'

Wednesday 5 May

Despite recent upsets, the polls suggest that the Tories retain a substantial lead over Labour and are poised to do well in tomorrow's elections. It is a measure of our decline that most voters have factored in the realisation that we are led by a rogue and a liar and they just don't care. Also, the working classes have not forgiven Labour for opposing Brexit. No point in beating ourselves up about it. It's just the way things are – and will remain for the foreseeable future.

Friday 7 May

As expected, the Tories – or should we now call them the English Nationalist Party? – have comfortably won the Hartlepool by-election, thereby triggering a lot of blather from Labour spokespersons about listening to the people and learning lessons. At least Corbyn can't be blamed this time round. It was Brexit, stupid. Chris Nicholson, with whom I played table tennis this morning, remarked that Keir Starmer doesn't play well outside the metropolitan areas. Also that the northern working classes rather like Boris Johnson. 'He is our Berlusconi.' As for the fuss about the wallpaper in the Downing Street flat, 'they don't care who paid for it, as long as it wasn't the taxpayer'. Also, says, Chris, the surly way in which the Europeans have reacted to Brexit has played into Johnson's hands. All true, alas.

This afternoon, to the cricket ground at Alnwick, where I received my second Covid jab, three months and one day after the first.

Saturday 8 May

Local election results are trickling in and they are dire. If there were a general election tomorrow, even my old seat in Sunderland would fall to the Tories. Meanwhile, from Labour spokespersons, much wailing and rending of garments. Keir Starmer talks vaguely of 'fixing it'. But what is this 'it' that needs fixing? Labour's dilemma is that the more it panders to the Brexiteers, the more it will alienate Remainers, who are now its base. As the BBC polling expert John Curtice says, that part of the working class that voted UKIP has shifted en masse to the Tory Party and they won't be coming back any time soon. And even if they do, it won't solve the problem of Scotland, where much of the Labour vote has defected to the SNP.

This evening to John Field's for a drink with former Attorney General Dominic Grieve, who is passing through en route from Scotland. I put it to him that I did not expect to see another non-Tory government in my lifetime. He thought one was an outside possibility, though it would require an alliance with the Lib Dems. Of course it will, but I doubt the penny has yet dropped with most members of either party. How bad does it have to get?

Sunday 9 May

'What is the point of a political party that began as the voice of the industrial proletariat when there is no more industrial proletariat?' asks Janet Daley in today's *Telegraph*.

Monday 10 May

Labour spokespeople running in circles trying to explain the debacle. Starmer has carried out a messy shadow Cabinet reshuffle, thereby adding to the turmoil and neatly deflecting attention from the mayoral results, where Labour has done well. He has removed his deputy, Angela Rayner, as campaign coordinator and replaced her with an excitable woman from Birmingham who on the radio this morning rabbited on at high speed without saying anything. One begins to hear mutterings about the position of Keir himself, though he is safe for the time being. Anyway, Labour never gets rid of failing leaders. Andy Burnham and Lisa Nandy will be eyeing the poisoned chalice, but if I were them, I wouldn't be in too much hurry to inherit. The downhill slide has still some way to go.

My thoughts: equanimity. Like it or not, for the foreseeable future we are now living in a one-party state. The way back for Labour, if there is one, is to 1. appeal to people's best instincts rather than their worst and leave flag-waving to the Tories; 2. continue to build a base among the younger, better-educated, outward-looking citizens while at the same time taking seriously issues of concern to the least prosperous – public health, the gig economy, 'levelling up' (let's see how that goes) and (yes) migration; 3. avoid disappearing down the rabbit hole of identity politics – that way lies ruin. Plus, we shall need to do some sort of deal with the Lib Dems and perhaps the Greens. At the very least we need to stop competing with them in marginal seats.

Tuesday 11 May

The Queen's Speech. A more bizarre pantomime than usual. Positively Masonic, in fact. Fifty red-robed peers wearing (mainly) black face masks. Only HM, a tiny woman in light blue, unmasked. Included in the proposed legislation, a new law requiring photo ID for voters, outlawing cancel culture in universities and an agriculture bill which among other things will outlaw live animal exports. This last, if it comes to pass, a welcome by-product of our departure from the EU.

Wednesday 12 May

A new war in Gaza. Hamas firing rockets into Israel, the Israelis massively retaliating.

Friday 14 May

Just when we thought it was all over… The Indian variant of Covid has arrived, triggering fears of a new lockdown. The big question: is the vaccine effective against this new version?

Saturday 15 May

We've finally got round to planting out our vegetables, about a month after Monty Don in the warmer climes of Herefordshire.

Sunday 16 May

No prizes for guessing how the Indian version of Covid managed to arrive here. It turns out that despite greatly reduced passenger numbers, the immigration service is still taking hours to process arrivals at Heathrow and making little or no effort to separate passengers from high-risk countries.

Wednesday 19 May

The *Telegraph* is obsessing about the impact of Covid on foreign holidays and the death of one of the Queen's corgis. Meanwhile the Israelis are still pounding Gaza to smithereens. Among the dead, a family of nine. Biden, who in so many respects is a breath of fresh air, is following the traditional US script: unconditional support for Israel.

Friday 21 May

The BBC is in big trouble over its famous Martin Bashir interview with

Princess Diana, following the Corporation's long-overdue admission that it was obtained by false pretences. Prince William has issued a furious statement saying that the interview contributed to his mother's distrust of those around her and further damaged the relationship between her and his father. This will provide yet further ammunition, were any needed, for the BBC's many enemies. Most of this could have been avoided if the top brass had owned up when doubts were first raised years ago.

Saturday 22 May

Panorama journalist John Ware has posted a detailed account of the BBC's cover-up of the truth about the Diana interview. Stand-out quote comes from an internal note by the Corporation's then chief political adviser, Anne Sloman: 'The Diana story is probably now dead unless [Lord] Spencer talks.'

Meanwhile, as the people of Gaza sift through the ruins of their homes, the *Telegraph* chooses to highlight a feature entitled 'As the Queen mourns a beloved puppy, experts share their tips on how to deal with the death of a pet'.

Sunday 23 May

The Eurovision Song Contest. UK score: nil, nought, zilch. Italy won with 524 points. Even Moldova got 115. What was it that Millwall fans used to chant? 'No one likes us, but we don't care.'

Wednesday 26 May

A marathon, much-anticipated evidence session by Dominic Cummings to a joint session of the science and health select committees. Attempts from some quarters to write him off in advance as an embittered ex-employee soon dissipated as the bombshells started exploding. Boris Johnson ('a shopping trolley smashing between aisles'), was unfit to be Prime Minister. Health Secretary Matt Hancock had 'lied' repeatedly. Tens of thousands of people had died unnecessarily as a result of government failures. As to the reasons for his own departure, they were primarily because his relations with the Prime Minister had broken down, but they were also 'connected to the fact that the Prime Minister's girlfriend was trying to change a whole bunch of different appointments at No. 10 and appoint her friends to particular jobs'. This was not the arrogant know-all we had been led to expect. Casually dressed in an open-necked white shirt, his demeanour was modest, respectful, apologetic. He will not easily be written off. Cummings is, after all, the man who put Boris Johnson where he is today.

Thursday 27 May

'An exercise in arrogant, self-delusional egocentricity from an intellectual narcissist' is the *Telegraph*'s considered view of yesterday's outing by Dominic Cummings. Although his allegations receive massive coverage, our free press has largely divided along predictable lines. The Brexit press either dismisses or downplays them and the Remain press takes them seriously. *The Sun* mocks up an optometrist chart which says in ever-diminishing characters, 'Do you need a hindsight test, Mr Cummings?' 'Too detailed and damaging to be left to a public inquiry that will not even start until next year,' says *The Times*. You pays your money, you takes your choice.

Joyce Quin and I drove to Lorbottle and walked up through the empty little valley that leads to our laird's shooting lodge at Sunbrough. During the recent local elections Joyce helped out in Blyth, once a Labour stronghold. She quotes former MP Ronnie Campbell as saying, 'The working classes are all voting Tory and the middle classes are all voting Labour.' The problem is, of course, that there isn't a big enough middle class in Blyth to make any difference.

Friday 28 May

To the Freeman Hospital in Newcastle for an X-ray of my kidneys. These days any outing beyond our little bubble is exciting. I walked up Grainger Street to Waterstones in search of the latest Robert Harris (which was out of stock) and then caught the Metro to South Gosforth. Despite what one hears about pockets of resistance, just about everyone was masked. The X-ray department was deserted. A cheerful young woman named Bryony asked me to lower my trousers and placed a white cloth over my nether regions. All over in a jiffy. 'Don't I recognise you?' asked a man behind the check-in desk at the hospital. Not bad considering I had my mask on. A man in the sandwich shop said the same but couldn't put a name to me. *Sic transit…* Back to Alnmouth on the 14.43. The sun still shining.

Saturday 29 May

To dinner in the south wing with Jonathan and Katherine Clark. The only other guests were Humphry and Katharine Wakefield. Much of the talk was of son-in-law Dominic's little outing three days ago. According to Humphry, he has documentary evidence for just about all of his allegations. Katharine recounted how in 1960 she and two male friends drove from Nairobi through Uganda and Rwanda into the Congo in a Morris Minor. Imagine doing that today.

Tuesday 1 June

For the first time in ten months no new Covid deaths have been recorded during the past twenty-four hours.

Wednesday 2 June

We harvested our first strawberries from the glasshouse.

Friday 4 June

Prospect have published my essay on the rise of English nationalism. Unfortunately the editor has chosen to highlight my suggestion that a future candidate for the Tory leadership – Priti Patel is the name that comes to mind – might promise a referendum on the return of the death penalty, which has created an unwelcome diversion.

Saturday 5 June

Most of the Twitter reaction to my *Prospect* piece is prompted by the stupid headline they put over it: 'From Hartlepool to the hangman: the flag-wavers now running the Tory Party could take Britain back to the gallows'. I kick myself for not offering stronger resistance.

Tuesday 8 June

The following letter from a retired GP, originally in *The Times*, is reproduced in the current issue of *The Week*:

> I have been vaccinating since January and our locality has now reached the thirtysomething cohort. Yesterday my colleagues and I were struck by the number of very anxious and 'needle-phobic' individuals, and witnessed refusals, tears, panic attacks and faintings. We concluded that this represents a generation of uber-anxious individuals or that there is an increasing fragility to the human psyche. It's a worrying trend because this group will be the leaders of the country in ten to twenty years' time.

More likely ten years, if the current cult of youth continues. Talking of fragility, I read that an MP – elected to Parliament aged just twenty-three – has taken leave of absence from Parliament, allegedly suffering from post-traumatic stress disorder. She is said to have been inundated with messages from fellow millennials praising her bravery, but my – no doubt politically incorrect – thought on the matter is that had she waited a few years until she had sorted out her own life, she might have been better placed to represent others. Snowflakes, please note, I intend no offence. I was myself a parliamentary candidate aged twenty-two, and with hindsight was utterly unready to represent others.

Sunday 13 June

My *Prospect* article has attracted a virulent denunciation ('bien pensant drivel') from the formidable Andrew Neil, whose Twitter following exceeds a million. 'There is no possibility', he asserts, 'that Britain will bring back capital punishment. Even America is moving away from it.' In response to which several people have posted pictures of Arizona's newly refurbished gas chamber. Mr Neil, by the way, has just launched GB News, a right-leaning, self-proclaimed anti-woke rival to the allegedly biased BBC. In keeping with the spirit of the times, the Union flag is much in evidence in promotional material for the new channel, though the launch seem to have been afflicted by technical difficulties.

Thursday 17 June
Millgate House, Richmond

Three days in North Yorkshire with our friends Diane and Martin Lee. Today a leisurely stroll around Fountains Abbey, tomorrow the great garden at Newby Hall. Martin recounted a visit he made just before the Brexit referendum to a working-class friend in Gateshead who was suffering from cancer. The friend proclaimed that he would be voting Leave on the grounds that there were 'too many Pakis in the country'. Martin, by the way, is of Chinese origin and therefore probably counts as a 'Paki' in the eyes of a certain type of Brexiteer.

Friday 18 June
Millgate House

Just when you think it's all over, politics springs a surprise. The Liberal Democrats have overturned a large Tory majority in the leafy Buckinghamshire seat of Chesham and Amersham, on a swing of 25 per cent. The by-election was caused by the death of the previous MP and attracted almost no attention. No one saw it coming. The upset is said to have been caused by a combination of HS2, Brexit, resentment at the relaxation of greenfield planning restraints and astute tactical voting. The Labour vote collapsed from about 7,000 to just over 600, said to be the lowest the party has ever recorded in a parliamentary election. Might this be the moment to talk about some sort of electoral pact (at least in marginal seats) with the Lib Dems – and if not now, when?

Monday 21 June

Sarah, Nick and the Little Lord fly to America today. Nick is due to take up a fellowship at a hospital in Boston. It is supposed to be for no more than a year or two, but I worry that we may lose them. People who go to work in the USA often don't come back.

The longest day. At 8 p.m., the sun still illuminating the mansion and the forested hills beyond.

Tuesday 22 June

The *Telegraph* is trying to arouse the indignation of its readers over the suggestion that the government may cut tax relief for the richest pensioners when the time comes to repay the vast debts we have accumulated as a result of Covid. It may just be me, but I find it hard to get worked up about comfortable Middle Englanders with pension pots of over £1 million and who have done extremely well out of the post-war house price boom. They are surely as well-placed as anyone to be first in line when it comes to paying the bill for the virus. Although not in that bracket myself, I suspect that many prosperous pensioners of my generation are not as mean as the *Telegraph* seems to think. Thank goodness the job of paying down the debt has fallen to a Tory Chancellor. Were Labour in office, mass hysteria would be organised.

Wednesday 23 June

Called on Bill Hugonin, the old Duke's former agent, at his home in the Hulne Park. A lovely old gent who never fails to remark on his good fortune and who continues to takes an interest in the state of the planet even though he is not long for this world, having recently been diagnosed with liver cancer. 'The nurse who broke the news was quite upset, but I told her that I am not in the least bothered. My only interest is in remaining in my own home.' Long may he do so.

Friday 25 June

Yet more evidence that the Conservative Party has been taken over by a cult. Joy Morrissey, who replaced that most intelligent and thoughtful Tory Dominic Grieve as the MP for Beaconsfield, is campaigning for a portrait of the Queen to be displayed in every home, company and institution. She tweets: 'I think this is a wonderful, patriotic and unifying campaign for our country. I will be writing to the Prime Minister to ask him to give it careful consideration and looking for opportunities to discuss further in Parliament.' Ms Morrissey is a 'core patron' of the British Monarchist Society. She's also an American by birth and upbringing. There is none so zealous as a convert.

Tuesday 29 June

Uproar over an assault on chief medical officer Chris Whitty by two apparently drunken yobs in St James's Park. Much more serious, however, is online footage from three days ago showing a crowd of anti-vaxxers gathered outside a block of flats in central London where he is said to live, chanting 'murderer' and 'traitor'. What's particularly chilling is how normal they look.

Wednesday 30 June

England has defeated Germany in the European Cup, thereby avenging fifty-five years of humiliation at the hands of the Hun. Tabloid celebrations have been mercifully restrained. No one has yet claimed this as a Brexit dividend, but there is still time.

Friday 2 July

Against expectations, Labour has clung on in the by-election at Batley and Spen. Labour were saved by the fact that their candidate, Kim Leadbeater, was the sister of the murdered MP Jo Cox and the only candidate to live locally. She won despite the disruptive presence of George Galloway. Too early to say whether this represents a one-off or a turning of the tide.

Sunday 4 July

We harvested our first crop of peaches. The trick, which we have only gradually caught on to, is to take them before they fall and leave them to ripen on the window sill.

Tuesday 6 July

To the Hexham Book Festival, my first public engagement for twenty months, where I delivered my 'Rise of English Nationalism' speech. A masked audience of about 120 people, half the usual turnout, but it amounted to a capacity crowd, taking into account that they had to be arranged into separate bubbles.

Wednesday 7 July

John Booth, an acquaintance from way back, stopped over for lunch en route to his home in Kirkcaldy. He told an amusing tale about being recruited into one of New Labour's focus groups which was supposed to consist of former Labour voters from the Hornsey and Wood Green constituency who had switched to the Lib Dems in the 2005 general election, but it turned out that most of them didn't live in the constituency and had never voted Lib Dem in their lives, although they all went along with the charade and duly collected their £40 participation fee. So much for focus groupery. John also quoted one of his grandmother's favourite sayings: 'Never trust men who dye their eyebrows.' 'It didn't mean anything to me until years later, when I met Robert Maxwell.'

Thursday 8 July

Growing nervousness at the government's plans to dispense with just about all Covid regulations despite a rapidly rising infection rate. A scientist was on the BBC the other night explaining that this could lead to new variants which may outwit the vaccine. As someone commented, 'God, this is so depressing.' I'll say.

Sunday 11 July

The UEFA Cup final. England versus Italy. The first time England has come within sight of a major international trophy since 1966. For days the bulletins have talked of little else. The tabloids have gone bonkers. The BBC's been leading on it for days. The Queen has sent a message of support. Boris Johnson is milking it for all it's worth – 10 Downing Street is decked out in the flag of St George. Mike White, formerly of *The Guardian*, tweeted, 'I shall be watching … and hope the team pulls it off. But "history"? No, it's a football game. This hysteria is unhealthy escapism reflecting deep national insecurity about our place in the world.' In the end we lost on penalties, whereupon the black players who failed to score were promptly showered with racist abuse.

Monday 12 July

Within five minutes of last night's defeat Boris Johnson deleted from his Twitter account the picture of himself in an England team shirt. Says it all.

Tuesday 13 July

The government has comfortably seen off a rebellion by Tory MPs against its decision to cut the aid budget, although it is claimed that the reduction is only temporary. An excellent speech from my friend Andrew Mitchell, one of the ringleaders of the uprising. 'There is an unpleasant odour wafting out from under my party's front door,' he said. In the event, twenty-four Tories, including Theresa May, voted against the government, which suggests there are marginally more one-nation Tories than I had previously thought but not enough to make a difference.

Thursday 15 July

A visit to Michael Ancram's garden at Mounteviot* bringing to mind happy memories of holidays past when we played hide and seek with the children amid his herbaceous borders. For the first time, we visited the house, which only opens in July. There, discreetly nestling among the family photographs, a group picture of young Ancram, dressed up to the nines, posing with the rich, entitled young louts of the Bullingdon Club. Dated 1964, a generation ahead of Cameron and Johnson.

The global death toll from Covid has passed the 4 million mark.

Friday 16 July

Keir Starmer says he will 'sweat blood over months and years to earn the respect of voters'. As part of which he is submitting himself to a long summer of purgatory touring the country, listening to surly, disaffected, whingeing allegedly ex-Labour voters. In the north he will have to endure complaints about Labour's resistance to Brexit (personified by Starmer). Further south, he will find equally dissatisfied Remainers. That is the core of Labour's dilemma and it doesn't require a PhD in psephology to work it out. Why submit oneself to this? A large part of me says that if most people want endless Tory government, let them have it. Oh, for the old certainties of the past.

---

* 13th Marquess of Lothian, former Conservative MP for Devizes and an occasional sparring partner of mine at Foreign Office Questions.

Monday 19 July

'Freedom Day'. From this day forth, masks and social distancing will be optional. Pubs and restaurants are to be permitted to operate normally. The *Telegraph* and other right-wing tabloids have been prattling on about it for weeks, but now that the great day has finally arrived, it doesn't seem quite so glorious. Despite the vaccine, infections are rising rapidly, a new and more potent variant has been detected and the Prime Minister and Chancellor are having to isolate, having been in contact with the Health Secretary, Sajid Javid, who has gone down with Covid. In fairness, there is a case for relaxing the rules. The success of the vaccination programme has lowered the numbers of deaths and hospital admissions and the economy urgently needs a boost. Either way, it is beginning to look as though the virus is going to be with us for the foreseeable future.

We harvested our first potatoes this morning, a healthy crop of Charlottes.

Tuesday 20 July

Dominic Cummings, in a long interview with the BBC's Laura Kuenssberg, says that within days of the 2019 election he and others in No. 10 were discussing getting rid of the Prime Minister. Why? 'He doesn't have a plan, he doesn't know how to be Prime Minister and we only got him in there because we had to solve a particular problem, not because he was the right person to be running the country.' Now he tells us…

Thursday 22 July

The government has announced a 3 per cent wage increase for health workers, while freezing the pay of many other public sector workers. Predictably, their union representatives and a number of the hotter heads in the Parliamentary Labour Party have denounced the offer as 'a slap in the face' and are demanding a 15 per cent increase. Exactly the sort of irresponsibility that led to the runaway inflation of the past and does no one any good in the end. It also plays into the narrative that Labour can't be trusted with the public finances.

Sunday 25 July

On the Twittersphere, footage from yesterday's anti-vaxxer rally in Tra-
falgar Square. Several of the usual suspects on the platform: David Icke,
Piers Corbyn etc. Plus, by far the scariest, Kate Shemirani, a struck-off
nurse asserting, with reference to Nuremberg, that doctors and nurses
who administer the vaccine could stand trial for genocide. The 5G mobile
phone network she alleged is 'a direct energy weapon ... In your injec-
tions hydrogel is a conduit, it has antenna that links you. It transmits and
receives. This is surveillance technology.' For good measure, she added
that face masks were 'subjugation tools' controlled by Freemasons. Another speaker asserted that 'demons' had persuaded millions around the
world to believe their plan by using a fake virus and fake death certificates
to give the illusion of a deadly disease that does not exist. Others said
that Covid was a hoax, 'just flu rebranded'. That the vaccine is a biological
and chemical weapon. That people who wear masks will be demented in
ten years' time. That what is happening in the UK is 'domestic terrorism'
and that the government's scientific advisory committee, SAGE, is 'a terrorist organisation'. All this to a cheering crowd several thousand strong,
though there must surely have been some present who, while sceptical of
government strategy, were beginning to wonder who they were mixed up
with.

Friday 30 July

The UK and Ireland are among five nations most likely to survive the
collapse of global civilisation, according to a report from the Global Sustainability Institute at Anglia Ruskin University. The others are Iceland,
New Zealand and Australia. I take no comfort. First because we are by
no means self-sufficient in food and second because one imagines that
many people in countries less fortunate than ours will want to make their
way here rather than sit at home and wait to die. A process already under
way: witness the huge increase in migration from failed and failing states
in Africa, Asia and the Middle East. No, the best way of surviving the
collapse of civilisation is surely to take whatever steps are necessary to
avoid it while there is still time. If indeed there is.

Saturday 31 July

A damp, grey, drizzly mist obscured the hills all day. I called on John Field at the Mill. 'Come in the back way,' he said. 'My cats have had a very stressful week and are composing themselves in the front porch.'

Thursday 5 August

To the Hulne Park to see Bill Hugonin. Physically he is fading, but intellectually still all there. 'I read *The Times* every day,' he said, 'though I find it less and less interesting. So much of it is about the past whereas I am interested in the future of our world.'

Friday 6 August

To the Harwood Forest with Tony Gates, Northumberland National Park chief executive, and a couple of officials to bear witness to the devastation caused by the planting of Sitka spruce in peat bogs. Tony is one of nine children brought up in Northern Ireland during the Troubles. His mother died recently aged ninety-six, in good health and still living in her own house. He described how on the last of her life day she went for an outing with those of his siblings who lived nearby. In the evening they had supper together. At about 6.30 p.m. Tony had a telephone conversation with her and she appeared to be on good form. Shortly afterwards she went to bed, complaining of a headache, and never woke up. How much merit she must have stored in heaven to be granted such a good death after so long a life.

Monday 9 August

Apocalyptic scenes from California and Greece, where vast forest fires are blazing out of control, consuming everything in their path. Even parts of Siberia and western Canada are on fire. In Greece the fires are threatening the suburbs of Athens, and thousands of people have been evacuated from one of the islands as fires drove them into the sea. The view from the ferry showed a vast red line of fire advancing along a black horizon. Such infernos are becoming annual events, no longer once-in-a-century happenings.

Tuesday 10 August

Amid the raging wildfires yet another warning from the UN panel on climate change, saying that time to avert catastrophe is running out. We have to change our lifestyles, they say. So, what contribution have the Mullins made? Although I like to think of myself as green and enlightened, the answer is very little. We have two cars, a wood-burning stove and the other day I had a new gas boiler installed, having ruled out a ground source heat pump on the basis that it was likely to cost several times the price of a boiler. True, we lead relatively modest lives by modern standards. We don't travel much, eat little or no meat, grow (some of) our own vegetables and take recycling seriously, but there is no escaping the conclusion that, like most first-worlders, we are part of the problem, not the solution.

A call from West Midlands Police to say that the Director of Public Prosecutions has declined to prosecute me for refusing to disclose my sources in the Birmingham pub bombings case. I should think so too. It would be beyond irony if the only conviction to arise from this latest investigation were to be of the person who exposed the vast edifice of lies that led to the collapse of the original convictions.

Monday 16 August

The Taliban have taken Kabul without firing a shot. No one anticipated the speed of the collapse. Afghan government forces simply melted away. Scenes reminiscent of the fall of Saigon as desperate crowds laid siege to the airport in the hope of escape. The abiding image: a huge US transport plane pursued by crowds as it rumbled towards the runway, bodies falling as it took off. Even after twenty years of bloodshed and the investment of billions, the regime was entirely artificial. Thus ends yet another ill-conceived Western intervention, though this one had better cause than most, given that the Taliban were hosting the perpetrators of 9/11.

Today's post brought another 1,000-page doorstopper – the second volume of Chips Channon's diaries. I am reviewing it for *The Spectator*.

Tuesday 17 August

No sooner had I received a letter from West Midlands Police confirming that the DPP would not authorise a prosecution for my refusal to disclose sources than there comes another threatening a civil action under the terrorism laws. This looks more ominous.

Wednesday 18 August

The NUJ has agreed to fund further legal advice as to how I should respond to the latest missive from West Midlands Police. 'What are the likely penalties for non-compliance?' I asked the lawyer. He thinks imprisonment is unlikely but unlimited fines are a possibility. A dark cloud is beginning to cast a shadow over my otherwise golden life.

Parliament has been recalled to discuss the Afghan crisis. Much impotent huffing and puffing from all sides, plus some moving speeches from veterans of the Afghan wars. Ultimately, though, it is futile. The bottom line is that once the Americans pulled the plug we had no choice but to follow suit. Interesting to hear Tory MPs leading demands that we accommodate more refugees. Tories were also in the lead last year when it came to offering asylum to several million Hong Kong Chinese. Remarkable considering that theirs is the party that plays the migration card at just about every general election. When the dust clears, how will this play with their newfound supporters in their recently conquered northern territories? Above all, the Afghan debacle surely marks the end of our pretensions to being a global power – clinging to America's coat-tails – though goodness knows what will happen when the Chinese come for Taiwan, as they surely will.

Tuesday 24 August

To London, my first visit in almost two years. On the train and at stations the British Transport Police are still endlessly broadcasting their fatuous 'See it, say it, sorted' slogan.

Wednesday 25 August

To Gray's Inn to consult Gavin Millar QC about to how to handle the latest threat from West Midlands Police. His opinion was that for all their bluster, they will be reluctant to take action against a journalist who is refusing to reveal his sources and that even were they to do so, a judge would be reluctant to issue an order. All very well, but supposing he did and I still held out? What is the likely penalty for defiance? A fine, he said. Unlikely to be more than £20,000, some or all of which we might be able to crowdfund.

Thursday 26 August

Home on the 09.30. The carriage was full of boisterous young people on their way to a music festival, not one of them wearing a mask. A nervous week ahead, waiting to see if my excursion has awarded me the virus.

Friday 27 August

Suicide bombers have killed more than ninety people at Kabul Airport, mostly Afghans, but also thirteen US Marines supervising the evacuation. Islamic State has claimed responsibility. Already the seeds of a new war are being sown. The Afghan mayhem is by no means over.

Saturday 28 August

The death toll from the Afghan bombing now stands at 170.

Sunday 29 August

A message from Nigel Vinson, who has finally got round to reading the copy of *Hinterland* I gave him three years ago: 'So enjoyed it … Oh, I so wish I had your easy pen.'

Monday 30 August

I dispatched a carefully worded response to West Midlands Police.

Tuesday 31 August

Finished Chips Channon's thousand-page blockbuster and tapped out a 1,400-word review for *The Spectator*. Extraordinary. Bombs falling all around, but he is still dining with political grandees and duchesses two or three nights a week at one or other of London's swishest hotels and, in between, entertaining lavishly. The war has forced him to reduce the number of servants at his house in Belgrave Square from fifteen to six, but otherwise his social life and that of his friends goes on much as before. Some amusing pen portraits. Lady Astor – 'an interfering termagant'. Sir Philip Sassoon – 'his teeth rattle like dice in a box', Churchill – 'that angry bullfrog, a slave of prejudice'. Duff Cooper – 'an inflated, conceited turkey cock' and so on. In some respects Channon reminds me of Humphry Wakefield. A great entertainer, a collector of interesting people, possessed of a savage wit. I'll always remember Humphry's magnificent put-down of someone who was writing a book about great British eccentrics, in which he featured: 'Captain of Boats at Eton. His mind's been in neutral ever since.'

Thursday 9 September

Awoke to find that I was sharing my bed with maggots. Upon investigation, they were found to be coming from the hatch in the bedroom ceiling, which, on being prised open, was found to contain a dead mouse. We removed the corpse and spent the best part of an hour clearing up.

Saturday 11 September

Twenty years today since the 9/11 attacks on New York's World Trade Center. A day never to be forgotten, after which nothing was ever the same again. I got out my well-thumbed copy of Richard A. Clarke's memoir. Clarke, a counter-terrorism adviser to three US Presidents, describes going into the White House the next day and being amazed to discover that Bush, Cheney and Rumsfeld were still fixated on blaming Iraq. Clarke and his colleagues had been trying for months to persuade them that the real enemy was Al-Qaeda, which had already been responsible for a series of terrorist incidents, including the attacks on the USS *Cole*, US embassies in Nairobi and Dar es Salaam and even the World Trade Center eight years earlier. He describes how, on the following day, he and several colleagues came across George Bush alone in the Situation Room. 'He grabbed us and closed the door ... "Look," he told us, "see if Saddam did this. See if he's linked in any way." I was taken aback … incredulous … "But Mr President, Al-Qaeda did this."*

Monday 13 September

Much of today's lunch – tomatoes, beans, mange tout, potatoes, plums – comes from the garden. 'Are you self-sufficient?' people sometimes ask. Ha! If we relied for survival on what we produce ourselves, we'd be dead by the end of October.

Wednesday 15 September

Cabinet reshuffle. Foreign Secretary Dominic Raab has been replaced by Liz Truss, who becomes the fourth holder of that office in five years – three of them duds. Jeremy Hunt, who lasted little more than a year, is the only one who wasn't. Morale at the FCO must be low. The new Culture Secretary is Nadine Dorries, whose best-known contribution to the preservation of our culture was moonlighting to Australia for a guest appearance in *I'm a Celebrity… Get Me Out of Here!* And our MP, Anne-Marie Trevelyan, fresh from her triumph in winding up DfID, returns to the Cabinet as trade minister.

Saturday 18 September

A little after 6 a.m. I was reading a light-hearted piece by Matthew Parris in *The Spectator* suggesting things we could live without; champagne and sex were mentioned. At which point the power failed, consigning us to twilight, and electricity became something we would have to live without, albeit for only a few hours. Unable to read, I went for a stroll around the lakes in my dressing gown and pyjamas, returning to find Ngoc, who spends much of the day on her iPhone, frantically trying to find a spot in the garden where she might find a signal. Who would guess that during her childhood in Vietnam she and her family survived without electricity for weeks on end? I spent the morning attempting to free our azaleas

---

* *Against All Enemies*, Simon & Schuster, 2004, p. 31.

from the accursed elder weed. We went to the cafe in the Ingram Valley for lunch. The power came back on in mid-afternoon. No harm done.

Friday 24 September

The Brexit bills are continuing to trickle in. First a shortage of care workers and now of drivers for heavy goods vehicle. Reports of petrol stations running out of fuel and empty shelves in supermarkets. In some areas rubbish is also going uncollected due to a shortage of drivers for the bin lorries. The Brexit tabloids are cautiously working themselves up into a frenzy about it ('We're running on empty,' says today's *Sun*), but somehow without much mention of Brexit. For the time being, this is all being swept under the Covid carpet – and it is true Covid is a factor, but it's by no means the whole explanation.

Saturday 25 September

The government is reluctantly considering temporary visas for HGV drivers from the EU in the hope that they can be persuaded to come back and bail us out of our present difficulty before being sent home again, but will they?

Sunday 26 September

Labour's mouthy deputy leader, Angela Rayner, has denounced Boris Johnson as 'Etonian scum'. This sort of puerile abuse demeans politics. I posted a note to this effect on Twitter and was duly assailed by a legion of headbangers who appear to think that this way of doing politics is entirely reasonable. One or two of the more learned referred to Nye Bevan's notorious denunciation of the Tories as 'lower than vermin'. As it happens, I don't regard that as the sainted Nye's finest hour either.

Tuesday 28 September

Headline in the *Telegraph*: 'How to escape paying £975,000 inheritance tax with this secret trick'.

Thursday 30 September

Signs of unrest in Brexitland. This from Allister Heath in today's *Telegraph*: 'What's wrong with this government? Why is it so passive, veering from crisis to crisis without a strategy, devoid of any meaningful plan?' He goes on:

> The Tory base, who are patriotic and proud of being British above all else, are increasingly worried that the rest of the world is mocking us. They look at the disgraceful queues at our petrol stations and wonder why we appear to be the only country to have imploded in such an embarrassing way.

Tuesday 5 October

'Businesses have become "drunk on cheap labour", say Tories'. Headline in today's *Telegraph*. Incredibly, the Tories are blaming their erstwhile friends for Brexit-related empty shelves and petrol shortages. A bold strategy.

Wednesday 6 October

Boris Johnson has addressed the Tory conference in Manchester. More shite about 'levelling up' and mendacious talk of the sixty-eight trade deals signed since Brexit, without mentioning that sixty-three of them are rollovers from the previous arrangements. The only one of any significance is with Australia, and any benefits from that will be easily eclipsed by the cost of exiting the single market.

Friday 8 October
Torpoint, Cornwall

These past three days were spent walking the coast of south Devon with my friends Chris Carter and Andy Carne. We started from Salcombe and worked backwards. Thirty-six miles with, on the first two days, a good deal of up and down. Past Burgh Island and the Mewstone. At the Flete Estate we paddled across the Erme estuary and trespassed as far as Nepean's

Cottage. Excepting Flete and Noss Mayo, which remain unspoiled, most of the little coves are crammed with ugly bungalows, vulgar hacienda and wooden chalets rising up the cliffs like Rio *favela*. Easier going on the third day, around the eastern edge of Plymouth Sound with its warships, ferries and little sailing boats. We paused for a drink at a pub on the Barbican and then made our way along the Hoe to the Torpoint ferry. Inland from these slivers of civilisation, most of Plymouth is a mess. It suffered horribly during the war, of course, but that does not begin to explain the damage inflicted by the planners. A touch of East Berlin, circa mid-'70s.

Monday 11 October

To London on the 09.00 and this evening to the Vintner's Hall in the City for the launch of Andrew Mitchell's memoir, *Beyond a Fringe*. Although Andrew claims to have 'resigned' from the Establishment, the place was crammed with grandees of all political denominations. From the Labour side, several old friends including Charlie Falconer and Clare Short. I was buttonholed by Sasha Swire, whose diaries caused a flutter in the Tory dovecotes last year. Did you lose many friends, I enquired? She claimed not, although David Cameron was 'a bit miffed'. I bet.

Saturday 16 October

Came across my neighbour Tony Henfrey, who is engrossed in the second volume of Chips Channon's diaries, with its lurid tales of how the idle rich lived during the war. 'Astonishing,' he says. 'The war seems only to be a mild inconvenience. Easy to see why the Tories lost the 1945 election so decisively.' Channon, by the way, asked only one question in Parliament in the five years covered by this volume of diaries and that was about an outbreak of mugging in Mayfair.

David Amess, a long-serving Tory MP, has been stabbed to death. The culprit appears to be a British citizen of Somali origin.

Sunday 17 October

Much talk of doing more to protect MPs in the wake of the David Amess murder, but in truth there is a limit to what can be done, although it would be helpful if the tabloids would stop monstering politicians they don't like. How many death threats must Jeremy Corbyn have received during his fraught five years as Labour leader? It would also be helpful if Labour politicians would stop using words like 'scum' to describe their opponents. Yesterday on the radio, an interview with a woman who had worked for Yvette Cooper, who claimed to have given up a job she enjoyed because she could not cope with the abuse and death threats directed at her employer. I may be wrong, but I don't think I ever had any death threats, though an irate constituent once smashed my office windows and I did receive a certain amount of abuse, which I stored in a box labelled A&A (Anonymous and Abuse). Of course, that was before the rise of social media.

Monday 18 October

Tapped out a note to Richard Benyon, the minister whose portfolio includes national parks, whom I came across at Andrew Mitchell's party last week, about the depredations of the Forestry Commission. On the one hand the government is giving public money for the restoration of peatlands while at the same time the Forestry Commission, a government agency, is destroying them.

Tuesday 19 October

Right on cue, the government has announced its plan for going carbon neutral. Among the promises, more money for the restoration of peat bogs, which soak up carbon.

Thursday 21 October

Less than a week after the murder of David Amess, a group of anti-vaxxers has erected a gallows in the park next to Parliament. The implication being that they want to hang MPs who take a different view from themselves. By no means their first offence. These lunatics have been parading around Westminster with a mock gallows for months while police looked on. Surely the time has come for some arrests.

Monday 25 October

From Afghanistan, dire warnings from the UN and aid agencies that millions face starvation without urgent help. Desperate parents are reported to be selling their children.

Wednesday 27 October

The budget. After a week of shameless leaking and innumerable photo opportunities, Chancellor Rishi Sunak finally got round to sharing the contents with the House of Commons. Turns out the economy is in better shape than expected, owing to a quicker-than-expected recovery from lockdown. He has begun to reverse George Osborne's dreadful legacy, with real-terms increases for every government department. 'The first such increase for ten years', he repeatedly boasted. Yes indeed. And whose fault is that? Ingeniously, and with the connivance of much of our free press, our masters are pretending that the party which laid waste to the public sector during much of the past decade is entirely different from the one now in power even though they share the same name and some of the same personnel. Sunak even had the gall to hold out the prospect of tax cuts, despite a mountainous public debt and despite having just increased the tax take to record levels. What's the betting the Tories go into the next election yet again proclaiming themselves to be the party of tax cutters? One can't be too cynical about these guys.

Thursday 28 October

According to an exchange of letters between Richard Hughes, chairman of the Office for Budget Responsibility, and shadow Chancellor Rachel Reeves, the long-term impact of Brexit is likely to be a 4 per cent reduction in GDP. About double the impact of Covid.

Friday 29 October

The ideologues at the *Telegraph* are working themselves into a frenzy over the budget. 'The Tories' nightmare conversion to Brownism will end in catastrophe,' rages Allister Heath. 'A complete trashing of the Osborne austerity agenda,' laments Jeremy Warner, calling it a 'smash-and-grab raid on our money'. Despite all the cheering and waving of order papers on the day, it appears that the Tory Party is not a happy ship. Meanwhile Kathleen Stock, a professor of philosophy at the University of Sussex, has been hounded out of her job by hooded trans rights 'activists'. Her crime? Expressing the view that biological sex is a fact of life that can't simply be overridden by 'identifying' as the opposite.

Sunday 31 October

'Plans for a third runway at Heathrow have been dealt a killer blow,' says a report in today's *Telegraph*. Nothing to do with saving the planet, of course. Just insufficient profit for shareholders. But hey, who cares. As one who was once the government's aviation spokesman in the Commons, I am delighted.

Monday 1 November

The rulers of the world (minus the Russians and the Chinese) have assembled in Glasgow for a massive climate change jamboree. Apocalyptic speeches and grand gestures combined with plentiful helpings of hypocrisy: witness the private jets and gas-guzzling armoured convoys. And beyond the wire several thousand baying 'activists', pouring scorn on the entire process. One has to ask, is this the best way to do business? But whatever the inadequacy of the process, lack of progress cannot be entirely blamed on our despised politicians. One way or another they are all beholden to domestic vested interests and their electoral base. Even in the UK, it is far from clear that the Great British Public are prepared to tolerate any more than the most marginal inconvenience to their lifestyles in the interests of saving the planet. This evening, a television report from Madagascar, where a huge climate change-related drought has been under way for months, unnoticed by the outside world. Emaciated children with swollen stomachs and stick-like limbs, some eating live insects to ward off hunger. 'I know we are all going to die,' said one mother. Another said of her little boy, 'He thinks we have hidden the food and keeps asking where it is.'

Tuesday 2 November

A CNN report from Afghanistan showing a weeping father handing over his nine-year-old daughter to a white bearded man who claims to be aged fifty-five but looks older. 'This is your bride. You are responsible for her now. Please don't beat her,' he says as the little girl is dragged away to a life of misery. I cannot suppress a tear as I compare this little person's fate to the golden lives that my Sarah and Emma enjoyed when they were that age.

Headline in today's *Telegraph*: 'How to avoid paying a higher rate tax (even if you earn £90,000 a year)'.

Wednesday 3 November

A huge row brewing over the government's use of a three-line whip to prevent the suspension of former Cabinet minister Owen Paterson following a unanimous finding that he had been energetically lobbying on behalf of companies paying him a total of £9,000 a month for his services. The vote was entirely along party lines: Tories on one side and everybody else in the opposite lobby. Interesting to observe how our free press are handling this. As one would expect, the *Express* and *The Sun* are doing their best to play it down. The *Telegraph* appears to take Paterson's side ('Paterson says MPs' watchdog must go…'). Most devious of all is the *Mail*: 'Shameless MPs sink back into sleaze'. The word 'Tory' conspicuous by its absence. I may be wrong, but it is – JUST – possible our masters may at last have over-reached themselves.

Thursday 4 November

Faced with a widespread backlash, the government has performed a screeching U-turn, abandoning plans to rescue Owen Paterson and re-write the parliamentary rulebook. Paterson, meanwhile, has announced his immediate resignation from Parliament. A by-election beckons in what would otherwise be an ultra-safe Tory seat but in the circumstances may be anything but safe.

This evening to the University of Sunderland, where I gave my 'Rise of English Nationalism' lecture. Afterwards someone tweeted, 'Just been to probably the best public lecture that Sunderland University has ever put on,' although she added that it was quite depressing. Indeed it was. And it would have been more so had I not deleted the final paragraph, which read as follows:

> Be warned: I have a tendency to err on the side of pessimism and so I may be entirely wrong. One should never say 'never' in politics. But as things stand I do not expect to see another non-Tory government in my lifetime. I am seventy-three and in good health.

Sunday 7 November

It is beginning to look as if our beloved Prime Minister may, just this once, have pushed his luck too far. Until now he has seemed to enjoy impunity. Nothing he did had adverse consequences, at least not for himself. No amount of bungling, blundering or blustering seemed to make any difference to his poll ratings – but the Owen Paterson business may have changed all that. Suddenly sleaze is back in the headlines. The media spotlight is starting to focus on other issues long overlooked, such as the umbilical link between peerages and donations to the Tory Party. Neither are Tory MPs best pleased at having been made to look complete fools: one minute ordered into the lobbies in defence of the indefensible, only for the retreat to be sounded twenty-four hours later. Johnson has never been popular with his MPs, who are all too well aware of what a charlatan he is. They have only tolerated him because he was a winner. If his star fades, they won't hesitate to dispose of him. Not that Labour will necessarily benefit. Like Sunderland's benighted football team, we remain firmly rooted to the bottom of the second division.

Tuesday 9 November

Geoffrey Cox, a million-a-year Tory lawyer, is the new name in the firing line. It seems he has been moonlighting in the British Virgin Islands and voting remotely (permissible during the pandemic). That, by the way, is the case for not permanently allowing digital voting, as some 'modernisers' demand.

Thursday 11 November

'In another life Boris Johnson might have spent his days trying the handles of parked cars,' writes Robert Shrimsley in today's *Financial Times*. 'The UK Prime Minister is a chancer, a man who believes in pushing his luck. He worries little about consequences because he trusts himself to get out of any scrape and conducts his politics with a smirk ... It has been a winning formula.' Indeed it has, so far.

The flow of migrants across the Channel is rising. Yesterday 695 arrived in twenty-two small boats. The figure for Tuesday was 504. So far this year 22,344 have reached the UK from France, compared with about 8,400 last year. Meanwhile several thousand migrants who have been enticed into Belarus on false pretences are laying siege to the Polish frontier. As the world beyond our borders disintegrates, it is becoming increasingly obvious that uncontrolled migration will be one of the great crises of future decades.

Friday 12 November

Yesterday a record 1,000 migrants crossed the Channel from France. The French don't seem to be trying very hard to stop them. One begins to wonder if they are playing a similar game to Belarus.

Saturday 13 November

A poll highlighted in today's *Mail* gives Labour a six-point lead over the Tories. Another puts Labour and the Tories on level pegging. Nothing to get too excited about, but it may begin to put the skids under Boris.

Tuesday 16 November

To Heathrow for the evening flight to Boston to stay with Nick, Sarah and the Little Lord. In the past fortnight we have had to jump through so many hoops that we shan't relax until we are on the plane, and even then there is the fearsome US immigration service to clear. In addition to visa waivers and insurance (costing as much as the airfare), we have to present our 'Fit to Fly' certificates and something called an Airline Attestation, of which we only became aware at the last minute. This is a device to absolve British Airways of responsibility for returning us to the UK if we fail to get through US immigration. To be on the safe side, Ngoc has printed out the form and filled it in manually. It turns out, however, that only a digital version is acceptable. No matter, the man at the BA desk takes our form and copies it manually into Ngoc's phone. All this at breakneck speed while conducting a conversation on his mobile in another language (Urdu?) while occasionally pausing to ask a question of us. He was still talking nineteen to the dozen as he waved us through.

Tuesday 23 November

Boris Johnson is reported to have made a car crash of a speech to a Confederation of British Industry conference in South Shields. 'Are you all right?' a reporter asked afterwards. Naturally he said he was, but one can't help wondering.

Wednesday 24 November

Beacon Hill, Boston

The Little Lord, now aged ten months, is a cheerful little chap who greets us each day with a radiant smile. He can crawl at high speed and clamber on sofas, but he can't quite walk yet. Already he can use the monitor to switch on the TV and usually makes a beeline for electricity wires and plugs, requiring a rescue party to be scrambled to intercept him. Sarah is an excellent, good-humoured mother, only occasionally showing the signs of strain that come from spending twenty-four hours a day in the company of a hyperactive little monster. Because the household revolves around his every whim, she refers to him as 'Sir'. 'Would Sir like his nappy changed?' 'Is Sir ready for his nap?' 'Sir, Sir, please don't do that.' And so on.

Thursday 25 November

News from home: twenty-seven migrants have drowned trying to cross the Channel in a small boat. Where will this end?

Friday 26 November

Like many of their generation, the lives of Nick and Sarah revolve around their iPhones. The most complex transactions can be accomplished in minutes. Buying, selling, map-reading. Anything is possible. Put them down anywhere in the world and they would soon find their way around. Shortly after we arrived, Nick announced that he was going to sell his car, a BMW. In no time at all, without moving from the living room, he surveyed the market and discovered a dealer within easy commuting distance who was offering a good price. By next evening the car had gone. Today we visited Newport, a twee coastal resort on Rhode Island, an hour or two south of Boston. For this, a Zipcar was required. Nick tapped into his iPhone and within minutes had discovered one available in the car park under Boston Common. He disappeared and twenty minutes later the car was parked at our door.

Saturday 27 November

Another day, another Zipcar. This time we headed north to Manchester-by-the-Sea and Rockport. The towns mostly have familiar names, Portsmouth, Bristol, Gloucester etc., but then, of course, this is New England. Classic wooden houses, all shapes and sizes, white wooden churches with sharp, pointed spires. Coastal mansions with towers, turrets and multiple balconies looking out over a blue sea. Lunch in a little diner at Rockport. From home, reports that a big storm has swept down through Scotland and the north-east, unleashing 100-mile-an-hour winds. Callaly seems to have been right in its path. I fired off half a dozen emails to neighbours, but no one has replied.

Sunday 28 November

The silence from Callaly is ominous. I rose at 4.30 a.m. and tapped out more emails. Eventually a reply came from a neighbour who has taken refuge in Newcastle and whose phone can therefore be charged. She reports that everyone is safe but the carnage considerable. The beautiful beech avenue which leads to the South Lodge has been devastated, phone lines are down and electricity is likely to be off for several days. Meanwhile, prompted by the arrival of the so-called South African Covid variant, the government has announced yet another sudden change in the travel rules. From 4 a.m. Tuesday, UK arrivals will be required to take a new PCR test and to quarantine until given the all-clear. Our plane will arrive two hours after the deadline. After a hurried conference, we decide to bring our flight forward by a day, thereby avoiding a new bout of hassle. Sarah and Nick get to work on their phones and in no time our flight has been rescheduled – albeit at an extra cost of £780. We departed for London at 18.55.

Tuesday 30 November
The Lycée, Kennington

Still no electricity at Callaly. Our neighbour Zoe, one of the few residents whose phone still works, reports that a large pine came down over the wall and narrowly missed our glasshouse. The good news is that no one has been injured and our homes are intact. This morning to the House of Commons for a coffee with Gary Gibbon of *Channel 4 News*, which I hope to interest in my difficulty with West Midlands Police.

Wednesday 1 December

To the West End offices of Simons Muirhead Burton for an audience with my solicitor, Louis Charalambous, who has finally taken delivery of the paperwork for the West Midlands Police application for an order requiring me to disclose the notes of my interview with one of the surviving pub bombers. It comes in four thick ring binders. The case will be heard at the Old Bailey on 23 and 24 February. Louis is optimistic. Me less so. This could be ruinous.

Thursday 2 December

Back to Callaly. On the train I read the first volume of West Midlands paperwork. It is detailed and repetitive. At first it consists mainly of a statement of facts, but somewhere along the way it morphs into a suggestion that I am lying about the existence of notebooks I long ago disposed of. I wish I had never cooperated with them.

Electricity was restored last night, but several nearby villages are still without it.

Friday 3 December

Daylight. I made a circuit of the estate to inspect the damage caused by Storm Arwen. The south drive has been cleared, but the gates remain locked since a large tree threatens to fall. The woods around the lakes are more or less intact. A couple of trees have come down in the burn, but the three giant redwoods are still upright. Surprisingly, the pine forest on the ridge looks intact, but the beech wood below is a sorry sight. At least twenty huge trees uprooted and lying flat, laying waste to all around them.

Saturday 4 December

From early morning, the sound of a chainsaw. Calum hard at work slicing up fallen timber. My neighbour John Nicholls has lost about twenty trees. Kate Donaghy at Lorbottle Hall says they are still without mains electricity and water, although they do have a generator which works intermittently. Among their losses, the magnificent cedar of Lebanon on the south lawn. Tony Henfrey, a man not easily intimidated, says the night of the storm was the most terrifying of his life. So violent that he feared the windows would come in or that the chimney stack would come through the roof. Next morning, the streets of Whittingham, our nearest village, were a spaghetti of telephone and electricity wires.

Monday 6 December

To the surgery in Rothbury to see a GP about a growth on my head which son-in-law Nick says is potentially cancerous. She agreed and promised to make an appointment with a dermatologist to have it removed and tested. So that's another little ailment to add to my growing list – crumbling teeth, arthritic knees, bronchial lungs – not to mention the occasional kidney stone. Gradually I am disintegrating.

Home via Eslington, where another scene of devastation greeted us. Massive beeches down over the avenue and on the Netherton road the 200-year-old wall breached in at least a dozen places. One large section entirely demolished. On the coast, at St Abb's Head, the storm is reported to have battered to death several hundred seal pups.

Matt Ridley has an excellent piece in today's *Telegraph* on the depredations of Forestry England (aka the Forestry Commission). I messaged him suggesting he bend Richard Benyon's ear on the subject. Almost by return he replied saying he was sitting in the Lords chamber and the minister was two rows in front of him. Eight minutes later I received another email saying that, as requested, he had bent the minister's ear. How's that for service?

Tuesday 7 December

A telephone conference with my esteemed lawyers. Gavin Millar QC advises that my notes are of no evidential value because they are no more than hearsay. However, he also advises caution on advance publicity – even a bald announcement – for fear of upsetting the judge. He is also reluctant to put me in the witness box. My instinct, however, is that this is as much about politics as it is about the legalities and that within reason we should do our best to up the ante in advance of proceedings.

Wednesday 8 December

To Chillingham to inspect the damage to the wild cattle park inflicted by Storm Arwen. The ticket office has been crushed by a vast pine and a large beech has fallen on the twelfth-century church, but the park itself is generally intact and the cattle have survived. Afterwards a cup of tea at the castle with Humphry and Katharine Wakefield. Humphry, whose morale is high despite the devastation, regaled me with tales of his dealings with Donald and Ivana Trump in the '80s and the inevitable difficulty of getting paid for his services. The castle is intact, but the grounds have suffered. Half the lime avenue is down, the glasshouse has been smashed and a chunk of the ancient wall by the rear entrance has been brought down by a huge beech which fell across the road.

Other news: a major row is under way following news of a Christmas party at No. 10 last year in defiance of the Covid lockdown imposed on the rest of the nation. Until now Johnson, who is said not to have been present, has been denying all, but a video has emerged which appears to undermine his position. Like the Cummings affair, this is damaging because it fuels the growing impression that the Tory elite are exempt from the rules that apply to the rest of us. By early evening the first head had rolled: Allegra Stratton, the Prime Minister's spokesperson, made a tearful apology and resigned.

Thursday 9 December

We are becoming so insular. The only foreign story on tonight's evening news is the Test match in Australia. Meanwhile in the rest of the world there are fears that Russia is about to invade Ukraine, the Israelis are threatening to bomb Iran's nuclear facilities, the Bosnian Serbs are threatening more mayhem in the Balkans and the Chinese may be gearing up for a possible invasion of Taiwan. Not to mention looming famine in Afghanistan, east Africa and Madagascar. On top of which the Ethiopians have decided to have another civil war. All the while we are obsessing about whether or not staff in Downing Street held a Christmas party last year in defiance of the Covid regulations. Yes, yes, I know it is part of a bigger picture, but it does seem awfully small beer.

Friday 10 December

The Appeal Court has ruled that Julian Assange should be sent to the American gulag, from which he may never emerge. The Extradition Act passed on our watch allows the courts very little leeway and is not reciprocal. One of the biggest regrets of my time as chair of the Home Affairs Committee is that we didn't offer stiffer resistance. Tony Benn, I recall, was scathing about our failure to oppose it and he was right.

Sunday 12 December

My seventy-fourth birthday. We drove to Embleton and walked along the beach to the Ship Inn for lunch. Ngoc took a photo of me, pint in hand, about to tuck into apple crumble and ice cream. A good picture, but I look rather decrepit. Maybe it's my untrimmed eyebrows.

Tuesday 14 December

A huge new panic under way prompted by the rapid spread of Omicron, the so-called South African variant. There seems no doubt that it is highly infectious, but it is far from clear that it is as lethal as earlier variants. Nevertheless, experts are sounding the alarm. Much talk of the NHS being overwhelmed. Government desperate to avoid another Christmas lockdown but at the same time anxious to avoid the charge of complacency. This evening, in the teeth of considerable resistance from the libertarian right – ninety-nine Tory MPs rebelled – they imposed vaccine passports as a condition of entry to events in large venues. The measure only went through with Labour support, which prompted an email from a former mandarin of my acquaintance: 'Can't help reflecting, in an entirely neutral way, that the first time Boris Johnson does something sensible half the Tory Party seems about to revolt.'

Wednesday 15 December

'A hammer blow to Boris Johnson's authority': the *Telegraph*'s verdict on last night's Tory uprising. Clearly Johnson isn't going to make it to the next election. No doubt the Tories will attempt to pull the same trick as they did in 1990 when John Major replaced Thatcher: 'You said you wanted change. We've given you change.' Meanwhile the *Mirror* has published a picture of a large group of Tory staffers and Shaun Bailey, their candidate in the recent mayoral elections, partying during last year's lockdown. More than ever, politics has become a game of gotcha.

Thursday 16 December

Labour posing shamelessly as the party of business. Health spokesman Wes Streeting was on the radio this morning, using the word 'business' about twenty times during his brief interview. He also had the nerve to assert that, unlike the government, Labour wasn't playing politics with Covid, but his every sentence reeked of opportunism. A low game, politics.

Friday 17 December

Awoke to the news that the Tories have decisively lost the North Shropshire by-election on a swing to the Lib Dems of 34 per cent. No question now: Johnson will not lead the Tories into the next election. Who next?

I put it to a former colleague in Parliament that it would be either Sajid Javid or Rishi Sunak, but she predicted it would be Liz Truss, who is shamelessly positioning herself. Lord spare us.

Saturday 18 December

Matthew Parris in today's *Times*: 'Since the European referendum campaign began, the Conservative Party has been poisoning itself, and the toxin is called populism. At first the experience was intoxicating, heady. Now the party's getting the shakes. The cure will require more than the removal of one man.'

Sunday 19 December

Lord Frost, the Brexit negotiator and a man who has done the UK a great deal of damage, has resigned. The latest of several Brexiteer ministers to flee the scene of their crimes.

Tuesday 21 December

Growing pressure from the scientists to impose another Covid lockdown. There is no doubt that the Omicron variant is spreading like wildfire, but it doesn't seem to be anything like as deadly as previous versions. Yesterday's Cabinet meeting divided on the issue, Johnson hoping to get past Christmas before he has to make a decision. This evening, a call from Emma to say that she and her boyfriend, Ed, will not be coming for Christmas after all. Ed's flatmate and two of Emma's work colleagues have gone down with the virus and they have decided it's just too risky. To bed feeling very down. We were so looking forward to seeing her.

Wednesday 22 December

Emma has tested positive for Covid.

Thursday 23 December

Calum has cut up the large ash tree that fell across Priests Walk. Ngoc and

I loaded the car boot with logs and took them to John Field's barn, where I started chopping while she stacked.

Friday 24 December

A grey, damp mist obscuring the hills. A couple of hours working in the garden. This afternoon Ngoc and I returned to John Field's barn for more log chopping.

Saturday 25 December

A second Christmas without family. We walked up to High Houses and back. Then video conference with Sarah, Nick and the Little Lord in Boston and Emma and Ed in London, after which Ngoc served up a splendid lunch of wild venison (more or less the only meat I eat), parsnips, sprouts and roast potatoes. We had intended to while away the afternoon watching the DVDs I recorded of the children when they were small, but I couldn't make the damn machine work, so instead I passed the afternoon in a chair by the fire reading A. J. P. Taylor's autobiography.

Sunday 26 December

Desmond Tutu, one of the great men of Africa, has died. I came across him twice, once when I was Africa minister and once when, to my amazement, I spotted him jogging up Brixton Road – he was apparently staying with one of my neighbours. Like his soulmate, the great Mandela, he never lost his sense of humour despite the horrors he had to confront. Witness the following: 'When the white man came to Africa, we had the land and he had the Bible. Then he said, "Close your eyes and pray." When we opened them again, he had the land and we had the Bible.'

Thursday 30 December

To Lorbottle Hall, where Jeremy and Kate were entertaining William Clouston, a pleasant, thoughtful man who claimed to be the leader of the SDP. I was under the impression that it had disappeared years ago. I googled him and sure enough the SDP has been reborn – this time round as a

Brexit party – and he is indeed the leader. Apparently it has about 18,000 members and has, unnoticed by the outside world, contested recent general elections. In 2019, their twenty candidates attracted a grand total of just 3,295 votes. We walked up to the crags while he outlined his plan for a grand anti-Tory coalition, which he reckoned might come to pass by 2030. The main snag is that it requires electoral reform, so in my view even 2130 would be a tad optimistic.

CHAPTER THIRTEEN

2022

Saturday 1 January

The Man is to be made a Knight of the Garter, thereby triggering yet another hail of fire and brimstone from his many enemies. They are getting up a petition asking the Queen to think again.

Tuesday 4 January

Keir Starmer delivered a New Year speech in Birmingham. It was actually rather good: Blair circa 1994–97, without the glitz. No more sniping at his own side. Highlighting the achievements of previous Labour governments. Guns pointed outwards. Shamelessly playing the patriotic card – an outsize Union Jack on display behind him. Addressed mainly to Labour's core voters – or at least those who used to be. Security, prosperity and integrity were the watchwords. Some good shots at the current management: 'I don't think politics is a branch of the entertainment industry.' No doubt that Starmer would be a competent, if dull and not very brave, Prime Minister. Maybe that's the best we can hope for in these difficult times.

Thursday 6 January

More than 600,000 people have now signed a petition to the Queen urging her to rescind the knighthood she recently awarded The Man owing to his getting us involved in Iraq. This is the product of an unholy alliance between opponents of the war and the right-wing media, who are playing it up for all it's worth, even though at the time most of them were keen on invading Iraq. Geoff Hoon's recent memoir in which he claims that he was ordered by Downing Street to burn an embarrassing memo from the Attorney General has stirred the pot. I have been asked by Middle East Eye for 2,000 words on Blair and Iraq. The stain that never goes away.

Friday 7 January

To Chillingham, where the debris from Storm Arwen will take years to clear. Half the lime avenue leading to the castle, planted in 1828, has been demolished. Humphry is philosophical. 'I look at it this way,' he said, 'I enjoyed Chillingham as it was for forty years and now I have a chance to plant trees for others to enjoy 200 years from now.'

Saturday 8 January

Signatories to the petition calling for Blair's knighthood to be withdrawn have now passed 1 million. The knighthood I would like to see rescinded is that of Sir Richard Dearlove, who presided over MI6 while it fed the government nonsense about Saddam's possession of WMD, failing to own up long after it became clear that it was nonsense.

The UK's Covid death toll has passed 150,000, putting us up there with the US, Brazil, India and Russia. All with much larger populations.

Monday 10 January

Ngoc has recently decreed that we need to hire a cleaner. I was opposed on the grounds that we are neither infirm nor too busy to clean up after ourselves, but inevitably it has come to pass. A cheerful local woman now comes each Monday for two hours and I find myself cleaning the bathroom sink and emptying the waste baskets in anticipation of her arrival.

Tuesday 11 January

The pit is getting deeper. An email sent from Boris Johnson's private office has emerged inviting No. 10 staff to a garden party ('Bring your own booze') on 20 May last year, at the height of the lockdown. About thirty people, including Boris himself, are said to have attended. On today's media, a parade of angry, tearful people who lost loved ones during the lockdown without being able to sit by their bedside or even have a proper funeral. Signs of growing exasperation within the Tory Party. No amount of bluster or even yet another grovelling apology is likely to explain this one way. The end is surely nigh.

Wednesday 12 January

Johnson has come down to earth with a bump. Gone the facetious, blustering, smirking Boris whose previous misdemeanours have been laughed off and which had no discernible impact on his poll ratings. This time it's different. At PMQs today Keir Starmer gave him a right going-over while his own side looked on in dismayed silence. Johnson read out what at first glance appeared to be a fulsome apology until, in the small print, he asserted that he had somehow been under the impression that he was attending a work meeting and that it was therefore above board. At that moment one realised that behind this newfound humility there lurked the same old Boris. The one to whom the rules that govern the rest of us do not apply. Chancellor Sunak was conspicuous by his absence, having discovered an urgent engagement elsewhere. Theresa May, seated four rows back, was struggling to keep a straight face. For her, this long-overdue unravelling must be a moment to savour. Until today I had thought Johnson would survive at least until the summer – and perhaps he will – but the end may come much sooner.

Thursday 13 January

Johnson is not the only prominent public figure in deep *shtook*. The Queen has stripped Prince Andrew of all his honorary titles in anticipation of a messy legal action in New York in which he is being sued for alleged sexual abuse by one of the young women recruited by the serial sex offender Jeffrey Epstein. Andrew has long been a national embarrassment. When I was at the Foreign Office, I recall one of our ambassadors complaining that a trade mission he had headed was 'like a rugby club outing'.

Friday 14 January

Another day, another No. 10 lockdown drinks party. This one by way of farewell to a Downing Street head of communications who was off to become deputy editor of – inevitably – *The Sun*. Reports of dancing and a suitcase full of booze. Johnson doesn't seem to be personally implicated, but given this took place on the eve of the Duke of Edinburgh's funeral it is a dangerous moment. A picture is beginning to emerge of a small elite who did not consider themselves bound by the rules they imposed upon the rest of us. By this evening Downing Street was offering yet more apologies, this time to the Queen.

Sunday 16 January

A new phrase has entered the English language: 'We must wait for Sue Gray', referring to the Cabinet Office civil servant who has been tasked with investigating the various parties held in Downing Street at the time of the lockdown. It has become the standard official response to all questions on the subject. So often has it been repeated that Ms Gray (who, by the way, was the civil servant who vetted the ministerial parts of my diaries) has overnight become a household name.

Monday 17 January

'Operation Red Meat' – a package of measures designed to placate the mob – is said to be under way as part of a 'Save Boris' strategy. Nadine Dorries, the Culture Secretary, has declared that the BBC licence fee will be abolished when it comes up for renewal five years from now, thereby reducing the Corporation to a subscription-only service, and the military are to be called in to repel cross-Channel migrants, foreigner-bashing always being a safe bet for a Tory government in trouble. So far only half a dozen MPs have publicly called for the resignation of their beloved leader, which suggests he is safe for the time being.

Wednesday 19 January

The nation still in the grip of 'Partygate'. Today one of the so-called Red Wall Tories defected to Labour, parking himself ostentatiously behind

Keir Starmer and looking ludicrous in his Union Jack face mask. How pleased should Labour be? In my view he should be treated as a prisoner of war and on no account allowed to stand as a Labour candidate.[*]

Friday 21 January

Came across the following in Geoff Hoon's recently published memoir, *See How They Run*:

> In the final few days before the attack on Iraq was to be launched, I was with Tony Blair in his small study in Downing Street together with Richard Dearlove, then 'C', the head of the British Secret Intelligence Service. Tony … asked him quite specifically and unambiguously whether Saddam Hussein had chemical weapons. His answer was unequivocal: the regime had them and would use them to defend Iraq if attacked.

Monday 24 January

The war drums are beating loudly in Ukraine, which is threatened with a Russian invasion. Today comes news that British and US embassies are evacuating non-essential staff. Putin is demanding that NATO stop messing about there, while the US and its allies insist on Ukraine's right to decide its own future. All very well in theory, but I do wonder whether it was wise to organise right up to the Russian border. According to Gorbachev, when he withdrew from Eastern Europe, he was privately assured that the US and its allies would not exploit the Soviet withdrawal, but no sooner were the Russians out of the door than most of Eastern Europe was recruited into NATO. Now we are signing up Ukraine. Hardly surprising that the Russians are paranoid. Imagine if France or Holland had joined the Warsaw Pact.

Tuesday 25 January

'I've already sold my daughters; now my kidney. Winter in an Afghan slum.' Headline in *The Guardian*.

---

[*] He was later imposed upon the Bury South Labour Party as their candidate without having to face a selection.

Wednesday 26 January

The Metropolitan Police have announced that they will be investigating Partygate, which means this nonsense could go on for months, by which time the public will be heartily sick of the subject. This plays straight into Johnson's hands. He will almost certainly live to fight another day.

Friday 28 January

A call from former Lord Chancellor Charlie Falconer to say that he is happy to put in a supportive statement re. my difficulty with West Midlands Police. Since it was he who took the Terrorism Act through the Lords, this is bound to carry weight.

Monday 31 January

The Times published a decent piece about the West Midlands Police action under the heading 'Birmingham Six police use terror act against writer'. The Tiny Lord and his entourage arrived from Boston. They will be staying for three weeks.

Tuesday 1 February

A helpful letter in today's *Times* from Jack Straw, Home Secretary when the Terrorism Act 2000 became law. It was, he says, never intended to catch a bona fide journalist. He adds, 'I have known Mr Mullin for forty years. Wild horses, thumb screws and a lengthy spell in jail would not make him break a confidence.' He is right about a spell in jail, but I am not so sure about thumb screws.

Thursday 3 February

The Tiny Lord has taken complete control of the household. The window sills in the living room have been cleared of all objects within his reach. The floor is piled with playthings, including various items of kitchenware which, when banged on the floor, make what, to him at least, is an agreeable noise. Meanwhile he races around on hands and knees under the watchful eyes of his many servants. A good-natured little fellow, always smiling.

A call from the practice nurse at the surgery with the results of my recent blood test. Kidneys, liver, cholesterol, all normal. Onwards and upwards.

Friday 4 February

The regime is crumbling. Today, not one but four resignations from No. 10. Three were expected in the wake of Partygate, but the fourth – Munira Mirza, director of the No. 10 Policy Unit, who left in protest at Johnson's refusal to apologise for a false smear against Keir Starmer – was a complete surprise. Meanwhile there are growing signs that Chancellor Sunak is on manoeuvres. The rumble of the guns draws closer by the hour.

Friday 11 February

Britain and the US are ramping up the rhetoric over Ukraine with repeated demands that it be allowed to join NATO. Yesterday we sent our flyweight Foreign Secretary, Liz Truss, to Moscow to read the Riot Act. Today it's the turn of our rather more substantial Defence Secretary, Ben Wallace. For Boris Johnson, the chance for a bit of posturing over Ukraine is a welcome distraction from his domestic woes. Joe Biden has called on American citizens to leave, warning that in the event of war the US will not be sending in troops to rescue them. The French and the Germans, meanwhile, are taking a more conciliatory approach. Broadly the same division of opinion as there was over Iraq. The Russian position is that Ukraine should adopt a policy of neutrality along the lines of its other neighbours, Finland and Sweden, which would be entirely reasonable were it not for the fact that they are already subverting eastern Ukraine.

Saturday 12 February

US government warning of 'imminent' Russian invasion of Ukraine. Embassies being evacuated. US and UK citizens being advised to leave. The Russians, meanwhile, say they have no such plans.

Wednesday 16 February

Prince Andrew has settled the long-running case being brought against him by an American woman who alleged she had been trafficked by the disgraced US financier Jeffrey Epstein, giving rise to the following ditty:

> The Grand old Duke of York,
> He paid 12 million quid,
> To someone he never met,
> For something he never did.

Friday 18 February

A new weevil is in the process of infiltrating the body politic – the Net Zero Scrutiny Group, made up of backbench Tory MPs. Its purpose being to persuade the government to abandon its recently proclaimed climate change commitments. So far only nineteen names are known. Needless to say, there is a considerable overlap with membership of the European Research Group, which has previously inflicted so much damage.

Sunday 20 February

The Queen has tested positive for Covid. The statement from the palace says, pointedly, that she 'will follow all the appropriate guidelines'.

Monday 21 February

Everything haywire. With only days to go until the hearing at the Old Bailey, the court now saying that the judge is unavailable for Thursday's session and that we may have to come back next week. Couldn't he sit for longer on Friday, I ask my lawyer? He laughs at my naivety. 'No, Chris. It doesn't work like that.' Later I hear that lawyers for West Midlands Police are applying for the case to be heard in secret. This evening the Russians annexed their two phoney 'breakaway' republics in Ukraine.

Tuesday 22 February

The airwaves are full of posturing politicians and the occasional retired general. 'Biggest crisis since Cuba,' say some. 'Biggest since 1945,' say others. Only the Ukrainians remain calm; they, after all, have lived with this situation for years. The real test would come if Putin were to attack the Baltic states and, fingers crossed, we are a long way from that.

Wednesday 23 February

To Gray's Inn for a meeting with my lawyers. West Midlands Police are retreating from their earlier suggestion that the hearing be in private. Actually, they have done us a favour. There is far more press interest now than there was two or three days ago. An alliance of media corporations including the *Mail* and *The Times* have hired a barrister to argue that the hearing should be in public. There is a possibility that it might be concluded in one day instead of the scheduled two. Counsel for the police is not interested in cross-examining any of our witnesses. A pity, I was looking forward to seeing him tangle with Charlie Falconer. The odds are that judgment will be reserved. I may be wrong, but I get the impression my lawyers are pessimistic. They seem to think we stand a better chance with the higher courts. 'It's eminently appealable,' remarked my esteemed Queen's Counsel, Gavin Millar, a veteran of many similar disputes. 'It could even go to Strasbourg,' he added with a glint in his eye. Oh please.

Thursday 24 February

The Russians have invaded Ukraine. Putin broadcast a deranged rant which only succeeded in illustrating the damage that twenty-two years of unbridled power can do to a man. The trouble is there is no one in Russia who is capable of saying 'no' to him and he has nukes. A dangerous moment. One wrong step and the whole of Europe could be sucked in.

Friday 25 February

To the Old Bailey, accompanied by Michelle Stanistreet, general secretary of the National Union of Journalists, which is paying my legal bill. I was last here thirty years ago on that memorable day when the Birmingham Six were released. Today a very different scene. No cheering crowds. No wall of cameras. Just three or four photographers and half a dozen NUJ activists with a banner and a few supportive placards. The first hour was taken up with representations from interested parties about whether to admit the press. In the end, common sense prevailed. It was agreed that the two men whose interviews are sought should be referred to only by letters of the alphabet. A low-key affair. No wigs, no histrionics. The tone was almost conversational. Much of the rest of the day was taken up with submissions. James Lewis QC for West Midlands Police, a mild-mannered man with a wispy, greying beard, took up most of the morning. In the afternoon it was our turn. The judge, a pleasant-looking man with impressive concentration, scarcely glanced at the court, focusing firmly on whoever had the floor and the documents before him, occasionally making notes on his computer.

The issue, although it has generated an enormous amount of paperwork and a certain amount of hot air, is fairly simple. Does the Terrorism Act 2000 give the police the power to oblige journalists to disclose their sources in a case involving terrorism? Although Jack Straw and Charlie Falconer, who saw the Act through Parliament, say that this was never their intention, it is not intention that counts. It is what the legislation actually says. Or at least what a judge believes it says. There are three main tests: first, does it involve serious terrorism? To which the answer is obviously 'yes'. And then the trickier ones: is the information sought likely to be of substantial value or is it a fishing expedition? And finally, and most important, is it in the public interest that I should be required to disclose, given the implications for investigative journalism? There are precedents, but none quite match my case. In truth, the law leaves the judge with a great deal of discretion.

Only two witnesses took the stand: Detective Constable Sutton, in whose name the West Midlands submission was made, and myself. My QC, Gavin Millar, used Detective Constable Sutton's appearance to dispose of a few canards. Were the police still alleging, as they did in their original submission, that I had lied about the existence of the original notebooks? Were they seriously suggesting that I had paid a clandestine visit to the Hull archive, where my papers are stored, and removed the documents the police are seeking? It turned out that they weren't. Another little retreat. When my turn came, I was expecting to be given a going-over by the mild-mannered Mr Lewis, but in fact I was only in the witness box for a few minutes. All he wanted to know was whether I was willing to name my sources and, of course, I wasn't. He asked the same question a couple of different ways, smiling gently as he did so. There was no argument. He had expected nothing less. As I left the court a couple of hours later, he wished me good luck.

Saturday 26 February

Ukraine dominates everything and the young President, Volodymyr Zelensky, is the hero of the hour, refusing to flee the capital, rallying his troops in the teeth of great odds, broadcasting eloquently to the world. 'I do not want my picture in your offices,' he told MPs soon after he was elected. 'The President is not an icon, an idol or a portrait. Hang your kids' photos instead and look at them each time you make a decision.' My kind of leader.

Sunday 27 February

The Russians are struggling in Ukraine. The one thing they have succeeded in doing is uniting the world against them. Germany, which was wavering, has cancelled the new gas pipeline, Russia has been cut out of the international banking system, the rouble is tumbling and interest rates have doubled. Even China has distanced itself from the invasion.

Monday 28 February

Lunch with Stephen Frears at our old haunt, Carluccio's on St Pancras Station. The great man, who is eighty, says he has more work than ever. His next project is likely to be a drama about the sub-postmasters whose lives were ruined by the refusal of the Post Office to admit its computers were up the creek. A scandal of some magnitude.

Tuesday 1 March

A forty-mile column of Russian tanks and other vehicles is said to be heading for Kyiv. Only a question of time till those poor brave souls are overwhelmed by their monstrous neighbour.

Wednesday 2 March

Forlorn talk of finding a 'golden bridge' enabling Putin to declare victory and withdraw without too much loss of face. Loath though one is to appease the tyrant, there is one obvious potential compromise: Ukraine could abandon its ambition to join NATO in return for being allowed to join the EU. A long shot, and maybe this is not the moment, but it may come to this in the end. The Ukrainians may also have to surrender territory in the Russian-dominated east.

Thursday 3 March

A million Ukrainians have crossed the borders into Poland and Hungary. Meanwhile the Russian blitzkrieg continues. As in Syria, the shelling and bombing is indiscriminate. The first city has fallen; Kyiv and Kharkiv are almost encircled. Another mad rant by Putin.

The National Union of Journalists has made me an honorary life member.

Saturday 5 March

Two weeks since the Russian invasion of Ukraine and gradually, ruthlessly, brutally, the net is tightening. Almost the entire Black Sea coast is in now in Russian hands. Yesterday a stray rocket came close to hitting a nuclear power station. Ukraine's brave young President is agitating for NATO to impose a no-fly zone over his country, but direct conflict with Russia is a road no one – outside of Ukraine – wants to go down. How isolated Putin looks. He seems to have little or no direct contact with any other human beings, preferring to do business remotely. When, occasionally, he is pictured in the company of others, he is at the far end of a ludicrously long table. In Russia itself almost all dissent has been suppressed. Yesterday the puppet Russian Parliament unanimously passed a resolution threatening anyone who spreads (in the words of Donald Trump) 'fake news' with up to fifteen years in prison. As a result most independent media outlets have been snuffed out.

Sunday 6 March

Today I did something for the last time. I got on my bicycle, which hasn't been ridden for seven years, and cycled out through the north gate, through the lanes to Whittingham and back via the South Lodge. A circuit of about four miles. In a week or two I propose to donate it to the bicycle recycling shop in Durham and that will be that.

Monday 7 March

It seems I am not the only one sceptical about NATO's eastward expansion. One doesn't have to look far to find foreign policy heavyweights who warned against it from the outset. George Kennan, architect of the cold war strategy of containment, described it at the time as 'a fateful error'. The respected US political commentator Thomas Friedman said it was 'the most ill-conceived project of the post-Cold War era'. Senator Daniel Patrick Moynihan remarked, 'We have no idea what we are getting ourselves into.' And Bill Clinton's Defense Secretary William Perry wrote in his memoirs that he nearly resigned over it.

Tuesday 8 March

Spare a thought for the wretched Afghans: they will be the biggest casualties of Putin's wicked invasion of Ukraine. The world can only concentrate on one disaster at a time. Ukraine is much closer to home and, besides, they look like us. Afghans are going to starve in their hundreds of thousands.

Thursday 10 March

Yesterday the Russians bombed a maternity hospital in Mariupol.

Friday 11 March

A message from 'Team Labour', part of a drive to recruit election candidates: 'Chris, have you ever wondered what it is like to be a Labour MP?'

Saturday 12 March

No doubt with one eye on a future Tory leadership election, Jeremy Hunt, whom I have always thought of as one of the more credible of the current crop of Tories, has called (in the *Telegraph*, where else?) for a 'massive' increase in defence spending. Many of the readers' comments are predictable ('foreign aid budget needs to go as a starter'), but one or two are surprisingly sensible: 'You have to say how you will pay for it…', 'Someone should write a list of the fantastic ways in which the Ministry of Defence wastes money. I'll start the ball rolling with £3 billion on Ajax tanks that don't work…'.

Monday 14 March

A message from a friend of Ngoc's in Brussels, a highly intelligent man who speaks maybe ten languages and once worked for the Canadian government refugee programme in Saigon. He says that he and his wife have packed their bags and are ready, in the event a nuclear strike is threatened, to get as far away as possible. What times we live in.

Wednesday 16 March

Ukrainian President Zelensky says negotiations with Russia are 'beginning to sound more realistic'. By evening, however, the Russians had bombed a theatre in the besieged city of Mariupol where a thousand people are said to be sheltering.

Monday 21 March

To Rothbury, where I gave a talk about my novels to members of the Coquetdale U3A, and then to London on the 1 p.m. train.

Tuesday 22 March

Judgment Day. People keep asking if I am worried, but I am calm. If we lose, we will appeal and the judges higher up the pecking order are likely to be friendlier than those at the Old Bailey, although thus far I have no reason to doubt the wisdom of Judge Lucraft. As before, I meet up with Louis, my solicitor, at Caffé Nero next to St Paul's Tube Station. He greets me with a broad smile and a thumbs-up. Unknown to me, the judgment has already been circulated to the lawyers – and we have won. We are sworn to secrecy, however, until judgment is formally delivered. So it is with straight faces that we make our way to the Old Bailey, past waiting cameras and a gaggle of journalists. This time we are in Court 10. The atmosphere is relaxed. The clerk smiles at us. Everyone except the journalists already knows the outcome. 'The court will be upstanding,' cries the usher, a blonde woman who takes her job very seriously. We stand. The judge enters. His judgment covers twenty pages, but the key sentence is in paragraph nine: 'I decline to grant the production order sought.' The judge departs. A big man asks to shake my hand. It is Dave Cook, the West Midlands Police officer with whom I was liaising for some time before they threw the book at me. 'Nothing personal,' he says. No indeed. I don't think the police will be appealing. They have already wasted quite enough taxpayers' money as it is. I suspect the chief constable was merely trying to get the victims' families off his back and on to mine. Even had he been successful, it wouldn't have made any difference. There is nothing in my notes that will enable a prosecution of the culprit.

Outside I read a brief and hopefully dignified statement to the waiting cameras. This is not an occasion for popping champagne corks. Beyond the professional classes there will be no public sympathy for my allegedly heroic stand. Within minutes the Twitter abuse starts to flow. The word 'scum' features frequently. 'You have as much blood on your hands as the actual murderer,' says one. 'He is as evil as the bombers,' says another.

Wednesday 23 March

I featured briefly on last night's news bulletins, but already attention is beginning to wane. Reports in today's papers are confined to inside pages. Predictably, only *The Guardian* shows any sign of excitement. Our free press is easily bored. Now that everything is broadcast online as it happens, most stories are regarded as old news by next morning. I suppose I would have had to be sent down to have aroused any serious interest.

Thursday 24 March

Well, well. A *Times* reporter has been in touch with Geoffrey Dear, the former West Midlands chief constable who once poured scorn on the idea that the wrong people had been convicted of the pub bombings and even went so far as to allege that those of us who took a different view were working with the IRA. In recent years Dear, now in the Lords, has kept his head well below the parapet, but it was high time he was smoked out. I expected him to maintain his silence, but not so. Instead he has responded with the following bald little statement: 'Although I and others saw Mr Mullin as an irrelevance and an irritation at the time, we were all proved wrong and he was proved right.' Some distance short of an apology. Damage limitation rather than repentance, but, hey, one can't have everything.

Tuesday 29 March

At Westminster Abbey a memorial service for the Duke of Edinburgh. Much speculation about whether the Queen, who is increasingly frail, would be well enough to attend, but in the event she was there, entering through a side door to avoid the long walk up the aisle. One commentator remarked that this may be one of the last occasions she is seen in public.

Monday 4 April

Ukrainian forces have re-entered a town north-west of Kyiv recently abandoned by the Russians. The streets are littered with bodies, some of whom appear to have been executed in cold blood. A mass grave has also been uncovered. Similar reports from other recently occupied towns. President Biden is calling for war crimes trials. All very well, but there is no prospect of Putin being arraigned at The Hague. War crimes trials are for little losers, not big ones.

A card from Hugh Callaghan, the lovely old gent who, aged ninety-two, is the oldest of the Birmingham Six. He writes, 'You worked so hard for us. I will never forget,' and encloses two £20 notes for 'a celebration drink', which I will donate to the Médecins Sans Frontières Afghan appeal.

Tuesday 5 April

For the first time, talk of supplying the Ukrainians with tanks, artillery and even fighter planes. On the radio this morning, a cautious retired general saying we need to think carefully where this is leading.

Friday 8 April

The latest horror from Ukraine: a Russian shell has landed on a crowded railway station, killing at least forty people who were waiting to be evacuated and seriously injuring many others. Tragic pictures of a platform scattered with the unclaimed luggage of the dead and injured, some obviously belonging to children.

Saturday 9 April

Our saintly Chancellor appears to have been holed below the waterline by the revelation that his Indian wife is a non-dom who stands to avoid paying tax on an inheritance that may one day be worth hundreds of millions. He is or was until recently also the holder of a US green card. Rather looks as if the golden couple just stopped over in the UK to govern us for a few years en route to California.

Wednesday 13 April

Yet another confected hoo-ha over the news that both Boris Johnson and his wife are among those fined for their presence at an impromptu birthday celebration involving a cake which, we are told, never left its Tupperware box and four cans of beer which remained unopened. It is painful to hear opposition spokespersons straining to sound indignant at a time when there is so much else to be upset about. Yet again distraught relatives of those who died alone during lockdown are being paraded before microphones in a cynical bid to make the offence sound worse than it was. Actually, this is among the least of Johnson's many sins. So far as one can tell, he had no notice of the event – as with the wallpaper, Carrie seems to have been the instigator. All the same, he is not yet out of the woods. Just one more Partygate fine could bring him down.

Meanwhile Joe Biden, increasingly reckless in his use of words, is talking genocide in Ukraine.

Thursday 14 April

Another ominous little straw in the wind. Nuclear weapons storage facilities at Lakenheath, which have been empty since 2008, are being upgraded in preparation for the return of US missiles.

Friday 15 April

> When a regime has been in power too long, when it has fatally exhausted the patience of the people, and when oblivion finally beckons – I am afraid that across the world you can rely on the leaders of that regime to act solely in the interests of self-preservation, and not in the interests of the electorate.

Guess who? Boris Johnson, writing in the *Telegraph*, February 2011.

Sunday 17 April

Priti Patel's latest wheeze, a hare-brained scheme to resettle asylum seekers in Rwanda, is attracting widespread derision, but the indignation of the righteous conceals an unpalatable truth. No one has the slightest idea how to stem the flow of migrants from the growing number of failed and failing states which, in the long run, has the capacity to bring down our fragile social systems and is driving our politics ever further to the right.

Tuesday 19 April

Starmer on devastating form today. The Tories looked miserable because they know that what he is saying is true. The skids finally seem to be under Johnson.

A visit to My Learned Friend John Field, who is off to Italy next week and has just booked himself into an expensive hotel in Mantua. 'As someone brought up in the era of post-war thrift,' he says, 'it has taken me eighty years to realise two things: one doesn't always have to be busy and one can occasionally spend money on oneself.'

Wednesday 20 April

Foreigners seem nonplussed by the fuss over 'Partygate'. 'Were there hookers?' enquired one bemused American.

Sunday 24 April

The Ukraine rhetoric grows steadily more extreme. For weeks now poor Zelensky has been accusing the Russians of genocide, a charge echoed by some Western politicians, including Joe Biden. Today Zelensky called the Russian regime 'Nazi'. Understandable given the pressure he is under and the ruin the Russians have brought upon his country, but in truth what is happening is awful enough without the need to exaggerate. In the circumstances, I cut Zelensky a lot of slack, but his supporters in the West have less excuse.

Monday 25 April

My neighbour Tony Henfrey has a friend in Denmark who lives close to the motorway that leads into Poland via Germany. Tony's friend reports that the road is clogged with huge quantities of American weaponry bound for Ukraine. Slowly but surely, the war is becoming a proxy conflict between the US and Russia. It could easily morph into a European war. To quote Chairman Mao, a single spark could light a prairie fire.

Thursday 28 April

Some of our leaders appear to be revelling in the Ukraine crisis. Foreign Secretary Liz Truss talks of 'doubling down' and restoring Ukraine's previous territorial integrity, which, as some have pointed out, would require Russia's unconditional surrender. A recipe for a long war, if ever there was one. Boris Johnson has also been indulging in war rhetoric, which of course has the benefit of distracting attention from his domestic woes. As Simon Jenkins said in yesterday's *Guardian*, 'The burning issue is not the awfulness of war. It is what can be done to stop it.'

Friday 29 April

A Tory has been caught watching porn on his phone in the House of

Commons chamber. Why on earth are MPs allowed to play with their phones in the chamber? It is supposed to be a forum for debate. If I were Speaker, I'd ban them.

Saturday 30 April

A growing air of decay increasingly reminiscent of the great 'sleaze' crisis of the mid-'90s. Neil Parish, the Tory MP caught watching porn, resigned today, thereby triggering what promises to be yet another tricky by-election despite a majority of 24,000. Each day brings a new crisis. Another Tory Member has been arrested after crashing his car into a lamp post and fleeing the scene. Meanwhile Boris Johnson is still deeply embroiled in Partygate, which could reignite at any moment. And yet, despite everything, I struggle to see how Labour can form a majority government, as long as the Nationalists continue to hoover up the Labour vote in Scotland.

Friday 6 May

Yesterday's local elections were not quite the Tory wipeout that some had been predicting. Labour did well in London, winning Barnet, Westminster and Wandsworth, but the so-called Red Wall seats remain surly. We ended up with 35 per cent of the vote while the Tories are on 30 and the Lib Dems on 19. Since most of the difference is accounted for by Tory midterm abstentions, it is unlikely that this will translate into a Labour government at a general election, although a hung parliament with Labour as the largest party is just about conceivable. Meanwhile Durham Police, after considerable prompting from the *Daily Mail*, have announced they are reopening their investigation into so-called 'Beergate', the allegation that Keir Starmer took part in an informal social event during the Covid lockdown following an afternoon's canvassing in Hartlepool. Starmer naturally denies all, but the announcement neatly turns the tables. Attempts to celebrate yesterday's local election gains were interrupted by shouts of 'Will you resign if you are fined?'

Saturday 7 May

Starmer has announced that, if fined, he will resign. What else could he say, given the fuss he has made about Johnson? Either a master stroke or a massive own goal. His fate – and perhaps Labour's – is now in the hands of Durham Constabulary.

Tuesday 10 May

The State Opening of Parliament. The Queen absent for the first time in more than fifty years.

Sunday 15 May

Home, after a visit to Orkney, to find the blue and yellow flag of Ukraine fluttering from the flagpole on the roof of the big house, courtesy of my neighbour Tony Henfrey. The flag of Ukraine has become a familiar sight in the past few weeks, in every town and village, in gardens great and small. A pleasant change from that ghastly cross of St George so beloved by English nationalists.

Wednesday 18 May

A man came to repair the shower. A former soldier, he'd served eight years in the Coldstream Guards. 'It may not be the general view,' he said, 'but I blame NATO expansionism for the war in Ukraine.'

Thursday 19 May

The Metropolitan Police have declared that their Partygate investigation is at an end. To general surprise and some disappointment, with the exception of the one fine they have already received, Boris Johnson and his wife are in the clear. All the same, 126 fines delivered to a single address in Whitehall, which also happens to be the place where the lockdown rules were made, is not a good look. For time being, however, Johnson is off the hook. Only Sir Keir remains in the frame. Oh the irony, were he to be the sole casualty.

Tuesday 24 May

The pit gets deeper. A photo has emerged, taken at a lockdown leaving party in Downing Street, showing our Prime Minister alongside a table littered with open wine bottles and other detritus, raising a glass to a departing colleague. Although, remarkably, his attendance at the event doesn't seem to have attracted the attention of the Met, the photo is destined to become one of the defining images of the Johnson era. Increasingly we resemble Berlusconi's Italy.

Wednesday 25 May

At last, Sue Gray's report. An anti-climax after so long a wait, but she illuminates a culture of partying and impunity in the heart of government which carried on shamelessly throughout the various Covid lockdowns. She talks blandly of 'failures of leadership' at the centre, 'both political and official'. Actually, it is officials rather than politicians who come out worst. They appear to have been well aware that much of this activity was in defiance of the lockdown rules. One internal message talks of 'not waving wine bottles around' while TV cameras were on the premises (the cameras in question were presumably there for a Covid briefing). Another talks of 'just about having got away with it', while yet another suggests that inviting 200 people to drinks in the No. 10 garden is 'somewhat of a comms risk in the current environment'. On occasion the partying went on far into the night under the noses of the cleaning and security staff, who were treated with disdain. And get this: at one event a karaoke machine was supplied by Sue Gray's successor, now a Deputy Cabinet Secretary. The most curious incident, which Ms Gray does not attempt to unravel, was an 'Abba-themed party' hosted by Carrie Symonds in the Downing Street flat which appears to have been celebrating the departure of Dominic Cummings. This afternoon, yet another brazen statement from the Lord of Chaos, professing humility and asserting that as team leader he was under an obligation to show his face at leaving parties for No. 10 staff. The official line is that, reprehensible though it may have been, all this is now in the past and an entirely different culture now prevails.

Tomorrow Chancellor Sunak is expected to announce a major spending splurge, the timing of which suggests it is designed to take our minds off other matters.

Thursday 26 May

Right on cue, Chancellor Sunak has announced another enormous bout of public spending to address the steep rise in the cost of living, particularly fuel prices. The package includes a windfall tax – or, as he delicately put it, 'an energy profit levy' (cf. Putin's 'Special Military Operation') – to which, until recently, the government and most Tory MPs were opposed. There are to be cash payments to every household, rich or poor, and extra for those in the greatest need. Two ways of looking at this: either a reasonable response to events beyond our control by a pragmatic, responsible Chancellor or a massive attempt to buy back votes by a party in deep political trouble. The cynics naturally take the latter view, neatly summarised in the following tweet from the makers of the BBC's *Have I Got News For You*: 'Vatican investigates possible miracle as UK government inexplicably finds £10 billion for energy bills just 24 hours after the Sue Gray report.' Either way, most opposition foxes have been shot for the time being.

Wednesday 1 June

A friend whose daughter used to work in the Cabinet Office reports that she described it as being full of entitled youths 'who thought they knew everything and in fact knew nothing'. Apparently they used to hold weekly parties known as 'champagne Fridays'.

Thursday 2 June

The jubilee. Yet more public holidays, fly-pasts, parades, street parties, flaming beacons, obsequious interviews. The tabloids have gone into overdrive. Predictably, the *Express* is the most servile – 'A Grateful Nation Salutes You, Ma'am'. Floating above it all, these days only occasionally glimpsed, the subject of this four-day jamboree. Radiant, cheerful, inscrutable. A feature of our lives for as long as most of us can remember. One of my earliest memories is watching the coronation on a neighbour's 9in. black and white telly, specially acquired for the occasion. Not long afterwards the Queen was driven past my primary school in London Road, Chelmsford, and we all had to go out and wave. I am now aged seventy-four, going on seventy-five, and she is still here, reigning benignly over us. Universally respected, if not always loved, having presided, albeit remotely, over an era of unprecedented prosperity and relative stability. How has she managed to navigate decades of social change, including various upheavals in her own family, and emerge unscathed? It is said that her father advised her to choose her words carefully because, when she became Queen, everyone she met would remember whatever she said to them for the rest of their lives. A lesson she appears to have taken to heart. In public at least, Elizabeth II has rarely said anything memorable. 'Have you come far?' 'For me? How kind,' are often the extent of her unscripted exchanges with ordinary mortals. Prime Ministers have remarked how well informed she is, but there is little known evidence. Dogs and horses are the only things that appear to excite her. And this strategy, if that is what it is, appears to have paid off. Just occasionally one glimpses evidence that behind that apparently bland exterior there lurks a sense of mischief, not to mention withering sarcasm. 'Someone important?' she enquired when Clare Short's pager went off during a Privy Council audience. And my favourite: the alleged reply from the palace to Margaret Thatcher's suggestion, after they appeared together in colours which clashed, that in future perhaps their private offices should liaise in order to avoid it happening again: 'Her Majesty does not notice what other people are wearing.' Would we be happier or better off if, as some suggest, we dispensed with the fairy tale and replaced the monarchy with a President Blair or Heseltine? Somehow I don't think so. Best leave well alone. After all, we are not short of bigger issues to worry about.

Friday 3 June

After two brief appearances yesterday, the Queen did not attend today's service in her honour at St Paul's. She is said to be suffering 'discomfort'. As to the nature of this discomfort, official statements are remarkably coy and our free press remarkably unenquiring.

This, by the way, is an extract from the lesson from St Paul's letter to the Philippians which Boris Johnson was asked to read at the service: 'Do nothing from selfish ambition or conceit, but in humility regard others as better than yourselves. Let each of you look not to your own interests but to the interest of others.' Someone up there has a sense of humour.

Sunday 5 June

HM has taken part in an amusing little skit with Paddington Bear, which some wag has amended by inserting speech bubbles. 'Would you like some tea, Ma'am?' enquires Paddington, leaning across the table, teapot in hand. To which HM replies, 'No. I'd like you to form a government.'

Monday 6 June

Down to earth with a bump. It was announced this morning that Tory MPs are to hold a vote of confidence in Boris Johnson. Within minutes up pops Sajid Javid, who will no doubt be a contender, pledging his un-wavering support. If you listen carefully, you can hear the cock crowing… Johnson, incidentally, won the vote, but the uprising was substantial. Much bigger than predicted. I'd be surprised if he sees out the year. Surely there must come a moment when the Tory Party regains its self-respect, if only for electoral purposes.

Thursday 16 June

The European Court of Human Rights has kiboshed Priti Patel's 'world-beating' plan to send asylum seekers to be processed in Rwanda. Yes, it's those dreaded Europeans again, although this one can't be blamed on the EU, since the convention is separate from the EU. And far from the Europeans having imposed it on us, we drafted it and persuaded them to sign up to it way back in 1951. But no matter, it's set off all the usual sus-pects. Meanwhile Allister Heath in today's *Telegraph* rages that, despite Brexit, Britain is still under the thumb of a left-wing elite. And this after twelve years of Tory government, with no end in sight.

Monday 20 June

A BBC interview with the chief of Britain's armed forces, General Sir Patrick Sanders. 'There is now', he says, 'a burning imperative to forge an army capable of fighting alongside our allies and defeating Russia in battle. We are the generation that must prepare the army to fight in Europe once again.' And NATO secretary general Jens Stoltenberg has told a German newspaper that the war in Ukraine could last for years. War without end. Talk of 'defeating' Russia. Where, oh where, are we heading?

On the home front, meanwhile, the teachers' union is gearing up to follow the rail workers' union into battle with a demand for a 12 per cent pay increase. Others will no doubt follow. All we need next is for the bin men to strike and then we will be back in the '70s.

Wednesday 22 June

To London via the annual meeting of the National Park Authority in Hexham. This evening to the *Prospect* summer party in Queen Anne's Gate, where I came across a reincarnated Jonathan Aitken, complete with dog collar and clerical garb, deep in conversation with his nemesis, former *Guardian* editor Alan Rusbridger. A funny old world.

Friday 24 June

The Tories have lost the Tiverton by-election to the Liberals on a swing of more than 30 per cent, said to be the largest ever against a sitting government. They have also lost Wakefield to Labour on a much lower swing and a very low turnout. The Tory chairman has resigned. Pressure on Boris Johnson grows, but he shows no sign of getting the message.

Saturday 25 June

This evening with the beautiful Emma Mullin to the Rolling Stones concert in Hyde Park, thereby fulfilling a lifelong ambition. We stood for four hours in a crowd of 50,000 people of all ages. By the end I could no longer feel my feet. Mick Jagger, aged seventy-eight, shows no sign of slowing down, cavorting around the stage, arms flailing, twirling his jacket around his head, while the crowd rocked and rolled more or less in time with the music. Only the young folk looked on bemused, not realising that they are in the presence of greatness.

Sunday 26 June

Boris Johnson has sent word from Rwanda, where he is attending the

Commonwealth conference, that he is aiming to go on indefinitely. A provocation if ever there was one. This evening back to Hyde Park with My Two Best Friends for an Eagles concert. A more sedate affair. None of Jagger's antics. Just gents of a certain age playing a selection of their greatest hits. The beauty of the Eagles is that their lyrics have a coherent narrative and the words make sense, which can't always be said of the Stones. 'Our mission', said lead singer Don Henley, 'is to offer you two hours remission from all the terrible things that are happening in the world. It's not that we don't care, but they will still be there in the morning.' For the second night running, a golden sunset. In the distance, every sixty seconds or so, a plane cruising silently across a clear blue sky towards Heathrow as the light faded, distinguished only by a flashing red tail light.

Tuesday 5 July

As Tony Blair once observed, British politics has become a game of gotcha. No day passes without some new scandal, real and alleged. The latest concerns the aptly named Chris Pincher, the government's Deputy Chief Whip, who has been obliged to resign after being accused of groping colleagues. Turns out he has previous form. Naturally Johnson denies knowing this, but this morning comes a damning letter from Simon McDonald, former Permanent Secretary at the Foreign Office, saying that Johnson was well aware of Mr Pincher's track record. Yet another ruinous by-election beckons. For how much longer can this go on? The regime is disintegrating before our eyes. Labour's role is confined to sitting on the sidelines, shouting, 'Ya boo.'

This evening, a new bombshell. Chancellor Rishi Sunak and Health Secretary Sajid Javid have resigned. Johnson, as ever, has vowed to fight on, but surely this is the end.

Wednesday 6 July

Resignations are coming in thick and fast. By noon thirty ministers and other office holders had gone. By nightfall the toll exceeded forty. From most of those who remain, an eerie silence. Nadine Dorries and Jacob Rees-Mogg are the only Cabinet members still prepared to go on record in defence of their leader. This evening Michael Gove was summarily dismissed after telling Johnson that he should go. A 'Downing Street source' described Gove as 'a snake'. That's something we can all agree on.

Thursday 7 July

7 a.m.: the list of the lately departed now stands at forty-eight. Their resignation letters are full of words like 'integrity' and 'competence'. Something they should have thought about when they chose this rogue to lead their party. It's not as though they didn't know.

12 noon: resignations in total now exceed fifty, including six members of the Cabinet.

12.30: it's over. Or is it? Boris Johnson, bullish, unrepentant, emerges from the front door of No. 10 and announces his resignation. But not just yet. He will stay until a successor is chosen, which could be as late as October.

Friday 8 July

The Office for Budget Responsibility has said the current level of debt is unsustainable and warned against unfunded tax cuts. This comes as candidates for the Tory leadership, urged on by their friends in the media, are entering a bidding war on tax cuts. The idea that these guys are better able to manage the economy than anyone else is bunkum.

Durham Police have cleared Keir Starmer and Angela Rayner of breaking the lockdown rules.

Saturday 9 July

A much-tweeted picture shows a woman in a bright yellow frock leaving Downing Street after being appointed a junior minister in the Education department giving the waiting crowd a middle-finger salute, which, as someone commented, is fast becoming the defining image of the modern Conservative Party.

Sunday 10 July

Today's headlines:

'Javid and Hunt call for massive tax cuts' (*Telegraph*)
'Liz Truss: I'll spike Sunak's tax hike' (*Mail*)
'Tories tear themselves apart over tax' (*Sunday Times*)

Over the next few weeks we are destined to hear a great deal about restoring integrity to government. One way of doing so would be to stop making irresponsible promises about tax.

Monday 11 July

Soon time to pull stumps. I feel no elation at this latest turn of events. It does not follow that Johnson's removal will excise the cancer from our increasingly febrile politics. Despite the government's present woes, it is hard to see how Labour can form a majority government without seats in Scotland, and that requires the implosion of the Nationalists, of which thus far there is no sign. They will also need some distinctive policies, and there is no sign of those either.

As for me, I am in reasonable health. With average good fortune I might expect another ten years. Even so, the shadows grow longer. I have a box file in which I store funeral notices and obituaries of late friends. It is full to overflowing. Lately I have had to open a second box. Although there are unlikely to be any more diaries after this volume, I do have some remaining literary ambitions: a book of essays and perhaps a slim collection of short stories. What I dread, above all, is having nothing useful to do. Running out of ideas. Waking up day after day to an empty diary. What is the point of life except to be useful? I am sure the Queen feels the same.

Wednesday 13 July

A new distinction has entered the political lexicon, courtesy of the Tory leadership election campaign. There are tax cutters and 'instinctive' tax cutters. Those who would slash taxes immediately tend to be some distance from power, whereas those such as Rishi Sunak who actually stand a chance of having to implement their promises are 'instinctive', which seems to mean actually increasing taxes while proclaiming their love of lower taxes.

Thursday 14 July

Candidates for the Tory leadership are now whittled down to five. By early next week there will be just two, whose names will be put to the elderly, wealthy, white membership, who dwell predominantly in the Home Counties.

Sunday 17 July

Amusing to watch candidates for the Tory leadership tearing lumps out of each other. Everyone except Rishi Sunak is demanding unfunded tax cuts and being denounced by Sunak as proponents of 'something-for-nothing economics'. Jeremy Corbyn, it appears, was not the only believer in the magic money tree.

Monday 18 July

A heatwave. Today's temperatures in the thirties. A record 40° in some parts is predicted for tomorrow. Elsewhere in Europe – Croatia, France, Greece, Italy, Portugal – huge wildfires. One would like to think this will focus minds on global warming, but it hasn't stopped candidates for the Tory leadership suggesting we should abandon the targets to which we only recently signed up at the Glasgow climate summit. Alok Sharma, the minister who presided at Glasgow, is threatening to resign if we do.

Tuesday 19 July

As predicted, the temperature across much of the country exceeded 40°, easily breaking previous records. Something that was not expected to happen for another twenty-five years. The bulletins are full heatwave mayhem. In Northumberland we scraped by on a mere 30°.

Wednesday 20 July

Tory leadership candidates now down to two: Sunak and Truss.

Monday 25 July

'Who will you be voting for?' I enquired of my neighbour Tony Henfrey, one of that small elite who will choose our next Prime Minister. 'Neither of the above,' he replied.

Thursday 28 July
Euphonia, Upper Street, Islington

Breakfast with Andrew Mitchell, who says, 'Boris is like the James Bond villain who quits the sinking craft in his escape pod, stroking his white cat, leaving the rest of us to clear up.' Which is more or less what is happening.

Friday 5 August

The *New Statesman* has obtained an extraordinary video clip of Rishi Sunak speaking to a gathering of Conservative Party members in a large garden in Tunbridge Wells, actually boasting of redistributing local government funding from the poor to the wealthy. These are his words:

> I managed to start changing the funding formulas, to make sure areas like this are getting the funding that they deserve. We inherited a bunch of formulas from the Labour Party which shoved all the funding into deprived urban areas. That needed to be undone. I started the work of undoing it…

Monday 8 August

One of my Tory neighbours complains that foreigners seem to have bought up much of our infrastructure as a result of privatisation. 'I suppose you blame Margaret Thatcher,' she said. Well yes, actually, I do.

Wednesday 10 August

A big crisis brewing over energy prices. Average gas bills on course to exceed £4,000 per household by early next year, threatening several million of our poorest citizens with destitution, and yet our masters, preoccupied as they are, have little or nothing to say on the subject.

Thursday 11 August

The heatwave is in its second month. Temperatures in the high twenties or low thirties. Much of southern Europe ablaze. In Germany, the Rhine is becoming impassable.

Sunday 14 August

A summer like no other. Work in the garden only possible in the early morning or evening, while the shadows linger. Between times, one can only sit and read, following the shade around the garden. A drought has been declared across much of southern England and the Midlands. The north-east still has a plentiful supply of water thanks to the Kielder reservoir, at least until the water companies find a way of diverting our water to fill swimming pools and sprinkle lawns in the Home Counties. Our water comes from a spring on the hill which thus far, touch wood, shows no sign of drying up.

Tuesday 16 August

The UK at the moment seems to have become an ungoverned space. While the nation frets about the upcoming cost-of-living crisis, our masters are preoccupied with their leadership election. Boris Johnson appears to have gone AWOL. He has recently been spotted on a beach in Greece and is planning to spend his remaining time in office chilling at Chequers. Meanwhile the mice do play. Nadhim Zahawi, our stop-gap Chancellor, has hired a luminary from the TaxPayers' Alliance to, as the *Telegraph* puts it, 'shake the tree at the Treasury'.

The weather has broken. Grey drizzle all day. In the space of two days the temperature has halved.

Saturday 20 August

Matthew Parris on Liz Truss in today's *Times*: 'Intellectually shallow, her convictions wafer thin…' He says that, despite a tendency by politicians and commentators to give winners the benefit of the doubt, first impressions are usually right. 'Save yourself the detour. She's crackers. It isn't going to work.'

Sunday 21 August

Who would want to be Prime Minister, faced, as we seem to be, with meltdown on all fronts? The Twitterati are circulating pictures of sewage pouring onto beaches, courtesy of our overpaid and underinvested privatised water companies, a fitting metaphor for the current state of the nation. Inflation is 10 per cent and rising. Vegetables are rotting in the fields because no one wants to pick them, many of the Eastern Europeans who formerly did the job having gone home in the wake of Brexit. Not for the first time, the NHS is talking collapse, with beds blocked and ambulances queuing for hours outside hospitals. Rail workers have been striking on and off for weeks. Today it was announced that workers at Felixstowe container port have turned down an offer of a 7 per cent increase plus a £500 bonus and opted instead for a strike. Meanwhile all the Tories, bogged down in their interminable leadership election, want to talk about is tax cuts and deregulation.

Tuesday 30 August

Mikhail Gorbachev, one of the great men of the twentieth century, has died, aged ninety-one.

Thursday 1 September

One third of Pakistan is under water, supposedly a once-in-a-century event but in fact a repeat of what happened as recently as 2010.

Monday 5 September

As expected, Liz Truss is the Chosen One. Tomorrow she will be anointed Prime Minister, our fourth in six years (we are becoming like Italy). Intellectually and perhaps morally, this marks a new low in British politics. Another step on the UK's long, gradual slide towards insularity and irrelevance.

Tuesday 6 September

Liz Truss flew to Balmoral to be anointed by the Queen, who is looking radiant but very fragile.

Thursday 8 September

Just after 12.30, a statement from the palace: 'The Queen's doctors are concerned for Her Majesty's health and have recommended she remain under medical supervision.' Widely interpreted as meaning that she is dying. Members of the family are reportedly travelling to Balmoral. The BBC has abandoned scheduled programming. This is a very big moment. I never thought I would, but I feel quite emotional.

Early this evening another statement: 'The Queen died peacefully at Balmoral this afternoon.' Amen.

Acknowledgements

Above all, I must thank my meticulous editor at Biteback, Olivia Beattie, who has rescued me from many a faux pas. Also Ruth Winstone, editor of my three previous volumes and who cast her eye over this one before it was offered for publication.

I also take this opportunity to remember some of the dear friends I have lost during the period covered by this volume: Martin and Mori Woollacott, whose generous hospitality at their beautiful house in Church Row, Hampstead, I enjoyed on many occasions. Ray Fitzwalter, sometime editor of *World in Action*, but for whom I would never have found the resources to investigate one of our most notorious miscarriages of justice, the Birmingham Six case. My brave friend Patricia Moberly, who lived a life of selfless public service and remained cheerful to the end. And John Williams, with whom I walked the length and breadth of Britain, who died in December 2022. I used to think he was immortal, but alas he proved not to be.

Finally, I hope that one day, after I am long gone, my children Sarah and Emma might dip into this and earlier diaries and remember their boring old dad with a smile.

Chris Mullin
April 2023

Index

'CM' indicates Chris Mullin. PM refers to
    Prime Minister.

A Walk-On Part (Chaplin play) 10, 16
Aaron (anti-racist tweeter) 463–4
Aaronovitch, David 296
Abbaye de Camon, Ariège 194
Abbott, Diane 41, 177
Abramsky, Jenny 8, 41
Active Northumberland 152
Adams, Gerry 42
Adie, Kate 221
Adonis, Andrew 308, 428
Afghanistan 228, 235, 388, 390, 489–91, 498, 500,
    517, 525, 528
Ahmed-Sheikh, Tasmina 99
Ainsworth, Bob 22
Aitken, Jonathan 538
Al Jazeera 223, 467, 471
Alderley Edge, Cheshire 19–22
Alexander, Danny 74, 89, 125
Alexander, Douglas 97, 219
Alexander, Heidi 165
Alnwick, Northumberland 56, 287
Alnwick Playhouse 64, 75
Amess, David 496
Ancram, Michael 485
Andrew Marr Show (BBC) 98, 148, 201, 222, 269,
    353, 388
Andrew, Prince 376, 515, 520
Andy and Sarah (walkers) 313
Antony House, Cornwall 313
Any Questions (BBC) 27, 36
Armistice Day 314–15
Arnold, P. P. 342

Article 50 199–200, 215, 357
Ashcroft, Lord 30, 40, 50, 132
Ashdown, Paddy 315, 320
Ashley, Jane 29
Ashworth, Jonathan 381
Assad, Bashar al- 139–40, 227
Assange, Julian 508
Astor, Lady 492
Astor, Lord 196
AstraZeneca vaccine 457
Atherton, Mike 14
Atomic Energy Authority, International 255
Attlee, Clement 297–8, 306, 328
Auckland Castle, Bishop Auckland 88, 102, 105
Australia 385
Austria 170, 249
Aye Write festival, Glasgow 334

Bailey, Andrew 442
Bailey, Colin 63
Bailey, Ric 372–3
Bailey, Shaun 509
Baker-Cresswell, Barbara 295–6
Baker-Cresswell, Charles 55, 64, 103
Baker, Kenneth 25, 129, 194
Baker, Steve 354
Bakewell, Joan 30
Balls, Ed 34–5, 42, 58, 62, 97, 202, 210
Bangkok, Thailand 329
Bangladesh 250, 251
Bank of England 188, 359, 421, 442
banking industry 102, 469
Banks, David and Gemma 249
Banks, Sally 100, 129, 164
Barcelona, Spain 246

Barclay, David and Frederick 33
Barnes, Julian 14, 234
Barnes Park, Sunderland 105, 173
Barnett, Joel 57
Barnett, Robin 398
Barnier, Michel 409, 446
Barter Books, Alnwick 88, 110, 113, 150, 219, 248, 270, 398, 433
Bashir, Martin 476–7
Beamish Hall Hotel, County Durham 105–6
Beamish Museum, County Durham 220
Beaverbrook, Lord 246
Beckett, Margaret 2, 357
Behr, Rafael 83, 432
Beith, Alan 49, 184
Belarus 502
Belfast Book Festival 291–2
Belger, Helen 400
Bell, Martin 43, 422
Bellingham, Henry 179
'Benji the Bin Man' (Benjamin Pell) 79
Benn, Caroline 123
Benn, David 39, 43, 123
Benn family 123, 386
Benn, Hilary 42, 142, 176, 189–90, 197, 365
  possible leader 2, 67, 150, 293, 357
  shadow Foreign Secretary 123, 124, 140
Benn, Joshua 42, 79
Benn, Melissa 39, 42, 150, 204, 331, 352
Benn, Sally 189
Benn, Stephen 39, 42, 123
Benn, Tony 38–9, 258–9
  CM on 9, 207
  CM's talks on 61, 62, 75
  death and funeral 41–2, 123
  diaries 331
  Extradition Act and 508
  on flames 386
  possible leader 31
Bennett, Alan 198, 219, 245, 369
Bennett, Catherine 13
Benyon, Richard 497, 507
Bercow, John 42, 116, 216, 330, 362, 395
  CM and 12, 15, 30, 81, 276, 315
Bercow, Sally 42
Bermann, Sylvie 461
Berwick, Bishop of 321
Bevan, Nye 68, 185, 494
Bevin, Ernest 428
Biden, Joe 400, 437–9, 441, 447, 455, 519, 528, 529

Bieber, Justin 472
Big Questions, The (BBC) 271
Birmingham 63, 196
Birmingham pub bombings (1974) 114–15, 153–4, 310–11
  anniversary 68
  Birmingham Six released 286, 464, 521
  Callaghan and 528
  civil action threat 490
  CM and Terrorism Act (2000) 518
  CM receives threats 345
  CM taken to court and wins 518, 520–23, 526–7
  Dear and 527–8
  inquest 172, 324, 330–31, 333, 335–6
  interview notes 338–9, 505
  Justice4the21 401–2
  media and 327, 449
  refusal to disclose sources 489–91, 505
  suspects 242
Blagdon Hall, Northumberland 33, 174, 292–3
Blair, Cherie 42
Blair, Ian 215
Blair, Tony
  on Brexit 217, 222, 242
  Brown and 1–2, 260
  business activities 85
  character 398
  Chilcot Report (2016) 180
  Corbyn and 112, 119
  freedom of movement and 157
  Iraq War and 513–14, 517
  Kennedys and 93
  Knight of the Garter 513
  on the Labour Party 307
  Leveson Report 27
  on McGuinness 223
  memoirs 1–2
  Nandy and 165
  on overseas aid 441
  as PM 14, 121, 327, 347
  on politics 539
  on the Tories 88
  and the WI 70
Blairites 144, 147, 156, 186, 293, 320
blame culture 240–41
Blomfield, Paul and Linda 312
Blunkett, David 375
Blyth, Northumberland 69
Boles, Nick 354
Booth, John 483–4

Borders Book Festival, Melrose 239, 346–7
Bormann, Martin 427
Boston, US 502–5
Boswell Book Festival, Dumfries House 287
Boulton, Adam 190, 194, 332
Bower, Tom 282, 328
Bowhill House, Selkirk 239
Bowie, David 147
Boyd, Anne 65
Bradshaw, Ben 27, 231
Bratt, Claes 171, 290, 330, 386
Brazier, Colin 464
Brazil 359
Breamish Valley, Alnwick 91–2, 155
Bremner, Rory 239
Brexit 155–6, 165–6, 187–8
    banking and 469
    Blair and 217, 222, 242
    deadline extended 337–8, 371
    divisive 243
    Irish backstop 325, 326
    Irish border 364
    last-minute deal 449
    May's deal 197, 295, 309, 315–16, 323–4, 334
    media obsession with 272
    no-deal Brexit 299, 319, 322, 351, 355–6, 361,
        435
    'Norway option' 318
    passports and 366
    and Polish taxi driver 335
    pound and 197
    resignations 315, 317
    right of residence 467
    shortages 494, 495
    'shouting match' between parties 359
    soft 300–301
    tariffs and 192
    travel rules 502–3, 505
    withdrawal 66, 127, 132, 134, 167, 369, 370
Brexiteers 256, 264, 318, 334, 340, 373, 385, 392,
    394, 481
Bridgeman, Lucia and Mark 48, 296
Brighton 158
British Library, London 331
British Steel 341
Broadcasting House (Radio 4) 412
Brooks, Charlie 23, 48
Brooks, Rebekah 23, 48
Brown, Gordon 1–2, 37–8, 259–60
    Chancellor 14, 33, 373
    on Corbyn 117

Covid-19 crisis 405
    E. Miliband and 6
    Edinburgh International Book Festival 191
    Hoon and 22, 195
    Jones and 93
    Milburn on 107
    as PM 5, 260
    Scottish referendum 55
Brown, John 191
Brown, Nick 62
Browne, Maj Simon 192, 229
Brownlow, Lord 472
Bruce (family cat) 47, 60–61, 68, 140, 141, 145
Brunert, Jonathan 39
Brussels explosions (2016) 161
Buccleuch, Richard, Duke of 239, 346–7
Bulgaria 131
Burma 100, 205, 262
Burnett, Ian, Lord Chief Justice 258
Burnham, Andy 475
Burrows, Saffron 42, 210
Bush, George W. 12, 34, 74, 135, 150–51, 203, 250,
    308, 398, 492–3
by-elections
    2014–17 52, 61, 68, 69, 142, 204, 219
    2019–22 343–4, 355, 481, 483, 500, 509, 532,
        538
Byers, Steve 34, 38, 100, 203
Bylaugh Hall, Norfolk 322
Byrne, Gabriel 18, 19, 21, 24
Byrne, Liam 95, 98

Cable, Vince 122, 125, 132, 237
Cain, Lee 439, 534
Callaghan, Hugh 528
Callaly Mill, Northumberland 53, 54, 300
Calum (CM's gardener) 127, 153, 268, 459, 506,
    510
Cambridge Analytica 280
Cambridge University 204, 257
Cameron, David
    EU referendum 155
    father's tax affairs 164
    and foreign leaders 135
    on H. Benn 197
    Laws on 162
    lobbyist 470
    memoirs 363, 454–5
    and migrant crisis 114
    Mitchell on 165
    and official ministerial cars 82

Cameron, David *cont.*
out jogging 373
on overseas aid 441
party conferences 4, 60
as PM 5, 40, 76, 327
publishes tax returns 164
regrets mishandling referendum 363
resignation 175, 361
and Scottish referendum 57, 132
Swire and 496
Syria and 138, 139
T. Benn and 42
tax cuts 60
Thatcher tribute 33
Campbell, Alastair 30, 42, 203, 286, 312, 354, 412
Campbell, John 40–41
Campbell, Ming 12, 219
Campbell, Nicky 271
Campbell, Ronnie 69
Candler, Jeana 436
Candler, Peter 337, 430, 436
Capitol riots (2021) 453
car industry 66, 173, 323, 327, 335, 362, 456
care homes/workers 75, 410, 413
caretaker government 357–8
Carew Pole, Sir Richard and Mary 313, 381
Carillion 268–9
Carne, Andy 495–6
Carney, Mark 187
Caro, Robert 88, 93, 99
le Carré, John 294, 446–7
Carrington, Lord 342
Carswell, Douglas 52, 61–2
Carter, Prof Chris 84, 190, 245, 313, 495–6
Carter, Jimmy 64, 450
Cash, Bill 149
Castle, Gordon 110
Castro, Fidel 204
Catalonia 256
Cathcart, Brian 280
Catherine, Duchess of Cambridge 38
Cavendish, Diana 297–8
celebrity culture 59, 150, 208, 398, 451
Change UK 329
Channel 4 News 124, 205, 232, 400, 427–8, 505
Channon, Henry 'Chips' 462, 489, 491–2
Chaplin, Michael 8, 10, 286
Chaplin, Syd 286
Charalambous, Louis 505, 526–7
Charities Commission 270
Charles, Prince of Wales 189–90, 408, 477

Charlie Hebdo attack (2015) 78
Cheltenham Literary Festival 14, 34
Cheney, Dick and Lynne 249
Chennai, India 353
Chester 197
Cheswick House, Berwick 207
Chilcot Report (2016) 180
Chillingham Castle, Northumberland 103, 186,
431, 438, 448
CM has dinner at 50, 57, 97, 196, 227, 273, 297
Storm Arwen 507, 514
China 182, 192, 250, 266, 393, 395–6, 406, 418,
423, 523
Christo (artist) 290
Church Row, Hampstead 156–7, 158, 218–19,
377, 378
Churchill College, Cambridge 257
Churchill, Sarah 428
Churchill, Winston 168, 492
CIA 74
Clark, Jonathan and Katherine 37, 316, 340–41,
448, 479
Clarke, Charles 204
Clarke, Kenneth 164–5, 215, 357, 361
Clarke, Richard A. 492
Cleeves, Ann 239
Clegg, Nick 53, 89, 93, 97, 125, 162, 237
climate change 359, 376, 471, 497
conferences on 311, 499
flooding 143, 145, 250, 545
heatwaves 294, 354, 359, 542, 544
Net Zero Scrutiny Group 520
Trump and 206, 212, 235
wildfires 294, 385, 488–9, 544
Clinton, Bill 42–3
Clinton, Chelsea 43, 305
Clinton, Hillary 43, 150, 163, 171, 186, 193, 198,
199, 208
Clouston, William 511–12
coalitions 5, 27, 161–2, 357, 474, 512
Cohen, Lt Col Mordaunt 262
College Valley, Northumberland 103
Collins, Philip 155, 279
Colston statue incident (2020) 429
Colville, Jock 257
Conservative Party
2015 election 77–8, 84, 86, 89, 94, 96–7
2017–19 elections 229, 375, 377, 380–83
donors 399, 472
by-elections 205, 538
human rights and 60

leadership candidates 343, 345, 355, 541–3, 542
legacies received 339
local elections 340, 473–4, 532
membership 347
migration policy 70
party conferences 60, 164, 254, 495
'Partygate' 507, 514–15, 516, 518, 529, 531, 533–4
racism 379
and raising taxes 94
on spending 90–91
'Tory sleaze' 470, 501
US diplomat resigns 379
Conway, Kieran 330–31
Cook, Dave 527
Cook, Robin 390
Cooke, Rachel 62
Cooper, Duff 492
Cooper, Rosie 294
Cooper, Yvette 101, 118, 120, 293, 357, 497
Corbyn, Jeremy 110–18, 125–6, 273–4, 440–41
2017 local elections 230
2017–19 general elections 233, 248, 372, 379, 380–82
Article 50 and 357
Bower on 328
Brexit and 159, 320
CM on 121, 231
conference speeches 128, 253, 309
constituency 312
on defence 149
on E. Miliband 123
Foster and 326
at Glastonbury 240
Guido Fawkes and 343
'IRA row' 233, 234, 235
Jews and antisemitism 169, 179, 281–4, 301–2, 345, 350, 352, 378–9, 435
journalists and 219
Labour leader 122–4, 148, 184–5, 187–8, 190–91, 193, 200, 360, 387, 474, 497
Maduro regime 245–6, 274
May and 286
Mitchell on 273
Mullin family and 110, 111, 112, 377
Munich Olympic massacre 303–4
Nandy on 165
Oborne on 292
PLO and 303
plots against 140

'as PM' 349, 377
PMQs 125, 133–4
poll rating 364
re-elected leader 195
Russia and 279–80
saying 'no' 255
shadow Cabinets 146, 147, 176–7
and shoot-to-kill policy 137
spy mania 274–5, 275
Starmer and 437, 441
and state dinners 133
Sutcliffe on 306
Syria and 140
in Tunisia 303–4
Watson and 124
Corbyn, Piers 487
Corston, Jean 81, 149, 210, 257
Cottage Garden Society 293
Coulson, Andy 8–9, 23, 48
council tax 397
courier companies, private 75
Covid-19 400–430, 439–40
anti-vaxxer rallies 487, 497
beginnings 393, 395–6, 399
Christmas cancelled 447–8
Dover trucks and 448, 449
easing of lockdown 433, 461, 468
'Freedom Day' 486
new variants 476, 484, 504–5, 508–9, 510
second lockdown 452, 456
travel and 450
vaccines 439, 445, 457, 459, 474, 509
Cowan, Rex 37
Cowen, Maj Robin 106
Cowper-Coles, Sherard 388, 390
Cox, Geoffrey 501
Cox, Jo 173, 174, 218, 296, 483
Coylumbridge Hotel, Aviemore 406
Crace, John 193
Cragside, Northumberland 314
Cram, Steve 139
Crawford, Judith 420
Cresswell Tower, Morpeth 216
Crick, Michael 28
Criminal Cases Review Commission 26, 258
Crosby, Lynton 228, 344, 356
Cryer, John 218
Culture, Media and Sport Committee 10, 15, 122
Cumbria 143
Cummings, Alan 35

Cummings, Dominic 354, 360–61, 363, 396, 426–7, 439, 470–71, 477–9, 486, 534
Cummings, John 211
Cunliffe family 183–4
Curran, James 84, 131
Curtice, John 362, 474

D-Day celebrations 343
Dacre, Paul 246
Daily Politics (BBC) 144, 193, 194, 252
Dale, Iain 40, 252
Daley, Janet 475
Dalrymple William 465–6
Dalton, Sir Richard 255
Dalyell, Tam 219
Damazer, Mark 36
Dance, Charles 19, 20, 21, 22, 24
d'Ancona, Matt 9, 421–2
Darling, Alistair 2, 22, 34, 67, 219
Darlington Council 173
Darroch, Sir Kim 352
Davey, Ed 341
d'Avigdor-Goldsmid, Maj-Gen Sir James 277
Davis, David 182, 293, 296
Davis, Evan 130
Dawnay, Caroline 59
Dear, Geoffrey 527–8
Dearlove, Richard 149, 180, 236–7, 377, 514, 517
Deedes, W. F. 256
defence budget 136, 526
Democratic Unionist Party (DUP) 237, 325, 364
Dench, Judi 129
Deng, Wendi 11
Denham, John 50
Desmond, Richard 431
Diana, Princess 477
Dimbleby, Jonathan 314
Dixon, David Dippie 468–9
Donaghy, Kate 51, 113, 172, 247–9, 407, 439, 442–3, 506, 511
Dorchester Hotel charity event (2018) 270
Dorkin, Mr (CM's surgeon) 47, 53, 54
Dorrell, Stephen 410
Dorries, Nadine 493, 516, 539
Douglas-Home, Alec 300
Douglas-Home, Caroline 227
Dowden, Oliver 465
Dowler, Milly 10
Doxford, John 8
Doyle-Price, Jackie 35
Drabble, Margaret 204

Dublin, Ireland 398–9
Dubs, Alf and Ann 55–6, 108, 109, 189
Duddridge, James 84
Duncan, Alan 296, 472
Duncan Smith, Iain 13, 180
Durham Book Festival 62, 132, 255
Durham Cathedral 105
Durham Police 532–3, 540
Durham University 35, 137, 255

Eagle, Angela 178, 183
East India Company 466
Easyjet 407
Eaton, George 272–3
Ebola epidemic (2014–16) 63, 81
Ed (Emma's boyfriend) 470, 510
Eddie (homeless man) 132–3, 138–9, 141, 143
Edgar, David 157
Edinburgh 171
Edinburgh International Book Festival 113, 116, 191, 305, 357
Edinburgh University Business School 84, 116, 190, 245
Education Maintenance Allowance 23
Edwards, Huw 464–5
Egremont, Max and Caroline 48
Egypt 135
Eliot, George 378
Elizabeth II, Queen 22–3, 535–6
    Churchill Trust and 83
    Covid-19 and 412, 445, 520
    death 546
    death of corgi 476, 477
    death of Prince Philip 469, 516, 528
    Morrissey on 482
    Paddington Bear skit 537
    PMs and 363, 365, 513, 545
    Queen's Speech 475, 533
    royal yacht 265
    support for England football team 484
    Thatcher and 33, 536
Elliott, Julie 25, 26–7, 176, 294, 380, 391
Elliott, Larry 4
Ellman, Louise 344
energy prices 543
England football team 177, 483, 484
English, Otto 456
Eno, Brian 361
Epstein, Jeffrey 515, 520
Erdoğan, Recep Tayyip 367
Essex lorry deaths (2019) 370, 371

Ethiopia 440
Eton College 24–5, 158, 360, 368
European Research Group (ERG) 318–19, 354, 520
Eurovision Song Contest 341, 477
Evans-Pritchard, Ambrose 456

Falconer, Charlie 181, 496, 518, 521, 522
Fallodon Hall, Northumberland 48–9, 296–7, 431
Fallon, Michael 89, 131, 152, 257, 258
Farage, Nigel 38, 97, 174, 265, 347, 371, 372, 375, 393, 394
fascism 209, 216, 272, 370–71, 421
FBI 198
Fearnley-Whittingstall, Hugh 348
Fellowes, Julian 129
Fellowes, Robert 83, 158
Felton Park, Morpeth 216
feminism 266
Field, Frank 243–4, 299
Field, John 326–7
    birthday 458
    character 53
    CM's walking companion 66, 91, 117, 146, 261, 394, 403, 406, 425, 439, 454
    comes to lunch 229
    drinks with 129, 160, 269, 474
    going to Italy 530
    Grieve and 53, 126, 300, 430
    has a fall 428, 429
    on his stressed cats 488
    on isolation 410
    present for CM 443
    supper with 126
financial crisis (2008) 7, 94–5, 105
Finland 519
Fiscal Studies, Institute for 90, 108
Fisher, Carrie 207
Fitzgerald, F. Scott 456
Fitzwalter, Ray and Luise 61, 98, 106, 160, 162, 163
Fixed Term Parliaments Act (2011) 165
Fleming, Renée 342
Fletcher, Paul 286
Fletcher, Tom 5–6
Floyd, George 428–30, 433
Flynn, Paul 140, 180
Foot, Michael 148, 232
Foot, Paul 378
Forbes, Lisa 344

Forbes, Nick 70
Foreign Affairs Committee 27
Forestry Commission 497, 507
Forgan, Liz 37, 64, 82, 174, 247, 353, 369, 414, 472
Formby, Jennie 441
Former MPs, Association of 352–3
Forsyth, James 252
Foster, Derek 326
Foster, Michael 188
Foster, Richard 26
Fox, Liam 391
Fraiman, Ed 18
France 78–9, 85, 183, 502, 519
Frank, Anne 281
Franklin, Andrew 128, 198
Fraser, David 99, 135–6, 172, 176, 235, 237, 288–90, 374–5
Fraser, Ian 339–40
Frears, Stephen 240, 283, 326, 327, 523
Freeman Hospital, Newcastle 53–4, 102–3, 204, 340, 358, 478
Freemasonry 320, 487
Friedman, Thomas 525
Frost, Lord 510
FTSE fat cats 80, 81, 86–7, 289

Gaddafi, Col Muammar 250
Galloway, George 169, 483
Gardeners' World (BBC) 182, 183, 188, 239
Gardner, Frank 285
Garel-Jones, Tristan 129
Garton Ash, Timothy 446–7
Gates, Tony 488
Gauke, David 376, 382
Gaza 169, 272, 283, 288, 476, 477
GCHQ 268
Geldolf, Bob and Jeanne 135, 275
general elections
    1826 469
    1997 230, 361
    2015 27, 56, 61–2, 68, 86–97
    2017 228, 229, 232, 236–7, 240, 378
    2019 372, 374
Germany 110, 207, 252, 300, 456, 519, 523
Gibbon, Gary 505
Gibson, Davie (CM's tree surgeon) 87, 262–3
Gilmour, Ian 96
global civilisation, collapse of 487
Goldsmith, Zac 170, 383
Gorbachev, Mikhail 545
Gore, Al 308

Gould, Philip 267
Gove, Michael 175, 178–9, 181, 319, 354, 363, 449–50, 539–40
Gow, Charlie and Ian 104
Grady, Patrick 255
Grant, Ann 99, 308
Graves, Rupert 20
Gray, Sue 516, 534
Great Ormond Street Children's Hospital 270
Greece 107, 110, 114
Green, Damian 259, 262, 264
Green Party 88, 99, 144, 158, 475
Green, Philip 244
Greene, Graham 265, 329–30
Grenfell Tower fire (2017) 238, 239, 240–41, 243
Grey, Sir Edward 48–9, 296–7
Grieve, Caroline 300
Grieve, Dominic 184, 300–301, 346, 365, 382, 430–31, 471, 474, 482
    Field and 53, 126, 300, 430
Grieve, James 430
Grillo, Beppe 46
Grocott, Bruce 134, 203, 276
Guido Fawkes 343, 418
Gummer, John 16–17

hacking scandal, phone 9, 48
Hague, William 116, 352
Ham, Adrian and Kathy 447
Hambleton, Julie and Brian 114–15, 333, 336–7
Hambleton, Maxine 114–15
Hamilton, Andrew and Diana 349, 351
Hamilton, Archie 293
Hamilton, Neil and Christine 19
Hamilton, Nick (CM's son-in-law)
    moves to America 481, 502, 504
    Mullin family and 65, 87, 87–8, 146, 209, 349, 377
    NHS surgeon 321, 406, 408, 414, 420, 506
Hamilton, Ralph Christopher James (CM's grandson) 454, 461, 466, 470–71, 473, 481, 502, 503, 518–19
Hammond, Philip 182, 220–21, 276, 313, 318, 352, 360
Hancock, Matt 409, 419, 477
Hann, Keith 460
Harman, Harriet 22, 109, 195, 357
Harmony House, Melrose 239, 346
Harris, Robert 32, 115, 230, 238, 294, 315
Harris, Tom 376
Harrison, Aidan and Jill 193

Harry, Prince, Duke of Sussex 389, 463
Harthope Valley, Northumberland 102
Hartley-Brewer, Julia 412
Hastings, Max 304–5
hate mail 121–2, 310, 365
Hatfield House, Hertfordshire 130
Hattersley, Roy 82
Hauxley wildlife centre, Northumberland 216
Hayes, Michael Christopher 242
Haymarket, Newcastle 67, 132–3
Healey, Edna and Denis 130–31, 238, 245
Heath, Allister 495, 498, 537
Heathcoat-Amory, David 50
Heathrow Airport 36, 248, 288, 476, 499
Hebden Bridge, West Yorkshire 232
Heffer, Simon 465
Hemingway, Ernest 435
Henfrey, Mary 194
Henfrey, Tony 91–4, 542–3
    Channon and 496
    CM's walking companion 66, 76, 153, 434, 436
    dinner with 194, 284, 360
    helps to remove silt from lake 90
    helps to remove trees 37, 49
    on A. Johnson 69
    on Mandelson 371
    on McDonnell 253
    Sarah's wedding day 351
    on Storm Arwen 506
    Ukraine flag 533
Henley, Don 539
Hennessy, Peter 149, 199, 331, 341, 343
Heritage Lottery Fund (HLF) 62–3
    appointments 41
    CM regional chairman 8, 10, 22, 36, 160, 173
    conference 50
    presentation by CM 185
    projects 79, 98, 102, 105, 167, 216
    regional chairs meeting 13, 132, 165, 196
Heseltine, Michael 42, 177, 352, 378, 390
Heslop, Charles 35
Hexham Book Festival 95, 231, 286, 339–40, 483
High Lorton, Cumbria 108–9
high street stores 291
Hill, Jonathan, Lord 338
Hill, Paddy 114
Hill, Susan 9
Hinterland Festival of Literature and Art, Kells 349–50
Hirsel Lodge, Coldstream 227
Hodge, Margaret 204, 241, 307, 344, 437, 440–41

Hodgkinson, John 10, 16
Hogan-Howe, Bernard 187
Hollande, François 214
Hollinghurst, Alan 12–13
Homan, Joe 162
homelessness 67, 74, 83, 132–3, 138, 231, 267, 288, 369–70
Hong Kong 395–6, 432, 437, 490
Hoon, Geoff 22, 181, 195, 514, 517
Hopkins, Kelvin 180
Hopper, Dave 35
Horne, David 37, 49
Hosenball, Mark 268
Hosking, Jeremy 172–3, 247–8, 249, 302, 407, 442, 511
Hôtel La Louisiane, Paris 212–13, 214–15
Howard family 293
Howard, Michael 270
Howard, Philip 108–9, 381
Howe, Geoffrey 373
Howell, David 35
Howick Hall, Alnwick 174
Hoyle, Doug 209
Hoyle, Lindsay 209, 373
Hughes, Dominic 312
Hughes, Richard 498
Hugonin, Bill 229, 256, 482, 488
Huhne, Chris 181
Hull History Centre 337
Humphrys, John 78, 121, 172, 328
Hung, Margaret 84, 131
Hungary 524
Hunt, Jeremy and Lucia 135, 181, 350, 493, 525–6
Hunter, Anji 37, 203
Hurd, Douglas 16–17, 218
Hurricane Katrina (2005) 250
Hurt, John 10
Husain, Mishal 223, 373
Hussein, Saddam 149, 514, 517
Hyman, Peter 144

Icke, David 487
identity politics 315, 473
Ilkley Literature Festival 367
IMF 91, 110, 131
INEOS 348
Ingrams, Richard 239
IRA 233, 234, 235, 330, 399
Iran 254–5, 387, 390–91, 404, 443
Iraq 59, 114, 138

Iraq War (2003–11) 1, 12, 148–9, 180, 185, 221, 513, 517
'WMD' 149, 514, 517
Islamist terrorist attacks
9/11 3, 74, 492–3
Afghanistan 491
American hostages 54
France 78–9, 137, 138, 183
Germany 207
Kenya 87
London 223, 235–6, 379, 380
Manchester 234, 244
Pakistan 75
Parliament and 59
Spain 246
Israel 169–70, 255, 259, 267, 271–2, 283, 287–8, 303, 399, 443, 476
Italy 291, 399, 401–6, 407, 409, 411

Jacobson, Howard 282
Jagger, Mick 538
James, Erwin 244
Janvrin, Robin 240
Japan 192, 250
Javid, Sajid
Chancellor 354, 371
Health Secretary 486
income tax plans 400, 408
possible leader 343, 510, 537
resignation 396–7, 539
Jay, Michael 148–9
Jay, Peter 84–5
Jenkin, Bernard 293
Jenkins, Roy 40–41, 68, 343
Jenkins, Simon 299, 314, 383, 531
Jenkyns, Andrea 540
Jenrick, Robert 431, 465
Jerusalem 288
Jo (CM's cousin) 210
Johnson, Alan 2, 34, 53, 67, 204, 293, 334
Johnson, Boris 155–6, 539–40
Article 51 and 369
Brexit 175
Cabinet reshuffle 493
Cain and 439
CBI speech 503
character and appearance 341, 348, 360, 397, 432, 461, 466, 471–2, 502, 536
CM on 181
conference speech 495
Covid-19 403, 409, 412–14, 419, 460–61

Johnson, Boris *cont.*
    Cummings and 426-7, 439, 477
    EU trade deal 445, 446
    Farage and 394
    and female journalist 365
    final offer to Brussels 365-6, 368, 371-2
    'flat renovation' 470, 471, 474
    Foreign Secretary 182, 296, 342
    goes AWOL 415, 544
    leadership campaign 344-6, 350, 355
    on long-term power 530
    Mayor of London 466
    on overseas aid 328
    Parris on 161
    'Partygate' 507, 514-16, 518, 529, 533-4
    Pick on 156
    as PM 353, 361-2, 370-71, 509
    possible leader 76, 165, 178, 340, 347
    promises prosperity 387
    proroguing Parliament 351-2, 359, 362-5
    Russia and 425
    in Rwanda 539
    on the Saudis 206
    support for England football team 484
    Ukraine and 519, 531
    wins vote of confidence 537
Johnson, Carrie (née Symonds) 416, 418, 472,
    478, 529, 533, 534
Johnson, Lyndon 88, 93, 99
Johnson, Rachel 323
Joicey, James 103
Jones, Digby 93
Jones, Owen 379
Jordan 30-31

Kaplinsky, Natasha 42
Kavanagh, Pat 378
Keegan, Bill 32
Kells, County Meath 349-50
Kelman, James 244
Kendall, Liz 98
Keneally, Thomas 129
Kennan, George 525
Kennedy, Bobby 93
Kennedy, John F. 93
KGB 275, 278, 279
Khan, Jemima 170
Khan, Sadiq 169
Khashoggi, Jamal 311-12
Kibasi, Tom 460
Kim Jong-un 245, 292

King, Prof Sir David 420-21
Kinnock, Neil 43, 246, 251, 312
Kinnock, Stephen 165
Kissinger, Henry 345
Klein, Carol 239-40
Knight, Andrew 174
Knight, 'Red Ted' 144
Krugman, Paul 104-5, 321
Kuenssberg, Laura 486
Kurds 59, 270, 367

Labour Party
    1997 election 230
    2015 election 77-8, 79, 85-6, 89, 93, 94, 96-7
    2017-19 elections 231, 237-8, 372, 385
    abolishing the monarchy 299-300
    antisemitism 169, 179, 272, 281-2, 307, 344,
        375, 378-9, 437, 447, 449
    by-elections 481, 483
    in crisis 176-7
    election candidates 525
    focus groups 484
    leadership candidates 66, 98, 100-101
    local elections 340, 473-4, 532
    manifesto 233
    membership 184, 188
    party conferences 58-9, 128, 253, 309
    Scottish 76, 97
    on spending 90
Lagarde, Christine 91
Lake District 55-6, 87, 285
Lamb, Christina 221
Lambton, Lucinda 33
Lansbury, George 306
Lansman, Jon 283-4
Laws, David 161-2, 163
Lawson, Nigel 174
Le Pen, Marine 176
Leadbeater, Kim 483
Leadsom, Andrea 180, 181, 373
Leave campaign 156, 172-5, 177-9, 324, 385
Lee, Christopher 342
Lee, Diane and Martin 481
Leigh-Pemberton, Caterina 442-3
Lepore, Jill 473
Les Allues, France 288-90
Letts, Quentin 395
Letwin, Oliver 365, 369
Leveson Inquiry/Report 15, 18, 27
Lewis, James 522
Liberal Democrats

2015 election 77, 94, 96–7
2019 election 372, 374–6, 378, 385
by-elections 481, 509
electoral pacts 89, 134, 158, 161–2
leaders 341, 354–5
local elections 340, 532
reversing Brexit 363
revival 267
voters and 40, 383
Liberia 265
Libya 167, 234
Libya migrant drownings (2016) 167
Lilburn, Northumberland 431
Lindisfarne Castle 287
Lineker, Gary 421
Lipman, Maureen 272
Live Theatre, Newcastle 8, 10, 95, 112
living/minimum wage 107–8, 134, 210, 218
Livingstone, Ken 124, 169
Lizzick Hall Hotel, Keswick 221
Lloyd, Anna 75
Lloyd George, David 297
Lloyd, Lord 149
Lloyd, Tony 22, 360
Lloyds Bank 233
local elections 170, 230, 287, 340, 473–4, 478, 532
Lockerbie disaster (1988) 126
London Bridge attack (2019) 379, 380
Long-Bailey, Rebecca 384, 391, 431
Longridge Tower School, Berwick 242
Loose Ends (Radio 4) 342
Lorbottle Hall, Northumberland 51–2, 172–3, 293, 442, 506, 511
Lowell, Robert 284
Lucas, Irene 182
Lucraft, Judge 526–7
Luff, Peter 41, 98, 105, 106, 185

McAvoy, Tommy 149
McCafferty, Christine 26
McCain, John 150
McCall, Sandy 346
McCluskey, Len 137
McCrory, Helen 473
McDermid, Val 239, 449
McDonald, Simon 539
McDonnell, John 203–4
    character 273
    Corbyn and 189
    demands general election 360
    'force another election' 238

Forgan on 353
on Grenfell 240
Henfrey on 253
interviewed by Humphrys 328
KGB and 275
possible leader 165, 301
shadow Chancellor 124, 128, 160, 187, 269
McElvoy, Anne 96
McEwan, Ian 33–4, 317, 322–3
MacGregor, Sue 114
McGuinness, Martin 42, 223
McIlkenny, Ann 114
McKee, Gina 19, 24
MacKenzie, Kelvin 249, 449
MacKinlay, Andrew 66
McKinty, Adrian 130, 165
MacMillan, Margaret 352
Macron, Emmanuel 309
Magee, Kevin 242
Maisky, Ivan 168
Major, John 27, 55, 165, 351–2
Man Booker Prize 6, 9–10, 12–14, 129, 234, 272
Manchester Arena bombing (2017) 234, 235, 244
Manchester University Alumni Association 327
Mandelson, Peter 32, 93, 371
    Brexit and 159
Manderston Hall, Scottish Borders 189
Manley, Stuart and Mary 248
Mann, John 169
Mansion House, Newcastle 362
March, Graham 391
Mardell, Mark 377
Margaret (CM's cousin) 44–6, 467
Margaret MacMillan 127
Marquis, Kevin 126
Marr, Andrew 98
Marris, Rob 165
Marsh, Henry 211
mass shootings, USA 173
Matterson, Jean 442–3
Mattinson, Deborah 6
Mattis, James N. 285
Maupin, Armistead 342
Maxwell, Robert 299, 414, 454
May, Theresa
    2017 general election 228, 233–4, 237
    Article 50 and 199
    Brexit plan 295, 309, 315–16, 323–4
    CM on 316
    conference speech 254
    grammar school expansion 193, 194

May, Theresa *cont.*
   Grenfell Tower fire 239
   Home Secretary 236
   Johnson and 515
   M. Howard on 270
   Mitchell on 277
   nickname 210
   overseas aid and 485
   plots against 332
   as PM 181, 182, 272, 280, 284, 286, 298, 327
   possible leader 179, 180, 181
   resignation 333, 340–41
   taxes and 222
   vote of no confidence 318–19
McDonald's 348–9
Meacher, Michael 16–17, 133, 136–7
Meale, Alan 237
Meckelen, Flanders 39–40
media village, College Green, Westminster 324, 332
Meghan, Duchess of Sussex 389, 463
Mensch, Louise 15
Mercer, Patrick 16–17
Merkel, Angela 5, 207, 252, 456
Merritt, David and Jack 380
Metropolitan Police 187, 517, 533
Meyer, Christopher 127
Meyer, Dr Hajo 301
MI6 5, 126
Michael, George 207
Middleton, Kate 38, 95
migration crisis, European 118–21, 151–2, 170
   Calais refugees 104, 113, 114, 193
   Essex lorry deaths 370, 371
   Germany 131, 207
   Hungary 124, 133
   Italy 291
   overseas aid 163
   small boats 92, 502, 503
   Syrians 143, 159
Milburn, Alan 107, 112–13
Milburn, Ruth 112
Miliband, David 2, 5, 6, 9, 33, 34, 37, 93, 301
Miliband, Ed 58–9, 66–7
   Benn's funeral 42
   CM advises 7, 11, 18
   Corbyn on 123
   David and 3, 6, 37
   and Ed Balls 62
   Fallon on 89
   granite pledges 96
   Labour leader 13, 50, 56, 79, 80, 94
   lack of confidence in 84
   on Murdoch 11
   possible leader 2
   resigns as leader 97
   The Sun photo 47
military rule 242–3
Millar, Fiona 385
Millar, Gavin 490–91, 507, 521
Millbank, Westminster 124, 144, 183, 252, 332
Millen, Robbie 68
Miller, Gina 200
Millgate House, Richmond 481
Mills, John 178
Mirvis, Ephraim, Chief Rabbi 378
miscarriages of justice 26, 183–4, 215
Mitchell, Andrew 71–2, 115–16, 276–7
   Brexit and 327
   CM and 97, 181, 447
   on Corbyn 273
   dinner with CM 135, 165
   on Johnson 353, 436, 543
   memoirs 496
   on migrants 121
   overseas aid and 391, 462, 485
   'Plebgate' 23, 24, 28, 36, 51, 259
   Yemen visit 212
Mitchell, Sharon 51, 71, 135, 181, 436
Mirza, Munira 519
Moberly, Patricia 65–6, 100, 129, 143–4, 157, 162
Moberly, Richard 66
Momentum 267, 273
Monbiot, George 221, 409
Montgomerie, Tim 30, 108, 412
Moore, Charles 131, 132, 366
Mordaunt, Penny 259
Mordey, Michael 261
Morgan, Piers 150, 398, 412, 419, 464
Mori, Martin 156, 157
Morrissey, Joy 482
Mountbatten, Louis, Lord 245, 399
Moynihan, Daniel Patrick 525
Mugabe, Robert 255
Mulholland, Hélène 157, 180, 287, 365
Mullin, Chris
   annual garden party 51, 295
   'The Art of Political Leadership' 116, 131, 168
   'The Challenges Facing Labour' 134
   'The Changing Face of Sunderland' 137
   Decline & Fall 22
   'In Defence of Politics' 94, 95, 218

diary talks 4, 16, 17, 24, 30
'Great Political Disasters I Have Known 245, 270, 333–4
'How to Be an MP' 393, 394–5
'My Walled Garden in Northumberland' 48, 130
'Remarkable Rise of Jeremy Corbyn' 279, 292, 305
'Rise and Fall of New Labour' 99
'Rise of English Nationalism' 479, 480, 483, 500–501
Tony Benn talk 61, 62, 75, 92
Decline & Fall 32
The Friends of Harry Perkins 113, 154, 157–8, 245, 295, 309, 324, 326, 327, 332–3, 335, 351, 355
Hinterland 115, 157, 192–3, 194–5, 202, 235, 239, 247, 252, 278, 296, 312, 315
A Very British Coup 9, 74, 115, 125–6, 128, 129, 134, 149, 244, 262, 323, 350
A Very British Coup spoof (R4) 115, 117
A View from the Foothills 113, 198, 251, 380
A Walk-On Part 12, 209
Mullin, David (CM's brother) 361
Mullin, Emma (CM's daughter)
    Christmas and Covid 510
    CM and 232
    concerts with CM 538
    on Corbyn 110, 112, 377
    in Cumbria 108–9
    dinner with CM 80
    family celebrations 47, 144, 281, 319, 349
    family life 53
    first-class degree 241, 243
    first jobs 232, 252, 253, 422
    at Goldsmiths 58, 75
    H. Wakefield and 51
    helps CM with Twitter 91
    in the Lake District 55–6
    meets with CM 252
    in Rome 43–4, 46, 47
    Sarah's diary entry 344
    turns vegan 175
    US visa application 265
    A View from the Foothills 113
    walks with CM 77, 87–8, 189, 227, 265, 303, 320, 357
Mullin family 72–3, 377, 389, 463, 470
    celebrations 76, 349, 351, 406, 511
    Covid-19 lockdowns 410, 414, 417, 436, 447–8, 449
Mullin, Liz (CM's sister) 76, 321, 349

Mullin, Sarah (CM's daughter)
    advises CM on Covid-19 405, 408
    Amsterdam with family 281
    on Brexit marches 318
    comes to stay 87, 321
    concert with CM 539
    on Corbyn 111
    diary entry about Emma 344
    dinner with CM 80, 374
    family celebrations 144, 349, 351, 373
    heritage 463
    iPhone and 504, 505
    on Labour 385
    living in London 65
    motherhood 448, 454
    moves to Boston, US 481, 502–4
    at Oxford 16, 42–3
    walks with CM 77, 87–8, 145, 146, 209
Munchetty, Naga 464
Munich Olympic massacre (1972) 303–4
Murdoch, James 10–11, 15–16
Murdoch, Rupert 10–11, 18, 81, 304–5
Murphy, Jim 97, 219
Murray, Judy 287
Murray, Michael 311, 331
Myanmar 461

Nandy, Lisa 165, 218, 384, 391, 392, 401, 411, 412, 475
Narey, Martin 4
National Action 294
National Front 449
National Garden Scheme 49, 431
National Park Authority 231, 251, 280, 285, 330, 363–4, 405, 443, 488, 538
National Trust 103, 237, 287, 314
National Union of Journalists (NUJ) 338, 452, 490, 521–2, 524
NATO 517, 524, 525, 533, 537–8
Naughtie, Jim 116, 239, 240, 332, 346
Naworth Castle, Cumbria 108–9, 381
Neil, Andrew 480
Nepal 250
Netanyahu, Benjamin 304
Netherlands 459
Newcastle City Council 70
Newcastle University 63–4, 74, 132, 211, 216, 223, 393, 394–5
Newmark, Jason 157
NHS 75, 76, 79, 90, 158, 204, 358, 381, 414, 486
    Covid-19 and 401, 406, 410, 418, 451

Nicholls, John and Gilly 103, 278, 403, 506
Nicholson, Chris and Christine 246, 474
Nicolson, Adam 302, 303
North Korea 153, 228, 245, 250
North of England Civic Trust 112, 185
North of England Refugee Service 67–8, 74
Northamptonshire County Council 273
Northern Ireland 325, 326, 347, 366, 467
Northumberland, Duchess of 167
Northumberland, Hugh, 10th Duke of 229
Northumbria University, Newcastle 271, 286
Nott, David 346
nuclear weapons 128, 148, 152, 163, 228, 245, 250, 255, 464, 530

Obama, Barack 153, 168, 208, 212, 255, 448, 450
Obama, Michelle 321
Obama, Sasha 321, 448
Oborne, Peter 292
Odey, Crispin 355–6
Office for Budget Responsibility (OBR) 402, 498, 540
oil and gas industry 84, 86, 101, 174, 358, 523, 543
Oldie literary lunches 9, 80, 244, 342
Osborne, George 110–11, 498–9
    autumn statements 73, 139
    BBC and 107, 444–5
    budget cuts 152
    budgets 107, 108, 109, 161
    Chancellor 19, 74, 84, 91, 124, 455, 458, 462
    defence budget 136
    on incomes 396
    Laws on 162
    party conference 4
    sacked 182
    second and third jobs 222, 458
    shadow Chancellor 458
    on Starmer 417
Ottaway, Richard 96
overseas aid budget 162–3, 441–2
    Foreign Office and 353, 391
    Mitchell and 277
    pressure on 145, 212, 328, 397, 485
    reduction 206
    refugees 120, 462
Owen, Wilfred 376
Oxford and Cambridge Club, London 218

Packwood, Alan 257
Pakistan 545
Palestine 169, 170, 283, 288

Palestinian Liberation Organization (PLO) 303
Palin, Michael 129
Palin, Sarah 150
Palmer, Adrian 189
Panorama (BBC) 418, 435
Papps, Alastair 263
Paris attacks (2015) 137, 138
Paris, France 148, 212–14
Parish, Neil 531–2
Park, Daphne 5, 136
Parkinson, Michael 239
Parris, Matthew 140, 161, 362, 493, 510, 544
passports 264
Patel, Priti 259, 354, 355, 397, 479, 530, 537
Paterson, Owen 174, 293, 500
Patten, Chris 371
Peake, Maxine 42, 431
Pearce, Ed 5
Pearson, Allison 413–14
Pen and Palette Club 362
Pence, Mike 228
pensions 88, 107, 229, 244, 268, 482
Peppiatt, Richard 15
Perry, William 525
Peru 428
Pessina, Stefano 79
Petworth, West Sussex 48
Philip, Duke of Edinburgh, Prince 23, 83, 230, 324–5, 331, 445, 462, 467–70, 516, 528
Phillips, Jess 387–8, 391, 392
Pick, Hella 156
Pincher, Chris 539
Pius V, Pope 46
Poland 131, 335, 524, 531
Political Book Awards 40
political correctness 211, 271
Political Science Association Awards 27
Pompeo, Mike 345
Portcullis House, Westminster 9, 15, 22, 98, 129, 180, 199, 276
Portillo, Michael 36
Powell, Anthony 242
Powell, Jonathan 34, 95, 203
Power, Breda 114
Prescott, John 326
press empires 247, 249, 280, 283, 305
Preston, John 454
Price, Chris 82
Prison Reform Trust 131, 195, 244, 309–10
Private Passions (Radio 3) 35
Profile Books 115, 262, 352

Project Fear (referendums) 166, 299, 358
Public Accounts Committee 241
Putin, Vladimir 208, 517, 521, 524
Puttnam, David 32–3, 34

Quin, Joyce 77, 293, 349, 478

Raab, Dominic 343, 354, 410, 493
RAF Boulmer, Alnwick 92
railway network 216–17
Randall, Nick 64
Rani, Anita 348
Raqqa, Syria 368
Ravens, Jan 346
Rawnsley, Andrew 111
Rayner, Angela 293, 429, 475, 494, 532–3, 540
Rees, Martin 33
Rees-Mogg, Jacob 273, 316–17, 349, 354, 539
Reeves, Rachel 475, 498
Reid, John 38
Remain campaign/Remainers 168, 172, 174–5,
    273, 302, 332, 362, 365, 369, 385
Rennard, Chris 162
Reunion (Radio 4) 114–15
Reynolds, Debbie 207–8
Richards, Gen Sir David and Caroline 31–2,
    181, 442
Richards, Steve 441
Ridley, Matt and Anya 33, 81, 97, 174, 292–3, 349,
    506–7
Riley, Bridget 80
Rimington, Stella 6, 9, 13, 14, 79
Robbins, Olly 329
Roberts, Julia 210
Roberts, Max 8
Robinson, Nick 78, 223
Robinson, Tommy 334
Rohingya people 100, 205, 251, 270, 422
Rolling Stones 538, 539
Romania 131, 415
Rome 43–47
Rose, David 174
Roussos, Saffie-Rose 234, 235, 244
Royal Bank of Scotland 339–40
Royal Institute of International Affairs 84
Rudd, Amber 362
Ruffer, Jonathan 102
Runciman, David 335
Rusbridger, Alan 538
Russia 92, 208, 217, 227, 250, 279–80, 284, 300,
    425–6

Ukraine and 517, 519–21, 523–6, 528–9, 531,
    537–8
Rwanda refugee plan 530, 537

Said, Edward 58
St Aubyn, Edward 269
St Peter's School, York 333–4
Salisbury, Dowager Marchioness of 130
Salisbury, Lord and Lady 130
Salisbury, Marquis of 5, 130
Salisbury poisonings (2018) 278, 279
Salmond, Alex 99
Sampson, Anthony 134
Sanders, Gen Sir Patrick 537
Sanderson, Glen 285–6
Sarkocy, Jan 275
Sassoon, Sir Philip 492
Saudia Arabia 127, 146, 206, 212, 255, 303, 311–12,
    339
Saunders, Bernie 400
Sawers, Sir John 350–51
Scarlett, John 180
Schovánek, Radek 275
Scotland 96–7, 99, 174, 347, 457–8
Scottish National Party (SNP)
    2015 election 77, 93, 94, 96, 99
    2017–19 elections 237, 372
    resurgence 84, 382, 474, 532
    support of 89
Scottish referendum (2014) 55, 57, 132
SDP 41, 511–12
Secret State (TV version of A Very British Coup)
    18–22, 24, 157
Seely, Bob 328
Seldon, Anthony 132
Shah, Naz 169
Sharples, Sir Richard 23
Shawdon Hall, Alnwick 106
Sheen, Michael 327
Shemirani, Kate 487
Shipman, Tim 240
Short, Clare 16–17, 328, 496, 536
Shrimsley, Robert 195, 457, 502
Sidaway, Bryn 360–61
Simmonds, David 176
Simon & Schuster 324, 332–3
Simpson, Alan 157, 287
Simpson, John 221
Singapore 346
Sisi, General Abdel-Fattah el- 135
Skidelsky, Robert 85

Skinner, Dennis 54, 62
Sky News 332
Slack, James 516
Sloman, Anne 477
Smith, Chris 258
Smith, John 12
Smith, Julian 397
Smith, Owen 183, 185, 187, 193
Smith, Sarah and Simon 239
Snow, Jon 27
'snowflake generation' 480
Soames, Nicholas 158, 230, 293, 361, 435
Social Democratic Party (SDP) 302
social housing crisis 318
Soderberg, Nancy 152
Somerville, Chris and Jane 221
Somme, Battle of the (1916) 179
Sommerville, Quentin 368
Sophie, Countess of Wessex 167
Sorrell, Martin 81
Soubry, Anna 382
South Downs Way walk 235-8
South Korea 250
space race 353
Spain 403, 404
Sparrow, Andrew 157
Spellar, John 140
Spencer, Michael 4
Spicer, Sean 212
Squawkbox 385
Sri Lanka Easter bombings (2019) 338-9
Stafford-Clark, Max 157
stalking 258-9
Stanistreet, Michelle 521
Star Inn, Netherton 160-61
Starmer, Sir Keir
    'Beergate' 532-3, 540
    Byers on 203
    character 392
    conference speech 309
    Corbyn and 437, 441
    Labour leader 411-12, 417, 435, 458, 460, 466,
        485, 530
    'landowner' 424-5
    leadership campaign 388, 391
    local elections 474
    New Year speech 513
    PMQs 423, 515
    possible leader 136, 165, 384, 385-6
    reshuffle 475
    'taking the knee' 429

Steel, David 219, 257-8
Steinberg, Gerry 436
Stevenson, Bryan 82
Stewart, Rory 27, 239, 259, 343, 352
Stiffkey, Rector of 202
Stock, Kathleen 499
Stockwell shooting (2005) 137
Stoltenberg, Jens 537-8
Storm Ali 308
Storm Arwen (2021) 504, 505, 506-7, 514
Stratton, Allegra 508
Straw, Jack 22, 31, 42, 123-4, 195, 518, 522
Streeting, Wes 509
Strictly Come Dancing (BBC) 202
Stuart, Douglas 457-8
Sturgeon, Nicola 87, 88
Summers, Larry 356
Sunak, Rishi
    budgets 402-3, 462, 498
    Chancellor 405, 408, 434, 442, 458, 515
    family financial affairs 529
    possible leader 510, 519, 541, 542
    public spending 533-4
    resignation 539
    Tunbridge Wells speech 543
Sunderland 147, 173, 175, 182, 185, 272, 360-61, 382
Sunderland AFC 101, 170, 230, 294, 501
Sunderland City Council 173
Sunderland University 133, 139, 262, 294-5,
    392-3, 500-501
Sutcliffe, William 306
Sutton, Detective Constable 522
Suu Kyi, Aung San 100, 251
Sweden 308, 519
Swift, Joe 184
Swinson, Jo 341, 354-5, 357, 363
Swire, Sasha 496
Syria 59, 121, 138, 140, 142, 205-6, 223, 227-8,
    284-5, 367-8, 395

Taliban 27, 390, 489
Tankerville Arms, Eglingham 64, 68
Tatchell, Peter 148
Taylor, Charles 265
Taylor, Matthew 199
teaching unions 424
Teather, Sarah 96
Terrorism Act (2000) 518, 522
Thailand 386
Thatcher, Margaret 17, 33, 35, 131-2, 219, 246, 303,
    366, 536, 543

Thornberry, Emily 69, 293, 384, 391, 397
Thorpe, Jeremy and Caroline 73, 283
Today (Radio 4) 75, 78, 124, 127, 147, 208, 272,
    318, 350, 356, 373
    CM dealings with 41, 71, 113, 223, 242
    CM interviewed by 11, 242, 335
Tony (CM's cousin) 72–3, 211
Torpoint, Cornwall 495–6
Toynbee, Polly 458
trade unions 3, 109
Travis, Tony 157
Trevelyan, Anne-Marie 329, 397, 465, 493
Trewin, Ion 9, 129, 134
Trident 152, 181, 183
Trollope, Anthony 410, 414
Trump, Donald 150–51, 211–12, 215–16, 254–5
    Assad and 228
    Capitol riots and 453
    Covid-19 crisis 403, 404–5, 411, 417
    Darroch and 352
    denies defeat 440, 441, 445, 447
    elected President 200–201, 208
    escapes impeachment 460
    Farage and 375
    Georgia tape 452
    on illegal immigrants 201
    Kurds and 367
    'leaves town' 455
    on the media 217
    meets Kim Jong-un 292
    and North Korea 228, 245
    policies 212
    as President 206, 217, 250, 268, 400
    presidential campaigns 163, 171, 186, 193, 196,
        198–9, 433, 438–9
    Putin and 298
    'state visit' to UK 296
    and Syria 284
    tweets 321
    visits Parliament 216
    Wakefield on 507
Trump family 352, 438
Truss, Liz 493, 510, 519, 531, 542, 544, 545
Tunisia 303, 304
Turkey 171, 209, 269–70, 311–12
Tutu, Desmond 511
TV licence fee (BBC) 107, 445, 516

U3A movement 168, 526
UKIP 61, 67–8, 77, 98, 219, 230, 334, 371–2, 393
Ukraine 517, 519–21, 523–6, 528–9, 531, 537–8

Ukrainian plane crash (2020) 389, 390–91
Umunna, Chuka 85, 98, 100, 293, 329
unemployment 202
Union Jacks 33, 292, 393, 458, 464–5, 513, 517
United Nations (UN) 167, 399, 422
United States (US) 201, 247, 356, 412–14, 418–19,
    473, 517, 531
universal credit 396
University Challenge (BBC) 64
University College Dublin 398–9

Vale of Lorton, Lake District 189
Valls, Manuel 151
Varoufakis, Yanis 305
Vaz, Keith 192
VE Day celebrations 421–2
Venezuela 245–6, 306–7
Venice, Italy 224–7
Vera (Star Inn landlady) 160
Versailles, France 213
Vietnam War 95, 300, 305, 308, 418, 489
Villiers, Theresa 397
Vinson, Nigel 172, 173, 184, 243, 457, 491
Vinson, Yvonne 184, 243, 457
Vintner's Hall 181, 496
von der Leyen, Ursula 445, 446

Waite, Terry 264
Wakefield, Sir Humphry
    carol service with 319, 384
    challenges Emma 51
    CM and 103, 448, 492
    evenings with 50, 57, 196, 273, 479
    hat incident 97
    on Storm Arwen 514
    tea with 186, 431, 507
    on test-firing cannon 438
Wakefield, Katharine 97, 186, 273, 431, 479, 507
Wakefield, Mary 57, 261, 426–7
Wakeford, Christian 517
Waldegrave, William 24–5, 359, 368
Walk-On Part (Chaplin play) 12
Wallace, Ben 519
Wallington Hall, Northumberland 103
Wallis, Jamie 532
Wansbeck Hospital, Ashington 49, 64, 197–8,
    259, 429
Ward, Sophie 21
Ware, John 115, 310, 435, 477
Warner, Jeremy 499
waste recycling 38, 39–40, 99, 181, 266, 348–9, 383

Waterhouse, Michael 49, 196–7
Waterstones 24, 144, 158, 340, 444, 478
Watson, James 33, 34
Watson, Paul 261
Watson, Tom 15, 122, 123, 124, 188, 352
Ways With Words Festival, Dartington 351–2
Weah, George 265
Welby, Justin 314
West, Adm Lord 152
West Bank 169, 422
West Bengal 250
West Ham United FC 72–3
West Midlands Police 337–9, 452, 489–91, 505,
    518, 521–3, 527
White, Michael 16, 408, 484
Whittingham Vale, Northumberland 468–9
Whitty, Chris 409, 482–3
WHSmith 223–4
Widdecombe, Ann 129
Wild Cattle Association, Chillingham 172
Wild, James 465
William, Prince, Duke of Cambridge 477
Williams, John
    CM stays with 148, 150, 183, 185, 200, 217, 342
    CM's walking companion 87, 261, 393
    recommend hotel to CM 212
    stays with Mullins 117
    Zoom with 447
Williams, Lia 20
Williams, Sheila
    CM and 16, 91, 116
    CM stays with 148, 150, 183, 185, 200, 217, 342
    recommend hotel to CM 212
    Zoom with 447
Williams, Shirley 257–8, 433–4, 468
Williamson, Gavin 279
Wilson, Harold 308
Wimbledon Literary Festival 131
Winchester Speakers Festival 235
Winfrey, Oprah 463
Winnick, David 237
Winston Churchill Memorial Trust 65, 82, 148,
    158, 199, 210, 257, 268, 389–90
Winstone, Ruth 32, 39, 42, 123, 157, 291, 331, 386
Wollaston, Sarah 356, 382
Wood, Gaby 9
Wood, Stewart 255
Wooler Parish Council 271
Woollacott, Katy 243, 465
Woollacott, Martin 4, 243, 433, 446, 459, 461,
    463, 465

Words by the Water Literary festival, Keswick
    31, 221, 278–9
Work and Pensions Select Committee 243–4
World at One (Radio 4) 324, 377
World Health Organization (WHO) 255
Worsthorne, Peregrine 33

Yemen 146, 205, 206, 212, 303, 462
YouGov polls 186, 322, 347, 383, 466

Zahawi, Nadhim 544
Zelensky, Volodymyr 523, 526, 531